MW01622785

The Comprehensive Forensic Services Manual

The Essential Resources for All Experts

STEVEN BABITSKY, JD

JAMES J. MANGRAVITI, JR., JD

CHRISTOPHER J. TODD, JD

S•E•A•K, Inc.
Legal and Medical Information Systems

Falmouth, Massachusetts

SUBSCRIPTION NOTICE

This SEAK product is updated on a periodic basis with supplements to reflect changes in the subject matter. If you purchase this product directly from SEAK, Inc., we have already recorded your subscription for this update service.

If, however, you purchased this product from a bookstore and wish to receive (1) the current update at no additional charge, and (2) future updates and revised or related volumes billed separately with a 30-day examination review, please send your name, company name (if applicable), address and the title of the product to:

SEAK, Inc.

P.O. Box 729
Falmouth, MA 02541
Phone: (508) 457-1111
Fax: (508) 540-8304
www.seak.com

The Comprehensive

Forensic Services Manual

The Essential Resources for All Experts

The Comprehensive Forensic Services Manual: The Essential Resources for All Experts

Second Impression 2001
ISBN: 1-892904-07-1

CONTENTS

Acknowledgments

The authors wish to acknowledge the following persons whose assistance in the production of this book was invaluable: Christopher R. Brigham, MD; Harold J. Bursztajn, MD; Mary L. Cataudella, Esq.; Nancy Coffone; David A. Dodge, CSP; Kathy Lamson; William Marletta, PhD, CSP; Dee Netzel; John M. Orlowski, PE, CSP, BCFE; Jerome H. Poliacoff, PhD; Gray Smith, AIA, AICP; and Melvin Tucker.

Related Products by SEAK, Inc.

<u>TEXTS</u>

The Independent Medical Examination Report: A Step-by-Step Guide with Models

How to Excel During Cross-Examination: Techniques for Experts That Work

The Comprehensive IME System: Essential Resources for an Efficient and Successful IME Practice

The Successful Physician Negotiator: How to Get What You Deserve

How to Excel During Depositions: Techniques for Experts That Work

<u>SEMINARS</u>

SEAK Law School for Physicians™

How to Be an Effective Medical Witness

How to Be a Successful Independent Medical Examiner

SEAK Negotiating Skills for Physicians™

SEAK Business School for Physicians™

National Expert Witness and Litigation Seminar

<u>AUDIOTAPE PROGRAMS</u>

Achieving Success as a Medical Witness

How to Be a Successful Independent Medical Examiner

<u>VIDEOTAPES</u>

The Expert Deposition: How to Be an Effective and Ethical Witness

Cross-Examination of the Expert: How to Be an Effective and Ethical Witness

The Most Difficult Questions for Experts: With Answers

For more information call SEAK at 508/457-1111. Inquiries may also be addressed to SEAK, Inc. at P.O. Box 729, Falmouth, MA 02541. Fax 508/540-8304; e-mail address: seakinc@aol.com; Internet address: http://www.seak.com

About the Authors

Steven Babitsky, JD, is the President of SEAK, Inc. He was a personal injury trial attorney for twenty years and is the former managing partner of the firm Kistin, Babitsky, Latimer & Beitman. Mr. Babitsky is the co-author of the texts *How to Excel During Cross-Examination: Techniques for Experts That Work,* and *How to Excel During Depositions: Techniques for Experts That Work.* Attorney Babitsky is the co-developer and trainer for the "How to Be an Effective Medical Witness" seminar, the seminar leader for the National Expert Witness and Litigation Seminar, and the scriptwriter for the videos "How to Be an Effective Medical Witness" and "The Expert Medical Deposition: How to Be an Effective and Ethical Witness."

James J. Mangraviti, Jr., JD, has trained hundreds of expert witnesses across the United States and Canada. He is a former trial lawyer with experience in defense and plaintiff personal injury law and insurance law. He currently serves as Vice President and General Counsel of SEAK, Inc. Mr. Mangraviti received his BA degree in mathematics *summa cum laude* from Boston College and his JD degree *cum laude* from Boston College Law School. His publications include the texts *SEAK Law School for Physicians, Law School for the Safety and Health Professional, The Independent Medical Examination Report: A Step-by-Step Guide with Models, The Successful Physician Negotiator: How to Get What You Deserve, How to Excel During Cross-Examination: Techniques for Experts That Work,* and *How to Excel During Depositions: Techniques for Experts That Work.*

Christopher J. Todd, JD, is the Assistant Vice President of SEAK, Inc. He is actively involved with expert witness issues as an author, editor, and trainer. He has researched extensively the law affecting expert witnesses and their role in American jurisprudence, has contributed to the *Expert Witness Journal*, and conducted much of the research underlying the development of *How to Excel During Depositions: Techniques for Experts That Work* (SEAK, 1999). Christopher has also developed internet- and audiotape-based training programs for SEAK, directs SEAK Web marketing efforts, and develops the SEAK Web site. He graduated from the University of California, Davis, School of Law, where he served as a Staff Editor for the UC Davis Law Review. He obtained his BA in Comparative Area Studies from Duke University.

Chapter 1 Overview

1.1 Introduction

The need for expert witnesses has never been greater than it is today. Litigants rely on expert testimony in approximately 80% of all civil cases and in one-half of all felony prosecutions."[1] Unfortunately, few experts receive formal training in such subjects as the expert's proper role in the legal system; how to communicate opinions effectively at deposition, at trial, and in a written report; the law and procedure dealing with experts; ethics; how to deal with attorneys; and how to better manage the business aspects of a forensic practice. This book has been written to provide information in all of these areas. It is the comprehensive resource for all experts.

The authors have illustrated the points made in this work by example. They have included over 440 examples in the twenty-four chapters of this book. In addition, there are lengthier examples and model documents in the twenty-five appendices. Many of the examples are summaries of actual court decisions. These are provided to give context to the principles discussed in this book as examples of how certain issues have been resolved by a court. **This book is in no way intended to give legal advice to the reader. Substantive and procedural law vary from jurisdiction to jurisdiction. Experts should consider seeking professional legal advice regarding any particular legal issue that may arise from their own forensic practices.**

The chapters in this book are grouped together in the following categories: procedure (2–4), evidence (5), qualifications (6–7), forming and expressing opinions (8–10), expert testimony (11–15), forensic practice management (16–20), and additional topics (21–24). A brief description of each of the chapters follows.

1.2 Procedure

Chapters 2–4 deal with the basic civil procedure that all experts should be familiar with. Included are an in-depth discussion of the broad-based discovery process, the limits thereto, and sanctions for its abuse. Also included is a discussion of basic trial procedure, including motions for directed verdicts and motions for judgment notwithstanding the verdict. Appendices E–J provide sample litigation documents including a complaint, an answer, answers to interrogatories, a request for production of documents, a sample schedule from a subpoena duces tecum, and a deposition transcript. Select Federal Rules of Civil Procedure are provided in Appendix Q.

---

[1] Marc S. Klein, "Why Judges and Juries Must Be Scientifically Literate," *NJL* 4 (Jan. 1995) 216.

1.3 Evidence

Chapter 5 provides an overview of the Federal Rules of Evidence. This includes a discussion of the key concepts of relevancy and unfair prejudice as they relate to expert testimony. Also explained are the "700" series of evidentiary rules that deal specifically with expert testimony. The chapter concludes with an explanation of the evidentiary rules that govern an attorney's attempt to challenge an expert's credibility by establishing bias and confronting the witness with prior inconsistent statements. The Federal Rules of Evidence are provided in Appendix P.

1.4 Qualifications

Chapter 6 explains in detail the legal requirements to qualify to testify as an expert witness. This explanation is supported by numerous case-based examples. The latter part of Chapter 6 explains how a cross-examiner may challenge an expert's qualifications even after that expert has qualified as an expert. Closely related to the issue of qualifications is that of the expert's curriculum vitae (CV). Chapter 7 provides practical suggestions for experts to make their CVs much more resistant to challenge on cross-examination. A CV quality control checklist is provided in Appendix A. Several model CVs are provided in Appendix T.

1.5 Forming and Expressing Opinions

Chapter 8 explains in detail the legal requirements for the expression and basis of an expert's opinion. This explanation is supported by numerous examples. Also included in Chapter 8 is an explanation of the methods a cross-examiner may use to challenge an expert's opinion. Chapter 9 explains in detail and with numerous examples the methodology requirements for expert testimony delineated by the U.S. Supreme Court in the landmark *Daubert, G.E.,* and *Kumho Tire* cases. Practical suggestions on how to defeat methodology challenges are provided. Chapter 10 discusses how to express an expert opinion in a written report in such a way that it will be less vulnerable on cross-examination. A report quality control checklist is provided in Appendix B. Several model forensic reports are provided in Appendix U.

1.6 Expert Testimony

An expert's function is to "assist the trier of fact." This can best be done when the expert communicates clearly and effectively with the trier of fact (usually the jury) at deposition and trial. Chapter 11 provides practical advice on how to "connect" with a jury of lay persons. Effective communication with the trier of fact requires preparation. How to prepare to testify at deposition and trial is covered in Chapter 12. Chapters 13–15 provide practical advice on how to better communicate while testifying. Expert depositions are discussed in Chapter 13. Because most civil cases never reach trial, depositions are the method by which the majority of expert testimony in civil cases is provided. Chapter 14 explains how to best communicate during direct examination. Chapter 15 explains specific techniques on how to deal with cross-examination and what an expert is likely to be asked. Included in Chapter 15 are numerous case examples on the extent of permitted cross-examination of an expert. Areas of common inquiry at deposition and trial are provided in Appendices C and D, respectively.

1.7 Forensic Practice Management

Experts who would like to be involved in more cases need to understand what attorneys are looking for from experts and how they select experts. This is explained in Chapters 16 and 17. Chapter 18 is a comprehensive explanation of expert witness marketing. Included are the benefits and drawbacks of various marketing methods including: word of mouth, speaking, writing, referral agencies, advertisements, and online marketing. Also included is a detailed discussion of how to test, track, and evaluate the effectiveness of each aspect of a forensic marketing campaign. Chapter 19 provides practical suggestions regarding how much to charge, what to charge for, and how to ensure collection of an expert's fees. Chapter 20 explains the protections and potential liabilities facing experts. Risk management techniques for experts are provided.

Substantial resources relevant to the business aspect of being an expert are provided in the appendices. Appendix K provides a compendium of expert witness referral organizations. Appendix L contains a list of online and print directories. Appendix M provides a list of legal journals and other publications. Key internet sites are provided in Appendix N and bar associations and other legal associations are provided in Appendix O. Appendix R contains model expert fee schedules and agreements. Appendix S contains model bills. A model consulting agreement has been provided in Appendix V and model marketing letters appear in Appendix W. Appendix X contains a fee survey of experts.

1.8 Additional Topics

The complex areas of privilege, work product, and expert discovery limits are discussed in Chapter 21. Numerous examples are provided to illustrate what testimony or information experts can or cannot be compelled to provide, including documents, communications with counsel, financial and tax records, and the situation where the expert was formerly employed by another party in the case. Chapter 22 covers how to communicate effectively with retaining counsel. Chapter 23 discusses expert ethics and provides concrete suggestions on how experts can avoid ethical violations. It is also important to understand the ethical rules that bind attorneys. Sample rules of ethics for attorneys are contained in Appendix Y. Chapter 24 describes the seventeen common abuses experts face and how to combat these abuses.

1.9 Updates

The authors have attempted to create a comprehensive and timely work on expert witnessing. Updates will be compiled on a periodic basis to keep experts current with new developments and changes in this area. If you have not purchased this book directly from SEAK, Inc., please contact SEAK, Inc.[2] to request that you be sent updates to this work when they become available.

1.10 Using This Book

The twenty-four chapters in this book have been placed in a logical order. Although all the chapters interrelate, the authors have attempted to make each chapter stand alone as much as possible. The design allows readers to quickly target the particular areas of concern they may have. To facilitate this process, a detailed table of contents and index have been provided. Where chapters closely interrelate, cross-references have been provided.

1.11 Conclusion

It is the authors' hope that this book will help the expert better assist fact finders. It is further their hope that the expert's forensic work will become more rewarding and less stressful. The reader's feedback is encouraged.[3]

---

[2] SEAK, Inc., P.O. Box 729, Falmouth, MA 02541; phone: (508) 457-1111; fax: (508) 540-8304; www.seak.com

[3] Feedback can be addressed to the authors at the contact information for SEAK, Inc., given in the previous footnote.

Chapter 2 Fundamental Elements of a Lawsuit

2.1 Introduction

The expert witness needs to be familiar with the procedures involved in the civil litigation process. Effective expert witnesses understand the civil litigation process. This chapter explains the fundamental elements of a civil lawsuit that all experts should understand.

A *lawsuit* has been generally defined by the United States Supreme Court as "any proceeding in a court of justice by which an individual pursues [a] remedy which the law affords."[1] *Civil procedure* is the body of rules and practices by which justice is meted out by the legal system.[2] Although the specific rules of civil procedure vary from jurisdiction to jurisdiction (for example, from state to state), they are generally based upon the Federal Rules of Civil Procedure (FRCP). The Federal Rules of Civil Procedure "govern the procedure in the United States district courts in all suits of a civil nature."[3] The Federal Rules will be the focus of the discussions in this chapter. (See Appendix Q for the full text of the most important Federal Rules of Civil Procedure.)

Example 2.1

You are involved in a products liability lawsuit that has been filed in the U.S. District Court for the District of Massachusetts, in Boston. The Federal Rules of Civil Procedure and any local rules of the District of Massachusetts will govern the lawsuit. Had the suit been filed in a Massachusetts state court, the Massachusetts Rules of Civil Procedure would have governed. Which rules apply could affect things such as what type of disclosure you as an expert will be required to make under discovery, which party is responsible for paying the fee for your expert deposition, and what information will be protected from discovery.

2.2 Complaint

A lawsuit begins or is *commenced* when a document called a *complaint* is filed with the court.[4] Generally, an attorney can file the complaint personally by going to the clerk's office in the courthouse, or she can mail the complaint to the clerk. The time of filing can be critically important because the statute of limitation tolls at the commencement of an action. To avoid being barred by the statute of limitations, a party needs to file the lawsuit before the statute runs.

---

[1] 91 U.S. 367, 375.

[2] Steven H. Gifts, *Law Dictionary,* (1984) 368.

[3] Fed. R. Civ. Pro. 1.

[4] Fed. R. Civ. Pro. 3.

A complaint is a document that sets out, in a plain and simple way, the facts on which the plaintiff's claim for relief is based. The complaint, as with all court documents, begins with the *caption,* which states the name of the court, the docket number, and the names of the various parties to the lawsuit. Next, the complaint contains numbered paragraphs stating the facts that the plaintiff alleges. The complaint concludes with a prayer for relief, a demand for a jury trial (if available), and the signature of the plaintiff's attorney or the plaintiff if the plaintiff is *pro se* (a pro se plaintiff is a plaintiff who represents himself). The purpose of the complaint is to define the lawsuit and put the defendant on notice as to why he is being sued. (A sample complaint from a personal injury case is included in Appendix E.)

Usually, the expert should request a copy of the complaint and other legal documents *(pleadings)* in the case from the attorney who retained him. By reviewing the complaint, the expert will be able to understand quickly who is being sued, by whom they are being sued, and what the plaintiff in the case is alleging. All of this information will allow the expert to have a better understanding of the case and can help him to be a more effective witness.

2.3 Service of Process

After the complaint is *filed* with the court, the plaintiff's attorney still needs to have it *served* on the defendant(s). The various methods of service of process vary from jurisdiction to jurisdiction. The methods include in-hand delivery by a sheriff or process server, deposit at the last and usual place of abode, and service via the U.S. Postal Service. Court rules will usually limit the amount of time the plaintiff's attorney can wait between filing the complaint and perfecting service of process. It is generally permissible, however, to serve the complaint after the statute of limitations has run. In such a case, the suit will generally not be barred as long as the case was commenced, prior to the running of the statute of limitations.

2.4 Answers and Pre-Answer Motions

Once the defendant has been served with a complaint, he has only a certain amount of time (20 days under the Federal Rules[5]) to file an *answer* or a pre-answer *motion to dismiss.*[6] Failure to respond in the applicable time period can result in a *default judgment* being entered against the defendant. A default judgment means that the defendant is held by the court to have lost the lawsuit for failure to respond in a timely manner. To avoid a default judgment, a defendant should immediately notify his personal attorney and insurance company if he is sued.

The various bases for pre-answer motions to dismiss include: lack of jurisdiction over the subject matter, lack of jurisdiction over the person,

[5] Fed. R. Civ. Pro. 12(a)(1)(A).

[6] Fed. R. Civ. Pro. 12(b).

improper venue, insufficiency of service of process, and failure to state a claim upon which relief can be granted. If any of these motions are granted, the complaint will be dismissed. (However, in some cases, the plaintiff could be allowed by the court to refile or amend the complaint and try again.) An example of circumstances where each of these motions may be a valid basis for dismissal of a suit is provided in Box 2.41

Box 2.41

1. **Lack of jurisdiction over the subject matter:** A plaintiff files a personal injury suit in the United States Tax Court.
2. **Lack of jurisdiction over the person:** A professional lives in New York, does no business in California and solicits no clients or business in California. The professional owns no property in California and has never even been to California. A former client who retained the professional in New York moves to California and files a malpractice suit against the professional in the U.S. District Court in Los Angeles.
3. **Improper venue:** A plaintiff and defendant live and work in county X of state A. The plaintiff sues the defendant by filing suit in county Y of state A.
4. **Insufficiency of service of process:** A defendant is sued. The complaint is left by the process server on the doorstep of a neighbor of the defendant's house.
5. **Failure to state a claim upon which relief may be granted:** A physician is working in an emergency room in 1998 and saves patient X's life. Two years later, patient X murders a father of three, Mr. Y. Mr. Y's family now sues the physician under the theory that the physician caused Y's death by saving X's life in 1998.

The *answer* is the document the defendant files as a response to the complaint. In the answer, the defendant responds to each and every numbered paragraph in the complaint by a) admitting the allegation, b) denying the allegation, or c) stating that he lacks sufficient knowledge to admit or deny the allegation. The answer will also list any *affirmative defenses* that the defendant may be asserting. These include defenses such as statute of limitations, consent, workers' compensation exclusivity, self-defense, and comparative negligence. A defendant asserting an affirmative defense is in effect saying, "Even assuming everything you allege is true, you still cannot prevail because...the statute of limitations has run, you were negligent yourself, I was acting in self-defense, etc." (A sample answer is provided in Appendix F.)

The expert should ask her retaining attorney to provide her with a copy of the answer. This document is part of the pleadings. By reviewing the answer, the expert will be able to understand which factual issues are in dispute in a case and will learn what affirmative defenses the defendant is asserting. For example, the expert may learn that one of the defendant's affirmative defenses is that he is alleging that the plaintiff herself was negligent, such that her claim should be barred.

2.5 Counterclaims, Cross-Claims, and Third-Party Actions

The defendant is allowed to sue the plaintiff back. If the defendant would like to assert a claim of his own against the plaintiff, he would include a *counterclaim* in the answer. For example, let's say a defendant is involved in an automobile accident at an intersection with a traffic light. The defendant claims that her light was green and the plaintiff claims that *his* light was green. Both the defendant and the plaintiff were injured in the accident. The plaintiff sues the defendant for his personal injuries. The defendant can now sue the *plaintiff* for the defendant's personal injuries by including a counterclaim in her answer.

There are two important things to remember about counterclaims. First, they can be very effective in leveraging concessions from a plaintiff. This is especially true if the plaintiff owns property and does not carry liability insurance covering the counterclaim. Second, some counterclaims are *compulsory*. A compulsory counterclaim is waived forever if not brought forward by the defendant as part of the lawsuit when he is being sued. Compulsory counterclaims are governed under Fed. R. Civ. Pro. 13, a portion of which is reprinted below in Box 2.51.

Box 2.51

Fed. R. Civ. Pro. 13. Counterclaim and Cross-Claim
A pleading shall state as a counterclaim any claim which at the time of serving the pleading the pleader has against any opposing party, if it arises out of the transaction or occurrence that is the subject matter of the opposing party's claim and does not require for its adjudication the presence of third parties of whom the court cannot acquire jurisdiction.

In the automobile accident example above, the defendant's personal injury claim against the plaintiff would be a compulsory counterclaim because it arose out of the transaction or occurrence that is the subject of the plaintiff's suit, namely, the automobile accident. The rationale for the compulsory counterclaim rule is that judicial economy is achieved by avoiding the relitigation of disputed facts.

If a defendant would like to assert a claim against a co-defendant, she would do so by means of a *cross-claim*. For example, let's suppose that three physicians who operated on a patient are sued for medical malpractice. The three physicians, depending upon the facts and circumstances of the case, may file cross-claims against one another for contribution and/or indemnification.

In effect, the defendants are trying to blame and collect money from each other if they are found to be liable to the plaintiff.

If a defendant feels that a person who is not a subject of the lawsuit is responsible for the plaintiff's harm, she can bring this person into the lawsuit by means of a *third-party action*. The person so brought into the case would then be called the *third-party defendant*. Let's reconsider the three physicians sued for malpractice. Suppose that four physicians had operated on the plaintiff, but only three were sued because the fourth physician was the plaintiff's father-in-law. If any of the other three physicians felt that the fourth physician was in any way responsible for the harm caused to the plaintiff, that defendant could bring the fourth physician into the lawsuit as a third-party defendant.

Counsel may seek an expert's opinion to assist in a claim, counterclaim, cross-claim, or third-party action. Many cases have all of these elements and multiple parties. An effective expert witness needs to understand which portion or portions of a lawsuit his opinion is being used in. He can gather this information from the pleadings and by asking retaining counsel to explain who the parties to the case are and who is suing whom for what.

2.6 Discovery

Discovery is the process by which a party to a lawsuit can find out information held by another party to the lawsuit or third-party witnesses. There are various methods of discovery including: depositions, interrogatories, requests for admissions, requests for production of documents, inspection of real evidence, and medical examinations. Once a lawsuit has been commenced, the parties to the suit are allowed to use these discovery methods to gather information. (The discovery process is discussed in greater detail in Chapter 3.)

2.7 Motions

A *motion* is an application to the court requesting an order or rule in favor of the applicant.[7] When attorneys ask the court to do something, they do so by making a motion. Motions can be either oral or written. There are certain common motions that all experts should understand. These include: motions to dismiss, motions for a directed verdict, motions for judgment notwithstanding the verdict, motions for continuances, motions in limine, and motions for summary judgment. The purpose of each of these common motions is briefly described in Box 2.71.

[7] See 347 S.W.2d 211, 216.

Box 2.71

Motion to dismiss: The moving party is requesting that a cause of action be dismissed because the alleged facts, even if proven, do not constitute a valid legal claim.
Motion for a directed verdict: The moving party requests at trial that a cause of action be dismissed because the party with the burden of proof has failed to establish sufficient facts so that a reasonable fact finder (e.g., the jury) could find in the claimant's favor. For example, in a complex toxic tort case, the plaintiff's only expert witness is barred from testifying as to causation under the *Daubert* rule. After the plaintiff rests, the defense moves for a directed verdict on the grounds that the plaintiff has not submitted sufficient proof of causation through an expert witness.
Motion for judgment notwithstanding the verdict: This motion is made by the losing party *after* an adverse jury verdict. The moving party is asking that the judge reverse the verdict of the jury. These motions may be granted if the judge determines that the jury verdict had no reasonable support in fact or was contrary to law.[8]
Motion for a continuance: The moving party is requesting that a scheduled event, for example a hearing or trial, be postponed or *continued* to a later date.
Motion in limine: The moving party is requesting that evidence that it expects the opposing side to offer be held inadmissible. For example, a party may make a motion in limine to exclude the testimony of an expert for failure to comply with the *Daubert* rule. (See Chapter 9 on the *Daubert* rule.)
Motion for summary judgment: The moving party is requesting, prior to trial, and based solely on documentary evidence (including expert deposition transcripts, reports, and affidavits), that the court grant judgment in its favor because no material facts are in dispute.[9] This is a device used to throw a case out of court without it ever getting to the jury. Many times a lawyer with a weak case will seek to survive summary judgment in order to be able to settle the case on favorable terms over the threat of a jury trial.

2.8 Trial

Cases that do not settle or are not resolved through a pre-trial procedure, such as a motion to dismiss or a motion for summary judgment, will need to be tried. To be effective, experts must be familiar with common trial procedures. (These procedures are discussed in Chapter 4, Anatomy of a Civil Trial.)

2.9 Remedies

The remedy that a litigant seeks in a civil lawsuit is usually money damages or court orders. In personal injury cases *special damages,* or "specials," refer to

[8] See 170 S.W.2d 303, 306.
[9] See Fed. R. Civ. Pro. 56.

easily determinable damages, such as medical bills and lost wages. *General damages* refer to all other damages, for example, damages for pain and suffering. Interest may also be applied to an award for money damages. *Punitive damages* are damages awarded for the sole purpose of punishing the defendant. These damages are not based on the harm suffered by the plaintiff but are based on the defendant's conduct and economic situation. Punitive damages are generally only available if they are specifically authorized by statute. Note that intentional tort damages and damages from drunk driving are generally *not* dischargeable in bankruptcy.

2.10 Interest and Costs

The prevailing party in a lawsuit seeking money damages may also be awarded interest and/or costs. Attorney's fees are generally not recoverable unless they are specifically authorized by a statute or a pre-existing contractual relationship between the parties. Interest is awarded, depending upon the jurisdiction, from the time of the accrual of a cause of action[10] or from the time of verdict. For example, suppose Dr. Jones, a physician, commits malpractice on a plaintiff/patient on January 1, 1998. On January 1, 2000, the plaintiff is awarded $1,000,000 in damages plus interest and costs. If interest is calculated at a simple 10% per year and accrues from time of accrual of the cause of action, then $200,000 will be added to this $1,000,000 judgment. This interest will continue to accrue until the judgment is paid. Costs could include out-of-pocket expenses, such as expert witness fees, filing fees, deposition costs, and photocopying.

2.11 Court Orders

Court orders are also known as *injunctions* or *equitable relief*. Equitable relief is not always available, but in some cases it may be the most appropriate remedy. For example, let's say a professional signs an employment contract including a two-year covenant not to compete. One year into the contract, the professional breaks his contract and sets up a competing practice across the street from his former employer. An appropriate remedy for the professional's former employer may be an injunction ordering the professional to refrain from running the competing practice. If the professional violates this order, he could be held in contempt and fined a certain amount of money for each day of violation. Note that there is generally no right to a jury trial when the plaintiff seeks equitable relief. It will be a judge, and not a jury, who grants an injunction.

2.12 Appeals

Generally, appeals may only be taken after a final judgment in a case. For example, say an expert is testifying in a case and is asked, over her retaining

---

[10] When it accrues from the accrual of the cause of action, this is known as *prejudgment interest*.

attorney's objections, to submit tax returns from the last three years into evidence. The judge overrules the objection and allows the question. The expert's retaining attorney will not be allowed to appeal this ruling until after the jury has reached an adverse judgment. *Interlocutory appeals* are appeals heard before a final judgment in a case. Interlocutory appeals are only allowed under limited circumstances.

Appellate courts generally only review questions of law, not of fact. They generally do not hear testimony and do not rule on the credibility of witnesses. Therefore, a case is not retried on appeal. The appellate court will decide if an error of law has been made based on the written arguments of the parties in their *appellate briefs,* the content of the record (i.e., the pleadings, exhibits, and testimony transcripts), and oral arguments of the attorneys (if allowed). The remedies granted by an appeals court include a vacated judgment with an order *remanding* the case back to the trial court for further action, usually another trial or a reversal or modification of the trial court's verdict of the judgment that was entered. **Because cases are not retried on appeal, expert witnesses need to be perfect at trial.** If an expert witness makes a mistake on the stand, she will not be afforded the opportunity to testify again before the appellate court.

Even if the appellate court determines that an error of law was made by the trial judge, this does not mean that the appellate court must reverse the trial court's judgment. Under the *harmless error rule* the appellate court will only reverse a judgment if a substantial right of a party was affected.[11] The harmless error rule is another reason why experts need to perform as well as possible at trial. Even if the case is appealed and the issue under appeal has merit, the appellate court could deny the appeal under the harmless error doctrine. Because appeals are difficult to win and are subject to the harmless error doctrine, it is important that experts minimize the mistakes they make at trial.

When a litigant is awarded money damages, this is done by means of a *judgment.* For example, let's say that a plaintiff wins a $1,000,000 action against a defendant. A judgment for $1,000,000 would be entered in the court records in favor of the plaintiff and against the defendant. A judgment is not a court order to pay the damages. For example, if the defendant does not have insurance or $1,000,000 in assets, he will not be held in contempt of court for failure to pay. In many cases, a defendant against whom a judgment has been entered can discharge his obligation to pay after filing for bankruptcy.

2.13 Conclusion

An expert who understands the fundamental elements of a lawsuit is well positioned to be effective and successful.

---

[11] Fed. R. Civ. Pro. 61.

Chapter 3 The Discovery Process

3.1 Introduction

The rules of civil procedure generally provide for very liberal, broad-based discovery. There are two rationales for the liberal discovery procedures that dominate today's civil lawsuit: the elimination of surprise at trial and the encouragement of settlement. The theory is that if all parties know all there is to know about the other side's case (including their experts and their experts' opinions), they will be able to evaluate rationally the merits and weaknesses of the case and settle the matter. Additionally, if the suit does go to trial, the outcome will be less dependent on gamesmanship because the possibility of unfair surprises has been minimized through the discovery process.

Expert witnesses need to understand and appreciate that the rules of civil procedure permit broad-based discovery. It is these broad-based and liberal discovery rules that allow counsel to ask far-ranging questions at deposition, to go on "fishing expeditions," and to subpoena documents and tangible things that are in one's care, custody, or control. It is presumed by the law that allowing liberal discovery will encourage settlement and eliminate surprises at trial. Because over 90% of cases settle before trial, these liberal discovery rules can be judged to be serving much of their purpose.

3.2 Scope

The scope of discovery is delineated in Fed. R. Civ. Pro. 26(b)(1).

Box 3.21

Fed. R. Civ. Pro. 26(b)(1).
Parties may obtain discovery regarding any matter, not privileged, which is relevant to the subject matter involved in the pending action, whether it relates to the claim or defense of the party seeking discovery or to the claim or defense of any other party, including the existence, description, nature, custody, condition, and location of any books, documents, or other tangible things and the identity and location of any persons having knowledge of any discoverable matter. The information sought need not be admissible at trial if the information sought appears reasonably calculated to lead to the discovery of admissible evidence.

The broad-based nature of Rule 26 must be kept in mind when one serves as an expert in a case. Note that under Rule 26 the information sought need not even be admissible at trial. The discovery rules permit the acquisition of a broad range of information.

Example 3.1
You are a sixty-two-year-old physician who has been retained by the defense to testify regarding an IME you performed on a plaintiff who has been involved in a motor vehicle accident. You are deposed by the plaintiff's attorney. The plaintiff's attorney spends forty-five minutes asking you every place you have lived and worked since you were sixteen years old. Such "fishing expedition" questions are generally allowable because of the broad-based discovery made available under Rule 26. The attorney asking such questions could argue that the questions may reveal information about your background that could be relevant to your credibility as a witness. If you serve as an expert witness in a case, your credibility is always a legitimate issue. Your experience and qualifications are relevant to your credibility.

Example 3.2
Ragge v. MCA/Universal, 165 F.R.D. 601 (C.D. Cal. 1995)
The purpose of discovery is to remove surprise from trial preparation so parties obtain evidence necessary to evaluate and resolve their dispute; toward this end, FRCP 26(b) is liberally interpreted to permit wide-ranging discovery of all information reasonably calculated to lead to discovery of admissible evidence, even though discoverable information need not be admissible at trial.

Example 3.3
Bockweg v. Anderson, 117 F.R.D. 563 (M.D. N.C. 1987)
Defendants in medical malpractice actions would be permitted to depose plaintiffs' expert witnesses regarding their prior or present involvement in other malpractice actions, in conformity with the purpose of Rule 26, which sanctions liberal discovery of expert witnesses, including information relevant only for impeachment.

Example 3.4
Michael v. Gates, 45 Cal. Rptr. 163 (Cal. App. 1995)
Personnel files of a retired Los Angeles police officer who was testifying as an expert witness were discoverable.

Example 3.5
Ceramic Corp. of Am. v. Inka Maritime Corp., 163 F.R.D. 584 (C.D. Cal. 1995)
Information regarding an expert's employment as master, including reprimands or disciplinary proceedings, were relevant and discoverable, but family, health, and financial documents were not.

3.3 Privilege

Rule 26(b)(1) provides that discovery may not be made of "privileged" matters. These include the attorney-client, husband-wife, and physician-patient privileges. An expert witness should check with an attorney in her jurisdiction if she is asked through discovery to disclose information that she feels may be privileged.

Example 3.6
You are an expert witness in a controversial case. At deposition, the opposing attorney asks you if you have discussed the case and the testimony you intend to give with your spouse. Such a question could call for information protected by the husband-wife privilege. The attorney who retained you might instruct you not to answer this question because it calls for such privileged information.

3.4 Other Limits to Discovery

Although discovery is broad-based, it is not unlimited. As has already been discussed, privileged information is not discoverable. There are further limitations to discovery as well. Consider Rule 26(b)(2).

Box 3.41

Fed. R. Civ. Pro. 26(b)(2).
The frequency or extent of use of the discovery methods otherwise permitted under these rules and by any local rule shall be limited by the court if it determines that: (i) the discovery sought is unreasonably cumulative or duplicative, or it is obtainable through some other source that is more convenient, less burdensome, or less expensive; (ii) the party seeking discovery has had ample opportunity by discovery in the action to obtain the information sought; or (iii) the burden or expense of the proposed discovery outweighs its likely benefit, taking into account the needs of the case, the amount in controversy, the parties' resources, the importance of the issues at stake in the litigation, and the importance of the proposed discovery in resolving the issues.

Example 3.7
You are sued by your office cleaning company. The cleaning company alleges that you haven't paid $3,000 of their bills. Your position is that the company's work was of very poor quality. The cleaning company serves your attorney with a discovery request requesting, among other things, "all invoices and canceled checks" to and from the cleaning company for the last five years and "any and all other documents relating to the running" of your office for the last five years. You may be able to use Rule 26(b)(2) to attempt to limit your disclosure to the invoices and canceled checks.

Attorney *work product* is generally nondiscoverable. This exception to discovery is designed to allow the adversary process to function properly. The work product exception to discovery is governed by Federal Rule 26(b)(3) and Rule 26(b)(4). An expert needs to remember that, generally speaking, if she is disclosed as an expert who will testify at trial, she will need to respond to the other parties' discovery requests for documents and other information. If, on the other hand, she is not disclosed as an expert who will testify at trial but is merely a *litigation consultant,* she will generally not be subject to discovery by the other parties in the case. Because the work-product doctrine provides little protection from discovery to experts who are to testify at trial, such experts should be very careful about creating any documents or correspondence that may damage their credibility. **If an expert expects to be called at trial, she should assume that everything she writes regarding the case, even if she labels it "confidential," will be subject to discovery and disclosure.** (Confidentiality and work product are discussed in greater detail in Chapter 21.)

Box 3.42

Fed. R. Civ. Pro. 26(b)(3). Trial Preparation Materials
Subject to the provisions of subdivision (b)(4) of this rule, a party may obtain discovery of documents and tangible things otherwise discoverable under subdivision (b)(1) of this rule and prepared in anticipation of litigation or for trial by or for another party or by or for that other party's representative (including the other party's attorney, consultant, surety, indemnitor, insurer, or agent) only upon a showing that the party seeking discovery has substantial need of the materials in the preparation of the party's case and that the party is unable without undue hardship to obtain the substantial equivalent of the materials by other means. In ordering discovery of such materials when the required showing has been made, the court shall protect against disclosure of the mental impressions, conclusions, opinions, or legal theories of an attorney or other representative of a party concerning the litigation.

Box 3.43

Fed. R. Civ. Pro. 26(b)(4). Trial Preparation: Experts
(A) A party may depose any person who has been identified as an expert whose opinions may be presented at trial. If a report from the expert is required under subdivision (a)(2)(B), the deposition shall not be conducted until after the report is provided.
(B) A party may, through interrogatories or by deposition, discover facts known or opinions held by an expert who has been retained or specially employed by another party in anticipation of litigation or preparation for trial and who is not expected to be called as a witness at trial, only as provided in Rule 35(b) or upon a showing of exceptional circumstances under which it is impracticable for the party seeking discovery to obtain facts or opinions on the same subject by other means.
(C) Unless manifest injustice would result, (i) the court shall require that the party seeking discovery pay the expert a reasonable fee for time spent in responding to discovery under this subdivision; and (ii) with respect to discovery obtained under subdivision (b)(4)(B) of this rule the court shall require the party seeking discovery to pay the other party a fair portion of the fees and expenses reasonably incurred by the latter party in obtaining facts and opinions from the expert.

Example 3.8
You are retained as a consultant (the attorney does not intend to call you as a witness at trial) by the plaintiff in a case. You review the records in question and issue a written report to the plaintiff's attorney stating that you have found no evidence of negligence. The plaintiff then discharges you and finds another expert witness who plans to testify at trial that negligence did in fact occur. Generally, your report will not be discoverable and the opposing sides will not be allowed to call you as a witness at trial.

Example 3.9
You are obtained as an expert witness and are expected to give testimony at trial. You send a confidential written report to the attorney that retained you. Generally, there is no protection against disclosure through discovery of this "confidential" report. The work-product doctrine does not operate to prevent discovery because the attorney intends to call you as a witness at trial.

Example 3.10
You are retained as a consultant on a case in which a victim has died. You perform an examination of the body and issue a report to the retaining attorney. The body is then interred and the plaintiff finds another expert to testify at trial. The defense may be able to use Rule 26(b)(4) to force discovery of your otherwise nondiscoverable report. The defense could argue that the "exceptional circumstances" mentioned in Rule 26(b)(4) apply to a case such as this one because the other side would need to disinter the body to obtain the information by other means.

3.5 Protective Orders

Protective orders are allowed to prevent possible abuses that could occur through the rules of discovery. The court has discretion to issue *protective orders* to protect a party or person from "annoyance, embarrassment, oppression or undue burden or expense."[1] The court can also issue protective orders to protect "a trade secret, or other confidential research, development, or commercial information."[2] Protective orders are issued after a motion is made by the person or party seeking the order. A person need not be a party to the lawsuit to seek a protective order. The granting of a protective order is within the court's sound discretion. When granting a protective order, the court may rule that the discovery be limited or disallowed, rule that the discovery only be made available to certain persons, or limit the method of discovery used.[3]

Example 3.11
You are a fifty-five-year-old professional who is to be called as an expert witness in a case. The opposing side subpoenas your personal income tax

---

[1] Fed. R. Civ. Pro. 26(c).
[2] Fed. R. Civ. Pro. 26(c)(7).
[3] Fed. R. Civ. Pro. 26(c).

returns from the last five years in an effort to establish bias. To protect yourself from the release of these sensitive documents, you can file a motion with the court for a protective order. In response to such a motion, the court could issue a protective order stating that you need not produce the returns or that the returns be held in confidence by the opposing side.

Example 3.12
State ex rel. Creighton v. Jackson, 879 S.W.2d 639 (Mo. Ct. App. 1994)
The court of appeals held that the trial court did not abuse its discretion by requiring an expert witness to produce portions of his federal income tax returns reflecting income received for service as an expert witness or consultant over a five-year period. However, the court did not determine the admissibility of the records at trial—rather, it noted that the information would be admissible at trial only if it reflected legitimately on the expert's objectivity.

Example 3.13
Grinnell Corp. v. Hackett, 70 F.R.D. 326 (D.C. R.I. 1976)
Showing that likelihood of harassment was "more probable than not" would be insufficient to warrant a protective order against discovery without concomitantly showing that the information sought was fully irrelevant and could have no possible bearing on issues.

3.6 Sanctions

If a party, deponent, or attorney unjustifiably refuses to disclose requested information, the party seeking the information can make a *motion to compel* the party or deponent to provide the requested discovery. If the motion to compel is granted, the party seeking the discovery may also seek sanctions against the party, deponent, and/or attorney refusing to provide the discovery. The potential sanctions include the costs of bringing the motion to compel, including attorney's fees. If the motion to compel is *denied*, the party and/or attorney bringing the motion to compel may be ordered by the court to pay the attorney's fees and costs of the person or party from whom discovery is sought. Sanctions can also be granted that affect the substance of a case. For example, if a plaintiff fails to answer interrogatories or produce requested documents in the time specified by the rules, the court could enter judgment in favor of the defendant or bar the plaintiff from introducing certain evidence.

Example 3.14
You have been retained by a plaintiff to provide expert testimony. The defendant is represented by the largest law firm in your city. The firm charges $350 per hour. At deposition, you are asked by the annoying defense lawyer in his $2,000 suit how much money you earned last year and what percentage of that income was derived from expert witness work. You are offended that he would ask such a personal question and respond, "That's none of your business." He asks again and you still refuse to answer. By refusing to answer this question, you are taking a risk of sanctions. If the defense files a motion to compel you to answer and this motion is granted, you may be forced to pay the

defense's attorneys' fees ($350 per hour) associated with bringing this motion to compel.

Example 3.15

Cooper v. Lewis, 719 So.2d 944 (Fla. App. 1998)

> Our inquiry is limited to what the appropriate sanction is, what the proper procedure for that sanction is, and against whom such sanction may be imposed when the expert fails to comply with a proper request. In our case, the doctor who performed the IME appeared at his deposition without the requested information relating to his past experience as one who provides IMEs. The doctor stated that because of short notice he did not have the information available.
>
> When it is disclosed or made apparent to the trial court that such a witness has falsified, misrepresented, or obfuscated the required data, the aggrieved party may move to exclude the witness from testifying, or further, move for the imposition of costs and attorneys fees in gathering the information necessary to expose the miscreant expert.
>
> Even if the doctor wrongfully withheld the requested information, there appears to be no authority for sanctioning an innocent defendant, particularly in a personal injury action. If the plaintiff, at the direction of his lawyer, goes to a doctor, knowing the doctor will find permanent injuries when there are none, then the plaintiff, his lawyer, and his doctor have conspired to work a fraud on the court and, upon proper proof, all should be subject to sanctions. But in this case, the defendant is not alleged to have committed any wrong. He didn't choose the doctor. For that matter, in a large majority of such cases, the defendant doesn't even choose the lawyer.
>
> The trial court erred in striking the doctor from defendant's witness list because of procedural irregularities and because the record does not support a finding of willful violation (contempt) or a violation of a court order. The court erred in assessing attorney's fees and costs against the defendant because the record does not support the imposition of sanctions against him.

Example 3.16

Rockwell International, Inc. v. Pos-A-Traction Industries, Inc., 712 F.2d 1324 (9th Cir. 1983)

If a motion to compel discovery of a deponent who is not a party is granted, the deponent may be required to pay the moving party's reasonable expenses unless opposition to the motion was substantially justified. Here, a nonparty witness agreed to have his deposition taken for use in two separate cases—a state action and a federal action by the same plaintiff. When the opposing attorney in the state action had completed his questions, the witness, on the advice of counsel, refused to answer questions by the opposing attorney in the federal action on the theory that no more than one attorney may propound questions on behalf of the same party at the taking of a deposition. The court found that the refusal to answer was unjustified and that the plaintiff could be awarded reasonable expenses incurred in obtaining an order compelling the witness to submit to discovery. These expenses were awarded against the witness and the witness's attorney, who had advised him not to answer.

Example 3.17
Waicis v. Superior Court, 226 Cal. App. 3d 283 (Cal. App. Dist. 1 1990)
In this medical malpractice case, the plaintiff's expert on standard of care, a DMD, refused to cooperate in the taking of his deposition. The expert forced a rescheduling of his deposition six times, often with little notice, and insisted that it be scheduled in the evenings and at awkward times. In the middle of a Saturday deposition, after "clear representation to the trial court that [the expert] would be available all Saturday," the expert claimed he had a personal appointment and left the deposition. The appellate court stated, "The trial court did everything it could to permit Dr. Frankel's deposition but the witness simply would not cooperate, even to the extent of directly violating the court's order that he be available for all of Saturday for his deposition." Additionally, it declared, "Not only is the evidence that [the expert] was uncooperative in permitting his deposition to be taken substantial, it is overwhelming."

The court approved the trial court's exclusion of the expert's testimony and awarded costs to the defendant, stating: "It is an affront to the orderly and expeditious disposition of cases for any witness, especially an expert witness, to be so uncooperative... [the expert's] conduct smacks of game playing."

3.7 Methods of Discovery

There are several forms of discovery allowed under the Federal Rules of Civil Procedure. These include interrogatories, requests for production of documents, depositions, subpoenas duces tecum, physical examinations, production of tangible things, and entry upon land. Each of these discovery methods is discussed below.

Interrogatories

Interrogatories are written questions that are served on another party in the case. They must be answered by the party (not the expert), in writing and under oath. Interrogatories generally are only served on parties to an action. Therefore, a witness who is not a party in a case will usually not have to answer the interrogatories. (A sample set of interrogatories, with answers, is provided in Appendix G.)

The number of interrogatories one party can propound to another is limited under the Rules of Civil Procedure. For example, under the Federal Rules, a party is limited to twenty-five.[4] There is also a fixed time period within which the interrogatories must be answered. Under the Federal Rules, this period is thirty days.[5] These time periods may be extended by agreement between the parties or a court order. The failure to answer interrogatories within the applicable time period can result in judgment being entered against the party who fails to respond.

In most lawsuits each party will ask, through interrogatories, certain questions about the other side's expert witnesses. The interrogatories will

[4] Fed. R. Civ. Pro. 33(a).
[5] Fed. R. Civ. Pro. 33(b)(3).

commonly ask for the name and address of the expert, a summary of her qualifications, and a summary of her opinions along with the facts upon which those opinions are based. The expert's interrogatories may also call for the expert's publications, a listing of any other trials the expert has testified in during the last four years, and the compensation paid to the expert for work in the case. Expert witnesses should be aware that they may have to provide this information to the retaining attorney so that he can advise his client on how to answer any interrogatory seeking said information. Failure to do so could result in a judgment being entered against the party who retained the expert or other sanctions, such as the expert being barred from testifying as an expert in the case.

Requests for production of documents

These may only be served upon a party to the lawsuit[6] and thus will generally not be served on experts. There is a time limit to respond of thirty days under the Federal Rules.[7] Failure to respond within the applicable time can result in sanctions being assessed against the party failing to produce the documents. The party requesting the documents only has a right to "inspect and copy" the requested documents, he does not have the right to keep the originals.[8] (A sample request for production of documents is provided in Appendix H.)

Depositions

Depositions are arguably the most powerful form of discovery allowed. Any person can be deposed, the person need not be a party in the lawsuit. In addition, depositions allow for all-important follow-up questions. The ability to ask follow-up questions makes depositions a far more powerful information gathering tool than interrogatories. (A sample deposition transcript of an expert witness is provided in Appendix J.) The vast majority of expert testimony is provided by way of a deposition rather than live testimony at trial. (Depositions are discussed in much greater detail in Chapter 13.)

Subpoenas duces tecum

A *subpoena duces tecum* is a legal document requiring the person on whom it is served to provide specified documents for inspection and copying. The person responding to the subpoena is usually allowed to charge the requesting party for reasonable copying costs. Subpoenas duces tecum are the discovery method that attorneys use to gain access to documents that are in the possession of persons who are not parties to a lawsuit, such as expert witnesses. As with any discovery, unjustifiable failure to comply with a subpoena duces tecum can result in sanctions against the noncomplying

---

[6] Fed. R. Civ. Pro. 34(a).
[7] Fed. R. Civ. Pro. 34(b).
[8] Fed. R. Civ. Pro. 34(a).

person. On the other hand, if the subpoena seeks confidential, sensitive, or statutorily protected documents, a person can seek a protective order to stop disclosure of the requested document. In addition, the disclosure may also otherwise be prohibited by law. An expert should consult with a local attorney to determine which records he must produce in response to a subpoena duces tecum and which documents are protected from disclosure. (A sample schedule specifying the documents to be produced from a subpoena duces tecum is provided in Appendix I.)

Example 3.18

Orkin Exterminating Company, Inc. v. Knollwood Properties, Ltd., 710 So.2d 697 (Fla. App. 1998)

Orkin retained C. Douglas Mampe, PhD, as an expert entomologist. Knollwood served a notice of taking deposition of Dr. Mampe, which included the request that Dr. Mampe bring with him a list of all cases for the past ten years, including court case numbers, in which he had testified or conducted an investigation or prepared the reports as an expert witness. In his deposition, Dr. Mampe was asked if he had brought such a list with him. Dr. Mampe responded: "No. That's just an impossible job. I probably have thirty a year. Go back seventeen years, that's a lot of cases; and I don't keep track of them once the case has been settled, closed, or disposed of in one form or another."

On further questioning, it was clarified that Dr. Mampe did not necessarily testify in all of the cases in which he was engaged as an expert. The expert must supply this information if requested and if the expert wishes to testify in a Florida court.

The court ordered the expert to produce a list, even if the only source was financial and business records.

Example 3.19

United States v. 25.02 Acres of Land, 495 F.2d 1398 (10th Cir. 1974)

Under Rules 26, 34, and 45(b), the trial court did not err in quashing a portion of the landowners' subpoena duces tecum that sought from the government's expert appraisal witness production of all appraisal reports that he had prepared for use of other private owners of property in the vicinity of the condemned property.

Physical examinations

The rules of discovery allow for the physical examination of a party "when the mental or physical condition (including the blood group) of a party" is in controversy.[9] These are most commonly requested by the defense in personal injury actions and are called *independent medical evaluations* or *IMEs*. IMEs are also allowed under most workers' compensation statutes.

---

[9] Fed. R. Civ. Pro. 35(a).

Production of tangible things and entry upon land

The rules allow parties to "inspect and copy, test, or sample any tangible things within the scope of Rule 26(b) and which are in the possession, custody or control of the party upon which the request is served."[10] The rules further provide "entry upon designated land or other property in the possession or control of the party upon whom the request is served for the purpose of inspecting and measuring, surveying, photographing, testing, or sampling the property or any designated object or operation thereon, within the scope of Rule 26(b)."[11] Experts commonly assist counsel in the inspection of land and other tangible things.

Example 3.20
You are an expert in a slip and fall or defective product case. The rules of discovery can be used to gain you access to the site of the slip and fall or the defective product in question.

3.8 Conclusion

Discovery is broad-based, but it is not unlimited. Discovery violations may result in sanctions against the expert. Experts should have a general idea of the limits allowed under discovery and seek legal advice when they feel those limits are being breached. Experts should understand how the various methods of discovery can be used by each party in a case to gather information.

---

[10] Fed. R. Civ. Pro. 34(a).
[11] Fed. R. Civ. Pro. 34(a).

Chapter 4 Anatomy of a Civil Trial

4.1 Introduction

Although all civil trials involve judges, not all civil trials involve juries. A trial in which the judge acts as the finder of fact is called a *bench trial.* A trial in which the jury acts as the finder of fact is called a *jury trial.* In either, the judge will run the courtroom and make all legal rulings, including the admissibility of evidence (including expert testimony). The fact finder in the case weighs the evidence presented by each side, evaluates the credibility of the witnesses involved, and comes to a determination as to the facts that are in dispute.

Example 4.1
In a negligence suit, the jury will decide, based upon the evidence the judge allows it to hear, whether the defendant acted unreasonably as well as all other disputed questions of fact. The jury also decides the factual question of the plaintiff's damages, including pain and suffering. The judge in the negligence suit runs the trial, makes all necessary rulings, and instructs the jury on the law to apply during deliberations.

When an expert gives testimony, he should keep in mind whether the trial is to be a bench trial or a jury trial. If the trial is in front of a jury, the jurors are likely to be unsophisticated in technical matters, may be less educated than the expert, and will have a short attention span. The expert will need to tailor the delivery of his testimony accordingly. In a bench trial, the audience—the finder of fact—will be a judge who will be far more sophisticated than the average juror. Whether testifying before a judge or a jury, the expert must remember that his role is to assist or educate the judge or jury in matters that are beyond their general experience or comprehension.

4.2 Jury Selection and Pre-Trial Motions

A civil trial begins with jury selection (if the trial is a jury trial) and any pre-trial motions. Jury selection procedures vary from jurisdiction to jurisdiction. Generally speaking, the lawyers in the case will be able to exclude from the jury pool certain persons who are perceived to be biased. The lawyers can also exclude a certain number of jurors without stating a reason for their exclusion by using *preemptory challenges.* The number of preemptory challenges per side varies from jurisdiction to jurisdiction. Jury selection will continue until there are enough jurors left in the pool to fill the jury panel.

Prior to opening statements, the attorneys may choose to make pre-trial motions. The most common of these motions is a *motion in limine.* It is very important that experts understand the purpose, effect, and availability of motions in limine. A motion in limine is a motion that can be used to ask the court to exclude reference to anticipated evidence claimed to be objectionable.[1] The motion is made out of the jury's presence. Its purpose is to prevent any unfair prejudice that may occur if the evidentiary issue was ruled on in the presence of the jury.

Example 4.2
Suppose you are a recovered alcoholic and have been retained as an expert witness in a case. Your retaining attorney doesn't want the jury to know or even suspect that you are an alcoholic. Instead of making an objection during the trial when you are asked during cross-examination, "You're an alcoholic, aren't you?," your retaining attorney may make the motion in limine prior to trial. If granted, it would prevent the opposing counsel from asking you about being an alcoholic. Thus, the jury would never be aware, even by inference, that you are an alcoholic.

If there is personal information that an expert does not want to come out at trial, she needs to tell her retaining attorney about it as soon as possible. The attorney may be able to successfully file a motion in limine that orders the opposing side not to ask the expert about the information in question. If an expert does not disclose such information to her retaining attorney, however, it will be much more difficult for the attorney to try to protect the expert.

4.3 Opening Statements

After selecting a jury, a trial begins with the plaintiff making an *opening statement.* During the opening statement the attorneys are allowed to outline their theories of the case and preview the evidence they intend to present. Attorneys are not allowed to argue during the opening statement, they can only preview the evidence. A defendant may give an opening statement or may defer the opening until the conclusion of the plaintiff's case. Failure of the plaintiff to outline all of the facts necessary to prove the plaintiff's case can result in a *directed verdict* being entered against the plaintiff.[2]

Example 4.3
A physician is sued for malpractice. During opening statements the defendant's attorney stands up and states, "Ladies and gentlemen of the jury, physicians are not God. They should not be held responsible just because a patient has not recovered." The plaintiff's attorney objects. The judge is likely to strike this statement as being argumentative. During opening statements, the lawyers are not allowed to make arguments, they can only preview what the evidence will or will not show.

Example 4.4
During a kidney transplant operation, a physician mistakenly removed his patient's one good kidney. He is sued for malpractice. At trial, the plaintiff's

[1] 220 N.W.2d 919, 922.

[2] In practice, this harsh rule is rarely enforced by the court.

attorney makes her opening statement, which is, "Ladies and gentlemen of the jury, my client has been caused to suffer greatly because of the action of Dr. Jones. We will prove that Dr. Jones should not be practicing medicine and ask that you carefully listen to the evidence in this case. Thank you for taking the time out of your busy lives to serve on this panel." The defense attorney rises and moves for a directed verdict. In this case, no specific instance of negligence was alleged in the opening statement. A judge could very well grant this motion for a directed verdict and dismiss the plaintiff's case because a plaintiff's attorney needs to lay out all the elements of a valid cause of action.

4.4 Burden of Proof

The burden of proof in most civil cases is a *preponderance of the evidence.*[3] To satisfy this burden, the fact finder must be convinced that it was more likely than not that the event in question occurred. In percentage terms, the fact finder would have to believe that there was a 51% or greater probability that the event in question took place. Some issues in civil cases must be proven to a higher standard. This standard is usually *clear and convincing evidence.* There is no percentage number that can be assigned to this higher standard. If a claim must be proven by clear and convincing evidence, this standard is usually specified in a statute or administrative regulation and is imparted to the jury via jury instructions.

It is crucial that expert witnesses understand the burden of proof in civil cases. For the opinion of an expert to be admissible, it must satisfy the 51%, preponderance of the evidence, more likely than not standard explained above. Commonly accepted phrases used by experts to express these concepts include stating that their opinion is based upon "a reasonable degree of scientific (or medical) certainty." It is absolutely crucial that experts state their opinions in a legally sufficient manner. Failure to do so could result in the opinion being stricken from evidence by the judge as being speculative. (See Chapter 8 on opinions.)

4.5 Presentation of Evidence

After opening statements, the presentation of evidence will begin with the plaintiff calling its first witness. The plaintiff's case will continue until the plaintiff has called its last witness. After the plaintiff has called its last witness, the defense will be given an opportunity to call witnesses and present its case. Generally speaking, the witnesses each side intends to call at trial need to be disclosed to the other parties in advance. This practice allows parties to depose and seek discovery from the proposed witnesses prior to trial and helps eliminate surprises at trial. Conversely, a party may be prohibited from calling a witness at trial, especially an expert witness, if the witness's identity has not been disclosed sufficiently before trial.

---

[3] 397 U.S. 358.

4.6 Directed Verdicts

A *directed verdict* is a verdict entered by the court in a jury trial without consideration by the jury because the facts elicited during the trial, together with the applicable law, made it clear that the directed verdict was the only one that could have been reasonably returned.[4] When the judge directs a verdict she is in essence saying that, based on the evidence submitted, the directed verdict is the only possible one a reasonable jury could have determined. Directed verdicts are governed by Federal Rule 50(a). They are granted most often against the plaintiff at the close of the plaintiff's case. When plaintiff's attorneys speak of "getting over the rail" or "getting to the jury" they are referring to avoiding a directed verdict by having the judge decide to let the jury decide the case. In weak cases, plaintiffs often seek to "get to the jury" to either encourage a settlement or take a chance on a favorable jury verdict. Defendants sometimes settle after a directed verdict is denied rather than chance a jury verdict.

Box 4.61

Fed. R. Civ. Pro. 50(a). Judgment as a Matter of Law

(1) If during a trial by jury a party has been fully heard on an issue and there is no legally sufficient basis for a reasonable jury to find for that party on that issue, the court may determine that issue against that party and may grant a motion for a judgment as a matter of law against that party with respect to a claim or defense that cannot under the controlling law be maintained or defeated without a favorable finding on that issue.

Many plaintiff cases depend upon certain expert testimony to avoid the entry of a directed verdict against the plaintiff. For example, let's say a plaintiff sues the manufacturer of a common shampoo claiming that the shampoo caused his hair loss. Ms. Johnson is the plaintiff's only expert witness and she is prepared to testify, based upon a reasonable degree of scientific certainty, that the shampoo did in fact cause the hair loss. When Ms. Johnson is called to the stand, the defense raises a *Daubert* challenge (see Chapter 9) and the judge rules that she cannot testify. At the close of the plaintiff's case, the defense attorney makes a motion for a directed verdict. This motion would likely be granted because the court would probably conclude that no reasonable jury could find for the plaintiff without expert testimony that established that the shampoo caused the hair loss.

Experts must be aware of and understand directed verdicts. An expert should ask his retaining attorney up front what minimum testimony is needed to avoid a directed verdict and get to the jury. An expert who is not able to provide such testimony should let the retaining attorney know as soon as

---

[4] 123 F.2d 438, 440.

possible so that she can look for another expert, settle the case, or take other needed action to protect her client's interests.

4.7 Closing Arguments

After the close of evidence, each party will be allowed to make a *closing argument* or *summation* to the jury. The amount of time each party can spend for summation is decided by the judge. During summation, the parties are allowed to make arguments as to how the evidence that was presented should be interpreted.

4.8 Jury Deliberation and Decision

After summation, the judge will instruct the jury on the law it should apply in its deliberations. This is called *jury instruction.* Each of the parties will usually submit suggested jury instructions for the judge to consider. Some states require that the verdict be unanimous, others require only a specified majority, for example, ten of twelve jurors. The number of votes necessary to return a verdict in federal civil trials is governed by Federal Rule 48. Jury instructions are governed by Federal Rule 51.

Box 4.81

Fed. R. Civ. Pro. 48. Number of Jurors—Participation in Verdict
The court shall seat a jury of not fewer than six and not more than twelve members and all jurors shall participate in the verdict unless excused from service from the court pursuant to Rule 47(c). Unless the parties otherwise stipulate, (1) the verdict shall be unanimous and (2) no verdict shall be taken from a jury reduced in size to fewer than six members.

Box 4.82

Fed. R. Civ. Pro. 51. Instructions to Jury: Objection
At the close of evidence or at such earlier time during the trial as the court reasonably directs, any party may file written requests that the court instruct the jury on the law as set forth in the requests. The court shall inform counsel of its proposed action upon the requests prior to their arguments to the jury. The court, at its election, may instruct the jury before or after argument, or both. No party may assign as error the giving or the failure to give an instruction unless that party objects thereto before the jury retires to consider its verdict, stating distinctly the matter objected to and the grounds of the objection. Opportunity shall be given to make the objection out of the hearing of the jury.

4.9 Verdict or Mistrial

After it is instructed by the judge, the jury will deliberate on each and every claim that is still in issue (that is, that hasn't been disposed of by a directed verdict or other means) until it reaches a verdict or becomes deadlocked. The jury's verdict may be general or special. A *general verdict* is merely a finding for the plaintiff or defendant. A *special verdict* is a verdict that answers specific questions of fact that were posed to the jury by the court. For example, "Was there a design defect in product x?" Special verdicts are often requested and used where there is a chance that the jury will misunderstand and misapply the law if they are just asked to find for the plaintiff or defendant with a general verdict. If the jury is deadlocked, the judge will eventually declare a mistrial and the case will have to be retried.

4.10 Post-Verdict Motions

After the jury returns its verdict(s), the parties may choose to make post-trial motions. A common post-trial motion is a motion for judgment notwithstanding the verdict. A motion for *judgment notwithstanding the verdict*, or *judgment n.o.v.*, is essentially a motion for a directed verdict made after the jury has returned an adverse verdict. Under the Federal Rules, a prerequisite for making a j.n.o.v. motion is that a motion for a directed verdict was made and not granted. Under the Federal Rules, the motion must be filed no more than ten days after entry of judgment.[5] When a party files a j.n.o.v. motion, it is essentially asking the court to throw out the jury's verdict because no reasonable jury could have come to such a verdict.

After a jury verdict, a party may also make a *motion for a new trial.* This may be granted for "any of the reasons for which new trials have heretofore been granted in actions at law in the courts of the United States."[6] These reasons include irregularities in the proceedings, misconduct of the jury, newly discovered evidence, and insufficiency of evidence. A motion for a new trial must also be made within ten days of entry of judgment.[7] Motions for new trials and j.n.o.v.s are checks on runaway juries and jury nullification. The availability of such a motion means that litigants can lose at the trial court level even if the jury loved their experts and finds in their favor. The granting of, or failure to grant, post-trial motions is a question of law that can be argued on appeal in an effort to reverse the judge's decision.

4.11 Alternative Dispute Resolution

It is important to keep in mind that many disputes are no longer resolved through formal civil litigation in state or federal court. The cost and time required to prosecute lawsuits have driven many prospective litigants to resolve their differences through *alternative dispute resolution* or *ADR.* The most common forms of ADR are mediation and arbitration. Expert witnesses are used in varying ways in all forms of ADR.

Mediation is a form of ADR that involves the appointment of an agreed-upon third party to facilitate settlement negotiations. This third party

---

[5] Fed. R. Civ. Pro. 50(b).

[6] Fed. R. Civ. Pro. 59(a).

[7] Fed. R. Civ. Pro. 59(b).

is called the *mediator*. Cases can be submitted to mediation before or after suit has been filed. Mediation is a useful tool to use to reach a settlement to a disagreement. An important advantage of mediation is that the parties control the outcome and all resolutions are voluntary. If the parties do not wish to settle through mediation, they can still go to court. The quality of the expert witnesses on each side and the content of the testimony they intend to give at trial are important factors that affect how much a case will be settled for during mediation.

Arbitration is a process by which the parties in a dispute submit the dispute for resolution to an agreed-upon arbitrator (or panel of arbitrators).[8] The arbitrator is then the fact finder and decision maker. Arbitration rules of procedure vary, but are usually far less formal and strict than the rules of civil procedure and evidence. Arbitration is usually faster and cheaper than formal litigation in a court of law. Arbitration can be binding or non-binding. In *binding arbitration* the parties agree that the judgment of the arbitrator is final and can be enforced through court action. *High-low* arbitration involves setting limits on the amount of the arbitrator's award and is a way to place some control over the outcome. Experts may participate in arbitration by testifying live at the arbitration hearing or by submitting written affidavits containing their sworn opinions. When testifying at an arbitration hearing, experts need to keep in mind that the decision maker is an arbitrator who is generally far more sophisticated than the average juror. Usually, the arbitrator has experience in the matter at issue, for example, construction or environmental litigation.

4.12 Conclusion

Experts should have a basic understanding of the procedures of a civil trial This will allow the expert to coordinate better with retaining counsel and communicate more effectively with the trier of fact.

[8] Under some forms of arbitration the parties do not need to agree upon an arbitrator.

Chapter 5 Evidence

5.1 Introduction

The rules of evidence vary from jurisdiction to jurisdiction. Federal courts use the Federal Rules of Evidence (FRE). State courts have their own evidentiary rules, but, generally, these are based upon the Federal Rules. The Federal Rules will be the basis of the upcoming discussion of evidence.

Experts should have a basic understanding of the rules of evidence. Evidentiary matters are questions of law that are decided by the presiding trial judge. The judge will be governed by whichever rules of evidence apply in that particular jurisdiction. The purpose of the Federal Rules of Evidence is stated in Rule 102.

Box 5.11

Fed. R. Evid. 102. Purpose and Construction
These rules shall be construed to secure fairness in administration, elimination of unjustifiable expense and delay, and promotion of growth and development of the law of evidence to the end that the truth may be ascertained and proceedings justly determined.

The purpose of the Federal Rules is therefore to seek justice and the truth, but to do so fairly and in a manner that does not result in unjustifiable expense or delay.

5.2 The General Structure of Evidence Law

Rules 401, 402, and 403 define the general structure of the Federal Rules of Evidence.

Box 5.21

Fed. R. Evid. 401. Definition of "Relevant Evidence"
"Relevant evidence" means evidence having any tendency to make the existence of any fact that is of consequence to the determination of the action more probable or less probable than it would be without the evidence.

Box 5.22

Fed. R. Evid. 402. Relevant Evidence Generally Admissible; Irrelevant Evidence Inadmissible
All relevant evidence is admissible, except as otherwise provided by the Constitution of the United States, by Act of Congress, by these rules, or by other rules prescribed by the Supreme Court pursuant to statutory authority. Evidence which is not relevant is not admissible.

Box 5.23

Fed. R. Evid. 403. Exclusion of Relevant Evidence on Grounds of Prejudice, Confusion, or Waste of Time
Although relevant, evidence may be excluded if its probative value is substantially outweighed by the danger of unfair prejudice, confusion of the issues, or misleading the jury, or by considerations of undue delay, waste of time, or needless presentation of cumulative evidence.

All relevant evidence is admissible, unless it is inadmissible due to another rule of evidence or law. Relevancy is very broadly defined in Rule 401. Rule 403 is the most important of the exclusionary rules. Under Rule 403, relevant evidence may be excluded by the trial judge if its probative value (tendency to prove or disprove a relevant fact) is *substantially outweighed* by the danger of unfair prejudice, confusion of the issues, misleading the jury, or by considerations of undue delay, waste of time, or needless presentation of cumulative evidence. "Unfair prejudice" means an "undue tendency to suggest decision on an improper basis, commonly, though not necessarily, an emotional one."[1] To avoid having testimony excluded under Rule 403, an expert may have to work closely with retaining counsel to flesh out every reason it is relevant and every reason it is not confusing or misleading. Consider the following examples dealing with expert evidence.

Example 5.1: Relevant expert evidence
Shekell v. Sturm, Ruger & Co. 14 Fed. Rules Evid. Serv. 1634 (CA.9 Mont. 1983)
In an action against a gun manufacturer arising from the discharge of a gun when it was dropped with the safety engaged, the testimony of an expert concerning accidents that occurred when an uncocked gun fired unexpectedly or when the position of the hammer was unknown was sufficiently probative on the issue of whether the gun was unreasonably dangerous to be relevant for purposes of Rule 401. The court found that a description of various ways in which a gun could accidentally fire was relevant if it promoted an understanding of how a firing mechanism works, aided in establishing whether the safety mechanism was defective, or assisted the jury in comprehending how the gun could have discharged when the plaintiff dropped it.

Example 5.2: Relevant expert testimony
Haney v. Mizell Memorial Hospital, 744 F.2d 1467 (11th Cir. 1984)
A medical malpractice defendant offered evidence regarding the plaintiff's intoxication and alcohol and drug use. The court found it admissible under Rule 401, concluding that it was relevant to the plaintiff's ability to communicate with medical personnel and their ability to restrain and obtain cooperation from him; relevant to the plaintiff's prayer for damages for future

[1] *Firemen's Fund Ins. Co. v. Thien,* 63 F.3d 754, 758 (8th Cir. 1995) (quoting *United States v. Dennis,* 625 F.2d 782, 796-797 (8th Cir. 1980)).

mental anguish, rehabilitation care, and loss of earnings; and relevant to rebut testimony offered by the plaintiff pertaining to his lifestyle and quality of life prior to the accident.

Example 5.3: Evidence not misleading
Edwards v. Liz Claiborne, Inc., 17 Fed. Rules Evid. Serv. 1316 (E.D. Pa. 1984)
In a product liability action, the plaintiff alleged that a terrycloth blouse retailed by the defendant was defective in design and in its failure to provide sufficient warnings of unusually hazardous burning characteristics. The defendant's expert witness performed an in-court experiment designed to show that the blouse would not have formed molten polyester drippings when burned, notwithstanding that the blouse material was 25 percent polyester and 75 percent cotton while the test material was 40 percent polyester and 60 percent cotton, and notwithstanding several departures from the standard testing procedure. The court admitted the evidence based on the facts that the experiment was specifically designed to illustrate one facet of the accident, it was highly unlikely that the jury mistook the experiment as an exact duplication of the accident itself, and the fabrics were sufficiently similar to enable the jury to find the experiment helpful to its determination of the likelihood that the fabric formed molten drippings when it burned.

Example 5.4: Relevant evidence
Ventura v. Titan Sports, 65 F.3d 725 (8th Cir. 1995)
A professional wrestler—and budding politician—sued a wrestling organization for compensation based upon illegal use of videotapes of his performance. The wrestler offered testimony by a damages expert. The court found it relevant to the wrestler's quantum meruit claim, because, regardless of whether the defendant's actions rose to the level of conscious tort, the expert's testimony concerning the market value of the wrestler's videotape license related to the material facts of the value of the license to the defendant and the value of the royalties to the wrestler.

Example 5.5: Danger of unfair prejudice outweighed probative value
White v. U.S., 148 F.3d 787, 792 (7th Cir. 1998)
In this malpractice action, the plaintiff sought to introduce the testimony of a credentials expert. The expert had reviewed the defendant physician's deposition testimony and the documents she provided regarding her degrees and licenses. The expert was prepared to testify that the physician could not have obtained certain degrees. The plaintiff wanted to show that the physician was not properly licensed. The court excluded the evidence, concluding there was no direct evidence of fraud or dishonesty, thus the probative value of the evidence was slight. The issue of credentials could have developed into a lengthy trial-within-a-trial.

Example 5.6: Irrelevant evidence
Campbell v. Vinjamuri, 19 F.3d 1274 (8th Cir. 1994)
The plaintiff sued the defendant anesthesiologist for malpractice. The plaintiff sought to introduce evidence that the defendant had failed board-certifying examinations in anesthesiology. The court excluded the evidence as irrelevant,

concluding that a person's performance on an examination is not determinative of that person's ability to meet a required standard of care.

Example 5.7: Irrelevant evidence
Barnes v. General Motors Corp., 547 F.2d 275 (5th Cir. 1977)
This was a products liability suit arising out of an automobile crash that allegedly resulted from the defective design of the car. The court found that the plaintiff's engineer expert's testimony regarding the results of an experiment he conducted on another automobile were irrelevant to the issue at hand and presented a real danger of unfair prejudice. The experiment was conducted under circumstances very different than those existing at the time of accident, thus the engineer's testimony had no probative value.

Example 5.8: Unfairly prejudicial expert testimony
Marcel v. Placid Oil, 11 F.3d 563 (5th Cir. 1994)
An oilfield worker sued the oil company for damages arising out of a slip-and-fall on an offshore rig. The oil company's expert economist testified on the issue of the worklife expectancy of an oilfield worker in an effort to show that the worklife was shorter than average. The defendant did not offer any other evidence comparing the worklife in the oilfield with the national average or with the worklife of any other occupation. The evidence was not admitted—its potential for unfair prejudice outweighed its probative value.

Example 5.9: Unfairly prejudicial expert testimony
Livingstone v. North Belle Vernon Borough, 91 F.3d 515 (3rd Cir. 1996)
In this proceeding, the court sought to determine whether the plaintiff's execution of an agreement to waive potential civil claims against the defendants in exchange for a dismissal of a criminal case against the plaintiff was voluntary. The plaintiff's attorney had advised her to concede the agreement. To show that the plaintiff's attorney in the underlying action had given erroneous advice that affected the voluntariness of the decision, the plaintiff's expert offered a report addressing the underlying liability of the defendants. The court found that the report presented detailed assertions that the defendants had violated the plaintiff's civil rights. The court concluded that the report would be unfairly prejudicial because the fact finders might rely on the assertions of civil rights abuses when making a decision on the voluntariness issue.

Example 5.10: Evidence potentially confusing
Rogers v. Raymark Industries, Inc., 922 F.2d 1426 (9th Cir. 1991)
The widow of a shipyard welder brought an action against an asbestos manufacturer, alleging asbestos exposure caused her husband's lung cancer. The plaintiff contended that her husband's work was less like a welder's and more like an insulation worker's. The plaintiff offered testimony from an expert in marine asbestos insulation techniques. The testimony was intended to describe the conditions under which the plaintiff's husband worked in the shipyard. The court excluded the testimony. It reasoned that the expert's description of shipyard insulation techniques would have been relevant only to that portion of the deceased's work experience that put him in close proximity

to insulators. Thus, the jury might have been confused into equating the expert's description of life as an insulator with life as a welder.

Example 5.11: Evidence unfairly prejudicial
Conti v. Commissioner, 39 F.3d 658 (6th Cir. 1994)
In this case, the plaintiffs voluntarily took polygraph tests to try and prove a cash hoard claim without the tax court's or IRS counsel's knowledge. The tax court held that the polygraph results were unreliable and refused to admit them. The tax court also excluded the results under Rule 403. The Sixth Circuit affirmed the tax court on the latter basis. The *Conti* court observed that the unfairly prejudicial effect of unilateral polygraph tests outweighs their probative value because the party offering them does not have an adverse interest at stake when taking the tests.

Example 5.12: Confusion
Monotype Corp., PLC v. International Typeface Corp., 43 F.3d 443, 449 (9th Cir. 1994)
In this intellectual property case, the court held that the district court properly excluded a report by a principal of a company that specializes in the design and production of digital typefaces. The report commented upon industry "moral code" and copied typefaces. The author was not testifying as an expert, nor had he seen the typeface at issue in the case. The court reasoned that even if the evidence were relevant, it would confuse the jury because the jury might give the typographical trade association's code too much weight for what it represented.

Example 5.13: Confusion
Paradigm Sales, Inc. v. Weber Marking Sys., Inc., 880 F. Supp. 1247, 1252-53 (N.D. Ind. 1995)
In this patent infringement action, the patent holder for a staple gun brought an infringement action against a competitor. Expert testimony by an engineer was offered by the defendant. This expert proposed to compare the physical operation of the alleged infringing gun to the operation of the staple gun manufactured by the patent holder. The court found the testimony irrelevant. "The issue for the trier of fact is whether the Weber device performs substantially the same function in substantially the same way to achieve substantially the same result as the device *disclosed in the patent,* not as the device manufactured by the defendant." The court held that expert testimony on this irrelevant matter would confuse the issues and was thus inadmissible under Rule 403.

Example 5.14: Confusion and waste of time
Tilton v. Capital Cities/ABC, Inc., 938 F. Supp. 751, 753 (N.D. Okla. 1995)
The court excluded an expert linguist's proposed testimony about how certain rhetorical devices or speech patterns convey implied meanings. It found the testimony would confuse the jury and that it was "a waste of time."

Example 5.15: Evidence relative and probative
Gilbert v. Cosco, Inc., 989 F.2d 399 (10th Cir. 1993)
In this products liability action regarding the design of child restraint seats, the manufacturer introduced evidence of tests it had performed. This evidence was offered to assist the manufacturer's expert in demonstrating the physical principals that formed the basis for his opinion. The court allowed the evidence, concluding that although it would be highly prejudicial to the plaintiff's case, the tests were relevant and the plaintiff had ample opportunity to attack the expert's conclusions on cross-examination.

Example 5.16: Evidence irrelevant
Brereton v. U.S., 973 F.Supp. 752 (E.D. Mich. 1997)
In the damages phase of this wrongful death action arising out of a fatal airplane crash, expert evidence was proposed to set the value of the survivors' loss of society and companionship. The expert, an economist, based his figures on the value that society might place on the safety and health of a statistically average individual. The court excluded the testimony, concluding it was irrelevant to the issue of the survivors' loss of companionship and society. The only way to determine this value was to assess the type of relationship the decedent had with the survivors, and the expert testimony was unhelpful in making such an assessment.

Example 5.17: Expert testimony relevant and probative
Stead v. F.E. Myers Co., 785 F.Supp. 56 (D. Vt. 1990)
This action was brought against the manufacturer of a submersible pump for injuries allegedly resulting from exposure to pump oil. The plaintiff offered expert testimony, by an MD and a PhD, that there was an increased risk of cancer resulting from the exposure. Neither expert could testify to a reasonable degree of medical certainty that the exposure caused cancer. This did not matter, however, because the plaintiff sought recovery for the cost of extensive medical monitoring that the increased risk of cancer made necessary. The court found the testimony relevant and probative to the issue of recovery of costs for future medical monitoring.

Example 5.18: Evidence unfairly prejudicial
Pinkham v. Burgess, 933 F.2d 1066 (1st Cir. 1991)
An attorney's former client sued him for intentional or reckless infliction of emotional distress. The attorney offered a psychologist's expert testimony that his mental state was such that he could not recognize the harm he was causing. The court found that such testimony had substantial potential to confuse or mislead because the jury might improperly consider the unsubstantiated psychological problem as an excuse for negligence. The evidence was not admitted.

Example 5.19: Evidence unfairly prejudicial
In re. Air Crash Disaster, 86 F.3d 498 (6th Cir. 1996)
Here, plaintiffs sued an airline after one of its planes crashed during takeoff. A human factors expert, also a pilot, was testifying for the plaintiffs. The defense sought to cross-examine the expert on a 1953 crash of a plane he piloted that

resulted in two deaths. The court found that the proposed line of questioning would result in testimony that was unfairly prejudicial and did not allow the cross-examination: "The time lapse, the different airport, the different technology, the dubious relevance to the witness's currently-claimed expertise, and the need to avoid detailed inquiry into a separate plane crash—these all spoke for exclusion."

5.3 Evidence Rules Dealing Specifically with Experts

Federal Rules of Evidence 702–705 deal explicitly with expert witnesses.

Box 5.31

Fed. R. Evid. 702. Testimony by Experts
If scientific, technical, or other specialized knowledge will assist the trier of fact to understand the evidence or to determine a fact in issue, a witness qualified as an expert by knowledge, skill, experience, training, or education, may testify thereto in the form of an opinion or otherwise.

The role of an expert is to "assist the trier of fact" through her "scientific, technical, or other specialized knowledge." If this opinion is not based upon reliable methodology, it may not assist the trier of fact and it may be excluded under the *Daubert* line of cases. (The *Daubert* line of cases and the legal requirements thereunder are discussed in Chapter 9 on methodology.)

To testify as an expert, an individual must be qualified by "knowledge, skill, experience, training, or education." Note the conjunction "or." An expert needs to be qualified under only one of these categories, not all. If the court holds as a matter of law that an expert is not qualified to testify in a certain area, then he will not be allowed to testify in that area. Note, however, that even if the judge does find the expert qualified to testify, his qualifications are still a legitimate line of inquiry in cross-examination because they will affect the weight to be given to the expert's testimony. (Qualifications are discussed in greater detail in Chapter 6.)

Box 5.32

Fed. R. Evid. 703. Bases of Opinion Testimony by Experts
The facts or data in the particular case upon which an expert bases an opinion or inference may be perceived by or made known to the expert at or before the hearing. If of a type reasonably relied upon by experts in the particular field in forming opinions or inferences upon the subject, the facts or data need not be admissible in evidence.

Rule 703 gives experts a fair degree of latitude regarding the facts or data upon which their opinion is based. This latitude is not, however, unlimited. These facts or data need not be admissible in evidence themselves (for example, hearsay) as long as they are of a type that is reasonably relied upon by experts in that field. ***If a court (i.e., the trial judge) holds that an expert's opinion is based upon facts or data that are not reasonably relied upon by experts in the same field, then the expert's testimony may be excluded.*** Consider the following examples.[2]

Example 5.20: Hypothetical question as basis for opinion
United States v. Mann, 712 F.2d 941 (4th Cir. 1983)
A weapons expert, called to give his opinion regarding the identity of a gun, heard this hypothetical question:

> I'm going to ask you to assume that the weapon in question was identical to that weapon [referring to a gun already in evidence as an exhibit]; having the infinity sign on it; having three selector positions on the selector switch; having a folding stock being the only difference; not having the word "Valmet" on it; not having the words "Inner Arms Company" on it; and I'm going to ask you to assume those facts and draw any conclusion you can as to what kind of gun [the defendant's was].

The description of the defendant's gun in this case was admitted into evidence through the testimony of one of the defendant's acquaintances who had seen the gun. The court noted, "The expert was free to rely on that testimony." The court concluded that,

> experts in weaponry may rest their opinions as to a weapon's identity on the markings and features of the weapon, whether witnessed firsthand or described by a layman. Of course, the credibility of the witness whose description underlies the expert's opinion may affect the weight ultimately accorded by the trier of fact to the expert's opinion, but it does not make the description a form of evidence not reasonably relied on by experts in the field.

Example 5.21: Evidence not reasonably relied upon
Redman v. John D. Brush & Co., 111 F.3d 1174 (4th Cir. 1997)
A metallurgic engineer's testimony that a safe was not burglar deterrent was properly excluded. The expert relied solely on hearsay information from store personnel to identify a standard of burglar protection capacity. Experts would not rely upon this hearsay as an indication of industry safety standards.

Example 5.22: Other professional reports
United States v. Posey, 647 F.2d 1048 (10th Cir. 1981)
In a drug prosecution, it was permissible for one chemist to rely upon tests run by another in testifying that the tested substance was cocaine. The court stated, "It is quite reasonable for a chemist to review another chemist's analysis when forming an opinion as to the veracity of the latter's test results."

Example 5.23: Other professional reports
Gong v. Hirsch, 913 F.2d 1269 (7th Cir. 1990)
In this medical malpractice suit, an expert relied upon a letter from the deceased's physician to a doctor at the medical department of the deceased's

---

[2] Chapter 8 on opinions contains further Rule 703 cases.

employer. The letter, stating that the deceased's perforated peptic ulcer was due to Prednisone, was not admissible as a type of information reasonably relied upon by an expert because it was merely a conclusory statement made by a doctor who was not the treating physician at the time of illness in question and the letter was for the presumed purpose of obtaining employment disability benefits.

Example 5.24: Hearsay

Ricciardi v. Children's Hospital Medical Center, 811 F.2d 18 (1st Cir. 1987)
In this medical malpractice action, the trial court was correct in ruling that the expert could not rely upon a note written in a patient's chart by a consulting physician when the consulting physician did not have personal knowledge of the alleged event and did not know where he obtained the information recorded in the note. Although an expert is not confined to admissible evidence in forming an opinion under Rule 703, the note in the chart was not of the type reasonably relied upon by experts in forming opinions or inferences upon a subject in this particular field.

Example 5.25: Reliance on expert report prepared for purposes of litigation

United States v. Tran Trong Cuong, 18 F.3d 1132, 1143-44 (4th Cir. 1994)
A family practitioner testified as an expert to the standard of care for a family physician. The expert testified that a nontestifying prosecution expert's report supported his conclusions. The nontestifying expert's report was prepared at the request of the prosecution and was thus a forensic opinion or report in a criminal case. The court doubted whether such a report "would qualify as data of a type reasonably relied upon by experts in the particular field...[w]e question whether [the expert] usually relies upon forensic medical opinions or reports in forming his opinions in his field of expertise—family medicine."

Box 5.33

Fed. R. Evid. 704. Opinion on Ultimate Issue

(a) Except as provided in subdivision (b), testimony in the form of an opinion or inference otherwise admissible is not objectionable because it embraces an ultimate issue to be decided by the trier of fact.

(b) No expert witness testifying with respect to the mental state or condition of a defendant in a criminal case may state an opinion or inference as to whether the defendant did or did not have the mental state or condition constituting an element of the crime charged or of a defense thereto. Such ultimate issues are matters for the trier of fact alone.

Experts are allowed under Rule 704 to testify on areas that embrace an ultimate issue to be decided by the trier of fact (for example, valuation of the property in a condemnation case).[3] Before the adoption of this rule, experts were allowed to offer factual opinions (the plaintiff's inattention caused the crash with the defendant's car), but not legal conclusions (the plaintiff's negligence caused the crash).[4] The rule no longer explicitly makes this distinction, but the difference remains: experts are not allowed to tell the jury how to apply the facts to the law.[5]

The one exception to this rule has to do with testimony regarding the mental state or condition of a defendant in a criminal case. This so-called "Hinckley Amendment" was enacted after the acquittal on the grounds of insanity of the attempted assassin of President Ronald Reagan.

Example 5.26: Testimony excluded
Burkhart v. Washington Metro. Area Transit Auth., 112 F.3d 1207 (D.C. Cir. 1997)
In this case, a deaf bus passenger became involved in physical fight with the bus driver. The passenger alleged that the transit authority discriminated against him under the Americans with Disabilities Act because it failed to ensure that communications with him were as effective as communications with others. The plaintiff's expert in police training and procedures testified regarding this allegation. His testimony concluded that the communications were not as effective as communications with others, which is the statutory requirement of the ADA. In effect, the testimony stated that the defendant did not comply with the ADA. The appeals court found that the testimony was an impermissible legal conclusion rather than a factual opinion.

---

[3] "The reasoning behind Rule 704(a) is that if an expert provides a solid foundation and explanation on an issue in which the factfinder needs assistance, the factfinder is simply left hanging if the expert cannot cap off the testimony with a conclusion about the ultimate issue to which the expert is testifying. Sometimes, a conclusion on the ultimate issue ties the expert's testimony together into a coherent whole, and as such it will be more helpful to state the conclusion along with the rest of the opinion. The Rule also recognizes that a distinction between 'ultimate' and other issues is elusive, and that common-law decisions attempting to draw such a distinction were often arbitrary and unpredictable." Stephen A. Saltzburg, et al., *Commentary to Federal Rule 704*, U.S.C.S. Fed. Rules Evid. 704 (1999) 134-135.

[4] "It would be disingenuous to suggest that the cases reflect a nationally uniform definition of the permissible parameters of expert opinions that stray near or across the line of legal opinions." Stephen D. Easton, "Yer Outta Here! A Framework for Analyzing the Potential Exclusion of Expert Testimony Under the Federal Rules of Evidence," 32 *U. Rich. L. Rev.* (1998) 1, 55.

[5] "Notwithstanding Rule 704(a), an expert cannot go beyond her proper role and intrude upon an important function of the Trial Judge, which is to instruct the jury as to the requirements of law that apply to the particular facts of the case." *Id.*

Example 5.27: Testimony admitted
Hoult v. Hoult, 57 F.3d 1 (1st Cir. 1995)
In this case, the plaintiff sued her father for assault and intentional infliction of emotional distress stemming from alleged childhood sexual abuse. The plaintiff based her allegations upon memories recovered during therapy. The expert psychiatrist testified regarding repression of memory caused by traumatic abuse. The psychiatrist came perilously close to testifying that the particular victim/witness could be believed. However, the appellate court did not overturn the trial court's admission of the testimony. The court noted that the psychiatrist was subjected to rigorous cross-examination; that defense counsel repeatedly attempted to elicit opinion testimony from the psychiatrist that she believed the plaintiff's allegations but she steadfastly refused to give an opinion; that the psychiatrist herself testified that she had no way of knowing whether the plaintiff's allegations were true; that the jury was presented with evidence contradicting or calling into question the psychiatrist's opinions; and that the court expressly instructed the jury that they were free to reject the psychiatrist's opinions. The psychiatrist stated no impermissible legal conclusion.

Example 5.28: Evidence admitted
United States v. Duncan, 42 F.3d 97 (2nd Cir. 1994)
The defendant was accused of bank fraud and conspiring to make corrupt payments to public officials. An IRS agent gave expert testimony regarding the type of transactions in question and the general functioning of the tax system. The court found that the agent's opinion testimony did not state a legal conclusion. The agent did not couch his opinions in terms that derived their definitions from judicial interpretations, his testimony was based on his personal knowledge, and, although he stated certain factual conclusions, he never expressed an opinion regarding the defendant's guilt of the offenses charged.

Example 5.29: Opinion on causation allowed
Miksis v. Howard, 106 F.3d 754 (7th Cir. 1997)
In this personal injury action arising out of a traffic accident, the plaintiff's sleep deprivation expert testified that the defendant was fatigued and that sleep deprivation was the primary cause of the accident. The court properly allowed the testimony. It noted that the expert did not attempt to reconstruct the accident and testified to the existence of fatigue, not just its role. Moreover, there was a factual dispute whether the driver was fatigued and whether that fatigue could have caused the driver to hit the plaintiff's construction bucket.

Example 5.30: Opinion not allowed
Owen v. Kerr-McGee Corp., 698 F.2d 236 (5th Cir. 1983)
In this personal injury action by a bulldozer operator against a gas pipeline operator, the plaintiffs alleged that the defendant's placement of a pipeline was negligent. This placement caused the bulldozer to strike the line. The expert was asked to opine whether the placement of the line was "negligent" rather than to state a conclusion that the placement of the line caused the accident. The court excluded the evidence because the question sought the witness's

opinion regarding the legal, rather than the factual, cause of the accident and there was no dispute in evidence regarding the factual cause.

Example 5.31: Mental state of accused, answer to hypothetical prohibited
United States v. Manley, 893 F.2d 1221 (11th Cir. 1990)
In this prosecution, defense counsel wanted to ask the expert psychiatrist a hypothetical question: whether a person with the described mental disease would "be able to appreciate the nature and quality of his actions." But the court of appeals upheld the trial judge's decision to preclude an answer to that hypothetical, on the ground that it would elicit testimony prohibited by Rule 704(b).

Example 5.32: Mental state of accused, opinion admitted
United States v. Conyers, 118 F.3d 755 (D.C. Cir. 1997)
In this case, the court decided whether the packaging of drugs and the possession of a firearm by the defendant were sufficient to support a finding of intent to distribute. The government expert testified that the packaging of the drugs found in the defendant's possession was consistent with the distribution in the area. He also testified that the weapon recovered from the defendant's person was the revolver of choice among local drug dealers. The court noted that an expert witness may testify about an established practice among individuals involved in the drug trade, provided that the witness does not speak directly to the guilt or innocence of the accused. The court then found that, although the testimony could support an inference of intent, it did not constitute an opinion on the ultimate issue of the defendant's guilt or innocence.

Example 5.33: Mental state of accused, testimony admitted
United States v. Brown, 32 F.3d 236 (C.A.7 Ill. 1994)
The defendant was charged with bank robbery and raised an insanity defense. The prosecution's psychiatrist testified that Brown suffered from a major depressive disorder and may have suffered some depressive episodes with psychotic features. Following the description of this diagnosis, the prosecutor asked the witness whether a person suffering from the disorder described was, by that reason alone, "unable to understand the wrongfulness of his acts." The witness answered in the negative. Brown objected that this was ultimate issue testimony as to his legal sanity, barred by Rule 704(b). The trial court allowed the testimony and the appellate court affirmed that decision. The court noted that the prosecution's expert "never testified to Brown's peculiar mental state" but rather "merely described Brown's mental disorder and that such an affliction does not preclude one from appreciating the nature or quality of his acts." The court declared that because the expert testimony was not "specific to Brown's mental state" but rather concerned "the characteristics of his mental disorder," it was permitted by Rule 704(b).

Example 5.34: Mental state of accused, evidence admitted
United States v. Thigpen, 4 F.3d 1573 (11th Cir. 1993)
Here, the court found no error in allowing the prosecutor to "ask a series of questions to elicit an opinion as to whether [schizophrenia] by necessity implies that a person would be unable to appreciate the nature and quality of his acts."

The court stated that these questions were permissible because "no question by the prosecutor asked the witness to opine whether [defendant] was able to appreciate his actions."

Example 5.35: Mental state of accused, evidence excluded
United States v. Kristiansen, 901 F.2d 1463 (8th Cir. 1990)
The defendant in this case was charged with escape from a halfway house. He claimed that he lacked willful intent due to insanity. The defendant's expert psychiatrist testified that he had been under the influence of cocaine and suffered from psychosis. On cross-examination, the prosecutor asked: "Would this severe mental disease. . .affect the individual's ability to appreciate the nature and quality of the wrongfulness of his acts?" The trial court sustained an objection, and the court of appeals affirmed, reasoning that this was a hypothetical question designed to elicit testimony on the ultimate issue of intent.

Example 5.36: Mental state of accused, evidence excluded
Salas v. Carpenter, 980 F.2d 299 (5th Cir. 1992)
Here, the Fifth Circuit explained its exclusion of proffered expert testimony as a matter inappropriate for expert opinions:

> As an expert in the field of hostage negotiation, Dr. Greenstone can properly offer evidence on effective methods and explain to a jury faults in the methods employed by a police force. On the other hand, Dr. Greenstone is not in a better position than a juror to conclude whether [defendant's] actions demonstrated such a lack of concern for [plaintiff's] safety as to constitute deliberate indifference or conscious disregard. Opening the door to ultimate issues did not 'open the door to all opinions.'

Box 5.34

Fed. R. Evid. 705. Disclosure of Facts or Data Underlying Expert Opinion
The expert may testify in terms of opinions or inference and give reasons thereof without first testifying to the underlying facts or data, unless the court requires otherwise. The expert may in any event be required to disclose the underlying facts or data on cross-examination.

Under Rule 705, an expert may be subject to cross-examination regarding the underlying facts or data upon which she has based her opinion. This is allowed because an expert's opinion is only as good as the facts and data upon which it is based.

Example 5.37: Bases for opinion
Lewis v. Rego, Co., 757 F.2d 66 (3rd Cir. 1985)
A products liability action was brought against the manufacturer of a propane cylinder's safety relief valve, seeking recovery in connection with the explosion of the propane cylinder. An expert in physical metallurgy was asked on cross-examination about the bases for his opinion. One of these was a conversation

he had with another metallurgist. The expert was not allowed to answer the question. This exclusion by the trial court was held to be improper. The appellate court stated: "Although it is not required that the bases for an expert's opinion be disclosed before the opinion is given, the bases of the opinion may be testified to on direct examination, and if inquired into during cross-examination, must be disclosed."

Example 5.38: Bases explored on cross-examination
Polythane Systems, Inc. v. Marina Ventures Intern., Ltd., 993 F.2d 1201 (5th Cir. 1993)
An employee sued his employer for constructive discharge under the Americans with Disabilities Act and for worker's compensation retaliation and defamation. The plaintiff's economics expert was to testify to back pay, using figures based upon employment history provided by plaintiff's counsel. The defendant challenged the bases of the testimony in a pre-trial motion. The court cited Rules 703 and 705 and denied the pre-trial motion to exclude the expert's testimony regarding the amount of compensation owed. The court then noted that the defendant could more fully explore the figures—and their bases—during cross-examination. The court then told the plaintiff to be prepared to proffer factual bases for the expert's assumptions during trial.

Example 5.39: Explanation of bases of opinion
Wilmington Trust Co. v. Manufacturers Life Ins. Co., 749 F.2d 694 (11th Cir. 1985)
The plaintiff sued an insurance company to recover proceeds under the insured decedent's life insurance policy. The insurer denied liability, claiming the insured had committed suicide within one year of the issuance of the policy. The court found that the plaintiff's experts should have been allowed to give testimony regarding the possibility of homicide. It reasoned that experts are entitled to give reasons for their opinions and to explain how and why they arrived at that result. The plaintiff's experts had considered homicide, but rejected it—this was part of their ideology in arriving at the conclusion that the death was accidental.

5.4 Credibility: Bias and Prior Inconsistent Statements

In the end, most trials boil down to one issue and only one issue—credibility. Therefore, the adverse party may try to subtly, or not so subtly, impeach or lessen the credibility of an expert witness. This is completely proper. This section is designed to teach, in a very basic way, some of the evidentiary rules dealing with an attorney's assault against an expert's credibility.

Bias

Although there is no Federal Rule addressing bias directly, the United States Supreme Court has held that a witness may be impeached on the ground of bias.[6] Judges usually give attorneys wide latitude to show a witness's potential

[6] *United States v. Abel,* 469 U.S. 45 (1984).

bias. If the witness being impeached denies the bias, the judge has discretion to allow extrinsic evidence to show the bias. ***An expert must expect that evidence that may tend to show her bias can and will be held to be admissible as it is relevant to her credibility.*** Please see the following examples of evidentiary questions regarding the potential bias of experts.

Example 5.40: Expert's relationship with counsel
Tiburzio-Kelly v. Montgomery, 681 A.2d 757 (Pa. Super. 1996)
The Pennsylvania Court dealt with a medical malpractice claim resulting when a child was born with disabilities. At issue was the proper scope of cross-examination of the defendant's expert medical witness in the case. Specifically, the plaintiffs sought to show bias by eliciting the fact that the expert was himself currently being represented by the defendant's law firm. The trial court did not allow the cross-examination, but the appellate court held that this information was the proper subject of a cross-examination designed to show bias. Plaintiff's counsel called the defendant's expert pediatric neurologist and sought permission to elicit from him the fact that he was then being represented in another matter by a member of the firm that was representing the co-defendant practice in the case at hand. The appellate court found that,

> ...it is proper to elicit from an expert the fee he is being paid to testify. Later decisions have further indicated that it is also proper to elicit whether a personal friendship exists between the expert and either the party calling him or that party's counsel....Certainly, evidence of an ongoing relationship between the witnesses and attorneys is information which the jury would want to know about and we believe is entitled to know about.

Note: The court held that the trial court's failure to allow cross-examination as to the expert medical witness's bias was so serious an error that it awarded the plaintiffs a new trial.

Example 5.41: Compensation in prior related cases
Coward v. Owens-Corning Fiberglass Corp., 729 A.2d 614 (Pa. Super. 1999)
A group of plaintiffs filed a products liability action against an asbestos manufacturer. The court considered whether an expert physician should have been subjected to cross-examination regarding the amount of money he was paid in other asbestos litigation over the previous twenty years. The court allowed the cross-examination. Cross-examining counsel specifically asked the expert whether that compensation influenced his opinions regarding the case at trial.

Example 5.42: Previous testimony for same party
Brantley v. Sears Roebuck & Co., 959 S.W.2d 927 (Mo. App. E.D. 1998)
The plaintiff, a homeowner, sued the seller of a dishwasher, alleging the machine caused a house fire. The court considered whether the fire expert could be cross-examined on the point that he had testified for the same insurer over one hundred and fifty times. The court found the cross-examination proper and allowed it to take place in order for the plaintiff to show bias.

Example 5.43: Expert witness income

State ex rel. Lichtor v. Clark, 845 S.W.2d 55 (Mo. App. 1992)

The plaintiff in this personal injury case objected to being examined by a physician selected by defense counsel, complaining that the doctor was biased. The particular orthopedic surgeon had a long history of employment by insurers and the defense bar. In the context of resolving that discovery dispute, the court discussed the problem of biased expert witnesses and held that "the trial judge in this case has discretion to allow testimony as to the amount of annual income derived from employment as an expert witness."

Example 5.44: Involvement in prior medical malpractice action

Underhill v. Stephenson, 756 S.W.2d 459 (Ky.1988)

In a medical malpractice action, it was proper for the plaintiff to cross-examine the defendant's medical expert regarding the expert's prior involvement in an unrelated malpractice action. The plaintiff, the court reasoned, had a right to cross-examine the medical expert on "all matters relating to every issue." Evidence to show bias of an expert witness, the court concluded, is relevant.

Example 5.45: Prior statements in different trial

Snyder v. Foote, 822 P.2d 1353 (Alaska 1991)

In this case, the court held that evidence that a doctor had made misstatements concerning his credentials in an earlier, unrelated lawsuit would not be admissible for impeachment purposes on a bias theory during a trial at which he was testifying as an expert. The defendant planned to impeach the expert by using the findings from a past trial court proceeding in which the judge found that the expert had misstated his credentials and that he had "knowingly and intentionally testified falsely at the trial." The court in this case refused to admit any evidence concerning the expert's prior misstatements for the purposes of demonstrating bias. The court commented that the defendant, for example, could have introduced evidence that showed the expert's favoritism toward the plaintiff, but evidence of the judge's findings concerning the expert's misstatements in the earlier case would not be admissible on a bias theory because such findings of fact had no tendency to demonstrate that the expert entertained a bias in regard to his testimony at the trial.

Example 5.46: Expert's relationship with counsel

Clements v. Stewart, 595 So.2d 858 (Ala. 1992)

In this medical malpractice case, the defendant's medical expert testified that the defendant had not deviated from the appropriate standard of care. The plaintiff made an offer of proof outside the presence of the jury that showed that the defendant's medical expert had been a defendant in a medical malpractice action; that the witness had been represented in that action by the same law firm that was representing the defendant in the current case; and that that action had been settled. The trial court did not allow cross-examination on the issue. The state supreme court heard the appeal of this decision and found that the plaintiff should have been able to cross-examine the expert with respect to any bias that he may have had against plaintiffs in medical malpractice actions. The court noted the rule: "Not only is there allowable great latitude on cross-examination of a witness, but this latitude is enlarged as to an expert witness."

Example 5.47: Relationship between expert and counsel
Jones v. Pizza Boy, Oxford, Inc., 387 So.2d 819 (Ala. 1989)
In this medical malpractice action, the court allowed the plaintiff to cross-examine the defendant's medical expert concerning defense counsel's representation of the witness in a pending malpractice suit.

Example 5.48: History of negligence cases
Mazzone v. Holmes, 557 N.E.2d 186 (Ill. App. Dist. 1 1990)
In this medical malpractice action, the plaintiff contended that the trial judge erred in refusing examination of a defense medical expert regarding the number of professional negligence cases brought or then pending against him. The plaintiff argued that the evidence was relevant to his interest or bias as the defendant physician's expert witness. The court concluded that it was proper to bar questions regarding the number of malpractice cases pending against the physician on the ground of relevancy. The only support for the plaintiff's position, the court observed, was the "general proposition that parties should have the opportunity to expose the interest or bias of medical experts through cross-examination." The court concluded, however, that such examination should be strictly limited to matters such as "the number of referrals, their frequency, and the financial benefit derived from them."

Example 5.49: Nonrenewal of privileges
Kane v. Ryan, 596 A.2d 562 (D.C. 1991)
The defendant physician in this malpractice case attempted to question the plaintiff's medical expert as to why her privileges at the hospital at which the plaintiff was treated were not renewed. During cross-examination, the defendant's attorney inquired as to whether the expert was upset with the subject hospital over the "manner" in which it did not renew her hospital privileges, to which the expert replied the matter was not relevant to the case at issue. The court denied any inquiry into the nonrenewal of the expert's privileges. It noted that the trial judge may properly limit bias cross-examination if it concludes that the evidence is too collateral. This rule, the court commented, allows the trial judge to direct the trial in a way that assures that the jury will focus on the central issues it must decide, rather than on a mini-trial of a marginally relevant or collateral issue. In the case at hand, the court reasoned, a further exploration of the reasons the expert was not renewed privileges would have required a "parade of witnesses on an issue that could have had only a remote bearing on possible bias against" the defendant physician, a doctor who had privileges at the subject hospital, but was apparently not among those who had a role in deciding the expert's future.

Prior inconsistent statements

Another important technique used to impeach an expert's credibility is through confrontation with a prior inconsistent statement of the expert. This is allowed under the rules and is a powerful form of impeachment because it shows that the expert has been inconsistent regarding an issue. The prior statements most commonly used to impeach an expert include the expert's published or unpublished writings and the expert's prior deposition or trial testimony. Because an expert's prior writings and testimony are becoming more and more easily available with the progression of technology, he should be well prepared for this form of impeachment.

Example 5.50
Q. And it's your testimony that Chemical X cannot, under any circumstances, cause pathology?
A. That's correct.
Q. Do you recall testifying in the *Todd v. Davis* case in 1993?
A. Vaguely.
Q. I have here your trial testimony from the *Todd* case. You were testifying under oath at trial and were asked, "Can Chemical X cause cancer?" Answer: "Yes." Am I reading that correctly, sir?

5.5 Conclusion

Experts should have a fundamental knowledge of the rules of evidence. These rules will allow relevant evidence unless there is a reason to exclude it. Evidence of bias and prior inconsistent statements are generally admissible because such evidence is relevant to the expert's credibility. The evidence the expert bases her opinion upon need not be admissible into evidence itself if it is of a type reasonably relied upon by experts in the expert's particular field.

Chapter 6 Qualifications

6.1 Introduction

To be effective, an expert witness must understand the requirements for his qualification as an expert. This chapter explains the requirements experts need and reviews recent cases regarding these qualifications.

6.2 Legal Requirements to Qualify as an Expert Witness

Qualifications of expert witnesses are governed by Federal Rule of Evidence 702.

Box 6.21

Fed. R. Evid. 702. Testimony by Experts
If scientific, technical, or other specialized knowledge will assist the trier of fact to understand the evidence or to determine a fact in issue, a witness qualified as an expert by knowledge, skill, experience, training, or education, may testify thereto in the form of an opinion or otherwise.

The role of an expert witness is to use "scientific, technical, or other specialized knowledge" to assist the trier of fact to "understand the evidence or to determine a fact in issue." The "trier of fact" is the jury in a jury trial and the judge in a bench trial (a trial without a jury). The rationale for Rule 702 is that the jury may not be able to understand or decide correctly a case without assistance from experts.

Experts are qualified to testify by their "knowledge, skill, experience, training, or education." Note the conjunction "or." Under Rule 702, the expert only needs to have "knowledge," "skill," "experience," "training," or "education." She need not have all five.

Expert witnesses will routinely be qualified at the beginning of direct examination by the counsel who has retained them. The expert can expect to be asked about her:

- profession
- education
- training
- employment
- experience
- certifications/licenses
- specialties
- present title
- practical experience
- number of examinations performed
- lecturing or teaching

- published works
- memberships in professional associations
- when and where she previously qualified to testify as an expert

Some experts may feel uncomfortable going over their credentials and professional accomplishments in open court. The extent of the "qualifying" testimony should be reviewed with counsel during pre-trial preparation. It is the responsibility of counsel to decide how much of the background, experience, and expertise of the expert to put before the jury. Counsel should attempt to impress the judge and jury without putting them to sleep.

Under Rule 702, it is the judge who initially determines if an expert's proposed testimony, as a matter of law, will satisfy the rule's requirements. If an expert's qualifications are challenged, the judge may have him *voir dired*. This means that the expert will provide preliminary testimony on his qualifications via direct and cross-examination. Based on the testimony he provides during the voir dire, the judge will then make her ruling on whether the expert is qualified to testify.

If the judge holds that the expert is not qualified to testify on a particular area, then the expert will not be allowed to testify on that area. The judge's decision in this regard is an issue that may be raised on appeal, but the standard of review is usually whether the trial judge abused her discretion in holding that the expert was not qualified. This is a difficult standard to meet.

If the judge finds that the expert is qualified, he will be allowed to state his opinion on the areas in which he was qualified.[1] Qualified experts are allowed to testify by expressing an opinion. This is in stark contrast to lay witnesses, who can usually only testify to firsthand personal knowledge. The issue of an expert's qualifications will be determined on a case by case basis.

The facts of a particular case will dictate the expertise needed by the proffered witness. The fact that a witness may have qualified previously in a particular case does not necessarily mean he will be found qualified in subsequent cases.

6.3 Factors Considered by the Judge

When deciding whether an expert is qualified to testify in a particular case, the judge will consider many factors. These include whether the witness has been qualified to testify on the issue in the past, the witness's specialized training and education (or lack thereof), whether the witness has published in the area in question, whether a firsthand inspection or examination was performed, the extent of the witness's real-world experience, and whether the proposed testimony is to be given in front of a jury or at a bench trial.

---

[1] Of course, the expert's proposed testimony could still be challenged under the *Daubert* line of cases. (See Chapter 9 on methodology.)

Previous cases

Was the expert's testimony previously accepted in a similar case? When counsel can demonstrate that the expert has previously been qualified in similar cases, this will be considered carefully by the trial judge.

Example 6.1
Dufrene v. Willingham, 702 So.2d 1026 (La. App. 5 Cir. 1998)
A retired police officer was qualified to testify as an accident reconstructionist. The witness had been testifying in state and federal courts since 1966 and had testified as an expert in accident reconstruction since 1964.

Example 6.2
Labit v. D. H. Holmes Co., Ltd., 721 So.2d 933 (La. App. 5 Cir. 1998)
A tire expert was found qualified in part because he had qualified as an expert in forty states and in over two hundred cases.

Example 6.3
Magnivision, Inc. v. Bonneau Co., 33 F.Supp.2d 1218 (C.D. Cal. 1998)
The court calls "significant" the fact that the witness had qualified to testify in a previous case.

Example 6.4
Colboch v. Uniroyal Tire Co., Inc., 670 N.E.2d 1366 (Ohio App. 8 Dist. 1996)
The court was dealing with a mechanic who was injured when the tire he was mounting exploded. The court found that the metallurgical engineer was qualified to testify, stating, "The other courts have reviewed Milner's qualifications and determined that he is qualified to testify as an expert in litigation regarding defective tires."

Education and training

Experts with appropriate training and education will be found to be qualified. However, when a judge finds that even a highly educated expert, such as a physician, lacks required additional specialized training, that expert may be found not to be qualified to testify. Frequently, experts who lack training in the area in question are found not qualified to testify.

Example 6.5
Dolen v. St. Mary's Hosp. of Huntington, 506 S.E.2d 624 (W.Va. 1998)
An oral surgeon qualified to testify to malpractice of physicians for failure to diagnose the plaintiff's jaw. The witness received a degree in dental surgery, a master's degree in biological sciences with a concentration in oral surgery, and had practiced in the fields of oral and maxillofacial surgery for the last 14 years.

Example 6.6

Everett v. Georgia-Pacific Corp., 949 F.Supp. 856 (S.D. Ga. 1996)
A family physician was found to be not qualified to testify about chronic obstructive pulmonary disease. The court found his lack of training in toxicology to be determinative.

Example 6.7

Cali v. Danek Medical, Inc., 24 F.Supp.2d 941 (W.D. Wis. 1998)
An orthopedic surgeon with thirty-five years of experience was found not qualified to testify in a pedicle screw case. The court noted that the witness had no experience or training in the area on which his opinion was to be offered.

Example 6.8

Wilson v. Woods., 163 F.3d 935 (5th Cir. 1999)
A mechanical engineer was found not qualified to testify as an accident reconstructionist. The witness did not have training or experience in this field.

Example 6.9

Kent v. Pioneer Valley Corp., 930 P.2 904 (Utah App. 1997)
A registered nurse was found not qualified to testify that an injection caused nerve damage. The court cited lack of formal education.

Example 6.10

Surace v. Caterpillar, Inc., 111 F.3rd 1039 (3rd Cir. 1997)
An electromechanical engineer lacked training in back-up alarms and habitation and was held not to be qualified.

Example 6.11

Waste Mgt. of Ohio v. Mid-America Tire, 681 N.E.2d 492 (Ohio App. 2 Dist. 1996)
An accident reconstructionist was found not qualified to testify on wheel explosion due to lack of training.

Example 6.12

Combs v. Norfolk and Western Ry. Co., 507 S.E.2d 355 (Va. 1998)
A biomechanical engineer with a PhD was found not qualified to testify regarding the cause of a ruptured disk. The witness did not have sufficient medical training.

Example 6.13

Kirker v. Nicolla, 681 N.Y.S.2d 689 (A.D. 3 Dept. 1998)
A surgeon was not permitted to testify on the standard of care of a physical therapist. The witness had no training or experience in the field of physical therapy.

Publications and writings

Judges frequently will find qualified and defer to experts who have published extensively in their fields.

Example 6.14
B.F. Goodrich v. Betkoski, 99 F.3rd 505 (2nd Cir. 1996)
The court found an argonomist who had written over 150 scholarly scientific articles eminently qualified to testify.

Example 6.15
Wood v. Minnesota Mining and Mfg. Co., 112 F.3d 306 (8th Cir. 1997)
A highway safety expert was permitted to testify on the safety of a railroad crossing. The expert was a contributing editor of an important text regarding traffic engineering as it applies to railroad crossings.

Expert's firsthand knowledge/inspection

In making their decision on qualifications, judges will consider whether the expert has firsthand knowledge of a machine, site, or condition due to an inspection.

Example 6.16
Burgess v. Harley, 934 S.W.2d 58 (Tenn. App. 1996)
The court was dealing with the dangerousness of an intersection. The judge relied in part on the fact that the civil engineer had firsthand knowledge due to his personal inspection and found him qualified to testify.

Example 6.17
Pelzer v. United Parcel Service, 484 S.E.2d 849 (N.C. App. 1997)
An engineer was found not qualified due to a delayed visit to an accident scene.

Example 6.18
West v. Sonke, 968 P.2d 228 (Idaho 1998)
A civil engineer did not inspect the actual tractor in question. The expert was held not qualified to testify.

Real-world experience

Judges may find experts with real-world experience qualified to testify, despite lacking formal education or training.

Example 6.19
Price ex. rel. v. NYC Housing Authority, 706 N.E.2d 1167 (N.Y. 1998)
The court found qualified an expert in criminal behavior who lacked a degree but had actual experience in the field.

Example 6.20
General Motors Corp. v. Pegues, 724 So.2d 489 (Miss. App. 1998)
An auto mechanic with forty years of experience but only a high school education was found qualified to testify on causation in a defective ball joint case.

Example 6.21
Guerrero v. Tarrant Cty. Mortician Servs., 977 S.W.2d 829 (Tex. App.-Fort Worth 1998)
As an official with the same goal as the defendant Mortician Services, the death investigator was competent to testify regarding what constitutes good faith in the collection of bodies at an accident scene. Because the witness was a former sheriff's deputy and is a death investigator, the witness was qualified to testify as an expert in the collection of bodies and their transport to the medical examiner's office.

Example 6.22
Hamilton Mut. Ins. Co. v. Ford Motor Co., 702 N.E.2d 491 (Ohio App. 6 Dist. 1997)
A fire and explosion investigator with twelve years of experience was found not qualified to testify regarding an allegedly faulty design or manufacturing defect of an automotive component. The witness had no experience in the design and manufacturing of automobiles.

Example 6.23
Sharon B.W. v. George B.W., 507 S.E.2d 401 (W.Va. 1998)
A psychologist was found qualified to testify in an alleged sexual abuse child-custody case even though his clinical practice did not encompass a great deal of sexually abused children.

Example 6.24
Price ex. rel. Price v. NYC Housing Auth., 706 N.E.2d 1167 (N.Y. 1998)
A criminal behavior expert was qualified by experience, skill, training, knowledge, and experience. Lack of academic training in behavioral sciences did not disqualify the witness.

Example 6.25
Johnson v. District of Columbia, 728 A.2d 70 (D.C. 1999)
A master plumber was found not qualified to testify regarding the required safety warnings on commercial heaters. The witness had no experience in the design of water heaters and their controls. His testimony showed that he was unfamiliar with and somewhat misinformed regarding regulations governing the permissible temperature ranges of hot water provided from commercial heaters.

Bench trial

The court may be more liberal in admitting expert testimony when the case is not before a jury. This is because the court does not have to worry about an unsophisticated jury being led astray.

Example 6.26
Endresen v. Scheels Hardware and Sports, 560 N.W.2d 225 (N.D. 1997)
An expert with questionable qualifications was allowed to testify. The court stated, "I think because it is a bench trial I have the luxury of being a little more liberal at least on the initial receipt of any evidence."

6.4 Case Examples by Type of Expert

There is a substantial body of reported cases dealing with the qualifications of expert witnesses. The following table provides a sampling of these decisions and is organized by type of expert. Although most experts are routinely found qualified, there has been a growing trend toward being more restrictive.

Table 6.41 Recent Cases by Type of Expert

Expert	Result	Citation
Accident Reconstructionist	Not qualified to testify regarding bodily symptoms from an auto accident.	*Azzano v. O'Malley-Clements,* 710 N.E.2d 373 (Ohio App. 8 Dist. 1998)
Accident Reconstructionist	Due to lack of training, not permitted to testify regarding cause of wheel explosion.	*Waste Mgt. of Ohio v. Mid-America Tire,* 681 N.E.2d 492 (Ohio App. 2 Dist. 1996)
Actuary	Not permitted to testify that victim's gross earnings would triple in 17 years.	*Williams v. Rene,* 72 F.3d 1096 (3rd Cir. 1995)
Appraiser (Real Estate)	Qualified to testify despite expired license.	*Watts v. Lawrence,* 703 So.2d 236 (Miss. 1997)
Appraiser	Not permitted to testify about impact of prior engineering report.	*Nesbitt v. Dunn,* 672 So.2d 226 (La. App. 2 Cir. 1996)
Attorney	Not permitted to testify on fair trade practices of Robinson-Patman Act.	*Wlasiuk v. Whirlpool Corp.,* 914 P.2d 102 (Wash. App. Div. 1 1996)
Attorney	Not permitted to testify on ultimate issue in ADA case.	*Kuehl v. Wal-Mart Stores, Inc.,* 909 F.Supp. 794 (D. Colo. 1995)
Auto Mechanic	Qualified to testify in defective truck part case.	*General Motors Corp. v. Pegues,* 724 So.2d 489 (Miss. App. 1998)

Automotive Expert	Not permitted to testify on ultimate issue (lack of starter interlock system rendered car defective).	*Puopolo v. Honda Motor Co., Ltd.*, 668 N.E.2d 855 (Mass. App. Ct. 1996)
Bacteriologist	Not qualified to testify regarding standard of care of blood-banking industry in HIV transfusion case.	*United Blood Services v. Longoria*, 938 S.W.2d 29 (Tex. 1997)
Biochemist	Not qualified to testify on the impact of artificial sweeteners.	*Ballinger v. Atkins*, 947 F.Supp. 925 (E.D. Va. 1996)
Biomechanical Engineer	Not permitted to testify regarding whether a twisting movement could have ruptured the plaintiff's disk.	*Combs v. Norfolk and Western Ry. Co.*, 507 S.E.2d 355 (Va. 1998)
Biomechanical Engineer	Qualified to testify regarding cause of TMJ.	*Baerwald v. Flores*, 930 P.2d 816 (N.M. App. 1996)
Biophysicist	Qualified to testify regarding if the slow speed, rear-end collision could have caused the type of injury claimed by the plaintiff.	*Nathanson v. Houss*, 717 So.2d 114 (Fla. App. 4 Dist. 1998)
Builder	Not qualified to testify on architect's standard of care.	*Walker v. The Bluffs Apartments*, 477 S.E.2d 472 (S.C. App. 1996)
Cardiologist	Not permitted to testify on heart attack from nicotine patch.	*Rosen v. CIBA-Geigy Corp.*, 78 F.3d 316 (7th Cir. 1996)
Certified Public Accountant	Permitted to testify on costs borne and profits enjoyed during alleged conspiracy to fix prices.	*City of Tuscaloosa v. Harcross Chemicals, Inc.*, 158 F.3d 548 (11th Cir. 1998)

Certified Public Accountant	Qualified to testify on telecom company's restructuring of rates.	*Oucc v. Citizen's Telephone Corp.*, 681 N.E.2d 252 (Ind. App. 1997)
Certified Public Accountant	Not qualified to testify on projected lost income.	*Maher v. Continental Cas. Co.*, 76 F.3d 535 (4th Cir. 1996)
Chemist	Testimony on cause of defective tire did not meet *Daubert* standard.	*Mitchell v. Uniroyal Goodrich Tire Co.*, 666 So.2d 727 (La. App. 4 Cir. 1995)
Chief Underwriting Officer	Qualified to testify regarding complexities of marine insurance policies.	*Johnson & Higgins v. Hale*, 710 A.2d 318 (Md. App. 1998)
Chiropractor	Permitted to testify about injuries to hand and arm.	*Winston v. Brodie*, 517 S.E.2d 203 (N.C. App. 1999)
Chiropractor	Not qualified to testify about TMJ.	*Fugett v. H.*, 669 N.E.2d 6 (Oh. App. 2 Dist. 1995)
Civil Engineer	Not permitted to offer opinion on cause of escalator accident.	*Jimenez v. GNOC Corp.*, 670 A.2d 24 (N.J. Super. A.D 1996)
Civil Engineer	Not qualified to testify on the useful safe life of a tractor.	*West v. Sonke*, 968 P.2d 228 (Idaho 1998)
Civil Engineer	Qualified to testify regarding landfill design despite never having designed a landfill.	*Sharp v. 251st Street Landfill, Inc.*, 925 P.2d 546 (Okl. 1996)
Civil Engineer	Not qualified to testify about the standard of care of a general contractor.	*IMR Corp. v. Hemphill*, 926 S.W.2d 542 (Mo. App. E.D. 1996)
Civil Engineer	Qualified to testify in hydroplaning accident case.	*Woollen v. State*, 593 N.W.2d 729 (Neb. 1999)
Clinical Psychologist	Opinion on custody rejected by trial judge.	*Warlick v. Warlick*, 661 So.2d 706 (La. App. 2 Cir. 1995)

Collector	Corvette collector qualified to testify as to value of 1961 Corvette.	*Mearns v. Mearns*, 946 S.W.2d 188 (Ark. App. 1997)
Construction Expert	Not permitted to testify regarding the cause and effect of delays.	*Jurgens Real Estate v. R.E.D. Constr.*, 659 N.E.2d 353 (Ohio App.12 Dist. 1995)
Coroner	Qualified to testify regarding the behavior of people under the influence of alcohol.	*Carter v. Febber*, 136 F.3d 1000 (5th Cir. 1998)
Correctional Expert	Qualified to testify on failure to protect inmate.	*Payne v. Collins*, 986 F.Supp. 1036 (E.D. Tex. 1997)
Death Investigator	Qualified to testify on body collection procedures.	*Guerrero v. Tarrant Cty. Mortician Servs.*, 977 S.W.2d 829 (Tex. App.-Fort Worth 1998)
Designer	Qualified to testify on eyeglass display system.	*Magnivision, Inc. v. Bonneau Co.*, 33 F.Supp.2d 1218 (C.D. Cal. 1998)
Detective	Not permitted to speculate on rape suspect.	*Gomez By Gomez v. N.Y.C. Housing Authority*, 636 N.Y.S.2d 271 (A.D. 1 Dept. 1995)
Economics Professor	Not permitted to testify regarding extent of investors' damages.	*Three Crown Ltd. Partnership v. Salomon Bros., Inc.*, 906 F.Supp. 876 (S.D.N.Y. 1995)
Economist	Not permitted to testify on enjoyment of life.	*Talle v. Nebraska Dept. of Social Serv.*, 541 N.W.2d 30 (Neb. 1995)
Economist	Not permitted to testify on value of enjoyment of life.	*Anderson v. Nebraska Dept. of Soc. Serv.*, 538 N.W.2d 732 (Neb. 1995)
Economist	Testimony on FELA injury inadmissible.	*CSX Transp. Inc. v. Casale*, 463 S.E.2d 445 (Va. 1995)
Electrical Engineer	Qualified to testify in patent suit despite not being an attorney.	*Endress & Hauser v. Hawk Measurement Systems Pty*, 122 F.3d 1040 (Fed. Cir. 1997)

Electromechanical Engineer	Not qualified to testify that backup alarms were prone to habituation.	*Surace v. Caterpillar, Inc.*, 111 F.3d 1039 (3rd Cir. 1997)
Emergency Room Physician	Not permitted to testify on head injury.	*Broders v. Heise*, 924 S.W.2d 148 (Tex. 1996)
Engineer	Not qualified to testify on standard of care for operating motor vehicles.	*Pelzer v. United Parcel Service, Inc.*, 484 S.E.2d 849 (N.C. App. 1997)
Engineer	Not permitted to testify on defective tire.	*Diviero v. Uniroyal Goodrich Tire Co.*, 919 F.Supp. 1353 (D. Ariz. 1996)
Engineer	Not permitted to testify on failure to mark curb.	*Guldy v. Pyramid Corp.*, 634 N.Y.S.2d 788 (A.D. 3 Dept. 1995)
Engineer	Not permitted under *Daubert* to testify on alternative design theory.	*Cummins v. Lyle Industries*, 93 F.3d 362 (7th Cir. 1996)
Engineer	Testimony of cause of spinout insufficient under *Daubert.*	*Pomella v. Regency Coach Lines Ltd.*, 899 F.Supp. 335 (E.D. Mich. 1995)
Environmental Engineer	Qualified to testify regarding "state of the art" on asbestos hazards.	*Anderson v. A.P.I. Co. of Minnesota*, 559 N.W.2d 204 (N.D. 1997)
Ergonomics Expert	Not permitted under *Daubert* standard to testify on CAD design.	*Bennett v. PRC Public Sector, Inc.*, 931 F.Supp. 484 (S.D. Texas 1996)
Ergonomist	Not permitted to testify on keyboard design.	*Dennis v. Pertec Computer Corp.*, 927 F.Supp. 156 (N.J. 1996)
Escalator Engineering Expert	Not permitted to testify on law.	*Weston v. Washington Metropolitan Area Transit*, 78 F.3d 682 (D.C. Cir. 1996)
Family Physician	Not qualified to testify on alleged release of harmful chemicals from pulp plant causing chronic lung disease.	*Everett v. Georgia-Pacific Corp.*, 949 F.Supp. 856 (S.D. Ga. 1996)

Family Physician	Not qualified to testify on aplastic anemia.	*Corsetti v. Koopers Co., Inc.*, 640 N.Y.S.2d 556 (A.D. 1 Dept. 1996)
Firearms	In bench trial, qualified to testify to alleged design defect.	*Endresen v. Scheels Hardware and Sports,* 560 N.W.2d 225 (N.D. 1997)
Fire and Explosives Investigator	Not qualified to testify as to an alleged design or manufacturing defect of an automobile component.	*Hamilton Mut. Ins. Co. v. Ford Motor Co.*, 702 N.E.2d 491 (Ohio App. 6 Dist. 1997)
Fire Captain	Not qualified to testify regarding alleged defect in baseboard heater.	*Weisgram v. Marley Co.*, 169 F.3d 514 (8th Cir. 1999)
Fire Investigator	Qualified to use lightning strike date from Bureau of Land Management to form opinion.	*Landham v. Idaho Power Co.*, 943 P.2d 912 (Idaho 1997)
Fire Safety	Qualified to testify that lack of smoke detector was contrary to national standard of care.	*Knoke v. South Carolina Dept. of Parks*, 478 S.E.2d 256 (S.C. 1996)
Forensic Consulting Engineer	Not permitted to testify about effect of degreaser on parking lot.	*Scheerer v. Hardee's Food Systems, Inc.*, 92 F.3d 702 (8th Cir. 1996)
Friction Expert	Not permitted to testify on bathtub fall.	*Fedorczyk v. Caribbean Cruise Lines, LTD,* 82 F.3d 69 (3rd Cir. 1996)
Gastroenterol-ogist	Not qualified to testify about gynecological malpractice.	*Hudson v. Arias*, 667 N.E.2d 50 (Ohio App. 8 Dist. 1995)
General Practitioner	Not qualified to testify on failed induced delivery.	*Chase v. Mary Hitchcock Memorial Hosp.*, 668 A.2d 50 (N.H. 1995)
General Surgeon	Qualified to testify regarding alleged medical malpractice of orthopedic surgeon.	*Hunter v. Bossier Medical Center,* 718 So.2d 636 (La. App. 2 Cir. 1998)

Gynecologist	Not qualified to testify about blood recycling systems.	*Hollingsworth v. U.S.*, 928 F.Supp. 1023 (D. Idaho 1996)
Hematologist	Not qualified to testify as to link between Benzene and leukemia.	*Sutera v. Perrier Group of America Inc.*, 986 F.Supp. 655 (D. Mass. 1997)
Heroin Addict	Not qualified to testify on withdrawals.	*Pedraza v. Jones*, 71 F.3d 194 (5th Cir. 1995)
Highway Safety Specialist	Qualified to testify on safety of railroad crossing.	*Wood v. Minnesota Mining and Mfg. Co.*, 112 F.3d 306 (8th Cir. 1997)
Horticulture Expert	Not permitted to testify about Benlate contamination.	*E.I. du Pont de Nemours & Co. v. Robinson*, 923 S.W.2d 549 (Tex. 1995)
Human Factors Psychologist	Not permitted to testify about unsafe gate.	*Chapman v. City of Virginia Beach*, 457 S.E.2d 798 (Va. 1996)
Human-Machines Interaction	Qualified to testify on cause of action at airline carousel despite lack of expertise in airline terminal area design.	*Stagl v. Delta Air Lines, Inc.*, 117 F.3d 76 (2nd Cir. 1997)
Industrial Psychologist	Qualified to testify in tire case despite lack of experience in tire industry.	*Cole v. Goodyear Tire & Rubber Co.*, 967 S.W.2d 176 (Mo. App. E.D. 1998)
Internist	Qualified to testify regarding nursing malpractice in cardiac catheter case.	*Hall v. Huff*, 957 S.W.2d 90 (Tex. App.-Texarcana 1997)
Internist	Not qualified to testify on whether PCBs caused personal injuries ranging from baldness to learning disabilities.	*Mancuso v. Consolidated Edison Co. of New York*, 967 F.Supp. 1437 (S.D.N.Y. 1997)
Internist	Qualified to testify despite retiring in 1982.	*McDougall v. Eliuk*, 554 N.W.2d 56 (Mich. App. 1996)
Internist	Not qualified to testify regarding cause of osteonecrosis.	*Nichols v. Hanzel*, 674 N.E.2d 1237 (Ohio App. 4 Dist. 1996)

Investigating Officer	Not permitted to testify on cause of accident.	*McMichen v. Moattar,* 470 S.E.2d 800 (Ga. App. 1996)
Mechanic	Not qualified to testify about battery design and explosion. Qualified to testify concerning adequate warnings.	*Tanner v. Shoupe,* 596 N.W.2d 805 (Wis. App. 1999)
Mechanic	Not qualified to testify on design defect (lack of park interlock device).	*Bogosian v. Mercedes-Benz of North America, Inc.,* 104 F.3d 472 (1st Cir. 1997)
Mechanical Engineer	Qualified to testify on tractor-trailer kingpin.	*Baldauf v. Arrow Tank and Engineering,* 979 P.2d 166 (Mont. 1999)
Mechanical Engineer	Not qualified to testify as an accident reconstructionist.	*Wilson v. Woods,* 163 F.3d 935 (5th Cir. 1999)
Mechanical Engineer	Qualified to testify in seat belt failure case.	*Gammill v. Jack Williams Chevrolet, Inc.,* 972 S.W.2d 713 (Tex. 1998)
Mechanical Engineer	Not qualified to testify on design of electric grill that allegedly caused electrocution.	*Trumps v. Toastmaster, Inc.,* 969 F.Supp. 247 (S.D.N.Y. 1997)
Mechanical Engineer	Not permitted to testify on sudden acceleration of auto.	*Lawrence v. General Motors Corp.,* 73 F.3d 587 (5th Cir. 1996)
Metallurgy Engineer	Qualified to testify on cause of exploding tire.	*Colboch v. Uniroyal Tire Co., Inc.,* 670 N.E.2d 1366 (Ohio App. 8 Dist. 1996)
Metallurgy Engineer	Not permitted to testify about sewer grate.	*Colston v. Southeastern Pa. Transp.,* 679 A.2d 299 (Pa. Cmwlth. 1996)
Neonatologist	Qualified to testify on alleged malpractice of obstetrician.	*Daniel v. Jones,* 39 F.Supp.2d 635 (E.D. Va. 1999)
Neurologist	Not permitted to testify about mental capacity based solely on the medical records.	*Tracy v. Steinberg,* 634 N.Y.S.2d 198 (A.D. 2 Dept. 1995)

Neuropsychologist	Qualified to testify about the cause of an organic brain injury.	*Huntoon v. TCI Cablevision of Colorado,* 968 P.2d 681 (Colo. 1998)
Neuropsychologist	Qualified to testify about plaintiff's cognitive defects after motor vehicle accident.	*Adamson v. Chiovaro,* 705 A.2d 402 (N.J. Super. A.D. 1998)
Neuropsychologist	Not qualified to testify on cause of organic brain damage.	*Standeford v. Winn Dixie of La., Inc.,* 688 So.2d 602 (La. App. 5 Cir. 1996)
Neuropsychologist	Not qualified to testify on toxic causation.	*Sanderson v. IFF,* 950 F.Supp. 981 (C.D. Cal. 1996)
Neurosurgeon	Not qualified to testify on chemonucleolysis procedure performed by orthopedic surgeon.	*Lawson v. Elkins,* 477 S.E.2d 510 (Va. 1996)
Neurosurgeon	Testimony on carpal tunnel syndrome insufficient under *Daubert*.	*Dukes v. Illinois Cent. R. Co.,* 934 F.Supp. 939 (N.D. Ill. 1996)
Nuclear Reactor Physicist	Testimony on TMI insufficient under *Daubert* standard.	*In Re TMI Litigation Cases Consolidated II,* 911 F.Supp. 775 (M.D. Pa. 1996)
Nurse	Not qualified to testify on causation of corneal burns.	*Arlington Mem. Hosp. Foundation v. Baird,* 991 S.W.2d 918 (Tex. App.-Fort Worth 1999)
Nurse	Not qualified to testify that a failure to give a preoperative hibiclens shower and antibiotics after surgery caused infection.	*Long v. Methodist Hosp. of Indiana, Inc.,* 699 N.E.2d 1164 (Ind. App. 1998)
Nurse	Not qualified to testify on alleged medical malpractice by a physician.	*Stryczek v. Methodist Hospitals, Inc.,* 694 N.E.2d 1186 (Ind. App. 1998)

Nurse	Not qualified to testify on whether a nurse's injection in the buttocks caused permanent sciatic nerve damage.	*Kent v. Pioneer Valley Hosp.*, 930 P.2d 904 (Utah App. 1997)
Nurse	Qualified to testify to standard of care of operating room technician.	*Healthtrust, Inc. v. Cantrell*, 689 So.2d 822 (Ala. 1997)
Nurse	Not qualified to testify in malpractice action against physician.	*Sigrist By and Through Sigrist v. Clarke*, 935 S.W.2d 350 (Mo. App. S.D. 1996)
Nurse	Not qualified to testify in medical malpractice claim.	*Flanagan v. Labe*, 666 A.2d 333 (Pa. Super. 1995)
Obstetrician	Qualified to testify about performance of episiotomy by a resident despite not being from same or similar community.	*Sheeley v. Memorial Hosp.*, 710 A.2d 161 (R.I. 1998)
Occupational Physician	Not permitted to testify on state of the art of asbestos hazards.	*Owens-Corning Fiberglass v. A.M. Centennial*, 660 N.E.2d 819 (Ohio Com. Pl. 1995)
Ophthalmologist	Not qualified to testify on water balloon toy's capability to cause eye injury.	*Naughton v. Bankier*, 691 A.2d 712 (Md. App. 1997)
Ophthalmologist	Not permitted to testify on chemical cause of cataracts.	*Grimes v. Hoffman-LaRoche, Inc.*, 907 F.Supp. 33 (D.N.H. 1995)
Oral Surgeon	Permitted to testify about malpractice of emergency room physician and radiologist for failure to diagnose broken jaw.	*Dolen v. St. Mary's Hosp. of Huntington*, 506 S.E.2d 624 (W.Va. 1998)
Orthopedic Surgeon	Qualified to testify on alleged malpractice by a podiatrist.	*Bennet v. Butlin*, 512 S.E.2d 13 (Ga. App. 1999)

Orthopedic Surgeon	Not qualified to testify about defects in pedicle screw.	*Cali v. Danek Medical, Inc.*, 24 F.Supp.2d 941 (W.D. Wis. 1998)
Orthopedic Surgeon	Qualified to testify on standard of care of referring patients to physical therapists.	*Joyce v. Boulevard Therapy & Rehab*, 694 A.2d 648 (Pa. Super. 1997)
Orthopedic Surgeon	Qualified to testify on alleged postoperative negligence by physiatrist.	*Poleri v. Salkind*, 683 A.2d 649 (Pa. Super. 1996)
Orthopedic Surgeon	Qualified to testify to alleged malpractice of physical therapist during postoperative care.	*Lee v. Visiting Nurse Health System*, 477 S.E.2d 445 (Ga. App. 1996)
Orthopedic Surgeon	Not permitted to testify on effect of litigation.	*Yingling v. Hartwig*, 925 S.W.2d 952 (W.D. Mo. App. 1996)
Orthopedic Surgeon	Not qualified to testify regarding chiropractic malpractice.	*Brodersen v. Sioux Valley Memorial Hosp.*, 902 F.Supp. 931 (N.D. Iowa 1995)
Pathologist	Not qualified to testify on standard of care of surgeon.	*Good v. Presbyterian Hosp. in City of New York*, 934 F.Supp. 107 (S.D.N.Y. 1996)
Petroleum Engineer	Not qualified to testify on suspension scaffold design.	*Ford v. Penzoil*, 974 F.Supp. 559 (E.D. La. 1977)
Pharmacologist	Not qualified to testify on alleged malpractice by ophthalmologist who allegedly prescribed the drug Feldene negligently.	*Bisset v. Renna*, 710 A.2d 404 (N.H. 1998)
Physiatrist	Qualified to testify on alleged malpractice by orthopedic surgeon regarding skin care.	*Smith v. Juneau*, 692 So.2d 1365 (La. App. 4 Cir. 1997)

Physician	Qualified to testify on standard of care of drug abuse counselors regarding sexual relationship with patient.	*Morgan v. Psychiatric Institute of Wash.*, 692 A.2d 417 (D.C. App. 1997)
Physician	Despite not being a board-certified OB/GYN, qualified to testify on alleged malpractice resulting from allegedly unnecessary hysterectomy.	*Ex Parte Sonnier*, 707 So.2d 635 (Ala. 1997)
Physician	Not qualified to testify on alleged malpractice by occupational therapist.	*Goring v. Martinez*, 479 S.E.2d 432 (Ga. App. 1996)
Physician	Not permitted to testify on effects of CCP.	*Rutigliano v. Valley Business Forms*, 929 F.Supp. 779 (D. N.J. 1996)
Physician	Not qualified to testify on polythermia.	*Muzzey v. Kerr-McGee Chemical Corp.*, 921 F.Supp. 511 (N.D. Ill. 1996)
Physician	Not permitted to testify that TCE caused birth defects.	*McKenzie v. Westinghouse Elec. Corp.*, 674 A.2d 1167 (Pa. Cmwlth. 1996)
Physician	Testimony insufficient to prove polysporin spray caused frostbite.	*Burroughs Wellcome Co. v. Crye*, 907 S.W.2d 497 (Tex. 1995)
Planning Regulator	Not qualified to testify on value of landowner's development rights.	*Suitum v. Tahoe Regional Planning Agency*, 80 F.3d 359 (9th Cir. 1996)
Plumber	Not qualified to testify on the required safety warnings on commercial heaters.	*Johnson v. District of Columbia*, 728 A.2d 70 (D.C. 1999)
Podiatrist	Not permitted to testify on defect in basketball shoe.	*Tucker v. Nike, Inc.*, 919 F. Supp. 1192 (N.D. Inc. 1995)

Police Investigator	Permitted to testify on cause of automotive accident.	*Dufrene v. Willingham,* 702 So.2d 1026 (La. App. 5 Cir. 1998)
Police Officer	Not qualified to testify on drug-sniffing dog.	*$18,800 in U.S. Currency v. State,* 961 S.W.2d 257 (Tex.App.-Houston 1st Dist. 1997)
Police Officer	Not permitted to testify about why motorist was negligent and why negligence caused accident.	*Robbins v. Buntrock,* 550 N.W.2d 422 (S.D. 1996)
Police Officer	Not permitted to testify on the cause of an accident.	*Madrid v. Robinson,* 906 P.2d 855 (Or. App. 1995)
Political Activist	Not permitted to testify on health risks of EMF.	*Banks v. Georgia Power Co.,* 469 S.E.2d 218 (Ga. App. 1996)
Power Line Construction	Qualified to testify on need to trim trees around power lines.	*BG & E v. Flippo,* 684 A.2d 456 (Md. App. 1996)
Professor of Biochemistry	Not permitted to testify on testing of lung tissue.	*Braun v. Lorillard, Inc.,* 84 F.3d 230 (7th Cir. 1996)
Professor of Civil Engineering	Qualified to testify as to safety of intersection.	*Burgess v. Harley,* 934 S.W.2d 58 (Tenn. App. 1996)
Professor of Criminology	Not permitted to testify about deadly force.	*Hattori v. Peairs,* 662 So.2d 509 (La. App. 1 Cir. 1995)
Professor of Economics	Despite lack of knowledge of recreational vehicle industry, qualified to testify on damages in stolen idea case.	*Olson v. Nieman's, Ltd.,* 579 N.W.2d 299 (Iowa 1998)
Professor of Securities Law	Not permitted to testify about statements not actionable under securities law.	*Ausa Life Ins. Co. v. Dwyer,* 899 F.Supp. 1200 (S.D.N.Y. 1995)
Psychologist	Qualified to testify on child custody.	*Sharon B.W. v. George B.W.,* 507 S.E.2d 401 (W.Va. 1998)

Psychologist	Not qualified to testify regarding sexual predator.	*In re Twining,* 894 P.2d 1331 (Wash. App. Div. 3 1995)
Psychologist	Not qualified to testify on warnings drug companies should give the public.	*Tyler By and Through Tyler v. Sterling Drug, Inc.* 19 F. Supp.2d (N.D. Okla. 1998)
Psychologist	Not permitted to testify about credibility.	*Westcott v. Crinklaw,* 68 F.3d 1073 (8th Cir. 1995)
Psychology Professor	Not permitted to testify about truthfulness.	*In Interest of S.J.M.,* 539 N.W.2d 496 (Iowa App. 1995)
Psychology Resident	Qualified to testify in custody case.	*State in Interest of G.Y.,* 962 P.2d 78 (Utah App. 1998)
Pulmonologist	Not qualified to testify about occupational asthma.	*Diaz v. Johnson Matthey, Inc.,* 893 F.Supp. 358 (D.N.J. 1995)
Quarter Horse Expert	Not qualified to testify about partially blind horse.	*Ansick v. Hillenbrand Industries, Inc.,* 933 F.Supp. 773 (S.D. In. 1996)
Race Car Driver	Qualified to testify about lost profits in breach of contract case regarding automotive driving school.	*Ishin Speed Sport, Inc. v. Rutherford,* 933 S.W.2d 343 (Tex. App.-Fort Worth 1996)
Radiation Expert	Not permitted to testify in Three Mile Island case.	*In re TMI Litigation Cases Consolidated II,* 910 F.Supp. 200 (M.D. Pa. 1996)
Railroad Maintenance Engineer	Qualified to testify as to safety of track in slip and fall case.	*Lauria v. National Railroad Passenger Corp.,* 145 F.3d 593 (3rd Cir. 1998)
Real Estate	Qualified to offer valuation opinion in condemnation case.	*West Virginia Div. of Highways v. Butler,* 516 S.E.2d 769 (W.Va. 1999)
Real Estate Broker	Qualified to testify on valuation.	*McGaffic v. Redevelopment Authority,* 732 A.2d 663 (Pa. Cmwlth. 1999)

Road Designer	Qualified to testify about road that changed from pavement to gravel and allegedly caused moped accident.	*Herman v. Will Tp.*, 671 N.E.2d 1141 (Ill. App. 3 Dist. 1996)
Roofing Expert	Not permitted to testify about negligence.	*Zens v. Hon*, 538 N.W.2d 794 (S.D. 1995)
Security Expert	Not qualified to testify about airport security.	*Shah v. Pan American World Services, Inc.*, 148 F.3d 84 (2nd Cir. 1998)
Sexual Harassment Expert	Not permitted to testify that plaintiff was a victim of sexual harassment.	*Fowler v. Kootenai County*, 918 P.2d 1185 (Idaho 1996)
Sports Experts	Not qualified to testify on danger recognition.	*McIntosh v. Omaha Public Schools*, 544 N.W.2d 502 (Neb. 1996)
State Trooper	Not qualified to testify about standard of care.	*Christiansen v. Silfies*, 667 A.2d 396 (Pa. Super. 1995)
Surgeon	Not qualified to testify on standard of care of physical therapist.	*Kirker v. Nicolla*, 681 N.Y.S.2d 689 (A.D. 3 Dept. 1998)
Surgeon	Qualified to testify on nursing malpractice despite not having practiced medicine in 13 years.	*Wolford v. St. Paul Fire & Marine Ins. Co.*, 961 S.W.2d 743 (Ark. 1998)
Surgeon	Not permitted to rely on discussions with doctors on national standard of care.	*Travers v. District of Columbia*, 672 A.2d 566 (D.C. App. 1996)
Thermodynamics Expert	Qualified to testify about failure to warn on dishwasher.	*Laramie v. Sears, Roebuck & Co.*, 707 A.2d 443 (N.H. 1998)
Tire Designer	Not permitted to testify about defective tire.	*Charmichael v. Samyang Tires, Inc.*, 923 F.Supp. 1514 (S.D. Ala. 1996)
Tire Engineer	Qualified due to vast experience and research and despite lack of extensive formal education.	*Bush v. Michelin Tire Corp.*, 963 F.Supp. 1436 (W.D. Ky. 1996)

Tire Failure and Analysis	Expert found qualified to testify in tire failure analysis and tire repair.	*Labit v. D.H. Holmes Co., Ltd.*, 721 So.2d 933 (La. App. 5 Cir. 1998)
Title Abstractor	Not qualified to testify on land ownership.	*Butler Crockett v. Pinecrest Pipeline*, 909 P.2d 225 (Utah 1995)
Toxicologist	Not qualified to testify on causation in *in utero* bromide exposure case.	*Wintz by and through Wintz v. Northrop Corp.*, 110 F.3d 508 (7th Cir. 1997)
Traffic Control Devices	Expert not qualified to testify about portable speed bumps.	*Goodyear Tire & Rubber Co., Inc. v. Ross*, 660 So.2d 1109 (Fla. App. 4 Dist. 1995)
Trainmen	Not permitted to testify on engine cab design.	*Rice v. Cincinnati, New Orleans & Pacific Ry. Co.*, 920 F.Supp. 732 (E.D. Ky. 1996)
Transportation Consulting Engineer	Not permitted to testify on who was driving vehicle in question.	*State Farm Mut. Auto. Ins. Co. v. Penland*, 668 So.2d 200 (Fla. App. 4 Dist. 1995)
Vocational Rehabilitation Counselor	Not qualified to testify about disability.	*Phillips v. Industrial Machine*, 597 N.W.2d 377 (Neb. 1999)
Vocational Rehabilitation Expert	Qualified to testify on employment opportunities despite lack of formal academic training.	*Waldorf v. Shuta*, 142 F.3d 601 (3rd Cir. 1998)

6.5 Qualifications and the Weight Given Testimony

If the judge finds an expert qualified, the expert will be allowed to testify as an expert witness in a case.[2] This, however, does not in any way eliminate the issue of qualifications. The expert's qualifications will remain a legitimate issue for direct and cross-examination because they are relevant to his credibility and to the weight the jury should give his testimony. A discussion of some of the more common areas of cross-examination inquiry regarding an expert's qualifications follows.

[2] Assuming the expert testimony is not excluded for another reason.

Gaps in the expert's CV

When trying to challenge an expert's credibility, counsel may focus on any gaps in the expert's CV. An expert witness should be prepared to explain any such gaps.

Example 6.27
Q. I see here a gap on your resume from May 1996 to September 1996. What were you doing at that time?
A. I took the summer off to backpack across Europe.

Licensing

Many records from professional licensing organizations may be available to a cross-examining attorney. These records could include college transcripts. An expert witness should be prepared to be questioned about any such records as they may affect her credibility.

Example 6.28
Q. I see here your license was suspended in 1997.
A. Yes, I was late paying the renewal fee.

Education

If an expert witness has a questionable academic background, he can expect to be questioned about this during cross-examination. He might also be questioned about any lacking education, especially if this contrasts with the opposing attorney's experts.

Example 6.29
Q. I have here your college transcript. Isn't it a fact that your GPA was only 2.2?

Example 6.30
Q. You don't have a graduate degree in this field, do you?

Professional writings

Publications may increase a witness's credibility with a jury. If a forensic expert "wrote the book" on a particular area, this may score points with the jury. If, however, an expert witness has not published in a particular area, this may be brought out on cross as a way to lessen her credibility. This is especially true if the opposing expert is well published.[3]

Example 6.31
Q. You haven't published anything in this area, have you?

---

[3] If an expert has published, then his writings can be used to impeach his testimony if they contradict what he says on the stand.

Experience

Practical, recent, relevant, hands-on experience—or the lack thereof—may be very relevant with a jury as far as an expert's qualifications are concerned. An expert witness should be prepared to answer any questions about his real-world experience. This is a particular area of concern if the expert is an academic or if he is retired and now only consults and testifies. It is also of particular concern when the expert's experience does not exactly match up with what's at issue in the case.

Example 6.32
Q. Doctor, when was the last time you actually delivered a baby?

Example 6.33
Q. I realize that you have a doctorate in mechanical engineering, sir. You don't have any experience regarding habituation, do you?

Training and certification

Any lack of training or certification can be brought out during cross-examination. Once again, this is most likely to occur if the opposing expert has more training or certification.

Example 6.34
Q. You're not board certified, are you?

6.6 Avoiding Qualifications Problems

Experts want to avoid being found to be not qualified to testify in a particular case because such a finding will be used against them in future cases. Experts can take steps to avoid being found not qualified.

1. Stay within one's area of expertise

The further an expert strays from her actual area of expertise, the more likely she is to be:

a. questioned about her qualifications;
b. found not qualified;
c. have her testimony limited; and
d. cross-examined at length.

2. Maintain an accurate CV

The expert should give his retaining attorney a complete and accurate CV without any mistakes, exaggerations, untruths, or material omissions. The expert should be honest with retaining counsel about any areas of concern he has regarding his qualifications to testify on a certain topic. The attorney can then decide if she needs to hire a different or an additional expert.

3. Discover the role of the expert
The expert should discuss with counsel what the expert's role will be and what issues and areas he will be asked to state his opinions on. An expert should decline cases in which he does not feel qualified.

4. Tell the truth
The expert should tell the truth when questioned about his qualifications, experience, and training by retaining counsel. He should be prepared to accept the fact that he may not be qualified in the case at hand.

5. Beware of large cases
Qualifications are most likely to be challenged in big cases where a lot of money is at stake. Experts should be especially careful about being truly qualified before agreeing to testify in such big cases.

6.7 Conclusion

The judge will initially decide, as a matter of law, whether an expert is qualified to testify. She will base her decision upon the expert's knowledge, skill, experience, training, and education. Even if an expert is found qualified by the judge, the expert's qualifications remain a legitimate area of inquiry during cross-examination. Experts should decline working on cases unless they are truly qualified to assist the trier of fact.

Chapter 7 Bulletproofing an Expert CV

7.1 Introduction

The expert's curriculum vitae (CV) is a very important document. It is usually the first document retaining counsel will review when she considers whether to retain an expert. It will also be scrutinized by opposing counsel. A poorly drafted CV can provide substantial ammunition to an attorney set on discrediting an expert. It is, therefore, extremely important that the CV be drafted carefully. This chapter provides specific advice on how to do this.

7.2 Currency

It is important to keep one's CV current and up to date. Failure to do so will make a forensic expert look sloppy. In some circumstances, it can even be used to make him look dishonest. Many experts fail to keep CVs up to date for the simple reason that they are too busy. To better maintain the currency of his CV, the wise expert should adopt a specific procedure for updating it and then stick to that procedure. The CV summarizes all of an individual's professional accomplishments. Experts need to find the time to keep their CVs up to date.

7.3 Accuracy

Mistakes, misleading impressions, and intentional or unintentional inaccuracies should be avoided. At best, these make an individual look sloppy and, at worst, they make her appear dishonest. In either event, her credibility will suffer.

It is especially important not to intentionally exaggerate, fabricate, or be dishonest in a CV. This means that the expert needs to describe items with sufficient detail, accuracy, and clarity so that the reader is not misled. Credibility is the key to one's value as an expert witness. Veracity on a CV can and will be used to prove or disprove an expert's credibility while testifying. As noted by this book's authors in a previous work:

> You can assume that counsel will have a copy of your latest as well as prior versions of your curriculum vitae (CV). It is extremely important that your CV contain no exaggerations or inaccuracies. If you did not graduate from MIT, summa cum laude, your CV should not indicate that you did. The date that you received a degree can also be used in cross-examination. If you list yourself as an author of a book or article and you were in fact only a co-author, you are opening yourself up to be damaged during cross-examination. If counsel can show that you exaggerated your CV, he can make the argument that you are exaggerating when giving your opinion.

> Even worse, if there is an obvious falsehood on your CV, counsel can portray you as a liar.[1]

7.4 Gaps in the CV

The first thing any lawyer will look for are any gaps contained in a CV. For example, are the years 1982 to 1983 unaccounted for? Did the expert actually graduate college in two years, or is she trying to hide the two years that she spent at a junior college? Counsel may create a timeline to determine if any periods on a CV do not match precisely with an expert's educational and work activities. Time gaps are red flags for opposing counsel. If there are gaps in an expert's CV, she can expect to face questions at deposition or trial such as those in the following example.

> **Example 7.1**
> When you left the years 1982 to 1983 out of your CV, you were attempting to mislead the jury, weren't you?

It is good practice to fill in the gaps in a CV. This is true even if a person is not particularly proud of what she accomplished during that time. An expert's most valued asset is her credibility. One's credibility is more likely to be damaged by an intentional omission on a CV than by whatever it was that the expert didn't want to report. Juries may forgive the fact that an expert failed out of the first college she went to thirty years ago. They will be far less likely to forgive their being intentionally deceived.[2]

7.5 Self-Designated Unearned Titles and Certifications

Experts should avoid listing certifications, titles, or designations that they in effect purchased and did not truly earn. Sophisticated counsel has access to lists of organizations that offer fancy sounding titles and designations in return for the payment of a fee. When, during cross-examination, it is revealed that an expert attended no courses, took no tests, and obtained the designation by being "grandfathered in," his credibility as an expert can be destroyed quickly.[3] Most sophisticated experts avoid this potential problem by leaving this kind of unearned title, designation, or certification off of their CVs.

---

[1] Steven Babitsky and James J. Mangraviti, Jr., *How to Excel During Cross-Examination: Techniques for Experts That Work* (Falmouth, MA: SEAK, Inc., 1997) 27.

[2] It may be good practice for experts to point out any gaps in their CV to retaining counsel. In this way, retaining counsel can ask the expert to explain the gaps during direct examination. The negative impact of these gaps should be diminished if they are brought out on direct rather than cross-examination.

[3] For example, "You took no test. All you did was pay the $800 and you got the designation. Isn't that the case?"

7.6 Multiple CVs

Many experts make the mistake of having multiple CVs. These could include a short one for quick and easy faxing, one that emphasizes certain kinds of experience or expertise, and (worst of all) one that is plaintiff- and another that is defense-oriented. Experts should assume that counsel has access to *all* their CVs. Counsel can use the existence of multiple CVs to damage one's credibility.

Example 7.2
Isn't it a fact that you intentionally omitted your work on behalf of the insurance industry from this CV?

As the above example illustrates, it is better practice to have one complete, accurate CV and to keep that CV up to date.

7.7 Memberships, Affiliations, and Licenses

One of the challenges for the expert who has a long, detailed CV is to keep it current. It is not uncommon for experts to list twenty, forty, fifty, or more scientific or professional societies that they are or have been involved with. The problem is that if an individual just lists the affiliations without dates, he leaves the impression that he is still actively involved in all of the societies or organizations. This will often come back to haunt the expert on cross-examination.

Example 7.3
Q. You listed the Managed Care Society of America on your CV under scientific societies. Are you a member in good standing of that organization?
Q. What about the next professional society you listed?

It is better practice to list the societies and organizations along with the dates of active involvement. When there is still active involvement, the expert can list the organization and note his membership from the date he first joined until the present.

Example 7.4
American Cancer Society 1989–Present.

Professional memberships are proper on a CV. One should not, however, place undue emphasis on a membership that only required a fee. Overly emphasizing such memberships can be used against experts during cross-examination.

7.8 Honorary Degrees and Memberships

To avoid misimpressions, *honorary* memberships or degrees should be listed as such.

Example 7.5
Honorary member California Research Committee in Nutrition (1991)

Example 7.6
PhD, Columbia University (Honorary) (1987)

Failure to do so may make an expert appear dishonest and can be used against her during cross-examination.

7.9 Self-Serving Comments

Some experts feel the need to enhance their CVs by including self-serving comments. Here is an example of such an inclusion.

Example 7.7
A nationally known teacher, lecturer, author, and consultant in risk management.

Such self-serving, subjective comments are an invitation for close scrutiny. They can also be a fertile ground for cross-examination by sophisticated counsel.

Example 7.8
Q. Who wrote this, sir?
Q. So you consider yourself nationally known?
Q. I wonder how many of the good men and women of the jury have heard of you?

It is better practice to leave any such self-congratulatory comments out of a CV. One can make the same point by listing one's books, articles, lectures, etc. A wise expert leaves the reader to draw his own conclusion that the expert is a "nationally known teacher, lecturer, author, and consultant in risk management."

7.10 Forensic Experience

Many experts make the mistake of listing the number of cases, states, and law firms they have been involved with in their forensic careers. They want readers to think that they must be good based on their volume of work. This type of inclusion in the CV may come in many forms, such as the following.

"Has served as an expert witness or consultant on cases in 42 states,"

or

"Consultant to the law firms of:

Kistin, Babitsky, Latimer, and Beitman
13 Falmouth Heights Road
Falmouth, Massachusetts 02540

and

Duff, Mangraviti, and Keefe
28 State Street
Boston, Massachusetts 02110,"

or

"Has performed in excess of 5,000 Independent Medical Evaluations."

This type of entry in a CV should be avoided. It is not relevant to one's expertise and it may provide counsel with ample ammunition for cross-examination. The potential areas of cross-examination inquiry that could result from such an inclusion include bias, hired-gun status, sources and amount of revenue earned, work on previous cases, personal relationship with counsel, and the propensity to testify only for plaintiffs or defendants. As such, these type of entries should not be included on a CV.

7.11 Writing and Publications

Forensic experts often get into trouble when listing their writings and publications on their CVs. Care should be taken to be completely accurate in all claims. Was the expert the "author," a "co-author," or one of fourteen contributors to an article, chapter, or book? The differences may at first seem subtle and perhaps even insignificant. Upon cross-examination, however, the forensic expert who exaggerates about his publications can be at risk.

Example 7.9
Q. So, when you testified that you authored six books on warning labels, you actually meant to say you contributed to these books. Would that be more accurate and less misleading to the jury?

An expert's attempts to increase the number of her publications by claiming responsibility for publications she did not write is a serious mistake. Consider the following example.

Example 7.10
Dr. Binder's research and educational activities concentrating in hematology have resulted in over 300 publications including some 60 chapters and books.

Such an item will open an expert up to numerous questions about what she actually wrote, why she inflated the number of publications on her CV, and why she was attempting to mislead the fact finder or jury. It is better practice to not inflate the number of publications, their importance, or their significance. The forensic expert who understates rather than overstates is in a much stronger position to withstand close questioning by counsel on cross-examination.

Another common mistake made by experts is to list a work that has only been accepted for publication as opposed to actually being published. This is an easy inaccuracy for attorneys to discover because the publication in question will not show up on electronic literature searches. Counsel will use such a mistake to show that the expert is misleading the jury. As such, it is better practice for experts to either only list a publication once it has actually been published or to specify in a separate section writings that have not yet been published but have been accepted for publication.

7.12 Form

There are many ways to lay out a CV. The form is mostly a matter of personal preference. (Appendix T contains some sample CVs.)

7.13 Conclusion

Forensic experts who are scrupulously accurate, complete, and honest in crafting their CVs enhance and protect their value as forensic experts.

Chapter 8 Opinions

8.1 Introduction

An expert is involved primarily in cases to render an opinion that will assist the trier of fact. This opinion needs to be stated in a legally sufficient manner and must be based upon reliable facts, data, and methodology. Experts can expect to be closely questioned on their opinions, how they were formed, and the facts and data upon which they are based.

8.2 Properly Stating an Expert Opinion

The legal requirements for stating an expert opinion in most civil cases is related directly to the burden of proof that exists in most civil cases. That burden of proof is a "preponderance of the evidence," "more likely than not," or "more than 50% likely." This is a much lesser burden of proof than the "beyond a reasonable doubt" standard with criminal cases.

The expert's opinion must satisfy the "preponderance of the evidence" burden of proof. This means that the expert must opine that it is more probable than not (there is more than a 50% probability) that his opinion is correct. Thus, an expert may give testimony in terms of an opinion that something could, or would, produce a certain result. The theory for admitting opinion testimony of this nature into evidence is that an expert witness's view regarding probabilities is often helpful in the determination of questions involving matters of science or technical or skilled knowledge.

The facts or scientific principles on which experts base their opinions must be sufficient to support reasonably accurate conclusions. Expert witnesses will not be barred from expressing opinions merely because they are not willing to state their conclusions with absolute certainty. However, expert opinions, if not stated in terms of the certain, must at least be stated in terms of the probable and not merely of the possible. The test of whether an expert's testimony expresses a reasonable probability is not based upon the use of "magic words," but is determined by looking at the entire substance of the expert's testimony. Although no magic words are required, certain phrases are commonly used by experts to express the idea that their opinions are based on at least a 51% probability. These phrases include:

- "based on a reasonable degree of medical certainty,"
- "based on a reasonable degree of scientific probability,"
- "based on a reasonable degree of scientific certainty,"
- "based on a reasonable degree of medical probability," and
- "more likely than not."

When an expert expresses opinions in a way that does not express the concept that she is at least 51% sure of her opinion, the opinion might be excluded by the judge. Thus, it is important to state an opinion in a way that clearly communicates that it is based upon a reasonable degree of probability and not just a mere possibility or speculation. Consider the following examples.

Example 8.1

Winntz By and Through Wintz v. Northrop Corp., 110 F.3d 508 (7th Cir. 1997)
Under Illinois law, to serve as the sole basis for a conclusion that an act was the proximate cause of the plaintiff's injury, an expert must be able to testify with a reasonable degree of medical certainty that a proximate cause existed. In light of the expert's statement on cross-examination that he was not stating with any degree of medical certainty that the plaintiff's problems had "at any time" been caused by bromide, the court concluded that his equivocal statement during direct that there was a "suggestion" that the symptoms were "related" to bromide was insufficient, standing alone, to raise an issue of fact as to proximate causation of the plaintiff's short-term problems.

Example 8.2

Nelson v. Ford Motor Co., 150 F.3d 905 (8th Cir. 1998)
The plaintiffs asserted that the district court erred by admitting testimony that there were no scratches in the notch where the jack was to be placed and that there was a tear elsewhere on the underbody of the car, indicating that the jack had been mispositioned. They contended that Ford's expert conceded in his deposition that it was not possible to state with absolute certainty that the jack had been incorrectly placed. The court held that the expert testimony was admissible and that any uncertainty in the expert's opinion was a factor the jury could consider in weighing his testimony.

Example 8.3

Kannankeril v. Terminix International, Inc., 128 F.3d 802 (3rd Cir. 1997)
Under New Jersey law, medical expert testimony must be made with a reasonable degree of certainty.

Example 8.4

Crawford v. Seufert, 388 P.2d 456 (Or. 1964)
The expert witness, an MD, admitted that his opinion rested upon speculation. The case was an action for damages arising out of an automobile collision. The plaintiff claimed that the accident caused her to suffer from severe perforations of the diverticulum. There was other evidence that the perforations were a result of a chronic degenerative ailment. The physician was to testify that the particular perforation was induced by the collision. On cross-examination, the doctor was asked about the three different types of perforated diverticula, and he admitted that there was no difference between that which he saw and the others.

Q. Diverticula do perforate into the mesentery?
A. Yes.
Q. And you don't know why?
A. No.

> **Q.** And then you necessarily had to speculate in this case, based upon the history of the accident that had been given you, that that would be a cause?
> **A.** Yes.

The court set aside the jury verdict in favor of the plaintiff. The court held that such speculative evidence, as a matter of law, could not support a finding that the accident caused the medical condition. It stated: "For medical opinion testimony to have any probative value, it must at least advise the jury that the inference drawn by the doctor is more probably correct than incorrect."

Example 8.5
Derrick v. Norton, 983 S.W.2d 529 (Mo. App. E.D. 1998)
At issue was why a full length mirror fell off a closet door and injured the plaintiff. The following exchange took place with the plaintiff's expert architect:

> **Q.** If there hadn't been any earthquake or some foreign object causing the mirror to fall, do you have an opinion as to the cause of the fall the mirror?
> **A.** Technically I don't know why the mirror fell because I was not there. I know that it was-
> **Counsel.** Your honor, let me object to any further editorialization as the witness has said he does not know why in answer to a question as to whether he has an opinion.
> **The court.** Sustained.

The court found that it was an abuse of discretion for the trial judge to exclude the opinion merely because of the above exchange. The court reasoned that although the expert used the words "I don't know," it was clear from the rest of his statement that he was merely noting that he had not personally observed the occurrence and was not denying that he had any opinion at all.

Example 8.6
Antoine-Tubbs v. Local 513, Air Transport Division, 50 F.Supp.2d 601 (N.D. Tex. 1998)
At issue was whether workplace stress caused preeclampsia in the plaintiff. The plaintiff's expert osteopath was asked if she could state with reasonable medical probability what caused the preeclampsia in the plaintiff. The witness replied, "You can't say that." The court found that the witness's testimony on this issue should not be admitted because it amounted to only subjective belief and unsupported speculation.

Example 8.7
Boudreau v. S/V Shere Khan C, 27 F.Supp.2d 72 (D. Me. 1998)
At issue was the cause of a fire aboard a yacht. The defendant's main attacks on the basis of the plaintiff's expert were the expert's lack of mathematical certainty about certain contributing fires in the leak and fire. The court held that the expert testimony was admissible because the expert testified credibly that such mathematical certainty was not necessary for him to render a competent opinion and explained credibly how he was able to determine the

cause of the fire from his two firsthand inspections of the vessel and the crew reports of the circumstances of the fire.

Example 8.8
Hawn v. Fritcher, 703 N.E.2d 109 (Ill. App. 4 Dist. 1998)
At issue was whether an auto accident caused a plaintiff's chondromalacia. The plaintiff's orthopedic surgeon testified as follows:

> **Q.** So, is your opinion, as to whether it might or could have been caused by the auto accident, is your answer yes or no?
> **A.** Yes, it could.

The court held the testimony admissible. It reasoned that the witness had testified to a reasonable degree of medical certainty that the accident "might or could" have caused the condition in the plaintiff's knees.

8.3 Facts and Data Relied Upon

The sophisticated expert understands what she is permitted to rely upon in forming an expert opinion. Federal Rule of Evidence 703 provides that the facts or data upon which the expert bases her opinion need not be admissible in evidence if of a type "reasonably relied upon by experts in the particular field in forming opinions or inferences upon the subject." The advisory notes to the rule give as an example a physician who relies upon others when practicing medicine.

> Thus, a physician in his own practice bases his diagnosis of information from numerous sources and of considerable variety including statements by patients and relatives, reports, and opinions from nurses, technicians, and other doctors, hospital records, and x-rays. Most of them are admissible in evidence but only with the expenditure of substantial time in producing and examining various authenticating witnesses. The physician makes life-and-death decisions in reliance upon them. His validation, expertly performed and subject to cross-examination, ought to suffice for judicial purposes.[1]

Thus, the expert may rely upon inadmissible information if:

1. it is reliable and assists the trier of fact (Rule 702) and
2. other experts would reasonably rely upon it.

The phrase "reasonably rely upon it" has been the subject of much discussion and litigation. Experts have been permitted to rely upon:

- consumer surveys,
- field agent reports,

[1] Advisory Committee Notes Rule 703.

- government-approved documents,
- affidavits of litigants,
- scientific studies, including those conducted in anticipation of litigation,
- trade publications,
- inspection of the scene,
- tests on products at issue,
- opinions of experts in the same or other fields,
- reports and testimony of expert witnesses in the same case,
- interviews, and
- other types of hearsay that the expert would normally rely upon in his/her work.[2]

Consider the following examples.

Example 8.9: Hypothetical question as basis for opinion
United States v. Mann, 712 F2d 941 (4th Cir. 1983)
A weapons expert, called to give his opinion regarding the identity of a gun, heard this hypothetical question:

> I'm going to ask you to assume that the weapon in question was identical to that weapon [referring to a gun already in evidence as an exhibit]; having the infinity sign on it; having three selector positions on the selector switch; having a folding stock being the only difference; not having the word "Valmet" on it; not having the words "Inner Arms Company" on it; and I'm going to ask you to assume those facts and draw any conclusion you can as to what kind of gun [the defendant's was].

The description of the defendant's gun in this case was admitted in evidence through the testimony of one of the defendant's acquaintances who had seen the gun. The court found that, "the expert was free to rely on that testimony." The court concluded that,

> experts in weaponry may rest their opinions as to a weapon's identity on the markings and features of the weapon, whether witnessed firsthand or described by a layman. Of course, the credibility of the witness whose description underlies the expert's opinion may affect the weight ultimately accorded by the trier of fact to the expert's opinion, but it does not make the description a form of evidence not reasonably relied on by experts in the field.

Example 8.10: Evidence not reasonably relied upon
Redman v. John D. Brush & Co., 111 F.3d 1174 (4th Cir. 1997)
A metallurgic engineer's testimony that a safe was not burglar deterrent was properly excluded. The expert relied solely on hearsay information from store personnel to identify a standard of burglar protection capacity. Experts would not rely on this hearsay as an indication of industry safety standards.

---

[2] *United States v. Arias* (C.A. 4 N.C. 1982) 678 F.2d 1202, 10 Fed. Rules Evid. Serv. 788, cert den (1982) 459 U.S. 910, 74 L. E.d 2d 173, 103 S. Ct. 218.

Example 8.11: Other professional reports

United States v. Posey, 647 F.2d 1048 (10th Cir. 1981)

In a drug prosecution, it was permissible for one chemist to rely upon tests run by another in testifying that the tested substance was cocaine: "It is quite reasonable for a chemist to review another chemist's analysis when forming an opinion as to the veracity of the latter's test results."

Example 8.12: Other professional reports

Gong v. Hirsch, 913 F.2d 1269 (7th Cir. 1990)

In this medical malpractice suit, a physician expert testified that the decedent's perforated peptic ulcer was due to Prednisone. The expert based this conclusion on a letter from the deceased's physician to a doctor at the medical department of the deceased's employer stating that the deceased's perforated peptic ulcer was due to Prednisone. The court rejected the testimony, finding that such a letter was not the type of information reasonably relied upon by an expert because it was merely a conclusory statement made by a doctor who was not a treating physician at the time of the illness in question. It was, in fact, an analysis made for the presumed purpose of obtaining employment disability benefits.

Example 8.13: Consumer surveys

President & Trustees of Colby College v. Colby College, New Hampshire, 508 F.2d 804 (1st Cir. 1975)

A survey of consumers may be used as the basis for expert testimony.

Example 8.14: Inspection of scene

Elgi Holding, Inc. v. Insurance Co. of North America, 511 F.2d 957 (2nd Cir. 1975)

An inspection of the accident scene may be used as the basis of expert testimony.

Example 8.15: Field agents' reports

United States v. Genser, 582 F.2d 292 (3rd Cir. 1978)

Reports from field agents are sources upon which an expert witness may reasonably rely for the basis of his opinions.

Example 8.16: Government-approved documents

Frazier v. Continental Oil Co., 568 F.2d 378 (5th Cir 1978)

Expert opinions as founded upon facts or data upon which experts may reasonably rely, such as governmentally approved tables or codes, are acceptable bases for expert opinions.

Example 8.17: Litigants' affidavits

In re Agent Orange Prod. Liab. Litig., 611 F.Supp 1223 (E.D.N.Y. 1985)

In this mass toxic tort case, physician experts based testimony on the affidavits of their clients. The court concluded, "Although Rule 703 permits experts to rely upon hearsay, the litigants' self-serving general affidavits and checklists prepared in gross for complex litigation are not material that medical experts would reasonably rely upon and so must be excluded under Rule 703." Also, the court found that the expert physician's failure to consider and discuss any studies that address the actual population and amount of exposure involved in the case at hand supported the conclusion that his opinion was legally incompetent.

Example 8.18: Opinions of experts in other fields

United States v. 1014.16 Acres of Land, 558 F.Supp 1238 (W.D. Mo. 1983)
In this land condemnation action, the court considered the admissibility of the opinions of a real estate appraiser, a hydrologist, and a forester. The court found that despite the opposition's contention that their opinions are improperly based upon opinions of other experts, it is reasonable to expect that experts will rely on opinions of experts in other fields as background material for arriving at an opinion.

Example 8.19: Scientific studies

Kelley v. American Heyer-Shulte Corp., 957 F.Supp 873 (W.D. Tex. 1997)
The court held that an expert's testimony regarding causation that was based on an epidemiology study should be excluded from a products liability case under Federal Rule of Evidence 703. The study had a lower-end confidence interval of less than one for the relative risk linking breast implants to Sjogren's Syndrome. The court found that it was unreasonable as a matter of law for an expert to rely on such a study to draw any conclusions regarding a Sjogren's implant link.

Example 8.20: Criticisms of scientific studies

Lynch v. Merrell-National Laboratories Div. of Richardson-Merrell, Inc., 646 F.Supp 856 (D. Mass. 1986)
The parents of a child with a birth defect attempted to introduce, through an expert, criticisms of the methodology of earlier studies of a drug's teratogenic effect and extrapolations of animal studies involving the drug. The court found that the evidence could neither form the basis for an expert opinion nor create a genuine issue for trial because such criticisms cannot be relied upon to establish causation and the animal studies were performed with far higher doses than those given therapeutically.

Example 8.21: Trade publications

United States v. Harpe, 802 F.2d 115 (5th Cir. 1986)
An expert in firearm origin, identification, and design classification could rely on trade publications and company catalogs in testifying on the origin of a firearm. Such publications were of the type reasonably relied upon by experts in the firearms field.

Example 8.22: Native American oral history

Cree v. Flores, 157 F.3d 762 (9th Cir. 1998)
A Native American elder testified as an expert regarding the meaning of a treaty to his tribe. His testimony was based on oral history passed down through generations of tribe members. Though this oral history was inadmissible hearsay, the court determined that it was of the type of data reasonably relied upon in the elder's field.

Example 8.23: Data provided by counsel

Deghand v. Wal-Mart Stores, 980 F.Supp 1176 (D. Kan. 1997)

The plaintiff's economic expert testified regarding the amount of damages. The defendant disputed the numbers and contended that the opinion lacked a factual foundation. The court concluded that it could presume that the plaintiff's counsel provided the expert with reliable data concerning the plaintiff's rate of pay at the time of her discharge and the average number of hours she worked per week. The court noted that the defendant's dispute with the numbers went to weight, not admissibility.

Example 8.24: Statements by subject of psychiatric examination

United States ex rel. Edney v. Smith, 425 F.Supp 1038 (E.D.N.Y. 1976)

Statements by the subject of a psychiatric examination may be used by an expert witness as the basis for his opinion.

Example 8.25: Investigator's reliance upon hearsay

First Nat'l Bank of Louisville v. Lustig, 96 F.3d 1554 (5th Cir. 1996)

A private investigator testified as an expert in civil fraud detection and investigation. This was a complicated bank fraud coverage case that required explanations of a lender's operations, loan approval procedures, and the transactions themselves. He reviewed documents and interviewed witnesses about the loans at issue. The district court admitted his testimony that the loan committee relied heavily on allegedly fraudulent misrepresentations in approving the loans even though he had no personal knowledge of this fact. The expert explained that his testimony in this case was derived from his conclusions from the knowledge he obtained through his investigation. The court held that the bases of the expert's opinion were proper.

Example 8.26: Hearsay

Doctor's Hosp. v. Southeast Medical Alliance, 878 F.Supp 884 (E.D. La. 1995)

In this action against a parish hospital service district for alleged violations of federal and state antitrust laws, an expert in the field of health care and economics testified on the general business practices of managed care plans. The expert, who testified for the defendant, based his opinion partly on interviews with representatives of managed care plans. The plaintiff hospital argued that these informal conversations did not adequately meet the requirements of a formal survey. However, the hospital did not show that the interviews held by the expert were not information-gathering devices reasonably relied upon by experts. Moreover, the court found that the interviews upon which the expert based his opinion went more toward the weight than the admissibility of his opinion.

Example 8.27: Hearsay

Ricciardi v. Children's Hospital Medical Center, 811 F.2d 18 (1st Cir. 1987)

In this medical malpractice action, the trial court ruled that a physician expert could not rely upon a note written by the consulting physician in the patient's chart where the consulting physician did not have personal knowledge of the alleged event and did not know where he obtained the information recorded in the note. The court found that, although an expert is not confined to admissible evidence in forming an opinion under Rule 703, the note contained in the chart was not of the type reasonably relied upon by experts in this particular field in forming opinions or inferences upon the subject.

Example 8.28: Limitation on evidence upon which expert's opinion is based
Engebretsen v. Fairchild Aircraft Corp., 21 F.3d 721 (6th Cir. 1994)
In this pilot's products liability action against an aircraft manufacturer for injuries sustained in an emergency landing, the reports of the defendants' experts who investigated the cause of the incident were not admissible under either Rule 702 or 703. The court noted that Rule 702 permits expert opinion testimony, not opinions contained in documents prepared out of court. It further noted that Rule 703 allows experts to rely upon materials, including inadmissible hearsay, in forming the basis of an opinion, but it does not permit the admission of materials relied upon for the truth of the matters they contain if the materials are otherwise inadmissible.

Example 8.29: Oil production figures
South Cent. Petroleum, Inc. v. Long Bros. Oil Co., 974 F.2d 1015 (8th Cir. 1992)
In this investors' suit arising out of an alleged breach of a purchase agreement for oil wells, the court properly admitted expert testimony to determine an offset amount. The court found that the production figures relied on by the experts were a type reasonably relied upon by experts in the field.

Example 8.30: Reliance upon expert report prepared for purposes of litigation
United States v. Tran Trong Cuong, 18 F.3d 1132 (4th Cir. 1994)
A family practitioner testified as an expert to the standard of care for a family physician. The expert based his conclusions on a nontestifying expert's report drafted at the request of the prosecution. The court noted that the nontestifying expert's report was a "forensic opinion" or a "report in a criminal case." The court doubted whether such a report "would qualify as data of a type reasonably relied upon by experts in the particular field…[w]e question whether [the expert] usually relies upon forensic medical opinions or reports in forming his opinions in his field of expertise—family medicine."

8.4 Ultimate Issue

Except in criminal cases where the issue is the mental state of a defendant, experts are permitted to give opinions that embrace "an ultimate issue to be decided by the trier of fact."[3] Experts who are qualified to testify are permitted to offer their opinions on ultimate issues, such as causation, negligence, speed, intoxication, handwriting, value, and damages.

8.5 Foundation of an Opinion

The expert's opinion is only as strong as the facts and data upon which it is based. The rules permit an expert to testify regarding her opinion without first

[3] Fed. Rule Evid. 704(a).

testifying to the underlying facts or data.[4] This does not mean, however, that the testifying expert will not have to disclose these facts or data. The facts and data upon which an expert bases her opinions are legitimate areas of cross-examination that she needs to be prepared to address. In attacking these facts and data, counsel will try to prove "garbage in, garbage out." Counsel may also try to show that the expert did not consider key information, did not have time to do an adequate analysis, and that the information considered was flawed. (Each of these lines of cross-examination attack is discussed below in Section 8.7 on cross-examination challenges.)

8.6 Methodology

Experts can expect to be scrutinized closely regarding the methodology they used in determining their opinions. In federal court, and in some state courts, the judge will act as a gatekeeper to exclude from evidence unreliable expert testimony that was not based upon sound methodology. Under the *Daubert v. Merrell Dow Pharmaceuticals, Inc.*[5] line of cases, a judge in a jurisdiction following *Daubert* will evaluate carefully the expert's methodology in forming her opinion. The judge will consider several factors, including:

1. whether the theory or technique used by the expert can be, and has been, tested,
2. whether the theory or technique has been subjected to peer review and publication,
3. the known or potential rate of error of the method used, and
4. the degree of the method's or conclusion's acceptance within the relevant scientific community.

Even if the judge does not exclude an expert's opinion under the *Daubert* line of cases, an expert's methodology will remain a legitimate area of inquiry on cross-examination. This is because the expert's methodology is relevant to the weight the fact finder should give the expert's testimony. (Methodology is discussed in much greater detail in Chapter 9.)

8.7 Cross-Examination Challenges to an Expert's Opinions

Experts can expect to be cross-examined extensively about their opinions. Areas of inquiry that the expert should anticipate and prepare for include the following.

---

[4] Fed. Rule Evid. 705, Disclosure of Facts or Data Underlying Expert Opinion: "The expert may testify in terms of opinion or inference and give reasons therefor without first testifying to the underlying facts or data, unless the court requires otherwise. The expert may in any event be required to disclose the underlying facts or data on cross-examination."

[5] 113 S. Ct. 2786 (1993).

OPINIONS

Sources of information

Were they reliable? Are they biased? For example, an oral history provided by the plaintiff or by counsel.

Basis for each opinion

Upon what facts and data is it based? Were there facts or data missing, or were any data or facts inaccurate?

When each opinion was formed

Was it before crucial information was available or before important tests were performed?

All assumptions upon which the opinions are based

If these assumptions can be shown to be false, an opinion may collapse.

The alternative opinions that were considered but rejected

Was the expert open minded? Does he have solid reasons for rejecting the other alternatives?

Degree of flexibility

Is the expert willing to change his opinion if he is presented with different/new facts or assumptions?

Degree of scientific certainty

Is the opinion a mere speculative "guess," and thus inadmissible, or is it based upon a reasonable degree of probability?

The methodology employed in arriving at the opinion(s)

Is the methodology sound and reliable, or is it a methodology that was created for the purpose of the current litigation?

Which documents were used/not used in forming the opinion(s)

These will indicate what facts and data the expert did and did not consider.

The equipment used

Was it appropriate to use? Was it used correctly? Is the equipment reliable? (For example, was it recently serviced, calibrated, tested, etc.?)

Tests relied upon

Did the expert do them personally? Were they done correctly?

Opposing experts

Why are the experts' opinions different?

8.8 Sample Opinions

Sample opinions from experts in different disciplines are provided below.

Sample 1: Physician's Opinion on a Car Accident

Based upon the available information, to a reasonable degree of medical certainty, there is probable causal relationship between Mr. Orrin's symptoms and complaints of neck pain and his 8/14/98 automobile accident.

Sample 2: Architect's Opinion on a Swimming Pool

It is my opinion, within reasonable architectural certainty that the "front" door and yard fence gate at 11950 Harvard Road were not locked or latched because they did not have self-closing and self-locking devices that would have prevented Lee Warren from passing through them. The door and gate also did not have alarms thereon that could signal their use to Lee Warren's parents. Lee Warren was unsupervised during his passage to the pool and into the pool. It was the Warrens' responsibility, at a minimum, to have self-closing and self-latching mechanisms on the yard fence gate. Moreover, it was the installation contractor's responsibility to be aware of the gate requirements and to advise the Warrens thereof, based on his extensive experience in pool installation.

The decision to backfill under and beside the fan deck, in light of the decision to excavate created the low fan deck configuration.

It is also my opinion that the *installation* of the subject aboveground pool at 11950 Harvard Road resulted in defective conditions. These conditions altered the safety factors designed in the pool's manufacture and stated in the installation manuals. The resultant position of the fan deck and the low height above the ground - less than 24 inches - of the fan deck created an accessible passageway onto the deck and into the pool, regardless of the placement of the step ladder. These conditions were hazardous and allowed Lee Warren to reach the pool. In the event that the filter/pump housing was used as a means to climb up to the deck (which is highly unlikely), its placement by the installation contractor was faulty, since it was located near a low point of the deck, a low height which the contractor created. ABC Pools, Inc., failed to construct a pool with a deck that was inaccessible to Lee Warren.

Sample 3: Engineer's Opinion on a Power Press

A.) The A.B. Stamp Press, serial number 104759, was sold to ACME Metal Stamp Company, Inc., with a defectively designed and manufactured latch and latch bracket. The defect caused the press, suddenly and without warning, to begin operating continuously while in the single stroke mode.

B.) The manufacturer failed to adequately notify and warn users about the extreme hazards associated with the defective latch bracket.

C.) The manufacturer failed to furnish the press with an appropriate point-of-operation interlocked barrier guard.

D.) The manufacturer failed to provide suitable warnings and instructions to insure that guards are in place, and interlocks functioning, prior to operating the press.[6]

Sample 4: Criminal Justice Expert's Opinion on Sexual Harassment

1. As a result of the failure of the supervisors of the Lincoln Police Department and its Chief to enforce its own directive, General Order 200-8 (Supervisor's Responsibilities), Officer Lynn Stephens was subjected to a violation of the law (sexual harassment) by Sergeant George Johnston and Lieutenant William Thomas while she was assigned as an officer in the Mounted Patrol Unit under the immediate supervision of Sergeant Johnston and the unit command of Lieutenant William Thomas.
2. Chief Tim Duncan's failure to insure the Lincoln Police Department's own directive system was followed (General Order 200-3 titled INVESTIGATION OF ALLEGED MISCONDUCT BY OFFICERS) in the investigation into the sexual harassment of Officer Stephens (that all complaints of serious misconduct be investigated by the Internal Affairs Division as a Class 1 complaint) sent a message to the employees of the Lincoln Police Department that sexual harassment is not considered a serious act of misconduct.
3. Chief Tim Duncan's decision to suspend for ninety days and to transfer Johnston and Thomas, but not to demote Johnston and Thomas as the Department's Administrative Disciplinary Committee had recommended, re-enforced the message already sent to the employees of the Lincoln Police Department that sexual harassment allegations would not be treated as seriously by the administration of the department as their Directives require or their employees (membership of Administrative Disciplinary Committee) expected.

   Chief Duncan's failure to terminate Thomas when another complaint was sustained against him after he returned to work from his ninety day suspension (as Chief Duncan had warned Thomas he would do) and the Department's performance evaluation of Thomas (very good) during the time period of his suspension again re-enforced this message.

   By neglecting to reflect the disciplinary actions taken against Lieutenant Thomas on Thomas's performance evaluation that covered the time period in which he was suspended for sexually harassing Officer Stephens, Chief Duncan and the supervisors of the Lincoln Police Department failed to insure General Order 300-8 (Performance Evaluations) was followed and properly enforced.[7]

Sample 5: Safety Professional's Opinion on a Slip and Fall

The area of Ms. Singh's accident was, indeed, too "dark" for safe pedestrian travel. It is inappropriate for a landowner to expect guests to remember the position of exterior pathways, therefore, they must be marked and lighted adequately so that pedestrians can see their way around and avoid

---

[6] See Appendix U for the complete report.

[7] See Appendix U for the complete report.

obstacles and follow the turns in a pathway. Ms. Singh was correct when she described the accident area as "dark", and "dark" is a quantifiable term.

Safety building codes used within the industry of rental property ownership require at least 1.0 foot candle of light at exterior walkways such as the one involved in Ms. Singh's accident (see exhibits #1, #2, and #3). Adequate lighting is very important on the accident pathway because of the 90° turn that must be negotiated and because of the 9-inch-high wall which becomes a tripping hazard if unseen. The light available at the bottom of the stairway at the time of Ms. Singh's accident was less than one-tenth that required for safe travel.

The building owner must accept responsibility for the safety of his or her tenants and invited guests and perform the necessary inspections to determine whether or not lighting fixtures which are necessary for safety are properly functioning.

Sample 6: Psychologist's Opinion on Emotional Distress Due to Battery
I can state with psychological certainty that:

(1) Mr. S. is suffering from emotional distress, including **depression (DSM IV: 296.22)** and **undifferentiated somatoform disorder (DSM IV: 300.81)**, but not from any **post-traumatic stress disorder (DSM IV: 309.89)**, and

(2) these conditions are **not caused by** or **attributable** to the alleged battery, rather

(3) Mr. S.' symptoms may be better accounted for by alternative stresses in his life experience.

8.9 Conclusion

Experts need to be prepared to deliver their opinions in a legally sufficient way. Speculation and guessing are not permitted. Opinions need to be based upon reliable methodology or they may be excluded from evidence. Cross-examination will challenge the expert's opinions, methodology, and the facts and data upon which the opinion is based. The expert should be prepared for such challenges.

Chapter 9 Methodology

9.1 Introduction

An expert's methodology can be challenged in two ways. First, it can be challenged as being unreliable "junk science" as a matter of law. This would be decided by the judge upon motion and would be based upon the *Daubert, G.E.,* and *Kumho Tire* cases discussed below.[1] In making her determination, the judge acts as a "gatekeeper" whose job it is to exclude from evidence unreliable expert testimony that will not assist the trier of fact. If the expert testimony is allowed by the judge, the expert's methodology will remain a legitimate area for cross-examination. This is because the methodology used is relevant to the weight the jury gives the expert's testimony.

> **Example 9.1**
> The defense makes a motion in limine to exclude causation expert testimony in a toxic tort case because the defense feels this testimony is unreliable. The judge finds that the expert's testimony is not unreliable and allows the testimony into evidence. The reliability of the expert's methodology may still be questioned on cross-examination because it is relevant to the weight to be given to the testimony.

9.2 Overview of the Case Interpretations of Federal Rule of Evidence 702

The *Daubert* line of cases interprets Federal Rule of Evidence 702.[2] *Daubert* established that a trial court judge is to act as gatekeeper under the Federal Rules of Evidence in order to ensure the scientific validity of the expert's testimony. *Daubert* set forth several factors a trial court should consider when evaluating scientific validity. (See the *Daubert* discussion below.) At the time, the case apparently applied only to novel scientific testimony—now its analysis applies to all expert testimony, scientific or otherwise.[3]

Four years after *Daubert,* in *General Electric v. Joiner,*[4] the Supreme Court limited appellate review of the trial court's decision to admit or exclude expert testimony to an abuse of discretion standard. The expert should realize that an appellate court will seldom reverse a trial judge's admissibility determination under this abuse of discretion standard. In effect, *Daubert*

---

[1] Not all jurisdictions follow these cases. Federal courts do, but state laws may vary.

[2] Fed. Rule Evid. 702, Testimony by Experts: "If scientific, technical, or other specialized knowledge will assist the trier of fact to understand the evidence or to determine a fact in issue, a witness qualified as an expert by knowledge, skill, experience, training, or education, may testify thereto in the form of an opinion or otherwise."

[3] In federal court and in states following this line of cases.

[4] *General Electric v. Joiner,* 522 U.S. 136, 139 L. Ed. 2d 508, 118 S. Ct. 512, 1997 U.S. LEXIS 7503 (1997), on remand, 134 F.3d 1457, 1998 U.S. App. LEXIS 1770 (11th Cir. Ga. 1998).

required a judge to scrutinize the validity of the expert's opinion. *Joiner* then offered increased protection and insulation of the judge's decision.

In 1999, the Supreme Court decided *Kumho Tire Company Ltd. v. Carmichael.*[5] *Kumho* directed that the *Daubert* factors be applied equally to nonscientific expert testimony as well as to scientific expert testimony.[6] The court also held that trial courts are free to apply other factors in addition to those set out in *Daubert.*[7] In effect, a trial court can now fashion the standard it uses to determine validity, subject only to review under an abuse of discretion standard. This further expands a trial judge's discretion in evaluating *all* expert testimony.[8]

9.3 *Daubert*

The landmark case of *Daubert v. Merrell Dow Pharmaceuticals, Inc.*[9] interpreted Federal Rule of Evidence 702. In *Daubert,* the court held that in order to meet the "specialized knowledge" requirement of Rule 702, the trial judge must make a threshold finding of whether the expert's methodology was sound. The *Daubert* court identified four factors bearing on that threshold finding. The judge will consider several factors, including (1) whether the theory or technique used by the expert can be, and has been, tested; (2) whether the theory or technique has been subjected to peer review and publication; (3) the known or potential rate of error of the method used; and (4) the degree of the method's or conclusion's acceptance within the relevant scientific community. Moreover, the Ninth Circuit added a fifth factor to the list upon hearing the remanded case: whether the expert's theory existed before litigation began. The expert should note that rarely will a court exclude testimony on the basis of one factor alone.

Procedure

An expert's reputation and viability for future work may ride on the outcome of a *Daubert* challenge to his testimony. It is therefore important to understand the process of how these challenges are made and what analysis is applied by the courts. *Daubert* challenges are usually raised in a *motion in limine.* This motion is commonly filed before trial or a motion for summary judgment. The motion may result in the judge holding a "*Daubert* hearing" outside of the presence of the jury. At the hearing, the expert will testify and the judge must decide, by examining the expert's methodology, whether the

---

[5] *Kumho Tire Co. v. Carmichael*, 143 L. Ed. 2d 238, 119 S. Ct. 1167, 1999 U.S. LEXIS 2189, 67 U.S.L.W. 4179 (1999).
[6] *Kumho*, 119 S. Ct. at 1175.
[7] *Id.* at 1176.
[8] Shubha Gosh, "Tires and Testimony: Judging the Junk: High Court Expands Trial Judges' Role in Evaluating Expert Witnesses," *Fulton County Daily Report,* April 29, 1999, 1.
[9] *Daubert*, 113 S. Ct. 2786 (1993).

expert has the "specialized knowledge" that will legally permit the witness to testify. These determinations will sometimes involve detailed and exhaustive proceedings. The expert's methodology in arriving at the opinion will be examined by the judge under the five *Daubert* factors.

Testability

The first *Daubert* factor is whether the scientific theory or technique at issue can be and has been tested. This is rooted in the notion that a scientific explanation must be capable of empirical test. *Testability* is central to the scientific method. Modern scientific methodology is based upon testing hypotheses to see if they can be falsified. The following are examples of expert opinions excluded because no evidence was offered to the court that the underlying scientific theory had been tested. Testability is often considered the most important *Daubert* factor.

Example 9.2
Bradley v. Brown, 42 F.3d 434 (7th Cir. 1994)
Two physicians, clinical ecologists, testified that the plaintiff suffered from MCS through exposure to the defendant's spraying of a pesticide. The court excluded the testimony because the experts' opinions were "hypothetical." The experts' opinions did not establish that the etiology of MCS was known or tested. The court found that the experts could not provide testimony explaining why a person contracts a chemical sensitivity—"The method leading to [the experts'] conclusions was merely anecdotal" (438). This case illustrates the proper court focus on principles and methodology, not conclusions.

Example 9.3
Schmaltz v. Norfolk & W. Ry. Co., 878 F.Supp. 1119 (N.D. Ill. 1995)
Physicians offered opinions that the plaintiff's respiratory condition was caused by exposure to the defendant's chemicals. The first physician's testimony was excluded because he offered no evidence of tests that support the theory.

Example 9.4
Zarecki v. National R.R. Passenger Corp., 914 F.Supp. 1566, 1574 (N.D. Ill. 1996)
A physician's proffered testimony on the cause of the plaintiff's carpal tunnel syndrome was excluded on the grounds that the physician offered no evidence that he had conducted any studies or analyses to substantiate his views. This case also confirms the following: "Of these four factors [listed in *Daubert*], the first—whether the proffered theory has been tested—has been deemed the most important."

Example 9.5
Stanczyk v. Black & Decker, Inc., 836 F.Supp. 565 (N.D. Ill. 1993)
This was a product liability action against a power-saw manufacturer for design defect. A mechanical engineer expert witness (who designed saws) testified that an alternative concept would have been safer. The court found that he

offered no testable design to support this concept and excluded the evidence on that ground.

Example 9.6
O'Conner v. Commonwealth Edison Co., 13 F.3d 1090 (7th Cir. 1994)
A physician's expert testimony that he could ascertain whether a particular cataract was caused by radiation just by looking at it was not admitted because no evidence was offered to prove that radiation-induced cataracts could be identified by mere observation.

Example 9.7
Wheat v. Pfizer, Inc., 31 F.3d 340, 343 (5th Cir. 1994)
This was a products liability action against manufacturers of drugs that allegedly caused the plaintiff's death. Expert witness testimony was excluded and the court noted that the expert's testimony would not have passed the first factor of a *Daubert* analysis. The expert hypothesized that the combination of two drugs may have caused the plaintiff's injury, but he admitted that no study of the combination had ever been done—"[T]hus his hypothesis lacked an empirical foundation."

Example 9.8
Kelley v. American Heyer-Schulte Corp., 957 F.Supp. 873 (W.D. Tex. 1997)
This was a products liability suit alleging the manufacturer's breast implants caused the plaintiff's injury. The epidemiologist expert witness's hypothesis, though testable, had never been tested. The court excluded the testimony on this ground, as well as others.

Example 9.9
Cabrera v. Cordis Corp., 945 F.Supp. 209 (D. Nev. 1996)
In this products liability suit against the manufacturers of a brain shunt, plaintiffs offered several experts to support the claim that the product caused the silicone toxicity present in the plaintiff. The immunologist expert witness testified to the results of a blood test he performed on the plaintiff that revealed the presence of antibodies allegedly resulting from the brain shunt. The court found several inadequacies with the test the expert employed. The internist expert witness opined that the plaintiff's medical complaints were a result of silicone toxicity. The court excluded the testimony in part because there was no way to test the validity of the opinions. Similarly, the physical chemist expert witness was to testify regarding the presence of a defect—the use of silicone—in the shunt. The court excluded the testimony because the expert had not tested, nor did he rely upon, any tests regarding the propriety of silicone as a material for brain shunts.

Example 9.10
City of Tuscaloosa v. Harcross Chems., Inc., 877 F.Supp. 1504 (N.D. Ala. 1995)
City water and public utilities sued several chlorine distributors for various antitrust violations. An economist expert witness offered an opinion that the defendants engaged in collusive behavior. The court excluded the opinion

because the theory upon which it was based ("conscious parallelism") had not been tested, nor was it capable of testing.

Experts should be prepared to explain the history of testing that supports the theory generating their conclusions. The opinion must not appear to be based upon speculation or pure hypothesis.

Peer review

Peer review refers to scrutiny by the scientific community. An expert's opinion based on information that cannot be independently verified may not be admissible because there is no guarantee that substantive flaws in the expert's methodology have been detected. Conversely, scrutiny by the scientific community is a component of good science because it increases the likelihood that substantive flaws will be uncovered. Although not dispositive, publication in a peer-reviewed journal is a relevant consideration in assessing scientific validity.

Example 9.11
Lust v. Merrell Dow Pharm., Inc., 89 F.3d 594 (9th Cir. 1996)
This products liability action was brought under the theory that the plaintiff's birth defect was caused by the plaintiff's mother's ingestion of the defendant's fertility drug. The plaintiff's expert, an epidemiologist, failed to subject his method of inquiry to peer review and to develop his opinion outside the context of litigation. His opinion was excluded.

Example 9.12
Wheat v. Pfizer, 31 F.3d 340 (5th Cir. 1994)
This products liability action was against manufacturers of drugs that allegedly caused the plaintiff's death. Expert witness testimony was excluded and the court noted that the expert's testimony would not have survived a *Daubert* analysis. The expert hypothesized that the combination of two drugs may have caused the plaintiff's injury, but admitted that no study of the combination had ever been done and that no study of the combined effects of the drugs had ever been subjected to peer review.

Example 9.13
Cuevas v. E.I. DuPont De Nemours & Co., 956 F.Supp. 1306 (S.D. Miss. 1997)
In this action against a herbicide manufacturer, the plaintiff's expert toxicologist opined that the herbicide caused the plaintiff's medical problems. The court excluded the opinion, noting that the expert "admitted that his opinion had not undergone any type of peer-review."

Example 9.14
Haggerty v. Upjohn Co., 950 F.Supp. 1160, 1164 (S.D. Fla. 1996)
In this products liability action against the manufacturer of a sleeping medication, the plaintiff's expert, a nonphysician pharmacologist, opined that the ingestion of the medication caused the plaintiff's injury. The court found

that the expert's causation opinion had never been subjected to peer review—her methodology had never been published nor discussed in front of a scientific audience.

Example 9.15
Cabrera v. Cordis Corp., 945 F.Supp. 209 (D. Nev. 1996)
In this products liability suit against the manufacturers of a brain shunt, the plaintiff offered several experts to support the claim that the product caused the silicone toxicity present in the plaintiff. The immunologist expert witness testified to the results of a "silicone antibody blood test" he performed on the plaintiff that revealed the presence of antibodies allegedly resulting from the brain shunt. The court excluded the opinion and noted that the methodology of this test had never been peer reviewed. Similarly, the physical chemist expert witness was to testify regarding the presence of a defect—the use of silicone—in the shunt. The court excluded the testimony, in part because the expert had never subjected his opinions to peer review.

Example 9.16
Stanczyk v. Black & Decker, Inc., 836 F.Supp. 565 (N.D. Ill. 1993)
This was a product liability action against a power-saw manufacturer for a design defect. A mechanical engineer (who designed saws) expert witness testified that an alternative concept would have been safer. The court found that he offered no testable design to support this concept, then went on to find: "One must consider whether there is peer review and publication of the technique. There is none." The court then excluded the evidence.

Example 9.17
Navarro v. Fuji Heavy Indus., 925 F.Supp. 1323, 1329 (N.D. Ill. 1996)
In this products liability action against the manufacturer of a vehicle, the plaintiff's engineering expert offered his opinion that the manufacturer's design was defective and this defect caused the structural failure that caused the plaintiff's injury. The court, declaring this testimony inadmissible, stated,

> [The expert] has not provided adequate scientific support for his damning conclusions. He cites no published journals, studies, reports, or treatises, nor has he set forth the methodology employed in reaching his conclusions. He does not identify testing or research techniques. There is no reference to peer review of any results reached by [the expert].

Rate of error and standards

The third *Daubert* factor the trial court must take into account is the known or potential rate of error in any scientific technique, as well as the existence and maintenance of standards controlling the technique's operation. Both the rate of error and controlling standards affect evidentiary reliability.[10]

---

[10] Courts consider "rate of error" less frequently than the other *Daubert* factors, however, because challenges to expert testimony often claim the underlying theory or technique is vague, untested, or overly subjective. In such cases, the court cannot

Example 9.18
In re TMI Litig. Cases Consol. II, 911 F.Supp. 775, 795 (M.D. Pa. 1996)
In this action, residents near Three Mile Island sought damages for alleged exposure to excessive amounts of radioactive gases during the reactor accident. The court excluded a chemistry professor's proffered testimony because his method of calculating radioactive half-life for soil samples, based on only two readings, had a very high potential rate of error. A meteorologist's testimony was also excluded. He proffered testimony about a plume movie and water model of dispersion of radioactive gases emitted during the reactor accident, and the court found that the methodology had a potentially high rate of error.

Example 9.19
Wade-Gereaux v. Whitehall Lab., Inc., 874 F.Supp. 1441, 1480 (D.V.I. 1994)
In this product liability action brought against the manufacturer of a nasal decongestant by a mother on behalf of her child, who was born with birth defects, the plaintiff's expert, a pediatric pathologist, testified that the decongestant was the cause of the birth defect. This opinion was based upon several animal studies. The court rejected the expert's opinion, stating: "The theory of plaintiff's expert witnesses that they can directly extrapolate from experimental animal studies without supportive positive human studies to opine as to causation in humans is one that has an extraordinarily high rate of error, and this fact weighs against the admissibility of opinions based upon those methodologies."

General acceptance

Widespread professional acceptance can be an important factor in ruling particular evidence admissible. On the other hand, a known technique that has attracted only minimal support within the related scientific community may be viewed properly with skepticism.

Example 9.20
Kelley v. American Heyer-Schulte Corp., 957 F.Supp. 873 (W.D. Tex. 1997)
This was a products liability suit alleging a manufacturer's breast implants caused the plaintiff's injury. The court rejected the epidemiologist expert witness's hypothesis because "his theory regarding general causation is not generally accepted in the medical community."

Example 9.21
Haggerty v. Upjohn Co., 950 F.Supp. 1160 (S.D. Fla. 1996)
In this products liability action against the manufacturer of a sleeping medication, the plaintiff's expert, a nonphysician pharmacologist, opined that the ingestion of the medication caused the plaintiff's injury. The court found,

---

ascertain a "rate of error." In other words, the proferred evidence will often fail to meet the other *Daubert* factors. Thus, the court will not undergo an analysis of "rate of error." For examples of this situation, see *Cartwright v. Home Depot U.S.A., Inc.,* 936 F. Supp. 900, 905 (M.D. Fla. 1996), *City of Tuscaloosa v. Harcross Chem., Inc.,* 877 F. Supp. 1504, 1526 (N.D. Ala. 1995).

"There is no general acceptance or support for [the expert's] causation methodology in the scientific community."

Example 9.22

Stalnaker v. General Motors Corp., 934 F.Supp. 179 (D. Md. 1996)
The court's words are illustrative.

> The Court agrees with the defendant that the plaintiff's expert witnesses do not present sufficient evidence from which a jury could reasonably conclude that there was a defect in the product, and that the so-called "skip-lock" theory is indeed a theory that is "scientific," in the sense that it relies on basic principles of physics and mechanics. Yet, it is in itself obviously so far afield from any recognized scientific principle to be completely inadmissible under the current standard for admissibility of expert testimony.

Example 9.23

Wade-Gereaux v. Whitehall Lab., Inc., 874 F.Supp. 1441 (D.V.I. 1994)
In this product liability action brought against the manufacturer of a nasal decongestant by a mother on behalf of her child, who was born with birth defects, the plaintiff supplied several experts to testify that the decongestant was the cause of the birth defect. The court found: "Each of plaintiff's expert witnesses [a teratologist/geneticist, a pathologist, a professor of cell biology, two toxicologists, and a pediatric physician] used a methodology not recognized by the relevant scientific community, and not subject to scientific verification. Therefore, each of their opinions was not helpful and must be excluded."

Example 9.24

Dennis v. Pertec Computer Corp., 927 F.Supp. 156 (D.N.J. 1996)
In this products liability action by keyboard operators against a keyboard manufacturer, a certified professional ergonomist opined that the defendant's keyboard design was likely to produce cumulative repetitive motion trauma. The court did not admit the testimony: "[The expert's opinion has] simply not gained general acceptance."

Example 9.25

Kurncz v. Honda N. Am., Inc., 166 F.R.D. 386 (W.D. Mich. 1996)
This was a personal injury action. The plaintiff sustained injury while riding a three-wheeler. The plaintiff offered testimony by an economist, purportedly to aid the jury in valuating the plaintiff's loss of future enjoyment of life caused by the defendant's negligence. The economist proposed a "willingness to pay" model for calculating these damages. The court rejected the testimony as unreliable: "[The] method has been subject to peer review and [the expert] is well published. The peer review, however, has not led to general acceptance—the fourth *Daubert* factor."

Example 9.26
American & Foreign Insurance Co. v. General Electric Co., 45 F.3d 135 (6th Cir. 1995)
Here, the court affirmed a district court's determination that the plaintiff's electrical engineering expert could not satisfy at least two of *Daubert's* four prongs. The expert's theories were not accepted by other experts in the same field and his testing and his theory were not of a type reasonably relied upon by others in his field. Moreover, his testing was woefully inadequate. He did not preserve the raw data from his tests and he never calibrated the instruments used to perform those tests.

Did the expert's theory exist before litigation began?

Testimony that is based upon methods specially employed in anticipation of litigation is viewed with particular suspicion. The opinions of experts should be based upon methods generally employed in their normal academic or professional endeavors. This stems from the notion that when an expert's findings flow from his own research or regular research activities, as compared to work performed at a litigant's direction or request, his testimony is less likely to be influenced or biased by promised compensation.[11]

Example 9.27
Lust v. Merrell Dow Pharm., Inc., 89 F.3d 594 (9th Cir. 1996)
This products liability action was brought under the theory that the plaintiff's birth defect was caused by the plaintiff's mother's ingestion of the defendant's fertility drug. The plaintiff's expert, an epidemiologist, testified that the drug caused the birth defect. The court rejected the expert's science as unreliable because he developed his theory while a "professional" expert witness, thus his opinion might have been influenced by litigation-driven financial incentives. The court stated: "'One very significant fact is whether the expert has developed [his] opinions expressly for the purposes of testifying,' since a scientist's normal workplace is the lab or the field, not the courtroom or the lawyer's office."

Example 9.28
Estate of Mitchell v. Gencorp, Inc., 968 F.Supp. 592 (D. Kan. 1997)
The estate of a worker who died of chronic myelogenous leukemia brought a products liability action against the manufacturer of chemicals that had been stored in a "flammable room" at the worker's place of employment. The plaintiff's experts—two physicians, each specializing in hematology and oncology—testified that the defendant's chemicals caused the decedent's leukemia. The court found it "significant" that the plaintiff's experts developed theory opinions expressly for the purpose of testifying, stating, "none of the witnesses has done any research on his theories outside the context of this

[11] Stephen D. Easton, "Yer Outta Here!: A Framework for Analyzing the Potential Exclusion of Expert Testimony Under the Federal Rules of Evidence," 32 *U. Rich. L. Rev.* (1998) 1, 34.

lawsuit." This fact, combined with other inadequacies in the experts' opinions, led the court to exclude the evidence.

Example 9.29
Braun v. Lorillard Inc, 84 F.3d 230 (7th Cir. 1996)
A smoker who had used cigarettes with an asbestos filter sued the manufacturers of the cigarette and filter under a theory of products liability, alleging that the products caused his mesothelioma. The plaintiff's expert, a professor of biochemistry, testified that lung tissue obtained from the plaintiff (who died before the conclusion of the litigation) contained asbestos fibers. The expert was also president of a consulting firm that does environmental testing for the presence of asbestos. The court found that the expert had never tested human tissues for the presence of asbestos before being hired by the plaintiff's lawyer and that the suggestion for using the particular testing method on humans had come from lawyers rather than scientists. The court excluded the testimony and characterized the situation as abuse by the plaintiff's lawyer: "That abuse is the hiring of reputable scientists, impressively credentialed, to testify for a fee to propositions that they have not arrived at through the methods that they use when they are doing their professional work rather than being paid to give an opinion helpful to one side of a lawsuit."

9.4 *G.E. v. Joiner*

G.E. v. Joiner[12] was the first Supreme Court case to follow up directly on *Daubert*. The *G.E.* decision established that appellate courts must review a trial judge's determination whether to admit or exclude expert testimony under an "abuse of discretion" standard. In practical terms, this means that it will be very difficult to overturn a trial court's determination.

In the case, plaintiff Robert Joiner alleged that he developed lung cancer as a result of exposure to polychlorinated biphenyls (PCBs). Joiner claimed that while his history of cigarette smoking and his family's history of lung cancer may have predisposed him to developing lung cancer, his exposure to PCBs and their derivatives (furans and dioxins) promoted the development of his cancer. The district court deemed inadmissible all of the plaintiffs' expert testimony that Joiner's exposure to PCBs, furans, and dioxins caused his cancer. After throwing out the expert testimony, the court entered summary judgment in the defendants' favor. The plaintiffs appealed to the Eleventh Circuit.

The Eleventh Circuit Court of Appeals applied *Daubert* to the plaintiffs' claims. The *Joiner* appeals court first determined that the plaintiffs' experts' methodology, procedures, and information supporting their opinions were scientifically reliable. The plaintiffs' two chief experts were Dr. Daniel Teitelbaum, a clinical toxicologist, and Dr. Arnold Schecter, a preventative

[12] *General Electric v. Joiner,* 522 U.S. 136, 139 L. Ed. 2d 508, 118 S. Ct. 512, 1997 U.S. LEXIS 7503 (1997), on remand, 134 F.3d 1457, 1998 U.S. App. LEXIS 1770 (11th Cir. Ga. 1998).

medicine specialist. Both doctors were well qualified. Both experts familiarized themselves with the specifics of Joiner's health history and disease, and both reviewed pertinent medical literature. Dr. Teitelbaum examined Joiner, interviewed him, reviewed his medical records, and reviewed the depositions of Joiner's family and his coworkers. Dr. Schecter interviewed Joiner, reviewed his medical records, and viewed a videotape of Joiner's working conditions related to his alleged toxic exposure. Each doctor employed scientific studies and authorities in formulating his respective opinions.

Moreover, each expert used scientifically reliable methods and procedures in gathering and assimilating all of the information forming his opinions. Each doctor asserted that the procedures he employed in arriving at his opinions were generally accepted in the medical community, a point that the defendants did not dispute. The doctors' extensive experience in their respective fields further augmented the reliability of their methodology and reasoning.

The appellate court especially criticized the trial court's review of the bases for Drs. Teitelbaum's and Schecter's opinions. For example, the district court rejected the plaintiffs' experts' two animal studies because of their limited number, because they used massive doses of PCBs, and because they were conducted on animals instead of humans. The appellate court found that none of these reasons was sufficient to render the experts' testimony unreliable—explaining that the question was simply whether the experts' use of challenged studies represents sound methodology. The appellate court proclaimed that the number of studies is irrelevant and it is improper to deem research unreliable solely because it employs animal subjects. In sum, this court reversed the trial court because:

> Instead of reviewing the bases for the experts' opinions to screen out mere speculation, the district court excluded the experts' testimony because it drew different conclusions from their research. This it should not have done. Courts should simply satisfy themselves as to the reliability of proffered expert testimony, "leaving the jury to decide the correctness of competing expert opinions."[13]

The United States Supreme Court reversed the Eleventh Circuit. It held (1) abuse of discretion is the proper standard for an appellate court to apply in reviewing a federal district court's decision to admit or exclude expert scientific testimony at trial; and (2) because it was within the discretion of the district court in the instant case to conclude that the animal studies and the four epidemiological studies upon which the experts relied were not sufficient, whether individually or in combination, to support the experts' conclusions that the electrician's exposure to PCBs contributed to his cancer,

[13] 78 F.3d 524 533 (11th Cir. 1996).

the district court did not abuse its discretion in excluding the experts' testimony.

9.5 *Kumho Tire*

The *Kumho Tire*[14] decision established decisively that the *Daubert* factors apply to the testimony of engineers and other experts who are not scientists. The decision also established that a trial court, in its discretion, may consider the *Daubert* factors in its analysis of expert testimony, but it may also consider other standards that it determines are better indicators of reliability of the specific circumstances of the case. The decision reaffirmed that a trial court's determination will be reviewed under *G.E.*'s abuse of discretion standard.

Kumho was a products liability case. A tire on the vehicle driven by one of the plaintiffs blew out, the vehicle overturned, one passenger died and the others were injured. The plaintiffs sued the tire's maker and its distributor (collectively Kumho Tire), claiming that the tire that failed was defective. Their case hinged in significant part upon the depositions of a tire failure analyst, Dennis Carlson, Jr., who intended to testify that, in his expert opinion, a defect in the tire's manufacture or design caused the blow out. That opinion was based upon a visual and tactile inspection of the tire and upon the theory that in the absence of at least two of four specific, physical symptoms indicating tire abuse, the tire failure of the sort that occurred here was caused by a defect. Kumho Tire moved to exclude the testimony on the ground that the expert's methodology failed to satisfy Federal Rule of Evidence 702. The district court granted the motion and acknowledged *Daubert*'s mandate that it should act as a reliability "gatekeeper." The court noted that the four *Daubert* factors argued against the reliability of the expert's methodology. The Eleventh Circuit Court of Appeals held that the district court had erred as a matter of law in applying *Daubert*. Believing that *Daubert* was limited to the scientific context, the court held that the *Daubert* factors did not apply to Carlson's testimony, which it characterized as skill- or experience-based. The Supreme Court reversed the Eleventh Circuit's ruling and held that the *Daubert* factors may apply to the testimony of engineers and other experts who are not scientists.[15] It explained that the evidentiary rationale underlying *Daubert*'s gatekeeping determination is not limited to scientific knowledge: "Rule 702 does not distinguish between 'scientific' knowledge and 'technical' or 'other specialized' knowledge, but makes clear that any such knowledge might become the subject of expert testimony."[16]

---

[14] 119 S. Ct. 1167 (1999).

[15] *Kumho*, at 7-13.

[16] The court further explained: "Finally, it would prove difficult, if not impossible, for judges to administer evidentiary rules under which a 'gatekeeping' obligation depended upon a distinction between 'scientific' knowledge and 'technical' or

The Supreme Court applied these standards to the case and found the trial court's decision to exclude the expert testimony proper. The Supreme Court explained that the trial court excluded the testimony because it initially doubted the expert's methodology and then found it unreliable after examining the transcript in some detail and considering the respondents' defense of it. The doubts that triggered the court's initial inquiry were reasonable, as was the court's ultimate conclusion that the expert could not reliably determine the cause of the failure of the tire in question. The question was not the reliability of the methodology in general, but whether the expert could reliably determine the cause of failure of *the particular tire at issue.* That tire, the expert conceded, had traveled far enough so that some of the tread had been worn bald, it should have been taken out of service, it had been repaired (inadequately) for punctures, and it bore some of the very marks that he said indicated not a defect but abuse. Moreover, the expert's own testimony cast considerable doubt upon the reliability of both his theory about the need for at least two signs of abuse and his proposition about the significance of visual inspection in this case. The plaintiffs argued that other tire failure experts, like their own, rely on visual and tactile examinations of tires. But there was no indication in the record that other experts in the industry used the plaintiffs' expert's *particular* approach or that tire experts normally make the very fine distinctions necessary to support his conclusions. Nor are there references to articles or papers that validate his approach. "[Plaintiffs'] argument that the District Court too rigidly applied *Daubert* might have had some validity with respect to the court's initial opinion, but fails because the court, on reconsideration, recognized that the relevant reliability inquiry should be 'flexible,' and ultimately based its decision upon Carlson's failure to satisfy either *Daubert*'s factors *or any other* set of reasonable reliability criteria."[17]

9.6 Treatment of Testimony by Specialty

The following table shows some of the cases in which the court has subjected expert testimony to a *Daubert* or *Daubert*-based analysis. The chart is organized by specialty type.

Table 9.61

Expert	Citation	Result
Accident Reconstructionist	*Perret v. Neson,* 722 So.2d 1118 (La. App. 5 Cir. 1998)	Force of impact based on the use of accelerometer to measure G forces on vehicle. Admissible—methodology was accepted industry practice.

'other specialized' knowledge, since there is no clear line dividing the one from the others and no convincing need to make such distinctions." *Kumho*, at 7-9.

[17] *Kumho*, at 13-19.

Accident Reconstructionist	*J.B. Hunt Transport v. General Motors,* 52 F.Supp2d 1084 (E.D. Mo. 1999)	Number of impacts upon vehicle. Admissible—methodology tested and generally accepted.
Agricultural Economist	*Blue Dane Simmental v. American Simmental Assn.,* 178 F.3d 1035 (8th Cir. 1999)	Causes of fluctuations in cattle market. Excluded—modeling method not generally used in field to support causation.
Agricultural Engineer	*James v. Beauregard Elec. Co-op., Inc.,* 736 So.2d 353 (La. App. 3 Cir. 1999)	Effect of electric cooperative's stray voltage on dairy herd. Admissible—theory exhaustively tested.
Agronomist	*B.F. Goodrich v. Betkoski,* 99 F.3d 505 (2d Cir.1996)	CERCLA suit. Costs incurred in clean up of hazardous substance. Admissible—opinion based on valid methodology.
Allergist	*Heller v. Shaw,* 167 F.3d 146 (3rd Cir. 1999)	Carpet caused respiratory illness. Inadmissible—no scientific studies presented. Methodology reliable, but did not "fit" conclusion drawn.
Anthropologist	*Grand Traverse Band of Ottawa & Chippewa v. U.S.,* 46 F.Supp.2d 689 (W.D. Mich. 1999)	Meaning of certain terms as applied by a government agency. Admissible.
Biomedical Engineer	*Guild v. General Motors Corp.,* 53 F.Supp.2d 363 (W.D.N.Y. 1999)	Theory of "inertial release" and its relation to crashworthiness of seatbelt system. Admissible—theory based on extensive testing.
Cardiologist	*Rosen v. CIBA-Geigy Corp.,* 78 F.3d 316 (7th Cir. 1996)	Nicotine overdose caused heart attack. Inadmissible—no scientific evidence presented to support theory, no reference to literature.

Cardiologists	*Knapp v. Northwestern University*, 942 F.Supp. 1191 (N.D. Ill. 1996)	Likelihood of future medical problems. Admissible—opinion based upon accepted scientific principles and proven data.
Ceramics Expert (PhD)	*Robertson v. Norton Co.*, 148 F.2d 905 (8th Cir. 1998)	Adequacy of warning label on grinder. Inadmissible—not based upon any scientific theory or empirical research.
Certified Public Accountant	*SEC v. Lipson*, 46 F.Supp.2d 758 (N.D. Ill. 1999)	Insider trading defendant found certain reports unreliable and did not pay attention to them. Inadmissible—methodology for opinion no more than speculation.
Chemical Engineer	*Burgess v. Abex Corp.*, 712 N.E.2d 939 (Ill. App. 4 Dist. 1999)	Asbestos manufacturers engaged in conspiracy. Admissible.
Chemist	*Loch v. Shell Oil. Co.*, 49 F.Supp.2d 1262 (D. Kan. 1999)	Farmer exposed to cattle larvacide and retained it in his tissue. Excluded on grounds of all *Daubert* factors, particularly "common sense" testing methods.
Chemist	*Mitchell v. Uniroyal Goodrich Tire Co.*, 666 So. 2d 727 (La. App. 4 Cir. 1995)	Cause of tire failure. Inadmissible—no evidence presented explaining methodology employed to support the theory or indicating the theory was tested under current manufacturing standards.
Civil Engineer	*Jiminez v. GNOC, Corp.*, 670 A.2d 24 (N.J. Super. A.D. 1996)	Preventative maintenance on injury-causing elevator was not properly done. Inadmissible—no evidence presented regarding any scientific basis for the opinion.
Clinical Ecologist	*Coffey v. County of Hennepin*, 23 F.Supp.2d 1081 (D. Minn. 1998)	Cause of MCS. Inadmissible—no reliable scientific basis for diagnosing MCS exists.

Clinical Social Worker	*America West Airlines, Inc. v. Tope,* 935 S.W.2d 908 (Tex. App.-El Paso 1996)	Terminated employee's mental anguish. Inadmissible—opinion not testable, peer reviewed. Accepted by community for nonjudicial use, but rate of error not explored.
Economist	*Cochrane v. Schneider Nat. Carriers, Inc.,* 980 F.Supp. 374 (D. Kan. 1997)	Loss figures for loss of guidance or counsel, in the context of parents' anticipated losses of financial support due to death of child. Inadmissible—not based on scientifically valid methodology.
Electrical Engineer	*Media Logic Inc. v. Xerox Corp.,* 689 N.Y.S.2d 762 (A.D. 3 Dept. 1999)	Theory that malfunction in copier caused fire, based on inspection of machine. Admissible.
Electrical Engineer	*Campbell ex. rel. Campbell v. Studer,* 970 P.2d 389 (Wyo. 1998)	Asphalt compactor was defective due to lack of automatic shutoff device. Inadmissible—"concept" related in opinion was untested.
Electrical Engineer	*Doyle Wilson Homebuilder, Inc. v. Pickens,* 996 S.W.2d 387 (Tex. App.-Austin 1999)	Electrical wiring started fire. Admissible—based upon reasoned elimination of other possible causes.
Electrical Engineer	*Maryland Cas. Co. v. Therm-O-Disc, Inc.,* 137 F.3d 780 (4th Cir. 1998)	Clothes dryer thermometer caused fire. Admissible—numerous works of technical literature supporting mode of analysis.
Electricity Expert (Physics PhD)	*Schlader v. Interstate Power Co.,* 591 N.W.2d 10 (Iowa 1999)	Stray voltage caused injury to dairy herd. Inadmissible—theory had no scientific support, theory untested.

Engineer	*Bartley v. Euclid, Inc.*, 158 F.3d 261 (5th Cir. 1998)	Vibrations in coal hauler due to design defect caused injuries in drivers. Admissible—"geometry" of haulers supports the opinion.
Engineer	*Demaree v. Toyota Motor Corp.*, 37 F.Supp2d 959 (W.D. Ky. 1999)	An airbag should only deploy at 20-25 mph in a frontal collision. Inadmissible—opinion was unpublished, untested, unverified.
Engineer	*Hanks by Old. Nat. Trust Co. v. Korea Iron and Steel*, 993 F.Supp. 1204 (S.D. Ill. 1998)	Identity of manufacturer of broken scoping line cable. Inadmissible—chemical analysis of wire rope based on unreliable methodology, no evidence presented regarding any of the *Daubert* factors.
Engineer	*Stibbs v. Mapco, Inc.*, 945 F.Supp. 1220 (S.D. Iowa 1996)	Explosion caused by small fragment of metal. Inadmissible—opinion based upon untested premises.
Engineer	*Rogers v. Ford Motor Co.*, 953 F.Supp. 606 (N.D. Ind. 1997)	Alternative seatbelt design feasibility and "inertial actuation." Inadmissible—design concept not subjected to peer review or testing.
Engineer	*Diviero v. Uniroyal Goodrich Tire Co.*, 919 F.Supp. 1353 (D. Ariz. 1996)	Cause of separation of tire belts. Inadmissible—did not incorporate any scientific authority.
Engineer	*Peitzmeier v. Hennessy Industries, Inc.*, 97 F.3d 293 (8th Cir. 1996)	Tire changer design defective. Inadmissible—expert never designed, built, or tested a changer that incorporated a different design based upon his alternative.

Engineer/ Accident Reconstructionist	*Waring v. Wommack,* 945 S.W.2d 889 (Tex. App.-Austin 1997)	Motorist caused accident and injuries to bicyclist. Admissible—theory based on physics, tests forming basis for opinion were sound and had nonjudicial uses.
Engineer/ Ergonomist	*Reiff v. Convergent Technologies,* 957 F.Supp. 573 (D. N.J. 1997)	Particular keyboard required excessive keying forces. Inadmissible—opinion not based on ergonomic analysis of factors affecting plaintiff.
Environmental Consultant	*Burns Philip Food v. Cavalea Continental Freight,* 135 F.3d 526 (7th Cir. 1998)	Results of confined testing to determine source of contamination by spilled diesel fuel. Inadmissible—testing methodology insufficient.
Epidemiologist	*Ambrosini v. Labarraque,* 101 F.3d 129 (D.C. Cir. 1996)	Depo-Provera caused birth defects. Admissible—methodology was conventional for expert's field.
Ergonomist	*Stasior v. Nat'l Railroad Passenger Corp.,* 19 F.Supp2d 835 (N.D. Ill. 1998)	Low repetition occupations are associated with cumulative trauma disorders. Inadmissible—testing underlying theory was insufficient.
Ergonomist	*Dennis v. Pertec Computer Corp.,* 927 F.Supp. 156 (D. N.J. 1996)	Biomechanics of keystroking, plaintiff's disorders, and the keyboard design. Inadmissible—no methodology presented, no evidence of peer review of theory.

Ergonomist	*Bennet v. PRC Public Sector, Inc.,* 931 F.Supp. 484 (S.D. Tex. 1996)	Computer-aided dispatch system caused repetitive motion disorder, workstation design unreasonably dangerous. Inadmissible—no evidence regarding source relied upon for relevant industry standards, no peer review or publication of conclusion.
Exercise Physiologist	*Olinger v. U.S. Golf Association,* 52 F.Supp.2d 947 (N.D. Ind. 1999)	Amount of energy an average person expended while walking a round of golf. Inadmissible—because no evidence of methodology disclosed.
Fire Expert	*Michigan Millers Mut. Ins. Corp. v. Benfield,* 140 F.3d 915 (11th Cir. 1998)	Fire was caused by arson. Inadmissible—conclusion came as a result of eliminating other factors, no testing took place, and an admitted lack of scientific basis for the hypothetical cause of the fire.
Forensic Chemist	*U.S. v. $141,770 in U.S. Currency,* 157 F.3d 600 (8th Cir. 1998)	Ninety-nine percent of U.S. currency is contaminated with drug residue. Inadmissible—no peer review of the test results underlying the opinion, tests are not replicable.
Gun Expert	*Bromley v. Garey,* 979 P.2d 1165 (Idaho 1999)	Gun malfunction caused hunting accident. Inadmissible—too speculative.
Immunologist	*Cabrera v. Cordis,* 945 F.Supp. 209 (D. Nev. 1996)	Brain shunt resulted in silicone toxicity, based upon "silicone antibody test." Inadmissible—test did not meet any of the *Daubert* factors.

Industrial Engineer	*Cummins v. Lyle Industries,* 93 F.3d 362 (7th Cir. 1996)	Alternative designs for braking system of trim press. Inadmissible—design had never been subjected to the scientific method, had never been tested.
Industrial Hygienist	*Mitchell v. Gencorp Inc.,* 165 F.3d 778 (10th Cir. 1999)	Level of exposure of worker to defendant's chemicals. Inadmissible—opinion based on photos of work site, methodology unreliable.
Industrial Hygienist	*Arnold v. Dow Chemical Co.,* 32 F.Supp.2d 584 (E.D.N.Y. 1999)	Exposure to trichloroethylene caused multiple myeloma. Admissible—methodology sound.
Industrial Hygienist	*Curtis v. M&S Petroleum, Inc.,* 174 F.3d 661 (5th Cir. 1999)	Exposure to excessive levels of Benzene caused injury. Admissible—generous scientific support for causation theory.
Industrial Hygienist	*Estate of Mitchell,* 968 F.Supp. 592 (D. Kan. 1997)	Toulene caused myelogenous leukemia. Inadmissible—expert knew no studies that showed that chemical caused the disease.
Industrial Hygienist and Environmental Engineer	*LaSalle Nat. Bank v. Malik,* 705 N.E.2d 938 (Ill. App. 2 Dist. 1999)	Ethylene oxide was entrained and circulated into plaintiff physician's office. Admissible—articles relied on were authoritative and methods accepted by the medical community.
Mechanical Engineer	*Juarequi v. Carter Mfg. Co.,* 173 F.3d 1076 (8th Cir. 1999)	Corn head device was unreasonably dangerous, should have had awareness barriers. Inadmissible—no testing of suggested device.

Mechanical Engineer	*Tassin v. Sears, Roebuck and Co.,* 946 F.Supp. 1241 (M.D. La. 1996)	Alternative design for safety device on table saw. Inadmissible—methodology "virtually nonexistent."
Mechanical Engineer	*Freeman v. Case Corp.,* 118 F.2d 1011 (4th Cir. 1997)	Pedal design of tractor was unreasonably dangerous. Inadmissible—opinion based on experience, but no evidence of scientific foundation offered.
Medical Toxicologist	*Nat'l Bank of Commerce v. Associated Milk Producers,* 22 F.Supp.2d 942 (E.D. Ark. 1998)	Exposure to contaminated milk caused laryngeal cancer. Inadmissible—no scientific literature drawing a connection between the type of exposure in this case and cancer, no human or animal study showing a connection.
Microbiologist	*Graham v. Playtex Products, Inc.,* 993 F.Supp. 127 (N.D.N.Y. 1998)	Certain tampons caused toxic shock syndrome. Admissible although not generally accepted.
Neurologist	*Minnesota Min. & Mfg. Co. v. Atterbury,* 978 S.W.2d 183 (Tex. App.-Texarkana 1998)	Exposure to silicone after breast implant caused multiple sclerosis. Inadmissible—scientifically unreliable theory, failed *Daubert* analysis.
Neurologist	*Colell v. Mentzer Investments, Inc.,* 973 P.2d 631 (Colo. App. 1998)	Causal relationship between stress and multiple sclerosis. Admissible—abundancy of specialized literature on the relationship.
Neurologist	*White v. Chicago Pneumatic Tool Co.,* 994 F.Supp. 1478 (S.D. Ga. 1998)	Device's vibration causes carpal tunnel syndrome. Admissible—theory subjected to numerous scientifically valid tests.

Neurologist	*Schudel v. General Electric Co.,* 120 F.3d 991 (9th Cir. 1997)	Neurological problems caused by exposure to solvents. Inadmissible—based on "whole person aggravation" theory, no evidence that theory had scientific basis, articles relied upon did not support neurotoxicity conclusions.
Neurosurgeon	*Dukes v. Illinois Cent. R. Co.,* 934 F.Supp. 939 (N.D. Ill. 1996)	Plaintiff developed carpal tunnel syndrome because he carried signal lights. Inadmissible—no investigation or research into causes of CTS, no articulation of methodology by which conclusions might be tested, testimony prepared specifically for litigation.
Nuclear Reactor Physicist	*In re TMI Litigation Cases Consol. II,* 911 F.Supp. 775 (M.D. Pas. 1996)	Plaintiffs were exposed to gases after a hydrogen blowout. Inadmissible—expert could not explain how he reached his conclusions.
Obstetrician	*Williams v. Hedican,* 561 N.W.2d 817 (Iowa 1997)	Administering chicken pox virus to mother would have protected a fetus that was born with defects. Admissible—opinion based on scientifically valid principle even though "science" has not fully tested expert's theory.

Occupational Physician	*Allen v. Pennsylvania Engineering Corp.*, 102 F.3d 194 (5th Cir. 1996)	Exposure to ethylene oxide caused brain cancer. Inadmissible—unreliable because based on inconclusive animal studies and insufficient epidemiological evidence.
Ophthalmologist	*Golod v. Hoffman-LaRoche,* 964 F.Supp. 841 (S.D.N.Y. 1997)	Ingestion of Tegison (for psoriasis) caused toxicity in plaintiff. Inadmissible—novel theory had not been tested, not accepted by medical community.
Ophthalmologist	*Grimes v. Hoffman-LaRoche, Inc.*, 907 F.Supp. 33 (D.N.H. 1995)	Therapeutic doses of Accutane caused cataracts. Inadmissible—no specific determination of how much of the drug actually reached plaintiff's lenses, nor how much need be present to produce cataracts.
Orthopedic Surgeon	*Smith v. Sofamor, S.N.C.*, 21 F.Supp.2d 918 (W.D. Wis. 1998)	Bone screw device used in spinal fusion caused injury. Inadmissible—no scientific basis for opinion presented, thus fails *Daubert* factors.
Orthopedic Surgeon	*Crafton v. Union Pacific R. Co.*, 585 N.W.2d 115 (Neb. App. 1998)	Keyboarding caused carpal tunnel syndrome. Admissible—based upon medical literature and nerve conduction tests, as well as experience.
Pediatrician	*Nat'l Bank of Com. v. Dow Chemical,* 965 F.Supp. 1490 (E.D. Ark. 1996)	Mother's exposure to Dursban caused birth defects in her child. Inadmissible—opinion not based on expert's own research or any animal or human studies.

Pharmacologist	*Ruiz-Troche v. Pepsi Cola of Puerto Rico,* 161 F.3d 77 (1st Cir. 1998)	Amount of drugs driver of vehicle consumed and time of consumption. Admissible—based on half-life methodology that has significant support in scientific community.
Pharmacologist	*Haggerty v. Upjohn Co.,* 950 F.Supp. 1160 (S.D. Fla. 1996)	Ingestion of Halcion caused psychological injury. Inadmissible—opinion based upon methodology not scientifically sound. Expert did not review epidemiological data or actual case studies underlying opinion.
Pharmacology Professor	*Willert v. Ortho Pharmaceutical Corp.,* 995 F.Supp. 979 (D. Minn. 1998)	Taking Floxin caused AIHA and GBS. Inadmissible—on all four *Daubert* grounds.
Physician	*Wesberry v. Gislaved Gummi AB,* 178 F.3d 257 (4th Cir. 1999)	Treating physician's medical opinion on causation can be based on differential diagnosis. Admissible.
Physician	*Coffin v. Orkin Exterminating Co., Inc.,* 20 F.Supp.2d 107 (D. Me. 1998)	Exterminator's negligence caused office worker's MCS. Inadmissible—theory of causation too speculative to satisfy *Daubert* factors.
Physician (Expert on Lead Poisoning)	*Dombrowski v. Gould Electronics, Inc.,* 31 F.Supp.2d 436 (M.D. Pa. 1998)	Use of "KXRF bone lead testing" to determine bone lead levels. Inadmissible—had not gained acceptance in the medical community, except for experimental purposes.
Physician	*Gess v. U.S.,* 952 F.Supp. 1529 (M.D. Ala. 1996)	Patient tampering took place. Admissible—based upon knowledge of toxicity derived from and supported by peer-reviewed articles.

Physician	*Lakie v. Smithkline Beecham,* 965 F.Supp. 49 (D.D.C. 1997)	Use of Oraflex (contaminated by Benzene) caused bone-marrow disorder. Admissible—three physician experts based theory on differential diagnosis methodology, clear connection in scientific literature of connection between Benzene and MDS.
Physician, PM&R	*Black v. Food Lion, Inc.,* 171 F.3d 308 (5th Cir. 1999)	Fall caused hormonal changes resulting in fibromyalgia. Inadmissible—no scientifically reliable basis for causation opinion.
Physicians	*Aldridge v. Goodyear Tire & Rubber Co.,* 34 F.Supp.2d 1010 (D. Md. 1999)	Occupational diseases caused by toxic chemical exposure. Inadmissible, no evidence proffered establishing *Daubert* factors.
Physicians, Toxicologist, Psychologists	*Frank v. State of New York,* 972 F.Supp. 130 (N.D.N.Y. 1997)	MCS caused by exposure to environmental pollutants. Inadmissible—inadequate scientific foundation for conclusions regarding MCS.
Polygraph Examiner	*Meyers v. Arcudi,* 947 F.Supp. 581 (D. Conn. 1996)	Results of polygraph exam, using control question technique. Inadmissible—rate of error undetermined, no general acceptance.
Professor of Materials, Science & Engineering	*Vassallo v. Baxter Healthcare Corp.,* 696 N.E.2d 909 (Mass. 1998)	Effects of silicone breast implants on the body. Admissible—based on expert's own research, chemical company studies, government studies, and other expert's testimony.

Psychiatrist	*Shahzade v. Gregory,* 923 F.Supp 286 (D. Mass. 1996)	Testimony relating to repressed memory. Admissible—theory had been tested, subjected to peer review, and accepted by clinical psychiatrists.
Psychologist	*Summers v. Missouri Pacific R.R. System,* 132 F.3d 599 (10th Cir. 1997)	Dementia caused by exposure to diesel fumes. Inadmissible—opinion based on testing still in the research stage.
Psychologist	*Tyus v. Urban Search Management,* 12 F.3d 256 (7th Cir. 1996)	Manner in which an "all white" advertising firm's campaign affects African-Americans. Admissible—based on peer-reviewed articles and sound methodology.
Radiation Geneticist	*In re TMI Litigation Cases Consolidated II,* 910 F.Supp. 200 (M.D. Pa. 1996)	Extent of radiation to which trees were exposed. Inadmissible—based upon dendrometric study, no evidence on the methodology employed.
Rheumatologist	*Kelley v. American Heyer-Schulte Corp.,* 957 F.Supp. 873 (W.D. Tex. 1997)	Breast implants caused Sjogren's Syndrome. Inadmissible—based upon literature that did not support theory, expert's own studies did not meet *Daubert* factors.
Safety Engineer	*Kirstein v. Parks Corp.,* 159 F.3d 1065 (7th Cir. 1998)	Instruction on adhesive remover rendered it hazardous. Inadmissible—insufficient testing, no studies presented.
Safety Engineer	*Doblar v. Unverferth Mfg. Co., Inc.,* 981 F.Supp. 1284 (D.S.D. 1997)	Gravity grain box was dangerous and unsafe. Admissible—based on commonly used design principles.

Toxicologist	*Louderback v. Orkin Exterminating Co.*, 26 F.Supp.2d 1298 (D. Kan. 1998)	Levels of exposure to termiticide. Admissible—in spite of the fact expert did not consider threshold levels of exposure. The opinion was consistent with accepted methods of toxicology.
Toxicologist	*Higgins v. Diversey Corp.*, 998 F.Supp. 598 (D. Md. 1997)	"Toxic reaction" caused by inhalation of powdered bleach. Inadmissible—expert never conducted any research to test the hypothesis, never saw the injury before, offered no scientific basis for the opinion.
Toxicologist	*Vardaman v. Baker Center, Inc.*, 711 So.2d 727 (La. App. 1 Cir. 1998)	Exposure to Chlordane caused injury. Inadmissible—affidavits containing expert's testimony offered no information about the methodology used or qualifications of the expert.
Toxicologist	*Matter of Sybers*, 583 N.W.2d 890 (Iowa 1998)	Potassium poisoning was used to murder decedent. Admissible—although theory was untested and novel. (This was a bench trial, which gave the court more latitude.)
Toxicologist	*Cuevas v. E.I. DuPont de Nemours and Co.*, 956 F.Supp. 1306 (S.D. Miss. 1997)	Herbicide caused injury. Inadmissible—opinion based on theory that had never been peer reviewed.

Toxicologist	*Cartwright v. Home Depot USA*, 936 F.Supp. 900 (M.D. Fla. 1996)	Latex paint exposure caused asthma. Inadmissible—expert's reports, affidavits, deposition testimony and supporting literature failed to identify what methodology he employed to reach his causation conclusion other than a temporal relationship.

9.7 How Experts Can Avoid or Deal with *Daubert* Challenges

An expert's opinion may be challenged at a *Daubert* hearing. If the challenge is successful before the judge, the expert's entire testimony could be excluded from evidence. This could result in the dismissal of the case and permanent damage to the reputation of the expert. What can an expert do to protect himself from a successful *Daubert* challenge?

General assessment

1. Prior to accepting the engagement, an expert should ask counsel if she anticipates a *Daubert* attack on the expert's testimony.
2. An expert should evaluate for himself if a *Daubert* attack is likely. Is the case novel? Is it complex? Is a substantial amount in controversy? Was the case filed in federal court?

Specific criteria

The expert should take a long, hard look at her work and methodology results under the *Daubert* criteria. To avoid rejection of testimony, an expert should do the following.

- Only use theories or techniques that have been tested and passed.
- Use theories or techniques that are objective.
- Specify the known error rate or potential error rate for the method.
- Use methods with acceptable error rates.
- Produce peer-review literature (i.e., journal studies, reports, and treatises supporting the expert's conclusions and opinions).
- Produce reliable scientific data to prove that her methods and conclusions are generally accepted in the scientific community.
- Demonstrate that her theories existed prior to the commencement of the litigation.
- Not develop novel theories to support conclusions for specific litigation.

- Demonstrate that she maintained standards and controls (for example, good laboratory practices and simultaneous blinded controls).
- Demonstrate that findings can and have been replicated by others.
- Demonstrate that her methodology followed the scientific method as it is practiced by at least a recognized minority of scientists in the expert's field.
- Offer testimony that is sufficiently tied to the facts of the case to help the jury to resolve a factual dispute.
- Avoid relying on the coincidence of temporality.
- Avoid extrapolating unjustifiably from an accepted premise to an unfounded conclusion.
- Adequately account for obvious alternative explanations.
- Demonstrate the same care and accuracy as in regular professional work.
- Use the real-world methodology of her field.
- Use an appropriate methodology to ensure that her opinion derives from and constitutes a form of specialized knowledge.

9.8 Conclusion

Expert opinions must be supported by reliable methodology. "Junk science" may be excluded from evidence for being unreliable. Even if it is not excluded by the trial judge, the expert's methodology may be subject to close questioning during cross-examination. Experts should base their opinions upon sound methodology that has been tested, is supported by peer-reviewed literature, has a known and acceptable rate of potential error that is generally accepted in the relevant community, and that was not developed solely for the purposes of litigation.

Chapter 10 Bulletproofing an Expert's Report

10.1 Introduction

Experts may be asked to draft a report that states their opinions and the bases for these opinions. To be safe, the expert needs to assume that anything he writes will be discoverable as part of ongoing or future litigation. (See Chapter 21 on confidentiality and work product.) ***An expert, therefore, should never draft a written report of any kind unless he has been expressly directed to do so by his retaining counsel.*** Counsel may remind the expert not to draft a written report when she retains the expert or when she sends the expert records or documentation. In any event, the expert should never draft a written report until after first checking with counsel.

10.2 Why Counsel May Want a Written Report

There are many reasons why counsel may want an expert to draft a written report. A written report may be required by the court or forum where the litigation is pending. For example, under Federal Rule of Civil Procedure 26(2)(B),[1] unless otherwise stipulated or directed by the court, an expert must prepare and sign a written report containing:

- a complete statement of all opinions to be expressed,
- the basis and reasons for the opinions,
- the data or other information considered,
- any exhibits to be used in summary of the opinions,
- any exhibits to be used as support for the opinions,
- the qualifications of the witness,
- a list of all publications authored by the witness in the preceding ten years,
- the compensation to be paid for the study and testimony, and
- a listing of any other cases in which the witness has testified as an expert at trial or by deposition within the preceding four years.[2]

The reason for requiring expert reports is the elimination of unfair surprise to the opposing party and conservation of resources.[3] Failure to comply with the requirements of Rule 26(2)(B) can result in the expert's testimony being stricken. The test of compliance is whether the report is sufficiently complete, detailed, and in compliance with the rules so that

---

[1] See Appendix Q for the full text of Rule 26.

[2] Fed. R. Civ. Pro. 26(2)(B).

[3] *Reed v. Binder,* 165 F.R.D. 424 (D.C. N.J. 1996).

surprise is eliminated, unnecessary depositions are avoided, and costs are reduced.[4]

Example 10.1
Salgado v. General Motors Corporation, 150 F.3d 735 (7th Cir. 1998)
The experts' reports were filed in an untimely manner and were markedly deficient—they appeared to be "preliminary" in nature. The first expert's report was "conclusionary" and thus insufficient. The court characterized the second expert's report as "devoid of any factual basis for its conclusionary opinions." Also, the second expert claimed the report was sparse because he had not been provided discovery materials. Then, he attempted to file a supplementary report containing the "factual bases" for his opinion. However, this supplemental report was based solely on materials already in his possession before the filing of the first report. The court barred both experts' testimony.

Example 10.2
Elgas v. Colorado Belle Corp., 179 F.R.D. 296 (D. Nev. 1998)
In this tort action, the plaintiff failed to provide a proper Rule 26 report for her designated expert witness. The court struck the designation of the expert, because "[the expert] has not listed other cases in which he has testified as an expert at trial or by deposition within the preceding four years. An expert's report must be 'detailed and complete.' The court explained:

> An expert's failure to maintain records in the ordinary course of his business sufficient to allow the disclosures to be made, does not constitute "substantial justification" for the failure to provide required disclosures as to any retained expert expected to testify at the trial of the case. The requirements of the Rule 26(a) are mandatory as to any expert retained to testify. If the expert is unable or unwilling to make the disclosures he should be excluded as a possibility for retention as an expert witness in the case.

The plaintiff argued that she was unable under her current financial situation to find another expert. However, the court rejected this and stated that "[a] party may not simply retain an expert and then make whatever disclosures the expert is willing or able to make notwithstanding the known requirements of Rule 26." The court reasoned,

> [T]he disclosure of prior recorded testimony is designed to give the other party access to useful information to meet the proposed experts' opinions. The proliferation of marginal or unscrupulous experts will only be stopped when the other party has detailed information about prior testimony. The list of other cases in which the witness has testified as an expert should include the court, the names of the parties, the case number, and whether the testimony was by deposition or at trial (298).

Because the plaintiff did not show how the failure to disclose was substantially justified or harmless, the court struck the designation plaintiff's expert.

---

[4] *Reed v. Binder,* 165 F.R.D. 424 (D.C. N.J. 1996).

Example 10.3
Nguyen v. IBP, Inc., 162 F.R.D. 675 (D. Kan. 1995)
The plaintiff's expert's report did not contain all the data required under Rule 26. The report identified patients about whom the expert had testified, but the report provided no identification of "cases" or courts in which the expert's deposition had been taken, had incomplete or missing attorney names, had missing phone numbers for attorneys, provided no witness signature, and offered entries for the last three, rather than four, years. The plaintiff maintained that all "reasonably available information" was disclosed, but the court found no substantial justification existed for the shoddy report. "An expert's failure to maintain records in the ordinary course of business sufficient to allow the disclosures to be made does not constitute 'substantial justification' for the failure to provide required disclosures as to any expert retained...." The court allowed the plaintiff the opportunity to submit a supplemental disclosure that corrected the deficiencies, then declared that the expert's testimony would be barred if the supplemental report did not suffice.

In some arbitration proceedings experts must present their direct testimony via a written report signed under the pains and penalties of perjury. Counsel may also want a written report to assist in settlement negotiations. A well-written and soundly reasoned report will improve the settlement value of a case. A written report may also be needed in support of or in opposition against a motion for summary judgment or as a vehicle to discourage costly expert depositions. Whatever the reason, the expert's report will become a crucially important document in a contested legal proceeding. It is, therefore, very important that it is drafted carefully.

10.3 Avoiding the Most Common Report Drafting Mistakes

When drafting a report, the expert should only address the issues that counsel has asked her to address in the report. If she is unsure of which issues to address, the expert should call counsel and ask him what he wants addressed. For example, when drafting an Independent Medical Examination (IME) report, an expert will need to know which issues and opinions should be included in the written report (for example, impairment, disability, symptom magnification, etc.).

The expert should address all the issues that counsel has requested her to address. Failure to do so can be very damaging to counsel's case. In some circumstances, for example, where the report was to be used to oppose a motion for summary judgment or where it was to be used in lieu of direct testimony, failure to address all the requested issues could result in the case being lost outright.

An expert should keep in mind that anything she writes in a report can and will be used against her when she testifies in the case at hand or even in some future case. A poorly written report can be used during cross-examination to damage an expert's credibility. There are several things to avoid when drafting reports because they could come back to haunt an expert during cross-examination. These include the following.

1. Sloppiness

The report should be proofed carefully. It's tough to pick up your own typos, so it may be a good idea for experts to have someone else proof their work. They should also use a computerized spelling and grammar checker. A good cross-examiner will point out each and every instance of sloppiness and typos in a report. Counsel can make the argument that if an expert was sloppy in drafting his report, he was probably rushed and sloppy when he formed his opinion. She will argue that an opinion based upon sloppy or rushed work is not credible. This problem is 100% avoidable if the expert takes his time and has his report proofed.

> **Example 10.4**
> It is therefore my opinion, based upon a reasonable degree of reasonable certainty that....

2. Remarks that make the expert appear to be an advocate

An expert needs to avoid making any remarks, even subtle ones, that counsel can use to show that the expert is really an advocate in the case for the party that retained him. The role of the expert in the case is as an expert, not an advocate. If counsel can successfully argue that the expert is an advocate, the expert will come off as a hired gun and will lose credibility with the jury. Examples of remarks to avoid include stressing key points with exclamation points, underlining, capitalization, and remarks addressing credibility.

> **Example 10.5**
> The defendant in this case was <u>clearly</u> GROSSLY Negligent!!!

> **Example 10.6**
> This report is based in part upon the deposition of the plaintiff, John Smith, who was not a credible witness.

3. Improperly stating an opinion

The expert's *only* reason for being involved in a case is to state an opinion that will assist the trier of fact in deciding the case. This opinion must be stated in a proper, legally sufficient way. The most commonly used phrase to properly state an expert opinion follows.

> **Example 10.7**
> Based upon a reasonable degree of (scientific or medical) (probability or certainty) it is my opinion that....

Experts need to avoid using words such as *may, could,* or *possible* when stating opinions.

Example 10.8
It's my opinion that it's possible that the tire that failed on May 9, 1999 had a design defect.

Failure to state an opinion properly in a report can result in major problems. First, in some cases, it can result in the expert's opinion being excluded by the court or other forum. Second, during cross-examination it will be used against the expert to damage her credibility.

4. Inartfully drafted sentences or phrases

Experts need to avoid using inartfully drafted sentences or phrases that could suggest incompetence or bias.

Example 10.9
Per your request, I have formed the opinion that....

Counsel will use anything and everything contained in an expert's report as ammunition against him during cross-examination. An expert should not give her any extra ammunition by using inartful sentences or phrases. Experts should read over their reports carefully before submission.

5. Prior drafts and notes

Counsel can use any and all prior drafts of an expert's report or handwritten notes as powerful ammunition during cross-examination. These prior drafts and notes can be extremely damaging to an expert's credibility. Seasoned experts commonly discard draft reports and notes and do not save the computer word processing files of their draft reports. This is done as part of their routine business practice to avoid the accumulation of unnecessary papers and materials. Experts should never discard anything that they have been subpoenaed to produce.

6. Drawing legal conclusions

Wise experts do not draw legal conclusions (for example, "The plaintiff was guilty of contributory negligence"). This is (usually) beyond the area of one's expertise and will get the expert into trouble during cross-examination.

Example 10.10
Can you please explain to the jury the four elements of negligence, Mr. Harding?

Experts should state their opinions in such a way that they do not reach legal conclusions.

Example 10.11
Based upon all of the evidence I have reviewed, it is my opinion, based on a reasonable degree of certainty, that the plaintiff was not operating her vehicle safely at the time of the motor vehicle accident in question.

7. Gratuitous information and opinions

Experts should not offer gratuitous information. Instead, they should address only the points they have been requested to address. Any additional information or opinions merely serve as cross-examination ammunition.

Example 10.12
I would also like to add that I am very happy that my involvement in this case will soon be coming to an end.

8. Failure to be clear and concise

The less clear and concise the report, the more an expert will be open to damaging cross-examination. Ambiguities fuel cross-examination.

Example 10.13
This is clearly a case of what you see is what you get.

9. Failure to check with counsel

An expert should put in a courtesy call to her retaining lawyer prior to drafting a report. During this call the expert can confirm that the attorney still wants a written report. It also provides a good opportunity to discuss findings prior to drafting the written report.

10. Being informal or "chatty"

The expert's report is a legally significant document that needs to be formally drafted. Informality or "chattiness" is to be avoided.

Example 10.14
Dear Teddy: Thank you for this referral. What a doozey of a case! I have reviewed....

11. Failure to review the report personally

The final step before signature should be the expert's personal review of the report. Experts should not provide clients or intermediaries with a pre-signed signature page or signature stamp.

10.4 Defending a Report at Deposition and at Trial

Experts need to know their reports cold. This includes dates, names, facts, and figures. The expert will lose credibility with the jury if he appears to not be thoroughly familiar with his own report. To become thoroughly familiar with the report, he will need to review it carefully and study it prior to testifying.

If an expert testifies in a way that is, or can be made to sound, inconsistent with his written report, he will be questioned about this. This is a process known as *impeachment*. Proper preparation is the key to surviving an impeachment attack. An expert needs to be prepared to justify any changes in opinion from what was described in his report or to correct any mischaracterizations that counsel may raise.

Example 10.15
Q. Your report stated that it was your opinion that the vehicle in question was traveling at 65–70 miles per hour at the time of impact. Now you're saying the speed was 75–80. You were obviously wrong once, when was it?
A. My opinion expressed in the report was based on all the information that was available to me when the report was drafted. Since then, new information, including…has become available to me. My opinion today is more valid than the one expressed in the written report because it is based on previously unavailable information.

If an expert is unable to explain during cross-examination, he will have an opportunity to explain himself adequately on redirect. The expert should prepare his retaining attorney in advance for the areas that may have to be explained on redirect.

The report in the case at hand is not the only one the expert needs to worry about. Counsel can and will use reports from prior cases to attempt to discredit an expert in front of the jury. This can be especially effective if counsel can show that the expert's opinion in this case is inconsistent from his opinion in a previous case (for example, in a previous case report he stated that fibromyalgia does not exist; in this case his testimony is that fibromyalgia was the diagnosis). There are two good ways to defeat this tactic. First, experts should call cases as they see them. This will greatly reduce potential problems with this tactic. Second, experts should keep their cool. There is most likely a very good reason why an expert's opinion has evolved ("Ah yes, that was before the landmark Colombaro study on the issue showed that…"). The expert should keep his head and make sure the reason for the change gets communicated to the jury. He shouldn't get rattled or else the jury may conclude that he has something to hide.

10.5 Formatting

A report that is organized into sections delineated by subject headings is the easiest to read. Commonly used headings include:

- Introduction, Overview, or Statement of Purpose
- Qualifications
- Prior Testimony

- Incident, History, or Facts
- Analysis or Discussion
- Supporting Data
- Test Results
- Materials Reviewed
- Exhibits
- References
- Opinion(s) or Findings
- Conclusion(s)

Reports should have an easy-to-read font size. This should be at least a size eleven because small print is very difficult for many people to read.

10.6 Further Resources

Several sample forensic reports have been provided in Appendix U. A report quality control checklist has been provided in Appendix B.

10.7 Conclusion

An expert should only draft a written report if she is explicitly requested to do so by retaining counsel. Everything in the report can be used as ammunition against the expert at trial. Therefore, experts need to draft and proof their reports very carefully and study them thoroughly prior to testifying.

Chapter 11 Connecting with the Jury

11.1 Introduction

In jury trials, the jury ultimately decides the case. Their job is to determine the facts of the case. A crucial part of this is determining the credibility of the witnesses.[1] This includes expert witnesses. As such, it is of the highest importance that experts are able to communicate with the jury in a credible and persuasive way. Everything else is secondary. To connect with the jury, an expert needs to understand what juries want and know the best ways to communicate with them.

11.2 What Juries Want

Attorney Jay W. Dankner, a highly experienced and successful litigator, explains that jurors want:

1. A relevant, coherent, understandable story.
2. To keep their interest at all times.
3. To be spoken to in clear, unambiguous terms.
4. Respect and sincerity.[2]

A relevant, coherent, understandable story

Sophisticated counsel will establish a theme or "story" for the entire trial that will appeal "to the jurors' standard of justice and fairness, be consistent with the evidence, and [be] easy to remember."[3] For example, the story could be "man gets in accident, fakes injury to get money," "big company makes dangerous product that doesn't perform as promised," or "company X breaks promise to company Y and company Y is devastated financially." The expert's testimony is a crucial part of the story. Many times, expert testimony is the glue that holds the story together. In any event, the expert needs to understand the story of the case and how her testimony fits into the story.

Keeping the juror's interest at all times

Boredom is likely to be an expert's number one obstacle to communicating effectively with a jury. Many jurors do not want to be on the jury and they

---

[1] The judge will give the jury the following typical expert witness jury instruction: "You have heard evidence in this case from witnesses who testified as experts. The law allows an expert to express opinions on subjects involving their special knowledge, training, skill, experience, or research. You shall determine what weight, if any, should be given such testimony, as with any other witness."

[2] Jay W. Dankner, *Communicating with the Jury.* Handout materials for the Fifth Annual National Expert Witness and Litigation Seminar, Hyannis, Massachusetts (June 20, 21, 1996) 2.

[3] Ibid., 2.

may have little or no interest in the case. Even more importantly, they may have an overwhelming desire that everyone concerned (the lawyers, the witnesses, and the judge) move the process along as quickly as possible so that they can all go home. To keep the juror's interest, an expert witness should:

- use powerful descriptive language that paints a picture,
- use phrases that the jury will remember, and
- use language that they will understand.

For example, the forensic expert might want to say (to describe a fractured neck), "It was like a finger getting caught in a door as it slammed shut. His spinal cord was cut and he'll be paralyzed the rest of his life." This is far more effective than saying, "I diagnosed a C3-C4 fracture with massive cord damage secondary to blunt trauma resultant from the MVA in question. Prognosis is for severe and permanent functional impairment." Technical language can be extremely boring. The expert should not fall into the temptation of using it to prove to the jury how smart she is. It is far more effective to use descriptive terms that they understand, can visualize, and will remember.

The expert witness should keep in mind that once she has "lost" the jury through boredom, it may be difficult or impossible to regain their attention. As such, it is good practice to communicate the major points of an opinion to the jury as soon as possible during direct examination. For example, let's assume an average juror has a 20-minute attention span.[4] Under this assumption, it is not good practice to spend 40 minutes talking about one's impressive experience, education, and publications *before* talking about the case at hand. By the time the expert gets to the case at hand, the jury may very well not be listening any longer.

Clear, unambiguous terms

It is best to avoid using technical terminology or jargon that is not likely to be understood by jurors. Such jargon is a major impediment to connecting with the jury. For example, the expert shouldn't say, "A comparison of the antemortem and postmortem records through the use of forensic odontology revealed endodential at tooth #1," when she can say, "I compared his dental records from before and after he died and found a root canal had been done on the upper right third molar...which is this tooth (demonstrating)." As part of the preparation process, the expert should lay out how she is going to explain her testimony in clear and unambiguous terms. Some experts practice their testimony with a lay person such as a teenage child or administrative assistant and then ask for feedback. This is a good technique to determine whether the expert will be able to communicate with the jury effectively. A little

[4] A valid assumption in the opinion of the authors.

forethought or advanced work in this area will pay major dividends on the witness stand.

Respect and sincerity

Most jurors do not have the education and technical knowledge of sophisticated experts. Collectively, however, they have hundreds of years of experience in spotting phonies. The expert witness, therefore, needs to avoid any comments or actions that can be interpreted as insincere or as showing a lack of respect for the jury.

> **Example 11.1**
> Well, I realize that most of the jury doesn't have a high level of technical education, so I'd like to explain by drawing a diagram. I think that would make it easier.
>
> **Advice for Experts:** There was probably no malice meant in a comment like this. However, reminding the jury of their lack of education is not a good way to connect with them.
>
> **Example 11.2**
> No, counselor, my $500/hour fee has nothing to do with why I'm here today. I'm here to help the jury. I really think my expertise will assist them.
>
> **Advice for Experts:** Jurors may not understand quantum mechanics or DNA testing, but they can spot a phony answer. Once the jury has labeled the expert as a phony, it is likely that his testimony will not be believed. This is not the way to connect with a jury.

11.3 Communicating with Jurors

Expert witnesses need to be able to communicate with the jury. The expert's role in the litigation is to assist the trier of fact. She cannot properly fulfill this role if the jurors cannot understand her testimony. To better communicate with the jury, Sonya Hamlin, one of the nation's leading jury consultants, recommends the following eight points.

1. During demonstrations print and do not abbreviate.

An expert cannot connect with the jury if they can't read her writing or if they don't understand her abbreviations.

2. Keep your language simple and recognizable.

Jurors are not persuaded by what they cannot understand.

3. Make sure the jury and judge can see your visuals.

Visual aids are useless if they can't be seen. A wise expert witness verbalizes his concern to the judge that the jurors be able to see. When the jury hears that he is concerned, this will score points with them. The expert will also find out whether they can see.

4. Practice with videotape.

The expert should see how he looks and determine where he needs to improve.

5. Self-edit and speak succinctly.

Wise experts get to the point. They assume that a juror's attention span is no more than 20 minutes. This time should not be squandered.

6. Tell the jurors what they need to know; not all that you know.

The expert witness should not run the risk of obscuring the important testimony or losing the jury's attention.

7. Understand the problems jurors have in assimilating a great deal of technical data when it is presented orally.

Effective experts make their presentations visual.

8. Visualize and demonstrate to reinforce your testimony.[5]

Today's "TV generation" is visually driven. When an expert witness lets the jurors see what he is talking about, they understand better and remember more.

Additional techniques for communicating with a jury that merit special attention are use of analogies and similes and employing verbal and nonverbal techniques.

Analogies and similes

Analogies and similes are powerful ways to connect with a jury.[6] The use of analogies and similes that relate to the jurors' personal experiences will, when done well, be remembered, discussed, and used during deliberations. The case of a young man who lost both arms in a farming accident comes to mind. The expert went to dinner with the plaintiff and his wife. When asked at trial to describe how the young man ate his dinner when the plate was put in front of him the expert stated, "He ate like a dog." This story was told to the author almost thirty years ago. He has not yet been able to forget it. Another memorable case involved a cardiologist who testified that an event made the

---

[5] Sonya Hamlin, *What Makes Juries Listen Today* (Glaser Legal Works, 1998) 556–591.

[6] Hamlin states: "…*if* you first use analogies based on *familiar* objects, experiences, or concepts. If you say, 'research is kind of like trying out the keys on your key ring until you can finally find the one that fits and opens the door,' jurors will have an instant image because they've done *that* a thousand times."[6]

heart attack inevitable and explained that it was "like lighting the fuse to a bomb. It was just a matter of time before it went off." An expert who can use analogies effectively is a formidable witness. This is true not because of her level of expertise, but rather due to her ability to communicate. Experts who make their testimony come alive are effective communicators.

Verbal techniques

Attorney Jay Dankner suggests that experts employ the following verbal techniques when testifying:

> Vary your pace. Keep the jury interested and awake. Use good vocal energy. Inspire confidence. Find your natural pace. Consider when to slow down or speed up. Don't rush because you're nervous. Use proper phrasing to make certain the jury understands your point. Vary your pitch. Create an impression of confidence and authority. Use proper articulation to convey competence. Use crisp language with ideas that are easy to follow. Regulate your volume for maximum impact.[7]

The expert witness also needs to remember to speak up and use his microphone correctly. The jurors can't believe a witness if they can't hear him.

Nonverbal techniques

An expert witness should dress appropriately. In most cases, this means formal business attire. The witness should be well groomed and not wear any ostentatious jewelry. A Rolex watch and a $2,000 suit will not help gain the sympathy of the jury. An expert witness should not chew gum. Everything a witness does can be seen by the jury and will affect how jurors evaluate the individual's testimony.

When walking in and out of the courtroom, the expert witness should not look at or acknowledge the party who has retained her. She should not stop to shake hands, etc. Doing so can make the expert look partisan and will lose her credibility with the jury. Furthermore, the expert witness should not invade the space of the jury by leaning on the railing to the jury box. Instead, she should maintain eye contact with the jurors and key in on any easily identifiable jury leaders.

The expert witness should try to appear calm and self-assured. It is important to use good posture while sitting in the witness box and to be serious and professional. Wise experts have all their documents and notes organized so that they do not have to fumble through them.

The jury scrutinizes body language closely. Therefore, effective expert witnesses will not appear uncomfortable or insecure. Signs of

[7] Dankner, 5.

insecurity include frequently moving a hand to one's mouth or face, fidgeting, toying with one's clothes or hair, and finger or foot tapping.[8] These signs present a negative image to the jury.

Things to avoid

There are a number of things that can impede one's ability to connect with the jury. The expert witness should not do the following.

- Act in a condescending manner
- Act pompous
- Appear egotistical
- Be pedantic
- Argue with counsel
- Praise oneself
- Be arrogant
- Be boring
- Be cute
- Be overconfident
- Overwhelm the jury
- Be sharp
- Be verbose
- Change her demeanor on cross-examination
- Confuse the jury
- Patronize
- Engage in nervous habits
- Fumble for papers or documents
- Look or act nervous, anxious, or worried
- Turn her back on the jury

11.4 Conclusion

Communication is key. An effective expert is one who can connect with and persuade the jury. Everything else is secondary.

[8] Harold A. Feder, "Methods of Challenging Forensic Fraud and Unethical Behavior," *Shepard's Expert and Scientific Evidence Quarterly* (Spring 1995) 3.

Chapter 12 Preparing to Testify at Deposition and Trial

12.1 Introduction

Experienced experts understand the need to prepare completely and thoroughly before testimony is given. Thorough preparation will most likely result in good performance. Inadequate preparation will most likely result in poor performance. Each time an expert testifies, her reputation and credibility are on the line. Any oversights, mistakes, or errors she makes due to a lack of preparation will become a permanent part of her "expert witness baggage." Not only will this affect the result in the underlying case, but the expert's future as an expert witness could be damaged permanently as well.

12.2 Preparation with Counsel

Experts who are preparing to testify at deposition or trial should meet with counsel who retained them to prepare. Such a meeting, however, is a legitimate area for inquiry during cross-examination. Any questions about the meeting with counsel before testifying should be answered truthfully, simply, and directly.

Example 12.1
Q. Isn't it a fact, Ms. Jones, that you met with Attorney Smith prior to your testimony here today?
A. Yes.
Q. Tell me everything you said and everything he said at this meeting.
A. I couldn't possibly recall that. We met to review the day's schedule, the relevant law, the procedures that would be used, and the questions I would likely be asked.

The following areas should be reviewed during the expert's meeting with counsel prior to testifying.

How to state an opinion correctly

The expert needs to understand the "magic words" necessary to render a legally sufficient expert opinion in the case at hand. There should be *no* confusion about this fundamental proposition. Ordinarily, "reasonable degree of scientific/medical certainty" is legally sufficient. The expert needs to understand fully the meaning of these terms of art (for example, "51% or more likelihood").

Example 12.2
At pre-deposition conference: Counselor, I am prepared to render my opinion based on a reasonable degree of scientific certainty. Is that sufficient in this jurisdiction?

Questions to be asked on direct examination

Experts can and should review the questions counsel intends to ask them during their direct examination at deposition or trial. A run-through of the answers with counsel is usually a good idea and is an accepted practice. The expert should anticipate, however, that counsel is likely to ask additional questions during the testimony if they are needed to flesh out the answers.

Questions likely to be asked on cross-examination

Experts should review with counsel what questions he anticipates the expert will be asked on cross-examination. (Please refer to Chapter 15 and Appendix D for listings of some of the possible areas of cross-examination inquiry.) Opposing counsel also prepares thoroughly and will attempt to discredit the expert's opinion during cross-examination. A run-through of the most difficult cross-examination questions that may be anticipated is a good idea.

The file that the expert intends to take to court or deposition

The expert should show counsel the entire file she intends to bring to the trial or deposition.[1] Counsel can then make suggestions about organization. The presence of any extraneous or privileged material may be better left back at the office.

Example 12.3
Counsel to expert: Is this your American Express bill from last month? Jimmy, this has no place in this file.

Information about the judge

Experts should discuss with counsel any habits, predilections, or biases of the presiding judge. It is a good idea to not unnecessarily antagonize the judge.

Example 12.4
Counsel to expert: Listen, Judge Jones is a real straight arrow. Don't even smile at him when you walk in. He once chewed out an expert in front of the jury for grinning at him on his way in.

Information about opposing counsel

Experts should ask counsel about the style, demeanor, tactics, tricks, standard questions, and predilections of opposing counsel at deposition and trial.

Example 12.5
Counsel to expert: Listen, let me give you the lowdown on Attorney Harris. He's got a standard routine and some standard zingers for experts. For example, he loves to ask....

---

[1] Of course, the expert should not bring any files unless he is asked to do so via subpoena or by counsel.

Theme of the case

Experts who are apprised by counsel of the theme of the case can, within the bounds of truth and ethical behavior, assist counsel in developing the theme. Once apprised of a case theme, experts may offer specific suggestions about areas of inquiry for direct or cross-examination, exhibits, or demonstrations to help counsel develop the trial theme.

Example 12.6
The theme of the trial may be that although the defendant may have made an error in judgment, there was no chance that this caused any harm to the plaintiff.

Testimony of other witnesses

Experts should be familiar with the testimony given by other witnesses in the case. This testimony of fact witnesses may affect the assumptions that were used to formulate the expert's opinion. The testimony of other expert witnesses will show the opposing side's theory of the case.

Example 12.7
In a medical malpractice case, the defense experts testified at deposition that causation was lacking, but they offered no opinions on breach of standard of care. Causation is likely to be the most hotly contested issue in this case when it goes to trial.

Information about the jury

The expert should know as much about the jury as possible. This includes their social, educational, professional, ethnic, and religious makeup. The expert's testimony needs to be tailored so that she can communicate most effectively with the jury. (See Chapter 11 on communicating effectively with juries.)

Example 12.8
Counsel to expert: We've got an African-American jury here in South Central Los Angeles. They are likely to be very mistrustful of the police. Keep that in mind.

Example 12.9
Counsel to expert: You're in rural Mississippi. Bury that damn Boston accent as much as you can—it won't go over well with this jury.

Exhibits and demonstrative evidence

The expert and counsel need to review together carefully all aspects of how, where, when, and which exhibits and demonstrative aids will be used during the trial. Failure to prepare can lead to delay, clumsiness, and in some cases, outright disasters. The sophisticated expert knows when the exhibits will be used, how they will be handled, where they will be placed, and what questions she will be asked about them. Most importantly, she makes sure prior to trial that everything functions properly.

Last-minute developments in the case

Counsel needs to share with the expert any last-minute developments in the case (for instance, witness unavailability, evidentiary rulings, or motions pending).

Timing issues

Trial delays are endemic to the legal system. The expert should review with counsel specifically when he is needed at the courthouse. Some experts ask to be "on call." In this situation, counsel will call or beep the expert, who promises to come quickly to the courthouse. In some cases, the expert may want to be present at the testimony of the other witnesses.

Dress

How does retaining counsel wish the expert to dress? This will vary depending upon where, when, and how the testimony will be given.

Other areas of concern

Any and *all* issues that concern the expert should be discussed with counsel at the pre-testimony conference. The stress of testifying at trial can be reduced significantly by eliminating any anxiety the expert may have due to unresolved areas of concern. A relaxed, well-informed expert is in the best position to testify effectively.

12.3 Independent Preparation

Experts also need to prepare thoroughly on their own. Experienced experts take the following actions when preparing to testify.

Read everything

The well-prepared expert reviews and reads every piece of paper in his file before the trial. This includes correspondence, witness statements, reports, the complaint, interrogatories, depositions, photos, videos, and exhibits. Frequently, an assignment has gone on so long that an expert may forget about crucial information without this review.

Memorize key facts

This includes the names of the parties. Not being able to recall a party's name may make a witness look callous or forgetful and can lessen the expert's credibility.

Recheck calculations, data, and test results

The sophisticated expert leaves nothing to chance prior to testifying. A review of calculations, data, and test results is necessary. If the expert is called upon to perform or explain these calculations or data, this review will prove to be invaluable.

Organize and index file

After reviewing the contents of her trial file with counsel, the experienced expert organizes and indexes the file to ensure ease of use while testifying. Unnecessary fumbling and searching through a file at trial is a rookie mistake and is to be avoided. The sophisticated expert summarizes voluminous data and has supporting data available.

Prepare responses for the hard questions

The experienced expert understands the need to anticipate, reflect upon, and be able to answer the difficult questions he will face on cross-examination. A wise expert takes time to think about the most difficult questions he could be asked and he determines how he would respond to them.

Example 12.10
Thinking to self: What if he asks me about why I don't defer to the opposition? What will I say?...I think I'll need to focus on the weight of my hands-on experience as being more valuable than the opposition's impressive academic credentials.

Re-examine the evidence

When an examination of evidence that may have changed was part of the basis of an opinion, the forensic expert should consider re-examining the evidence immediately prior to testifying.

Example 12.11
You will be testifying on the prognosis for an individual you last examined 18 months ago. It may be a good idea to set up a brief meeting to see the person prior to testifying so that your information is up to date.

Update research

Experts should perform a literature search to see if any new research has been published that may change their opinions.

Visit the courtroom

Visiting the courtroom prior to the day of the trial is a good idea if time permits. This pre-trial visit will acquaint the expert with the physical facility and its limitations and will increase his comfort level when arriving for trial.

Removing one aspect of the fear of the unknown will help reduce the anxiety level of the expert.

Reread deposition and reports

Most sophisticated experts read their own deposition and reports one or more times immediately prior to the trial. It is an absolute necessity for the expert to have a complete mastery of her prior testimony and reports in the case. Cross-examiners will use any inconsistency between deposition testimony and trial testimony to impeach a witness. Failure to master one's own testimony and reports will often result in a devastating cross-examination.

Review the important dates

Successful expert witnesses review the crucial dates in the case. Many commit them to memory. These dates include:

- When the expert was first contacted by counsel
- When the expert was retained
- When the expert received the records and from whom they were received
- When the expert formed his opinion(s) in the case
- The date of the accident in question
- The date(s) key tests were performed

Failure to be familiar with key dates will make an expert look sloppy and will affect his credibility negatively.

Keep CV up to date

The expert may be asked to produce her CV. She should therefore make sure that it is updated and proofed.

Work out any demonstrations

The wise expert makes sure her audiovisual and other demonstrations work flawlessly. If they don't, she will lose credibility and the jury will lose interest. The "higher tech" the presentation, the more one needs to be concerned over whether it will work properly when needed. Having a backup plan in the event of system failure is a good idea.

Relax

The expert should *not* work and study until the moment he is called to the stand. He should complete his preparation and set aside time to relax and reflect on the task ahead. Taking a walk in the park, going for a run, or doing those things that one finds relaxing are important parts of a witness's preparation. The relaxed, confident, and prepared expert will do his best at trial.

12.4 Lack of Preparation

Most expert testimony is given by way of deposition. Sophisticated experts make the time necessary to prepare for deposition. If they cannot do this, they should ask that the deposition be rescheduled. If the request is made sufficiently in advance, retaining counsel should be able to reschedule the deposition. Depositions are commonly rescheduled. This is one way experts can avoid testifying unprepared.

Trial testimony is much more difficult to postpone because it will be the judge who ultimately decides when the trial will start. However, attorneys can request that trials be postponed or *continued.* If a case is set for trial during a time of year when it will be difficult to prepare properly, the expert may want to ask counsel if he can get a better trial date. The expert should let counsel know up front about any scheduled vacations or unavailable dates. This allows counsel to act before a trial date is set and helps avoid counsel having to ask for a continuance. The expert can also request that counsel call the other witnesses first, to give herself additional time to prepare.

12.5 Conclusion

Effective testimony is dependent upon proper preparation. Experts should properly prepare before giving testimony.

Chapter 13 The Expert Deposition

13.1 Introduction

Well over 90% of civil cases settle prior to expert witnesses being called at trial. As such, the forensic expert can expect that the majority of testimony that he gives will be given at deposition. It is important to be effective during expert deposition. This chapter provides a brief overview of expert depositions and provides some tips for being more effective at deposition.[1]

13.2 Deposition Basics

The ability of counsel to ask follow-up questions and pursue many lines of inquiry make the deposition counsel's most potent discovery tool in a case. (For more information, please refer to Chapter 3 on the discovery process.) As Fish and Ehrhardt note,

> It is only the oral deposition which permits the spontaneity and conflict necessary for testing perceptions by follow-up questions and immediate inquiry into peripheral matters. Most importantly, it is the only opportunity to obtain admissions directly from parties, rather than from the written words of attorneys. It provides a chance to determine the credibility and demeanor of a witness and the impression he or she is likely to create upon the jury. Under most circumstances in the personal injury case the oral deposition should be the focal point of the discovery plan. All other discovery devices should be utilized, at least partially, for deposition preparation.[2]

At deposition, the expert who is being deposed is called the *deponent*. The deponent's testimony is taken under oath. The deposition may be scheduled in counsel's office or in the expert's office. The two kinds of depositions that experts face are:

1. preservation of evidence depositions and
2. discovery depositions.

In *preservation of evidence depositions*, the expert will be deposed by counsel who retained him. These depositions are commonly videotaped. (See Section 13.9 for a discussion of videotape depositions.) Preservation of evidence depositions are taken because counsel may want to use the deposition

[1] For comprehensive coverage of expert depositions, see Steven Babitsky and James J. Mangraviti, Jr., *How to Excel During Depositions: Techniques for Experts That Work* (Falmouth, MA: SEAK, Inc., 1999).

[2] Raymond M. Fish and Melvin E. Ehrhardt, *Malpractice Depositions: Avoiding the Traps* (Montvale, NJ: Medical Economics Co., Jan. 1987) 3.

at trial in lieu of having the witness appear live. Preservation of evidence depositions are usually taken if counsel feels the witness might be unavailable at trial and/or to avoid the cost of paying the expert to appear at trial. In this type of deposition, the expert can expect a full direct examination by retaining counsel and a close cross-examination by opposing counsel. What is happening in effect is that the witness's trial testimony is merely being taken outside of the courtroom. Because preservation of evidence deposition testimony resembles trial testimony closely, the expert witness should follow the advice in Chapter 14 (on effective direct examination testimony) and in Chapter 15 (on effective cross-examination testimony) when faced with a preservation of evidence deposition.

In *discovery depositions,* the expert will be deposed by opposing counsel. Most or all of the questioning will come from the opposing attorney. The expert witness will generally not be questioned by the attorney who retained him because she already knows what the expert is going to say at trial.

The opposing attorney at a discovery deposition may have many goals. The most important ten goals of the questioning attorney are discussed below.

13.3 Discovery Deposition Goals

To be effective during a discovery deposition, an expert witness needs to understand the goals of the deposing attorney. Generally speaking, counsel has one or more of the following ten goals.[3]

1. Learn the expert's opinions

The only reason the expert is testifying is to render an opinion. Counsel will almost certainly want to learn precisely what the expert's opinion is, the basis for her opinion, how the opinion was formed (i.e., the methodology used), when she arrived at the opinion, what future tests and evaluations she is planning, and whether she is willing to change or modify her opinion.

Example 13.1

Q. Please state any and all opinions you will be giving at trial and the bases for each of these opinions.

Q. When did you form your opinion?

Q. Would your opinion change if it was shown that the lab report of 9/28/99 was inaccurate?

Q. Are you planning on doing any further tests?

Advice for Experts: Counsel has a right to this information. Opinions should be well founded and answer counsel's questions truthfully and directly.

---

[3] Steven Babitsky and James J. Mangraviti, Jr., *How to Excel During Depositions: Techniques for Experts That Work* (Falmouth, MA: SEAK, Inc., 1999) 17–36.

However, experts should not volunteer information that was not asked for. If asked if his opinion would change if presented with new or additional facts, the expert witness should provide an open-minded, honest answer. If the expert is inflexible when presented with new facts, he runs the risk of losing credibility.

2. Explore the expert's qualifications

Qualifications are relevant to an expert's credibility and are a legitimate area of inquiry. Opposing counsel will want to learn as much as possible about an expert's qualifications. Specifically, the expert may be questioned about her background, education, training, and experience.

Example 13.2
Q. How many of these types of machines have you designed over the last ten years?
Q. Please detail for me your educational background from high school to the present.
Q. Why did you leave your first college after only two years?
Q. Has your license ever been suspended or revoked?
Q. Have you received any awards for your work in this field?
Q. What have you published in this field?

Advice for Experts: Exaggeration of qualifications is not honest and can come back to haunt an expert. An expert should not obsess over these questions. What is usually far more important to a jury in terms of credibility is whether they like the witness, how well the expert communicates, and whether the expert witness is in a reasonable position to offer a valid opinion. The fine details and points of qualifications may be very important to experts and their peers, but they may be of little interest to a jury.

3. Lock down the expert

One of the main purposes of depositions is to get an expert's testimony *on the record.* The stenographer at the deposition will do just that—record sworn testimony onto a written transcript. This written transcript serves to "lock down" testimony because a witness can be impeached by the deposition transcript if she later contradicts her opinion at trial.

Examples 13.3
Q. Are there any other opinions you will be offering at trial?

Advice for Experts: Everything said on the record at deposition is recorded by the stenographer. The transcript of the deposition can be used against a witness who changes his testimony at trial. Counsel may also attempt to take deposition testimony out of context. Therefore, expert witnesses need to consider carefully their answers at deposition and make sure their answers are truthful and phrased artfully.

4. Evaluate an expert's probable credibility

The expert's demeanor and communication skills will also be evaluated by counsel during the deposition. The ability to communicate and persuade is a crucial piece of information that counsel needs to prepare for trial and to evaluate properly the settlement value of a case. Counsel will want to determine the likely effect of an expert's testimony if she were to testify before a jury or fact finder. Will the expert be credible, likeable, believable, and remain calm under fire?

Example 13.4
Q. How much are you being paid for your testimony here today?
A. Not nearly enough.
Q. Where did you go to college?
A. Ahhh…well…, that's a tough one. I…ahhh, did two years at RPI, then I went into the army. Ahhhh…and I transferred into…no, strike that, I went back to MIT, I believe that was in 1968….

Advice for Experts: Experts should concentrate on presenting themselves well at deposition. One's value as an expert witness is based more on the ability to communicate and persuade than on technical and professional qualifications.

5. Probe for possible bias

Generally, questions concerning potential bias are allowed at deposition because they are relevant to the credibility of a witness. Counsel will attempt to discover any potential biases that a witness may have, which, if revealed to the jury or fact finder, may detract from one's credibility. Common areas of inquiry on the subject of bias include expert witness fees and income, the propensity for testifying only for plaintiffs or defendants, and any personal interest or relationship the witness may have with the subject matter of the litigation or the parties and attorneys involved in it.

Example 13.5
Q. How much are you being paid for your testimony?
Q. What percentage of your income do you earn from expert witness and forensic work?
Q. When was the last time you testified for a defendant in a case?
Q. You're Attorney Keefe's brother-in-law, correct?
Q. How many cases have you been involved in over the last five years?

Advice for Experts: Bias is a legitimate area of inquiry. Expert witnesses should answer these questions simply and directly. Evasive answers will only compound any bias damage and further damage an expert's credibility. Simple and direct answers will force counsel to move on to new lines of questioning.

6. Determine the factual assumptions that are the basis of the expert's opinion

An opinion is only as good as the facts and assumptions upon which it is based. Counsel will attempt to learn and explore the assumed set of facts upon which an expert based her opinion(s). If counsel can undermine these assumptions, the reliability of any and all of the expert's opinions will be called into question.

Examples 13.6
Q. On what assumptions is your opinion based?
Q. Would you change your opinion if you were to learn that your assumptions were invalid?

Advice for Experts: Factual assumptions must be reasonable and accurate. An expert should be prepared to give ground if he is asked if his opinion would change under different assumptions.

7. Gather as much information as possible

Deposition is a golden opportunity for counsel to gather information about the expert, the science upon which her opinions are based, how her opinions will be presented to the jury or fact finder, and many other areas of inquiry.

Example 13.7
Q. What are the major texts in this area?
Q. Please tell me each and every place you have been employed since high school.
Q. Do you plan on using any demonstrative evidence at trial?

Advice for Experts: Counsel has the right to try to gather information. The expert must answer truthfully, but should not volunteer information.

8. Use the expert's opinion to bolster counsel's case

Counsel may attempt to use the expert's opinion to bolster his own case. This is commonly done in three different ways. First, counsel may point out where experts for the opposing sides are in agreement. Second, counsel may try to demonstrate that if the underlying factual assumptions are changed, the expert's opinion will change to support their case. Finally, counsel may attempt to push an expert's opinion to the extreme in an attempt to make it look ridiculous.

Example 13.8
Q. You would agree that there is significant impairment, would you not?
Q. Let's assume that the plaintiff lied to you when describing these events. Under this assumption, would you consider changing your opinion?
Q. Does your opinion hold true in all cases, without exception?

Advice for Experts: A wise expert avoids extreme, all-encompassing opinions. He defends his opinions with conviction, but gives ground when appropriate.

9. Intimidate the expert

Counsel may use pointed questioning at the deposition to demonstrate the professional and personal price the expert will have to pay for continued involvement in the case. This may be designed to keep the expert off balance, make him fearful of a trial appearance, or encourage him to end his involvement in the case.

Example 13.9
Q. Are you prepared to tell the jury that your license was suspended?
A. Absolutely. I'm not ashamed that I had an alcohol problem and I am extremely proud of my recovery.

Advice for Experts: Dealing with an aggressive attorney is like dealing with an aggressive dog. It is best not to show fear.

10. Learn as much as possible about the opponent's case

Depositions are all about gathering information. Counsel will attempt to pump expert witnesses dry of whatever useful information they may possess.

Example 13.10
Q. Who did you consult with prior to forming your opinion?
Q. Did you meet with counsel prior to this deposition?
Q. What did you examine at the scene of the accident?

Advice for Experts: Answer the questions truthfully and do not volunteer information.

13.4 Preparing for Expert Depositions

Effectiveness at deposition may depend upon whether an expert prepared properly for deposition. As part of the preparation process, the expert is well advised to require a full and complete pre-deposition conference with the lawyer who has retained her. Because trial lawyers are typically very busy, it may be necessary to insist on this conference taking place. Prior to the conference, the wise expert does the following.

1. Reads all materials counsel has sent.
2. Completes tests, experiments, and other necessary work.
3. Fully thinks through all of the important aspects of the case, in particular possible questions from the opposition and how to respond to them.[4]

---

[4] Henry L. Hecht, *Effective Depositions* (Chicago, American Bar Association: 1997) 417.

At the pre-deposition conference with counsel, the expert should cover any areas she is concerned about. At this conference, the expert may want to do the following.

- Review the type of questions that opposing counsel is likely to ask. In complex or challenging cases, it is not unusual to have a "run-through" with a vigorous cross-examination by counsel or an associate. In a run-through, the expert will be asked the most difficult questions and be given an opportunity to reflect on the questions and answers.
- Review the questions (if any) retaining counsel will ask.
- Review the pertinent legal standard for liability and causation. Review the applicable jury instructions and become familiar with any "magic words" that must be used to make testimony legally sufficient.
- Identify any privileged information or work product contained in the expert's file.
- Review what should and should not be brought to the deposition. This includes responses to any subpoenas the expert may have received.
- Be updated on the current status of the litigation by having counsel share documents, interrogatories, and pleadings. If these are not forthcoming, the expert may request them for review prior to deposition.
- Share with counsel any prior contrary opinions the witness may have rendered in other cases.
- Review the day's schedule and the procedures that will be followed.
- Review the expert's qualifications and opinions. Discuss the bases of these opinions and how these opinions fit into the case.[5]

In addition to the pre-deposition conference with counsel, the expert should consider taking the following actions to prepare properly for deposition.

- Review her CV to make sure that it is completely accurate and up to date.
- Review and master the crucial dates in the case.
- Review and master the important facts in the case, including names and places.
- Review and master her own reports and records.
- Get enough sleep the night before the deposition.

---

[5] Steven Babitsky and James J. Mangraviti, Jr., *How to Excel During Depositions: Techniques for Experts That Work* (Falmouth, MA: SEAK, Inc., 1999) 39–40.

- Set aside adequate time for the deposition itself.

Depositions are commonly rescheduled. An expert who has not had sufficient time to prepare for a deposition should strongly consider asking counsel to reschedule it. Depending upon the amount of notice and the status of the litigation, he will likely be successful in doing so. In any case, it doesn't hurt to ask. The worst thing that the other side can say is no.

13.5 Subpoenas and Documents

The notice of deposition is frequently accompanied by a *subpoena duces tecum*. This type of subpoena requires that the expert produce certain documents that are specified in a schedule attached to the subpoena. (Appendix I provides a sample subpoena duces tecum schedule.) When served with this type of subpoena, the expert should do the following.

1. She should review her file for extraneous material and remove these from the file. If the expert has any questions about what should or should not be removed, she should ask retaining counsel.
2. In the pre-deposition conference, she should have counsel review her subpoena and her file to see if some of the information requested need not be produced under the discovery rules.
3. She should not remove or try to hide potentially damaging documents.
4. She should not produce requested documents that are not properly discoverable under the rules of discovery.[6]

When confronted with or asked to comment on documents during the deposition, the expert witness should take all the time necessary to read the entire document before responding. She should not worry about taking too much time—that's the problem of the attorney who asked the question, not of the expert. When referring to a document, experts should use its exhibit number, followed by a brief description of the document. This will help ensure an accurate transcript.

Example 13.11
Exhibit 1, the September 6, 1999, FAA report.

13.6 Transcript

The most important result of the deposition is the transcript or videotape. This is the "record" that can be later used as part of a summary judgment motion and at trial. Expert witnesses may have the right to verify the accuracy of the transcript by reading and signing the deposition transcript. This right should be affirmatively asserted by the expert when counsel is

---

[6] Determining this may require getting legal advice.

agreeing to the stipulations at the beginning of the deposition. Stating, "I will not waive the reading and signing and would like to read and sign" should preserve this right. Failure to affirmatively assert the right to read and sign may result in a waiver of that right.

The Federal Rules allow deponents to make changes in form or substance to their testimony. If changes are made, they need to be explained on an *errata sheet.*[7] The Rules place no limitations upon the type of changes that may be made. However, the original answer to a deposition question remains part of the record and can be read at trial.[8] If significant changes are made, these can even result in the deposition being reopened.[9]

13.7 Deposition Advice for Experts

The authors recommend the following.

Experts should tell the truth.

This is an expert's legal and ethical duty.

Experts should act naturally.

An expert is likely to make a better witness if he doesn't try to be someone he is not.

It is wise for an expert to say he doesn't know if he doesn't know.

This is a perfectly legitimate response. No one is expected to know everything about everything. An expert should not be too proud to say, "I don't know."

It is best to avoid arrogance.

Juries don't like arrogant witnesses. Arrogance makes for a less valuable witness.

Wise experts avoid absolute words.

Experts should avoid *always* and *never*. Counsel will employ a counterexample to make the expert who uses absolute words look silly.

It is important to avoid hedge words.

Experts should avoid *could, I suppose,* and *possibly.* If a witness uses hedge words, her opinion might not be legally sufficient.

---

[7] For example, a witness who said "1977" at a deposition, but meant to say "1997." The expert would state "mistake in date" on the errata sheet.

[8] *Podell v. Citicorp Diners Club,* 112 F.3d 98 (2nd Cir. 1997).

[9] *United States ex rel. Burch v. Piqua Eng'g,* 152 F.R.D. 565 (S.D. Ohio 1993).

Experts should take breaks when needed.

Witnesses perform best if they do not allow themselves to get worn down.

It is essential to read documents before testifying about them.

Experts should take their time. A witness can't testify accurately about a document unless he takes the time to read it carefully.

Experts should not argue with counsel.

The expert's role is to be an expert, not an advocate. An expert who appears to be an advocate will lose credibility.

Experts should not assume, exaggerate, speculate, guess, or estimate.

Expert testimony needs to be based on a reasonable degree of medical or scientific certainty. Guessing is not permitted.

An expert should not joke.

The expert should show respect for the process or the jury will not respect her. Joking is not appropriate at deposition.

It is best for an expert to say he doesn't remember if he doesn't remember.

This is a legitimate response.

It is unwise to interrupt the questions.

Doing so runs the risk of providing information that was not going to be asked for.

Experts should listen to all questions carefully.

Listening carefully allows an expert witness to confine her answers to what was asked.

It is important to pause before answering.

This gives the witness a chance to consider his response carefully and gives counsel a chance to object to the question if she chooses to do so.

Experts should avoid slang.

Use of slang diminishes credibility.

Effective experts will not lose their temper.

An expert witness who loses her temper is likely to say something on the record that she will later regret.

13.8 Fees and Billing

See Chapter 19 for a detailed discussion of fees and billing.

13.9 Videotape Depositions

Videotaped depositions are permitted by the Rules of Civil Procedure[10] and are being used with increasing frequency. To excel at videotape depositions, the authors recommend the following. Expert witnesses should:

1. Prepare with counsel and practice before a video camera to correct annoying, distracting, or unfavorable mannerisms, methods of answering questions, or nervous habits.
2. Dress conservatively.
3. Men should try to get a close shave.
4. Look directly into the camera when testifying.
5. Avoid long, pregnant pauses that may make them look evasive or uninformed.
6. Hold exhibits so they can be seen by the judge and jury.
7. Avoid eating, drinking, or chewing on gum, pens, or pencils.
8. Turn off pagers and cell phones.
9. Avoid making unnecessary noise by rustling paper or touching the microphone.
10. Avoid being goaded into flashes of anger, arrogance, or combativeness.
11. Use make-up and powder.
12. Watch their body language.
13. Try to not appear evasive, suspicious, nervous, or anxious.
14. Not be distracted by counsel.

13.10 Handling Abuse at Deposition

Chapter 24 discusses how to best handle abusive tactics and conduct of counsel.

---

[10] Fed. R. Civ. Pro. 30(b)(4) provides: "Unless otherwise agreed by the parties, a deposition shall be conducted before an officer appointed or designated under Rule 28 and shall begin with a statement on the record by the officer that includes (A) the officer's name and business address; (B) the date, time, and place of the deposition; (C) the name of the deponent; (D) the administration of the oath or affirmation to the deponent; and (E) an identification of all persons present. If the deposition is recorded other than stenographically, the officer shall repeat items (A) through (C) at the beginning of each unit of recorded tape or other recording medium. The appearance or demeanor of deponents or attorneys shall not be distorted through camera or sound-recording techniques. At the end of the deposition, the officer shall state on the record that the deposition is complete and shall set forth any stipulations made by counsel concerning the custody of the transcript or recording and the exhibits, or concerning other pertinent matters."

13.11 Conclusion

Most expert testimony is given by way of deposition. Experts need to be effective when testifying in this format.

Chapter 14 Direct Examination

14.1 Introduction

Direct examination is all about persuasion and communication. It is a forensic expert's opportunity to persuade the jury (or judge at a bench trial) that her opinion should be believed. The goal during direct testimony is to persuade the jury to find one's opinion credible. To achieve this goal, the witness will need to concentrate all of her energies on communicating persuasively with the jury or fact finder. If she does not communicate effectively with them, they will not value her opinion. The expert needs to persuade the jury to agree with her opinions. Everything else is secondary.

14.2 Preparing to Testify

What will be asked

It is far easier to prepare for direct examination than it is to prepare for cross-examination. During direct examination, the expert witness will be asked questions by the attorney who retained him. By meeting with that attorney prior to testimony, the expert can go over exactly what he is going to be asked. Because he knows what he will be asked, he can then prepare his responses. Common areas of inquiry on direct examination include:

- qualifications,
- fees and other difficult areas (to defuse cross-examination on these issues),
- investigation and methodology (the bases of the expert's opinions), and
- opinions.

When preparing his responses, the expert should keep in mind that he will be attempting to persuade a scientifically unsophisticated jury of lay people. It is during this preparation process that he can formulate the analogies and explanations that he will use to speak in terms that the jury will understand. The expert should review the analogies and explanations that he intends to use with his retaining attorney prior to testifying. The retaining attorney may have some good advice on how to better communicate with the jury.

A wise expert meets prior to trial with the attorney that is going to examine him. The expert should insist upon meeting with the actual attorney, not one of her associates. It is only by meeting with the attorney who will question him that the expert witness can get a feel for the attorney's style in asking questions. He should therefore practice and try to develop a smooth rhythm with the examining attorney.

Experts should prepare for testimony and think in advance of their responses. They should not memorize their responses, however. The jurors may pick up on memorized responses and may judge the testimony as staged. It is likely that such testimony will then be discounted.

The successful witness gets his facts straight before trial. He needs to know his facts cold. He also needs to know *everything* upon which he based his opinion. He should be prepared to discuss any and all of his written reports. If the expert witness is unprepared and forgets or is slow to remember key facts or key bases for his opinions, he will lose credibility with the jury.

Visual aids

The expert witness should always show retaining counsel any and all visual aids she intends to use during testimony. Visual aids that are simple and easy to read are the best. Complicated or "busy" aids may not be appreciated by the jury. Experts now commonly use various high-tech audiovisual aids as demonstrative evidence to help them better communicate with the jury. Such aids can be extremely effective. During the preparation process, experts need to check and recheck their equipment. It is unwise to get into a situation where one's testimony is heavily dependent upon high-tech audiovisual equipment that fails to work.

Dress

The jurors will have an emotional reaction to how a witness dresses. For example, they may be offended if they notice a flashy Rolex watch on an expert's wrist. These jurors probably earn a very small fraction of what a forensic expert earns. Additionally, they are generally being forced to serve as jurors against their choice. Experts should not wear any flashy clothes or jewelry that will either offend or distract the jurors. An expert witness wants the jurors to consider her testimony carefully, she does not want them to think about how much her watch costs.

Witnesses should dress neatly. A witness should make sure that his shirt is tucked in. Men should get a good shave the morning of the trial. Expert witnesses want to look as though they have their act together. A witness who doesn't look personally well organized and well kept may lose credibility with the jury.

The expert should meet with retaining counsel prior to the trial to discuss how she would like the witness to dress. This will depend in large part upon where the trial is being held and who is on the jury. For example, cowboy boots might be the best way to dress for a trial in Texas, but they would probably distract the jury if the trial were held in New York City.

Mannerisms

People often employ various nervous mannerisms when they are in a stressful situation.[1] This is commonly true of experts when they are in the stressful position of testifying in front of a jury. Nervous mannerisms are distracting and weaken one's ability to persuade the jury. They need to be avoided or the jury may think that the witness is nervous because she is not telling the truth.

To eliminate nervous mannerisms, one needs to first identify what they are. A witness who has given videotaped testimony in the past should review this testimony and try to pick up any nervous or distracting mannerisms. If a witness hasn't given videotaped testimony in the past, she should consider giving some mock testimony in front of home videotaping equipment. She might consider having a relative or friend watch the tape(s) with her. Once the expert has identified her distracting mannerisms, she should practice testifying while attempting to eliminate these mannerisms. By eliminating as many distracting mannerisms as possible, an expert witness will be in a much better position to communicate with and to persuade the jury.

Documents

A wise expert organizes his files and documents before going to court. He does not want to take the stand with a file spilling out with loose and dog-eared documents. If an expert is asked to find a document on the stand, he needs to be able to find it right away. If he looks disorganized, he will lose credibility with the jury. The forensic expert should think about the jury deliberations. He wants the jury talking about his opinions, not the fact that his file was a mess and that it took him five minutes to locate a document.

14.3 Testifying Techniques

Communicating with the jury

As a rule of thumb, expert witnesses should think of the jury as a group of eighth graders. Like eighth graders, jurors are generally not highly educated and generally have a very short attention span. They can, however, be extremely adept at determining when someone is being dishonest with them. First impressions are important. If a jury's first impression is that an expert is arrogant, the entire testimony will likely be tainted. Jurors respond best to analogies and visual aids. An expert should therefore try where possible to use analogies and visual aids in order to better communicate with and persuade the jury.

Jurors make decisions based largely on emotion. Experts need to recognize this fact in order to properly communicate with them. If an expert is biased, arrogant, or pompous, jurors may be offended by him and, based on emotion, discount his opinion. If, on the other hand, an expert appears

---

[1] For example, tapping fingers, twirling hair, shaking a leg or knee, etc.

likeable and unbiased, the jurors' emotions will tell them to listen carefully to what is said and to give it credence. To a large extent, *how* an opinion is presented can be far more important in communicating to the jury than the scientific or technical basis of the opinion.

Qualifications

An expert's direct testimony will usually begin with a discussion of her credentials. She should work with counsel to make the testimony about credentials as brief as possible. When explaining credentials to the jury, the expert should stress the credentials that tend to show an expertise in the particular area where she will be testifying. Experts should not fall into the trap of being overly longwinded about their credentials. Doing so runs two major risks. First, the expert may come off as being cocky and self-centered and the jury may hold this against her. Second, and much more importantly, a jury usually has a very limited attention span unless what they are listening to is very interesting. If the jury is only going to pay attention for twenty minutes, an expert doesn't want to spend all of those twenty minutes discussing each and every paper she has published. If she does, the jury won't pay close attention when she gets to the meat of her testimony—her opinions and their bases.

Demeanor

Experts should try to be themselves while on the witness stand. This will make them more relaxed and help them make a better impression on the jury. If an expert makes a good impression on the jurors, they will be more likely to believe him. There is an important exception to this rule. That exception applies to those who are abrasive (for example, cocky and arrogant). An individual with a personality or style of presentation that tends to rub people the wrong way needs to try adopting a different approach when taking the witness stand. It cannot be overemphasized that a witness is less likely to be an effective communicator with the jury if the jury doesn't like him. Having the jury like an expert is generally far more important to his credibility as a witness than are his credentials, awards, and his professional and financial success.

The successful expert witness won't look worried or anxious. The jurors will pick up on this. If a witness looks worried or nervous, the jurors will ask themselves what he is worried about. The answer to this question is unlikely to enhance one's credibility.

Appearing confident is also important. An expert witness should sit up and use good posture. He should maintain eye contact with the jurors, but should not stare at them. Moreover, he needs to appear as though he truly believes in his opinion. If an expert does not appear to believe in his own opinion, he will be unlikely to persuade the jurors to believe it.

Expert witnesses should avoid distracting mannerisms, such as gum chewing, hair twisting, hand rubbing, nose picking, beard rubbing, etc. These mannerisms distract from one's effectiveness. When the jurors go back to the jury room, the witness wants them to discuss how impressed they were by him and how his opinion affects the case, not how his mannerisms distracted them. As discussed above, experts should attempt to identify distracting mannerisms prior to testifying. Videotapes of one's prior testimony may help.

Expert witnesses should be polite, serious, professional, and courteous to everyone in the courtroom. This includes the litigants, judge, jury, attorneys, gallery, and courtroom personnel. The jurors will pick up on this and it will help bolster one's credibility. Expert witnesses should avoid jokes and flippant remarks. These will lessen one's credibility. If, however, something happens in the courtroom to make everyone laugh, including the judge and jury, an expert should laugh along with them. If he doesn't, he'll look like a robot and will lose credibility with the jury.

Appearing unbiased is critical. This means avoiding even subtle actions that could tend to imply that an expert is biased. For example, when his testimony is complete, he should leave the courtroom directly. He should not stop to shake hands with his retaining attorney and her client.

A wise expert will not talk about the case in the hall or bathroom before or after testifying. One never knows who might overhear the conversation. When an expert finishes testifying, he should leave the courthouse. He does not want to be seen hanging around because it may appear that he has a personal interest in the outcome of the case.

Teach and explain

The jury is made up of lay people. As such, the forensic expert needs to assume that everything needs to be explained to them. What seems to be a common term or concept to an expert can be a mystery to the jury. People like to learn and generally like interesting teachers. An effective expert is one who can teach and thus communicate effectively with the jury.

Experts should use commonly understood terms whenever possible. For example, one should say "collarbone" instead of "clavicle." Using commonly understood terms allows the expert to better communicate with the jury (they can more easily understand what is said), making her a more sympathetic figure in the eyes of the jury (the jury can more readily identify with a person who speaks as they do).

Analogies and examples can be very effective in communicating and explaining complicated opinions to the jury. For example, let's say an expert is trying to explain DNA matching to a jury. A good way to explain DNA matching might be, "DNA is a chemical found in every cell of a person's body. You might call it a chemical 'fingerprint.' Like fingerprints, the odds against any two people having identical DNA are absolutely astronomical, in the order of billions to one. It's nearly impossible." Jurors understand fingerprints and are more likely to remember a testimony with the soundbite of "chemical fingerprint." Counsel can also use the "chemical fingerprint" soundbite from the analogy during her summation. Analogies are a very effective way to explain complicated concepts to a jury. A wise expert plans her analogies and runs them by counsel before she uses them on the witness stand.

Demonstrative aids

Experts should strongly consider using visual aids to assist them in giving testimony. If appropriate, one may ask for permission from the judge to leave the witness box in order to use the visual aid. Getting out of the witness box has several advantages. First, it gives the jury something more interesting to focus on than a "talking head" in the witness box. Second, an expert will probably be more relaxed, and thus a better witness, when she gets out of the witness box. Finally, by getting out of the witness box, the expert removes a psychological barrier between herself and the jury.

It is important to make sure that everyone on the jury can see the visual aid. An expert witness may consider asking the judge to ask the jurors if they can all see. This serves two purposes. First, to determine whether all the jurors are able to see the visual aid. Second, the jury should like the fact that the expert cares about them. If the jurors feel that the expert cares about them, they may be more likely to pay close attention to her and give her testimony greater credence.

Jurors are becoming more and more visually oriented. Most have grown up with television. Many have grown up with video games, computers, and the Internet. Experts can capitalize upon this by using visual aids to explain their testimony whenever it helps. A picture says a thousand words. It also breaks up the monotony of testimony, arguments, and motions, and it provides the jurors with a form of information that they are more likely to pay close attention to and remember when they retire to deliberate.

Answering counsel's questions

An expert witness should tell the truth. He is under oath. Telling the truth is a legal and ethical duty. After an expert witness presents his testimony on direct examination, he will be subject to cross-examination. Cross-examination is a remarkably effective tool that can be used to expose dishonest experts. An expert witness should not assume that because he is more intelligent than the cross-examining lawyer and smarter than the jury that he can get away with being less than truthful.

Experts should not memorize their testimony. Memorized testimony looks rehearsed or as though words were put into one's mouth by the lawyer. Jurors can pick up on this. Experts should pause before answering counsel's questions. They need to actively listen to the questions and answer the question they are asked, not the question they expected to be asked.

A successful expert explains why she is in a position to provide a valid opinion. She communicates all that she did, the tests she performed, the documents, articles and evidence she reviewed, etc. An opinion is only as good as the facts and work upon which it is based. If the jury sees that an expert has done her homework, she will be a more credible witness.

Finally, expert witnesses should direct their answers to the jury, not to the lawyer who is questioning them. They should make eye contact with the jurors and speak clearly and loudly enough to be heard. If there is a microphone on the stand, the witness must speak into it properly. Jurors can't be persuaded to believe an opinion if they cannot hear what a witness has to say. Lastly, an expert should not turn his back on the jury. This is disrespectful and the jurors probably won't be able to hear what the expert has to say.

14.4 Conclusion

The key to direct examination is connecting with the jury. If an expert connects with them, her opinion will hold weight with them. If she does not connect with them, her opinion will not be given substantive weight.

Chapter 15 Cross-Examination

15.1 Introduction

Cross-examination is one of the most difficult and challenging aspects of being an expert. Counsel for the opposition will read and study the entire case file and prepare for hours or days for his cross-examination of an expert. To perform well under cross-examination, an expert witness needs to understand the goals of the cross-examining attorney, follow the fifteen golden rules of testifying under cross-examination, and anticipate the likely areas of inquiry.

15.2 Goals of the Examining Lawyer

Generally speaking, opposing counsel will have two major goals during his cross-examination of a forensic witness. These are to lessen the credibility of the witness and to use the witness, where possible, to bolster his own case. Let's examine each of these goals in more detail.

All trials ultimately boil down to one issue and one issue only. That issue is *credibility*. An expert's opinion is only as strong as her credibility. Opposing counsel will use cross-examination as a vehicle to lessen one's credibility. This is most commonly done by attacking an expert's qualifications and expertise, exposing her bias, impeaching her with prior statements or writings, and by challenging her opinions, methodology, facts, and data.

Example 15.1
You're not board certified in obstetrics, are you?

Example 15.2
Isn't it a fact, Ms. Jones, that you've testified for this defendant as an expert in twelve cases in the last four years?

Example 15.3
That's not what you testified to at deposition, is it?

Example 15.4
You never took samples from the accident scene, did you?

Sometimes it may be difficult for opposing counsel to successfully undermine an expert's credibility. Opposing counsel may also feel that attacking an expert witness would not be a good strategic move or may not sit well with the jury. As such, counsel may seek to use the witness's expertise to support his own theory of the case. The most common way this is done is by pointing out the areas in which the witness agrees with the other experts in the case. In many cases, there is quite a large area of agreement. When using this technique, counsel is using the expert to bolster his own case.

Example 15.5
And you agree, do you not, that the plaintiff will never be able to walk again?

Counsel may also attempt to use hypothetical questions. Experts should always remember that their opinions are only as good as the factual assumptions upon which they are based. During cross-examination, counsel may present an alternate set of assumptions and ask if this would change the expert's opinion. It often does. If counsel can then prove the existence of the alternate set of assumptions, he has successfully used the witness to bolster his case.

Example 15.6
Let's assume for a moment that the velocity data provided to you was false. If the true velocity was 45 mph, would that change your opinion?

From one trial lawyer's perspective, the ideal cross-examination is one:

1. That to an extent was entertaining, which can be a method of controlling the momentum and maintaining the jury's interest;
2. That to an extent impugned the credibility and/or exposed the adverse witness's true bias or attitude while he/she was on the witness stand;
3. That to an extent destroyed or weakened the adverse witness's observations or the force of his/her harmful testimony, and particularly the opinions or conclusions, if an expert;
4. That to an extent obtained beneficial information or admissions as a predicate for cross-examination of other adverse witnesses and/or supported your theory of the case and/or one of your witnesses (lay or expert) and/or was important for your summation.[1]

15.3 The Fifteen Golden Rules of Testifying under Cross-Examination

The authors suggest fifteen rules to follow while testifying on cross-examination.

1. An expert witness should tell the truth simply and directly.

Telling the truth is a legal and ethical duty. Experts should not be evasive. If a witness appears evasive, he will lose credibility with the jury. A good trial lawyer will be persistent and eventually get at the information she was seeking. Evasiveness will only serve to highlight this information to the jury.

[1] Bob Gibbins, Advanced Evidence and Discovery Law Course, Chapter K: "Arts and Science of Impeaching Witnesses on Cross-Examination" (Nov. 1995). State Bar of Texas: State Bar of Texas Professional Development CLE Online, Austin: 1997, Section III.

Example 15.7
Q. Isn't it true that you earned in excess of $35,000 as an expert witness this year?
A. Yes.

2. An expert witness should stay within his area of expertise.

The further a witness strays "out of his sandbox," the more vulnerable he becomes to cross-examination and to successful attacks on his credibility. An expert should not be afraid to tell his retaining counsel early in the case which areas he will offer his expert opinion on. Questions by counsel for either side that attempt to push an expert beyond the area in which he feels comfortable can be answered, "I can't answer that question. It is beyond my area of expertise."

Example 15.8
Q. With this level of impairment, she's going to be permanently and totally disabled, isn't she?
A. I can't answer that question. It is beyond my area of expertise.

3. If an expert doesn't know an answer, the appropriate answer is, "I don't know."

There is nothing wrong with this response. Even the most educated people in the world do not know the answer to everything. An expert witness should not let her ego get in the way of making this response. She should not be tricked by counsel who asks a series of questions that the expert is forced to answer, "I don't know." Counsel is just trying to rattle the expert or trying to force her to make a mistake.

Example 15.9
Q. What was the time of death?
A. I don't know.

4. An expert witness should not volunteer information.

He should answer the question that is asked and only the question asked. The expert's role is to transmit his specialized knowledge honestly and objectively to the fact finder. The expert is not to act as an advocate. Volunteering information may open up new lines of inquiry that may undermine the expert's credibility.

Example 15.10
Q. Have you ever been qualified to testify in the state of Massachusetts as an expert?
A. No, but I was qualified in Rhode Island.

5. An expert witness should not argue with counsel.

Arguing with counsel will detract from an expert's credibility because she will no longer appear to be impartial. However, when appropriate, one can and should disagree with counsel.

Example 15.11
Q. Do you agree that the cause of the accident was excessive speed?
A. No, I do not.

6. An expert witness should not be arrogant, hostile, or condescending.

Such behavior can and will destroy rapport with the fact finder or jury. It will thus lessen the expert's persuasiveness.

Example 15.12
Q. Did you examine the accident scene?
A. Counsel, you know very well I was out to the accident scene three times. Why would you even ask a stupid question like that?

7. An expert witness should pause before responding to a question.

This gives the expert time to consider the question carefully. It also gives the witness's retaining attorney an opportunity to object if she chooses to do so. Even so, an expert witness should not overdo this because it can be a distraction and it may affect one's credibility.

Example 15.13
Q. Did you graduate from Boston College, sir?
A. Well, (pause) yes.

8. An expert witness should not exaggerate, speculate, or guess.

This type of testimony is objectionable and will invite additional cross-examination.

Example 15.14
Q. How far was the car from the intersection when it started to brake?
A. I would guess about 110 feet.
Q. When you say *guess* and *about*…

9. An expert witness should remain cool, calm, and collected.

If a witness loses his cool, he is likely to blurt out a response that has not been considered carefully.

Example 15.15
Q. In light of the fact that your opinion on causation stands in stark contrast to

those of the three prior experts, do you still maintain the cause of the fire was electrical in nature?
A. Yes.

10. An expert witness should actively listen to the question.

The witness should answer the question he was asked, not the question he anticipated or that he should have been asked.

Example 15.16
Q. Do you have an opinion as to causation?
A. It's causally related?
Q. Do you have an opinion?
A. Yes.

11. An expert witness should get all her facts and data straight before taking the stand.

An unprepared witness will lose credibility.

Example 15.17
Q. What was the terminal velocity?
A. Ah...Ummm...Let me look in my report...Ummm...It's here somewhere....

12. An expert witness should use accepted methodology.

If an expert's methodology is suspect, her credibility can be challenged. Opposing counsel may even be able to have her opinion excluded from evidence in its entirety. (For further information, please refer to Chapter 9.)

Example 15.18
Q. Can you please cite the peer-reviewed studies which support your opinion?
A. I can't think of any.

13. If interrupted, an expert witness should finish his answers.

Expert witnesses should assert themselves and not let counsel cut off their answers.

Example 15.19
Q. There were no objective findings of impairment, were there?
A. Actually—
Q. Doctor, how much are you being paid for your testimony here today?
A. You didn't let me answer your previous question. Actually, there were many objective findings of impairment. These included....

14. If questioned about a document, an expert witness should ask to see it.

An expert witness should never comment on a document without asking to see it. Counsel may very well be mischaracterizing what the document states. Wise experts take the time necessary to read documents carefully before commenting on them.

Example 15.20
Q. The 8/1/99 EPA report concluded that the contamination began in 1979. Are you saying that the EPA is wrong and you're right?
A. Could I please review the report you are referring to?

15. An expert witness should not use slang.

This detracts from one's expertise and one's credibility.

Example 15.21
Q. You never examined her again, did you?
A. Nope.

15.4 What the Expert Will Be Asked

On cross-examination, the expert should anticipate and prepare for intense questioning on the following areas of inquiry.

1. Qualifications

Qualifications are relevant to credibility. Typical areas of inquiry regarding qualifications include the following.

Example 15.22: Education
Q. You do not have a PhD in engineering, do you?

Example 15.23: Skills
Q. You have never personally performed this procedure, have you?

Example 15.24: Experience
Q. You haven't performed this procedure in twenty-eight years, have you?

Example 15.25: Training
Q. You never completed a residency in obstetrics, did you?

Example 15.26: Knowledge
Q. You really don't know what you're talking about, do you?

2. Bias

Bias is relevant to credibility. Counsel may attempt to show that because a witness is biased, her opinions should be discounted. Typical areas of inquiry regarding bias include the following.

Example 15.27: Expert witness fees
Q. How much are you being paid for your testimony here today?

Example 15.28: Expert witness marketing activities
Q. This is a copy of the ad you placed in *Trial Magazine,* isn't it?

Example 15.29: Relationship with a party or attorney
Q. In fact, you've testified on behalf of Attorney Lamson six times in the last three years, haven't you?

Example 15.30: Prior testimony
Q. You've testified for plaintiffs twenty-eight times in the last four years. Can you name one defendant that you testified for during that time period?

Example 15.31: Personal and professional writings
Q. Once again referring to your letter to the editor of the *New York Times,* dated 3/6/99, and I quote, "The tort system is nothing but a sham to keep the trial lawyers rich." Am I reading that correctly?

Example 15.32: How much an expert testifies
Q. Isn't it a fact that 75% of your income comes from your work as an expert witness?

3. Challenges to an opinion

Experts can expect counsel to try to undermine their opinions. Typical methods for doing so include the following.

Example 15.33: Showing that the facts the expert relied upon were inaccurate
Q. The age you based your opinion on was 48 years. The true age was 58 years, wasn't it?

Example 15.34: Showing that the facts the expert relied upon were unreliable or biased
Q. You got all the data you relied on from Attorney Coffone, didn't you?

Example 15.35: Showing that the expert failed to consider certain key facts
Q. You never reviewed the rehabilitation records from Dr. Siciliano, did you?

Example 15.36: Presenting the expert with new facts
Q. If you were to assume that the plaintiff was drunk, would that change your opinion on the proximate causation of this accident?

Example 15.37: Impeaching the expert's opinion with a prior contrary opinion
Q. That's not what you testified to at deposition, is it?

Example 15.38: Impeaching the expert's opinion with a learned treatise
Q. Referring to Smith's text on this subject he quotes....That's contrary to what you did in your investigation, isn't it?

15.5 Extent of Cross-Examination

The extent of cross-examination allowed will be determined by the trial judge. The judge will consider the relevancy and probative value of the subject matter that the line of questioning explores. Often, counsel will attempt to impugn an expert's credibility by expanding the cross-examination into areas that are marginally relevant. Sometimes, the judge will allow questioning into damaging subjects if it is determined that these facts speak to an expert's credibility or bias. On occasion, the judge may prevent the line of questioning because it is not relevant to the matter of credibility and counsel is simply trying to get unpleasant testimony before the jury. Other times, the subject matter will be technically relevant, but the judge will not allow the cross-examination because its prejudicial value outweighs its probative value. However, on many occasions, the judge will allow extensive cross-examination into many facets of one's professional past. The expert should not count on the judge to limit the cross-examination. Consider the following examples.

Example 15.39: Compensation in prior related cases
Coward v. Owens-Corning Fiberglass Corp., 729 A.2d 614 (Pa. Super. 1999)
A group of plaintiffs filed a products liability action against an asbestos manufacturer. The court considered whether an expert physician should have been subjected to cross-examination regarding the amount of money he was paid in other asbestos litigation over the previous twenty years. The court allowed the cross-examination. Cross-examining counsel specifically asked the expert whether that compensation influenced his opinions regarding the case on trial.

Example 15.40: Authoritative article
Courtney v. Taylor, 708 N.E.2d 1053 (Ohio App. 1 Dist. 1998)
This was a medical malpractice case filed after physicians failed to diagnose a pulmonary embolism. The court considered whether a physician expert could be cross-examined with a medical journal article. The court found the cross-examination proper because the expert had mentioned the article in the bibliography of a textbook chapter he had co-authored.

Example 15.41: Failure to obtain board certification
Jackson v. Buchanan, 996 S.W.2d 30 (Ark. 1999)
This was a medical malpractice suit against the defendant-expert. The court found that it was improper for him to be cross-examined about his failure to obtain board certification, including his three failed attempts to pass the exam. The court excluded the evidence because of its prejudicial nature—it feared that the jury would consider it evidence of negligence, rather than impeachment material.

Example 15.42: Impeachment by statutes and regulations
Schmidt v. Royer, 574 N.W.2d 618 (S.D. 1998)
This was a wrongful death action brought by the estate of a truck driver killed in a collision with another truck. The expert, an accident reconstructionist, was to be cross-examined about braking force statutes and regulations and their prescribed methodology. The court found that this was proper—without the cross-examination, the jury would be misled.

Example 15.43: Previous testimony for same party
Brantley v. Sears Roebuck & Co., 959 S.W.2d 927 (Mo. App. E.D. 1998)
The plaintiff, a homeowner, sued the seller of a dishwasher, alleging the machine caused a house fire. The court considered whether the fire expert could be cross-examined on the point that he had testified for the same insurer over one hundred and fifty times. The court found the cross-examination proper and allowed it to take place in order for the plaintiff to show bias.

Example 15.44: Employment status
Cunningham v. McDonald, Del. Supr., 689 A.2d 1190 (De. 1997)
This was a personal injury suit arising out of an automobile accident. The court considered whether the cross-examination of the blood alcohol expert regarding his employment status was proper. The court found that the cross-examination should have been allowed. The court noted that the jury learned that the expert was on paid administrative leave but was never permitted to learn what that meant. The court also deemed it important that the jury learn that the expert's employment status was the subject of pending litigation.

Example 15.45: Commonality of insurance with the defendant
Warren v. Jackson, 479 S.E.2d 278 (N.C. Ct. App. 1997)
This was a medical malpractice case. The court considered whether the expert physician could be cross-examined regarding the fact that he shared the same medical malpractice carrier as the defendant. The court did not allow the cross-examination. It noted that policyholders in a mutual insurance company have a greater stake in the company than do policyholders in other types of insurance companies. It then found that the connection was too "attenuated" and that the evidence's prejudicial value outweighed its probative value to the jury.

Example 15.46: Commonality of insurance with the defendant
Wallace v. Leedhanachoke, 949 S.W.2d 624 (Ky. Ct. App. 1997)
In this malpractice case, the court considered the very same question it did in the previous case, *Warren*. The court found that the expert could not be cross-examined about the fact that he shared the same medical malpractice carrier as the defendant. The court found no evidence of any connection to the insurance company (i.e., limited insurance pool, fractional ownership interest). It concluded that the mere fact that the expert, as an insured, might experience rising insurance rates in the case of an adverse verdict would be too prejudicial.

Example 15.47: Accident reconstruction expert
Ratliff v. Schiber Truck Co., Inc., 150 F.3d 949 (8th Cir. 1998)
This was a wrongful death suit against a truck driver's employer for his attempts to avoid an unknown wrong-way driver. The court considered whether the accident reconstruction expert could be cross-examined about a report he read before he prepared his own report, although he rejected the conclusion presented in the report. The court allowed the cross-examination because the report in question—an accident report prepared by a state trooper—was the type of document accident reconstructionists reasonably rely upon when forming an opinion. "Counsel was free to cross examine the expert as to all documents he reviewed in establishing his opinion."

Example 15.48: Compensation as expert
Wrobleski v. de Lara, 727 A.2d 930 (Md. 1999)
In this medical malpractice case, defense counsel questioned one of the plaintiff's medical expert witnesses as to how much money the witness had earned in 1995 from testifying as an expert. The doctor in this case practiced principally in New York but had testified, mostly for plaintiffs, in fourteen states, ranging from Maine to Louisiana and Illinois. The court allowed inquiry into the expert's income, and stated:

> The allowance of the permitted inquiry, both at the discovery and trial stages, should be tightly controlled by the trial court and limited to its purpose, and not permitted to expand into an unnecessary exposure of matters and data that are personal to the witness and have no real relevance to the credibility of his or her testimony. Second, the fact that an expert witness devotes a significant amount of time to forensic activities or earns a significant portion of income from those activities does not mean that the testimony given by the witness is not honest, accurate, and credible. It is simply a factor that is proper for the trier of fact to know about and consider.

Example 15.49: Compensation and frequency of testimony
Trower v. Jones, 520 N.E.2d 297 (Ill. 1988)
Trower was a medical malpractice case in which defense counsel was allowed to cross-examine the plaintiff's medical expert as to (1) the frequency with which he testified for plaintiffs rather than defendants, and (2) the annual income he derived from services related to testifying as an expert witness. The witness had testified in over a dozen states on a variety of medical subjects. The court stated:

> Adding to the importance of effective cross-examination is the proliferation of expert "locator" services which, as a practical matter, can help the litigants of either side of most any case find an expert who will help advocate the desired position. As this case helps illustrate, many experts today spend so much of their time testifying throughout the country that they might be deemed not only experts in their field but also experts in the art of being a persuasive witness and in the art of handling cross-examination.

The plaintiff argued that inquiry regarding an expert witness's financial interest should be limited to the remuneration received for testifying (1) in the particular case, (2) for a particular party, or (3) for a particular party's attorney. The court rejected those limitations, noting that "[a] favorable verdict may well help [the witness] establish a 'track record' which, to a professional witness, can be all-important in determining not only the frequency with which [the witness] is asked to testify but also the price which [the witness] can demand for such testimony." The court found wanting the additional arguments that allowing such an inquiry would inject collateral issues into the trial, such as the reasonableness of the fees charged by the witness, and that it would complicate the discovery process by creating conflicts between the need to discover impeachment evidence and various evidentiary privileges, such as the physician-patient privilege. Both of those problems, it held, could be controlled by the trial court and did not suffice to keep relevant information from the jury.

Example 15.50: Frequency of testimony
Strain v. Heinssen, 434 N.W.2d 640 (Iowa 1989)
In this action for medical malpractice, the plaintiff's counsel could cross-examine expert-witness doctors concerning the frequency with which they had previously testified on behalf of doctors in other malpractice cases. However, cross-examination concerning the experts' employment by the co-defendant insurance company was improper absent evidence in the record disclosing that the relationship between the witnesses and the defendant's malpractice liability insurance company was closer than that of any other experts or of the insurer calling them in malpractice cases.

Example 15.51: Number of referrals
Norfolk & W. R. Co. v. Sonney, 374 S.E.2d 71 (Va. 1988)
In an action involving a work-related injury to a railroad worker, it was proper for the railroad to show on cross-examination of the plaintiff's doctor the number of injured railroad client referrals the plaintiff's attorney had made to the plaintiff's expert witness.

Example 15.52: Compensation
Spino v. John S. Tilley Ladder Co., 671 A.2d 726 (Pa. Super. 1996)
In this case, it was proper for the defendant to question the plaintiff's medical expert witness, who was a principal of a forensic consulting company, as to whether he was earning $100,000 a year from that business.

Example 15.53: Involvement in prior medical malpractice action
Underhill v. Stephenson, 756 S.W.2d 459 (Ky. 1988)
In a medical malpractice action, it was proper for the plaintiff to cross-examine the defendant's medical expert regarding the expert's prior involvement in an unrelated malpractice action. The plaintiff, the court reasoned, had a right to cross-examine the medical expert on "all matters relating to every issue." Evidence to show bias of an expert witness, the court concluded, is relevant.

Example 15.54: Accusations of malpractice
Wischmeyer v. Schanz, 536 N.W.2d 760 (Mich. 1995)
In this medical malpractice action, the plaintiff's expert—a surgeon—was properly cross-examined regarding poor surgical results in back surgeries by a

technique different from that used by the defendant physician. The expert's competency was before the court and the evidence pertained to his credibility. However, the cross-examination regarding prior medical malpractice claims against the expert that were unrelated was not proper—it was not probative of truthfulness or competency.

Example 15.55: Suspension
Gasinowski v. Hose, 897 P.2d 678 (Ariz. App. Div. 1 1994)
Here, the court permitted the cross-examination of an anesthesiologist about his subsequent suspension from the hospital.

Example 15.56: Drug addiction
Winant v. Carras, 617 N.Y.S. 2d 487 (A.D. 2 Dept. 1994)
Here, the court permitted counsel for the defense to cross-examine the plaintiff's expert on the issue of alleged drug addiction.

Example 15.57: Bankruptcy and professional discipline
Ad-Vantage Telephone Directory Consultants, Inc., v. GTE Directories Corporation, 37 F.3d 1460 (11th Cir. 1994)
In an antitrust and intentional interference with advantageous business relationships case, the plaintiff called a CPA-lawyer for expert testimony about the plaintiff's lost profits. On cross-examination, the defendant's counsel questioned the expert extensively on his methods and calculations. The defendant then moved away from the expert's lost profit estimates and into the expert's past. The personal questioning concerned three events, (1) the expert's bankruptcy several years before trial, (2) the disciplinary proceedings of the state bar and state institute of CPAs against the expert in 1990 and 1991, and (3) his censure by the state board of accountancy in 1969. The court found that the first line of questioning was improper on the ground that, unlike forgery, fraud, and perjury, application for bankruptcy does not show a "disregard for truth that would cast doubt on a witness's veracity." The court also found improper the cross-examination on the second two issues: "Given the absence of any sanctions from the 1990 accusation and the temporal remoteness of the 1969 sanction, we doubt the evidence's relevance. Nonetheless, the evidence—even if relevant—was certainly too weakly probative to survive Rule 403's balancing test."

Example 15.58: Fees, licensing, and malpractice claims
Maria R. Navarro De Cosme, et al., v. Hospital Pavia, et al., 922 F.2d 926 (1st Cir. 1991)
In this medical malpractice action, the defendant was allowed to cross-examine the plaintiff's medical expert about another case, in which the doctor testified under oath that he had submitted an inflated invoice for fees earned as an expert witness. The defendant also questioned the doctor about the suspension of his license as a notary for failure to submit the required reports and about the fact that he had been a defendant in three medical malpractice cases. The court stated,

> An expert is a person who, due to his training, due to his education, due to his standing in the community, is allowed to come before a court to give an opinion on something after the fact. . . .The person under those circumstances has to come to court and has to submit to the rigor of qualifications which includes not only the technical aspects; but also on . . .his standing in the community and his performance as a physician,. . .all the things that we have been discussing here. I think that these lawyers on the defense side are more than entitled to cover these areas.

Example 15.59: Professional negligence claims pending
Mazzone v. Holmes, 557 N.E.2d 186 (Ill. App. 1 Dist. 1990)
In this medical malpractice case, the court held that relevancy principles precluded the cross-examination of an expert witness regarding his personal involvement in medical malpractice cases. The cross-examination of the defense medical expert regarding the number of professional negligence cases brought or then pending against him was intended to show interest or bias as the defendant physician's expert. The court noted the "general proposition that parties should have the opportunity to expose the interest or bias of medical experts through cross-examination." The court concluded, however, that such examination should be strictly limited to matters such as "the number of referrals, their frequency, and the financial benefit derived from them."

Example 15.60: Suspension of privileges
Whisenhunt v. Zammit, 358 S.E.2d 114 (N.C. Ct. App. 1987)
Here a physician testified as an expert for the patient in a professional negligence action alleging the defendant's failure to monitor the effects of prescription medication. The court allowed the cross-examination of the physician regarding his suspension of staff privileges from two separate hospitals. It found the questioning relevant and probative and determined that the question of reasons for the witness's suspension would allow the jury to decide how much weight to give his testimony. The circumstances of the suspension, the court continued, may have also had a bearing on the bias of the witness, which was a proper consideration for the jury.

Example 15.61: Nonrenewal of privileges
Kane v. Ryan, 596 A.2d 562 (D.C. App. 1991)
Here, the court did not allow cross-examination of a patient's medical expert regarding why the expert's privileges at the hospital at which the plaintiff in the medical malpractice action was treated were not renewed. The court found that the evidence had but a remote bearing on possible bias the expert might have had toward the physician being sued as a defendant in the case. During cross-examination, the defendant's attorney inquired as to whether the expert was upset with the subject hospital over the "manner" in which it did not renew her hospital privileges, to which the expert replied the matter was not relevant to the case at issue. The court reasoned that a further exploration of the reasons why the expert was not renewed privileges would have required a "parade of witnesses on an issue that could have had only a remote bearing on possible bias against" the defendant physician, a doctor who had privileges at the

subject hospital but was apparently not among those who had a role in deciding the expert's future.

Example 15.62: Suspension of professional license
Morrow v. Stivers, 836 S.W.2d 424 (Ky. Ct. App. 1992)
In this medical malpractice action, cross-examination of the medical expert was not allowed. The court determined that the cross-examination into two matters—(1) the expert had had his license suspended for five years because he had passed hepatitis to several patients, and (2) the expert could only have transmitted hepatitis through dirty instruments, sexual intercourse, or other exchange of bodily fluids—was improper. It concluded that having hepatitis and thus not practicing for a time did not reflect on the expert's knowledge or ability to testify on matters at hand and that the inflammatory effect of the jury's hearing that the expert may have had sex with patients, although unproved, would have outweighed any probative value it might have had.

15.6 Conclusion

To perform well during cross-examination, an expert should always keep in mind the fifteen golden rules explained above. Experts who follow these rules will be on their way to performing well during cross-examination.

Chapter 16 What Attorneys and Clients Look for in an Expert

16.1 Introduction

Experts who are going to successfully work with and promote themselves to attorneys need to understand what attorneys look for in an expert witness. Attorneys are paid to win. When an attorney goes back to his firm after a trial, he is only asked one question: "Did you win?" The successful attorneys are those who win.

What attorneys look for in expert witnesses are individuals that can help them win. There are many characteristics in an expert that will help an attorney win. The sophisticated expert understands what attorneys and other clients really look for in an expert. These characteristics are as follows:

- Qualifications
- Credibility
- Availability
- Preparation
- Communication, articulation, and persuasion
- Personal attributes
- Reaction to adversity
- Temperament
- Good suggestions

16.2 Qualifications

Education

The attorney and client will look at an expert's background to see if the expert was educated at reputable universities. An expert with a blue-chip education is generally more valuable than one who attended a less prestigious school. Attorneys will also look for any "missing" education that may make the expert less qualified than the opposing experts.

Example 16.1
You are an expert witness who holds an undergraduate degree in your specialty but the opposing expert holds a graduate degree in that specialty. The opposing expert may be given more credibility by the jury.

Training, licenses, and certification

The training an expert received, his past and current licenses, and his certifications will be reviewed. The failure to obtain appropriate licenses or certifications may be questioned. Such a failure could lessen the expert's credibility with the jury and make it more difficult for the retaining attorney to persuade the jury.

Example 16.2
You hold an accounting degree but are not a certified public accountant.

Practical, real-world experience

Many attorneys and clients look to see what practical, real-world experience the expert has. Jurors generally find experts with real-world experience to be more believable than "ivory tower" academicians. The more relevant and recent an expert's real-world experience, the more valuable he will be as a witness. "Professional witnesses" who haven't had any recent real-world experience are much less valuable.

Example 16.3
An automotive mechanic with twenty years of experience may be more valued in a defective repair case than a retired automotive design engineer with a PhD who never repaired an engine and hasn't worked in the field in ten years.

Literature published and research projects

Publication generally brings credibility. An expert who has published in her field or who has been active in research projects may be viewed as more qualified than an expert without these credentials. The most valued experts are often those who "wrote the book." Jurors believe that if an expert wrote the book on a subject, she most likely knows what she is talking about.

Example 16.4
You recently had a text published entitled *Causation of Catastrophic Failure in Passenger Aircraft*. You will be a very valuable witness in a case where the cause of a passenger airplane crash is at issue.

Professional memberships and affiliations

Membership in appropriate professional organizations and the additional status of a diplomat or fellow will be another indication of qualifications of an expert. The lack of such affiliations could be used against an expert to lessen his credibility with the jury. There is one caveat: if the diplomat or fellow status was purchased by simply paying a fee, this can and will be used against an expert.

Example 16.5
Q. You don't belong to any professional societies and you haven't worked in the field in seven years. Isn't it a fact that you haven't kept up in this area since your retirement?

Litigation experience

Many attorneys and other clients look for experts who are experienced and who have been battle-tested. Counsel then has an idea that the expert will perform well on the stand, will be able to communicate effectively, and will not get rattled easily. If an expert has too much experience, however, some attorneys will shy away because the opposition may be able to portray him as a professional witness who is nothing more than a hired gun.

Example 16.6
Q. You've testified eighteen times in the last three years. Now, you wouldn't want to say anything that might hurt Attorney Thome's case and jeopardize your lucrative litigation business, would you?

16.3 Credibility

Credibility is the ultimate issue at every trial. A valuable witness is one who will be credible to the jury. No matter how qualified an expert is, if he is not believed by the jury or fact finder, he is of little value to counsel. To help maintain credibility, experts should:

Avoid being or appearing to be biased.

Jurors may not understand astrophysics, but they can and will see through someone who may be biased. An expert should not think that she can outsmart the jury on this issue.

Answer questions directly, without being evasive.

Jurors are very adept at perceiving when someone is being evasive. They will conclude that an expert witness is trying to hide something and is not honest (for example, "That depends upon what the meaning of *is* is").

Be an expert, not an advocate.

Jurors may discount experts who appear to have an ax to grind.

Call cases as they see them and readily make concessions where appropriate.

If an expert is strong in defense everywhere, she is strong nowhere. Experts should give ground where called for. They will lose credibility if they never agree with the opposition on any point.

Refuse cases where they cannot honestly provide the opinion that is being sought.

This, in the long run, is best for the expert and for the attorney seeking her assistance.

16.4 Availability

An expert, no matter how qualified and credible, is of little value to counsel if she is not available. Experts will be more valuable if they are not too busy and manage to make themselves available for conferences, reviews, testing and examinations, depositions, and trials. Attorneys get to choose who their experts are and many will refuse to work with experts who are difficult to deal with.

16.5 Preparation

Peak performance requires proper preparation. Performing well in a courtroom or deposition is accomplished through perspiration, not inspiration. Attorneys value experts who are willing (and able) to devote the time necessary to prepare properly. Proper preparation for deposition and trial involves studying all relevant documents, anticipating the questions that one will be asked, preparing analogies, and pointing out gaps and inconsistencies to counsel. (More detailed advice on preparation is provided in Chapter 12.)

16.6 Communication, Articulation, and Persuasion

The only reason an expert is testifying in a case is to proffer an opinion. This opinion is worthless to counsel unless the expert can communicate it to the jury of lay persons. This is true even if an individual is the world's leading expert in a particular field. If the jury cannot understand an expert, does not listen to her, or does not like her, they may not be persuaded by her opinion. (Communicating with a jury is discussed in Chapter 11.) Some of the things that will help an expert to be a better communicator and persuader include the following points.

Experts should communicate the truth in an ethical, objective, and effective way.

Experts are well advised to give ground where called for and to not be evasive. This makes for a more persuasive witness.

Example 16.7

Q. Is it possible that you were provided with false documents?

A. Anything's possible, counselor.

Experts should not overemphasize uncertainty.

There is no need to overemphasize uncertainty.

Example 16.8

Again, I want to stress that nothing in this world is 100% certain and especially in science. We deal with probabilities based upon past observances.

It is best to speak to the jury and observe their nonverbal feedback.

An expert witness should address his remarks to the jury—they're the ones who will decide whether to believe the witness. Remarks should be adjusted based upon the jury's reaction.

Example 16.9
If the jury responds well to being somewhat informal, continue using that style while testifying.

Experts should not use jargon.

There's no quicker way to lose a jury than by using technical jargon that they do not understand. Once the jury is lost, it may be difficult or impossible to regain their attention.

Example 16.10
Jargon: My diagnosis was that the patient suffered a fracture of the clavicle secondary to the MVA of 9/18/99.
More effective: She broke her collarbone as a result of the car accident that happened on September 18, 1999.

A wise expert maintains eye contact with the jury.

This makes a witness more credible. One shouldn't stare, however.

Experts should speak with confidence.

If a witness doesn't appear to believe in his own opinion, why should the jury?

Effective experts use visual aids.

A picture says a thousand words. Good visual aids can be a very effective way to communicate with a jury. However, the expert should make sure the visual aids work.

It is good to teach the jury.

A wise expert witness acts as a teacher and assumes the jurors know nothing. She uses terms that they understand. Jurors like to learn and should respond favorably.

An expert should use analogies and similes.

This is the most effective way to communicate technical ideas to a jury.

Example 16.11
Q. After both of his arms were amputated, how did the plaintiff eat?
A. Like a dog.

16.7 Personal Attributes

If an expert is likeable, he is more likely to be believed by a jury. If, on the other hand, he is gruff, arrogant, or condescending, he is not likely to do well with a jury. Attorneys prefer likeable, sympathetic experts.

16.8 Reaction to Adversity

Things almost never turn out exactly as anticipated when dealing with expert testimony. Experts who are able to react to difficult and, in many cases, unexpected adverse situations and developments are sought out by counsel. The ability to think on one's feet and stay calm, collected, and professional while under fire is one of the most sought-after attributes in an expert.

Example 16.12

Q. You never reviewed the report of Dr. Jones dated August 6, 1999, did you?
A. Would you mind if I review the document you are referring to?...As you can see here from page three of the report, review of this document at the time wouldn't have changed my opinion in the least because....

16.9 Temperament and Cooperation

Nobody wants to work with a temperamental or difficult expert. This is especially true if the expert thinks he is smarter and better than everyone else. Counsel will seek out and value experts who are cooperative and not condescending, arrogant, and pompous. Counsel values experts who return phone calls promptly. Furthermore, attorneys understand that "nice" experts are more likely to do well in front of a jury.

16.10 Good Suggestions

The truly valuable expert will be proactive in attempting to educate retaining counsel. Sophisticated experts assist counsel by not only answering the questions asked, but by making valuable suggestions as well. Suggestions by experts regarding demonstrative aids, questions for depositions, and realistic evaluation of theories, reports, and proposed evidence all make an expert more valuable to counsel.

16.11 Conclusion

Attorneys try to win their cases. Therefore, they look for experts who help them win. Such an expert is one who can persuade the jury effectively. This does *not* require a witness to be the world's leading expert in a particular field. An expert with a likeable personality who will work hard before testifying, who can teach the jury without jargon and with the use of analogies, who will make concessions where called for, who will assist counsel with suggestions, and who will call cases honestly will be a highly sought-after expert.

Chapter 17 How Attorneys Locate and Select Experts

17.1 Introduction

It is important to understand how attorneys locate and select experts to assist them in their cases. Those who understand how attorneys and other clients go about selecting experts for their cases will be in the best position to make themselves accessible and available. The common resources used by counsel and other clients to locate experts include:

- Other attorneys
- Expert locator and referral services
- Associates
- Literature searches
- Certifying agencies
- Universities
- Experts used in the past
- Jury verdict reviews
- Referrals from the client (in-house experts)
- Internet Web pages
- Directories
- Advertisements and direct mail

Each of these will be discussed in this chapter.

17.2 Referrals from Other Attorneys

Lawyers talk to each other all the time, asking for advice and tips on how to handle certain matters. This includes recommendations on expert witnesses. For example, a lawyer undertaking a bad faith case against a certain insurance company will look to a lawyer who has litigated a similar case recently. First, she will look inside her own firm. If that fails, she will call colleagues in other firms.

Example 17.1
(Intra-office E-mail): To: All Attorneys/Paralegals
Re: Blood Alcohol Expert Needed
I'm defending a new dram shop matter. Anybody know of any good blood alcohol experts?

Experts who have excelled in previous cases are in the best position to be recommended. Being a good expert means being knowledgeable, cooperative, well-prepared, and most importantly, being able to communicate effectively and persuasively at deposition and trial. It does not mean simply telling the retaining attorney what she wants to hear.

When an expert is recommended, the attorney receives a colleague's opinion as to the strengths of an expert witness. This is one of the two principal advantages of being recommended.[1] Most other ways of finding experts do not allow attorneys this most important bit of information—how effective the person is as a witness. For example, a literature search may reveal that Ms. Smith is the world's leading expert in a particular area. That same literature search would not, however, say anything about how good a witness Ms. Smith is. For example, counsel wants to know if juries like a witness. Does the witness prepare thoroughly? Can the witness communicate effectively with a lay jury?

A good witness will often be recommended to others regardless of which side he worked for in the previous case. It is very common for attorneys to recommend or seek out experts who have testified against them in a previous matter. One of the greatest compliments an expert can receive is to have the opposing attorneys ask for their business card at the conclusion of a deposition. Because all the attorneys in the case will be evaluating the expert's performance in a case, it is doubly important to be a good witness. At the conclusion of the case, an expert should ask his retaining attorney to recommend him to other attorneys. Finally, the expert should send the attorney two or three copies of his business card and his curriculum vitae.

17.3 Expert Locator and Referral Services

Many attorneys turn to expert locator/referral services for assistance. There are several reasons that attorneys may turn to these services. These include the following.

- They are unable to get a recommendation for an expert.
- They do not have the time or inclination to search for an expert by some other means.
- Their first-choice experts have been retained by the opposition.
- Their first-choice experts are unavailable.
- They need an out-of-state expert and can't get a recommendation on an expert in that locale.
- The area of specialty is very narrow (for example, arctic exposure) and there are very few experts in that field.

Locator and referral services are usually not an attorney's first choice in choosing an expert. There are three main reasons for this. First, they do not get a trusted colleague's opinion as to the effectiveness of the potential expert. Second, there may be a fee involved in using the service. Finally, the

[1] Cost-effectiveness is the other.

fact that the witness is registered with a referral agency may be brought in front of the jury to show bias.

Although not usually the attorney's first choice, referral services are very commonly used by attorneys to locate and retain experts. They can be especially effective in generating business for experts in narrow fields. The sheer number of referral services available is a testament to how much attorneys use these resources. (A list of referral sources is provided in Appendix K.)

Many attorneys also look to professional organizations and their referral services. One of the largest and most established is the Defense Research Institute.[2] This database is for members only and services the defense bar.

17.4 Associations

Counsel looking for a specific type of expert will often contact a particular discipline or profession's association. Many of these associations provide lists of experts and consultants, literature searches, and recommendations. These services may be complimentary to the attorney and may be provided as a free service to the association's members. Experts may contact the professional organizations that they belong to to find out if they have these services available. Experts should also make sure to be on the organization's panel of experts. They may also consider joining other relevant professional associations that may have these services.

17.5 Literature Searches

Many lawyers seek out experts who have published texts and articles. They consider such experts to have inherent credibility. Experts who have published in a certain field are very easy to find through computer-based literature searches. A published expert can expect to be contacted by attorneys who have found her name through literature searches.

17.6 Certifying Agencies

Counsel may turn to certifying organizations when searching for experts. For example, the American Board of Independent Medical Examiners (ABIME) lists approximately 1,500 physicians who have passed a rigorous exam. Most certifying agencies provide counsel with a directory or list of members for use in selecting experts. Experts who desire to increase their accessibility to counsel should consider obtaining the appropriate certifications and being listed in the available directories.

There is a note of caution, however, regarding certification. Experts who obtain certifications by purchasing them through diploma mills decrease their value and marketability. By *diploma mill,* the authors mean a certifying

---

[2] DRI may be contacted at (312) 944-0575.

agency that has very weak certification standards and is probably most interested in the applicant's money. These facts can be brought out during cross-examination and can harm an expert's credibility before the jury.

Example 17.2
Q. I see here that you are board certified by the Fictional Board of Forensic Experts?
A. Yes.
Q. Very impressive.
A. Thank you.
Q. What requirements did you meet to obtain this board certification?
A. The requirements of the board.
Q. What were they?
A. I forget.
Q. Did you take an examination?
A. No.
Q. Did you complete a specified training program?
A. No.
Q. You paid your fee and they gave you the certification, didn't they?
A. Yes.

17.7 Universities

Lawyers may try to tap into universities when looking for experts. Professors and other instructors may have increased credibility with a jury. Those experts who act as professors, instructors, or even adjunct instructors at colleges and universities increase their visibility to counsel. Many of the nation's leading experts and consultants have affiliated themselves with colleges and universities. Not only does this help in their being contacted first, it adds a great deal of credibility to their qualifications.

17.8 Experts Used in the Past

Lawyers may contact experts they have used in the past to obtain recommendations on an expert in an allied or even in a different field. For example, a lawyer may call a psychiatrist he has worked with in the past for a recommendation on a psychologist. Experts in a specialty may be willing to refer a colleague cases when they are unavailable or are conflicted out of a case. It is wise to network with as many experts as possible. This is word-of-mouth marketing at its best.

17.9 Jury Verdict Reviews

Settlements and jury verdicts are reported in legal publications. These reports contain the results of the case and the names of the expert witnesses in the case. Counsel will frequently contact experts reported in jury verdict reports when undertaking a new case. Jury verdict reports are another way that being effective in one case can generate additional referrals.

17.10 Client Referral of In-house Experts

The client itself is often looked to by counsel when searching for an expert. These in-house experts, usually the employees of the company, are available, experienced, and will testify without additional payment. The impartiality of these in-house experts will often be questioned, however. An individual who is given the opportunity to testify as an expert on behalf of her employer should consider taking it. Testifying for an employer is a good opportunity to gain experience and establish a reputation of being a good expert. Both may be invaluable to someone who later leaves her employer and desires additional forensic work. However, an in-house expert may be asked to sign a confidentiality, nondisclosure agreement limiting her future testimony as an expert. The expert should consult with counsel before signing such an agreement.

17.11 Internet Web Pages

Attorneys are turning with increasing frequency to the Internet to locate experts. Many Internet sites provide attorneys with the opportunity to search for expert witnesses. (Some of the more important sites are listed in Appendix N.) These sites may charge the expert or attorney a fee, or they may be free to both. The Internet is fast and easy to use, and it may be a very economical way for attorneys to locate experts.

17.12 Directories and Source Books

Counsel may use directories and source books to locate experts. Most of these publications require the payment of an annual listing fee for the expert to be listed. Directories and source books can be a cost-effective way for experts to promote themselves. (A listing of expert witness directories is provided in Appendix L.)

17.13 Advertisements

Many lawyers look in the professional services or classified section of state and national legal publications in their search for experts. (The national publications consulted by counsel most frequently are listed in Appendix M.) Many experts find it is cost-effective to advertise in these and other state and national legal publications to increase their visibility and to obtain additional forensic work.

17.14 How Attorneys Choose Among Experts

Often, attorneys will locate more experts than they need in a particular matter. They will then be in a position where they can choose from amongst these experts the one that they would like to retain. In making this selection, attorneys consider many factors. These include the following points.

Reputation as an effective expert

Does the witness have a reputation as an effective witness? That is, is this a witness who can persuade the jury and help the attorney win? This information may only be available if the attorney is able to get a colleague's recommendation on a particular expert.

History of past cases

Was the expert associated with favorable verdicts/settlements in the past? This can be determined from jury verdict reports and may be relevant to one's ability to persuade and communicate effectively.

Strength of CV/qualifications

Are there any missing credentials? Are there any time gaps or holes in the CV?

Publication

Has the expert published? Such experts often carry more credibility with a jury.

Academic positions

Experts affiliated with colleges and universities may carry more weight with a jury.

Perceived ability to communicate and persuade

In preliminary verbal contacts with the expert (on the phone or in person), did she have good communication skills? Was she likeable and even-tempered? Can she explain complicated concepts effectively in laymen's terms? Is she likely to do well in front of a jury?

Baggage

Is there anything in the expert's past that can be used against her? Controversial writings? Unprofessional marketing activities? Bias to one side or industry? Is she a "professional" witness who no longer works in the field in question? Was she disqualified in the past? Were there any disciplinary or legal problems?

Geography

It is less expensive to use an expert who is local to the venue of the litigation. Paying an expert to travel gets very expensive.

Fees

This is not the primary consideration, but it will come into play. The more at stake in the case, the less cost-sensitive the attorney is likely to be.

Relevant, recent experience
This plays well with a jury.

Easy to work with, reasonable
This information will be determined from initial contacts. Is the expert easy to deal with? Does she return phone calls? Are her retention terms reasonable? Is she pompous and arrogant or have a chip on her shoulder regarding attorneys?

The more an individual can distinguish himself in these areas, the more likely it is that he will be the preferred expert who is consulted and who can charge a premium fee for his time.

17.15 Conclusion

To properly promote oneself, an expert needs to understand how attorneys locate and select expert witnesses.

Chapter 18 Marketing a Forensic Practice

18.1 Introduction

Marketing a forensic practice can be challenging. Forensic experts are faced with the daunting task of marketing their services without compromising their integrity, credibility, professionalism, or reputation. A legitimate concern about marketing is how it will play to juries, potential clients, and colleagues.

The type of questioning one can expect to face on cross-examination with regard to marketing efforts will go something like this:

Q. Who first contacted you in regard to this case?
A. Robert Smith.
Q. Doesn't Robert Smith work for National Forensic Science Locator, Inc.?
A. Yes.
Q. And Mr. Smith called you on behalf of NFSL, Inc., did he not?
A. Yes, he did.
Q. Now, NFSL is a service that finds expert witnesses for attorneys, is it not?
A. Yes, it is.
Q. An attorney needs an expert in a field and he calls up NFSL, correct?
A. I would assume so.
Q. And NFSL advertises in various lawyers' publications, does it not?
A. I'm not sure.
Q. Now, sir, you have listed yourself with NFSL as an expert on the topic of helicopter design, have you not?
A. Yes, I have.
Q. That's between "heating and air conditioning" and "hot air balloons," is it not?
A. I wouldn't know that.
Q. Here is their brochure. "Helicopter" is between "heating and air conditioning" and "hot air balloons," is it not?
A. It appears to be.
Q. And the reason you listed yourself with NFSL is so that you could get more work testifying as an expert witness, is it not?
A. Yes.
Q. Would you tell the jury about where else you advertised your services as an expert witness for hire and your other marketing efforts, sir?

These types of questions must be kept in mind in reference to each of the marketing methods that will be discussed in this chapter.

18.2 The Three Rules of Marketing

In the authors' opinion, there are three rules of marketing that hold true in most circumstances. These rules are simply:

1. Nobody can tell an expert what will work to market his forensic practice.

A person who can, with certainty, predict what will work to market a product or service can be compared to a person who can, with certainty, predict the stock market. It just doesn't happen. What a marketing expert can do, however, is look at the ways that similarly situated businesses have successfully sold their products and services. This chapter reviews and explains the techniques that the authors know have worked for experts.

2. The way to see if something works is to try it.

The only way to know for certain what will work is to try it out. Testing can tell an expert whether direct mail, speaking, writing, or another technique will generate cases.

3. Track results. Repeat what works. Discontinue what does not work.

It is essential for an expert to track where her cases come from. The first thing she should ask a new attorney is, "Where did you get my name?" Only through tracking can an expert make an intelligent decision as to which marketing methods work and which do not. An expert should repeat what works and discontinue what doesn't work. For example, if Mr. Lopez wrote a scholarly article for a legal publication and that got him fourteen cases, he should probably try to write more articles for legal publications. On the other hand, if he advertised in a legal publication for a full year and got no cases from that ad, that is something he should probably discontinue. A good tracking system will tell an expert that after four years of placing an ad, she received not one new client or piece of business. Thus, it might be time to rethink the notice.

18.3 Identify the Target Market

Before undertaking any marketing effort, an expert needs to identify his target market. That is, he must ask who his potential clients are. This should be the start of any marketing plan. The market for an expert's services will depend upon what services he is willing and able to provide. It will also depend upon in which geographic area he will seek to market his services. A key to cost-effective marketing is to identify the market with as much precision as possible. For example, if Ms. Browne is a medical malpractice expert, from a marketing standpoint she may be much better off if she speaks at a conference on malpractice for 150 attorneys than if she spoke at a general bar association meeting of 1,200 attorneys.

Once an expert identifies her market, the next step will involve reaching the market in a cost-effective way. We will discuss the various ways to reach a target market later in this chapter.

18.4 The Value of a Client

For each marketing technique that we will discuss, we will stress that the expert needs to do a cost-benefit analysis. The cost of each method will vary by marketing technique and will be a function of the time involved and the out-of-pocket expenditures that must be made. The benefit of a marketing method is a function of how much a client is worth.

Forensic experts are highly compensated. If an expert charges $350 per hour and bills 50 hours on the average case, each case then generates $17,500. If the average client will retain an expert a total of three times or will refer him to two new clients, then the average client is worth $17,500 x 3 = $52,500. When new clients can be extremely valuable, in many cases it makes economic sense to spend time and money to obtain new clients.

18.5 Personal Reputation—Word of Mouth

Most forensic experts would agree that the most cost-effective, efficient, and least offensive marketing method is by personal reputation—word of mouth. As former trial lawyers, this point was driven home time and time again to the authors at depositions of experts. All of the lawyers would file in dutifully and then two, three, or more hours of intense questioning of the expert would follow. Each time the expert was prepared, knew the facts and science cold, was organized, and testified in a cool, calm, professional manner, the same thing would happen at the conclusion of the deposition. Each lawyer would shake the expert's hand and reach over to the desk and take two to three business cards for future use. This is personal reputation/word-of-mouth marketing in action.

Lawyers constantly communicate with one another and share information. The first stop for a lawyer in search of an expert is usually his colleagues. If an expert does a good job on a case, lawyers will recommend him when asked, "Do you know any experts in the field of...?" Lawyers also frequently discuss the good and bad expert witnesses they have used. It is very common to hear advice such as, "If you ever need a cardiologist, Dr. Davidson, who I deposed last week, was dynamite!" from a colleague.

The lesson is clear. Doing an excellent job on current cases and developing a reputation for professionalism can be an expert's most effective marketing tool. It is also extremely cost-effective in that it costs nothing. If an expert does a good job, lawyers will recommend him to their colleagues and will use him again on other cases.

The converse, however, is also true. If an expert does a poor job on a case, his retaining lawyer is not likely to use him again and the word will spread quickly through the legal community. Attorneys will share information about which experts not to use as readily as they share information about which experts to use. Once the word gets out about an expert, his work can dry up quite quickly.

Word-of-mouth referrals will increase if an expert provides exceptional service. Many long-term relationships with clients are forged not because of lengthy CVs or impressive credentials, but are due to excellent service and responsiveness by the expert. Most clients look for similar types of things. They want an expert who is prompt, courteous, cooperative, reasonable, and who exceeds expectations.

Promptness

An expert who does things promptly—for example, issuing initial oral reports—is highly valued. Trial attorneys face many court-imposed deadlines. The number one reason lawyers get sued for malpractice is for missing deadlines. They appreciate experts who allow them to meet their deadlines.

Courtesy

Trial lawyers are involved in an adversarial litigation process. The expert who is courteous to the client and especially to their support staff will tend to be selected more often than his curt or arrogant counterparts. One comment by a staff member ("Dr. Jones is so nice") may go a long way in forging a long-term relationship with a new client. If a lawyer has a choice between two equally qualified experts, he will retain the expert who is easier to deal with. Trial lawyers deal with big egos all day long. The last thing they want to deal with is an arrogant expert witness.

Cooperation/availability

The world-renowned expert who is never available to talk to, who is booked up for six months of appointments, and who is in Europe touring during the summer months is of little value to most clients. Experts who go out of their way to be cooperative and available are highly valued. Going out of one's way to demonstrate cooperation and availability is usually an excellent marketing technique.

Reasonableness

Attorneys prefer to work with reasonable people. Unreasonable attitudes will discourage future referrals and will be publicized by the victimized attorneys. Some common conduct that attorneys may consider unreasonable include a too restrictive nonrefundable deposition cancellation policy and unreasonable expense reimbursement requests (for example, insisting on a limousine for all ground transportation).

Exceed expectations

The ability to exceed the expectations of the client by the expert is perhaps the most important service/marketing technique. When the client is "blown away" by the level of completeness, the excellence of a report or recommendation, or the research done by the expert, his expectations have been exceeded. This client will place such an expert at the top of the list for future expert witness/consulting work.

Backlash

There is very little backlash potential from word-of-mouth referrals. This is one of its chief advantages.

Cost-Benefit Analysis

Word-of-mouth referrals cost nothing out of pocket. They work very well. Under a cost-benefit analysis, this type of forensic marketing is always a winner.

18.6 Speaking Engagements

Most forensic experts understand that it is good for business to speak professionally. The idea is that by being seen and recognized, an expert picks up new clients and business. Being a valuable expert is all about one's ability to communicate verbally. If a forensic expert can communicate well with juries and judges, she can help an attorney win his case. If she cannot communicate well, all of her expertise and credentials will be useless to the attorney.

Speaking is an opportunity to show off one's communications skills and is a very effective way to manifest one's skills as a forensic expert. Attorneys seek out and will pay a premium for experts that they think will connect with a jury. As such, experts who speak to legal groups should spend as much time preparing the delivery of a talk as they do its content. If an expert can make the topic interesting and easy to understand for the lawyers, they will conclude rapidly that she would probably make a good witness in front of a jury.

Experts need to be prepared to capitalize on their appearances as speakers. They should bring plenty of business cards in case they are asked for them after the talk. If possible, they should also bring a handout with valuable information that the audience will want to keep. The handout material should contain the expert's contact information. A lawyer can't hire an expert if he can't find her.

In order to use speaking as an effective marketing tool, the forensic expert should consider:

- to *whom* he will speak,
- *where* he will speak,
- *when* he will speak,
- *what* he will speak about, and most importantly,
- *why,* specifically, he will speak.

To whom the expert will speak

Forensic experts should keep in mind who their target market is when deciding to seek out or accept speaking engagements. To obtain business from attorneys, one needs to contact and speak to local, state, and national bar associates at meetings of lawyers. (See Appendix O for a listing of state and national bar associations.) If, on the other hand, the target market is insurance companies and claims adjusters, one needs to talk to insurance professionals, including claims adjusters' associations.

It is a common mistake to assume that a bigger audience will provide more clients. In the authors' experience, some of the most effective marketing presentations we ever gave were to small groups of key people. For example, we gave a presentation for a local union group on workers' compensation law. We had only thirty-five attendees. Almost every union person there came for a reason (either they had a case or their friend, who couldn't be there, needed help). We had enough foresight to hand out extra information packets. We received clients and calls for information and help for many years after the presentation. The key wasn't the number of people, but reaching the right people.

These should be an expert's first major considerations: who will attend the presentation, will the audience members be in a position to retain the expert's services, and are the audience members in a position to recommend the expert's services to others? If the answer to these questions is no, then perhaps it is a waste of valuable time to speak to that particular group.

Where the expert will speak

An expert who has to travel from his home base should consider:

- How many days of work will he miss? Traveling over 1,500 miles may need three days—one to get there, one to do the presentation, and one day to get back home. Will the presentation be worth missing three days of work? How many cases would the expert need to generate to make it cost-effective?
- Is the presentation outside of the expert's geographic target market? Does someone who practices in Boston really want to solicit work in

San Francisco? Some national presentations may require substantial travel time and effort. Evaluation of the type of exposure one will get is critical when deciding if a speaking engagement will be cost-effective.

In the end, an expert may be better off speaking at a local bar association meeting forty miles from his office than traveling thousands of miles to give national presentations to larger groups.

When the expert will speak

A speaker's place in the program may well determine how much exposure and business she picks up. Ideally, one wants to speak as early as possible in the program to the largest group possible. When solicited to speak, an expert should ask the following questions.

1. *When* will I speak? What are the date and time?
2. Will it be a *general session*, a *breakout*, or a *workshop?*
3. *How many* attendees are likely to attend my session?
4. What kind of people are likely to attend my session? For instance, lawyers, adjusters, nurses?
5. What other sessions will I be up against?

It's important to remember that an expert's exposure will be significantly reduced if she speaks at the same time as a well-known speaker.

Finally, the wise expert knows that a meeting planner wants and needs her to speak. Otherwise the planner would not have called the expert. Therefore, when considering a speaking engagement, one should feel free to request good placement early on in the program.

What the expert will speak about

What one is asked to speak about is important to determining the cost-benefit of giving the presentation. If the talk an expert is asked to give is already prepared, it will cost him very little time to prepare for the speaking engagement. If, on the other hand, a talk will require considerable preparation time, he should take this into account before deciding if it is worthwhile to agree to give the presentation. In addition, an expert wants to select the topic related most closely to the types of cases he is looking for.

Why the expert will speak

It is important for experts to always determine and keep in mind specifically why they are considering speaking. Is it to pick up clients and business? Is it to flesh out a CV? Is it for a nice trip where someone will pick up the airfare? It is wise to consider the cost in terms of time lost from work in determining if the proposed speaking engagement will be cost-effective and makes sense from a business development standpoint.

Backlash

Speaking engagements can and will be used during cross-examination to show an expert's bias. Speaking at well-balanced educational programs will not be a problem. If, however, an expert speaks exclusively at insurance defense conferences or at plaintiff bar association meetings, she can expect to have her impartiality questioned as a result of these speaking engagements.

Example 18.1
Q. I see here on your CV that you do a lot of speaking to groups of lawyers.
A. I do speak to groups of lawyers.
Q. You've spoken for the Association of Trial Lawyers of America, the Massachusetts Trial Association, the Barnstable County Trial Lawyers' Association, and the New England Trial Lawyers' Association?
A. Yes, I have.
Q. When was the last time you've spoken to any lawyer's groups that weren't plaintiff's lawyers?
A. I don't recall.

Cost-Benefit Analysis

Speaking engagements involve personal contact and can be very effective in generating referrals. They offer a very attractive cost-benefit ratio if travel expenses are reimbursed and travel time is kept to a minimum. The cost-benefit ratio is even more attractive if the speaker can obtain an honorarium and if the talk is ready and does not require substantial preparation time.

18.7 Writing Articles

The analysis forensic experts should undertake before agreeing to write articles, book chapters, etc., is similar to the analysis for speaking engagements. Before deciding to spend the time to write an article for publication, one should consider the following carefully.

1. *Where* the article will be published.
2. *Who* will read it.
3. *When* it will be published.
4. Whether *contact information* will be provided.
5. *Why* the expert will be writing.
6. What the potential *backlash* might be.
7. Whether writing makes sense after a *cost-benefit analysis.*

Where will the article be published?

Before submitting an article for publication, one should consider the publication itself. Is it considered a prestigious peer-reviewed journal? Or is it a publication with few publication requirements that advocates a distinct point of view? There may be a backlash associated with writing only for publications that have slanted views. This could be used against an expert to show bias. The article will generally be more valuable from a marketing standpoint if it is published in a prestigious journal.

Who will read the article?

It is helpful to check the circulation (audited or unaudited) and the number of people who actually read the publication. Is it a publication professionals pay to subscribe to or is it sponsored by a grant and mailed free of charge to one or more categories of professionals? Again, the key may not lie only in the number of people who subscribe or read it, but in the specific type of readers. If, for example, Mr. Lee is marketing his services as a reinsurance expert/consultant and the five hundred key reinsurance professionals read an influential journal or newsletter, he might be better off publishing in that journal than in one with five hundred times the circulation. (See Appendix M for a listing of major legal publications.)

At a minimum, one should make sure articles in the publication are indexed in electronic search engines. Many attorneys will search for experts by doing a literature search. Articles are much more valuable from a marketing standpoint if they are electronically indexed.

When will the article be published?

To paraphrase Vince Lombardi, "Timing isn't everything, it's the only thing." If an article is published in July or August, when many professionals are on vacation, or if it appears in December when most people are too busy with the holidays to read anything, there will be much less of an impact and interest. If the article is in a peer-reviewed journal, the review process may delay publication. Many editors will hold and save articles for when they are needed to fill in space. An author should attempt to get an agreement in advance for exactly when his article will be published. It is unwise to spend valuable time writing an article that will sit in an editor's file for nine months before she publishes it.

Contact information

It is useful to try to insist that the magazine or journal either list the author's phone number or provide an easy way to contact him. The more difficult it is for the reader to track down an author, the less calls and business he can expect. If they will not list contact information, it may be possible to subtly work into the article information that can be used to find the author (where he lives or works, etc.). Having a personal Web site with the author's name registered in the proper search engines is another good back up.

Why the expert will write

An expert needs to identify specifically what she hopes to achieve before she will have any realistic chance of achieving it. Is she trying to beef up her CV? Is she hoping potential clients will see the article and call for consultations and to retain her services? Clearly identifying her goals will force an expert to consider if the article, chapter, or book is a cost-effective marketing method. While there will be little if any out-of-pocket cost, the time it will take to write the article should be factored into one's decision.

Backlash

Balancing who one writes for avoids the appearance of partiality and bias. If, on the whole, an expert will not be better off professionally having published in a particular journal or newspaper, why do it? It is also critical to keep in mind that anything an expert writes can be used against her during cross-examination. With electronic search engines, attorneys can easily develop a fairly comprehensive list of an individual's publications. These publications can be used against an expert to show bias and to show any inconsistencies with the testimony she provides on the witness stand.

Example 18.2

Q. You are here giving your unbiased opinion, are you not?

A. Of course.

Q. In July 1997, in the publication *The Forensic Specialist,* you wrote an article entitled, "Progression of Litigation-related Injury."

A. Ahh. Yes.

Q. Is this a copy of that article?

A. Yes.

Q. I direct you to page 3, paragraph 3, the fourth sentence, and I quote, "Of course, it's common knowledge that once an injured person retains a lawyer, his recovery will almost always be delayed." Am I reading that correctly sir?

Cost-Benefit Analysis

As with any marketing effort, a cost-benefit analysis is necessary. Writing can be very time-consuming. It's also important to remember to track referrals. If an expert's tracking reveals that her article generated a number of cases, she should strongly consider spending the time to write more articles.

18.8 Writing Texts

An expert who "wrote the book" on a particular topic can become a very highly valued witness. As an example, Mr. Babitsky wrote a book on the legal implications of the American Medical Association's *Guides to the Evaluation of Permanent Impairment.* A few years ago, he was asked to testify in Eagle Pass, Texas, in a case dealing with the *Guides.* Mr. Babitsky lives in Cape Cod. Because he wrote the book and because they wanted him, he was able to arrange a fee whereby he was paid a high portal-to-portal hourly fee from the time he left his house in Cape Cod until the time he returned.

Writing a book makes an expert easy to find. Many attorneys will search for experts by doing a literature search and seeing who comes up on the particular topic in question. Coming up on such a search is great marketing with little or no backlash.

Backlash

Anything written by an expert can be used against him during cross-examination. This is especially true of comments that may tend to show bias or comments that can be construed as being inconsistent with the testimony the expert presents on the witness stand.

> **Example 18.3**
> **Q.** And you based your opinion, Doctor, partly on the tests that you performed to detect malingering?
> **A.** Yes.
> **Q.** I have here the book you authored, *Symptom Magnification and Malingering*. Page 189, line 3, and I quote, "Most, if not all, of the tests to detect malingering have serious deficiencies in validity and reliability." Am I reading that correctly?

Cost-Benefit Analysis

When deciding whether to write a book, it is critical to remember that writing a book is a very big project. As such, it may be a risky proposition. It is much less costly to "test" whether speaking or writing an article will generate business than to write a book. Of course, depending upon the topic, an author may be able to recoup some or all of the time spent on writing the text through royalties from its sale. As noted above, if an individual "wrote the book" on a particular subject, her time may be worth considerably more to the referring attorney.

18.9 Referral Agencies, Locator Services, and Brokers

There are dozens of referral agencies, locator services, and brokers who can help market an expert's services. These organizations vary in geographic scope. Some are local or statewide while many are national. How these organizations get paid also varies. Prior to deciding whether to be listed with one or more of these services, it is necessary to do one's homework. Due diligence is important. Some of the questions the forensic expert needs to ask follow.

1. How long has the organization been in business?

Is this a start-up or fly-by-night group? It is critical that attorneys have heard of the organization, that they use it, and that it will be in business in the near future.

2. How does the organization publicize itself?

What do copies of their materials look like? Are they professional and classy? Would it be embarrassing to be confronted with them on the witness stand? Are they spending any money to reach clients?

3. Is there a contract? If so, what does it say?

One should always read all the fine print. The devil is in the details. Experts who need help should get a lawyer to review the contract.

4. Is the contract exclusive or nonexclusive?

In the authors' opinion it is not usually a good idea to sign an exclusive contract.

5. What are the financial arrangements?

Is there a flat fee for a listing for a time period (similar to an ad)? Do they surcharge the complete fee? Do they take a portion of the fee? Who does the billing? Who bears the loss if the client decides to default? When does the expert get paid?

6. How do they select which expert to offer to the client?

Is it based upon expertise, experience, a rotating system, or some other criteria?

7. Do they provide insurance or a hold-harmless agreement if an expert is sued?

8. How many times has the organization been sued over the past five years?

For what were they sued? What were the result(s)?

Many experts we know have had very positive and financially rewarding experiences with referral agencies. The sophisticated forensic expert will, however, exercise caution before signing up with one or more referral agencies, locator services, or brokers. The wise expert understands that his credibility, professionalism, and reputation could be affected adversely by the activities of these agencies. Calling the agency to see how they respond to telephone inquiries and even meeting the people in charge and viewing the premises, personnel, and facility are highly recommended. (See Appendix K for a listing of referral organizations.)

Backlash

As can be seen from the first example in this chapter, an affiliation with a referral agency can be used against an expert during cross-examination. One should accept this fact before deciding to sign up with an agency. An expert should also do his homework on the agency to find out if there is anything about the organization that he wouldn't want to be asked about on cross-examination.

Cost-Benefit Analysis

Registering with referral agencies usually requires little time and involves little or no out-of-pocket expense. These agencies allow experts to reach potential clients that they could not reach by any other reasonable means. They therefore offer a very attractive cost-benefit ratio, especially for those who possess expertise in a rare area. Attorneys are most likely to use referral agencies for these rare areas of expertise. If, on the other hand, an expert is one of 50,000 chiropractors in the United States, an attorney will probably not have to resort to a referral agency to locate her. The benefit of referral organizations increases if they provide services, such as handling billing, sifting out inappropriate cases, and guaranteeing collections.

18.10 One-on-One Meetings

One of the most effective marketing techniques is meeting in-person with potential clients or those responsible for selecting and retaining experts. When using this technique, the potential client will be able to evaluate the expert's ability to communicate and his experience, training, and knowledge in his field. The client will be able to evaluate the type of impression the expert is likely to make on the jury or fact finder. Intangibles, such as whether the expert appears to be credible and likeable, are best learned in face-to-face meetings.

These meetings can also be useful in that they help experts bond with potential clients. During the meeting, the expert has an opportunity to get the potential client to like him. If the client likes the expert, she will be much more likely to retain him.

One of the best ways to set up a meeting with a potential client is to offer to take the client to lunch. Attorneys are hesitant to turn down a free meal, especially if the person who is treating can help them win their next big case. Obviously, no one can take every attorney in the country out to lunch. The key to making the one-on-one meeting technique cost-effective is to narrow down a target market and try to meet with the lawyers who are the best prospects. For example, a tobacco expert should meet with the lawyers doing the tobacco litigation in her geographic area.

The client will use the meeting to try to see if the expert would be useful to her. Specifically, she will look at the following seven points.

1. Qualifications

Is the expert truly qualified in the area where he claims expertise?

2. Credibility

Is the expert a hired gun? Is testify all he does?

3. Track record

How many cases has the expert been involved in? What has been the result of these?

4. Ability to communicate

Would the expert do well in front of a judge and jury?

5. Availability

Is the expert available if a case goes to trial, or is he always traveling?

6. Honesty

Does the expert "call them as he sees them," or is he biased?

7. Cost

Based upon the size of the case, is the expert affordable? Is the expert local such that there will not be large travel costs?

An expert should bring to the meeting his business card, his current CV, and any letters of reference from satisfied clients. He may also want to bring along copies of articles he has written. His goal is to have the attorney remember him and to be able to easily contact him. The expert can also learn, if he asks, about other attorneys who may be interested in his services.

Cost-Benefit Analysis

The cost of this marketing technique is very small. It is, therefore, an easy method to test. A support person can set up the meetings. The meetings themselves should take less than an hour and lunch is not an expensive meal. Two additional advantages are immediate feedback and ease of tracking. When meeting one-on-one with someone, an individual can usually get a good idea of whether he is connecting with the other party. Finally, tracking meetings is easy. If an expert gets a case from an attorney he met with, he can probably assume it was a result of that meeting.

18.11 Directories

One effective method for marketing services as an expert is to pay to be listed in a printed directory of experts. Directories can be local, state, or national in scope. Some directories are limited as to the type of experts listed (for example, IME physicians or medical experts), while others combine experts from all fields in the same directory. (A listing of online and print directories is provided in Appendix L.) As in most forms of advertising, the expert should determine the following when deciding on being listed in a directory.

- What is the *fee* to be listed and how often is the fee due?
- What is the *circulation* of the directory and is this *guaranteed* in writing?
- Who will *receive* the directory? (Will it be lawyers, insurance companies, etc?)
- What is the *geographic breakdown* of the *circulation* of the directory? (If an expert lives in Maine, is it wise to participate in a directory where 70% of the distribution is on the West Coast?)
- How *large is the directory?* How many pages is it? What is its trim size? If possible, it is a good idea to obtain a past directory to see the quality and feel of the publication.
- How *often* does the directory come out? Is it annual? Semi-annual? When will the expert be listed?
- *What information and how much information will the expert be permitted to list* in the directory? Is the directory arranged alphabetically by specialty, by the name of the expert, geographically, or in some other fashion?
- *What will be the surrounding directory listings?* For example, an arborist may not feel comfortable following an abortion specialist. One can just imagine the cross-examination possibilities.
- *Who has already signed up* for the directory? Who has signed up for the directory in the past?
- Is the *directory indexed?* If so, how is it indexed?
- How *long has the publishing company been in existence* and what is their reputation?
- Is there any *guarantee or money-back offer* if one is not satisfied with the results?
- Will there be advertising in the directory? If so, how much will there be and who is likely to advertise?
- If the directory is online, do other online directories link to it? This may be explored by examining the links that the directory lists (often the links are there because of reciprocity agreements, and there will be a corresponding link in the other directory) and by exploring the links at other directories. When an attorney conducts a search on one online directory and fails to find the expert he wants, the attorney may move on to another directory—the first ones he will try will be the ones listed in the initial directory.
- If the directory is online, how much effort and money does the publisher spend to promote the site? If they do not promote the site aggressively, it will not be visited and the individuals listed will not get referrals.

Due diligence on the part of the expert is highly recommended. She should know what she is getting into and make an informed decision as to its likely cost-effectiveness. As with all marketing techniques, experts should take care to track the results so that they can determine if continued listing in a particular directory is cost-effective.

Backlash

As with any advertisement, a listing in a directory can be used against an expert on cross-examination in an attempt to show bias. To minimize this risk, the expert needs to be careful in who he lists with and in what his listing actually says. It is critical to avoid any imprecise language that could tend to indicate bias.

Cost-Benefit Analysis

Directory listings require a relatively small amount of time to complete. The cost will vary, but will generally be recouped with the first referral. Because the out-of-pocket risk and the time commitment are small, directory listings are a good candidate for testing. If an expert has done his due diligence and has a good feel for a particular directory, he should try a listing. If it works, he has made some money and gained a valuable client. An expert should only renew the listing because it keeps on working. If the listing doesn't work, he shouldn't renew it. The losses will be very limited.

18.12 Advertisements

Advertising may be a cost-effective way to market a forensic practice. There are two general types of advertising, classified ads and display ads. Each is discussed below. For any advertising to be effective, the publication it is in must reach the target audience of attorneys. Before advertising in a publication, one should verify the total distribution of the publication (how many copies of the ad will get into the marketplace?), whether it is free or paid for (attorneys are more likely to actually read something they had to pay for), the geographical distribution (does it zero-in on attorneys in a region, or is it spread from coast to coast?), and the specialty of the attorneys that read it (is it a publication for trial attorneys only, or is it for all attorneys, many of whom never hire experts?).

After placing an ad, the expert needs to follow up on it by reading the publication in question. It is not uncommon for publishers to make mistakes in typesetting or publishing an ad. If there is a mistake, the expert should inform the publisher immediately. Otherwise, the expert may have difficulty in obtaining a refund.

Classified advertisements

Classified advertisements can be a cost-effective way to market services. Classified ads are usually sold by the line or word. To save money, an expert may chose not to repeat the category she is listed under in the classified section. For example, if Dr. Jones is a toxicologist and is listed under "Toxicology," she could probably omit "toxicology" from her advertisement.

The most important factor that will determine whether a classified ad will work is duration. A classified ad must run for a long time if it is to have any reasonable chance of success. This cannot be overemphasized. The authors recommend a one-year minimum to properly test this marketing media. When listing for long periods, an expert should be sure to ask the publisher for any applicable discounts.

A classified ad need *not* be an attention-getter. Basic information is usually sufficient to generate leads. What usually transpires is that an interested attorney will call every listing in the category. Whether the expert gets the referral will then be up to the strength of his CV and communication skills. The shortness of a classified ad has the added benefit of reducing the potential backlash from advertising. A good classified ad has basic information and may highlight the area that makes an expert stand out in his field.

Example 18.4
Economist. M.I.T. Faculty. Nancy D. Marinelli. 617-555-1234.

Display advertisements

Display ads are typical ads found in any publication. They are usually sold by the size of the ad. A display ad must have a "hook" to draw the reader's attention. Because display ads are expensive and may easily miss the expert's target audience, they are not recommended by the authors.

Backlash

An expert can, of course, be confronted with her advertising on cross-examination. The shorter the ad, the less ammunition the cross-examiner will have. This is another advantage of a short, basic classified advertisement. When confronted with questions concerning whether one advertises, it may be best to answer the question simply and directly. This avoids being evasive and forces counsel to move on.

Example 18.5
Q. Isn't it a fact that you advertise in *National Law Day?*
A. Yes.

There is nothing unseemly about dignified advertising and there are very few types of professionals who do not advertise. One only needs to pick up any Yellow Pages directory in the country. The largest section of advertisers will probably be for lawyers. To minimize the potential backlash from advertising the expert needs to 1) keep it short and 2) be very careful about what is written in the ad.

Cost-Benefit Analysis

Display ads are usually not cost-effective for experts. Classified ads, on the other hand, may be very cost-effective. The time involved in drafting the ad is small and the ongoing time commitment is negligible. The cost of a one-year ad may be justified to test whether classified ads will work. The expert should keep the ad simple and run it for a year. He shouldn't waste money by advertising in a publication that doesn't reach his target audience. Also, an expert shouldn't forget to track his referrals by asking contacts how they found out about him. If experts don't track referrals, they'll never know if their ads worked.

18.13 Direct Mail

Direct mail is another way that experts can market their services. (Some sample marketing letters are provided in Appendix W.) There are several points to remember about direct mail.

1. The most important factor in any direct mail campaign is the mailing list.

The list is everything. The advantage of direct mail is that an individual can put her material in front of her target audience—if she has the proper list.

2. Direct mail is expensive and time-consuming.

Total costs include drafting, designing, printing, mailing, list rental or assembly, postage, and proofing. Depending upon the size of the piece and the volume of the mailing, the final cost could be well over $1 per piece.

3. Lawyers and other busy professionals usually throw out 99% of the mail they identify as junk mail.

4. Direct mail pieces in envelopes usually work the best.

5. Direct mail campaigns can be repeated and remain effective.

6. Direct mail is a good medium to test new markets.

7. Attorneys will save their expert witness direct mail and CVs and file them for the future.

8. First-class, personalized, stamped mail in envelopes gets opened the most.

It's also the most expensive type of direct mail.

Backlash
Anything said in a direct mail piece can and will be used against an expert on cross-examination. To minimize the potential damage, experts should make sure that whatever they write is objective and does not indicate bias. It is also wise to keep it short. The best designed pieces are 100% objective and professional.[1] If asked whether she markets by direct mail, an expert should defuse the situation by answering yes. She should not make matters worse by being evasive.

Cost-Benefit Analysis
Because of the tremendous time and cost of direct mail campaigns, they are usually not the best option for individual experts.[2] One exception could be, however, extremely personalized and targeted direct mail. This would involve an expert identifying his best target market. For example, the one hundred best, most active medical malpractice attorneys in a particular state. It could be very effective to send each a personalized letter saying, for example, "I am enclosing for your convenience a copy of an article of mine which was recently published in....I have also enclosed an updated CV reflecting this publication and other recent accomplishments." This is professional and gives value to that attorney.

The key here is always the mailing list. A *small, well-targeted* mailing list may very well be cost-effective. Mass mailings, on the other hand, generally aren't cost-effective. An expert should develop and maintain a list of key attorneys. As always, an expert should track referrals, otherwise he'll never know what worked and what didn't. Finally, one shouldn't give up if there isn't an immediate response. Attorneys will often save a direct mail piece for the future when they may need it.

18.14 Newsletters
Newsletters are a subset of direct mail. The creation, development, and mailing (distribution) of a complimentary newsletter to potential clients can be effective in generating referrals. Because the newsletter is of value to the recipient, it is much more likely to be read than junk mail. It also is professional and may be less susceptible to backlash than a typical direct mail solicitation. Newsletters can be retained as a reference and help reinforce one's expertise. The expert's goal is a well-researched, fully documented, practical, cutting-edge newsletter that leads to the inescapable conclusion that

---

[1] "Dear Attorney Jones. I was referred to you by Attorney Tom Smith, who I met at a recent bar association meeting where I had been invited to speak. Attorney Smith suggested that I send you a copy of my CV, which I have enclosed for your convenience. Please call me if you have any questions, comments, or concerns."
[2] This may be different for a large group of experts. Also, national referral agencies use direct mail to promote their groups of experts cost-effectively.

the expert knows her field and should be considered for consultations and retention.

Backlash

If a newsletter is designed as a true newsletter, there will be very little backlash. Two areas to look out for are *puff pieces* and controversial issues. Experts should avoid puff pieces that are merely self-promotions. Instead, it is best to stick to real stories of interest to the reader. Also, one must be very careful about writing about controversial issues. Anything an expert writes can and will be used against him on the witness stand. This includes opinions expressed in his newsletter.

Cost-Benefit Analysis

The key to making newsletters cost-effective is keeping the time and out-of-pocket expenses down. Both can be controlled by strictly limiting the number of issues written and the number of copies mailed each year. Some recommendations for creating a cost-effective marketing newsletter follow.

1. Limit the number of pages and the number of issues each year

Many experts underestimate the time and effort that is required to put together a newsletter. Limiting the newsletter to four pages published four times a year will be enough to achieve marketing goals without overburdening oneself with work.

2. Make the newsletter useful

Newsletters that contain puff pieces about degrees the expert has obtained are not retained and, in most cases, are not even read by potential clients. Newsletters that contain breaking stories and practical information are more likely to be read and retained.

3. Three-hole punch the newsletter

By three-hole punching a newsletter, the expert encourages the retention of the newsletter in a binder.

4. Encourage feedback

By encouraging feedback through the readers' questions, letters, and phone calls, the expert will, in effect, encourage potential clients to contact him.

5. Distribution

The key to success will be to create a useful, easy-to-read newsletter distributed to potential clients. The distribution can be by direct mail, handing out at seminars and meetings, or any other way one can get the newsletter into the hands of potential clients. With the increasing use of the Internet and

World Wide Web, experts should consider distributing their newsletter electronically as well as by mailing.

18.15 Online Marketing

Lawyers and other potential clients are using the Internet more and more to find experts. Thus, the expert can use the Internet to market his forensic services. Strategies the expert should consider include:

1. Create and maintain a Web site.
2. List with online expert directories.
3. Use e-mail to disseminate information or newsletters to potential clients.

Web sites[3]

A recent analysis of a leading national legal publication found that approximately 40% of the expert classified advertisers list a Web site in their ad. This percentage will continue to grow. The reasons are obvious: the Web site provides a potential client with immediate, 24-hour access to the expert's CV, publications, and other information.

William G. Dobson, an expert who developed and ran an online expert marketing service, recommends the following with regard to an expert's Web page:

What Should Be on Your Web Page

1) A brief description of what you offer
2) Your current CV (absolutely!) and associates
3) Your picture
4) Your fees and payment requirements
5) Anything else you think is appropriate, such as articles or reprints
6) Provide content!
7) Link to other Web sites - don't be a dead end!

(Keep it low key, professional in appearance and tone).[4]

---

[3] We will use the terms *Web site* and *Web page* interchangeably. A Web site begins as a collection of Web pages and can contain other tools and features. One can put as many Web pages as needed—or as many as fit within the size limit—on the Web site.

[4] William B. Dobson, *Marketing Services Online.* Outline presented at the 5th Annual National Expert Witness and Litigation Seminar in Hyannis, Massachusetts (June 20-21, 1996).

Designing and maintaining a Web page is straightforward. The software is inexpensive—usually free—and it operates like a word processor. This is the *design* portion of maintaining a Web site that almost anyone can do at a rudimentary level.

The Web site will need to be "put" somewhere. Usually, this means one needs a *Web host*. The Web host maintains a server on which the Web site resides. Web hosting services have become quite inexpensive—again, some are now free. *Internet service providers* (the companies that provide connections to the World Wide Web, often the same companies that provide e-mail service) may provide Web hosting services.[5]

Sophisticated experts who develop Web sites understand that the sites are of limited value if no one can find them. Without promotion an expert will simply be lost in cyberspace. Experts should not rely on *search engines* (discussed below) to generate traffic to their Web sites. Instead, they should place their Web page address on their letterhead, correspondence, advertising, and all other marketing materials.

Linking is also crucial if an expert wants to get traffic on her page. Linking a Web page to aligned experts, groups, associations, nonprofits, and discussion groups will help drive potential clients to an expert's site. Original content, such as articles, or links to related sites or discussion groups on an expert's Web page will help retain the interest of potential clients once they find the page. Finally, experts should make sure that their contact information is easy to find. The authors suggest displaying it on each page of the Web site. It is best to avoid bells and whistles. The wise expert keeps her site simple, professional, and useful.

<u>Search engines.</u> The expert can increase the visibility of the page by registering with Internet *search engines*. This process will help with Web site promotion, but will rarely be as important as promoting the site address and linking to other sites. Attorneys don't have time to surf the Web.

[5] Many Web hosting options exist. An individual may place her site on the "personal Web page" that her ISP may provide with her account. Or, she can place a Web page on a free-page Web site, a few of which are maintained by certain online expert witness directories. These simply offer to place (and, usually, maintain) an individual's Web page on their Web site. This arrangement will limit what an expert can do with her Web site and limits how much information about her services and professional history she can provide, but it will fulfill the main purpose of the Web site—namely, unlimited access to information about one's forensic services. The best option, however, is to obtain a *virtual Web site* from one's Web host. This involves renting space on the Web host's server. Then the expert can create and register her domain name (the part before the .com, .org, .net, etc.). Essentially, the expert will then own the name. Moreover, the Web site will appear more professional. Www.networksolutions.com offers more information about registering domain names. Web hosts can also register the name.

Furthermore, it's time consuming for experts to keep updating their search engine registrations.

A search engine searches the Web for sites and pages that contain the keyword or words entered by the person conducting the search. For example, a Web user enters the keywords *expert witness* into a search engine, such as Yahoo!. The search engine then displays a list of Web sites and Web pages containing the term *expert witness*. Many search engines only display sites that have been registered with that specific search engine. Thus, the expert must register her page with the search engine to ensure that it will appear in that list of search results. The home page of various search engines will supply information on how to register a Web site or a Web page. However, this "do-it-yourself" site registration can be quite time-consuming because there are hundreds of search engines. Experts should consider using a registration service to register their sites for them.[6] Most services charge a fee, but an expert will save countless hours by using the service. The authors suggest manually registering with the ten major search engines,[7] then choosing and using a registration service to maximize coverage.

Search engine directories. Many search engines contain *directories* (again, Yahoo! is an example). These directories categorize sites and allow a searcher to explore the Web by following increasingly specific categories. Registering with search engines as discussed above will generally get the expert's site into that engine's directory.[8]

Link directories. Another avenue through which an expert can promote her site is the *link directory*. Link directories are Web sites that contain directories and lists of links to related sites. Some of these sites are run by individuals, but in the expert witness field many more of them exist as part of large compilations of legal resources. Both variations of link directories get mentioned in discussion groups (Internet mailing lists and newsgroups), in the press, and by word of mouth. Thus, the expert should find these directories and add them as links to her site. (A list of legal research indices in Appendix N contains several sites that maintain link directories of expert witnesses.) Usually, the Web site will provide contact information and/or instructions on how to add a link to a site. When submitting a link or a request to be listed,

---

[6] For example: www.worldsubmit.com

[7] These are: Alta Vista (www.altavista.com), Excite (www.excite.com), HotBot (www.hotbot.com), InfoSeek (www.infoseek.com), LookSmart (www.looksmart.com), Lycos (www.lycos.com), Northern Light (www.northernlight.com), Snap (www.snap.com), WebCrawler (www.webcrawler.com), and Yahoo! (www.yahoo.com).

[8] However, the expert should probably register manually with the directories at these three sites: Excite, Yahoo!, and NetGuide Live. See Peter Kent, *Poor Richard's Web Site* (Lakewood, CO: Top Floor, 1998).

an expert should provide a short description of her site along with the URL she wants listed. Examples of link directories include:

- *Larry Anderson's Expert Witness Page* at `www.home.earthlink.net/~laanderson/experts.htm`

- or the *WashLaw WEB* at `www.washlaw.edu`

Online expert directories

The second method used to market expert services online is by paying a fee (or without payment, in some cases) to be listed in an online directory of experts. As with any printed directory, the questions experts need to ask the publisher/provider are:

- How is the site promoted?
- What is the cost to be listed?
- How often is the fee due?
- How many experts are listed?
- How long have you been in business?
- How many hits does the directory get each month and is the number increasing or decreasing?
- What is your retention/renewal rate of experts? (This will be indicative of client satisfaction.)
- How often is the site updated?
- How often does the site go down?
- How is the site indexed?
- How easy is it for a potential client to locate an expert? (The potential client should try it for herself.)
- With which other directories is the site linked?
- Is there a money-back guarantee?
- Can an expert link into her personal Web site to enhance her listing?
- Does the attorney pay to use the site? (He'll be more likely to use it if it's free.)

By far the most important question to ask is how the site is promoted. How much is the site sponsor spending on marketing the site, where are they advertising, and what links do they have to related sites? The World Wide Web has millions of Web pages. The key question is how will a potential client find the online directory and the expert's contact information? If they do not sponsor it by promoting and advertising the site, the expert is probably wasting his money. Generally speaking, promotion and linkage are required to generate traffic. Search engines themselves aren't generally effective. The expert should look at the resources and the sites that attorneys use, such as legal research sites (refer to the examples in Appendix N), legal publications (examples are provided in Appendix M), and bar associations (listings appear in Appendix O) and verify any prospective expert witness directory's marketing presence.

Due diligence is the key to marketing services with an online directory. Experts should visit the site, assess whether it is user friendly, and review the extent of its coverage. Does the directory contain numerous experts in a wide array of fields? Clients will be less inclined to use an online directory if coverage is thin and fails to offer experts that meet the needs of clients. As with previous marketing techniques, tracking the results of any online marketing effort is necessary to make informed decisions regarding renewals. (Appendix L lists several online directories.)

E-mail

E-mail can be used to deliver newsletters and direct-mail type messages inexpensively. However, there are obvious problems with the use of e-mail as a marketing tool. Junk e-mail ("spam") is more likely to annoy recipients than to result in referrals. For experts, the use of e-mail is most effective if what is delivered is substantive and useful to the recipient. For example, if an expert developed a database of e-mail addresses, she could deliver her newsletter online in e-mail format. This would greatly reduce her out-of-pocket newsletter expenses.

E-mail can also be used to send "ad hoc" newsletters of substance. This gives an expert publicity and credibility without wedding her to a printed newsletter and its deadlines. For example, one could send an e-mail with "RE: *New Study on Second-hand Smoke*" as the subject. Then, in the body of the e-mail, the expert could provide a synopsis of the study and a link to her Web site. The Web site would have more information on the subject as well as links to relevant sites.

As Seth Godin notes, "The Internet is the greatest direct marketing medium ever invented. It is not TV."[9] To capitalize on this technology, experts may want to use e-mail in conjunction with their Web sites. An interactive combination is effective—it allows experts to notify and *maintain* contact with clients by low-cost e-mail, allows them to offer these clients useful, relevant information, and then provides clients with a way to contact the expert and to offer commentary.

<u>Networking.</u> E-mail can also be used as a quick and easy follow-up to networking. "Jim, it was nice meeting you at the recent bar meeting. Attached is my CV. Regards, Steve Joyce." An expert who stays in someone's mind is the one who is most likely to get referrals.

---

[9] Seth Godin, *Permission Marketing* (New York: Simon & Schuster, 1999) 155.

Backlash
Like any form of marketing, anything an expert says or writes online can be used against him. Some rules of thumb may help. Experts should:

1. keep it objective and avoid puffery,
2. not appear biased,
3. provide content, not ad copy, and
4. answer cross-examination marketing questions directly.

Cost-Benefit Analysis
Online marketing can be a cost-effective, low-risk marketing technique. If an expert's Web site is well promoted and well linked, it will serve as a 24-hours a day/seven-days a week resource for attorneys. The development and maintenance costs of a small Web site are not overwhelming. Online directories that are well promoted and linked can be as, or more, effective than print directories. Their relatively low cost is such that they might be worth a try. E-mail can be a very cost-effective way to deliver content and to keep in touch with potential clients.

18.16 Conclusion

There are many different techniques that experts can use to market their forensic services professionally. Experts who wish to increase the amount of time they spend in forensic work should consider trying one or more of these techniques. They should then repeat the techniques that were shown to be cost-effective and discard the others. An expert's marketing activities can, however, be used against him on the witness stand. Therefore, all marketing material should be drafted carefully and should not indicate any bias.

Chapter 19 Fees, Billings, and Collections

19.1 Introduction

An expert witness is entitled to be paid a reasonable fee for her time and expertise.[1] The successful expert understands the engagement process, how much to charge, what to charge for, and how and when to collect her fees.

19.2 The Engagement Process

Experts should have the key financial terms of their engagement clearly laid out in writing before agreeing to work on a case. (Sample fee schedules, letters, and agreements are provided in Appendix R.) The key terms that these documents need to specifically cover include fees, billings, retainers, travel, expenses, and interest for overdue accounts.[2]

Fees

This is the hourly rate charged for the expert's time. Some experts charge an increased hourly rate for deposition and trial. Some experts also charge a minimum rate for depositions (for example, two hours) and trial (for example, a half day or four hours). Contingency fee agreements by experts—those that are in whole or in part contingent upon success in a case—are unethical and illegal in most states and should be avoided.

Billings

This is how often the client is to be billed—usually every 30 days. Also included are payment terms, also usually 30 days or net 30.

Retainers

1. How much of a retainer is required in order to commence the engagement? Sophisticated experts require, at a minimum, an initial retainer. The required payment of an initial retainer may help to weed out bad credit risks.

2. Is the retainer refundable? The nonrefundable portion of a retainer compensates the expert for those cases in which he is "conflicted out" of other work or for those situations where the case settles after the expert is designated by counsel.

3. Is the retainer replenishable? Sophisticated experts ask for a replenishable retainer. A replenishable retainer is where the expert is always paid in advance and will do no further work until the amount of the retainer will cover the anticipated time he will spend on the case. Replenishable

[1] As an expert, an individual is paid for her time, not for her testimony.

[2] Most fee letters also contain the expert's taxpayer ID number.

retainers eliminate all collections problems dealing with fees for an expert's time.

Travel

How an expert charges for travel. Some experts charge portal-to-portal, especially for local travel. This means that they charge their hourly rate from the moment they leave their office until the moment they return. Some experts charge a flat rate for out-of-state travel (for example, ten times their hourly fee).

Expenses

What the expert will seek reimbursement for. This may include, but is not limited to, photocopying, couriers, research, telephone (including wireless calls and fax charges), and travel expenses.

Interest

This is the interest that will be added to overdue accounts.

Using a fee letter or agreement will protect experts against troublesome attorneys. There are two reasons for this. First, the document will serve as evidence of what was agreed to. Second, the document will be diagnostic in nature. If the attorney balks at sending a retainer in response to a document, she is an attorney an expert probably does not, from a practice management standpoint, want to get involved with. Sophisticated experts also investigate potential clients to check on their reputation in the legal community. One or two phone calls to fellow experts or attorneys can help avoid problematic engagements.

19.3 Setting the Correct Rate

One of the most important decisions an expert needs to make is setting the correct rate for her time. If an expert charges too much, she may price herself out of the market. If she charges too little, she may not seem credible and may be charging less than her true value. In many years of dealing with this issue, the authors have developed two steadfast rules.

Two rules of fee setting

1. **Far more experts undercharge than overcharge.** This is usually the result of inexperience and a psychological hesitancy to charge a rate of hundreds of dollars per hour for the expert's time.
2. **When experts increase their fees, the volume of work they receive increases.** Attorneys are paid to win and seek out the best possible experts. Many assume that because an expert charges more, she is a better expert. This assumption results in increased demand for the best experts who charge a premium for their services.

There are many factors that affect how much an expert can charge in a certain case. These include the expert's qualifications, his reputation as a witness, his communication skills, the amount at stake in the litigation, the availability of other experts, how much the expert's time is worth objectively, and legal limits to expert fees. (A 1998 fee survey of medical experts, by specialty, is provided in Appendix X.)

Qualifications

The world's leading expert on a particular topic will generally be able to command a higher fee for his time.

Example 19.1
Recently, the authors were retained by a client to find the leading experts on a particular type of pharmaceutical. We conducted a world-wide literature search and developed a list of 5–7 names. When it came time for these individuals to negotiate fees, they were in a very strong bargaining position.

Reputation as a witness

Someone with the reputation of being a formidable witness will be able to command a higher fee. An expert's value to the attorney is very much determined by how well the expert performs in front of a jury—the people who ultimately decide the case. One's reputation as a witness can be established by word of mouth and through jury verdict reporters. The converse is also true. Someone with a reputation as an ineffective witness will not be able to command a premium fee and might not be offered any work at all.

Example 19.2
In a certain type of toxic tort litigation that the authors used to practice, there was a particular expert witness who usually testified for the defense. The witness was a petite woman in her sixties. Juries *loved* her and she was very effective. Her reputation as a witness was so strong, in fact, that merely naming her as a witness in a case had a substantial effect on its settlement value. As such, she was in a very strong bargaining position regarding her fees.

Communication skills

If an expert does not yet possess a reputation as being a good witness, attorneys will estimate how well they think he will be able to communicate with and persuade a jury. This will usually be done while the attorney is interviewing the expert during their initial discussions of the case. If the expert can demonstrate that he is a superior communicator and that a jury would probably like him, he will be able to command a higher fee.

Example 19.3
An attorney has done a literature search to locate two or three individuals that have published in a particular field of expertise. The expert that will be in the most demand will be the one that demonstrates the best communication and persuasion skills. In the end, the expert's ability to communicate with and persuade the jury is what makes the expert valuable.

The amount at stake in the litigation

If a case is worth a significant amount of money, the amount paid for expert witness time will be a very minor consideration. For example, in a $2.5 million malpractice case, the top concern of the lawyers will not be whether the experts are paid $350 or $450 per hour. The lawyers want and need to win and will usually be willing to spend whatever it takes to get the expert they need. On the other hand, if a case involves a small amount of money, say a $5,000 property dispute, the attorneys may be very cost-sensitive regarding fees for expert witnesses. There is usually no point in winning a $5,000 case if you run up $7,000 in expert witness fees in the process.

Availability of other experts

The rarer an individual's expertise, the higher the fee she will command. If, on the other hand, there is an oversupply of an individual's expertise, she will command a lower fee.

Example 19.4
A chiropractor in New York City will generally not be able to command an exceptionally high fee. The reason is simple. There are plenty of other chiropractors in New York City for attorneys to use.

Example 19.5
One of the authors is the country's most recognized experts on a particular legal topic. At one point there was a major case taking place in a rural part of the country 2,000 miles from where he lived. He was able to command a high fee and such concessions as portal-to-portal billing for his entire two-day trip. The reason for this was simple. Under the law of supply and demand, he was the only "supply."

How much an expert's time is worth objectively

An expert will command a higher fee for forensic work if she can show that she is forgoing other lucrative work in order to devote time to the case. She will be in a stronger bargaining position with the attorney when it comes time to negotiate her fee because she can point to the income she is forgoing.

Example 19.6
Attorney: As I understand it, you're looking for $500 per hour for your time. How can you expect me to pay that much?

Expert: The microsurgery opportunities I give up and my ongoing overhead demand that I charge $500 per hour.

Legal limitations

Experts appearing in certain administrative forums may be limited by statute, regulation, or custom as to how much they may be permitted to charge. For example, in workers' compensation cases some states limit the amounts experts can charge. Experts should check with the agencies and/or counsel prior to accepting these assignments. When an opposing party is legally required to pay for the expert's time, for example, in depositions in most jurisdictions, there may be a legal requirement that the expert's fee be reasonable.[3]

Example 19.7: "Reasonableness" of the expert witness fee
Anthony v. Abbott Laboratories, 106 F.R.D. 461 (D.R.I. 1985)
The plaintiff's medical witness requested a deposition fee of $420 an hour. The defense contested the request on the grounds that the fee was unreasonable. The court held that there must be a reasonable relationship between the services rendered and the amount to which an expert is entitled, then reduced the fee to $250 an hour. The court also found the following factors noteworthy:

1. the expert charged a "friendly" litigant $250 per hour;
2. the expert had little or no discernable overhead;
3. annualization of the requested fee resulted in an exorbitant yearly income; and
4. the requested rate was not merely high, but "astronomical."

Example 19.8: "Reasonableness" of the expert witness fee
Goldwater v. Postmaster General of the United States, 136 F.R.D. 337 (D. Conn. 1991)
In this case, a postal employee sued for wrongful termination. During discovery, the defendant deposed the plaintiff's expert, a psychiatrist. The defendant contended that the expert's fee was unreasonable. The court established and applied the criteria that should be considered in determining the reasonableness of an expert's fee:

1. the witness's area of expertise;
2. the education and training required to provide the expert insight sought;
3. the prevailing rates of other comparably qualified experts;
4. the nature, quality, and complexity of the discovery responses provided;
5. the cost of living in the particular geographic area; and
6. any other factor likely to assist the court in balancing Rule 26 interests.

Then, the court found the psychiatrist's fee to be extravagant and reduced it from $450 per hour to $200 per hour.

[3] Fed. R. Civ. Pro. 26(b)(4)(c).

Example 19.9: "Reasonableness" of the expert witness fee
Jochims v. Isuzu Motors, Ltd., 141 F.R.D. 493 (S.D. Iowa 1992)
Goldwater was refined in *Jochims v. Isuzu Motors, Ltd.* The case was a products liability action and the plaintiff's main liability expert—a PhD—was an associate professor of mechanical and aerospace engineering. The expert had been charging the plaintiff between $150 and $250 for activities such as computer modeling and crash avoidance research. However, the expert requested $500 for time spent at deposition. The court in *Jochims* relied on the factors set forth in *Goldwater*, with the exception of the fifth factor, believing that the cost of living in a particular geographic area is not directly relevant to a reasonable fee and is "frequently, at least indirectly, calibrated into prevailing market rates." The court also added the following two factors:

1. the fee actually being charged to the party retaining the expert; and
2. fees traditionally charged by the expert on related matters.

After applying these factors, the court reduced the fee to $250.

Example 19.10: Annualized income
(Courts will often take the rate requested by an expert, multiply it by a forty-hour work week and annualize the income to illustrate the extravagance of the fee.)
Hose v. Chicago & North Western Transportation Co., 154 F.R.D. 222 (S.D. Iowa 1994)
The expert, a physician specializing in neurology and disability evaluations, was deposed by the defendant in a Federal Employer's Liability Act action. The expert billed the defendant $800 an hour—in addition to $160 for reviewing medical records. The court declared that neither the expert's background, training, nor the status of his location entitled him to the rate sought. The court then multiplied $800 an hour by 40 hours a week to show that the expert would earn $1.6 million a year at $800 an hour. The court then reduced the fees to $400 an hour.

Example 19.11: Conduct of the witness at the deposition
(Where the witness is evasive or argumentative in the deposition, a court may find that this conduct warrants a reduction in an exorbitant fee.)
Goldwater v. Postmaster General of the United States, 136 F.R.D. 337 (D. Conn. 1991)
Here, a postal employee sued for wrongful termination. During discovery, the defendant deposed the plaintiff's expert psychiatrist. The defendant contended that the expert's fee was unreasonable. The court noted that the expert was at times evasive and argumentative. "The quality of the answers noted in the portions of the transcript perused by the court hardly warrants a fee more than twice that requested by other comparably respected psychiatrists."

Example 19.12: The time and place of the deposition
(A court may consider the inconveniences that a deposition poses upon an expert's professional practice and the losses to the expert stemming from that inconvenience.)

Hose v. Chicago & North Western Transportation Co., 154 F.R.D. 222 (S.D. Iowa 1994)
The deposition in this case was conducted at the offices of the expert after normal business hours. The court found no "disruption" or "inconvenience" to the expert's regular practice, thus a premium fee was not warranted.

Example 19.13: Fee charged to other clients
(The court may consider how much the expert charges his patients or professional clients and compare that rate to the rate sought in litigation.)
Dominguez v. Syntex Laboratories, Inc., 149 F.R.D. 166 (S.D. Ind. 1993)
The plaintiff's expert, a neurologist specializing in smell and taste disorders, requested $860 an hour for deposition testimony. The court noted that he charged his patients only $94 an hour for office visits, which "presumably" cost more to conduct than a visit with an attorney. The court reduced the expert's deposition fee to $341 an hour.

Hose v. Chicago & North Western Transportation Co., 154 F.R.D. 222 (S.D. Iowa 1994)
A neurologist requesting $800 an hour for his deposition charged his patients the same rate for neurological testing, but this did not make his fee request reasonable.

Example 19.14: Fee schedule
(If the expert has a fee schedule that lists a variety of rates for various litigation services, a court may be persuaded to find that the fee for "responding to discovery" bears no reasonable relationship to the expert's services or credentials.)
Kirby v. Ahmad, 63 Ohio Misc. 2d 533, 635 N.E.2d 98 (Ohio Com. Pl. 1994)
In a medical malpractice case, the plaintiff's medical expert, an MD, set out on his fee schedule fees of $500 per hour for a discovery deposition and $750 per hour for a video deposition. "What rational basis exists for the disparity of the hourly rate between a written deposition and a visual deposition is incomprehensible to this court."

Example 19.15: Affidavits from comparable witnesses or attorneys
(A court may consider affidavits from comparable experts setting forth their standard fees for expert witness services, or counsel can provide the court with an affidavit setting forth the attorney's experience in retaining comparable experts and the fees charged in connection with other litigation.)
Dominguez v. Syntex Laboratories, Inc., 149 F.R.D. 166 (S.D. Ind. 1993)
The defendant's expert witness, a neurologist specializing in smell and taste disorders, was described by the plaintiffs' expert as one of the "gurus" in his field. The defendant's expert provided an affidavit setting forth his maximum fee of $300 per hour, which was $560 per hour less than the rate sought by the plaintiffs' expert witness. The court considered this discrepancy when reducing the plaintiff's fee to $341 an hour.

Mathis v. Nynex, 165 F.R.D. 23 (E.D.N.Y. 1996)
The plaintiff's expert, a psychiatrist, charged the defendant $250 per hour for time spent at deposition. The defense argued that $150 was reasonable. The court deemed $250 reasonable and noted that the plaintiff's expert was as qualified as the defendant's expert, whom the defendant was paying $300 per hour. The court also noted that the plaintiff's expert charged the plaintiff $250 per hour, regularly charged the same rate for his consultative services, and only testified twice as an expert in the prior thirty-two years.

Example 19.16: The expert's deposition testimony on fees
(The court may consider an expert's testimony at deposition, if it has already been taken. Testimony regarding fees may reveal inconsistencies in prior charges, differences in the amounts charged for the same or different services, and charges that vary depending on the party requesting the services.)
Dominguez v. Syntex Laboratories, Inc., 149 F.R.D. 166 (S.D. Ind. 1993)
The plaintiff's expert, a neurologist specializing in smell and taste disorders, requested $860 an hour for deposition testimony. The expert had already testified at deposition that his charge for reviewing records varied from a low of $200 to maybe $260 per hour or $300 per hour. The court considered this testimony, among other factors, when deciding to reduce the expert's deposition fee to $341 per hour.

Example 19.17: The nature of the service performed
(When the expert performs a service that did not need to be performed by the expert, the court may set a lower expert witness fee. For example, a court may reduce fees for a service that is clerical in nature.)
Dominguez v. Syntex Laboratories, Inc., 149 F.R.D. 166 (S.D. Ind. 1993)
The court rejected the plaintiff's expert's claim for $460 an hour for retrieving medical records, which he had to perform himself because his records were not computerized and his handwriting was illegible. The court observed that the expert was asking the defendant not to pay for his medical skills but for his personal clerical skills "which are clearly not as good."

Rosenblum v. Warner & Sons, Inc., 148 F.R.D. 237 (N.D. Ind. 1993)
The court noted that it does not take an expert to make copies of videotapes or photographs. Thus, the court held that fees for one and a half hours claimed by an expert witness for copying videotape and photographs were not reasonable.

Example 19.18: The nature of the expert's business
(If the expert witness is a "professional" expert and provides no services other than expert witness or consulting services, the court may subject an excessive expert witness fee to greater scrutiny.)
Bowen v. Monahan, 163 F.R.D. 571 (D. Neb. 1995)
The plaintiff's medical toxicology expert had an extensive and impressive resume. Additionally, he was exclusively employed in his own corporation as an expert witness and consultant in medical toxicology. The court considered his fee unreasonable and reduced the fee by half, stating, "While plaintiff may contract with any expert of plaintiff's choice and, by agreement, that expert

may charge unusually high rates for services, the discovery process will not automatically tax such unreasonable fees on the defendant."

Example 19.19: How the expert bills expenses
(A court may consider billing practices or requirements that appear extravagant or excessive.)
Bowen v. Monahan, 163 F.R.D. 571 (D. Neb. 1995)
The plaintiff's medical toxicology expert provided an engagement letter establishing that he required reimbursement for first-class airfare, rather than coach, "time and a half" rates for weekends and holidays, and a mileage rate one and a half times the rate utilized by the IRS. The court reduced the fee by one half.

Example 19.20: Concessions of discovering party
Hose v. Chicago & North Western Transportation Co., 154 F.R.D. 222 (S.D. Iowa 1994)
The court set the expert's "reasonable fee" at $400 per hour, instead of the $800 per hour requested, but noted that it would have set the fee at $220 per hour (twice the rate of the expert's record review fee) were it not for the defendants' concession that $400 is a reasonable fee.

Example 19.21: Stress of the deposition
(Subjective fears and stress that a deponent may experience as a result of being deposed do not support the enhancement of an hourly rate.)
U.S. Energy Corp. v. NUKEM, Inc., 163 F.R.D. 344 (D. Colo. 1995)
The plaintiff's expert, an attorney, employed a bifurcated fee structure—$170 for support services and $300 per hour for depositions. The defense contended that the upper end of the scale was unreasonable. The reason presented for this structure was that the adversarial nature of depositions, and the resulting stress, justified the higher rate for appearances at depositions. The court rejected this reasoning and reduced the deposition fee to $235 per hour.

Jochims v. Isuzu Motors, Ltd., 141 F.R.D. 493 (S.D. Iowa 1992)
The court stated that "subjective concerns and fears about the stress of a painstaking and carefully taken deposition by a skilled adversary—while perhaps justified—do not, on this record, support an enhancement of [the expert's] hourly rate by a factor of two."

Example 19.22: Preparation time
Rhee v. Witco Chem. Corp., 126 F.R.D. 45 (N.D. Ill. 1989)
The issue of compensation for the time spent by a deponent in preparing for a deposition was addressed extensively in this case. The court stated "the real issue is raised by plaintiff's demand that defendant pay plaintiff's expert for the time spent by plaintiff's expert 'preparing' for his deposition." The court continued:

> Many courts addressing Rule 26(b)(4)(C) have ordered compensation of experts without elaborating on what constitutes "time spent in responding." *See e.g., Eliasen v. Hamilton,* 111 F.R.D. 396, 404 (N.D. Ill. 1986); *Keith v. Van Dorn*

> *Plastic Machinery Co.*, 86 F.R.D. 458, 460 (E.D.Penn. 1980). Some have limited compensation to time spent in the deposition. *See Cotton v. Consolidation Coal Co.*, 457 F.2d 641, 646-47 (6th Cir. 1972); *Herbst v. Int'l Telephone & Telegraph Corp.*, 65 F.R.D. 528, 531 (D.Conn. 1975). One court has awarded compensation for "preparation" time. *See Carter-Wallace, Inc. v. Hartz Mountain Ind., Inc.*, 553 F. Supp. 45, 53 (S.D.N.Y. 1982). Others, without specifically excluding preparation time, have ordered the seeking party to pay the responding party's expert for time spent travelling to and from, as well as at the deposition. *See, e.g., Henlopen Hotel Corp. v. Aetna Ins. Co.*, 33 F.R.D. 306, 308 n. 6 (D.Del. 1963) (decided prior to 1970 amendment of rule 26). None of these decisions is binding on the court. However, exclusion of "preparation" time is supported by the lack of a provision for compensation for time spent by experts in responding to interrogatories under Rule 26(b)(4)(A)(i). *See, e.g., Keith*, 86 F.R.D. at 460.

Example 19.23: Preparation time
Hurst v. United States, 123 F.R.D. 319 (S.D. 1988)
Reasonable expert witness fee includes time spent preparing for deposition and time during deposition, but not time spent waiting for deposition to conclude.

Example 19.24: Surcharge disallowed
Draper v. Red Devil, Inc., 114 F.R.D. 46 (E.D. Ark. 1987)
Finding no evidence or explanation supporting a $10 "surcharge" that the expert, an engineer, imposed on the discovering party, the court reduced the rate from $120 per hour to $110 per hour.

Example 19.25: Unreasonable fee
Magee v. The Paul Revere Life Ins. Co., 172 F.R.D. 627 (E.D.N.Y. 1997)
In this action, an insured brought suit against a disability insurer for breach of contract by failure to pay benefits. The defendant's expert, a psychologist, was noticed for deposition. The expert sought $250 an hour for preparation time, $350 per hour for travel, and $700 for time spent at the deposition. The court reduced the fees to $250 across the board. The court conceded that the expert was well qualified, but found the fee request unreasonable because he charged the defendant $250 per hour for an examination of the plaintiff, he did not provide evidence of what similar experts charged, and because the plaintiff's experts charged $130 and $250 per hour, while the defendant retained similar experts at $150 and $100 per hour.

Example 19.26: Is $430 per hour reasonable?
Drake v. Wal-Mart, Inc., 876 P.2d 738 (Okla. App. 1994)
In this wrongful death suit against a department store for selling a handgun to a nineteen-year old who later committed suicide using the weapon, the defendant challenged the reasonableness of the plaintiff's expert psychiatrist. The court construed an Oklahoma statute modeled after Rule 26(b)(4)(C). The expert advised the defendant that her fee would be $1,250 if the deposition lasted less than four hours and $2,500 if it lasted more. It lasted four hours and twenty minutes and the expert billed $2,500 and an additional amount for time spent answering interrogatories after the deposition. The court held that the $430 an hour effective rate of the plaintiff's expert witness was reasonable. The court looked to several grounds in making the decision: because the defendant failed

to provide evidence of what the expert charged plaintiffs or other parties, what the expert charged for other depositions or what other similar experts would charge, and because the deposition caused the expert inconvenience and financial loss (the expert's child was ill and required 24-hour care).

When last-minute assignments are accepted, many experts charge a premium fee for weekend or overtime work. Experts can and do commonly charge 150% of their hourly rates for these last-minute assignments. This is, in most cases, reasonable and will be agreed to by the attorney who doesn't have time to find another willing and able expert.

Some expert witness brokers mark-up the experts' fees to clients. Some experts have reduced their fees to reflect this mark-up. This is not ordinarily necessary and is not good business practice. The fact that attorneys still hire an expert despite the mark-up may be an indication that one's fees are too low.

19.4 What to Charge For

Not charging for all that they can and should is a common mistake made by many experts. Experts are usually retained by attorneys. There is no reason, therefore, that an expert should not bill a retaining attorney the same way an attorney would bill *him* if the expert had retained the attorney's services. This means charging for the following.

1. Any and all time spent on the case

This includes preparation time, portal-to-portal travel time, and time spent on brief telephone conversations. It is helpful for experts to keep a notepad at their side to keep track of all of the time they spend on the case.

2. Reasonable out-of-pocket expenses

These include travel expenses, telephone charges, copying expenses, meals, electronic research fees, and all other reasonable out-of-pocket expenses.

3. Reasonable cancellation fees

It is important to establish, in writing, reasonable cancellation fees. Such fees will protect an expert from the loss of time for last-minute cancellations of depositions and other testimony. Sophisticated experts charge reasonable cancellation fees.

Most attorneys would charge for all their time and expenses if an individual retained their services. There is no reason why an expert shouldn't charge them the same way. What she will charge for should be clearly spelled out in her written retention letter or written fee schedule. This will help prevent any misunderstandings concerning what the expert will charge.

19.5 Collecting Fees

Replenishable retainers

Collecting their fees from attorneys is a common problem faced by many experts. By far the best way to avoid collections problems is to collect the fee up front in the form of a replenishable retainer. This is a common technique employed by many experts. When the retainer is used up, the expert can demand further payment before conducting more work or testifying in the case. The single biggest mistake inexperienced experts make in this area is not requiring prepayment of their replenishable retainer. If counsel is hesitant or reluctant to make these payments, the expert should seriously consider *not* accepting the assignment.

The best way to collect out-of-pocket expenses is to have these paid for directly by the retaining attorney in advance of the expert's testimony.

> **Example 19.27**
> Your engagement requires taking a commercial airline flight to attend a deposition out of state. Have the attorney charge your airline tickets to his credit card. You will then not have to worry about your ability to collect for this out-of-pocket expense. You also won't lose any float on the money you fronted for this expense.

Billings

Monthly itemized bills to counsel are highly recommended. (See Appendix S for model expert bills.) The expert witness bills that frequently go unpaid are those presented for the first time at the conclusion of the assignment or case. If an expert's monthly bills are not being paid, he can consider doing no further work on the case until they are satisfied. An expert will have much less leverage to collect his billings if he waits to bill until after a case concludes.

Interest

It is wise to have a written policy that assesses interest on all past-due bills. Charging interest is a good way to discourage slow payment of one's bill.

Depositions

In most jurisdictions, the opposing side is responsible for paying the expert a reasonable fee for taking her deposition. Collection difficulties can arise as a result of this arrangement. To avoid such problems, it is best to insist on payment of the deposition fee up front. Some experts refuse to even schedule a deposition until they have received payment. In cases where the deposition prepayment is used up as a result of the deposition going longer than expected, the expert should, at a minimum, get counsel to agree on the record to pay the expert's hourly rate for the remainder of the deposition within seven business days.

Legal actions

When faced with an outstanding bill for services that counsel or the client refuses to pay, the expert has the following legal options.

1. Retain counsel and file suit based upon the contract or bill for services.
2. File a lawsuit in small claims court (if the amount is fairly small).
3. File a complaint with the local bar association or bar fee arbitration board.
4. Walk away from the bill and refuse to do work for the client again.

None of the above options is nearly as good as getting paid for one's time in the first place. Prevention is the key. A sophisticated expert uses a replenishable retainer and asks to be paid for depositions up front. At a minimum, she bills monthly and insists that her bills be paid before continuing to work on a case.

19.6 Conclusion

Carefully considered fee setting, billing, and collection policies can greatly benefit an expert's bottom line.

Chapter 20 Expert Witness Liability and Risk Management

20.1 Introduction

The expert has in the past rarely faced civil liability for actions performed while serving as an expert witness. However, the potential liability of experts may be growing. The law generally affords immunity to a witness from civil liability stemming from testimony or communications made in the course of litigation. This immunity has limits, however. Moreover, an expert may face liability for inadvertently or intentionally losing or destroying evidence (*spoliation* of evidence) or for negligent acts. Of course, the expert may also face civil or criminal liability for lying under oath. This chapter will provide an in-depth discussion concerning the potential liability of expert witnesses and will conclude with risk management advice on how to avoid suffering a loss as a result of providing forensic services.

Generally speaking, most cases initiated against expert witnesses have involved defamation lawsuits against opponents' witnesses. Lawsuits against friendly hired witnesses occur infrequently. The suits are not based on defamation, but rather on negligence claims where disappointed clients assumed their experts would assist them in winning their claim.[1]

The expert should know that very few states have considered the issue of expert witness liability, and fewer still have stripped experts and their testimony of immunity and privilege.[2] Nonetheless, the expert may face a lawsuit—and occasionally the expert may lose that lawsuit. Also, privileges and immunities are applied differently in each state, which prevents a definitive answer to the expert's questions of liability. The expert should also note that several legal commentators have pointed out an emerging trend toward increased expert witness liability.[3]

---

[1] Randall K. Hanson, "Witness Immunity Under Attack: Disarming 'Hired Guns,'" 31 *Wake Forest L. Rev.* (1996) 497, 498.

[2] Six states have decided recent cases involving lawsuits against expert witnesses. Four of these six states have held expert witnesses accountable for their actions and have narrowly construed the protection of witness immunity. Only Washington and Pennsylvania have held an expert witness immune from liability. California, Missouri, New Jersey, and Texas courts have held expert witnesses liable. *Id.* at 498.

[3] See, for example, Douglas R. Richmond, *"The Emerging Theory of Expert Witness Malpractice,"* 22 *Cap. U. L. Rev.* (1993) 693; Randall K. Hanson, "Witness Immunity Under Attack: Disarming 'Hired Guns,'" 31 *Wake Forest L. Rev.* (1996) 497, 498; Christopher M. McDowell, "NOTE: Authorizing the Expert Witness to Assassinate Character for Profit: A Reexamination of the Testimonial Immunity of the Expert Witness," 28 *Mem. St. U. L. Rev.* (1997) 239.

20.2 Litigation Privilege and Witness Immunity

Litigation privilege and witness immunity are related—if not quite synonymous—protections. Both have traditionally protected expert witnesses from civil liability for acts and statements made while serving as experts. The *litigation privilege* has traditionally shielded trial participants, including expert witnesses and trial consultants, from liability for statements or work product related to a trial. *Witness immunity* has traditionally shielded expert witnesses from liability for defamation[4] and negligence.[5] (In this chapter, we will use the terms *privilege* and *immunity* interchangeably.) The rationale for this legal protection is to encourage witnesses to make full disclosure of all pertinent information, to assuage fears of retribution for giving testimony, and to save courts from an endless spiral of suits brought by parties allegedly injured in trial.[6]

As a result of this immunity, actions for libel, slander, malicious prosecution, negligence, and breach of contract were traditionally of little concern to the expert. However, some courts have begun to carve out exceptions to expert witness immunity. Accordingly, malfeasance by an expert today may in fact subject him to civil liability. He may face suits by the people against whom he testified and by the party that hired him. Even if ultimately vindicated, an expert who is sued and does not carry applicable liability insurance may be faced with large legal bills associated with successfully defending the suit.

Example 20.1

The Restatement (Second) of Torts §588 states the general rule that absolute privilege generally applies to statements made in the course of judicial proceedings and acts as a bar to any civil liability:

> A witness is absolutely privileged to publish defamatory matter concerning another in communications preliminary to a proposed judicial proceeding or as a part of a judicial proceeding in which he is testifying, if it has some relation to the proceeding.

The comments of the Restatement emphasize that the privilege does not provide blanket immunity to all statements, and the comments limit the scope

---

[4] The rationale is to encourage frank testimony.

[5] The rationale is that under oath the witness has an obligation to speak the truth.

[6] "Without absolute immunity for their testimony, the objectivity of witnesses might be threatened. If an expert witness could be sued based on her performance in the courtroom, her testimony might be distorted by a desire to avoid a subsequent lawsuit. In addition, holding expert witnesses liable might discourage anyone but a full-time expert from testifying. Only 'professional witnesses' could afford malpractice insurance to protect against such liability." Leslie R. Masterson, "Witness Immunity or Malpractice Liability for Professionals Hired as Experts?" 17 *Rev. Litig.* (1998) 393, 397.

of the privilege to statements that have some relation to the proceeding or to a party to the proceeding.

Example 20.2
An example of the litigation privilege appears in the California Civil Code §47(b):

> A privileged publication or broadcast is one made:...In any (1) legislative or (2) judicial proceeding, or (3) in any other official proceeding authorized by law, or (4) in the initiation or course of any other proceeding authorized by law and reviewable pursuant to Chapter 2 (commencing with Section 1084) of Title 1 of Part 3 of the Code of Civil Procedure....[7]

Absolute versus qualified immunity

It is important to understand the distinction between absolute and qualified immunity. Some states provide for absolute immunity for experts while others provide for qualified immunity. *Absolute immunity* serves as a shield from liability, even where willful misconduct occurs. *Qualified immunity* differs from absolute immunity in that it does not protect those who act with malice.

20.3 Negligence

The protection from liability to the retaining party afforded expert witnesses has eroded somewhat in recent years. A party may be able to conclude an action against its own expert successfully in some jurisdictions. This section provides notable case examples, including the $42 million *Mattco Forge* case.

---

[7] Several policies underlie the privilege. First, it affords litigants free access to the courts to secure and defend their rights without fear of harassment by later suits. Second, the courts rely on the privilege to prevent the proliferation of lawsuits after the first one is resolved. Third, the privilege facilitates crucial functions of the trier of fact.

The statutory privilege protects attorneys, judges, jurors, witnesses, and other court personnel from liability arising from publications made during a judicial proceeding. Although originally enacted in the context of defamation actions, the privilege now applies to "any communication, whether or not it amounts to a publication [citations], and all torts except malicious prosecution. [Citations.] Further, it applies to any publication required or permitted by law in the course of a judicial proceeding to achieve the objects of the litigation, even though the publication is made outside the courtroom and no function of the court or its officers is involved. [Citations.]" *Mattco Forge v. Arthur Young & Co.*, 6 Cal. Rptr. 2d 781, 787 (Cal. Ct. App. 1992).

As usually formulated, "the privilege applies to any communication (1) made in judicial or quasi-judicial proceedings; (2) by litigants or other participants authorized by law; (3) to achieve the objects of the litigation; and (4) that have some connection or logical relation to the action. [Citations.]" *Mattco Forge*, 6 Cal. Rptr. 2d 781, 787.

Example 20.3

Mattco Forge v. Arthur Young & Co

The case *Mattco Forge v. Arthur Young & Co.* made a major impact on expert witness liability for negligence. The court declared that the expert, an accounting firm, was not protected from liability for testifying from negligently prepared data. Mattco Forge was awarded $42 million.

Allowing expert witness negligence clearly prevailed in a California case in which the California court of appeals explicitly permitted a plaintiff to bring a negligence claim against a "friendly" expert witness.[8] In *Mattco Forge v. Arthur Young & Co.,* Mattco Forge, a manufacturing company, sued Arthur Young, an accounting firm, for negligently providing accounting services.[9] In the underlying case, Mattco filed a federal civil rights action against General Electric ("GE"), claiming that GE had eliminated Mattco as an approved subcontractor for racial reasons. Mattco hired Arthur Young as a damage consultant and expert witness to assist in calculating lost profits. Among other discovery disputes, GE alleged that Mattco had fabricated documents with the assistance of Arthur Young. Stalled by the discovery disputes, the federal case finally ended before trial in mutual dismissals.[10]

Mattco subsequently sued Arthur Young, alleging, *inter alia*, for accounting malpractice.[11] Arthur Young moved for summary judgment, raising as a defense a California statute that provided a "litigation privilege."[12] The trial court granted Arthur Young's motion, holding that the statutory litigation privilege barred Mattco's claims as a matter of law. Mattco appealed.

The court of appeals reversed the summary judgment,[13] refusing to apply the litigation privilege to a "friendly" expert witness. The court reasoned that extending the litigation privilege to protect Arthur Young from professional malpractice would not further the policy of encouraging truthful testimony.[14] In addition, the procedural safeguards that provide a compelling rationale to protect experts from liability are not present when the witness has not testified at trial—she has not sworn an oath, faced the hazard of cross-examination, or the threat of a prosecution for perjury.[15] The court pointed out that the

---

[8] *Mattco Forge v. Arthur Young & Co.,* 6 Cal. Rptr. 2d 781, 789-790 (Cal. Ct. App. 1992) (reversing trial court and permitting a claim for expert witness negligence); 45 Cal. Rptr. 2d 581 (Cal. Ct. App. 1995) (reversing trial court's ruling on settlement agreement); 60 Cal. Rptr. 2d 780 (Cal. Ct. App. 1997) (reversing trial court and requiring trial-within-a-trial measure of damages).

[9] See *Mattco Forge,* 60 Cal. Rptr. 2d at 783 (discussing the background of the case).

[10] *Id.*

[11] *Mattco Forge*, 6 Cal. Rptr. 2d at 783.

[12] *Id.* at 787 (citing California Civil Code 47(b) (West 1996), which provides: "A privileged publication or broadcast is one made: ...In any (1) legislative or (2) judicial proceeding or (3) in any other official proceeding authorized by law and reviewable pursuant to Chapter 2 (commencing with Section 1084) of Title 1 of Part 3 of the Code of Civil Procedure....").

[13] *Id.* at 790–791.

[14] *Id.* at 789–790.

[15] *Id.* at 789.

litigation privilege is not "absolute."[16] The court analogized to malpractice suits brought by a party against his former attorney, noting that the litigation privilege does not entirely protect attorneys from suit by a former client.[17]

In order to recover on a claim of expert witness negligence, the plaintiff may be required to prove that the professional's conduct was the cause-in-fact of her injuries. In *Mattco,* Arthur Young argued throughout the trial that in order to prevail on its claim of professional negligence, Mattco had to prove that it would have prevailed in the underlying federal suit against GE.[18] The trial court rejected this approach.[19] In the liability phase of the trial, Mattco merely had to show that Arthur Young had caused Mattco to suffer "harm." Its burden in the damages phase was to prove its case against GE had "value." The jury awarded Mattco $42 million in damages, and Arthur Young appealed.[20]

In this appeal, the main issue was whether the trial court erred in refusing to apply the "suit within a suit" requirement to a claim of accountant malpractice.[21] Mattco, similar to a client who brings a malpractice action against her attorney, complained that it lost its claim against GE due to professional negligence. When an attorney is sued for malpractice relating to the litigation of the underlying suit, the plaintiff must prove that the attorney's conduct was the cause-in-fact of her injury. This burden is called the "suit within a suit" requirement. In effect, two separate lawsuits are tried in the malpractice action. Where the attorney's negligence caused the plaintiff to lose her claim, she must show that she would have prevailed on her claim and the amount that would actually have been collected. Where the attorney's negligence caused the plaintiff to lose a defense in the underlying suit, she must show that the defense was meritorious.

The court of appeals in *Mattco* noted criticism of the suit within a suit requirement, but explained that "it is the most effective safeguard yet devised against speculative and conjectural claims in this era of ever-expanding litigation."[22] The court reversed the award of damages and remanded the case for a new trial. In order to prevail, Mattco would have to establish that but for Arthur Young's negligence, Mattco would have won its case against GE. The court stated that, "Like other defendants in negligence lawsuits, litigation support professionals are only responsible for the losses they cause."[23] Thus, where the alleged negligent conduct results in the plaintiff's loss of the underlying case, the plaintiff is held to the same burden as an attorney who has mishandled litigation.[24]

---

[16] *Id.* at 790.
[17] *Id.* at 789–790.
[18] *Mattco Forge v. Arthur Young & Co.,* 60 Cal. Rptr. 2d 780, 786 (Cal. Ct. App. 1997).
[19] *Id.*
[20] *Id.* at 784.
[21] *Id.* at 784.
[22] *Id.* at 788.
[23] *Id.* at 789.
[24] *Id.*

Example 20.4
Murphy v. A.A. Mathews, 841 S.W.2d 671 (Mo. 1992)
The Missouri Supreme Court has held that witness immunity does not shield professional experts from negligence claims brought by their former clients. In *Murphy v. A.A. Mathews,*[25] Murphy hired Mathews, as professional engineers, to testify at an arbitration proceeding regarding expenses that arose from construction problems. Mathews testified at the arbitration proceeding, but Murphy was awarded an amount substantially less than his requested compensation. Murphy sued his experts, alleging that Mathews had negligently prepared and documented Murphy's claim. In the malpractice proceeding, Mathews moved to dismiss based on witness immunity.

Mathews asked the court to extend witness immunity, which Missouri courts had traditionally applied to protect witnesses from defamation actions brought by adverse parties to bar malpractice claims against professionals hired to perform litigation support services.[26] Following *James* (Texas) and *Mattco* (California), the Missouri Supreme Court declined to extend witness immunity to protect a privately retained professional who negligently provides pre-trial litigation support services.[27] Experts are not unbiased court servants, but instead sell their professional services for a fee.[28] By their very nature, experts are not objective witnesses, and immunizing their testimony does not further the policies underlying witness immunity.[29]

20.4 Knowing Misrepresentation

An expert may not be immune from liability for knowingly misrepresenting her opinion to her own client—even if the underlying matter never resulted in a lawsuit. Consider the following example in which the court held that expert immunity does not protect an expert from liability for knowingly misrepresenting his opinion.

Example 20.5
Hart v. Browne, 163 Cal. Rptr 356 (Cal. App. Dist. 1 1980)
In this case, a patient, Hart, was treated by Dr. Nork. Hart underwent nine operations and eleven hospitalizations. She was unsatisfied with the treatment

---

[25] *Murphy v. A.A. Mathews,* 841 S.W.2d 671 (Mo. 1992).
[26] *Id.* at 674.
[27] *Id.* at 680. The court explained: "Witness immunity is an exception to the general rules of liability. It should not be extended unless its underlying policies require it be so. In Missouri, this immunity generally has been restricted to defamation, defamation-type, or retaliatory cases against adverse witnesses. This narrow restriction is consistent with the historical development of immunity.

"While witness immunity might properly be expanded in other circumstances, we do not believe that immunity was meant to or should apply to bar a suit against a privately retained professional who negligently provides litigation support services."
[28] *Mathews,* 841 S.W.2d at 681.
[29] *Id.*

and retained a lawyer to investigate a medical malpractice case. The attorney retained an expert witness, Dr. Browne, who rendered an opinion that there was no medical malpractice. As a result, the malpractice case was not filed and the statute of limitations ran out. Ms. Hart then sued Dr. Browne. The court rejected Dr. Browne's immunity defense. It then found that the doctor made representations that he knew to be false. The court explained:

> There was abundant testimony that gross malpractice had been committed by Dr. Nork. This subnormal treatment was evident from [Hart's] narrative and her hospital records, both of which were used by [Dr. Browne] in rendering his opinion to appellant's attorneys. [Dr. Browne] enjoyed a reputation as a highly regarded orthopedic surgeon and a teacher of orthopedic surgery at a prestigious medical center. Given the man's reputation and the nature of the information and materials on which he was basing his opinion, the jury could well have inferred that [Dr. Browne] knew his opinion was a misrepresentation. Such a misrepresentation of opinion is actionable when the [expert] holds himself out to be specifically qualified in the area on which he gives the opinion.

20.5 Negligence: Court-Appointed Experts

Even a court-appointed expert can be liable for negligence. Consider the following case where the expert accountant allegedly negligently appraised the value of a certain quantity of stock.

Example 20.6
Levine v. Wiss & Co., 478 A.2d 397, 398 (N.J. 1984)
In this divorce action, an accountant was hired to evaluate assets. The parties to the divorce agreed, in anticipation of an equitable distribution, that an "impartial expert" would be retained to value the husband's interest in a corporation and that the parties would be bound by the accountant's valuation. The accountant completed his evaluation and submitted a report to the divorce court that estimated the husband's equity interest in the corporation and the company's cash basis income for the four previous years. Before trial, and after receiving the expert's report, the husband and wife reached a pre-trial settlement. This settlement encompassed property, alimony, and child support. Then, both parties jointly moved to vacate the settlement. The trial court denied the motion to vacate and entered a judgment of divorce that incorporated the earlier property settlement.

The husband then brought suit against the accountant, alleging negligence in the valuation of the business. The husband asserted that he was forced to pay his ex-wife an excessive amount because of the incorrect values submitted by the accountant. The accountant argued that he was entitled to immunity because he acted in the role of an arbitrator, he was court-appointed, and his decision regarding valuation was binding. The court rejected this argument. Although the court recognized that arbitrators, like judges, are generally afforded immunity for the consequences of their decisions, the court refused to extend immunity to shield experts performing limited professional services that involved neither testimony nor the exercise of judicial discretion. In contrast to an agreement for arbitration, which generally encompasses the entire controversy between the parties, an appraisal simply resolves the actual cash value of a particular item. The court stated that the

> defendants were expected to apply their professional accountancy skills....They can appropriately be considered "appraisers"....Consequently, the standards of reasonable care applied to lawyers, doctors, engineers, and other professionals charged with furnishing skilled services for compensation attach with equal force and justification to defendants here.

Note: The immunity claimed by the accountant here was based on the notion that arbitrators, because they frequently proceed quasi-judicially, are generally afforded an immunity from liability for the consequences of their decisions or awards that is comparable to that accorded judges. This is why the court discussed whether the accountant was an arbitrator or a professional furnishing skills for compensation. The point of this case can be summed up in the oft-quoted line penned by the judge in *Levine:* "A court-appointment is not a talisman for immunity."

20.6 Defamation

Expert witnesses will usually be protected from defamation liability by immunity. This immunity is provided in order to encourage full and frank disclosure by the expert. Experts need to keep in mind, however, that there is no immunity for communications made outside the context of the lawsuit and that they may be subject to other liability (for example, negligence, professional discipline, and perjury) for making defamatory communications in the context of a lawsuit. Please consider the following cases.

Example 20.7
Twelker v. Shannon & Wilson, Inc., 564 P.2d 1131 (Wash. 1977)
In this case, a soil engineer brought a defamation suit against a fellow soil engineer who allegedly defamed his professional reputation by sending a letter to an insurance company regarding the cause of a landslide. The letter was directed to the cause of a landslide that damaged a building completed two months earlier. The insurance company insured the general contractor in charge of the construction of that building and the plaintiff prepared the soil report for the project. Apparently concerned with the possible exposure to the liability of its insured, the insurance company retained the respondent to investigate the slide and issued a statement of its findings with regard to its cause. A three-page report prepared pursuant to that request and forwarded to the insurance company contains the allegedly defamatory remarks.

The defendant prepared his letter following two inspections of the landslide site and a review of various documents, including the plaintiff's soil report, which were pertinent to the construction project. The plaintiff argued that the letter contained several specific false statements regarding the contents of the original soil report, and that those statements concerning the report were made with knowledge of or reckless disregard for their falsity.

The defendant raised the defense of absolute immunity in an attempt to bar the suit. In essence, the court found that the defendant's report was made in the course of judicial or quasi-judicial proceedings, and thus the defendant was eligible for protection. However, the protection was not absolute. The court decided that it was questionable whether the statements were made after a fair and impartial investigation or upon reasonable grounds for belief in their truth. Because of this, the defendant may have abused his privilege and absolute immunity could not extend to protect his statements. The court explained that the privilege of immunity is a judicially created privilege founded upon the belief that the administration of justice requires witnesses in a legal proceeding to be able to discuss their views without fear of a defamation lawsuit. The privilege of absolute witness immunity creates an "extraordinary breadth" of protection and should not be extended absent the existence of compelling public policy justifications. The court remanded the case for a trial on the merits of the suit.

Example 20.8

James v. Brown, 637 S.W.2d 914 (Tex. 1982)

In 1982, James sued several doctors who had filed reports with a Texas probate court concerning James's mental competency.

James had been hospitalized for observation. During the course of this observation, she was examined by several doctors who filed reports stating that the plaintiff was not of sound mind, was not competent to handle financial affairs, and was likely to cause injury to herself if she were not restrained.

James later obtained a court order that released her from the hospital's custody. The competency proceeding was then dropped and James sued the doctors who had indicated that she was incompetent. In her complaint, James alleged libel, negligent misdiagnosis, medical malpractice, false imprisonment, and malicious prosecution. Under the libel claim, the Texas court applied witness immunity to the doctors, protecting them from liability for allegedly defamatory statements. The court held that no statements in a judicial proceeding can give rise to a civil action for libel or slander, regardless of negligence or malice as long as the statement has some relation to the proceeding.[30]

However, the court noted that the witness immunity protection does not provide blanket immunity from all civil liability. Specifically, the court stated that James was not precluded from suing the doctors for negligence resulting from their misdiagnoses just because their diagnoses were later communicated to a court in the course of a judicial proceeding.

The court explained, "While the doctors' communications to the court of their diagnoses of [the plaintiff's] mental condition, regardless of how

---

[30] *James v. Brown,* 637 S.W.2d 914, 917 (Tex. 1982) "A witness is absolutely privileged to publish defamatory matter concerning another in communications preliminary to a proposed judicial proceeding or as a part of a judicial proceeding in which he is testifying, if it has some relation to the proceeding." Restatement (Second) of Torts, section 588 (1981).

negligently made, cannot serve as the basis for a defamation action, the diagnoses themselves may be actionable on other grounds."

The expert should note that although the court here allowed the suit against the experts for negligent misdiagnosis to proceed, the basis of the suit was a Texas statute that imposed a duty on the psychiatrists to conduct their examinations with the degree of skill ordinarily employed under similar circumstances by similar specialists in the field.

Example 20.9: Immunity upheld

Aequitron Medical Inc. v. Joseph P. Dyro, et al., No. 96-2187 (E.D.N.Y. 1998) The plaintiff, a manufacturer of infant heart and breathing monitors, sued the defendant biomechanical engineer for trade libel, defamation, and tortuous interference with prospective business advantage. The defendant had testified previously as an expert in two products liability actions involving the plaintiff's monitors.

In its complaint, Aequitron claimed that a videotape of the defendant's test of the monitor was false and misleading because the defendant failed to disclose that he found no defect in an earlier test, that he previously testified that the alarm functioned, and that the device was not returned for factory certification. The plaintiff also alleged that the defendant circulated the videotape in order to get hired as an expert in cases against Aequitron and in other product liability cases.

The U.S. District Court for the Eastern District of New York found that statements by parties and their attorneys are absolutely privileged under any circumstances if they are pertinent to the litigation.

"Moreover, and contrary to plaintiff's position, the absolute privilege attaches not only at the hearing or trial phase, but to every step of the proceeding in question, even if it is preliminary and/or investigatory," the court said.[31] The privilege, the court continued, has been found to extend to letters, settlement offers, statements in a magazine article, and subpoenas.

The court added:

> It should also be noted that a retained expert is more than just the average witness, but acts as an agent for the attorney whose reports to the attorney based on information from the client can be subject to attorney-client privilege. Although the videotape was later disclosed to Aequitron's counsel and not subject to any attorney-client privilege . . . the Court finds that a retained expert's role in trial preparation and the privileges accorded to those experts weighs in favor of providing absolute immunity for statements made in the course of those preparations, so long as the statements are pertinent to the ongoing litigation.

The court also mentioned,

> While [the defendant's] prior testing and deposition testimony would have been excellent fodder for cross-examination in those actions, they do not form the basis of a defamation of trade libel claim under New York law as they are absolutely

[31] The district court cited *Herzfeld & Stern v. Beck*, 175 A.S.2d at 691, 572 N.Y.S.2d at 685 (1st Dep't. 1991) for this proposition.

privileged. The fact that the statements were made during trial preparation rather than in open court is of no moment, as the above-discussed cases clearly indicate.

20.7 Effect of Immunity upon Professional Disciplinary Action against the Expert

An expert should assume that he will not be able to successfully invoke immunity if his alleged misconduct results in a professional disciplinary proceeding. In the following case, the court rejected the psychologist expert's immunity claim and suspended his license for ten years.

Example 20.10

Deatherage v. Examining Bd. of Psychology, 948 P.2d 828 (Wash. 1997)
A state board of psychology (Board) brought disciplinary proceedings against a psychologist, alleging he failed to meet professional ethical standards in work that formed the basis of his expert testimony in several child custody suits. The Board found the psychologist's failure to qualify statements, his mischaracterization of statements, his failure to verify information, and his interpretation of test data were adequate grounds for initiating disciplinary proceedings under state regulations. After an extensive hearing, the Board found that the expert had committed misconduct in three custody evaluations, and suspended his license for ten years. The psychologist sought, and was granted, judicial review of the Board's decision.

The psychologist raised the defense of absolute witness immunity, which, he argued, prevents the Board from initiating disciplinary proceedings against him based upon his work and conduct as an expert witness testifying in a court proceeding. The state supreme court held that absolute witness immunity does not exist in the context of a professional disciplinary proceeding.

20.8 Absolute Immunity

Some courts have held that an expert witness enjoys absolute immunity from civil liability. The rationale for this view is to encourage full and frank testimony—the threat of a potential lawsuit might persuade an expert to be less than fully candid. Consider the following examples.

Example 20.11

Bruce v. Byrne-Stevens & Assocs. Engineers, Inc., 776 P.2d 666 (Wash. 1989)
In this case, the Washington Supreme Court broadly applied witness immunity to a "friendly" expert witness.

Bruce involved an engineer who, as an expert, testified it would cost $10,020 to stabilize the soil on the plaintiff's property. The trial court found in the plaintiff's favor and awarded the plaintiff a judgment for exactly that amount. The actual cost of the repair was twice the amount the expert witness testified to at trial. The plaintiff attempted to sue the expert witness in negligence. The plaintiff contended but for the expert witness's negligent analysis and testimony they would have been awarded the true cost of repair. The court did not agree and held absolute witness immunity barred the suit.

In reaching this result, the plurality in *Bruce* stated that as a general rule witnesses in judicial proceedings are absolutely immune from civil liability based on their testimony. The plurality's application of the immunity rule extended the traditional rule, but the plurality's justification for granting absolute immunity to expert witnesses was supported by traditional public policy considerations—the most important of which was "to preserve the integrity of the judicial process by encouraging full and frank testimony."

The primary argument against providing immunity to expert witnesses is the threat of liability encourages prudence in testimony. The court explored the argument and weighed the benefit of testimony subject to liability against the threatened loss of objectivity. It concluded that civil liability for expert witnesses was "too blunt an instrument" to gain much reliability in testimony because liability would result in testimony motivated by litigants' interests and not professional standards.

Ultimately, the court was concerned that if immunity was lifted, a witness could testify in a manner that would prevent the potential lawsuit, but would deprive the court of the benefit of candid, unbiased testimony. The court felt that the benefits gained by extending witness immunity were counterbalanced by safeguards inherent in the judicial system. It noted that witness reliability is ensured by oath, cross-examination, and the threat of criminal prosecution for perjury. The court found that those safeguards insured truthful and accurate testimony.

Example 20.12
Darragh v. Superior Court, 183 Ariz. 79, 900 P.2d 1215 (Ariz. Ct. App. 1995)
Here, landowners whose land a city was attempting to buy sued the city's expert for undervaluing the land—allegedly as part of a conspiracy to encourage the city to underpay the landowners.

In the underlying case, a city was attempting to buy property in order to redevelop an area. The city hired an expert to prepare written appraisals of the fair market value of the subject properties and to testify as an expert witness at trial if condemnation proceedings became necessary. Owners of a particular piece of property within the designated area rejected the city's offer, which was based upon the expert's appraisals. The city then instituted a condemnation proceeding. The city's expert testified that the land was worth $486,650. The jury disagreed and found the value to be over a million dollars. The property owners then filed a suit against the city and the expert claiming that they conspired to give perjured testimony and submit false and fraudulent documents in an attempt to acquire the owners' property at less than fair market value. The expert asserted immunity from the suit because both his appraisals and subsequent testimony were services rendered while the city was seriously contemplating eminent domain litigation, and thus the services occurred in the course of litigation. The court held that the expert witness had absolute immunity for his testimony at trial and deposition. The court also found that the expert's appraisals were absolutely privileged as communications made in connection with judicial proceedings because, at the time the expert was hired, the city was seriously contemplating litigation.

Example 20.13
Bird v. W.C.W., 1994 Tex. LEXIS 13, 868 S.W.2d 767 (Tex. 1994)
In this case, a psychologist, Esther Bird, examined a child for signs of sexual abuse. After examining the child, the psychologist concluded that the child had been sexually abused and that the natural father, W.C.W., was the abuser. The psychologist then signed an affidavit reporting these conclusions. The affidavit was filed by the child's mother, B.W., in the family court in an effort to modify child custody and visitation orders. All matters, criminal and civil, predicated upon the assertion that the natural father was a child abuser were eventually dropped. The natural father then sued the psychologist. The issue was whether the psychologist owed a professional duty of care to the natural father to not negligently misdiagnose the condition of the child. In defense, the psychologist asserted that there is no professional duty running to third parties as a matter of law, and regardless, the affidavit asserting the natural father to be the abuser of the child was used as a part of the court litigation process, and consequently, the statement was privileged as a matter of law. The court held that as a matter of law there is no professional duty running from a psychologist to a third party to not negligently misdiagnose a condition of a patient. The court "further reaffirm[ed]" that a statement in an affidavit filed as a part of a court proceeding is privileged.

Example 20.14
Lindemann v. Falk, 1999 Wash. App. LEXIS 85 (Wash. Ct. App. Jan. 19, 1999)
David Lindemann obtained a temporary domestic violence restraining order against Kimi Lindemann, as well as temporary custody of their children, after she assaulted him with a 12-gauge shotgun. Kimi Lindemann's counsel employed Richard Falk, EdD, to interview the children and prepare a recommendation for use in the show cause hearing related to that court order. Falk recommended that the children be immediately placed in the residential care of their mother because his interviews with the children allegedly disclosed that they had been inappropriately touched by their father. After Falk's recommendation was given to the court, the children were temporarily placed with their aunt. David Lindemann claims that Falk failed to act in good faith and alienated the affection of his children by preparing that recommendation. David Lindemann's suit against Falk was dismissed upon summary judgment on the basis that Falk is absolutely immune from suit for preparing his recommendation.

Example 20.15
Clark v. Grigson, 579 S.W.2d 263 (Tex. Civ. App.-Dallas 1978)
Here, a convicted felon sued a psychiatrist who had testified adversely in the punishment stage of the plaintiff's criminal trial. The plaintiff sought damages on the theory that the psychiatrist negligently made an improper diagnosis, which resulted in heavier sentences than the plaintiff would have received if the psychiatrist had made an accurate diagnosis. In support of liability for expert witness negligence, the plaintiff argued that "improper expert testimony would occur less frequently if experts [were] civilly liable for damages for negligence in reaching the conclusions to which they testify." The court of appeals

rejected this argument, finding it "more than counterbalanced" by the policy of affording witnesses absolute immunity in order to encourage unrestrained testimony.

Example 20.16

Laub v. Pesikoff, 979 S.W.2d 689 (Tex. Civ. App. Dist. 1-Houston, 1998)
Here, a state court of appeals addressed a party's novel attempt to impose liability upon the opponent's expert witnesses for their affidavit testimony.

Laub was a divorce proceeding. Mr. Laub alleged that his wife signed certain documents that conveyed real property and transferred securities to him. Mr. Laub filed a motion requesting the court to uphold these gifts. Mrs. Laub responded by arguing that at the times in question, she did not possess the requisite donative intent to make the alleged gifts. She supported her response with affidavit testimony from her treating psychiatrist and psychologist, who both opined that due to the husband's physical abuse of the wife, she lacked the mental capacity to make the gifts. Soon after the response was filed, Mr. Laub filed a separate lawsuit against both experts, alleging that they had committed intentional libel and slander, intentional infliction of emotional distress, conspiracy to defraud, denial of constitutional due process, and tortious interference. The trial court granted summary judgment in favor of the experts on all theories.

On appeal, the state court of appeals addressed whether Mr. Laub's claims were barred by the judicial communications privilege. The court acknowledged the absolute immunity of parties and witnesses from liability for their testimony in judicial proceedings, noting that "even perjured testimony, made in a judicial proceeding, cannot serve as a basis for a suit in tort." The court also noted a concern for the "full and free disclosure from witnesses unhampered by fear of retaliatory lawsuits."

The *Laub* court held that, regardless of libel, the essence of Mr. Laub's claims against the experts was that he suffered injury as a result of the communication of allegedly false statements during a judicial proceeding. The court found such communications to be absolutely privileged as judicial communications and, therefore, affirmed summary judgment in favor of the experts.

Example 20.17

Serchia v. MacMillan, PICS Case No. 97-0734 (E.D. Pa. March 20, 1997)
A federal judge interpreting Pennsylvania law threw out a medical malpractice claim lodged against a doctor who examined a criminal defendant on behalf of federal prosecutors and said the man was fit to stand trial. The man later died, and his surviving spouse filed a wrongful death suit against the physician.

Ronald Serchia—the decedent—was indicted in 1992 on federal drug charges. His attorney said the proceedings should be delayed because of his health. Serchia's doctor said that because of Ronald's health problems, it would be dangerous for him to endure the stress of a trial.

MacMillan examined Serchia twice in 1993 and testified in September 1993 that while Ronald did have an abdominal aortic aneurysm and high blood pressure, he was fit to stand trial. Proceedings began, and then Ronald Serchia died in May 1994. Serchia's wife sued MacMillan, arguing that he ignored Ronald's medical condition "in order to curry favor" with the government.

The U.S. District Court judge dismissed the suit after concluding that the physician expert witness was absolutely privileged and thus immune from malpractice liability. The judge said that when a person's health is an issue in litigation, the opposing party should be able to "explore" the person's medical condition without fear of being sued at a later date.

"Because [Serchia's] claims for wrongful death and malpractice are based solely on MacMillan's examination of Mr. Serchia in his capacity as the government's expert witness in the criminal proceedings against Mr. Serchia, MacMillan is entitled to immunity in the present action." The judge noted that, although the Pennsylvania Supreme Court had not directly ruled on the issue, it has recognized that that trial participants can't be sued for defamation based on statements they make during litigation. The judge then cited a case in which the Pennsylvania Superior Court had extended immunity beyond defamation.[32]

20.9 Presenting False Evidence

The policies supporting witness immunity are so strongly favored that even a witness who offers perjured testimony may be immune from liability for damages. However, such an expert would still be subject to criminal prosecution and to discipline within his profession (for example, potential loss of an expert's professional license). Consider the following case.

Example 20.18

Carden v. Getzoff, 190 Cal. App.3d 907, 235 Cal. Rptr. 698 (Mar. 1987)

The plaintiff here sued an expert accounting witness. The underlying case was a marital dissolution between the plaintiff and his wife. The wife's accounting expert allegedly manufactured false evidence in the dissolution action when he prepared a medical practice valuation of the appellant's anesthesiology practice to be used in the negotiation of a settlement agreement. Allegedly, he examined the appellant's anesthesiology practice to determine the goodwill therein and to compare the evaluation of the goodwill found in the appellant's practice to that of "other similar practices" that he had also examined. The plaintiff alleged that those representations were false and that no evaluation was made of the appellant's anesthesiology practice and no comparison was made. Moreover, the plaintiff claimed that the expert misused the process of the court when he testified that he had made an appraisal of the anesthesiology

[32] The judge cited the state Superior Court's decision in *Clodgo v. Bowman,* 601 A.2d 342 (Pa. Super. 1992), in which the court held that a plaintiff couldn't sue a court-appointed doctor for medical malpractice for incorrectly identifying the parent of a child in a custody hearing. The federal judge said the *Clodgo* court determined that while the case involved medical malpractice and not defamation, the traditional privilege against liability should apply. The judge also stated that the *Clodgo* court warned that carving out an exception would create a dangerous precedent, making experts afraid to testify because of potential liability. The federal judge also stated that the fact that the expert in *Clodgo* was court-appointed and MacMillan was testifying on behalf of an adverse party was irrelevant.

practice based upon an examination of the practice and a comparison of the evaluation of the goodwill of the practice to that of three other comparable anesthesiology medical practices.

The plaintiff then sued the expert. The court dismissed the plaintiff's suit by applying the privilege:

> We in no way condone the alleged perjury. If the allegations in the complaint are true, respondent's conduct is indeed outrageous. However, when there is a good faith intention to bring a suit, even malicious publications "are protected as part of the price paid for affording litigants the utmost freedom of access to the courts." [Citations.] Otherwise, adverse witnesses would always be fearful of subsequent civil suits and would be extremely hesitant or unwilling to testify. Appellant's potential remedies are to assist in the prosecution of criminal charges; to report any allegations of dereliction to the Board of Accountancy; and to attempt to litigate any claims he might have against his trial attorney.

20.10 Changing an Opinion

Experts are expected to tell the truth. Courts have found that experts are not liable to their retaining parties if, during the course of a trial, they change their testimony. Consider the following examples.

Example 20.19

Panitz v. Behrend, 632 A.2d 562 (Penn. 1993)

In the underlying case, the expert was retained by a law firm on behalf of clients whom the law firm represented in a personal injury action. On direct examination, the expert testified that the injuries at issue had been caused by formaldehyde. However, on cross-examination, the expert could not explain some inconsistencies in her testimony and admitted that her reasoning was inaccurate. The plaintiffs received an unfavorable verdict, and the law firm refused to pay the expert the balance of her fee. The expert sued to recover her fee, and the law firm counterclaimed alleging gross negligence. The trial court granted the defendant expert's demurrer and dismissed the counterclaim. The law firm appealed.

In refusing to hold the expert liable for her testimony, the appeals court reasoned that "[t]o allow a party to litigation to contract with an expert witness and thereby obligate the witness to testify only in a manner favorable to the party, on threat of civil liability, would be contrary to public policy." The appeals court in this case took the position that "[t]he primary purpose of expert testimony is not to assist one party or another in winning the case but to assist the trier of facts in understanding complicated matters." The court also stated that an expert witness "will not be subjected to civil liability because he or she in the face of conflicting evidence or during rigorous cross examination, is persuaded that some or all of his or her opinion testimony has been inaccurate." Rather than malpractice liability, the court relied on procedural safeguards, such as judicial discretion on admissibility pursuant to Rule 702, to ensure the reliability of expert testimony.

Example 20.20
Schaffer v. Donegan, 585 N.E. 2d 854 (Ohio App. 1990)
In this case, the court rejected liability for an expert who changed his testimony during the underlying medical malpractice trial. In the underlying case, the plaintiff brought suit against two surgeons. The plaintiff's expert, another surgeon, reviewed the medical records and agreed to testify that the dentists were negligent and that the negligence caused the plaintiff's injury. On the seventh day of the trial, the expert reported to the plaintiff that he could no longer testify favorably on the issue of liability. He explained that while he was still of the opinion that the two physicians who treated the plaintiff were negligent in failing to diagnose the particular fracture involved, he was no longer able to say that that negligence was the proximate cause of the injuries and losses claimed by the plaintiff. The plaintiff then settled the case, then claimed that the expert, by reason of changing his opinion, breached his contract to testify and his duty to provide the other parties to his contract with timely notice of his change of opinion.

The appellate court affirmed the trial court's judgment in favor of the expert. The court recounted the rule: "As a general principle a witness has a duty to appear and testify truthfully concerning his knowledge or belief and a person who violates this duty may be required to respond in damages to the person injured by the violation." It then stated, "We see no liability on the part of [the expert] for changing his opinion on the liability issue if he did so for valid medical reasons as he testified." The court based its opinion on the notion that the plaintiff had no right to expect the witness to say anything but the truth. The contract was for the expert to testify to the truth, thus the expert did not breach it—a contract to testify in a certain way would have been void and unenforceable.

20.11 Breach of Contract

There is a strong public policy to support the view that experts should not be liable for breach of contract if they fail to testify as they had originally intended. The courts do not want to sanction an agreement to testify favorably. Consider the following case.

Example 20.21
Griffith v. Harris, 116 N.W.2d 133, 136 (Wisc. 1962)
Here, the plaintiff sued a physician for malpractice. While preparing this malpractice case for trial, the plaintiff's attorneys contacted the two defendants, who were both physicians, with the intention of getting them to testify in support of the plaintiff's malpractice case. The plaintiff's attorneys furnished the two doctor-defendants with hospital records on which the malpractice charge was in part based. The hospital records were not sufficient to establish the plaintiff's case without supporting expert medical testimony. The defendants were requested to testify in response to hypothetical questions. They were told that the plaintiff's attorneys would not proceed to trial without supporting expert medical testimony. The defendants took the matter under advisement and subsequently notified the plaintiff's attorneys that they would

testify favorably for the plaintiff. Later, the defendants were furnished copies of the proposed hypothetical questions.

Less than 24 hours before they were to be called to testify, the defendants informed the plaintiff's attorneys that they would not testify without a subpoena and, if subpoenaed, they would not testify in any way that would benefit the plaintiff. Because of this latter fact, the defendants were not subpoenaed. They did not appear and testify on behalf of the plaintiff. Because of the absence of favorable expert medical testimony, the plaintiff failed to establish a *prima facie* case of malpractice.

The plaintiff sued the experts for breach of contract. The court found that the essence of the plaintiff's complaint was that the experts broke their contract—not merely to testify, but to testify in the plaintiff's favor. Therefore, the court declared that "under no circumstances would an agreement to give favorable testimony be sanctioned by the courts."

20.12 Spoliation of Evidence

Spoliation of evidence is the destruction of relevant evidence by a party or his agent. The doctrine generally imposes some sanction on the party responsible for the destruction of the evidence.[33] The law regarding spoliation is vastly different in each jurisdiction. In some, an expert may face tort liability for negligent, as well as intentional, spoliation—although successful civil suits against an expert based on the tort of spoliation are rare. The expert may also face sanctions, such as the exclusion of the expert's testimony or dismissal of the case, for acts of spoliation.

Example 20.22

Vodusek v. Bayliner Marine Corp., 71 F.3d 148 (4th Cir. 1995)

In this products liability suit, a boat exploded, injuring the plaintiff. The plaintiff sued the manufacturer. The plaintiff sought to establish the defendants' liability through the testimony of an expert witness, offered as an expert in marine vessel safety and the causes of fires on vessels. In examining the boat to discover the cause of the explosion and fire, the expert, along with the plaintiff's two sons, employed destructive methods that rendered many portions of the boat useless for examination by the defendants and their experts.

Under the spoliation of evidence rule in this jurisdiction, an adverse inference may be drawn against a party who destroys relevant evidence. The plaintiff argued that she and her expert did not act in bad faith in destroying portions of the boat, but acknowledged that those portions were permanently

[33] "The most remarkable aspect of the doctrine of spoliation of evidence is that it has been held to be: (1) a cause of action in tort (for either intentional or negligent spoliation of evidence); (2) a defense to recovery; (3) an evidentiary inference or presumption; and (4) a discovery sanction. Furthermore, the doctrine of spoliation of evidence has been held in some jurisdictions to constitute a substantive rule of law, while other courts have held it to be a procedural evidentiary rule." Robert L. Tucker, "The Flexible Doctrine of Spoliation of Evidence: Cause of Action, Defense, Evidentiary Presumption, and Discovery Sanction," 27 *U. Tol. L. Rev.*(1995) 67, 68.

destroyed as part of the expert's deliberate investigative efforts. While the expert may have decided that the destroyed portions of the boat were not relevant to his theory of the case, that conclusion ignored the possibility that others might have entertained different theories to which destroyed portions might have been relevant. In this case, both the defendants and the district court concluded that the destroyed portions were significant to the effort to explain where and why the boat explosion occurred. The jury was allowed to "draw an inference adverse to the plaintiffs based on the spoliation," and did so. Ultimately, the jury found in favor of the defendants. However, in this instance, the expert did not face civil liability for his spoliation.

Example 20.23
Gootee v. Lightner, 274 Cal. Rptr. 697 (Ct. App. 1990)
In this case, the California Court of Appeals held that the protective mantle of a testimonial privilege embraces not only the courtroom testimony of witnesses, but also work product prepared for the testimony of witnesses. Therefore, the failure of a witness to preserve work product generated in preparation for testimony is not subject to the spoliation tort as long as the destruction of the work product does not involve pivotal physical evidence. *Pivotal evidence* consists of evidence that is independently significant, distinct from the witness's report and testimony. Absent this independent significance, third persons such as expert or lay witnesses and adverse parties are immune from spoliation claims.

The *Gootee* court reasoned that considerations, such as access to the courts, encouragement of witnesses to testify truthfully, and finality in litigation would suffer if a witness was exposed to civil litigation "merely because the witness failed to retain every note or paper, generated in anticipation of testifying, which an unhappy litigant surmises would have benefited his cross-examination of the witness."

Example 20.24
Nally v. Volkswagen of America, Inc., 405 Mass. 191, 539 N.E.2d 1017, 1021 (Mass. 1989)
An expert hired by the plaintiff had conducted some tests on parts of an automobile that had been involved in an accident. During the course of the testing, the expert had destroyed those parts. Those parts thus were no longer available for later examination and replicate testing by the defendant. The defendant, in effect, moved to dismiss the case and that motion was allowed in the trial court. On appeal, the Supreme Judicial Court reversed but, in the process, set out the remedy that is to be used in the event of an expert's intentional or negligent spoliation of evidence that is material to a case in which the expert has been hired to testify. The court's explanation is clear:

> We conclude that, in a civil case, where an expert has removed an item of physical evidence and the item has disappeared, or the expert has caused a change in the substance or appearance of such an item in such circumstances that the expert knows or reasonably should know that the item in its original form may be material to litigation, the judge, at the request of a potentially prejudiced litigant, should preclude the expert from testifying as to his or her observations of such items

before he or she altered them and as to any opinion based thereon. The rule should be applied without regard for whether the expert's conduct occurred before or after the expert was retained by a party to the litigation. The reason for the rule is the unfair prejudice that may result from allowing an expert to deliberately or negligently to put himself or herself in the position of being the only expert with first-hand knowledge of the physical evidence on which the expert opinions as to defects and causation may be grounded. Furthermore, as is possible in this case, the physical items themselves, in the precise condition they were in immediately after an accident, may be far more instructive and persuasive to a jury than oral or photographic descriptions of them. As a matter of sound policy, an expert should not be permitted to intentionally or negligently destroy or dispose of such evidence, and then to substitute his or her own description of it.

Example 20.25

Patton v. Newmar Corp., 538 N.W.2d 116 (Minn. 1995)

The plaintiffs were traveling across California in their motor home when it caught on fire. The driver pulled off the road, and the plaintiffs attempted to get out by way of the passenger side door. While doing so, one of the plaintiffs tripped and allegedly sustained an injury to her back.

After the fire, the vehicle was towed to an auto salvage yard. Six months later, the plaintiffs' counsel retained an expert fire investigator to conduct an examination of what remained of the vehicle. During the course of this investigation, the expert extensively photographed the vehicle and removed and retained several unidentified components.

The plaintiffs commenced this action, alleging that the injuries were the result of the defendant's negligence in its design of what they characterized as a faulty dual fuel system. When the defendant requested to inspect the vehicle, it was informed that the location of the motor home was not known and that the unidentified components removed and retained by the plaintiffs' expert had been lost.

The trial court excluded the expert witness's testimony and other evidence derived from his investigation. As a result, the plaintiff could not prove its case, and the court dismissed the action.

Example 20.26

Hamann v. Ridge Tool Co., 539 N.W.2d 753, 757 (Mich. Ct. App. 1995)

The fifty-year-old plaintiff, an ironworker, broke his knee during a bridge reinforcement project when the cable hoist holding the cable supporting the plaintiff broke. When the hoist handle frame broke, it shattered into several pieces, three of which were retrieved. One of the plaintiff's experts examined two of the pieces. The plaintiff's attorney then delivered the pieces to another of the plaintiff's experts. While in the custody of this second expert, those pieces were lost. Of the parties' experts, therefore, only the first had the opportunity to examine the pieces. The trial court allowed the plaintiff to offer expert testimony about the evidence. The appellate court reversed that decision, concluding that the trial court erred in permitting the plaintiff to offer testimony about evidence that was lost, even though it was lost unintentionally.

Example 20.27
Gentry v. Toyota Motor Corp., 471 S.E.2d 485, 488 (Va. 1996)
Here, the Supreme Court of Virginia considered the circumstances under which a party may be sanctioned for spoliation of evidence by that party's expert. The case involved claims arising out of an accident that occurred when one of the plaintiffs lost control of her Toyota truck and crashed into a ravine. The plaintiffs' attorney hired a self-styled sudden acceleration expert who, without receiving authorization from anyone, used a hacksaw to cut into the truck's instrument panel and removed a temperature control cable. At a hearing, Toyota's expert testified that the plaintiffs' expert's conduct had prevented him from evaluating whether the temperature control cable had been involved in causing the accident. The plaintiffs then alleged a new cause of the accident based on the anticipated opinion of a new expert. That new opinion attributed the cause of the crash to a carburetor problem unrelated to the tampered-with temperature control cable. Toyota's expert acknowledged that his evaluation of the plaintiffs' new theory was not affected by anything the plaintiffs' first expert had done to the vehicle.

Nevertheless, the trial court dismissed the case based on the first expert's spoliation of evidence. The Supreme Court reversed and held that, because neither plaintiffs nor their counsel acted in bad faith, and because the first expert's conduct did not prejudice Toyota, the trial court had abused its discretion in dismissing the plaintiffs' action.

20.13 Risk Management for Experts

There are many techniques that can minimize an expert's exposure to loss as a result of her work as an expert witness. These techniques include the following.

1. Testifying honestly

Truth is a defense to defamation actions. Truthful testimony is not perjurious. If an individual is untruthful, the law may offer her fewer protections from civil liability. Additionally, she could be subject to professional discipline and her reputation can and should suffer.

2. Doing one's homework and being competent

Experts should double- and triple-check their data, computations, and conclusions. Many experts get into trouble because of sloppy work. It is best to be careful and do a good job.

3. Not discussing cases

Expert immunity only applies to statements made in the course of the litigation. It does not apply to statements made outside of the context of litigation, such as statements to the press.

4. Maintaining insurance

Experts should consider maintaining liability insurance against the risks associated with serving as an expert. Even if actual expert civil liability is relatively rare, such insurance will provide peace of mind and will pay the legal costs of defending claims.

5. Not destroying, losing, or misplacing evidence

Experts must be very careful with evidence. They should not use destructive testing techniques unless all counsel and parties approve.[34] In many cases, spoliation of evidence will result in the expert's retaining party losing the case and it may subject the expert to civil liability.

6. Calling cases as one sees them

This is true even if the testimony would be unfavorable to the party that retained the expert and contrary to how she originally intended to testify. Honesty and truthfulness are paramount.

7. Avoiding conflicts of interest

Experts should not get involved in any cases where there may be a conflict of interest.

20.14 Conclusion

The potential liability of expert witnesses varies from jurisdiction to jurisdiction. To help avoid potential liability, experts should practice sound risk management.

[34] Destructive testing is done frequently, but it is usually coordinated among all parties so they have a chance to get involved.

Chapter 21 Privilege, Work Product, and Expert Discovery

21.1 Introduction

Experts should understand privilege, work product, and the limits to expert discovery.

21.2 Attorney-Client Privilege

The attorney-client privilege protects confidential communications between a client and an attorney and the attorney's agents, made for the purpose of obtaining legal services or advice from that attorney. **Because an expert is not the attorney's client, the attorney-client privilege generally *does not* protect communications between the expert and the retaining attorney.** Therefore, experts should assume that any oral or written communication they make with their retaining attorney will be discoverable and can and will be used against them and their clients.

Attorney-Client Privilege Generally

The attorney-client privilege is held by the attorney's client.[1] Generally, an attorney has a privilege to refuse to disclose and to prevent any other person from disclosing communications intended to be confidential and made for the purpose of facilitating the rendition of professional legal services to the client.[2] The privilege is designed to encourage full and truthful communication between client and attorney in order to improve the quality of the advice that a client receives. Only the communication is privileged, not the underlying facts. In essence, the privilege means only that *what a client says* about events to her lawyer is protected, not what the client may know about the events in controversy in the lawsuit.[3]

The Expert and the Attorney-Client Privilege

Generally, the privilege encompasses confidential communications made to a *representative* of the lawyer—that is, a person employed by the lawyer to

---

[1] The work-product privilege, in contrast, belongs to the attorney.

[2] The Federal Rules of Evidence do not spell out particular privileges. Rather, Fed. Rule Evid. 501 provides for the application in federal court of federal common law privileges and state law privileges when state law governs the case. Federal common law and every state recognize the attorney-client privilege.

[3] Stanley D. Davis and Thomas D. Beisecker, "Discovering Trial Consultant Work Product: A New Way to Borrow an Adversary's Wits?" 17 *American Journal of Trial Advocacy* (1994) 580, 592.

assist in the rendition of professional legal services.[4] Thus, an expert who is a representative of a lawyer may fall within the privilege. Whether an expert falls into the category of "representative" turns on the distinction between an expert hired to testify and an expert consulted as an advisor. An expert hired as a witness will not be a representative and will be precluded from invoking the privilege.[5] This is because the testifying expert will be presenting evidence rather than assisting the attorney in "render[ing] legal services."[6] However, a nontestifying expert retained to assist counsel may qualify as a representative. The privilege will, however, only shield knowledge obtained from the lawyer, who obtained it from the client. Knowledge that the expert obtains from sources other than the communication by the client to the attorney will not be protected by the privilege.

Although the attorney-client privilege is very deep, it is very narrow. When it applies, it is very difficult to overcome. However, it applies in very limited circumstances. The privilege will rarely arise in matters involving experts. This is because nontestifying experts are, for the most part, immune from discovery and because attorneys will not provide testifying experts with confidential information because they know that this kind of disclosure might jeopardize the privilege.

Example 21.1: Communications between attorney and litigation consultant
Baxter Travenol Laboratories, Inc. v. Lemay, 89 F.R.D. 410 (S.D. Ohio 1981)
In this case, a plaintiff's attorney hired a former associate of the defendant as a litigation consultant. The attorney hired the consultant to aid in an investigation to supply the basis for evaluating the plaintiff's legal rights, including potential litigation. The defendants sought to discover the substance of the conversations between the consultant and the attorney. The court applied the attorney-client privilege to the conversations and held them undiscoverable.

Example 21.2: Communications between lawyer and nontestifying expert
Oines v. State, 803 P.2d 884 (Alaska App. 1990)
In this criminal prosecution for drunk driving, the defendant's attorney secured a blood alcohol expert as an expert witness regarding blood test results. The court held that the results of the tests performed by the defense expert were

---

[4] Jack B. Weinstein and Margaret A. Berger, 2 *Weinstein's Evidence* 503(c)[01](1989) 503–516. An example of the formulation of the privilege appears in what is now known as Supreme Court Standard 503: "A client has a privilege to refuse to disclose and to prevent any other person from disclosing confidential communications made for the purpose of facilitating the rendition of professional legal services to the client."

[5] Daisy Hurst Floyd, "A 'Delicate and Difficult Task': Balancing the Competing Interests of Federal Rule of Evidence 612, The Work Product Doctrine, and the Attorney-Client Privilege," 44 *Buffalo L. Rev.* (1996) 101.

[6] Another related basis for excluding testifying experts from the definition of representative is that their communications are subject to disclosure at trial and therefore cannot be considered confidential.

privileged. It reasoned that the expert was a representative of the lawyer representing the client, and the results of the blood test were confidential communications between the lawyer and the lawyer's representative. The rationale for this protection in this particular case was to allow the attorney freedom to make an informed judgment regarding the best defense for his client without creating a witness for the state.

Example 21.3: Privilege applied to expert's environmental audit report
Olen Properties Corp. v. Sheldahl Inc., 1994 W.L. 212135 (C.D. Cal. April 12, 1994)
Here, a company had requested an environmental audit report, which it then provided to its in-house counsel. The court found that the report had been prepared for the purpose of securing an opinion of law, and thus the court applied the attorney-client privilege to the disclosure of the report.

Example 21.4: Nontestifying expert within the privilege
Bailey v. Meister Brau, Inc., 57 F.R.D. 11 (N.D. Ill. 1972)
In this case, the defendant sought to discover documents. The plaintiff's attorney hired a financial expert to analyze the financial situation of a company. One of the documents was prepared by the plaintiff and summarized discussions between the client, the attorney, and the expert. A second document summarized similar conversations and was prepared by the attorney. A third document, prepared by the plaintiff, contained projections and was read by an accountant retained by the attorney. The court found the privilege to apply to all the documents, based on the principle that confidentiality is not destroyed if a third party privy to the confidential communication is someone hired by the attorney to facilitate the rendition of legal services. The court held that both the expert and the accountant were hired to do so.

Waiver

An adverse party may discover materials within the attorney-client privilege if the privilege is waived. *Waiver* can occur when the client discloses the information in a nonprivileged setting, most often a setting in the presence of a third party. An attorney, as the client's agent, may also waive the privilege for the client by disclosing information in a nonprivileged setting.[7] Such a waiver may take place purposely or inadvertently, although the standards vary from jurisdiction to jurisdiction. Waiver usually occurs when the client or lawyer discloses the confidential communication to someone other than those included within the scope of the privilege. As discussed in the previous section, a consulting expert generally falls within the scope of the privilege, while a testifying expert falls outside. In other words, if the client or the attorney discloses confidential information to a third party who happens to be a consulting expert, there has been no waiver. The same cannot be said for a disclosure to a testifying expert.

---

[7] Many jurisdictions will find that the disclosing attorney, as the client's agent, had implied authority to waive the privilege.

Example 21.5: Waiver of privilege in patent infringement case
Multiform Dessicants v. Stanhope Products Co., 930 F.Supp. 45 (W.D.N.Y. 1996)
In this patent infringement/validity case, a party designated the attorney who prosecuted the patent as an expert witness. The court held that, by doing so, the party waived any attorney-client or work-product protection from the disclosure of all information pertaining to the subject matter of the expert's opinion.

Example 21.6: Circulation of memo waives privilege
Bituminous Cas. Corp. v. Tonka Corp., 140 F.R.D. 381 (D. Minn. 1992)
Here, counsel for the plaintiff copied the plaintiff's environmental consultant on memoranda regarding the environmental consultant's report. The court found the attorney's action to have waived the client's attorney-client privilege regarding the memoranda.

Example 21.7: Defendant waives privilege
Daniels v. Hadley Memorial Hospital, 68 F.R.D. 583 (D.D.C. 1975)
In this medical malpractice action, the defendant anesthesiologist spoke with an insurance adjuster regarding the claim against her. The adjuster was an agent of the defendant's attorney because he was hired by the attorney to investigate. The adjuster conveyed some of the doctor's statements to the plaintiff's attorney. The plaintiff then sought to depose the agent regarding the defendant's statements. The court found that these statements would have been protected under the attorney-client privilege because the adjuster was a representative of the attorney. However, the defendant waived the privilege by testifying about the statements in her own deposition.

21.3 Work Product

Work product is essentially trial preparation material. This includes facts and information "hidden" in the attorney's file and the thought processes—and related notes, drafts, or discussions—of an attorney or an expert that lead up to an opinion or a theory. *Core,* or *opinion, work product* refers to analysis, while *fact,* or *ordinary, work product* refers simply to factual information underlying an analysis. The work-product privilege held by the attorney attaches to materials prepared by counsel or counsel's representatives in anticipation of litigation and allows them to be discovered only upon a showing of need. The need that the discovering party must show varies and depends upon whether the materials sought are fact or opinion work product. The privilege is waivable.

An expert's opinions provide the attorney with invaluable insight into the best way to pursue a case. To get to this insight efficiently, the attorney may furnish to the expert witness documents that detail the underlying facts of the litigation, or she may disclose her analysis of the case to the expert through memoranda, highlighted or condensed witness statements, correspondence, or some other type of background document she prepared.

This trial preparation material ("work product") is, to varying degrees, protected from discovery.[8]

Conflictingly, the discovery rules say that the "things" that an expert considers when forming an opinion are discoverable. This is a conflict that the courts have resolved inconsistently. These inconsistencies make it difficult to present a clear picture of the discovery rules as they relate to work product. They make it more difficult still to answer the expert's ultimate question here: what is discoverable? An overview of the general rules appears below.

Overview

Generally speaking, there is little protection given to expert witnesses who are expected to testify at trial. Much more protection is given to experts who will not be testifying at trial. Expert witnesses, therefore, should *assume* that any document they create or review and any conversation they have with retaining counsel will be subject to discovery.

The general breakdown of the work-product privilege and the expert discovery rules follows.

1. The opinions of and the facts known by an expert retained in anticipation of litigation but not expected to testify (a nontestifying expert) are exempt from discovery unless the other side makes a showing of exceptional circumstances under which it is impracticable for them to obtain facts or opinions on the same subject by other means.

2. Experts who will testify (testifying experts) must disclose opinions, the bases for them, and all information considered in forming them. The testifying expert can be deposed. Moreover, the other side can discover documents and tangible things prepared in anticipation of litigation by the expert, if the other side can show a substantial need for the materials and an inability to obtain the substantial equivalent of the materials elsewhere without undue hardship. However, the rule says that after the required showing has been made, the court must still protect against the disclosure of the mental impressions, opinions, or legal theories of the attorney or the expert regarding the litigation (opinion work product). Some courts apply the conflicting rules by the analysis set forth in a, b, and c below. Others, however, dispense with this analysis and allow the discovery of all documents an attorney discloses to the expert.

---

[8] The rationale of this protection is to allow the attorney the freedom to examine the case from numerous angles and to consider all possible theories. The basic formulation of the protection—traditionally called the "work-product privilege"—is found in *Hickman v. Taylor,* 329 U.S. 495 (1947).

a.) The testifying expert's "documents or tangible things prepared in anticipation of litigation," such as drafts or margin notes, will be discoverable once the showing of substantial need has been made. The showing of substantial need will need to be more compelling if the document contains the expert's opinions than if it merely contains facts underlying the opinion.

b.) If these materials contain the opinion work product of the attorney, then the protection is even stronger. In some jurisdictions, the showing of substantial need will need to be even more compelling. In other jurisdictions, the expert's materials that contain attorney work product will not be discoverable, or at least the portions of the documents containing the opinion work product will be absolutely protected.

c.) If the attorney waives the privilege by improperly disclosing the work product, then no showing of need and undue hardship will be necessary. Whether it is possible to waive the protection for opinion work product is still an open question.

Usually, a work-product discovery controversy will center upon the attorney's work product disclosed to an expert because the attorney's freedom to develop the case is the underlying rationale for the protection. Experts will, of course, have their own work product, but the protection of opinion work product in practice applies only to the *attorney's* mental impressions.

Nontestifying experts

Whether the expert is retained to testify or merely to consult is a crucial distinction, because Rule 26(b)(4)(B) exempts the opinions of and the facts known by an expert retained in anticipation of litigation but not expected to testify from discovery. There are many confidentiality-related considerations that may push retaining counsel to use an expert as a consulting witness only. Counsel can protect the expert's identity, as well as her work product, much more readily and for a longer time than that of a testifying expert. Thus, counsel can consult with the expert freely. The expert might assist counsel in preparing for trial, in evaluating opposing experts' reports, in critiquing and preparing for the depositions of opposing experts, or simply in reminding the opposition that their expert's opinion will be scrutinized carefully.

Nontestifying experts: anticipation of litigation

If the document or tangible thing was not created in anticipation of litigation, then the discovery exemption does not apply. Consider the following example.

Example 21.8: Insurer's investigation not conducted in anticipation of litigation
Harper v. Auto-Owners Ins. Co., 138 F.R.D. 65 (S.D. Ind. 1991)
The plaintiff-insured sued the defendant after the defendant denied his claim for coverage resulting from a fire that destroyed his business. The plaintiff sought production of several documents produced in relation to his claim. The defendant asserted that all documents related to the claim, from the date of the fire, were privileged. The insurance company had hired counsel and arson investigators after the fire department's report indicated that the fire was incendiary in origin. The reports of the fire experts and of counsel's examination of the claimant were included in the file. The defendant asserted that the notice of the possibility of arson, based upon the fire department's reports, was in itself a threat of litigation and that all actions taken after that notice were in anticipation of litigation. The court rejected the claim of privilege. It found that the insurer's investigations were a routine business practice, thus they were not motivated because of the anticipation of litigation.

Nontestifying experts: exceptional circumstances

An opposing party can overcome the discovery protection afforded nontestifying experts by showing *exceptional circumstances* under which it is impracticable for them to obtain facts or opinions on the same subject by other means.[9] Exceptional circumstance, in the words of one court, means simply a basic lack of ability to discover the equivalent information.[10]

Example 21.9: Circumstances not exceptional
Hartford Fire Ins. Co. v. Pure Air on the Lake Ltd., 154 F.R.D. 202 (N.D. Ind. 1993)
In this litigation arising out of a subsurface collapse that resulted in extensive property damage to a construction site at a generating plant, the defendant sought to discover the reports of the plaintiff's nontestifying engineer expert. The reports contained information on the cause of the cave-in and attendant property damage. The court found that the subject of discovery was the cause of the collapsed pipes and that the defendant had ample opportunity to investigate and evaluate these pipes during the excavation process and, in fact, did undertake an investigation. Thus, the defendant made no showing that it could not discover equivalent information regarding the cause of the pipes' collapse.

Example 21.10: Circumstances exceptional
Delcastor, Inc. v. Vail Assoc., Inc., 108 F.R.D. 405 (D. Colo. 1985)
In this case, a mudslide destroyed a construction site. The next day, the defendant's consulting expert was at the site and subsequently prepared a

[9] This rule is designed to prevent an opposing party from using the experts of its adversary in an effort to prepare for litigation. *Hartford Fire Ins. Co. v. Pure Air on the Lake, Ltd.*, 154 F.R.D. 202, 207 (N.D. Ind. 1993).
[10] *Eliasen v. Hamilton,* 111 F.R.D. 396 (N.D. Ill. 1986).

report. The plaintiff's expert was unable to inspect the site until five days later, when the conditions had considerably changed and the conditions of the site immediately after the mudslide could not be reconstructed. The court found exceptional circumstances and ordered the nontestifying expert's report disclosed.

Example 21.11: Circumstances exceptional
Heitmann v. Concrete Pipe Machinery, 98 F.R.D. 740 (E.D. Mo. 1983)
In this case, a consulting expert engineer prepared a report for the defendant. The defendant then designated another engineer as a testifying expert. This expert was then deposed and at deposition noted that he had read the report when developing his opinion. The plaintiff sought production of the report. The court found that exceptional circumstances existed because the plaintiff needed the report in order to effectively cross-examine the testifying expert as to the bases of his opinion.

Example 21.12: Circumstances not exceptional
Shoemaker v. General Motors Corp., 154 F.R.D. 235 (W.D. Mo. 1994)
The plaintiffs' counsel could not attend testing performed by the defendant. The presence of the plaintiffs' counsel would reveal protected attorney work product and nontestifying expert information. The plaintiffs' fears regarding the integrity of the testing did not constitute exceptional circumstances justifying disclosure of information about facts known and opinions held by nontestifying experts.

Testifying experts

If an expert has been retained to testify, significant discovery is allowed. However, FRCP 26(b)(3), which codified the work-product privilege, protects from discovery documents and tangible things prepared in anticipation of litigation by the expert unless the other side can show a substantial need for the materials and an inability to obtain the substantial equivalent of the materials elsewhere without undue hardship. The rule also directs the courts to protect against the disclosure of "the mental impressions, conclusions, opinions, or legal theories of an attorney or other representative of a party concerning the litigation." In other words, the party seeking discovery must show substantial need to get to a testifying expert's fact work product. If the party seeks to discover opinion work product, the court should protect against discovery.

Testifying experts: documents or tangible things, conversations

The work-product protection of 26(b)(3) extends only to documents and tangible things. In some jurisdictions, the expert may be required to testify to conversations between the expert and the party's attorney containing work product because the conversation is neither a document nor a tangible thing, or because the expert considered information contained in the conversation when forming an opinion.

Example 21.13: Conversation discoverable
BCF Oil Ref., Inc. v. Consolidated Edison Co., 171 F.R.D. 57 (S.D.N.Y. 1997)
Here, the court considered a request by the defendant to discover the substance of conversations between a testifying expert and counsel that contained the attorney's mental impressions. The court noted that "data or other information" means documents or conversations, and that an expert could be asked about such conversations at deposition. However, the court held that an attorney's notes recording such conversations, which were never shown to the expert, were not discoverable. The expert could not have "considered" the documents if he never saw them.

Example 21.14: Conversation not a tangible thing, not discoverable
Maynard v. Whirlpoool Corp., 10 F.R.D. 85 (S.D.W.Va. 1995)
Here, the plaintiffs sought to compel the defendant's expert to respond to deposition questions inquiring about statements defense counsel made to the expert regarding a former expert. The plaintiffs hoped to show that defense counsel was dissatisfied with the former expert. The court found that the conversation was not a document or tangible thing, thus Rule 26(b)(3) was not applicable. It found that the conversation contained counsel's mental impressions and looked to the common law to determine that these impressions were privileged. The court did not allow the discovery of the conversation.

Testifying experts: documents prepared in anticipation of litigation

A document must have been prepared in anticipation of litigation or for trial in order to benefit from work-product protection. Thus, documents prepared after a potential cause of action arises, even if actual litigation has not yet begun, are usually work product. However, documents prepared in the regular course of business might not be protected. Courts generally look at the primary purpose for the preparation of the document to determine this element.[11]

Example 21.15: Prepared in anticipation of litigation
Magee v. Paul Revere Life Ins. Co., 172 F.R.D. 627 (E.D.N.Y. 1997)
Here, an insurance company hired a psychiatrist to review a claims file that included correspondence between outside counsel and the claims manager. The expert was designated a testifying expert and the plaintiff sought discovery of several pieces of correspondence that the expert had considered in forming his opinion. The court explained that if a document was prepared exclusively or principally to assist in anticipated or ongoing litigation, then the documents would meet this prong of the work product analysis. However, if the materials are assembled in the ordinary course of business, they are not shielded. The court then noted that this distinction is especially difficult to ascertain in insurance cases. Then it held that the document that was generated after

[11] Connie C. Sandifer and Timothy J. Chung, "Ethics and Professional Responsibility Work Product Doctrine." ALI-ABA Course of Study Materials SC45: Eminent Domain and Land Valuation Litigation (January 1998) 117.

litigation had begun was prepared in anticipation of litigation. The second two documents were created after the claimant's counsel had threatened litigation. The court found that because of this, it was reasonable for defendants to anticipate litigation. Thus, work-product protection was triggered.

Example 21.16: Prepared in anticipation of litigation
Logan v. Commercial Union, 96 F.3d 971 (7th Cir. 1996)
In this case, a plaintiff-insured sued the insurer based upon a denial of coverage. The plaintiff sought to discover documents composed by the insurer relating to the processing and disposition of his claim. The insurer had produced much of the claim file, but withheld several documents that had been created after the plaintiff's claim had been denied on the grounds that they were protected by work-product protection. The court inspected the documents in chambers and found that the work-product doctrine applied. It found that the documents were not only created after the initial claim had been submitted, investigated, and denied, but after the plaintiff filed suit with the state workers' compensation board. Moreover, the court found that the general subject matter of the documents concerned how the insurer planned to defend against the plaintiff's workers' compensation claim. The court noted, however, that "the mere fact that litigation does eventually ensue does not, by itself, cloak materials…with the work product privilege; the privilege is not that broad."

Example 21.17: Anticipation of litigation—investigation by federal agency
Martin v. Monfort, Inc., 150 F.R.D. 172 (D. Colo. 1993)
In this case, the Department of Labor sought to compel the discovery of studies conducted by the corporate employer under investigation. Counsel for a corporate employer was contacted by the Department of Labor concerning the corporate employer's potential violations of the Fair Labor Standards Act. The studies were then conducted. The court found that the work-product privilege protected the documents and that "[I]nvestigation by a federal agency presents more than a remote prospect of future litigation, and provides reasonable grounds for anticipating litigation sufficient to trigger application of the work-product doctrine."

Example 21.18: Anticipation of litigation—insurance documents
Henderson v. Zurn Industries, Inc., 131 F.R.D. 560 (S.D. Ind. 1990)
Here, the defendant's employee sued for injuries sustained when a ladder fell on him. The defendant asserted work-product privilege for its insurance company's files regarding the claim at issue. The court found that these documents were privileged because they had been prepared after the insurance company had received a very detailed letter from the plaintiff's attorney regarding settlement negotiations. The letter also contained a threat to file a lawsuit. The court applied privilege to all insurance documents prepared after the receipt of this letter.

Example 21.19: Documents not prepared in anticipation of litigation
Taroli v. General Elec. Co., 114 F.R.D. 97 (N.D. Ind. 1987)
Here, the plaintiff brought a products liability action against the manufacturer of a light bulb that exploded and injured the plaintiff. The plaintiff sought to

discover documents prepared by the defendant's insurance carrier. These documents contained statements of third parties taken by the carrier and a report prepared by an independent adjusting company at the request of the insurance carrier. The defendant claimed work-product privilege. It asserted that the insurance company had conducted its investigation (and hired the independent adjuster) in anticipation of litigation, because it had received a letter of subrogation and also because the report was prepared after the decision to deny coverage had been made. The court denied the work-product protection. It noted that the mere fact that the plaintiff has consulted an attorney is not enough to trigger a reasonable anticipation of litigation and that a subrogation notice cannot be used to create a work-product privilege in every instance.

Example 21.20: Not in anticipation of litigation
Coastal States Gas. Corp. v. Dept. of Energy, 617 F.2d 854 (D.C. Cir. 1980)
In this case, the plaintiff sought to discover memoranda from the Department of Energy's regional counsel to auditors working in the DOE's field offices pertaining to interpretations of regulations. The court found that the work-product privilege did not apply to these memoranda because no claim had arisen—there was no specific charge or allegation—during the audits before the memoranda had been written. The court pointed out that the audits were not investigations, they were merely measuring compliance with certain regulations. The court compared the case to several in which governmental agencies had successfully protected documents with the privilege, but that in each case a specific allegation was under investigation. Here, the court found, a mere audit could not create anticipation of litigation.

Example 21.21: Not in anticipation of litigation
Binks Mfg. Co. v. Nat. Presto Industries, Inc., 709 F.2d 1109 (7th Cir. 1983)
In this contract dispute over payment for a paint system that did not work, the plaintiff compelled discovery of two memos written by the defendant's in-house counsel to the defendant assessing the conflict. On appeal, the court considered whether the privilege should have protected the memos. The court looked to the exchange of correspondence between the parties before the memos were composed to determine whether the memos were prepared in anticipation of litigation. The court found no explicit threats of litigation in the pre-memo correspondence. Rather, the letters were intended to persuade the plaintiff to correct the alleged problem. The court then declared that although the pre-memo correspondence may have evidenced the remote prospect of litigation, the memos were not prepared *because* of that prospect or because of some articulable claim *likely* to lead to litigation. The work-product privilege was found to be inapplicable.

Example 21.22: Not in anticipation of litigation—routine business practice
Harper v. Auto-Owners Ins. Co., 138 F.R.D. 65 (S.D. Ind. 1991)
The plaintiff-insured sued the defendant after the defendant denied his claim for coverage resulting from a fire that destroyed his business. The plaintiff sought production of several documents produced in relation to his claim. The

defendant asserted that all documents related to the claim from the date of the fire were privileged. The insurance company had hired counsel and arson investigators after the fire department's report indicated that the fire was incendiary in origin. The reports of the fire experts and of counsel's examination of the claimant were included in the file. The defendant asserted that the notice of the possibility of arson, based upon the fire department's reports, was in itself a threat of litigation and that all actions taken after that notice were in anticipation of litigation. The court rejected the claim of privilege. It found that the insurer's investigations were a routine business practice, thus they were not motivated because of the anticipation of litigation.

Work-product protection extends only to materials prepared by or for another party, or by or for that other party's representative—including the other party's attorney, consultant, surety, indemnitor, insurer, or agent. Accordingly, expert witnesses fall within the scope of the rule. In determining this element, the court will weigh the motivation behind the production of the document more heavily than the classification of the person who prepared it.[12]

Testifying experts: fact work product

Fact, or ordinary, work product generally refers to situations in which counsel furnishes to the expert witness documents that detail the underlying facts of the litigation. Though ostensibly subject to the protection of 26(b)(3), most courts do not require the showing of substantial need and undue hardship when the documents sought contain fact work product. Most simply declare the fact work product to be "data or other information considered" by the expert and order its disclosure. Consider the following.

Example 21.23: Fact work product discoverable
B.C.F. Oil Ref., Inc. v. Con. Edison Co., 171 F.R.D.57 (S.D.N.Y. 1997)
Here, an oil refiner brought an action against an electric utility and oil transporters, alleging that the utility distributed, and the transporters delivered, contaminated oil to the refinery. The defendants sought production of numerous documents by the plaintiff, which the plaintiff claimed were protected by the work-product privilege. A group of documents provided to the testifying expert by counsel contained facts and "assemblages of facts." The court discussed the notion that an attorney must be able to sift relevant from irrelevant facts and must be able to provide the relevant facts to the expert. The court found that this factual information did not deserve as much protection as opinion work product. It cited the need for the adversary to know the basis of the expert's opinion as overriding, then it held the information discoverable as "data or other information considered" by the expert. The court engaged in no substantial need analysis.

[12] *Id.*

Example 21.24: Fact work product discoverable at deposition, opinion work product not discoverable
Haworth, Inc. v. Herman Miller, Inc., 162 F.R.D. 289 (W.D. Mich. 1995)
In this patent infringement action, the defendant deposed the plaintiff's trial expert. Defense counsel asked the expert to testify about discussions he had with plaintiff's counsel regarding the defendant's product manuals. The plaintiff's counsel had provided these manuals to the expert. The court noted that all factual information considered by an expert must be disclosed in the expert's report. It went on to say that attorneys should no longer be able to make work-product privilege arguments regarding materials containing facts or assemblages of facts because they are obligated to disclose all factual information on their own. The court then discussed which questions regarding the conversations were allowed. If the question tests whether certain facts had not been provided to the expert for his consideration, it would be allowed. The court did not allow questions regarding opinion work product.

Testifying experts: How can the opposing party overcome work-product protection?

Parties seeking discovery of work product materials may defeat the protection 26(b)(3) offers if the parties meet two requirements. First, they must show that a *substantial need* for the documents exists. Second, they must show an inability "to obtain, without undue hardship, the substantial equivalent of the materials by other means." If the party seeks discovery of opinion work product, it will likely need to show an even more compelling need and an even more burdensome hardship. This standard is vaguely defined, and some courts grant absolute protection to opinion work product.

Substantial need and undue hardship

Courts have either applied the requirement of substantial need unevenly or they have completely glossed over any discussion of it. Generally, the importance of the materials, whether the party needs them to prove its case, and whether the information will be useful for impeachment purposes are the usual factors a court considers.[13] To meet the undue hardship requirement, a party must show that it has tried and been unable to obtain the information contained in the requested documents without going to great lengths; that it lacks knowledge of where else to obtain it; or that the information is completely unavailable elsewhere.[14]

---

[13] Daisy Hurst Floyd, "A 'Delicate and Difficult Task': Balancing the Competing Interests of Federal Rule of Evidence 612, The Work Product Doctrine, and the Attorney-Client Privilege," 44 *Buffalo L. Rev.* (1996) 101, 112.

[14] Kevin M. Clermont, "Surveying Work Product," 68 *Cornell Law Review* (1983) 755, 802.

Example 21.25: No substantial need
Magee v. Paul Revere Life Ins. Co., 172 F.R.D. 627 (E.D.N.Y. 1997)
Here, an insurance company hired a psychiatrist to review a claims file that included correspondence between outside counsel and the claims manager. The expert was designated a testifying expert and the plaintiff sought discovery of the correspondence that the expert had considered in forming his opinion. The plaintiff claimed substantial need based upon his observation that the documents related to a review of the defendant's handling of the claim, including the manner in which an independent medical examination was conducted and the denial of benefits. The plaintiff also claimed the documents were essential to his proof of related intentional tort claims. The court found no substantial need in light of the fact that the tort claims had been dismissed. The court did, however, order the documents to be reviewed in camera so that the court could determine if they contained discoverable factual information.

Example 21.26: No need
Hamel v. General Motors Corp., 128 F.R.D. 281 (D. Kan. 1989)
Here, the plaintiff requested the production of documents from the defendant's expert witness. There was no question that the material was opinion work product. The plaintiff sought the documents in order to use them to suggest that the expert developed his opinions by the statements of the defense counsel. However, the plaintiff made no showing of which of the forty-two documents requested were relied upon by the expert. The plaintiff merely assumed that the expert would lie if asked about the documents upon which he based his opinion. The court found that the plaintiff did not show why he could learn, himself, from the witness, which documents the witness examined; nor did he show why the requested documents would be necessary to impeach the witness. The court concluded that the plaintiff based the request on "little more than speculative need," which did not rise to the level of substantial need.

Example 21.27: No substantial need
Rail Intermodal Specialists v. Gen. Electric Capital Corp., 154 F.R.D. 218 (N.D. Iowa 1994)
In this contract interference action, counsel for the defendant sent identical letters to two testifying expert witnesses. The experts were to testify regarding loss of business and damages. At deposition, each expert testified that he had relied upon the letters in formulating an opinion. The plaintiff contended that the discovery rules required production because the experts relied on the letters and that effective cross-examination of the experts required disclosure. The defendant objected to production of the letters, claiming that they contained counsel's mental impressions. The court reviewed the letters in camera. It found that the plaintiff had no substantial need for production of the letters, even for cross-examination purposes. The court concluded that the information in the letters was available to the plaintiff from the experts themselves or from other documents already available as a result of the extensive discovery already conducted.

Example 21.28: Substantial need, danger of undue hardship
State ex. rel. Butterworth v. Industrial Chemicals, Inc., 145 F.R.D. 585 (N.D. Fla. 1991)
Here, the state of Florida filed an antitrust action against the defendant. The defendant sought discovery of civil investigation demand depositions that the plaintiff had collected during a two-year investigation of the defendant. The court found that even if the documents contained attorney mental processes, the defendant made a showing of substantial need. The court noted that the documents contained the very evidence upon which the state based its case. Without discovery, the defendant would have no idea of the particulars of the state's action. Regarding the undue hardship prong, the court stated that the complexity of the case and the massive amounts of documentation amassed would render it difficult for the defendant to replicate the state's investigation when the information was readily available in the documents at issue.

Mental impressions and legal theories of attorney

When the documents or information sought contain the attorney's mental impressions or legal analysis of the case, the law governing discovery is quite muddled. The discovery rules conflict: the expert is required to disclose "all data or other information considered by a testifying expert in forming the opinions,"[15] yet the court is directed to protect against disclosure of the mental impressions, conclusions, opinions, or legal theories of an attorney.[16] In other words, when the material "considered" by the expert includes opinion work product, the court will face the opposing dictates of the two discovery rules.[17] Some jurisdictions have concluded that attorney-expert mental impression communications are outside the scope of disclosure because "data or other information" connotes only facts. Others have decided that the disclosure requirements override the work-product shield.

Example 21.29: Opinion work product protected
Haworth, Inc. v. Herman Miller, Inc., 162 F.R.D. 289 (W.D. Mich. 1995)
In this patent infringement action, the defendant deposed the plaintiff's trial expert. Defense counsel asked the expert to testify about discussions he had with plaintiff's counsel regarding the defendant's product manuals. Plaintiff's counsel had provided these manuals to the expert. The court noted that all factual information considered by an expert must be disclosed in the expert's report. It went on to say that attorneys should no longer be able to make work-product privilege arguments regarding materials containing facts or assemblages of facts because they are obligated to disclose all factual information on their own. The court then discussed which questions regarding the conversations were allowed. If the question tests whether certain facts had

[15] Fed. R. Civ. Pro. 26(a)(2)(B).
[16] Fed. R. Civ. Pro. 26(b)(3).
[17] Lee Mickus, "Discovery of Work Product Disclosed to a Testifying Expert Under the 1993 Amendments to the Federal Rules of Civil Procedure," 27 *Creighton L. Rev.* (1994) 773.

not been provided to the expert for his consideration or whether the expert's report reflects accurately all the facts actually considered, it would be proper.

The court did not allow questions regarding opinion work product. It specified that any question that created a danger of revealing the lawyer's mental impressions would not be proper.

Example 21.30: Opinion work product protected

Magee v. Paul Revere Life Ins. Co., 172 F.R.D. 627 (E.D.N.Y. 1997)
Here, an insurance company hired a psychiatrist to review a claims file that included correspondence between outside counsel and the claims manager. The expert was designated a testifying expert and the plaintiff sought discovery of the correspondence that the expert had considered in forming his opinion. This included the mental impressions of both in-house counsel and outside counsel to the defendant. The court held that the opinion work product was not absolutely privileged, but that the substantial need/undue hardship test was much harder to meet for opinion work product than for fact work product. The court did not allow discovery of the documents and approved the rule that "opinion work product enjoys a nearly absolute immunity and can be discovered only in very rare and extraordinary circumstances."

Example 21.31: Opinion work product discoverable

Musselman v. Phillips, 1997 U.S. Dist. Lexis 16898 (D. Md. Oct. 14, 1997)
In this intentional tort case, the defendant sought production of two letters written by the plaintiff's counsel to expert psychiatrists retained by the plaintiff to testify at trial. The court found that the experts had considered the letters, which contained counsel's mental impressions and legal theories. The court held that when an attorney communicates otherwise protected work product to an expert witness retained for purposes of providing opinion testimony at trial, whether factual in nature or containing the attorney's opinions or impressions, that information is discoverable.

Example 21.32: Opinion work product discoverable

Karn v. Rand, 168 F.R.D. 633 (N.D. Ind. 1996)
In this personal injury action, the defendant sought production of a medical chronology concerning the plaintiff's injury. The chronology was prepared by the plaintiff's attorney's staff and was reviewed by the plaintiff's vocational expert. The defendant also sought production of a letter from the plaintiff's counsel to the plaintiff's liability expert. The court held that "data or other information considered" by the expert means all materials containing work product. Thus, both documents were discoverable. The court noted that this "bright line" rule actually preserved work-product protection because there would be no uncertainty as to what was discoverable. However, the court did mention that oral communication containing work product is not discoverable.

Example 21.33: Opinion work product discoverable

B.C.F. Oil Ref. v. Consolidated Edison Co., 171 F.R.D. 57 (S.D.N.Y. 1997)
Here, an oil refiner brought an action against an electric utility and oil transporters, alleging that the utility distributed, and the transporters delivered,

contaminated oil to the refinery. The defendants sought production of numerous documents by the plaintiff, which the plaintiff claimed were protected by the work-product privilege. The expert was hired not only to give testimony regarding contamination, but also to assist the plaintiff's counsel with technical issues during the discovery process. The court considered four sets of documents.

The first set of documents was produced by or considered by the expert in his consulting role, rather than his testifying role. Thus, they were not discoverable.

The second set of documents was written by the expert during the preparation of his report and his expert testimony. The court found that all documents, including drafts and memoranda, produced by an expert as he develops his opinions to be presented at trial are discoverable. It ordered production of this set of documents.

The third set of documents contained facts and "assemblages of facts" provided to the expert by counsel. The court found that this factual information did not deserve as much protection as opinion work product and that it was discoverable as "data or other information considered" by the expert.

A fourth set of documents contained the mental impressions and explicit litigation strategies of the plaintiff's counsel. The court held that these were discoverable, relying on the open discovery policies underlying Rule 26 and granting much weight to the 26(a)(2) "data or other information considered" language.

Finally, the court discussed oral communications between the expert and counsel that contained the attorney's mental impressions. The court noted that "data or other information" means documents or conversations, and that an expert could be asked about such conversations at deposition. However, the court held that an attorney's notes recording such conversations, notes that were never shown to the expert, were not discoverable. The expert could not have "considered" the documents if he never saw them.

Example 21.34: Opinion work product discoverable
Lamonds v. General Motors Corp., 180 F.R.D. 302 (W.D. Va. July 2, 1998)
Here, the plaintiff brought a products liability action against an automobile manufacturer, alleging that a design defect in the automobile caused her to be severely injured in an accident. The defendant sought production of two documents that were created by the plaintiff's legal team and shared with the plaintiff's experts. The court declared that everything "considered" by the experts in forming their opinions was discoverable—in effect, stating that Rule 26(a)2 "trumps" the work-product protection of Rule 26(b)(3). Thus, the court held that the plaintiff must produce the documents, even though they contained opinion work product.

Example 21.35: Opinion work product discoverable
Nationwide Mut. Fire Ins. Co. v. Smith, 174 F.R.D. 250 (D. Conn. 1997)
In a counterclaim by claimants alleging that their insurance carrier, the plaintiff, acted in bad faith when denying coverage for a fire loss, the defendants sought to ask the plaintiff's fire investigator several questions at

deposition. They sought responses to questions about conversations and meetings between the investigator and a fire protection engineer who the plaintiff had retained to testify. The court found that even had the conversations occurred in anticipation of litigation (they did not), the plaintiff was entitled to answers even if they contained opinion work product. The defendants were entitled to discover how the insurer processed its fire claim and why the insurer denied the claim. The court based this on the fact that the facts and information considered by the testifying expert were discoverable. Moreover, the court stated that if it were required to consider a showing of substantial need, the defendants would have made the showing. This is because evidence of how an insurer processed a claim goes to the very heart of a bad faith action.

Waiver of work-product protection

An attorney may inadvertently waive work-product protection if she improperly discloses work product. Disclosure of opinion work product to an expert by an attorney traditionally has not operated as a waiver.

Example 21.36: Inadvertent waiver of work-product protection
Kennedy v. Baptist Memorial Hospital, 179 F.R.D. 520 (N.D. Miss. 1998)
In this medical malpractice action, the defendant retained an OB/GYN physician as a testifying expert. The expert sent a letter to the defendant's counsel that he was not qualified to opine regarding the cause of death and that the defendant was the victim of a miscommunication by another physician. The next day, the expert sent another letter to counsel in which he stated a cause of death, but he did not mention any communication between the defendant and the other physician. Counsel disclosed the two letters as reports, then the plaintiff sought production of any data and information considered by the expert in order to understand the significant changes in the expert's opinions. The court held that normally communications between counsel and a retained expert are protected by the work-product rule; in this case, the rule did not apply. The court explained that counsel "opened the door" to discovery of all communication, even work product, when he inadvertently disclosed the first letter, then the second letter with substantial revisions.

A rule of evidence provides that an opposing party may discover any document used by a witness to refresh his memory during or before testifying.[18] In the past, some courts held that by showing a testifying expert work product that the expert uses to testify, the attorney waives the privilege. This waiver, however, does not extend to opinion work product. Courts have shown great inconsistency and confusion as to where this rule fits with regard to work product.

[18] Fed. Rule Evid. 612.

21.4 Documents Produced by Experts

All written statements prepared by a testifying expert should be assumed to be discoverable. This includes administrative documents, such as time sheets, bills, engagement letters, and fax cover sheets. It bears repeating that experts and their staffs should commit to writing only what is necessary to assist in the preparation of a report or testimony. Retaining counsel will often try to reinforce this by asking an expert not to write a report until the expert has discussed his initial findings with her.

21.5 Draft Reports

Although the specifics of the law are unsettled, the legal realities can be stated generally as follows. First, drafts are generally discoverable. Second, a document is generally not privileged from discovery if it is a draft of a document, the final version of which is intended to be disclosed to third parties. Moreover, "since the weight of authority is that testifying experts and the attorneys do not share any privileges, it can be persuasively argued that any draft which is circulated is discoverable, regardless of its marginalia."[19]

Although Rule 26(a)(2) allows opposing counsel to discover everything that led to the formation of the expert's opinion (subject to the previously discussed work-product doctrine), communications between an expert and an attorney are often difficult to explore. Opposing counsel often attempts to get to these communications through drafts of expert reports that were circulated between the expert and the retaining attorney—the attempt is intended to shed light on the extent and nature of the attorney's influence on the formation of the expert's opinion. Experts and attorneys can, perhaps, minimize the discoverability of drafts by communicating over the phone, rather than in writing. Also, then, the expert can answer truthfully that no prior draft ever circulated. Opposing counsel will look for an analysis being removed from the expert's report because the result was not favorable, thus establishing bias and the unreliability—or falsity—of the expert's opinion. She would love for the expert to say to the jury that he "destroyed" previous drafts of the report, which might get the jury wondering why the expert would destroy something that should bolster his testimony. Opposing counsel would also love to see a trail of drafts to show that an expert's opinion was directed by the retaining attorney.

Kim K. Burke, an environmental lawyer, discusses the discovery of drafts:

> The first risk of alteration is obvious: trial counsel for the other side will ask for all drafts of the report, will focus upon any differences in the text, and will ask why those changes were made.

[19] Alan B. Rich, Advanced Evidence and Discovery Course, Chapter L: "Discovery of Expert Materials" (Nov. 1996). State Bar of Texas: State Bar of Texas Professional Development CLE Online, Austin.

> When the testimony is elicited that the attorney was responsible for the change in the document, this will seriously affect the credibility of the expert witness, and his/her independent opinion concerning technical matters. Typically, opposing counsel is baffled when no draft report has been prepared and that counsel would have enough confidence in his or her experts to allow a report to go directly to final. The final reports typically look less lawyer-like, and more like the product of a consultant, which they are. Again, the ability to follow this approach depends upon the trust that the trial attorney has in the experts, and the experts in each other.[20]

Another of the attorney's considerations regarding drafts:

> I am always delighted to have opposing counsel take the opportunity to carefully mark up every draft prepared by an expert so that I can show that the opinions rendered by the expert are not those of the expert, but rather the expert acting as the mouthpiece for the lawyer.[21]

The following examples illustrate the extensive scope of draft discovery.

Example 21.37: Drafts discoverable
B.C.F. Oil Refin. v. Consolidated Edison Co., 171 F.R.D. 57 (S.D.N.Y. 1997)
In this case (discussed earlier in the chapter), an oil refiner brought an action against an electric utility and oil transporters, alleging that the utility distributed, and the transporters delivered, contaminated oil to the refinery. The defendants sought production of numerous documents by the plaintiff that the plaintiff claimed were protected by the work-product privilege. The expert was hired not only to give testimony regarding contamination, but also to assist the plaintiff's counsel with technical issues during the discovery process. The court considered a set of documents which was written by the expert during the preparation of his report and his expert testimony. These included drafts. The court found that no work-product protection applied to documents generated by experts in connection with litigation. The court confirmed that this rule applied to all documents, including drafts and memoranda, that experts generate as they develop the opinions they will present at trial. It then ordered the production of the documents.

[20] Kim K. Burke, "The Use of Experts in Environmental Litigation: A Practitioner's Guide," 25 *N. Ky. L. Rev.* (1997) 111, 136.
[21] Kim K. Burke, "The Use of Experts in Environmental Litigation: A Practitioner's Guide," 25 *N. Ky. L. Rev.* (1997) 111, 136.

Example 21.38: Drafts of expert reports discoverable
Quadrini v. Sikorsky Aircraft Div., United Aircraft Corp., 74 F.R.D. 594 (D. Conn. 1977)
In this case arising out of a helicopter crash, both sides relied heavily on expert testimony. The defendant requested production from the plaintiff's expert of

> all reports, memoranda, papers, notes, studies, graphs, charts, tabulations, analyses, summaries, data sheets, statistical or informational accumulations, data processing cards or worksheets, and computer generated documents, including drafts or preliminary revisions of any of the above, prepared in connection with this litigation by or under the direction or supervision of any witness...

expected to testify at trial. The court held that effective cross-examination of experts would be essential in this complex and very technical case. Thus, the court ordered production of the documents.

21.6 Document Retention Policy

A carefully considered document retention policy can help alleviate many potential discovery headaches. During discovery, opposing counsel will ask something like, "What were the instructions, or communications, from the party that hired you?" Counsel might instead ask to see everything the expert has considered, including all correspondence with the attorney who retained her and all draft reports. These questions are designed to discover the extent to which counsel has made changes to the expert's report and influenced the formation of her opinion. Thus, not only should experts keep written communications to a minimum, they should develop a rational document retention policy. For example, draft reports might be discarded when no longer useful. When a second draft is prepared, the first might be discarded. An expert's motivation for this is quite rational: one discards drafts because no one working on the matter, such as a staff member, has to wonder whether they are looking at the most current version of the document. Early drafts might also be discarded simply because they are no longer needed. A reasonable and consistent document retention policy can mitigate opposing counsel's attempt to portray discarding drafts as manipulative and dishonest. Most sophisticated experts use the term *discarded* and not *destroyed* when describing documents that are no longer in their file according to their document retention policy.

21.7 Financial Records

A general distrust of expert witnesses, who are viewed as "professional witnesses," leads attorneys to often request the discovery of an expert witness's financial records in order to establish interest, bias, or prejudice. These may include income tax returns, receipts, journals, balance sheets, income statements, billings to law firms for testifying as an expert, and other records that show income earned from an expert's nonlegal services. Once discovered, attorneys will attempt to use financial records to show how much of an expert's income is generated from testifying, how many times an expert has testified, and an expert's previous associations with the retaining attorney in the current lawsuit.

Generally, opposing counsel may ask the expert questions relating to the expert's financial records and previous associations with participating attorneys. Less well settled is whether opposing counsel can require the production of the actual records. Courts have wide discretion to order disclosure of materials during discovery. As long as the materials are within the scope of discovery, the courts can at least consider ordering production. Moreover, under the Federal Rules, the testifying expert's report must contain not only the opinions and data considered in formulating it, but also a listing of cases in which the expert has testified. This is intended to allow some inquiry into the expert's history of expert witnessing. A court may easily find that an expert's financial records are "relevant" to the pending action. Indeed, many federal courts have permitted the discovery of information to be used to impeach the opposing party's expert witness. Many states have adopted rules identical to the federal discovery rules and have interpreted them similarly. On the other hand, several state courts have ruled that an expert witness's financial records are not within the scope of discovery when used as impeachment evidence to show that the expert has a history of testifying for a particular party—on the grounds that the records are not relevant.

The device opposing counsel will usually use to access an expert's financial records is the subpoena duces tecum. Interrogatories will seldom, if ever, be used to probe an expert's financial records. They are directed at parties. More importantly, the information obtained in an interrogatory will be less reliable than the information an attorney can get from an expert at her deposition.

Example 21.39: Financial records protected

Syken v. Elkins, 644 So.2d 539 (Fla. Dist. Ct. App. 1994)

Here, the court considered certain discovery orders directing a proposed medical expert in a personal injury action to produce an array of financial records. Specifically, the information sought numerous documentation regarding past IMEs performed by the expert. Also, a subpoena duces tecum was issued for all bills generated by the physician as a defense expert examiner to any insurance company or law firm, all journals, ledgers, and 1099 forms pertaining to payments received by the physician during a certain period for examinations performed at the request of any insurance company or law firm.

In setting out guidelines regarding what could be compelled and what could not, the court held that an expert "may be asked to give an approximation of the portion of their professional time or work devoted to service as an expert," but the witness "need not answer how much money he or she earns as an expert or how much the expert's total annual income is." The court's guidelines, by no means nationally followed, are nonetheless helpful as an example of one state's treatment of the issue:

1. The medical expert may be deposed either orally or by written deposition.
2. The expert may be asked as to the pending case, what he or she has been hired to do and what the compensation is to be.
3. The expert may be asked what expert work he or she generally does. Is the work performed for the plaintiffs, defendants, or some percentage of each?
4. The expert may be asked to give an approximation of the portion of their professional time or work devoted to service as an expert. This can be a fair estimate of some reasonable and truthful component of that work, such as hours expended, or percentage of income earned from that source, or the approximate number of IME's that he or she performs in one year. The expert need not answer how much money he or she earns as an expert or how much the expert's total annual income is.
5. The expert may be required to identify specifically each case in which he or she has actually testified, whether by deposition or at trial, going back a reasonable period of time, which is normally three years. A longer period of time may be inquired into under some circumstances.
6. The production of the expert's business records, files, and 1099's may be ordered produced only upon the most unusual or compelling circumstance.
7. The patient's privacy must be observed.
8. An expert may not be compelled to compile or produce nonexistent documents.

The Florida Supreme Court found these factors to strike a reasonable balance between a party's need for information concerning an expert witness's potential bias and the witness's right to be free from burdensome and intrusive production requests.

Example 21.40: Party's payments to expert discoverable from party
Allstate Insurance Co. v. Boecher, 24 Fla. L. Weekly S187 (Fla. April 22, 1999)
The court in this case held that the insured claimant could seek discovery from the party insurer regarding the extent of its relationship with a particular expert. Thus, the claimant could discover how often a particular expert testified on an insurer's behalf and how much money the expert made from its relationship with the insurer.

The alleged victim of an accident sued the defendant, his uninsured motorist carrier. The defendant intended to call an accident reconstruction and injury causation expert in the case. The claimant then propounded interrogatories to the defendant concerning the relationship between the defendant and the expert. The questions sought the identity of cases in which the expert had performed analyses and rendered opinions for the defendant, as well as the fees paid, nationally and in the preceding three years. The trial court overruled the defendant's objections of undue burden because the interrogatories were directed to the party and not to the expert. The appellate court affirmed the ruling, reasoning that the relationship between a particular expert and a party is directly relevant to a party's efforts to demonstrate the witness's bias. Limiting this discovery could potentially undermine the fairness of the trial. As such, the court held that a party may attempt to discover facts known directly by a party concerning the extent of that party's relationship with an expert witness.

Example 21.41: Financial records
Wrobleski v. de Lara, 727 A.2d 930 (Md. 1999)
In this medical malpractice case against a gynecologist, the defendant sought the production of numerous financial records from the plaintiff's physician expert. At deposition and at trial, the expert refused to reveal the amount of income he had received from testifying in 1995. The trial court allowed the question but did not force the expert to answer. The jury then found for the defendant. On appeal, the court found that the question was proper and that the jury could infer what they wished from the expert's refusal to answer it. The court limited its holding, explaining that,

> harassment of expert witnesses through a wholesale rummaging of their personal and financial records under the guise of seeking impeachment evidence is not permitted; rather, the allowance of the permitted inquiry, both at the discovery and trial stages, should be tightly controlled by the trial court and limited to its purpose, and not permitted to expand into an unnecessary exposure of matters and data that are personal to the witness and have no real relevance to the credibility of his or her testimony.

Example 21.42: Financial records discoverable
Orkin Exterminating Co., Inc. v. Knollwood Properties, Ltd., 710 So.2d 697 (Fla. App. 5 Dist. 1998)
Here, a trial court's order requiring an expert witness in a civil trial to provide a list identifying prior cases in which he had testified during the past three years was proper. No list identifying such cases existed. The only documents the expert had that would comply with the order were financial and business records. The expert was required to produce these records.

Example 21.43: Financial records discoverable
Rowe v. State Farm Mut. Auto. Ins. Co., 670 So.2d 718 (La. App. 3 Cir. 1996)
In this action by insured-plaintiffs against their uninsured/underinsured insurer, the plaintiffs sought production of financial and medical records of the medical expert retained by defense counsel. They sought the records in order to discover how much work the expert did for the defense counsel and the insurer. The court held that the plaintiffs should have been able to discover those records and that cross-examination alone was not effective to show the expert's possible bias.

Example 21.44: Financial records discoverable
McAdoo v. Ogden, 573 So.2d 1084 (Fla. App. 4 Dist. 1991)
In this personal injury suit, the plaintiff sought to examine copies of bills to individuals or companies for whom the defendant's expert had served as a defense expert in the previous year. The court allowed the discovery. It weighed the burden of the request and the confidentiality interests of the doctor with the relevancy of the information. It found that the expert's only burden was producing an estimate as to the approximate cost of compiling the information and subsequently supervising that procedure. The court held that the information sought was relevant in that it might serve to demonstrate the

expert's potential bias, if, as the plaintiff suggested, a significant part of the expert's income was derived from insurance company business.

21.8 Income Tax Records and Returns

Opposing counsel may seek an expert's tax returns or tax forms provided by clients in an attempt to discover the amount of compensation the expert has received for expert consulting and witnessing. The law varies state by state, but in many instances the trial judge may allow discovery of the documents but will first inspect the forms and returns in order to protect any information not directly relevant to the case.

Federal trial courts might also order production of tax records. Many follow a two-pronged test to determine whether to allow discovery of the tax records. The test requires (1) a finding that the returns are relevant to the subject matter of the action, and (2) a compelling need for the tax returns because the information is not otherwise readily obtainable. Some courts, both state and federal, have weighed in with the opinion that courts have gone too far in allowing inquiry into the private financial affairs of expert witnesses. Moreover, a qualified privilege is emerging that protects disclosure of a person's income tax records.

Example 21.45: Income tax returns not discoverable
Hawkins v. South Plains Intern. Trucks, Inc., 139 F.R.D. 679 (D. Colo. 1991)
The plaintiff, a mechanic, sued the manufacturer of a truck after the truck's oil unit's allegedly defective design caused injury to the plaintiff. The plaintiff retained an engineer as a testifying expert witness who would testify to the defective design of the piece of the defendant's truck at issue. The defendant sought to discover the income the expert had received as an expert witness. They sought production of the expert's income tax returns for the previous eleven years. The court applied the two-prong relevancy and compelling need test. The records were relevant to the expert's credibility, but there was no compelling need. The defendant could have obtained the information elsewhere. The court concluded that the plaintiff did not need to produce the records, but would be required to produce information regarding the expert's income at his consulting firm or allow him to be further deposed on the matter.

Example 21.46: Tax returns not discoverable
Wacker v. Gehl Company, 157 F.R.D. 59 (D. Colo. 1994)
In this case, the defendant sought the production of the plaintiff's testifying expert witness's tax records. The request was for a copy of the portions of his tax returns for the past five years reflecting the income he had received in expert consultant and witness matters. The defendant claimed that the information requested might demonstrate the financial interest, bias, or prejudice of the expert. The court found that, although the returns might lead to such information, the request was not "reasonably calculated" to lead to the discovery of such evidence. The court refused to allow such a "fishing expedition," noting that the defendant offered no factual information "whatsoever" that the returns would lead to admissible evidence.

Example 21.47: Tax returns discoverable
State ex rel. Creighton v. Jackson, 879 S.W.2d 639 (Mo. Ct. App. 1994)
Here, the court held that the income tax returns reflecting the income an expert received during the past five years from services as a consultant or witness were within the scope of discovery as impeachment information.

The court discussed the considerations, noting that the trial court should restrict such discovery so that it is no more intrusive than necessary. It went on to say that counsel should never be permitted to "harass, badger and humiliate" the witness with inquiries not strictly necessary to the discovery of matters relevant to professional objectivity. It charged the trial court with the responsibility of delicately balancing privacy interests against the need for accountability. However, the court maintained that the fees earned by an expert witness for testifying in cases bears materially on the witness's credibility and is appropriate impeachment evidence. The trial judge has discretion to allow testimony regarding the amount of annual income derived from employment as an expert witness. Evidence that a witness makes substantial income from testifying illuminates the financial interest that the expert has in giving such testimony.

Example 21.48
In re Doctor's Hosp. of Laredo, Ltd. Partnership, 2 S.W.3d 504 (Tex. App.-San Antonio 1999)
Here, a medical malpractice action was brought against a hospital regarding a child's birth. The trial court ordered the medical experts' depositions and ordered discovery of the experts' income tax schedules and one expert's calendars. The appellate court held that: (1) the hospital properly redesignated the doctor from a testifying expert to a consulting expert, and thus the trial court abused its discretion in ordering the doctor's deposition, and (2) the new state discovery rules, which provided for the discovery of any bias evidence of testifying witness, did not allow the discovery of personal financial records and appointment books of a nonparty witness.

Example 21.49: Tax returns not discoverable
Olinger v. Curry, 926 S.W.2d 832 (Tex. App.-Fort Worth 1996)
In this personal injury action, the plaintiff sought production of the federal tax returns of the defendant's medical expert. The expert admitted in deposition that approximately 90% of his expert consultation services had been provided for defendants, as opposed to personal injury plaintiffs. The court found that the records requested were neither relevant nor reasonably calculated to lead to the discovery of admissible evidence, and therefore the plaintiff was not entitled to discovery of such returns. Otherwise, the court reasoned, such discovery would have irreparably violated the expert witness's privacy.

Example 21.50: Tax returns not discoverable
Young v. Santos, 611 So.2d 586 (Fla. App. 4 Dist. 1993)
In this case, a physician expert was asked to produce tax records for the last three years. The court found that the federal income tax returns showing the overall income of the expert were not discoverable. It reasoned that the

relevant information was the amount of income the physician received from work as an expert consultant or witness, and neither the trial court nor the opposing party had explored less intrusive means of obtaining the information, even though the physician had ignored other attempts at discovery.

21.9 E-mail

E-mail can be discoverable. To protect themselves and their clients regarding e-mails, experts should consider the following.[22]

1. Don't write anything in an e-mail that you wouldn't want to be in front of a jury.
2. Label all e-mails as confidential or privileged information.
3. Develop an e-mail retention policy—based upon your document retention policy—and follow it. Routinely delete e-mail messages from your computer's wastebasket, diskettes and hard drive.
4. Avoid offering opinions on cases using e-mail.
5. Look at how your computer software routes e-mail. Understand it so that you can protect yourself. Learn its idiosyncrasies.
6. A candid, conversational tone in e-mails may be used to discredit you on the stand.
7. When sending e-mail, remember that you lose immediate control of its distribution.

21.10 The Nontestifying Expert: Contact by Opposing Attorneys After Discharge

After an individual has been hired as a nontestifying expert, has rendered an opinion on a matter, and has been discharged by his client, he may be approached by the other side and asked to testify regarding the matter. The expert may want to testify or the other side may try to force him to testify.

Example 21.51: Testimony voluntary
The plaintiff in a medical malpractice action retains you, a physician, to review the case. You determine that the defendant's conduct conformed to the standard of care required. The attorney thanks you for your opinion, pays your fee, and goes on her way. Then, an attorney representing a medical malpractice defendant calls and hires you to review a case. While reviewing the records, you recognize that they belong to the same case. You offer to testify for the defendant.[23]

---

[22] These suggestions were made by Joan Feldman, president of Computer Forensics, Inc, www.forensics.com. Portions of this list appeared in "Protect Yourself When Sending E-mails by Following These Tips," *The Testifying Expert*, March 1996. Ms. Feldman also contributed to *An Attorney's Guide to Protecting, Discovering and Producing Electronic Information* (by Michael J. Patrick, Danvers, MA: LRP Pub., 1995).

[23] *Healy v. Counts,* 100 F.R.D. 493 (D. Colo. 1984). The court did not allow the expert to testify.

Example 21.52: Testimony compelled

You are a physician with an expert witness practice. In a medical malpractice action, you are retained by counsel for the defense as a consulting expert to evaluate the case. You do so and prepare a report in which you opine that the defendant committed malpractice. The plaintiff obtains a copy of this report during pre-trial discovery and subpoenas you to testify at trial despite your unwillingness to testify and without regard to the fact that your expert witness practice depends upon your loyalty to clients.[24]

Court decisions addressing these issues have created a maze of case law. Neither the discovery rules nor the evidence rules give explicit guidance. Thus, the expert should be aware of each of the possible outcomes, although there is little an expert can do to influence the outcomes. If an expert is subpoenaed and does not wish to testify, the expert's personal attorney can file a motion to quash the subpoena. There may be flaws in the subpoena. An expert can also notify her client—the retaining attorney—who will very likely oppose the subpoena through various measures or she may attempt to have the testimony limited. On the other hand, if the expert wishes to testify for the other side, a court, responding to objections from the original retaining attorney, might use a combination of discovery rules, attorney-client privilege, and the work-product privilege to limit or prevent the expert's testimony. Even so, there is no inviolate law against "switching sides."[25]

Example 21.53: Testimony not allowed

Durflinger v. Artiles, 727 F.2d 888 (10th Cir. 1984)

In this wrongful death action against several doctors employed by a hospital, the plaintiffs retained a psychiatrist as a consultant and designated him a probable witness. They subsequently elected not to use him as a witness. The defendants then contacted the expert and asked for and obtained a copy of the report he prepared for the plaintiffs. The defendants then sought to call him at trial as their expert. The court did not allow it, stating that it would have violated the principle of fairness by allowing unreasonable access to an opposing party's diligent trial preparation. It reasoned that there was no hardship worked on the defendants by this ruling: they had another expert testify on the same issue and could have easily found others.

---

[24] *Fenlon v. Thayer,* 506 A.2d 319 (N.H. 1986). The court allowed the plaintiff to question the consulting expert about his prior employment with the defendant.

[25] For example, the court in *Industrial Risk v. M.A.N.,* 141 F.3d 1434 (11th Cir. 1998) responded to a party's assertion that federal and Florida cases uniformly prohibit testimony against a party's interest by an expert witness formerly retained by that party. It stated, "The effect of these rules [FRCP 26, the attorney-client privilege, and the work-product doctrine] taken together, is that parties will rarely be able to avail themselves of the services of the other side's expert witnesses—but that is merely the effect of these rules and not a rule unto itself. In the absence of any precedent, we decline to recognize any blanket rule or policy against 'side-switching.'"

Example 21.54: Testimony not allowed
Campbell Indus. v. M/V Gemini, 619 F.2d 24 (9th Cir. 1980)
Here, the seller of a boat sued the buyer to recover costs of repairs allegedly not covered by the warranty. The defendant counterclaimed, alleging that the boat was defective. The plaintiff retained an expert to inspect the vessel, which he did. The plaintiff then designated him as a testifying expert. The defendant also hired experts to inspect the boat and called one of them to testify. The defendant sought to take the expert's deposition. Before trial, it was learned that defense counsel had contacted the plaintiff's expert, and that the expert wanted to testify on behalf of the defendant. The court did not allow it, citing the impropriety of the defense counsel's contact with the expert and the fact that the defendant already had experts who could testify to the same issue.

Example 21.55: Testimony not allowed
Rubel v. Eli Lilly and Company, 160 F.R.D. 458, 460 (S.D.N.Y. 1995)
In this products liability case, the plaintiff sued a drug manufacturer for injuries sustained after ingesting the drug. The defendants hired an expert to examine the plaintiff and render a report, which he did. The defendant did not designate the expert as a trial witness. He submitted to a deposition by the plaintiffs. The plaintiffs tried to introduce portions of his testimony in their case in chief. The defendant objected, so the plaintiff subpoenaed the expert to testify. The court quashed the subpoena on the grounds that the plaintiffs had access to other experts, the evidence was cumulative, the plaintiffs had been aware of the issue addressed in the deposition for a long time, and the plaintiffs had never relied on the admissibility of the deposition or testimony.

Example 21.56: Testimony allowed or compelled
Lazorick v. Brown, 480 A.2d 223 (N.J. Super. Ct. App. Div. 1984)
Here, a medical malpractice action was brought against two doctors. After being treated by the two doctors, the plaintiff received care from two more doctors. The issue here was whether the defendants should be barred from calling the two treating physicians as witnesses because defense counsel spoke with them and received reports from them without the patient's consent. The court allowed the doctors to speak with the defendant's counsel. It cited the general policy of allowing all competent, relevant evidence to be produced, subject to privileges. However, the court stated that the doctors were not obliged to voluntarily serve as the patient's adversary's experts, and that they could have refused to divulge any information unless compelled to do so by judicial process.

Example 21.57: Testimony allowed or compelled
Cogdell v. Brown, 531 A.2d 1379 (N.J. Super. Ct. Law Div. 1987)
In this medical malpractice action, the plaintiffs sought to call as their witness an examining physician who was initially consulted by one of the defendants. The defendants objected to this on the grounds of breach of loyalty. The issue for the court to decide was whether a plaintiff can call as a trial witness an examining physician who submitted a report on behalf of a defendant. The report was favorable to the plaintiffs, so plaintiffs' counsel decided to call the expert as his witness. The witness had no objection to this designation, which

occurred well over a year before the trial date. The court found no intent to mislead the plaintiffs or any cause for surprise that would mandate exclusion of the testimony. Moreover, the court rejected any claims of a "duty of allegiance." The court allowed the testimony and allowed the fact that the expert was initially consulted by the defendants to come out at trial.

Example 21.58: Testimony allowed or compelled
Levistky v. Prince George's County, 439 A.2d 600 (Md. Ct. Spec. App. 1982)
In this condemnation action, the county called the appraiser who had been retained by the condemnee to testify. The court not only allowed the county to use the expert in their case-in-chief, but also to elicit from the expert in front of the jury that he had been formerly employed by the condemnee.

Example 21.59: Testimony admitted, but limited
Sun Charm Ranch, Inc. v. City of Orlando, 407 So.2d 938 (Fla. Dist. Ct. App. 1981)
Here, the city-defendant employed an appraiser. The plaintiff called the expert to testify. The court allowed the plaintiff to question the appraiser, but did not allow any questioning about his previous employment with the city.

Example 21.60: Testimony admitted, but limited
Peterson v. Willie, 81 F.3d 1033 (11 Cir. 1996)
In this case, a prisoner sued the correctional facility's medical care provider for injuries sustained in an attack by other inmates under the provider's care and supervision. In the pre-trial process, the plaintiff retained a psychiatrist and designated him as an expert witness expected to testify at trial. Shortly before his scheduled deposition noticed by defendants and not objected to by the plaintiff, the expert reexamined the plaintiff without the plaintiff's attorneys' instruction or knowledge. The psychiatrist then testified at the deposition that, as a result of his second examination, his opinion concerning the plaintiff's damages had changed. The plaintiff then changed counsel, and the new attorney subsequently withdrew the designation of the psychiatrist as a trial expert and filed a motion in limine seeking to preclude him from testifying on behalf of the defendant. The trial court permitted the psychiatrist to testify concerning his opinion as well as the fact that he had been previously retained by an attorney representing the plaintiff. The appeals court found that it was proper to have admitted the expert's testimony regarding his opinion, but it was improper to permit the defendant's counsel to elicit the fact of his previous employment by the plaintiff. The court reasoned, "Once a witness has been designated as expected to testify at trial, there may be situations when the witness should be permitted to testify for the opposing party." It found that this decision was committed to the sound discretion of the district court, "While it may generally be possible to permit a party to call a witness without disclosing the fact of his or her prior engagement by the opposing party, there may be little reason to require this effort if other expert witnesses are readily available." The court continued, "In such situations, however, we believe that a party should not generally be permitted to establish that the witness had been previously retained by the opposing party. While there may be situations where

this fact should be disclosed to a jury, we believe that the unfair prejudice resulting from disclosing this fact usually outweighs any probative value."

21.11 Guidelines for Protecting Unwanted Disclosure of Attorney Work Product, Expert Work Product, and Confidential Information

To protect unwanted disclosure of attorney work product, expert work product, and other confidential information, experts should heed the following advice.

1. An expert should assume that anything an expert writes, reviews, or says can and will be used against him and his client.
2. An expert should not commit anything to writing that he wouldn't want a jury to see.
3. All opinion work product provided by retaining counsel is potentially discoverable. Thus, retaining counsel may not communicate her legal theories to an expert.
4. Counsel may attempt to be evenhanded in providing selected background materials about the case to an expert. She does not want opposing counsel to discover only materials that tend to produce a favorable opinion.
5. An expert should realize from the outset that any drafts, notes, investigative materials, or correspondence to him are likely to be discovered.
6. Experts should refrain from annotating or highlighting materials, particularly in the early stages of the opinion formulation process. These notes will be discoverable and are a legitimate area of inquiry at deposition.
7. An expert should not record preliminary conclusions until the nature and scope of the testimony have crystallized and he has called retaining counsel to discuss.
8. It is best to avoid drafts if possible.
9. An expert should be aware that counsel will want to discuss in detail the content of any report before it is committed to writing.
10. An expert should check his retainer agreement for a confidentiality provision.
11. The expert should be aware that counsel will not want the expert to prepare his demonstrative trial exhibits if counsel does not want to have them disclosed before trial.
12. Experts should keep an accurate record of all documents provided by counsel. This allows experts to disclose easily and accurately a list of all documents considered when preparing an opinion.
13. Experts should be aware that counsel will attempt to balance two competing interests. She will try to avoid the disclosure of expert

opinions and will thus instruct the expert not to commit them to writing until later in the process. At the same time, she is trying to establish for the benefit of opposing parties the strength of the expert opinions that will be rendered at trial. A written expert report will convey that strength.

14. An expert should mark materials containing privileged communications with the legend "CONFIDENTIAL AND PRIVILEGED, DO NOT COPY OR DISTRIBUTE."

15. An expert should not disclose or discuss case information with anyone other than counsel—even an inadvertent disclosure may waive a privilege.

21.12 Conclusion

Some legal protection is available to shield documents from discovery. To be safe, however, experts should assume that anything they write or consider will be discoverable.

Chapter 22 Communicating with Counsel

22.1 Introduction

It is important to be able to communicate effectively and properly with retaining counsel. Communication between counsel and experts is complicated by the differences in technical backgrounds, jargon, and the standards of proof used by each profession. The role of the expert witness is to help counsel in understanding, evaluating, and if necessary, proving his case. Communication between them must be a two-way street. Both the expert and the attorney need to listen actively and understand clearly what the other person is saying and, in some cases, what they are not saying.

22.2 Avoiding Jargon

When experts and attorneys talk to each other, they should avoid technical jargon as much as possible. Use of jargon by either the expert or the attorney may cause unnecessary misunderstandings. An expert should talk to the retaining attorney as she would talk to the jury on direct examination. She should act as a teacher and use analogies and similes. Not only will this help the expert to communicate more clearly with the attorney, it will also demonstrate that she will be an effective witness on the stand. It will also permit her to practice the testimony she may provide during direct examination.

Example 22.1
Q. By counsel: Can you testify to a reasonable degree of scientific certainty that the fire was the result of the arson?
A. Expert: No, because you have not yet provided me with verification of trailers, alligatoring of wood, depth of char, and spalling.

Example 22.2
Q. By expert: When would you need a written report on this?
A. Counsel: That depends what they do vis a vis Rules 26 and 56 and whether we get a stipulation.

When experts and counsel truly understand what the other party is saying, actual communication has begun.

22.3 Discoverability of Communications

All communications with counsel should be oral unless the expert is instructed specifically by his retaining attorney to create a written document or an e-mail. This rule is followed because the discovery rules may allow the production of any and all written communications between retaining attorneys and experts. The rules governing this possible disclosure vary (see Chapter 21 on confidentiality and work product), but it is best to assume that any written communication will be subject to discovery.

The same is true of oral communication between an expert and retaining counsel. Some oral communication may be protected. However, one should assume that any communications between an expert and counsel will be a legitimate area of inquiry at deposition and trial.

Example 22.3
Q. Resuming the deposition of Dr. Jones. Dr. Jones, during our ten-minute break I saw you conferring in private with Attorney Smith. Please tell me everything you said and everything she said.

22.4 Areas to Cover

The topics that need to be covered between retaining counsel and the expert include the following.

- How the attorney intends to use the expert's testimony
- Conflicts of interest/bias
- Status of the litigation
- Agreement on fees, expenses, and methods of payment
- Initial opinion sought
- Setting reasonable timeframes for the completion of the work to be undertaken
- Instructions in scientific principles
- Opinions the expert can express
- Opinions the expert cannot express
- Opinions to be expected by opposing experts
- Demonstrative evidence
- Approval of expert discovery
- Written vs. oral reports

How the attorney intends to use the expert's testimony

Prior to accepting an assignment, the expert should discuss with counsel the nature of the case, the parties involved, and how counsel intends to use the expert's testimony. A frank initial discussion will enable the expert to avoid conflicts of interest and those cases in which he does not feel comfortable getting involved in. This discussion is the first step in valuable communication between counsel and the expert. As Eric Swan notes,

> It is critical to have an understanding of what the attorney is using your testimony for and how this is used during the litigation. Once you fully understand how the attorney intends to use your expert testimony, then you can clearly communicate with the attorney and provide help and guidance.

> You can work together to present the most persuasive and compelling testimony possible given the facts and circumstances of the case.[1]

Conflicts of interest/bias

Any potential conflicts of interest or potential bias should be brought to the retaining attorney's attention immediately. Such conflicts could include a financial or personal relationship to an opposing party or lawyer in the case. A potential bias could include a financial or personal relationship to the party or lawyer who is retaining the expert in the case. Experts should not get involved in cases where a potential conflict of interest exists. Bias can and will be brought out before the jury to discredit an expert. An expert should only get involved if he and the retaining attorney are both willing to risk having the expert's credibility challenged due to the potential bias.

Example 22.4
Q. From expert: Who is the defendant in the case?
A. Smith and Jones, LLP.
Q. I'm sorry, I can't get involved. My sister is an equity partner in that firm.

Example 22.5
Q. From expert: What firm are you with again?
A. Robinhood and Coleson.
Q. I have to inform you that my niece, Mary Jones, is an associate at your firm and they could use that against me to show bias.

Status of the litigation

It is wise to inquire about the status of the litigation or the claim counsel is inquiring about. The case may be:

1. contemplated but not yet filed,
2. filed without discovery,
3. in the initial discovery stage,
4. completed the initial discovery stage and in the process of taking depositions,
5. marked ready for trial, or
6. scheduled for trial.

A specific understanding of how far the case has proceeded is required before an expert can make an informed, intelligent decision regarding whether she wants to get involved in the case. The farther along the case is, the less time one will have to work on the matter. Experts who get involved in

---

[1] Eric J. Swan, Esq., *Communication with Counsel and Jury.* Handout materials from the SEAK Seventh Annual Expert Witness and Litigation Seminar, Hyannis, Massachusetts (June 18–19, 1998) 200.

cases at the last moment should anticipate vigorous cross-examination on this issue.

Fees

There must be no misunderstanding about fees, retainers, and expense reimbursements. To prevent this, a written fee schedule or agreement is recommended. (Fees are discussed in detail in Chapter 19. Model fee schedules and agreements are provided in Appendix R.)

Initial opinion sought

After an expert has been retained and has reviewed the available evidence, documents, reports, and studies, he may be asked by counsel for an *initial opinion.* As Harvey Cohen discusses, the expert will usually give counsel one of the following five responses:

> i. Yes, not only can I be helpful, but I am familiar with the particular issue and will be able to testify on your behalf.
> ii. I need more information and must assess the particular facts in order to reach a conclusion on what I could testify to. At the least, I can help you to put the case into perspective with respect to the scientific issues, show you the strengths and weakness of your case, and help evaluate the opponent's case against you.
> iii. I understand the technical issues, but you should be aware that my position on some of the issues may be contrary to those you would like to prove. Alternatively, I can agree with your theory to some extent, but have some reservations, and if cross-examined on certain issues, I would have to state opinions that may not be helpful. In any event, I can help you in the evaluation of your case and can assist you in understanding both the positive and negative aspects.
> iv. I cannot help you because my position on the issues is completely at odds with your theories.
> v. I prefer not to get involved because the issues are not in my areas of expertise (or an area in which I do not want to become involved).[2]

Clear communication and full disclosure at this stage are important. Such communication will prevent, or at least help deter, the retaining attorney from pressuring an expert later to testify to more than she may feel truly comfortable with.

---

[2] Harvey Cohen, PhD, CIH, *Communication with Counsel.* Handout materials for the Sixth Annual SEAK National Expert Witness and Litigation Seminar, Hyannis, Massachusetts (June 19–20, 1997) 119–120.

Reasonable timeframes

The expert should first determine the status of the litigation. Then the expert will want to discuss with counsel a reasonable timeline for the completion of the assignments. Before accepting any assignment, the expert should make an honest appraisal of whether she will have the time to do her best work. Counsel who refuses to communicate a timeline or tells the expert "not to worry" should be questioned closely by the expert on realistic timeframes.

The sophisticated expert will refuse assignments in which he is not given adequate time to do a professional job. These experts have a healthy suspicion of such last-minute assignments. Such assignments could result in substandard work with resultant damage to the expert's reputation and potential civil liability. (See Chapter 20 on expert liability and risk management.)

Instruction on scientific principles

The successful expert instructs counsel on the scientific principles, literature, and its ramifications for the case at hand. The ability of the expert to gather all of the literature and explain it to the attorney so that she truly understands it is the key to successful communication in this area. Even attorneys without scientific backgrounds can be made to understand the science involved when they take adequate time to be prepared by the expert. The ability of the expert to make the attorney understand and appreciate the scientific principles, ramifications, nuances, and opposing scientific opinions will often determine the outcome in the case.

Opinions the expert can express

The opinions the expert can express need to be communicated to the retaining attorney. This should be done orally after the expert has completed the investigation, research, documents review, and other work. A phone call is the preferred method of communication. The expert should communicate:

1. the areas on which he will offer opinions,
2. the exact parameters of the opinion,
3. the degree of scientific certainty and reliability of the opinions, and
4. the strengths and weaknesses of the opinion.

It is only after the initial oral report that an expert should create a written report. Such a report should be written *only* if the expert is specifically requested to do so by counsel.

Opinions the expert cannot express

Equally important is for counsel to know and understand the opinions an expert *cannot* express. Counsel may have a different agenda than an expert.

Counsel wants to win. The expert should want to tell the truth and maintain his credibility. If counsel attempts to push, cajole, trick, or intimidate an expert into giving opinions he does not feel comfortable with, the expert should flatly and clearly (but politely, of course) refuse to do so. The expert's role in the case may end, but his reputation will remain intact.

Opinions by opposing experts

Experts who use their experience and familiarity with opposing experts and provide counsel with their writings, presentations, prior testimony, and likely testimony communicate invaluable information. Frequently the expert, due to her experience and familiarity with the field and other experts, is in an excellent position to offer this assistance to counsel. Experts can also help to prepare counsel to cross-examine and otherwise question the opposing experts' opinions.

Demonstrative evidence

Demonstrative evidence can be very effective in communicating complex information to a jury or other fact finder. The expert is in an excellent position to recommend to counsel demonstrative evidence, such as charts, videotapes, equipment, and other aids, for use at trial. Likewise, counsel may make similar suggestions to the expert to help her testimony come alive and be memorable for the jury. By working together and communicating with each other, the attorney and the expert can help assure that the expert will be able to communicate properly with the jury.

Approval of expert discovery

A sophisticated expert asks to read, approve, and sign-off on all discovery responses or disclosures concerning the expert, her qualifications, opinions, and the factual basis for her opinions. If counsel does not communicate this information to the expert before it is provided to opposing counsel, unnecessary errors can be made. Experts should anticipate being questioned about discovery disclosures at deposition and at trial. A failure of communication between counsel and the expert concerning the discovery process can be a serious mistake with negative consequences.

Written vs. oral reports

Experts should communicate with counsel orally to determine if a written report is desired *before* preparing or sending out any reports. It is best to assume that all written reports by experts are discoverable by opposing counsel. It is common practice for experts to orally discuss with counsel their findings and conclusions before preparing any written reports. In addition, it is crucial that experts clearly understand the parameters of the questions to be addressed in any written reports. Additional areas should not be addressed in written reports.

22.5 Communications at Deposition and Trial

An expert can generally communicate with counsel prior to deposition or trial or during breaks in these proceedings. Of course, the content of these oral communications is usually a legitimate area of inquiry. An expert is generally not allowed to take a break from either for the specific purpose of consulting with his retaining attorney.

Communication at deposition or trial may, however, still take place. When an objection is made at deposition or at trial, counsel might also be communicating certain key points to an expert. When an objection is made, the expert should immediately stop talking and listen intently to the objection.

Example 22.6
Counsel: Objection. Misleading and confusing. He's taking that statement out of context.
A. That's not what I meant. If you read the entire document you can see....

The repetition of certain questions on direct examination may be an attempt to communicate with the expert. One noted trial attorney explains:

> You generally can tell when there is a glitch in communication in court because there are signs of a problem. If the attorney asks you the same or virtually the same question repeatedly there is a problem. Take a step back and try to see why the answer you are providing is not satisfying the attorney. You may want to tell the attorney that you are not sure what he is asking for or getting at. This can force him to rephrase the question so you can learn what the problem may be.[3]

The repeating of a question is a red flag that the expert may have forgotten to include some part of the testimony that he had intended to provide.

Example 22.7
Q. What did you base your opinion on, doctor?
A. The history provided by the examinee, the medical records, a review of the depositions, and a review of the relevant medical literature.
Q. Anything else?
A. Yes, of course, my examination of Ms. Jones on December 3, 1999, and again on February 14, 2000.

---

[3] Swan, 208.

22.6 Conclusion

Clear and honest communication with counsel is required. Such communication will prevent many potential problems and will enhance the effectiveness of an expert witness. Even so, experts should avoid communicating with counsel in writing unless specifically requested to do so by counsel.

Chapter 23 Ethics and the Expert

23.1 Introduction

Experts need to understand the moral, legal, and financial reasons for acting in an ethical manner. If an expert operates unethically, she can be and, in many cases, will be subject to a variety of sanctions including prosecution for perjury, civil suits, professional discipline, loss of future referrals and damage to her reputation. This chapter will identify some of the most common ethical violations by experts and explain how these can be avoided.

23.2 Sample Ethical Codes of Professional Groups

In addition to their legal obligations, experts are subject to the ethical standards and codes of conduct of their professional organizations and certifying bodies. An expert should review the ethical rules governing litigation support with all his relevant organizations. Experts with multiple affiliations and certifications should take care to comply with all of the applicable standards and codes of conduct they are subject to. An instructive sampling of relevant standards and codes is provided below.

Deceit

"Engineers shall avoid deceptive acts." (National Society of Professional Engineers (NSPE) code of ethics for engineers, I, 5)

Competence and qualifications

"Engineers shall perform services only in the areas of their competence," and "engineers shall undertake assignments only when qualified by education or experience in the specific technical fields involved." (NSPE, 2, a)

"A computer professional has a duty to be honest about his or her own qualifications and about any circumstances that might lead to conflicts of interest." (Association of Computer Machinery (ACM) Code of Conduct, 1.3)

"Engineers shall perform services only in areas of their competence." (American Society of Civil Engineers (ASCE) Code of Ethics, 2)

"ISA appraisers should accept only appraisal assignments which fall within their field of expertise unless they are willing to take steps to see that the necessary research is done." (International Society of Appraisers—Code of Ethics and Professional Conduct, Rule 4.07)

"Medical experts should have recent and substantive experience in the area in which they testify and should limit their testimony to their sphere of medical expertise." (American Medical Association, Code of Medical Ethics: Current Opinions of the Council on Ethical and Judicial Affairs of the American Medical Association, Opinion E-6.01)

Honesty and truthfulness

"Medical witnesses should be adequately prepared and should testify honestly and truthfully to the best of their medical knowledge." (Code of Medical Ethics: Medical Testimony: Current Opinions of the Council on Ethical and Judicial Affairs of the American Medical Association)

"Be honest in all communications." (American Board of Independent Medical Examiners Guidelines of Conduct, 1)

"Relate honestly and ethically in all professional relationships." (American College of Occupational and Environmental Medicine (ACOEM) Code of Ethical Conduct)

"Being honest, impartial and serving the public, employers and clients with fidelity." (American Society of Safety Engineers Code of Professional Conduct, 21)

"Honesty is an essential component of trust. Without trust an organization cannot function effectively. The honest computing professional will not make deliberately false or deceptive claims about a system or system design but will instead provide full disclosure of all pertinent system limitations and problems." (ACM, 1.3)

"Engineers shall be guided in all their relations by the highest standards of honesty and integrity." (NSPE, III, 1)

"Truthfulness and Candor. (A) In forensic testimony and reports, psychologists testify truthfully, honestly, and candidly and, consistent with applicable legal procedures, describe fairly the bases for their testimony and conclusions. (B) Whenever necessary to avoid misleading, psychologists acknowledge the limits of their data or conclusions." (American Psychological Association: Ethical Principles of Psychologists and Code of Conduct, 7.03)

Conflicts of interest

"Engineers shall disclose all known or potential conflicts of interest which could influence or appear to influence their judgment or the quality of their services." (NSPE, 4, a)

"To avoid real or perceived conflicts of interest whenever possible, and to disclose them to affected parties when they do exist." (Institute of Electrical and Electronics Engineers—Code of Ethics, 21)

"Conflict of Interest—ISA members must avoid situations which represent a conflict of interest." (ISA, Rule 4.06)

"Conflict of Interest: Members should avoid conflicts of interest in their professional practices and fully disclose all unavoidable conflicts as they arise." (American Institute of Architects, Code of Ethics 3.2)

"A prior professional relationship with a party does not preclude psychologists from testifying as fact witnesses or from testifying to their services to the extent permitted by applicable law. Psychologists appropriately take into account ways in which the prior relationship might affect their professional objectivity or opinions and disclose the potential conflict to the relevant parties." (APA, 7.05)

"In most circumstances, psychologists avoid performing multiple and potentially conflicting roles in forensic matters. When psychologists may be called on to serve in more than one role in a legal proceeding—for example, as consultant or expert for one party or for the court and as a fact witness—they clarify role expectations and the extent of confidentiality in advance to the extent feasible, and thereafter as changes occur, in order to avoid compromising their professional judgment and objectivity and in order to avoid misleading others regarding their role. (APA, 7.03)

Contingency fees

"A physician's fee should not be made contingent on the successful outcomes of medical treatment. Such arrangements are unethical because they imply that successful outcomes from treatment are guaranteed, thus creating unrealistic expectations of medicine and false promises to consumers." (American Medical Association, Code of Medical Ethics: Current Opinions of the Council on Ethical and Judicial Affairs of the American Medical Association, Opinion E-6.01)

"Never accept a fee for services which are dependent upon writing a report favorable to the referral service." (ABIME, 6)

"No engagement shall be undertaken on a contingent fee basis." (American Society of Questioned Document Examiners, Code of Ethics, Rule 7)

Confidentiality

"To treat information received from a client as confidential; and when a matter has already been undertaken, to refuse to perform any services for any person whose interests are opposed to those of the original client, except by express consent of all concerned, or where required by established administrative procedure or by law." (ASQDE Code of Ethics, Rule 3)

"Confidentiality—ISA members shall maintain the confidentiality of their relationship with the client regarding the property that is being appraised. The ISA members shall safeguard all appraisal reports and documents from unauthorized scrutiny and/or seizure, unless compelled by court order to make such disclosure." (ISA, Rule 4.06)

"Confidentiality: Members should safeguard the trust placed in them by their clients." (American Institute of Architects, Code of Ethics and Professional Conduct, Ethical Standard, 3.2)

"Maintain confidentiality consistent with the applicable legal jurisdiction." (ABIME, 7)

"Keep confidential all individual medical information, releasing such information only when required by law or overriding public health considerations, or to other physicians according to accepted medical practice, or to others at the request of the individual." (ACOEM, 5)

"The principle of honesty extends to issues of confidentiality of information whenever one has made an explicit promise to honor confidentiality or, implicitly, when private information not directly related to the performance of one's duties becomes available. The ethical concern is to respect all obligations of confidentiality to employers, clients, and users unless discharged from such obligations by requirements of the law or other principles of this Code." (ACM, 1.8)

Impartiality

"To act at all times both in and out of court in an absolutely impartial manner and to do nothing that would imply partisanship or any interest in the case except the proof of the facts and their correct interpretation." (ASQDE, 5)

"Being honest and impartial and serving with fidelity the public, their employers and clients." (ASCE, 2)

"The medical witness must not become an advocate or a partisan in the legal proceeding. The medical witness should be adequately prepared and should testify honestly and truthfully. The attorney for the party who calls the physician as a witness should be informed of all favorable and unfavorable information developed by the physician's evaluation of the case." (AMA)

Reports and opinions

"(b) Except as noted in (c), below, psychologists provide written or oral forensic reports or testimony of the psychological characteristics of an individual only after they have conducted an examination of the individual adequate to support their statements or conclusions...(c) When, despite reasonable efforts, such an examination is not feasible, psychologists clarify the impact of their limited information on the reliability and validity of their reports and testimony, and they appropriately limit the nature and extent of their conclusions or recommendation." (APA, 7.02)

"Engineers shall be objective and truthful in professional reports, statements or testimony. They shall include all relevant and pertinent information in such reports, statements or testimony, which should bear the date indicating when it was current." (NSPE, 3a)

"To render an opinion or conclusion strictly in accordance with the physical evidence in the document, and only to the extent justified by the facts. To admit frankly that certain questions cannot be answered because of the nature of the problem, the lack of material, or insufficient opportunity for examination." (ASQDE, 4)

23.3 Lawyers' Ethical Obligations

The lawyers involved in a case are subject to their profession's ethical rules. Sophisticated experts understand not only their legal and ethical obligations but those of counsel who has retained them as well. Unfortunately, experts may be subjected to intense pressure by counsel to reach the result that counsel desires. Knowledge of lawyers' legal and ethical obligations gives the expert valuable information, which can and should be used to help them stand their ethical ground.

The ethical obligations of lawyers are controlled by their state rules of professional conduct or code of professional responsibility. The American Bar Association's model rules of professional conduct, which have been adopted by the majority of states provides:

> Rule 3.3 ABA Model Rules of Professional Conduct
>
> A lawyer shall not knowingly:
>
> 1. Make false statement of material fact or law to a tribunal.
> 2. Offer evidence that the lawyer knows to be false. If a lawyer has offered material evidence and comes to know of its falsity, the lawyer shall take reasonable remedial measures.

. . .

Rule 3.4 ABA Model Rules of Professional Conduct

A lawyer shall not:

1. Unlawfully obstruct another party's access to evidence or unlawfully alter, destroy or conceal a document or other material having potential evidentiary value. A lawyer shall not counsel or assist another person to do any such act.
2. Falsify evidence, counsel or assist a witness to testify falsely, or offer an inducement to a witness that is prohibited by law.

. . .

Rule 8.4 ABA Model Rules of Professional Conduct (1992)

It is professional misconduct for a lawyer to:

1. Violate or attempt to violate the Rules of Professional Conduct, knowingly assist or induce another to do so, or do so through the acts of another.
2. Commit a criminal act that reflects adversely on the lawyer's honesty, trustworthiness or fitness as a lawyer in other respects.
3. Engage in conduct involving dishonesty, fraud, deceit or misrepresentation.
4. Engage in conduct that is prejudicial to the administration of justice.

The exact rules that govern the conduct of attorneys vary from state to state. (As an example, see the rules that govern Massachusetts attorneys in Appendix Y.) The thread that binds all ethical rules governing attorneys is honesty. If an expert feels that she is being asked or pressured to provide false testimony, she should strongly consider discretely reminding the attorney that she is aware of the ethical rules that the attorney is subject to and that she would never provide false testimony, reports, or data. If the expert still feels that she is under pressure to provide dishonest testimony, reports, or data, it may be time to end the relationship with the attorney in question.

23.4 Common Ethical Violations by Expert Witnesses

Harold Feder notes that the most common ethical violations committed by experts include:

- Outright false data
- Investigation not done
- Data altered
- Conditional engagement undertaken
- False testimony

- Intentional ignoring of available data
- Recanting prior contra positions
- Assignment beyond competence
- Accepting unauthorized attorney influence
- Inadequate support or time to complete assignment
- Conclusion reached before research
- Conflicts of interest[1]

Other ethical violations include *trimming* (smoothing irregularities to make data look accurate and precise), *cooking* (retaining only those results that fit the theory and discarding others), and *forging* (inventing research data).[2]

23.5 Results of Expert's Dishonesty on Litigation in Question

Experts who testify dishonestly can be subject to criminal, civil, and professional legal action. Dishonest expert testimony may also result in the setting aside of the verdict in the case the expert testified in.

Example 23.1
Trapp v. American Trading & Production Corp., 414 N.Y.S.2d 11 (1st Dept., 1979)
In an action by a seaman to recover damages for personal injuries, alleging unseaworthiness and common law negligence, the jury verdict in the plaintiff's favor was properly set aside by the trial judge and a new trial was properly granted on the ground of newly discovered evidence. Such evidence being that one of the plaintiff's expert witnesses lied about his academic and occupational qualifications, where the trial judge thought perjury so infected the verdict as to require the verdict to be set aside in the interests of justice.

In giving his qualifications, the expert lied. He said that he holds a Bachelor of Science degree in mechanical engineering from Brown University; that he holds a Master of Science degree in electrical engineering from the University of California; that he had taken advanced studies at Rensselaer Polytechnic Institute and Old Dominion University; that he had served for twenty-two years in the United States Navy achieving the rank of captain; that he had commanded destroyers, cruisers and ultimately the aircraft carrier *Saratoga*; that he holds a master's license in the merchant marine for unlimited tonnage on all oceans; that he had sailed in the merchant marine for about seven years principally as chief officer and master; that he had been a marine surveyor, as vice-president in charge of the Norfolk office of Fraser Marine Surveyors, a company of which he and apparently his brother were part owners.

On the motion for a new trial on the ground of newly discovered evidence, it was conclusively established that these qualifications were wholly false; that

---

[1] Harold A. Feder, *Shepard's Expert and Scientific Evidence Quarterly,* 2, no. 4 (Spring 1995) 7–10.

[2] Steven Babitsky and James J. Mangraviti, Jr., *How to Excel at Cross-Examination: Techniques for Experts That Work* (Falmouth, MA: SEAK, Inc.) 14.

he held no degrees, graduate or undergraduate; that he had not completed his freshman year in college; that although he was a "member of the Navy" for twenty-five years, he served on active duty for only nine years; that the highest rank he ever held was chief warrant officer; that he had never reached the rank of captain or commanded the *Saratoga*; that he holds no licenses in the merchant marine, master or even third mate; and that he has no connection with his brother's marine surveying firm and has no business connection with his brother, although without authority he apparently uses his brother's name on his letterhead.

Example 23.2

Oxendine v. Merrell Dow Pharmaceuticals, Inc., 563 A.2d 330 (Dist. Col. App. 1989)

In a products liability case, the plaintiff's expert testified that (1) he was presently, on May 3 and May 11, 1983, a member of the Wayne State University Medical School faculty, when, in fact, he had submitted a letter of resignation from Wayne State dated April 24, 1983, to the Dean of the University, which the Dean accepted on April 29, 1983; (2) he was, at the time of the trial, Chairman of the Formulary Committee at Children's Hospital, a hospital affiliated with the Wayne State Medical School, when, in fact, he had ceased in January 1982 to be Chairman, and in March 1982 to be a member of the committee; (3) he was presently responsible for a fully staffed laboratory at Children's Hospital that conducted ongoing research at his request and direction, even though he had no laboratory assigned solely to him for the two years prior to his testimony and had conducted no research projects at any laboratory during that time; (4) he was presently responsible for the care and treatment of patients, even though after his resignation he had no such responsibilities; and (5) he was a Professor of Pharmacology and Toxicology at the Wayne State Medical School, when no such faculty rank existed and his correct title was Professor of Pediatrics and Pharmacology.

Judge Wolf also found that Dr. Done implied at trial that he was an expert in teratology (the study of birth defects and malformations) and epidemiology (the study of disease incidence and control in a population), but he later stated at the evidentiary hearing that he was not an expert in those entire fields.

The trial judge reversed a jury verdict in the plaintiff's favor solely because of the expert's false testimony, although the jury verdict was later reinstated.

Example 23.3

State v. DeFronzo, 394 N.E.2d 1027, 1034 (Ohio Ct. App. 1978)

The state's expert, a police laboratory technician, testified at the defendant's trial for drug possession, possession of an illegal firearm, and falsifying prescriptions. He purported to qualify himself as an expert in drug analysis by stating under oath that (1) he had a four-year bachelor's degree in Pharmacy from the University of Toledo (when he did not); (2) he had a license from the Drug Enforcement Administration that allowed him to analyze and test controlled substances and drugs (when, in fact, nowhere in the expert's personnel file was there a license from the Drug Enforcement Administration, nor was any such license produced at any hearing); (3) that he had received certain on-the-job training (when the training he had received was from various police captains who served as heads of the crime laboratory); (4) he had attended various state and federal seminars regarding the analysis of drugs (when, in fact, he did not attend any state seminars conducted by the Ohio Bureau of Criminal Identification and Investigation, nor did he produce any evidence that he attended any federal drug seminars).

Moreover, the expert testified that he had analyzed the substance found in the foil packet and determined that cocaine was present. In a later hearing, a civilian crime lab technician testified that the expert related to him that he, the expert, had not performed the drug analysis in the Nicholas DeFronzo case, but that a local doctor made the analysis. The expert testified that he attended the FBI Academy on the subject of handwriting, as well as BCI-sponsored handwriting analysis seminars. He did not. Based upon this, and other, false testimony, the court awarded a new trial.

Example 23.4
Herington v. Smith, 485 N.E.2d 500 (Ill. App. 4 Dist. 1985)
The plaintiff won a negligence action for personal injury arising out of an auto accident, but the damages fell far short of the plaintiff's medical costs. Later it was learned that the defendant's expert witness, a chiropractor, had lied under oath concerning his credentials, and the plaintiff requested a new trial. The expert was presented to the court and the jury as a licensed chiropractor and a licensed medical doctor. He testified that he had graduated from the University of Iowa in 1966, when in fact he graduated from Upper Iowa University in 1979. He testified that he received an MD degree from the University of Santo Domingo, when, in fact, he had an MD from the Universidad Cetec in the Dominican Republic. Finally, he testified he was licensed to practice medicine in the state of Florida, when, in fact, his only Florida certificate relates to homeopathic medicine. The court granted the plaintiff a new trial, based upon a rule that mandates where perjured testimony so permeates the process as to constitute a fraud upon the court, false testimony by a material witness may alone be sufficient to warrant a new trial.

Example 23.5
Peteet, et al. v. Dow Chemical Co., 868 F.2d 1428 (5th Cir. 1989)
In a products liability action, the plaintiffs' expert, a toxicologist, testified that the product at issue, a herbicide, caused the plaintiff's death. The defendant claimed that the expert testified falsely at trial about knowing a man named Joseph Moss. Before the expert's deposition, his assistants collected three boxes of medical records regarding this case for the deposition. In one box of documents, the medical records of Mr. Moss, another of the expert's patients, were mistakenly included. The defendant's counsel noticed the error and asked the expert what records he relied upon in forming his opinion that the herbicide caused the plaintiff's cancer. The doctor expansively responded that he had relied upon all the documents in the room, and the defense counsel marked all the records as exhibit number 2. At trial, counsel produced exhibit 2 and asked the expert if he had relied on those records. The expert apparently became confused when he saw the Moss records contained in exhibit 2 and stated that

he did not know Joseph Moss. This testimony was false because Moss was a patient of the expert.

Counsel admitted that he realized during the deposition that the expert's assistants had mistakenly included Moss's medical records, which had nothing to do with the plaintiffs' case, and was simply trying to show that the expert made a mistake. The expert reiterated that his opinion was based on the plaintiff's medical records. The court found that this "false" testimony could not have affected the jury's decision and then refused to overturn the defense verdict based on this "false" testimony.

23.6 Avoiding Ethical Violations

The sophisticated expert takes the following steps to avoid potential ethical violations.

Experts should tell the truth simply and directly.

Honesty is *always* the best policy. Honesty is a legal, ethical, and moral duty.

An expert should avoid deceitful acts.

Experts should not cook, trim, ignore, or forge data. They should review all available material prior to offering an opinion.

Experts should not accept assignments outside of their area of competence.

This is a disservice to everyone involved in the case, including the expert. Experts should not let counsel push them into areas outside of their true area of expertise and should never hold themselves out to be what they are not. Such conduct is unethical and short-sighted. Expert opinions will usually be examined under cross-examination and a lack of true expertise will probably be exposed publicly.

An expert should undertake assignments only when she is able to perform them in a professional and timely manner.

An expert should not take an assignment if she does not have time to consider her opinion carefully and to review all of the relevant information.

A wise expert is honest in all assignments.

Experts should disclose any and all potential conflicts of interest.

If an expert is subject to a real or perceived conflict of interest that might bias her opinion, this needs to be disclosed. Examples are direct or indirect financial interest in the case or prior work for another party in the case.

Experts should maintain confidentiality.

This is not only good ethics, it is also good business. If word ever gets out that an expert disclosed confidential information improperly, her days of being retained as an expert witness will come to a close rapidly.

Experts should act with impartiality at all times.

An expert is not an advocate. An expert should call them as she sees them and avoid advocacy. The attorneys, not the experts, are the advocates.

It is important to be objective and truthful in all reports, testimony, and statements.

A wise expert provides opinions based upon the evidence and a reasonable degree of scientific certainty.

In most civil cases, an expert's opinion must be based upon a "reasonable degree of scientific or medical certainty." In other words, it is more likely than not that the expert's opinion is valid. An expert is not required to say more, but if she gives an opinion based on less than this minimal threshold, it will be found to be legally insufficient.

Experts should avoid contingent fees.

These are not only unethical, but they may open an expert up to a potentially devastating cross-examination.

Experts should always act with integrity, competence, and moral, professional, and scientific responsibility.

Whenever in doubt, an expert should take the high road. The case at hand may soon end, but an expert's reputation will stay with her for the rest of her life. One should not risk damaging one's reputation.

23.7 Conclusion

Experts should be aware of their ethical obligations and conduct themselves in an ethical manner at all times. Experts also need to be aware of the ethical obligations of attorneys. It may sometimes be prudent to remind attorneys of their ethical obligation of candor.

Chapter 24 Handling Abuse

24.1 Introduction

Expert witnesses are commonly subject to various forms of abuse. The purpose of this chapter is to identify the most common of these forms of abuse and to provide courses of action.

24.2 The Most Common Forms of Abuse

The seventeen most common forms of abuse are reviewed below.

Abuse 1. Pirating an expert's name and reputation

In this form of abuse, counsel, without first contacting the expert, settles or attempts to settle the case based on the expert's reputation. In effect, the lawyer is misappropriating the expert's name and reputation. This may be done in a purposeful attempt to avoid having to pay an expert's fee. More likely, however, is the scenario where the attorney discloses the name of an expert witness to opposing counsel without the expert's knowledge or permission. This is frequently done because he would like to deny the other parties in the case the opportunity to retain the expert but didn't want to spend the time and money necessary to contact her.

> **Example 24.1**
> You are a highly regarded lead paint expert. In a lead paint poisoning case, defense counsel discloses your name as an expert who will testify to the other parties. Subsequently, the case settles on favorable terms. You are never notified of any of this, are never retained, and are never compensated.

This type of action by counsel may violate the rules of professional conduct of lawyers that prohibit attorneys from engaging in dishonest behavior. If faced with this situation, an expert could report the potential misconduct of the attorney to opposing counsel, the judge, or the state organization responsible for disciplining attorneys. Alternatively, the expert could bill the attorney for the use of his name.[1] The problem with each of these courses of action is that the expert would first need to detect the fact that his name is being used without his consent. One way to do this is to run periodic computer searches of court documents, settlement reports, and other legal publications.

---

[1] Some experts have come so far as to require a check for a retainer before even sending out their CV to counsel.

Abuse 2. Nonpayment or slow payment of fee

In this form of abuse, counsel retains an expert and then delays or never pays his fee. This is an all too common form of abuse. When retained by the defense, insurance companies often pay for the expert witness fees. Unfortunately, it is common for insurance companies to be very slow in paying expert bills. When retained by plaintiffs, plaintiff's counsel often advance the fees of expert witnesses out of their own pockets. Many plaintiff's attorneys would obviously like to avoid taking the risk that their client will be unable to pay them back.

Example 24.2
When you send a bill after your first thirty days of an engagement, the plaintiff's attorney responds that he cannot pay you until the case settles.

One way to minimize this problem is for experts to check out counsel and his reputation prior to accepting the assignment. This can be done by consulting with other experts and attorneys. **A fool-proof way to avoid this problem is to get paid in advance through the medium of a replenishable retainer.** If all else fails, the expert may be forced to stop additional work or even, in extreme cases, may refuse to testify without payment of her fees. After an expert testifies and the case is over, she has very little leverage over the retaining attorney. The time to act to ensure payment is before the attorney gets what he wants. In any event, early diagnosis of this form of abuse is very helpful. This can be done simply and effectively by billing the retaining attorney every thirty days. (For a complete discussion of fees, billings, and collections, please refer to Chapter 19.)

Abuse 3. Missing records or information

Here counsel of the party retaining the expert intentionally fails to send the expert crucial records, notes, studies, or other underlying data. Counsel, or the client, then pushes the expert for a report or opinion based on the incomplete or limited information provided.

Example 24.3
You are retained as an expert medical witness on behalf of the plaintiff, and counsel intentionally fails to provide you the medical records that deal with the plaintiff's pre-existing condition.

This type of action by counsel may violate the rules of professional conduct of lawyers that prohibit attorneys from engaging in dishonest behavior and presenting false testimony before a court. An expert should remind the attorney of this fact and demand that he be provided with complete documentation. He should refuse to issue an opinion or report until given access to the missing information. Failure to do so can result in damage to one's professional reputation, credibility, and viability as an expert in future cases. If an expert suspects game-playing, he should ask counsel to verify in writing that the expert has been provided with all the records.

Abuse 4. Pushing the expert outside his area of expertise

Here counsel asks, cajoles, or demands that the expert testify on matters outside his true area of expertise. This usually happens after the expert has been retained and is working on the case for some time. It happens for two reasons. First, counsel may have been too lazy or not had time to locate and retain another expert. More commonly, counsel is trying to save money by, in effect, getting two experts for the price of one.

Example 24.4
You are an orthopedic surgeon who has been retained by the plaintiff in a broken leg case. On the way into the courtroom, the retaining attorney states to you, "Oh, by the way, I'll also need you to causally relate her depression to the broken leg."

Experts should not be tricked, cajoled, or forced into testifying in areas that are outside their true areas of expertise and in which they do not feel comfortable. Experts who allow themselves to be pushed into an area beyond their true area of expertise are likely to get destroyed on cross-examination. This won't do the expert or the retaining attorney any good.

If an expert is pushed into testifying beyond the area of her expertise, she can tell counsel that, "I am not an expert in that area and I will so testify if you pose those questions to me." If pushed on the stand, one can simply reply that, "That's outside my area of expertise and I don't have an opinion on it." In any event, the solution to this common form of abuse is "just say no."

Abuse 5. Unrealistic time demands

Here counsel or the client asks that the expert "drop everything" and work up a preliminary report or opinion quickly. The expert is frequently either intentionally (to save money) or unintentionally (due to poor planning or late notice) given inadequate time to assimilate the facts and documents, conduct research, and operate in a professional manner.

Example 24.5
You are an engineer. An attorney calls you up and asks for your report and opinion regarding a particular surface where a slip and fall took place. He states, "And I'll need your signed affidavit in the form of an expert report in 48 hours because I have to file an opposition to a motion for summary judgment."

Many people do not like to say no. Unfortunately, when one is not given adequate time to do a professional job, saying no is probably the best course of action. Last-minute assignments will likely result in substandard work and resultant damage to an expert's reputation. If an expert feels that he can do a professional job in the timeframe allowed, he should consider charging a premium fee. This is only fair because he was given a "drop everything" assignment. Counsel is unlikely to refuse because she may not be able to find another expert in time.

Abuse 6. Tying preliminary opinion to being retained

Counsel may inquire directly or indirectly as to what an expert's opinion is likely to be before she retains and pays the expert. Frequently, counsel will give the expert a version of the facts and ask, "What do you think?" The implication is clear—if the expert supports the lawyer's position, he will be retained. If he doesn't, he won't.

Example 24.6
Yes, Doctor, I represent the plaintiff in a case where there was a broken ankle and the issue in question is the long-term impairment likely to be resultant thereto. What do you think?

If an expert does not have enough information to form a very preliminary opinion, he should say so. Failure to do so could box him into a corner that may be difficult to get out of later on. When faced with a situation like this, an expert should tell counsel that, based upon the amount of material she would like the expert to review, he can get her a preliminary opinion in *x* hours. To make sure that he is not subject to even subconscious bias in his initial opinion, an expert can even consider asking that the attorney not reveal which party she represents.

Abuse 7. Refusal to prepare the expert for deposition or trial

While almost all of the abuse at deposition takes place at the hands of opposing counsel, a failure or refusal to prepare the expert is abuse or neglect by counsel who has retained that expert. The typical last-minute hurried meeting is usually the result of counsel who has been too busy to focus properly on the case or who is trying to save money.

In all but routine, simple, or small cases, an expert should insist that counsel have an in-depth pre-testimony (deposition or trial) conference with him. In this conference, counsel should brief the expert fully on the issues, on the status of the litigation, on the discovery, and be prepared to answer any and all questions the expert may have. It is in everybody's best interest that the expert be briefed fully and that her testimony goes well.

Abuse 8. Providing an uncomfortable environment for deposition

Counsel may try to make an expert uncomfortable at deposition in an attempt to distract or break her concentration. The theory here is that if counsel can make the expert uncomfortable enough, she will say anything to get out of the room.

Example 24.7
A deposition that is held in a small, poorly lit, poorly ventilated room with no writing surfaces and hard, uncomfortable chairs is all part of this tactic. Opposing counsel smokes during the deposition and the room is kept at a temperature of 80 degrees. You are forced to sit facing bright sun and there are no blinds on the window.

The expert can ask, and if necessary, demand that she be made comfortable while being deposed. Experts need not be subject to smoke-filled rooms for depositions that drone on endlessly. If the request is not complied with, the expert should make sure that it is repeated on the record (that is, recorded on the deposition transcript by the stenographer). The expert should state on the record that she will be forced to terminate the deposition if she is not provided with a comfortable setting. It is wise to specify on the record what is wrong with the setting. If an expert chooses to terminate the deposition, she should make sure that a protective order from the court is filed for promptly.

Abuse 9. Repetitive questioning at deposition

Here counsel tries to get under the expert's skin by asking repeatedly and deliberately the same questions over and over again. Counsel will attempt to get the expert to "blow up" or to change his answer. In a lengthy deposition, this may be part of the overall strategy of trying to break the expert's will by wearing him down.

Example 24.8
Q. Is the plaintiff's condition causally related?
A. Where the hell do you get off? You've asked me that question seven times already. No. No. Noooooooo. All you plaintiff's attorneys are the same. Nothing but damn scheisters. They need to pass tort reform and get rid of the whole lot of you bastards.

Counsel is granted great leeway with regard to cross-examination of the expert at deposition. Additionally, there is no judge present to cut off repetitive questioning. Thus, the expert will be best served by exercising tireless patience and politeness and just answering the questions. Repetitive questions should not get under the expert's skin, especially because he is being paid by the hour. Once counsel realizes the expert's answers are not changing and he is not getting flustered, she will usually move on and drop this tactic.

Abuse 10. Threats of counsel for failing to answer improper questions at deposition

Counsel will attempt to get the expert to answer improper questions (for example, a question asked in bad faith to annoy, embarrass, or oppress the expert) by threatening to go to the judge and seek a contempt finding and sanctions, such as court costs and legal fees.

Example 24.9
You are asked at deposition about the financial details of your divorce that occurred seven years previously. This was three years before you were retained as an expert in your very first case. You refuse to answer.

It is important to understand that judges are never happy to be bothered with these types of discovery disputes. An expert should not be bullied into answering questions that he knows or strongly suspects to be improper. Although the expert's retaining counsel is not the expert's lawyer, she will frequently pose objections and assist by instructing the expert not to answer. While these objections are technically incorrect, they usually will resolve the matter. In the rare instance when the expert is left alone to deal with this abuse, he can terminate the deposition and seek a protective order.

Abuse 11. Lack of breaks at deposition

This form of abuse involves counsel keeping the deposition questioning going for hours without permitting any breaks. It is designed to wear down the expert so that she will begin to provide answers that have not been considered carefully.

Example 24.10
You are questioned for five hours at deposition. After every hour of questioning you ask for a five-minute break to stretch. All of these requests are refused.

An expert can and should demand occasional breaks to use the restroom, telephone, or to just gather herself mentally. However, anything that the expert discusses with retaining counsel or with opposing counsel during a break can and often will be brought up when the deposition resumes. If counsel unreasonably refuses to grant breaks during a lengthy deposition, the expert should make the record clear, terminate the deposition, and seek a protective order.

Abuse 12. Harassing questions at deposition

Counsel may attempt to intimidate, distract, or break an expert's will by asking a series of harassing questions at deposition.

Example 24.11
Have you had any homosexual sexual relationships in your life?

Counsel is not permitted to ask bad faith questions that are designed to unreasonably annoy, embarrass, or oppress experts.[2] Counsel is, however, given a good amount of latitude in asking questions at deposition. In *Gasinowski v. Hose*, 897 p.2d 678 (Ariz. App. Div. 1 1994), the court permitted the cross-examination of an anesthesiologist about his subsequent suspension from the hospital. In the case of *Winant v. Carras*, 617 N.Y.S. 2d 487 (A.D. 2 Dept. 1994), the court permitted counsel for the defense to cross-examine the plaintiff's expert on the issue of alleged drug addiction. The courts have gone as far as permitting counsel to inspect the personnel files of a retired Los Angeles police officer who was testifying as an expert witness. See *Michael v. Gates*, 45 Cal.Rptr. 163 (Cal. App. 1995).

If counsel who retained the expert does not put a stop to the harassment, the expert should warn opposing counsel about his actions on the record: "Note for the record that counsel is harassing me and if it continues, I will have no alternative but to terminate the deposition." If the harassment continues, the expert can consider terminating the deposition and seeking a protective order from the judge. The judge will most likely find in the expert's favor if the question was in no way relevant to credibility. If the question was relevant to the expert's credibility (which is always a legitimate issue in a case), then the expert will be more likely to lose before the judge. The losing party may be subject to sanctions.

Abuse 13. Hostile personal attacks at deposition

Here the attorney crosses the line with sarcastic, hostile, or profane remarks.

Example 24.12
So how many other wops do they have on faculty at Harvard?

If an expert is sure that counsel has crossed the line, the expert should warn counsel on the record. If the behavior continues, it is best to terminate the deposition and seek the protection of the judge through a motion for a protective order.

Abuse 14. Nonpayment of deposition fees

Under the Federal Rules of Civil Procedure, the party seeking to depose an expert is liable for his reasonable fees.[3] Under this form of abuse, counsel will schedule the deposition and not arrange for payment of the expert.

---

[2] Fed. R. Civ. Pro. 30(d)(3).

[3] Fed. R. Civ. Pro. 26(b)(4)(c) states: "Unless manifest injustice would result, (i) the court shall require that the party seeking discovery pay the expert a reasonable fee for time spent in responding to discovery under this subdivision; and (ii) with respect to discovery obtained under subdivision (b)(4)(B) of this rule the court shall require the party seeking discovery to pay the other party a fair portion of the fees

Experts should ask to be paid prior to the deposition. Failure to do this may result in collection problems. If the deposition goes longer than was estimated (which is not uncommon) sophisticated experts have counsel agree on the record (recorded by the stenographer) to make the additional payments required.

Abuse 15. Wasting the time of the expert at deposition

There are three ways that this is commonly done. These are:

1. dragging on the deposition with endless questions,
2. canceling the deposition on short notice, or
3. requiring the expert to travel substantial distances.

An expert can counteract this abuse easily by charging by the hour (including travel time) and requiring a nonrefundable retainer in the event of the last-minute cancellation of a deposition. When counsel realizes that she is being charged for all of the expert's lost time, the wasted-time problem frequently resolves itself quickly. If counsel would like to ask endless questions, an expert should let her because the expert is being paid for his time by the hour.

Abuse 16. Abusive questioning at trial

Counsel may ask a series of difficult, pointed, or embarrassing questions at trial.

Example 24.13
Isn't it a fact that your professional license was suspended seven years ago?

Unfortunately, counsel is given a good deal of latitude in asking relevant questions about credibility. Many pointed questions will be relevant to an expert's credibility. The only surefire way to avoid being asked tough questions on the stand is to choose not to become involved in expert witness work in the first place.

Some questions do, however, cross the line. In these instances, it will be up to the attorney who retained the expert to object. The judge (who is present, unlike at a deposition) will then be able to rule on the objection and either direct the expert to answer or will sustain the objection and force counsel to move on.

Retaining lawyers can also protect their experts from certain lines of questioning at trial by filing what is known as a *motion in limine* before the expert testifies. If this motion is granted, the other lawyers will be precluded

---

and expenses reasonably incurred by the latter party in obtaining facts and opinions from the expert."

from asking the expert questions regarding whatever was covered under the motion in limine. Motions in limine are a good technique to remove the uncertainty of how a judge will rule on an evidentiary matter that is expected to come up at trial. (A further explanation of motions in limine is provided in Chapter 4.)

Example 24.14
Your ex-wife took out a restraining order on you three years ago. You don't want to be asked about this at trial. The lawyer who retained you can file a motion in limine asking the judge to order, before you testify, that the other parties cannot question you about the restraining order.

Abuse 17. Trying to "steal" the expert's opinion by calling him as a fact witness and then asking his opinion

This is where the expert may have some independent factual knowledge relevant to the case, but has not been retained as an expert witness. An attorney may attempt to subpoena such a witness as a fact witness (who is not entitled to more than a nominal fee for her time) and then ask the witness questions that call for an opinion. When subpoenaed as fact witnesses under these circumstances, experts should ask the attorney for their usual and customary expert witness fee. If this is refused, experts should get legal advice on whether they can refuse to offer opinions and limit their testimony to facts.

Example 24.15
Mason v. Robinson, 340 N.W.2d 236, 242 (Iowa 1983)
The issue presented in this action was whether a trial court has discretion to relieve an unwilling expert witness, who is a stranger to the litigation, from providing opinion testimony during a pre-trial discovery deposition. The court determined that a litigant does not have an absolute right to compel an unwilling expert to give an opinion on facts outside the expert's personal knowledge and held that a trial court has discretion to either relieve or compel such testimony depending on the circumstances presented in a particular case. This case arose out of a medical malpractice action. The plaintiff learned that one of the defendant doctors had provided factual information about the surgery and its subsequent complications to the expert, who was a professor of surgery at the University of Iowa College of Medicine. The plaintiff subpoenaed the expert, who refused to be deposed. The judge directed him to answer questions about the facts given him, but refused to compel any discovery regarding his expertise. The plaintiff then named the doctor as a witness, sent him the statutory fee, and filed a motion to compel him to give his expert opinion. The court granted the motion to compel. The supreme court adopted a balancing test and stated that generally an expert witness, absent some other connection with litigation, is free to decide whether or not he wishes to provide opinion testimony for a party. The court still has discretion to compel testimony, but:

> Before the court compels an expert to testify solely on the basis of his expertise and in the absence of any other connection to the litigation, the compelling party should affirmatively demonstrate some compelling necessity for an expert's testimony that overcomes the expert's and the public's need for protection. Additionally, an adequate plan of compensation must be presented. Finally, an expert only can be compelled to give previously formed opinions and can not be required to engage in any out-of-court preparation.

The court then found that because the plaintiff did not affirmatively demonstrate a compelling necessity for the particular witness's expert testimony, the trial court erred in granting the motion to compel.

Example 24.16
In re Imposition of Sanctions Alt. v. Cline, 589 N.W.2d (Wis. 1999)
The court held that, absent a showing of compelling circumstances, an expert cannot be compelled to give expert testimony, whether the inquiry asks for the expert's existing opinions or if it would require further work.

24.3 Fighting Back

In some cases, counsel has been sanctioned for abusing an expert witness. In others, expert witnesses have successfully sued. Consider the following examples.

Example 24.17
In re Petition for Disciplinary Action against James Malcolm Williams, Attorney at Law of the State of Minnesota, 414 N.W.2d 394 (Minn. 1987)
This action for disciplinary action arose out of a fraud case against a lending institution and its attorney. The plaintiff cross-examined the defendant attorney's expert witness, the former chief justice of the Minnesota Supreme Court, who was testifying as an expert for the defendant on the standard of care required of an attorney. The plaintiff's counsel converted a proper inquiry regarding "the real party in interest status of liability insurers in personal injury litigation where the insurer retains counsel to represent the insured" into a false personal attack on the witness. Excerpts follow:

> WILLIAMS: Well, Mr. Sheran, you regularly appeared before the juries as a defense lawyer and told the juries that you were representing an individual when in truth and fact you were representing an insurance company, isn't that true?
> OPPOSING COUNSEL: Argumentative, your honor.
> COURT: Objection sustained.
> SHERAN: It is an untrue statement in addition.
> WILLIAMS: Well, don't you think that a juror would want to know whether or not you were representing an insurance company as well as a client who you were professing to represent?
> OPPOSING COUNSEL: Same objection, your honor.
> COURT: Objection sustained.
> WILLIAMS: And yet you went through case after case for a number of years as a former FBI agent, knowingly misrepresenting to the juries time and time again that

> you were representing an individual when in truth in fact you were representing insurance companies in those cases?
> SHERAN: That statement is false and scandalous.
> * * *
> WILLIAMS: Didn't you, on several occasions, while you were on the court rule that if in fact a jury was told that there was an insurance company involved behind the defense lawyer, that you would take that jury verdict away from the plaintiff and send it back for a new trial because you felt that the jury is not entitled to know the truth about who in fact was being represented in the lawsuit?
> OPPOSING COUNSEL: I object, your honor, but I would ask the witness to be permitted to answer.
> * * *
> SHERAN: The statement is inaccurate and it is scandalous.

The trial court chastised the attorney and stated, in *Sievert v. First National Bank in Lakefield*, 358 N.W.2d 409 (Minn. App. 1984): "[I]t is not in keeping with the role of the advocate to try to humiliate a witness for self-gratification" (at 416). Similarly, the court that disciplined the attorney stated: "[Attorney] asserts he has a right, indeed an obligation, to represent his clients vigorously, aggressively, and zealously. To be vigorous, however, does not mean to be disruptively argumentative; to be aggressive is not a license to ignore the rules of evidence and decorum; and to be zealous is not to be uncivil." The attorney was publicly reprimanded and suspended for 6 months.

Example 24.18
In the Matter of Lester T. Vincenti, 704 A.2d 927 (N.J. 1998)
An attorney was disbarred for repeated ethics violations. One of these occurred during the course of a proceeding to terminate parental rights of the natural mother of a minor for whom the attorney acted as a guardian at law. Selected treatment of the witnesses follows.

> Attorney's treatment of the State's witnesses was equally obnoxious. He was abusive and tried to intimidate the witnesses, with some success. [Attorney] personally attacked the witnesses during his unreasonably long and confrontational cross-examinations. He called the witnesses insulting names and belittled the credentials of the expert witnesses.
>
> Dr. Douglas Haymaker, a psychologist, treated J.D.'s son, A.R.S. During cross-examination, when Haymaker did not immediately answer [attorney]'s question, [attorney] snapped:
>
> > Do you want time to think about it, Doctor? Because I mean there seems to be a habit in this case of witnesses who don't know what to say to simply sit there and think and come up with some cockamamie response to a very serious question. Now I'd like you to answer the question without thinking about it ad nauseam for the next five minutes.
>
> [Attorney] harassed Haymaker by asking him irrelevant questions, such as whether he was an aficionado of pornography, a militarist and whether he believed in military solutions to political problems. When Haymaker testified that a statement made by A.R.S. could not necessarily be attributed to his foster mother, [attorney] sarcastically asked, "Oh, it could have come from the froggies or the

horsies or some other non-living thing, is that right?" [Attorney] also accused Haymaker of having a highly selective memory and of being "in cahoots" with the foster parents.

In reply to one of [attorney]'s questions, Haymaker used the word "assume," prompting [attorney] to interrupt him:

> A. I assume, I assume it was a work similar—
> Q. No, don't make assumptions, I mean that's all you've done so far is make assumptions and speculations and give us your opinions and conclusions. I'm not interested in your opinions and conclusions, speculations or assumptions, Doctor. I'm interested in having you search your memory, think if you can come up with what was stupid, et cetera. Make your best effort, Doctor. It's only a year ago. As a matter of fact, it's not even a year ago. It's eight months ago. That's not such a long time ago. Tell us. I challenge you to tell us.

[Attorney]'s comments were particularly inappropriate because he previously had demanded that Haymaker express his opinions and conclusions.

During the trial, [attorney] referred to Haymaker as a "liar," "so-called psychologist," "busy body do-gooder" and "so-called therapist." He belittled Haymaker's therapy sessions with A.R.S. as "your so-called game therapy, play therapy so-called." [Attorney] accused Haymaker of condoning violence, insults to women, pornography and brutality.

Another witness called by DYFS was a social worker. At the request of James Valenti, law guardian for A.R.S., the social worker conducted a bonding evaluation to address the issue of where A.R.S. should reside permanently. The social worker, too, was the victim of harassment and intimidation by [attorney]. At the ethics hearing, the social worker testified as follows about [attorney]'s courtroom behavior:

> A. The thrust of his questions as I experienced them had less to do with the content than with an attempt to demean me, to ridicule me. I felt the nature of his cross-examination was highly personalized and had very little to do with the content or with trying to uncover the truth of the issues. For example, in the voir dire, he took a tremendous amount of time asking me what specific courses I had taken when I was in graduate school. At the time that I testified, I had - it had been fifteen years since I completed my doctorate and over twenty years since I completed my Masters degree. He wanted to know the specific names of the courses I had taken. I said I couldn't remember the specific names, but I could talk about the kinds of courses I took and how they were related to the work that I was doing. He ridiculed me for the fact that I could not remember the course name and went over that over and over again.

[Attorney] also made insinuations about the social worker's sexual orientation. He suggested that she inappropriately touched his client, J.D., during a bonding-evaluation session with J.D. and A.R.S. [attorney] attached significance to the fact that the social worker used purple paper for taking notes in her office, despite her explanation that it was the easiest color for her eyes. [Attorney] even said that he would bring in an expert to talk about the meaning of using purple paper. [Attorney] also used sashaying and other body language to question her sexuality.

In addition, [attorney] took the social worker's notes from her during her testimony. He then toyed with her, refusing to return the notes. When she asked Judge Hanifan to instruct [attorney] to return the notes, [attorney] berated the judge for talking to the witness.

> Unfortunately for the social worker, the conclusion of the A.R.S. trial did not signal the end of [attorney]'s harassment toward her. About six months after the trial ended, she and Dr. Hagovsky, another witness who had testified in the A.R.S. matter, were invited to participate at a conference sponsored by the Association of Trial Lawyers of America. There was no connection between the trial and the conference. However, in a letter to Cary B. Cheifetz, the conference coordinator, [attorney] contended that the social worker and Hagovsky held "Nazi views" and suggested that it would be helpful if [attorney] attended the conference to denounce them. Although the letter could not be introduced into evidence because Cheifetz discarded it after receiving it, both Cheifetz and the social worker testified at the ethics hearing about the contents of the letter. While [attorney] complained that the letter was not produced, he did not deny having sent it.

Example 24.19
Florida v. Schaub, 618 So.2d 202 (Fla. 1993)
A prosecutor was suspended for thirty days after he insulted the defense expert, elicited irrelevant information from the expert, and expressed his own derogatory opinions of the expert's field.

Example 24.20
In the case of Lexecon v. Milberg Weiss[4]
A Chicago-based economic consulting firm filed an abuse of process suit against a well-known law firm. One of the chief allegations in the suit was that an attorney at the defendant law firm sued an expert/consultant at Lexecon because he wanted to "put the little fucker out of business." The expert/consultant and the attorney had done battle in several previous high-profile cases. At the conclusion of the trial, the jury awarded the plaintiff expert/consulting firm $45 million. While the jury was out considering punitive damages, the defendant law firm settled the case for $50 million. The law firm had reportedly earned $679 million in profits since 1988.

24.4 Conclusion

Experts may be subject to various form of abuse. They should know how to deal with each in a professional, constructive manner.

---

[4] See Karen Donovan, "Milberg Weiss' $50M Mistake," *National Law Journal,* April 26, 1999 at A1. See also Richard B. Schmitt, "Milberg Weiss Agrees to Pay $50 Million to Settle Lexecon Case," *Wall Street Journal,* April 14, 1999, at B17. The firm had represented a class of plaintiffs who had lost savings in a savings and loan failure. The suit named numerous defendants, one of which was the consulting firm Lexecon. The firm also named a principal at the consulting firm in the suit—this same principal had testified as an expert previously against the law firm's clients. Lexecon later filed the abuse of process lawsuit, alleging that the law firm used the legal process to drive the expert out of business. The chairman of the federal jury that heard the abuse of process suit said, "The biggest single factor for us was that they went after [the expert] personally."

Appendix A CV Quality Control Checklist

The expert's CV is the first place opposing counsel looks to gather information for deposition, trials, and cross-examination purposes. Preparation, attention to detail, accuracy, and precision can help the expert avoid unnecessary difficulty.

Accuracy

__ Was your CV 100% accurate when written?
__ Has anything changed since your CV was written?
__ Was your CV 100% accurate when presented to counsel?

Timeline and Gaps

__ Have you listed your inclusive dates of work, education, and other activities?
__ Do you have gaps in your CV timeline?

Prior CVs

__ Are your prior CVs consistent with your current one?
__ Are there material changes, omissions, or alterations that open lines of inquiry?

Multiple CVs

__ Do you have more than one current CV?
__ Are your multiple CVs prepared and used for different clients?

Professional Societies and Certifications

__ Are the affiliations listed current?
__ Have you removed those organizations in which you merely paid a fee and obtained the credentials?

Writings

__ Are the dates, titles, and claims to authorship accurate?
__ Have you listed co-authors?
__ Have you exaggerated the importance of the publication or your role in it?

Self-serving Comments

__ Have you made self-serving comments that can be taken out of context and used to cross-examine you?

Previous Cases

__ Do you list the cases you have worked on?
__ Should you consider removing these from your CV?

Attorneys Worked With

__ Do you list the attorneys you have worked with/for?
__ Should you consider removing these from your CV?

Dating

__ Is your CV dated so that it is easy to update and keep current?

Appendix B Report Quality Control Checklist

__ Has a written report been expressly requested by counsel at this time?
__ Have you covered all the issues counsel wanted addressed?
__ Have you avoided covering any issues counsel did not want addressed?
__ Is your report dated?
__ Pursuant to your routine business practice regarding documents that are no longer needed, have you discarded preliminary drafts of the report?
__ Have you had the report proofed for spelling and grammar mistakes?
__ Have you removed any inappropriate remarks from your report?
__ Have you specified upon which facts, data, standards, and information your opinions are based?
__ Is the tone of the report formal?
__ Have you formatted the report with subheadings for ease of reading?
__ Opinions
	__ When did you form your opinion?
	__ Upon what underlying facts and data is your opinion based?
	__ What are your opinions?
	__ Have you stated that you may have additional opinions if additional material is provided?
	__ Are your opinions expressed in a legally sufficient manner?
__ Have you included a summary of conclusions and opinions?
__ Have you included appropriate appendices?
	__ Correspondence
	__ Copies of documents
	__ Photos
	__ Charts
	__ Test results
	__ Drawings
	__ Underlying data
	__ Codes
	__ Records
	__ Ordinances
	__ Statutes
	__ Licenses
	__ Permits
	__ Other documentary material
__ Does your report comply with the Federal Rules of Civil Procedure Rule 26 2(B) and contain the following?
	__ A complete statement of all opinions to be expressed by the expert.
	__ The basis and reasons for the expert's opinions.
	__ The data or information considered by the witness in forming the opinions.
	__ Any exhibits to be used as a summary of or support for the opinions.
	__ The qualifications of the witness, including a list of all publications in the preceding ten years.

__ The compensation to be paid for the study and testimony.
__ A list of any other cases in which the witness has testified as an expert (at trial or in deposition) within the preceding four years.

Appendix C Deposition Areas of Inquiry

Experts should prepare for deposition with their retaining counsel. An understanding of the common areas of inquiry is helpful.

Subpoena Duces Tecum

__ Have you received a subpoena?
__ What were you requested to produce?
__ Is the material in your file?
__ Do you have copies of the materials?
    __ Have you in fact produced all of the material subpoenaed?
__ Have you removed anything from the file?

General Background Information

__ Name
__ Date of birth
__ Where you were born and raised
__ Your home and professional address

CV

__ Is it correct and accurate?
__ Do you have copies for the attorneys and stenographer?
__ Do you use any other versions of your CV?

Educational Background

__ What schools have you attended?
__ What were your major areas of study?
__ What degrees did you obtain?
__ What are the dates for your attendance and degrees?
__ What additional training courses have you attended?
__ What continuing education courses have you attended in the past ten years?
__ Have you been the subject of any disciplinary actions?
__ Have your licenses ever been suspended or revoked?
__ What were your grades?
__ What did you do between any gaps in your education?

Relationship with Counsel

__ What is your personal/financial relationship with counsel who has retained you in this case?

Employment

__ What were the dates of each position?
__ What are all the positions you have held?
__ What were your titles?
__ What were your duties at each position?
__ What did you do during gaps in your CV?

Teaching at Schools
__ Have you taught at any educational facility?
__ Where and when did you teach? What was taught?

Teaching at Seminars
__ Have you been on the faculty of any seminars, conferences, or workshops?
__ What did you speak on?
__ Were there outlines, course materials, or other handout materials?

Fees
__ How much have you been paid to date in this case?
__ What is your hourly rate?
__ Do you have any outstanding bills in the case?
__ How much do you expect to bill in the future in the case?

Forensic Income
__ Who are your major clients?
__ How much income did you obtain for forensic work in the past three years?
__ What percentage of your professional time is devoted to forensic work?
__ What percentage of your income is from forensic work?

Bias
__ Do you have any biases in this case?
__ Are you impartial?
__ Do you have a direct or indirect financial interest in the case?
__ Are you a friend or relative of an attorney/party?

Witness Experience
__ How often do you testify?
__ What percentage for plaintiffs? Defendants?

Publications
__ State all of the articles, chapters, books, reviews, abstracts, and other writings that you have had published.
__ When and where were these published?
__ Have any of your writings not been accepted for publication? Specify.

Organizations
__ Of what professional organizations and societies are you a member?
__ What is your status in the organization(s)?
__ Have you ever paid a fee to obtain additional credentials?

Involvement in Case
__ When were you first contacted concerning this case?
__ By whom were you contacted?
__ How were you contacted: Phone, letter, e-mail, other?

Acceptance of Case
__ When did you accept this case?

DEPOSITION AREAS OF INQUIRY

What materials or records were you provided? By whom and when were they provided?

__ Correspondence
__ Reports
__ Messages
__ Notes
__ Computer disks
__ Police reports
__ Investigative reports
__ Medical and hospital records
__ Literature
__ Tables
__ Standards
__ Contracts
__ Photographs
__ Videotapes
__ Other materials

Pleadings

__ Which of the pleadings have you read in this case?
 __ Complaint
 __ Answer
 __ Interrogatories
 __ Depositions
 __ Motions
 __ Other

Research

__ What research did you do prior to forming your opinions?

Authorities

__ What do you recognize as authoritative in your field?
 __ Books
 __ Treatises
 __ Articles
 __ Journals
 __ Other experts
 __ Others

Site Inspection

__ Have you visited the site of the accident?
 __ When?
 __ With whom?
 __ Did you take or have you taken:
  __ Sketches?
  __ Photos?
  __ Videotapes?
  __ Any other depictions of the site?

Standards of Care

__ What is your understanding of the standard of care in this case?
__ From what are they derived?

Standards

__ What are the industry standards in this case?
__ Where are they derived from?

Work You Have Done in this Case

__ Records and documents reviewed: Which ones and when?
__ Examination of the product: When and what was done?
__ Testing: What was done, when was it done, and what were the results?
__ Is all of this work reflected on your bills and invoices?
__ What additional work do you anticipate doing prior to the trial?

Equipment

__ What equipment did you use in this case? Who were the manufacturer and calibrator? How was the equipment used?

Computers

__ What computers did you use to test or formulate your opinion? How did you use them?

Demonstrative Aids

__ Have you produced or used, or do you intend to produce or use, any of the following demonstrative aids at the trial? If so, specify:

__ Graphs
__ Charts
__ Models
__ Illustrations
__ Computer animation
__ Other

Opinions

__ What are the facts and assumptions upon which your opinions are based?
__ What are the opinions you will be testifying to?
__ What is the methodology employed in reaching the opinion?
__ What areas will you not be offering opinions on?

Concluding Remarks

__ Have you stated all of your conclusions and opinions in this case?

Appendix D Areas of Inquiry During Cross-Examination

Experts need to be effective when questioned by opposing counsel during cross-examination. Anticipating the areas of likely inquiry and preparing accordingly will increase an expert's effectiveness. The following outline describes some of the most important lines of inquiry opposing counsel may follow.

Initial Consultation

__ When you were first contacted
__ By whom you were contacted
__ When you were retained
__ What you were requested to do

Qualifications

__ Accuracy of CV
__ Knowledge
__ Skill
__ Education/Degrees/Licenses
__ Training
__ Memberships in societies
__ Awards
__ Practical experience
  __ Recentness of experience
  __ Relevancy of experience
__ Credibility
__ Marketing activities
__ Relationship to retaining party or attorney
__ Affiliation with an insurance company
__ Conversations with retaining attorney
__ Indirect monetary interest
__ Prior testimony
__ Professional presentations
__ Professional and personal writings

Opinions

__ Documents and pleadings reviewed
__ Validity of underlying facts
__ Validity of underlying assumptions
__ Sources of information
__ Reports of other experts reviewed
__ Your opinion's foundation
__ Reliance on tests not personally performed
__ Reliance on other experts' records
__ Reliance on self-reported history
__ Omitted facts
__ When you formed your opinions

__ Opinions you will be offering
__ Opinions you will not be offering
__ Prior contrary opinions

Fees and Billing
__ Hourly rate
__ Amount billed to date
__ Amount anticipate billing
__ Amount paid in prior cases by client

Forensic Work
__ Percentage of your time spent on forensic work
__ Amount for plaintiffs
__ Amount for defendants
__ Percentage of your total income derived from forensic work
__ Consulting work where not retained to testify

Bias
__ Impartiality
__ Inflexibility
__ Personal/social relationship with party/attorney
__ Professional witness
__ Advocate
__ Fees and compensation
__ Direct or indirect financial interest in the case

Reports
__ Dates of reports
__ Oral vs. written
__ Revisions
__ Information in report
__ Inaccuracy in reports
__ Preliminary vs. final
    __ Additions, alterations, corrections
    __ Prior drafts

Tests Performed
__ When, where, at whose request
__ Results
__ Equipment used
__ Similarity of conditions
__ Photos, videos, or sketches taken
__ Tests not performed
__ Accuracy of calculations, tests

Visit to Accident Scene
__ When and at whose request
__ Similarity of conditions
__ What was done during visit

AREAS OF INQUIRY DURING CROSS-EXAMINATION

Skeletons in Closet

__ Professional discipline
__ Loss of job
__ Failing certification exams
__ Criminal convictions
__ Suspension/revocation of licenses
__ Testimony rejected by other courts or administrative agencies
__ Findings of being not qualified to testify
__ Prior professional or testifying mistakes

Subpoenas

__ Fully complied with subpoena
__ Removed documents from your file

Learned Treatises

__ Which texts, treatises, and articles are authoritative
__ Contrary statements in treatises

Prior Testimony

__ One-sidedness
__ Inconsistencies (impeachment with prior testimony)

Legal Standards

__ Degree of probability required
__ Standards of practice
__ Pertinent statutes, rules, regulations, and codes

***Daubert* Issues**

__ Has your technique or theory been tested?
__ Has your technique or theory been subject to peer review and publication?
__ The known or potential rate of error of the technique or theory
__ The existence of standards and controls
__ The degree to which the technique or theory has been generally accepted by the scientific community
__ Theory developed "for litigation only"

Appendix E Complaint

COMMONWEALTH OF MASSACHUSETTS SUPERIOR COURT

NORFOLK, SS: No. 90-00447

CHARLES SMITH; PATRICIA SMITH; and KATELYN SMITH, KYLE SMITH, and MATTHEW SMITH, Minors by Their Mother and Next Friend, PATRICIA SMITH, Plaintiffs	)))))	
	)	COMPLAINT
VS.	))	
ABC CONSTRUCTION CO., INC., Defendant	)	

PARTIES

1. The Plaintiff, Charles Smith, is an adult individual and is a resident of Jackson, Rhode Island.
2. The Plaintiff, Patricia Smith, is an adult individual who at all times relevant has been the lawful spouse of Charles Smith, and is a resident of Jackson, Rhode Island.
3. The Plaintiffs Katelyn Smith, Kyle Smith and Matthew Smith are minor children of Charles Smith; are residents of Jackson, Rhode Island; and are represented in this action by their mother and next friend Patricia Smith.
4. The Defendant, ABC Construction Co., Inc., is a business corporation, duly organized under the laws of the Commonwealth of Massachusetts, having the powers and purposes, *inter alia,* of developing real property and buildings thereon; and has a locus in Milton, Norfolk County, Massachusetts.

DECLARATION OF FACTS

5. On or about February 24, 1988, the Defendant ABC Construction Co., Inc., was the owner of certain real property in Wilder, Norfolk County, Massachusetts, being known as 10 Maple Drive, in the Wilder Farms subdivision.
6. On or about February 24, 1988, the Defendant was then engaged as general contractor for the construction of a dwelling house on the property at 10 Maple Drive, Wilder, Massachusetts.
7. The Defendant had a subcontract with ACME Construction Company, of Fairfield, Massachusetts, in effect as of February 24, 1988, to furnish carpentry services for the construction of the dwelling at 10 Maple Drive.
8. The Plaintiff, Charles Smith, was an employee of ACME Construction Company as of February 24, 1988; and was employed by said company as a carpenter.
9. On or about February 24, 1988, the Plaintiff Charles Smith was lawfully on the Defendant's premises at 10 Maple Drive, for the purpose of acting within the scope of his employment with ACME Construction Company, to provide carpentry services to Defendant on said property.

10. While on said premises on February 24, 1988, the Plaintiff Charles Smith was at all times exercising due care for his personal safety.
11. While on Defendant's premises on February 24, 1988, the Plaintiff did step upon a plywood covering placed over a floor opening, which cover was not properly constructed or adequately secured; and as a result the Plaintiff Charles Smith did then and there fall through the floor opening sustaining severe personal injuries.
12. The injuries sustained by Plaintiff from such fall on February 24, 1988, include a herniated lumbar disc which has required surgery. By reason of such injury, Plaintiff has suffered such pain and will suffer such pain in future.
13. By reason of such injury, Plaintiff has suffered loss of bodily function and disability, with consequent loss of earning capacity which is in excess of $44,800 at present; and such disability with loss of earning capacity continues and will continue in future.
14. By reason of such injury, Plaintiff has incurred reasonable medical expenses to date in excess of $10,000.00 and Plaintiff continues to require medical care and will require further medical care in the future.
15. By reason of such injury, Plaintiff Charles Smith has also suffered the loss of the ability to enjoy life and to attend to daily activities, and such loss continues and will continue in future.
16. By reason of the physical and mental injuries sustained by Charles Smith, the Plaintiff Patricia Smith has suffered loss of her husband's full care, society, companionship, service, comfort and spousal consortium, and she has been damaged thereby; and Plaintiff Patricia Smith continues to suffer such loss and will suffer such loss in future.
17. By reason of the physical and mental injuries sustained by Charles Smith, the minor Plaintiffs Katelyn Smith, Kyle Smith and Matthew Smith, have suffered loss of their father's full care, society, companionship, service, comfort and parental consortium, and they have been damaged thereby; and said minor Plaintiffs continue to suffer such loss and will suffer such loss in future.
18. The proximate cause of the injury, loss and damage sustained by the Plaintiffs was the negligence and lack of due care of Defendant, ABC Construction Co., Inc., in the following particulars.
a) The Defendant did cause to exist on its premises an unreasonably dangerous and defective condition, i.e., the improperly constructed floor hole covering;
b) The Defendant did, by failure to reasonably inspect its premises, suffer or permit the unreasonably dangerous and defective condition to remain on its premises;
c) The Defendant failed to provide adequate warnings or other safeguards to prevent injury to persons such as Plaintiff from the unreasonably dangerous and defective condition on its property; and
d) The Defendant failed to take reasonable action to correct the dangerous and defective condition existing on its property.

COUNT I: CHARLES SMITH, PERSONAL INJURY

19. By reason of the matters stated in Paragraphs 1 to 18, above, the Defendant ABC Construction Co., Inc., is liable for its negligence to the Plaintiff Charles Smith, for damages to compensate for his injury and loss, to include pain and suffering, lost earning capacity and medical expense, as stated above.

COMPLAINT

COUNT II: PATRICIA SMITH, LOSS OF SPOUSAL CONSORTIUM

20. By reason of the matters stated in Paragraphs 1 to 18 above, the Defendant ABC Construction Co., Inc., is liable for its negligence to the Plaintiff Patricia Smith, for damages to compensate for her injury and loss, to include loss of spousal consortium, as stated above.

COUNT III: KATELYN SMITH, LOSS OF PARENTAL CONSORTIUM

21. By reason of the matters stated in Paragraphs 1 to 18 above, the Defendant ABC Construction Co., Inc., is liable for its negligence to the minor Plaintiff Katelyn Smith, by her mother and next friend Patricia Smith, for damages to compensate for her injury and loss, to include loss of parental consortium as stated above.

COUNT IV: KYLE SMITH, LOSS OF PARENTAL CONSORTIUM

22. By reason of the matters stated in Paragraphs 1 to 18 above, the Defendant ABC Construction Co., Inc., is liable for its negligence to the minor Plaintiff Kyle Smith, by his mother and next friend Patricia Smith, for damages to compensate for his injury and loss, to include loss of parental consortium, as stated above.

COUNT V: MATTHEW SMITH, LOSS OF PARENTAL CONSORTIUM

23. By reason of the matters stated in Paragraphs 1 to 18 above, the Defendant ABC Construction Co., Inc., is liable for its negligence to the minor Plaintiff Matthew Smith, by his mother and next friend Patricia Smith, for damages to compensate for his injury and loss, to include loss of parental consortium, as stated above.

WHEREFORE, Plaintiffs demand relief as follows:

First, Judgment for Plaintiff Charles Smith, on Count I above, for damages to include $44,800 for lost earning capacity to date, and such further amounts as may be determined by the jury for continuing and future lost earning capacity; to include $10,000 for medical expense incurred to date, and such further amounts to be determined by the jury for continuing and future medical expense; to include damages to be determined by the jury to compensate Plaintiff in full for his physical and mental pain and suffering, and loss of ability to enjoy life and attend to daily activities; plus interest and costs of the action.

Second, Judgment for Plaintiff Patricia Smith, on Count II above, for damages in an amount to be determined by the jury to compensate for her past, present and future loss of spousal consortium; plus interest and costs of the action.

Third, Judgment for Plaintiff Katelyn Smith, on Count III above, for damages in an amount to be determined by the jury to compensate for her past, present and future loss of parental consortium; plus interest and costs of action.

Fourth, Judgment for Plaintiff Kyle Smith, on Count IV above, for damages in an amount to be determined by the jury, to compensate for his past, present and future loss of parental consortium; plus interest and costs of the action.

Fifth, Judgment for Plaintiff Matthew Smith, on Count V above, for damages in an amount to be determined by the jury, to compensate for his past, present and future loss of parental consortium; plus interest and cost of the action.

<u>**Sixth**</u>, Judgment for such other relief as the Court may be empowered to grant Plaintiffs for the loss.

PLAINTIFFS DEMAND JURY TRIAL ON ALL ISSUES.

For the Plaintiffs,
by their Attorney,

____

Daniel P. Larsen
Hamlin, Rose, Larsen & Nicholson
Box 111, 20 Doyle Road
Fraser Lake, MA 01234
(000) 555-1111
BBO #987654

Dated: February 12, 1990

Appendix F Answer

COMMONWEALTH OF MASSACHUSETTS

NORFOLK, SS.

SUPERIOR COURT DEPARTMENT
CIVIL ACTION NO. 90-00447

CHARLES SMITH; and KATELYN SMITH, KYLE SMITH, and MATTHEW SMITH, Minors by Their Mother and Next Friend, PATRICIA SMITH, Plaintiffs	ANSWER AND JURY CLAIM OF THE DEFANDANT, ABC CONSTRUCTION CO., TO THE PLAINTIFFS' AMENDED COMPLAINT
VS.	
ABC CONSTRUCTION CO., INC., Defendant and Third-Party Plaintiff	
VS.	
ACME CONSTRUCTION COMPANY, INC. and 123 CONCRETE, INC. Third-Party Defendants	

FIRST DEFENSE

The Complaint of the Plaintiff fails to state a claim against the defendant upon which relief can be granted.

SECOND DEFENSE

Now comes the Defendant, ABC Construction Co., Inc., and responds to the allegations in the Plaintiff's Complaint, paragraph by paragraph, as follows:

1. The Defendant admits the allegations contained in paragraph 1 of the Plaintiff's Complaint.
2. The Defendant admits the allegations contained in paragraph 2 of the Plaintiff's Complaint.
3. The defendant, ABC Construction Co., Inc. does admit that it is a business corporation duly organized under the laws of the Commonwealth of Massachusetts, but suggests that it has greater powers than suggested in paragraph 3 and admits it has a locus of business in Newberry, Massachusetts.

Therefore, the defendant admits part of paragraph 3 and denies a part of paragraph 3, as stated in its response.

4. The Defendant alleges that it is without knowledge or information sufficient to form a belief as to the truth of the allegations contained in paragraph 4 of the Plaintiff's Complaint.
5. The Defendant denies the allegations contained in paragraph 5 of the Plaintiff's Complaint.
6. The Defendant denies the allegations contained in paragraph 6 of the Plaintiff's Complaint.
7. The Defendant denies the allegations contained in paragraph 7 of the Plaintiff's Complaint.
8. The Defendant alleges that it is without knowledge or information sufficient to form a belief as to the truth of the allegations contained in paragraph 8 of the Plaintiff's Complaint.
9. The Defendant alleges that it is without knowledge or information sufficient to form a belief as to the truth of the allegations contained in paragraph 9 of the Plaintiff's Complaint.
10. The Defendant alleges that it is without knowledge or information sufficient to form a belief as to the truth of the allegations contained in paragraph 10 of the Plaintiff's Complaint.
11. The Defendant alleges that it is without knowledge or information sufficient to form a belief as to the truth of the allegations contained in paragraph 11 of the Plaintiff's Complaint.
12. The Defendant alleges that it is without knowledge or information sufficient to form a belief as to the truth of the allegations contained in paragraph 12 of the Plaintiff's Complaint.
13. The Defendant alleges that it is without knowledge or information sufficient to form a belief as to the truth of the allegations contained in paragraph 13 of the Plaintiff's Complaint.
14. The Defendant alleges that it is without knowledge or information sufficient to form a belief as to the truth of the allegations contained in paragraph 14 of the Plaintiff's Complaint.
15. The Defendant denies the allegations contained in paragraph 15 of the Plaintiff's Complaint.
16. The Defendant denies the allegations contained in paragraph 16 of the Plaintiff's Complaint.
17. The Defendant denies the allegations contained in paragraph 17 of the Plaintiff's Complaint.
18. The Defendant denies the allegations contained in paragraph 18 of the Plaintiff's Complaint.
19. The Defendant denies the allegations contained in paragraph 19 of the Plaintiff's Complaint.
20. The Defendant denies the allegations contained in paragraph 20 of the Plaintiff's Complaint.
21. The Defendant denies the allegations contained in paragraph 21 of the Plaintiff's Complaint.
22. The Defendant alleges that it is without knowledge or information sufficient to form a belief as to the truth of the allegations contained in paragraph 22 of the Plaintiff's complaint.

ANSWER

COUNT I

23. The Defendant denies the allegations contained in paragraph 23 of the Plaintiff's Complaint.

COUNT II

24. The Defendant denies the allegations contained in paragraph 24 of the Plaintiff's Complaint.

COUNT III

25. The Defendant denies the allegations contained in paragraph 25 of the Plaintiff's Complaint.

COUNT IV

26. The Defendant denies the allegations contained in paragraph 26 of the Plaintiff's Complaint.

THIRD DEFENSE

The defendant says that if the plaintiffs suffered damages as alleged in the Plaintiff's Complaint, such damages were caused by someone or something for whose conduct the defendant was not responsible.

FOURTH DEFENSE

The plaintiffs are barred from recovery because this action has not been brought within the time allowed by the appropriate statue of the Massachusetts General Laws.

FIFTH DEFENSE

The defendant says that at the time and place alleged in the Plaintiff's Complaint, the plaintiff so carelessly and negligently conducted himself so that he, by his own negligence, contributed directly and approximately to his own alleged injuries and damages.

SIXTH DEFENSE

The defendant says that the negligence of the plaintiff was as great or greater than the alleged negligence of the defendant and that such negligence of the plaintiff contributed to his damages and that, therefore, the plaintiff is barred from recovery under M.G.L., C. 231, Sec. 85 as amended.

SEVENTH DEFENSE

The defendant says that the plaintiff is guilty of contributory negligence and that damages, if any, recovered by the plaintiff should be reduced in proportion to the negligence of the plaintiff in accordance with M.G.L., C. 231, Sec 85 as amended.

EIGHTH DEFENSE

The defendant says further that the plaintiffs have no standing to sue the defendant in tort.

NINTH DEFENSE

The defendant says that the alleged incident resulted from dangers, the risk of which the plaintiff assumed.

TENTH DEFENSE

The defendant says that the plaintiffs have suffered no damages as a result of the alleged accident.

ELEVENTH DEFENSE

The defendant denies that any agents, servants or employees of his business were involved in any incident at the time and place alleged, as a result of which the plaintiff claims damages.

TWELFTH DEFENSE

The defendant says that at the time and place alleged in the Plaintiff's Complaint, the plaintiff was on the premises of the defendant without the permission or consent of the defendant, and was a trespasser.

THIRTEENTH DEFENSE

By way of affirmative defense, the defendant states that the plaintiffs are prohibited from making any claim against the defendant pursuant to General Laws, Ch. 152, as amended, and, therefore, the claims of the plaintiffs are barred.

WHEREFORE, the defendant requests this Honorable Court to dismiss the Plaintiff's Complaint and to award the defendant reasonable costs and attorney's fees for the defense of this action.

THE DEFENDANT DEMANDS TRIAL BY JURY ON ALL ISSUES.

By the Attorney for the Defendant,

____

Ronald A. Patton, Jr., Esquire
PATTON, DESOTO & HALL, P.C.
1 Inverness Place
Hillsborough, MA 23456
555-9999
BBO No. 777777

Dated: ____________

CERTIFICATE OF SERVICE

I, Ronald A. Patton, Jr., Attorney for the defendant in the foregoing action, do hereby certify that I have, this day, served a copy of the foregoing:

ANSWER AND JURY CLAIM OF THE DEFENDANT, ABC CONSTRUCTION CO., INC. TO THE PLAINTIFFS' AMENDED COMPLAINT.

to the attorneys of record by mailing same postage prepaid to:

Daniel P. Larsen, Esq.
Hamlin, Rose, Larsen & Nicholson
P.O. Box 111, 20 Doyle Road.
Fraser Lake, MA 01234
BBO #987654
(000)555-1111

Loren DeMol, Esq.
Michael A. Bruce, Jr., Esq.
Law Offices of Michael A. Bruce, Jr.
222 Benton Ave.
Baileys, MA 22666
(000) 555-8844

Richard Logan, Esq.
Logan, Coens, and Richey
100 Randolph Street
P.O. Box 789
Boston, MA 02000
(000) 555-4567

____
Ronald A. Patton, Jr., Esquire
PATTON, DESOTO & HALL, P.C.
1 Inverness Place
Hillsborough, MA 23456
555-9999
BBO No. 777777

Dated: ____________

Appendix G Answers to Interrogatories

COMMONWEALTH OF MASSACHUSETTS

NORFOLK, SS.

SUPERIOR COURT DEPARTMENT
CIVIL ACTION NO. 90-00447

CHARLES SMITH; PATRICIA SMITH; and KATELYN SMITH, KYLE SMITH, and MATTHEW SMITH, Minors by Their Mother and Next Friend, PATRICIA SMITH, PLAINTIFF, CHARLES SMITH'S Plaintiffs	
	ANSWERS TO DEFENDANT'S INTERROGATORIES
VS.	
ABC CONSTRUCTION CO., INC., Defendant	

Q. 1. Please identify yourself by stating your full name, date of birth, social security number, residence, employer, business address, occupation and, if married, the name of your spouse.

A. 1. Charles Smith; 4/6/48; 039-28-5945; 27 Harbor Road, Jackson, RI; Unemployed; Not applicable; Framing Carpenter/Disabled; Patricia Smith.

Q. 2. Please describe in full detail how the alleged accident occurred, stating what you saw, heard, did and what happened to you in order in which the events took place.

A. 2. We returned to the job site at 10 Maple Drive in Wilder, Massachusetts, on the morning of February 24, 1988. I went over to the area of the cellar hole opening that we had covered with plywood laid down on framing timbers and I saw it had been covered over with plastic since we were there the previous week. I went over to remove the plastic sheet and I stepped on the plywood covering the hole. When I stepped on the plywood my foot went through and I fell 3 feet or so when I got hung up on a steel center beam which was below the opening. I came down on to this steel beam with my back and my right shoulder making contact.

Q. 3. Please state the exact hour, day and date and when the alleged accident occurred.

A. 3. The accident occurred on February 24, 1988, at about 7:00 A.M.

Q. 4. Please give a complete description of the injuries you received as a result of the alleged accident.

A. 4. As a result of this accident I suffered herniated disc in my lower back with right leg pains resulting from the sciatic nerve. This has been diagnosed as herniated nucleus pulposis at L5-S1, with sciatica.

Q. 5. Please give a complete description of the injuries which you believe to be permanent as a result of the alleged accident.

A. 5. I believe the injury of herniated disc with residual back pain and sciatic pain as described in answer to question 4 permanent. I have suffered symptoms continuously from the date of the accident through the present by reason of such injuries.

Q. 6. If, as a result of any injuries received with regard to this alleged accident, you received medical and/or other treatment, state:

a. The name and address of any and all persons or institutions from which you received such medical or other treatment;

b. The number of treatments so received, setting forth as accurately as possible, all dates of treatment and a description of said treatments;

c. The number and description of treatments received at a doctor's office or institution and the number at your home; and

d. An itemized account of all expenses incurred for the above referred to treatments.

A. 6. My medical treatment has included the following:

	V.A. Hospital Epworth, RI	
2/25/88	Orthopedic Clinic, X-ray	$ 127.00
3/1/88	Orthopedic Clinic	127.00
4/20/88	Orthopedic Clinic	127.00
5/4/88	Orthopedic Clinic, X-ray	127.00
6/29/88	Orthopedic Clinic	127.00
7/5-7/8/88	Inpatient: CT and Myelogram	1,419.00
7/27/88	Orthopedic Clinic	127.00
8/22-8/26/88	Inpatient Care	1,892.00
8/29-9/3/88	Inpatient: Disc Surgery	3,055.00
9/19/88	Orthopedic Follow-up	127.00
10/17/88	Orthopedic Clinic	110.00
11/28/88	Orthopedic Clinic	110.00

12/5-12/10/88	Inpatient: CAT Scan, Myelogram	2,415.00
8/14/89	Orthopedic Clinic	110.00
10/4/89	Orthopedic Clinic	116.00
10/6/89	Physical Therapy	116.00
10/11/89	Physical Therapy	116.00
10/16/89	Physical Therapy	116.00
10/20/89	Physical Therapy	116.00
10/23/89	Physical Therapy	116.00
10/25/89	Physical Therapy	116.00
11/1/89	Physical Therapy	116.00
11/3/89	Physical Therapy	116.00
1/11/90	Orthopedic Clinic, X-ray	116.00
4/4/90	Orthopedic Clinic	116.00
4/10/90	Physical Therapy	116.00
10/23/90	Orthopedic Clinic	116.00

More detailed information is contained on my medical records, copies of which are being provided to Defendant in response to request for production of documents.

Q. 7. a. Please state the dates between which you were confined to your home as a result of the alleged accident;

b. Please state the dates between which you were confined to your bed as a result;

c. Please state the dates between which you were absent from work as a result of the alleged accident.

A. 7. a. After seeing the doctor on February 25, 1988, I went home and stayed home for one week. On March 1, 1988, I went out again, to see the doctor.

Following this visit, I went back to work for a period of weeks between March 5, 1988, and April 15, 1988. I worked only a few days each week, and I missed many days due to back pain. I did not keep a record of these days. I last worked on April 15, 1988. On those days that I missed, I was confined to home, at bed rest.

After seeing the doctor on April 20, 1988, I stayed home at bed rest for 2 weeks, and I have remained at home since that time. Gradually, I have increased my ability to get out of the house, to where I now can be up and about from one to two hours per day. The remainder of the time, I am still confined to home, with frequent bed rest.

b. I was confined to bed, at home from February 25, 1988, after seeing the doctor, to March 3, 1988. I was confined to bed at home, on doctor's orders, from April 20, 1988, through May 3, 1988. I was confined to bed, in hospital, from July 5, 188, to July 8, 1988. I was confined to bed at home from July 9, 1988, to July 27, 1988, when I returned to the doctor. I remained at bedrest, at home, from July 28, 1988, to August 21, 1988. I remained at bedrest, in hospital, from August 22, 1988, to August 26, 1988, to August 28, 1988. I remained at bedrest, in hospital, from August 29, 1988, through September 3, 1988. I remained at bedrest, at home, from September 4, 1988, to September 19, 1988, when I returned to the doctor. I remained at bedrest, at home, from September 20, 1988, to October 17, 1988, when I returned to the doctor. I remained at bedrest at home, on doctor's orders, from October 18, 1988, to November 28, 1988, when I saw the doctor again. I was confined to bedrest, in hospital, from December 5, 1988, through December 10, 1988.

At all other times, from and after April 20, 1988, I have remained sedentary, spending most of my time at home sitting or reclining, with gradual increase in my ability to get up and about.

c. I have been out of work, as follows:

February 25, 1988 through March 4, 1988; and April 18, 1988, to present.

Also, I missed several days between March 5, 1988, and April 15, 1988, but I have not record of these days.

Q. 8. Describe fully and in complete detail any illnesses, injuries, diseases, defects or operations which you may have or suffered from:

a. within five years prior to the date of the alleged accident;

b. at any time subsequent to the date of the alleged accident; and

c. at any time after the date of the alleged accident not caused by or arising from the same, setting forth the dates upon which each of the above was had or suffered from.

A. 8. a. With the exception of the occasional cold or flu, I had no illness, injuries, diseases, defects or operations within 5 years prior to February 24, 1988. In 1969, while serving in Vietnam, I injured my back, and since that time, over the years, I did experience occasional backaches, for which I was treated at the VA Hospital Orthopedic Clinic. Also, in 1987 or 1988, I experienced some ankle swelling, but I do not know of any accident or injury that caused the swelling.

b. With the exception only of the occasional cold or flu, and the residual affects and/or treatment for the injury I sustained on February 24, 1988, I have had no further illness, injuries, diseases, defects or operations since that time.

c. With the exception only of the occasional cold or flu, and the residual affects and/or treatment for the injury I sustained on February 24, 1988, I have had no further illness, injuries, diseases, defects or operations since that time.

Q. 9. State the name and residence, business address, occupation, and specialty of each person you expect may be called by you as an expert witness at the trial of this action, setting forth:

a. the subject matter in detail on which each such person may be expected to testify;

b. in detail, the substance of all facts about which each such person may be expected to testify; and

c. in detail, the contents of all opinions to which each such person may be expected to testify.

A. 9. Patrick McDonald, MD
15 Kildeer Blvd.
Providence, RI 02907

(a) Dr. McDonald will be asked to testify as to Charles Smith's injuries, including diagnosis, causation, prognosis, symptomology, loss of function and disability.

(b) Dr. McDonald will testify as to the following facts and opinions.

REPORTED HISTORY: The patient is a 42-year-old male who had been employed for three and a half years of Acme Construction as a carpenter prior to his injury. The injury occurred on February 24, 1988 at about 10:00 A.M. He fell through an opening In the floor, falling about four feet and landing diagonally across a metal beam. He struck his lower back and injured his upper back and shoulder as well. He was able with some difficulty to sit and wait out the rest of the day. He did very little work. Since it was a Friday, he went home.

The following Monday because of increasing pain, he was seen at the VA Hospital. He was evaluated over a period of months. He did not improve and, in fact, he began developing right leg pain for which he underwent a lumbar laminectory by Dr. Lynne in August of 1988. He says the numbness and some of the pain in his right leg improved briefly after that but then his low back pain became more severe and his right leg pain returned. He is now using crutches for stability. He has physical therapy ongoing three times a week and he sees the VA people back about every three months.

Current Complaints: He has basically pain which is quite extreme in his low back, into both groins and into his right leg down to the ankle. He denies any pain on the left side. He is able to drive a car but does so only rarely. He is anxious to try and get better but is also concerned that another operation may not help him anymore than the first.

PAST MEDICAL HISTORY: Medications: Percocet, Tylenol No. 3 and Motrin. Medical problems: None. He smokes one half pack of cigarettes a day for 20 years. He admits to no alcohol use. Surgical history is for tonsils and adenoids and lumbar laminectomy.

PHYSICAL EXAMINATION: On examination, he is 6'1" tall and weighs 230 pounds. He is able to move with an antalgic gait around the room. There seems to be some weakness on dorsiflexion on the right side compared to the left. His EHL on the right is slightly weak as well. His reflexes are 1+ Achilles tendon and patella tendon. Straight-leg raising sitting is negative on the left side to about 60 degrees.

On the right side, it is positive at about 40 degrees sitting with pain down the right lower extremity below the knee. When he is recumbent, I can get the right leg only up to about 20 degrees before again he has right radicular type of pain. On the left side, I can get it to about 40 degrees before he has significant low back pain. He has a well-healed incision in the lumbar spine which is about two inches in length which is minimally tender to palpatin. SI joints are slightly tender but the sciatic notch on the right is exquisitely tender compared to the left side.

Forward bending of the lumbar spine is perhaps 20 degrees at best, and extension is neutral. Lateral flexion is about 3 degrees at best and rotation is really not possible.

DIAGNOSIS: Status-post herniated lumbar disc with chronic low back pain and radicular pain, right lower extremity, suggestive or recurrent disc.

ASSESSMENT: It is Dr. McDonald's opinion that the patient's injury occurred acutely as a result of his job on February 24, 1988.

Based on examination of 6/22/90, it is Dr. McDonald's opinion that Plaintiff is not capable of returning to his regular work. He is capable of minimal sedentary work.

Dr. McDonald concurs with the need for aggressive therapy, also for the evaluation for facet blocks and work up to see if the patient has indeed another fragment of disc where he is in need of further surgery would be appropriate as well.

Dr. Danes would concur that there is a functional overlay here which is almost expected given a two year history of out of work with significant back injury.

(c) The bases of Dr. McDonald's opinions include the history taken from Plaintiff and the observations made during examination on June 22, 1990.

Steven Danes, MD

(a) Dr. Danes will be asked to testify as to Charles Smith's injuries, including diagnosis, causation, prognosis, symptomology, loss of function and disability.

(b) Dr. Danes will testify as to the following facts and opinion:

REPORTED HISTORY: The patient was seen on November 3, 1988 and on January 23, 1990. Patient is 41-year-old male who worked as a framing carpenter for ACME Construction for about two and a half years. He sustained an injury to his low back on February 24, 1988, when he was on the deck of a building and walked onto a piece of plywood covering a fireplace opening which gave way. He fell approximately two feet backwards and his back hit a steel center beam. He was unable to hold himself from fall further by grabbing the beam.

He was initially seen at the Veterans Administration Hospital and was subsequently seen in the orthopedic clinic there by Dr. Lynne. He underwent lumbar spine surgery on August 31, 1988. Post-oppressively, he states that he continued to have symptoms.

ANSWERS TO INTERROGATORIES

Interval History: The patient states that his right leg numbness and deadness have resolved approximately 90 percent. However, he continues to have severe low back pain and some difficulty with the right lower extremity. He has been to physical therapy for about two weeks but could not tolerate the therapeutic regimen.

Complaints are of persistent severe pain in the low back with difficulty moving at all out of a recliner chair or bed. He states that he spends most of his day lying or sitting in a recliner chair or in his bed and has used two crutches for ambulation, having progressed to two canes, and having the feeling of instability and increasing back pain. He takes two Percocet every six hours, 800 milligrams of Ibuprofen every six hours and two Soma tablets every six to eight hours.

Post-operatively, the patient did undergo a myelogram and CT Scan. He remains under the care of Dr. Lynne. A second operation is under consideration.

PAST HISTORY: The patient denies any interval injury since last seen or since his injury of February 24, 1988. Past history is positive for some low back pain with his work. He never had leg pain or missed any work because of this.

PHYSICAL EXAMINATION: Height is 6'1" tall and weight is 235 pounds. Patient enters the building and the exam room with two crutches and a very slow and cautions gait, limping on the right lower extremity. He has a two inch mid-line lumbar scar and tenderness over the scar.

There is no paraspinous spasm although he does withdraw on palpation of his scar. Lumbar range of motion is quite limited with 30 degrees of flexion, 15 degrees of left and right side bending and 5 degrees of extension. Deep-tendon reflexes are trace at the knees bilaterally and absent at the right ankle and trace at the left ankle. Sensation is preserved to light touch in the lower extremities. Motor testing shows 5/5 strength of extensor hallucis longus, tibialis anterior and quadriceps bilaterally.

The sciatic stretch tests on the right in the seated position is positive for his radiating pain as well as in the supine position. However, the sciatic stretch test is aggravated by knee flexion. Also of note is a positive patella tilt sign with complaints of low back pain aggravation by manipulation of the right patella. This is indicative of significant non-anatomic pain. He also has a slightly positive axial compression test.

DIAGNOSIS: Severe back pain and status post failed lumbar disc surgery.

ASSESSMENT: The onset of this patient's problem was the injury at work as stated above.

A subsequent course and failure to improve stems from that original injury.

The patient does show objective signs of limitation of lumbar motion and decreased right ankle jerk. He is not capable of regular or light work at this time.

In addition, he shows significant overlay of psychophysiological pain experienced as demonstrated by exacerbation of his pain by knee flexion and patella tilt sign.

Prognosis is extremely guarded given his progress to date.

(c) The bases of Dr. Danes's opinions include the history taken from Plaintiff and the observations made during examinations on November 3, 1988, and January 23, 1990.

Q. 10. State whether or not there were any witnesses to the alleged accident and, if so, state the name and address of all such witnesses other than the parties involved in this suit.

A. 10. Yes, there were witnesses present. They include:

John Williams, 900 Correy Street, Pawtucket, RI.
Karl Amons, 416 Kaspar Lane, Pawtucket, RI.
Thomas Andrews, 40 W. School Rd., Pawtucket, RI.

Q. 11. State what, if any, you consumed by way of any alcoholic beverages or drugs for a period of 24 hours prior to this accident, setting forth in detail where same were consumed, the type of alcohol or drugs, the amounts thereof consumed by you, and at what time intervals.

A. 11. I had no alcohol nor any medications or drugs within 24 hours prior to this accident.

Q. 12. Give an itemized statement of all monetary loss sustained by you as a result of the alleged accident.

A. 12. My economic loss to date is as follows:

Medical Expense:

V.A. Hospital
2/25/88 to present
As itemized at No. 6, above:
$11,506.00

Lost Earning Capacity:

Total disability from 4/15/88 to present,
$57,640.00
131 weeks at $440

Both medical expense and lost earning capacity continue to accrue, and these sums are expected to increase accordingly through the date of trial.

Q. 13. Please state in detail and as fully as possible, all conversations or the substance thereof that any defendant had with you or others in your presence concerning the alleged accident, stating as accurately as you are able, what was said by each.

A. 13. I do not recall any conversations with ABC Construction Company, Inc. Nor do I recall any conversations with ABC's owner, individually.

Q. 14. State with reference to the time of the alleged accident, the occupation in which you were engaged, setting forth the name of your employer, the particular capacity in which you were employed, and the wages, salary or profit you were receiving at that time.

A. 14. At the time of this accident I was employed by ACME Construction Company Inc. I was employed as a framing carpenter. I was earning $11.00 an hour, and I was averaging 40 hours a week.

Q. 15. If as a result of this accident you have received compensation from workers' compensation or other insurer, please identify the insurer and state the amounts received on a weekly basis and/or lump sum basis.

A. 15.
a. Workers' Compensation, Goode Insurance Co. $213.84 per week.

b. Other insurance
Social Security Disability, Title II
$171 per month

Q. 16. If you allege that the occurrence resulted in whole or in part from a defective condition involving the defendant's equipment or premises, please:
a. describe the alleged defective condition in complete detail;

b. state how long to your knowledge the alleged defective condition had existed prior to the alleged occurrence;

c. state whether or not you had observed or otherwise become aware of the alleged defective condition prior to the alleged occurrence.

A. 16. a. The defective condition consisted of a makeshift covering over the floor hole which was not properly secured by nailing and/or cross bracing. This consisted solely of half inch plywood laid across the opening. There were two sheets of plywood which were laid side-by-side over the hole and were not lapped over each other. This plywood was not adequate to support the weight of a 210-pound adult male. Additionally, the plywood was covered by plastic sheeting which obscured the edges of the plywood where it lapped over the perimeter of the hole, so I could not see that the 2x4 cross bracing had been removed.

b. The condition existed at least 24–48 hours to the best of my knowledge and information.

c. No. I was unaware of the defective condition prior to the accident. I was aware that when the ACME crew for whom I was working left the job site approximately one week earlier, we left the floor opening properly covered by laying 2x4's on the flat across the floor opening and then covering it with half-inch plywood which was nailed through to the decking.

Q. 17. Please give the date and time of day when you first saw the defect or defective condition in existence.

A. 17. I first became aware of the defective condition when my foot went through and I fell into the hole.

Q. 18. If you claim that the negligence of any person or persons, including the defendant, contributed to cause the alleged occurrence, please state their names and the manner in which each contributed to cause the alleged occurrence.

A. 18. The negligence of ABC Construction Co., Inc. (Defendant) arose in two contexts:

(a) as owner and party in control of the premises at 10 Maple Drive, Wilder, MA; and

(b) as general contractor, in charge of all construction activities at that location.

The specific negligent conduct of Defendant included:

(a) As owner or party in control of the premises, Defendant was negligent in failing to maintain the premises in a reasonably safe condition for lawful visitors by creating or permitting to exist an unreasonably dangerous and defective condition: i.e., an inadequately and improperly covered floor opening on the premises.

(b) as general contractor, Defendant was negligent in creating or permitting to exist on premises under construction an unreasonably dangerous and defective condition: i.e., an inadequately and improperly covered floor opening.

Also, as general contractor, Defendant failed to warn of the dangerous and defective condition.

Also, as general contractor, Defendant failed to designate suitable, competent persons to inspect the premises for safety hazards, such as the improperly covered floor opening.

Also, as general contractor, Defendant failed to assign to a suitable and competent person the task of covering or otherwise guarding the floor opening in a proper manner after Defendant's employees last used the floor opening for access to the basement, prior to the morning of February 24, 1988.

There may be others whose negligence contributed to my injury, to include other contractors on the site during the week prior to February 24, 1988, who had occasion to use the floor opening to the cellar and who may have been directly responsible for not covering the floor opening in a proper manner. Plaintiff's discovery, still unanswered by Defendant, seeks the names of any such other parties as may exist. In any event, as general contractor, Defendant was ultimately responsible for overall safety on this job site, even if the dangerous and defective condition had been directly created by such others.

Q. 19. Please describe the weather at the time of the alleged occurrence and during the 24 hours prior to the alleged occurrence, including whether it was clear, cloudy, raining lightly or sprinkling, raining hard, sleeting, snowing or otherwise, and whether or not there was an accumulation of any type of precipitation around the area of the occurrence.

A. 19. The weather was cold and clear.

Q. 20. Please state fully and in complete detail all that the defendant did or failed to do which in any way caused or contributed to cause the alleged occurrence, including every act or omission of the defendant which you allege constitutes negligence.

A. 20. See answer to Question 18, above, and Question 23, below.

Q. 21. Please identify by name, title, and business address the person with whom you dealt as being the person responsible for, in charge of or supervising the performance of your work on behalf of the owner of the premises at which you were performing your work at the time of the alleged accident.

A. 21. My work was supervised by Mr. Thomas Andrews as president and principal of ACME Construction Company Inc. Mr. Andrews did not supervise the performance of my work as a servant of the owner of the premises but was, on my information, an independent contractor.

Q. 22. If on the day of the alleged accident you were part of a work crew or group, please identify each member of the crew or group by name and residential and business address stating the identity of the person in charge of or in the position as the supervisor of the group and whether any of such persons were present at the time and place of the accident and witnessed the accident.

A. 22. The work crew consisted of the following individuals:

John Williams, 900 Correy Street, Pawtucket, RI.
Karl Amons, 416 Kaspar Lane, Pawtucket, RI.
Thomas Andrews, 40 W. School Rd., Pawtucket, RI, Supervisor.

Q. 23. If you claim that the defendant in any way violated any trade standards, safety standards, state, local or federal governmental regulations in the production or construction of the dwelling house at which the accident occurred, please state:

a. the exact standard which it is claimed that the defendant violated and the respect in which the standard was violated;

b. how and in what manner this violation caused or contributed to cause the alleged occurrence.

A. 23. (a) Defendant, as general contractor, violated the following provisions:

Mass. Division of Industrial Safety
Prevention of Accidents in Construction Operations
411 CMR 10.00 (Effective 1/1/78)

10.03 (1)	Protection of Health & Safety
10.03 (5)	Requirements of Competence
10.03 (7)	Safety Inspections
10.04 (6)	Falling Hazards
(a)	Prevention; and
(b)	Floor Security

Current regulations, 454 CMR 10.00, became effective on 7/8/88, after Plaintiff's accident, and therefore Defendant's violations arose under the previous regulations at 441 CMR 10.00.

OSHA Safety & Health Standards
Construction Industry Standards

29 U.S.C. Part 1926

Subpart C
Sect. 1926.20 Contractor Requirements for Accident Prevention

Subpart G
Sect. 1926.200 (b) Danger signs
(c) Caution signs

Subpart M
Sect. 1926.500 (9) (b) (8), and (f) (5) (ii) Floor hole guards

(b) These violations caused or contributed to the accident as follows:

Mass. DIS Violations

(1) 441 CMR 10.04 (6) (a) required that every hold or opening in any floor through which a person may fall shall have all exposed sides guarded by a barrier sufficient to prevent falls. This was not done at 10 Maple Drive. If Defendant had complied with this section, Plaintiff would not have fallen through the floor opening.

(2) 441 CMR 10.04 (6) (c) required that when floor openings are covered by solid temporary construction, such cover shall be properly anchored to prevent accidental

displacement. When ACME left the site a week before the accident, they had left the floor opening secured in compliance with this section, by laying 2x4s across the opening and then nailing plywood onto the 2x4s and through to the decking. This cover was removed when Defendant's employees or others used the floor opening to gain access to the cellar when the concrete floor was poured. This cover was replaced by loose sheets of 1/2 in. plywood laid across the opening, with no timber supports and no nailing, in violation of 10.04 (6) (c). When Plaintiff stepped on the unsecured 1/2 in. plywood, this was not adequate to support his weight, and he fell through the hole. If Defendant had complied with 10.04 (6)(c), the accident would have been prevented.

(3) 441 CMR 10.03 (5) required that the general contractor designate a person of suitable competence to perform in all work. Defendant permitted an incompetent person or persons to perform the task of covering the cellar hole opening after the basement floor was poured.

Also, if Defendant had arranged for daily inspections on the site, Defendant did not designate a person of suitable competence to perform such inspections.

Had a competent person been designated to cover the floor hole after the basement floor was poured, or had a competent person been designated to inspect the site, this accident could have been prevented.

(4) 441 CMR 10.03 (1) (a) required that all work sites be so arranged as to provide reasonable and adequate protection for the safety of employees and others. And 441 CMR 10.03 (1) (b) provided that it is the responsibility of both owners and contractors to provide for such safety. Defendant, both as owner and as general contractor, violated this section by causing or permitting to exist on the job site a dangerous and defective condition, which consisted of an inadequately constructed floor-hole cover. And this was compounded by Defendant's causing or permitting to exist a plastic sheet which covered and obscured the hazardous condition.

<u>OSHA Violations</u>
29 U.S.C. Part 1926

(1) Subpart C, sect. 1926.20 (b) (1), provides that it is an employer's responsibility to initiate and maintain safety programs on a job site. And sect. 1926.20 (b) (2) provides that this must include frequent and regular inspections. If a competent inspection had been performed at 10 Maple Drive, the accident would have been prevented, where the unsecured and inadequate floor hole cover was a hazard to employees.

(2) Subpart G, Sect. 1926.200 (b) requires that danger signs be posted at dangerous locations on a job site, and Sect. 1926.200 (c) requires that caution signs be posted where potential hazards exist. If, for any valid reason, it was not possible to re-secure the floor hole cover with adequate cross bracing and nailing down, then such danger or hazard should have been signaled by the placement of an appropriate sign. Had such sign been posted, Plaintiff would have been alerted to the fact that the solid floor hole covering had been replaced by an inadequate cover, and this

accident could have been prevented. Instead of providing such warning, Defendant caused or permitted to exist a plastic sheet over the floor hole cover, which obscured the hazard.

(3) Subpart M. Sect. 1926.500 (b) (8) provides that floor holes into which a person may fall must be guarded by either a railing and toe board, or a floor hole cover of standard strength and construction that is secured against accidental displacement. When ACME left the job site a week before the accident, they left the floor hole covered with a secure cover, in compliance with this section. When Plaintiff returned on February 24, 1988, the secure cover had been removed, and it was replaced with one that was of less than standard construction and which was not secured properly. If the floor hole had been properly covered after Defendant's employees or others had worked on the cellar floor, this accident would have been prevented.

Q. 24. Please describe any and all written or oral warnings or instructions given to you in relation to the defect, its existence or use, giving the name and address of each person who gave each such warning or instruction.

A. 24. None.

Subscribed on pain of perjury this 6th day of November, 1990.

____

Charles Smith

Appendix H Request for the Production of Documents

COMMONWEALTH OF MASSACHUSETTS

NORFOLK, SS.

SUPERIOR COURT DEPARTMENT
CIVIL ACTION NO. 90-00447

CHARLES SMITH; PATRICIA SMITH; and KATELYN SMITH, KYLE SMITH, and MATTHEW SMITH, Minors by Their Mother and Next Friend, PATRICIA SMITH, Plaintiffs VS. ABC CONSTRUCTION CO., INC. Defendant	REQUEST OF THE DEFENDANT FOR THE PRODUCTION OF DOCUMENTS UNDER RULE 34 TO THE PLAINTIFF, CHARLES SMITH

Now comes the defendant, ABC Construction Co., Inc. in the above entitled action through its attorney and pursuant to Rule 34 of the Massachusetts Rules of Civil Procedure, requests that the plaintiff, Charles Smith, produce and permit the said defendant to inspect, copy, and/or photograph all documents and things in the possession, custody, or control of the plaintiff, or any agent of the plaintiff, other than writing, documents, and tangible things prepared in anticipation of litigation or for trial, which embody, refer to, or relate in any way to the subjects listed below.

The said defendant requests that these documents and things herein requested be produced at the law firm of PATTON, DESOTO & HALL, P.C., 6 1 Inverness Place, Hillsborough, Massachusetts 22222, on or before the 30th day after service of this request, except that compliance with this request may be made by mailing copies of said documents to the defendant's attorney, but mail, postage prepaid, such mailings to be postmarked prior to the 30th day following service of this request.

NOTE: With respect to the hospital records, signed hospital authorization slips will suffice.

REQUESTS

1. Any and all hospital and medical records and reports regarding the injuries and damages and treatments thereof, received by the plaintiff with reference to the injuries alleged to have been sustained by the plaintiff in his Complaint.
2. True copies on the plaintiff's and Patricia Smith's Federal income tax returns for the years 1986 through 1989, and copies of all forms W-2 received by the plaintiffs for those years.
3. Full and complete records of any and all hospitals and other medical facilities at which the plaintiff was examined and/or treated in the past five-year period prior to the date of the alleged accident.
4. All employers' written confirmation or verification of the time and/or earnings lost as result of the accident.
5. Any and all written or documentary evidence which relates to the issue of the plaintiff's damage.
6. All signed and/or unsigned statements made by the defendant which are in the possession of the plaintiff or under his control and which relate directly or indirectly to any subject which is the basis of this complaint.
7. Any and all photographs in the possession, control and custody of the plaintiff which relates in any way to the accident alleged in the plaintiff's Complaint and amended Complaint, including all photographs showing the scene of the alleged accident, showing that the injuries sustained by the plaintiff or any effect thereof, and photographs of the scene of the accident and any components or parts of the equipment or dwelling house which caused the accident alleged in the plaintiff's Complaint.
8. Any and all written or other documentary evidence which relates to the issue of the defendant's liability.
9. And all written or other documentary evidence which tends to exonerate or exculpate the defendant.
10. Any and all written or other documentary evidence which tends to show that the conduct by act or omission of some third person or persons caused or contributed to the happening of the event or injuries which form the subject matter of this complaint.
11. Any and all photographs which the plaintiffs intend to offer at the time of trial.
12. Any and all documentary evidence which the plaintiffs intend to offer at the time of trial.
13. All financial records, bills, invoices or other such documents relating to amounts charged to or expended by or on behalf of the plaintiff as a result of the occurrence referred to in the plaintiff's Complaint.
14. All employment records of the plaintiff including, but without being limited to the names and addresses of all employers the records of the dates lost from work for any reason whatsoever, and the employment income loss during the period of time commencing five years before the date of the occurrence alleged in the plaintiff's Complaint and amended Complaint up to and including the present day.
15. Copies of any and all written statements, signed or unsigned, of any and all witnesses to the accident and/or copies of all verbatim written transcripts of any and all statements of such witnesses taken on a recording device prior to the

filing of the suit herein, which are in the possession, custody or control of the plaintiff or the plaintiff's attorney.

16. Copies of all written statements, signed or unsigned, of any and all witnesses to the subject of the plaintiff's alleged allegations of both liability and/or damages from the incident as alleged in the plaintiff's Complaint and/or copies of all verbatim written transcripts of any and all statements of such witnesses taken on a recording device prior to the filing of this suit herein which are in the possession, custody or control of the plaintiff or the plaintiff's attorney.
17. Copies of all accident reports made by the plaintiff which relate to the accident alleged in the plaintiff's Complaint and amended Complaint.
18. If the plaintiff applied for or received workers' compensation as a result of the accident, which is the subject of the plaintiff's Complaint, the entire file maintained by the workers' compensation carrier with respect to the loss.
19. Each investigation report relating to the accident which is the subject of the plaintiff's Complaint and which was prepared by any agency, bureau or commission of the Federal government, or any state, local or municipal government.

By the Attorney for the Defendant,

____

Ronald A. Patton, Jr., Esquire
PATTON, DESOTO & HALL, P.C.
1 Inverness Place
Hillsborough, MA 23456
BBO No. 777777

Dated: _____________

Appendix I Sample Schedule from Subpoena Duces Tecum

SCHEDULE A.

You are requested to bring with you any and all materials of the following descriptions which (a) you referred to in preparing your report of November 28, 1995; and/or (b) to which you may refer in giving testimony at trial.

1. Notes prepared by you in the course of your inspection of the 480DM screener and/or in the course of your research (excluding notes which memorialize communications with counsel or which may otherwise be privileged).

2. Diagrams, blueprints, plans, drawings and sketches.

3. Graphs and/or charts.

4. Records and reports from other persons or entities.

5. Photographs, films and/or videotapes.

6. Deposition excerpts to which you referred in preparing your report.

7. Governmental regulations, including OSHA.

8. Published standards of any industrial or professional associations, including ANSI and ASME.
9. Non-published written standards from any industrial or professional source.

10. Product brochures and/or manuals.

11. Written or transcribed statements of any person.

12. Treatises and/or publications.

13. Test results and survey reports.

14. Physical objects, to include without limitation any exemplar wrenches used by you in performing any test or experiment on the 480DM screener and any instruments used by you in performing any such test or experiment.

Appendix J Deposition Transcript

COMMONWEALTH OF MASSACHUSETTS

Norfolk, ss. Superior Court

CHARLES SMITH, ET AL.

vs. Civil Action No. 90-00447

ABC CONSTRUCTION COMPANY, INC.

Deposition of PATRICK EDWARD MCDONALD, MD, taken on behalf of the Plaintiff pursuant to the Rhode Island Rules of Civil Procedure, on December 17, 1990, at the offices of Group Medical, Inc., at 15 Kildeer Boulevard, Providence, Rhode Island, before Grace T. Van Melca, Notary Public, convening at 5:00 P.M.

APPEARANCES:

HAMLIN, ROSE, LARSEN & NICHOLSON
BY: DANIEL P. LARSEN, ESQ. . . . . Counsel for the Plaintiffs

PATTON, DESOTO & HALL
BY: MARC S. NICITA, ESQ. . . . . .Counsel for the Defendants

STENO ASSOCIATES
Shorthand Reporters
Suite 124 - 300 Downey Street
Kingston, Rhode Island 02000

INDEX

Plaintiff's Exhibits

MR. LARSEN: Are we going to do the same stipulations?
MR. NICITA: Yes.
MR. LARSEN: Okay. Doctor, do you want to reserve the right to read and sign this deposition, or do you want to waive that right?
THE DEPONENT: No. I'll waive that.
MR. LARSEN: Okay. And we will stipulate to waive the signing and reading?
MR. NICITA: Yes. Sure. That's fine.
MR. LARSEN: Okay. The doctor needs to be sworn.

PATRICK EDWARD MCDONALD, MD, first having been duly sworn by the Notary Public, testified as follows:

EXAMINATION BY MR. LARSEN

Q: Dr. McDonald, will you please state your present address.
A: The address for this is 15 Kildeer Boulevard, Providence, Rhode Island. My office address is 215 Scenic Drive, Warwick, Rhode Island.
Q: What is your occupation?
A: Orthopedic surgery.
Q: And for how long have you been in that occupation?
A: Seven years.
Q: Do you hold any licenses?
A: I'm licensed to practice medicine in Rhode Island and Massachusetts. I'm board certified in orthopedic surgery, a member of the American Academy of Orthopedic Surgeons.
Q: Dr. McDonald, let me ask you to slow down a second.

MR. LARSEN: Off the record.
(A discussion was held off the record.)
MR. LARSEN: We can go back on the record.

Q: Are you licensed to practice medicine, Dr. McDonald?
A: Yes
Q: And what licenses do you hold and what dates of issue?
A: In Rhode Island, Doctor of Medicine, July 1983; and Massachusetts, 1985, also Doctor of Medicine.
Q: Do you have a board certification, Doctor?
A: Yes.
Q: And what is that?
A: American Board of Orthopedic Surgery.
Q: When did you get the board certification?
A: 1985.
Q: What has been your undergraduate and graduate education?
A: Undergraduate, Pennsylvania State University, 1969 through 1973; medical school, University of Michigan, 1974 through 1978.
Q: What training or education have you had after your graduation from medical school?
A: Internship and general surgery at North Central Hospital. That's in Michigan.
Q: In what field?
A: General surgery.
Q: And what degree did you take in Michigan?
A: That was the MD degree.

Q: What work experience have you had in the field of medicine, and particularly, in the field of orthopedics?
A: Four years of orthopedic residency, also at North Central Hospital.
Q: And how long have you been in your current position?
A: I was employed with Group Health, Inc. from July 1983 through December 1989, in private practice from that date until the current date.
Q: And do you specialize in your current private practice?
A: I do general orthopedics.
Q: Do you have any hospital associations, affiliations?
A: I'm on staff at the Good Shepherd Hospital and at County Hospital.
Q: Dr. McDonald, are you familiar with a patient by the name of Charles Smith?
A: Yes.
Q: And would you describe how you came to know Charles Smith?
A: I was requested by Goode Insurance to evaluate the patient as an independent medical expert on July 22, 1990.
Q: Was this on behalf of his employer, ACME Construction?
A: I presume it was on behalf of the insurance company.
Q: Did you conduct an examination?
A: Yes.
Q: And would you describe the procedure, just an overview of the procedure, that you undertook on June 22, 1990?
A: I asked the patient how long he had been employed by ACME Construction and what his job was. He described it as being a carpenter. Then I asked him to detail the injury including the date and time that it occurred, how he was injured, and what treatment he was rendered for that injury.
Q: Did Charles Smith give you a history?
A: Yes.
Q: Would you tell us what the history was.
A: That on February 24, approximately 10:00 A.M.—this was in 1988—he fell through an opening in the floor where he was working and landed diagonally across a metal beam that was below him, with an injury to his lower back and his upper back. He continued to work that day, but as he states, was not able to perform all his work. He simply went home, rested over the weekend, and was seen at the V.A. Hospital the following Monday morning. Do you want me to continue with the—
Q: Yes. Please continue with the history that you took from him.
A: He states he had persistent right leg pain that developed over an undetermined period of time, underwent some conservative treatment, and ultimately underwent a lumbar laminectory for excision of a herniated disk by Dr. Lynne in August of 1988. This was for right leg pain predominantly and lower back pain. At the time of my exam, July 22, 1990, he still had persistent lower back and right leg pain. Although he had a period of time when his leg pain had improved, it had now gotten worse. He had had some treatment from a conservative standpoint, facet blocks, and further surgery on his back was being considered at that time. His main complaint at that time was low back pain and the pain in the right leg and ankle and into the groin region, with no pain on the left side.
Q: Was that the main complaint as of the time of the examination?
A: That's correct.
Q: Did he give you an account of his typical daily activities?
A. He did not detail to me, no.

Q: Did he give you a past medical history?
A: I inquired as to medications, and he detailed that as well as medical problems, cigarette, and alcohol history and surgical history.
Q: Did you conduct a physical examination of Charles Smith?
A: Yes.
Q: Would you describe what you did and what you observed on that examination.
A: I evaluate the patient as he ambulates in the room, and noted that he was limping. He had weakness of the muscles going to his right great toe and also to his foot on the right side, compared to the left. His reflexes were symmetrical, and he had a—what we call a positive straight-leg raising sign, meaning when I would lift his right leg, he would get pain duplicating his pain down the right lower extremity, which is significant for a herniated disk or nerve root inflammation. I examined his back, measured the scar that he had, and examined him for areas of tenderness, and he was tender over the sciatic notch on the right side which is directly over the nerve that would be affected by a herniated disk; also checked his range of motion, which was quite limited.
Q: Doctor, what is the clinical significance, in your view, of the weakness determined on strength testing?
A: It's indicative of a particular nerve root that may be affected as opposed to another nerve root.
Q: And in this case, what would that be indicative of with respect to the particular nerve roots involved?
A: It would probably be the L5-S1 disk space which would then be hitting the S1 nerve root. Unfortunately, it could also be the disk space just above it and still be catching that same nerve root. It's significant, however, that it coincided with the same leg that he was having the pain in.
Q: And what is the significance of the straight leg raising findings?
A: It's a provocative test intended to stretch an already irritated nerve root even further to see if, indeed, you can reproduce his symptoms. The significance is then stretching the same nerve root on the opposite leg and eliciting none of the same symptoms.
Q: And what does that indicate for diagnostic purposes?
A: It would tend to cooperate the complaints with the finding, meaning his right leg pain fits the provocative test on the right leg.
Q: What does the term "exquisitely tender" mean in, I would say, layman's terms, referring to palpation of the sciatic notch on the right.
A: The sciatic notch is the area where the sciatic nerve passes by, and palpating a nerve that's already inflamed and irritable causes even more pain and irritability; and again, this fits his findings, and in fact, it was tender on the right and only minimally so on the left side.
Q: Did you make a diagnosis on this examination, Doctor?
A: It was a herniated disk—. I'm sorry. Status post-herniated disk excision with chronic back pain and persistent radicular pain suggestive of current—
Q: What does "post-herniated lumbar disk" mean, Doctor?
A: That was my way of describing the fact that he had one herniated disk that had been successfully operated on.
Q: What does "radicular pain" mean?
A: Radicular pain means pain that follows the radicular nerve going down into the leg.

Q: And that is suggestive in your diagnosis of recurrent disk. What does that refer to, in layman's terms?
A: Recurrent disk would be either a re-rupture of a disk at that same level that had been previously removed, or perhaps a disk at another level. Recurrent, obviously, suggests a disk at the same level that had previously been operated.
Q: Did you make an assessment of causation of this injury?
A: It was my opinion that the patient's injury, as he described to me on February 4, 1988, was the cause of his current symptoms.
Q: Did you make an assessment of his capacity for any type of work activity on your examination?
A: Based on my exam and understanding the work of a carpenter, I did not feel he was capable of returning to that, and in fact, mentioned that he could only return to minimal sedentary work.
Q: Would you expand just a bit on "minimal sedentary work" as what limitations you might feel would be appropriate?
A: Based on that examination, less than a full day sitting for a major portion of that day, no lifting or carrying, no stair walking.
Q: You have stated that you concur with the need for aggressive therapy and for evaluation for facet block. Would you explain what that involves?
A: A physical therapy program would be indicated to try and reduce the inflammation around the nerve and improve his motion and hopefully avoid the need for another surgery. The facet blocks are an invasive procedure that is sometimes helpful in reducing people who have primarily back pain as opposed to leg pain, and it was my opinion that this might help to reduce some of his back pain.
Q: Now, when you prepared your notes on this examination, Doctor, did you have a chance to refer to a report by Dr. Danes of this office?
A: Yes.
Q: And were there any significant differences between your finding and Dr. Danes's findings?
A: Specifically with respect to the range of motion, mine were not significantly different than his.
Q: Prior to testifying today, were you furnished with copies of records from the V.A. Hospital, being CAT scan reports and myelogram reports?
A: Yes.
Q: Have you reviewed those reports, particularly the ones from January 1989 and December of 1988?
A: I have reviewed all of those, and the two in questions, in fact, I reviewed I have circled, indicating I read it.
Q: And does your review of those reports in any way alter the diagnosis of recurrent disk that you made in June of 1990?
A: No. It does not alter my diagnosis.
Q: Are these findings as stated on those reports, being CT scan and myelogram of 12/9/88 and January 6, '89, are they consistent with your diagnosis—
A: Yes.
Q: —of recurrent disk?
A: Yes, they are.

MR. LARSEN: I'd ask that these two documents be marked as Exhibits 1 and 2.

MR. NICITA: I'm going to object to their admission through this witness. Just note my objection that on the grounds that this is the improper witness to get those medical reports through.

(So noted.)

Q: Doctor, in your education as a physician, did you have occasion to take any course work in the field of psychiatry or psychology?
A: Yes.
Q: Would you describe what training you have had?
A: Well, rotations in the medical school setting through psychiatry encompassing two or three months. I forget how long.
Q: In the practice of orthopedic medicine, do you have occasion to look out for symptoms that may have a more psychological basis than a physiological basis?
A: Yes.
Q: And in this case, did you do so?
A: In reviewing anyone who has had back pain for over a year, there would be a need to be cautious of symptoms such as depression; and so whenever you examine a back pain patient who has had a history for that length of time, yes, you're always looking for other signs of psychiatric illnesses, if you will.
Q: Referring to your notes on June 22, 1990, did you take account of Dr. Danes's reference to functional overlay?
A: I made mention of that in my report.
Q: And what was your assessment of that condition in Mr. Smith's case?
A: That that was not inconsistent with someone who had had a two-year history of being out of work, undergone a significant back operation, and still left with some residual leg pain.
Q: And what is "functional overlay," by the way, Doctor?
A: Meaning that he may be overplaying some of his symptomatology or that one cannot blame all of his pain strictly on the anatomic findings of the disease, in this case, a herniated disk. In other words, depression can play a major role in his recovery and in the prognosis.
Q: Does it play any role in augmenting complaints of pain?
A: It can, yes.
Q: Does it play a role in augmenting perception of pain on the part of the patient?
A: It can.
Q: In this case, was it your opinion that that had been occurring, in terms of being a functional overlay?
A: I think I only indicated that this type of thing can occur—would not be unexpected in a history of this type in this particular patient. I was not struck that he was particularly overt in exhibiting any of these symptoms, however.
Q: Did you have occasion to again examine Mr. Smith?
A: Yes.
Q: And when was that, Dr. McDonald?
A: December 3rd, 1990.
Q: And just in general terms, what was your procedure on that examination?
A: I would examine the patient after reviewing the history with him and making certain that the previous history obtained was consistent. I would ask the patient what his current complaints were, and also ask him what the medical plan was, as he perceived it to be, for continuing treatment.
Q: Did you take a history at this time, on December 3, 1990, Doctor?

A: I reviewed the previous history with him to make sure it was consistent.
Q: What history did you take?
A: That he, again—. Would you like me to review the history from the initial injury?
Q: Was it similar to—. Well, what additional history did you take from him at this time that you hadn't taken?
A: I asked him where his pain was specifically at that time and he stated that it was in his lower back, that he was having even more difficulty ambulating than on previous exam. He again did not complain of any pain down his left leg. He indicated that there was some consideration for a repeat operation and he gave me the date when he was going to follow up with the physician who had done the previous surgery, and that studies had been completed to—or going to be completed to determine if, indeed, a repeat operation will be necessary.
Q: Who was that physician?
A: Dr. Lynne, L-Y-N-N-E.
Q: Did you conduct a physical examination on the December 3rd visit?
A: Yes.
Q: And what observations did you make and what findings did you make?
A: The pertinent findings then were that he was using a cane in his left hand to help him in ambulating because he had a significant antalgic (phonetic spelling), or limping, to the right side. His spine range of motion was restricted even more than on previous exam. His tenderness over the sciatic notch that I had noted earlier was still present. He still had the positive straight leg raising that I had noted on the previous exam.
Q: What significance, if any, do you attach to the finding of lateral flexion being essentially nonexistent as is rotation? Would you describe what those findings involve?
A: I have the patient standing and I attempt to have him lean to the side, both to the right, to the left, and then to rotate as if you were going to turn his shoulders and look behind him, and his pain was such that he really could not perform any of those movements. He could simply stand and bend forward slightly and bend backwards slightly.
Q: Did you make a diagnosis at this time?
A: The diagnosis was again recurrent herniated disk versus scar formation and the differential between those two is always in question whenever somebody has had a previous operation, you can't tell which it is.
Q: Would the reports that you reviewed prior to coming in here today have any role in shedding some light on that question, Doctor?
A: The M.R.I. can occasionally help in distinguishing a scar from a disk, but it is not always consistent. This is a report of a lumbar myelogram and then a CAT scan.
Q: Computer tomography?
A: And between those two, you still can't tell if it is disk or scar.
Q: And scar would refer to the scar from the previous operation?
A: No. It's actually the scar that the patient develops which is something that occurs individually and cannot reasonably predicted, but presumably would not occur unless he had a previous operation, yes.
Q: It occurs in the area or the site where the operation occurred?
A: Yes.
Q: Did you make an assessment of the patient at this time?

A: I stated that he was not capable of returning to his regular work, meaning a carpenter; and I also indicated that consideration for repeat surgery was certainly appropriate, in my opinion. I also indicated that return to anything more than a sedentary occupation, at least in the near future, was not likely.
Q: And did you make any observation as to the course of treatment he had undergone up to December 3, 1990 with Dr. Lynne?
A: It was my opinion that his treatment up until that date had been in an appropriate fashion.
Q: Did you make a determination whether up to that point he had reached a reasonable medical end result?
A: It was my opinion that barring another surgical intervention, he—I could not foresee him improving, so yes, I stated he probably reached a medical end result.
Q: Dr. McDonald, do you have an opinion now, based upon examination of Mr. Smith, as to the cause of Mr. Smith's complaints of back pain and leg pain?
A: Both were related to the injury which occurred at work, in my opinion, February 24, 1988.

MR. LARSEN: Thank you, Doctor. I have no further questions. (Pause) Oh, before I close, I would like to offer as exhibits both of these reports dated June 22, 1990, and December 3, 1990.

MR. NICITA: No objection.

(A PHOTOCOPY OF A THREE-PAGE MEDICAL REPORT DATED JUNE 22, 1990, WAS RECEIVED AND MARKED PLAINTIFF'S EXHIBIT 3 FOR IDENTIFICATION.)

(A PHOTOCOPY OF A THREE-PAGE MEDICAL REPORT DATED DECEMBER 3, 1990, WAS RECEIVED AND MARKED PLAINTIFF'S EXHIBIT 4 FOR IDENTIFICATION.)

Q: Doctor, just for the record, I'm going to show you a document that's now been marked Plaintiff's Exhibit 2 and I'd ask you, is that a true copy of your notes from the examination?
A: Yes.
Q: I show you another document that's now been marked as Plaintiff's Exhibit 4, and I ask you if that is a true copy of your notes from the December 3, 1990, examination?
A: Yes.

MR. LARSEN: Thank you.

EXAMINATION BY MR. NICITA

Q: Doctor, your opinion that Mr. Smith has reached a reasonable medical end result could be different if, in fact, he has further surgery; isn't that true?
A: That's correct.
Q: And with regard to your training, sir, other than the two or three months or training in psychiatry that you had in medical school, you have had no further training in that area; have you, sir?
A: That's correct.
Q: And you do not possess a degree in psychiatry or psychology, do you?
A: No.
Q: Now, you testified earlier that you were in agreement with Dr. Danes that there was a nonanatomic component to Mr. Smith's condition and ongoing disability; isn't that correct?
A: I'm sorry. Could you state the questions again?
Q: Isn't it true, sir, that you testified that there was a nonanatomic component, specifically a functional overlay, which was contributing to Mr. Smith's condition; isn't that true?
A: Yes.
Q: And is it possible to differentiate between a patient's anatomic condition and this, the extent of the functional overlay, which he exhibits?
A: Probably a psychiatrist might make an attempt at that. I would not make an attempt. I would only mention that I think there is some element of functional overlay.
Q: And the presence of that functional overlay could be contributing not only to his subjective pain but his attitude in resolving that condition, couldn't it?
A: I think that's possible.
Q: Did you consider the functional overlay of Mr. Smith to be a significant component of his disability?
A: No.
Q: But you do consider it to be a factor in the disability?
A: I don't know as I considered that a significant factor. I mentioned it, as I testified before, as being a part of nearly everyone who has been out of work for a two-year period of time with an injury, subsequent surgery, and persistent pain. It's almost always present in those situations.
Q: And that assessment doesn't take into account other factors that may also be contributing to his emotional state that you were not aware of, does it?
A: That's true.
Q: In your opinion, what type of surgery would be contemplated at this point for Mr. Smith?
A: A reexploration of the disk space, a possible fusion and an exploration of the nerve root. Again, this would all be predicated on getting sufficient preoperative studies that would corroborate those studies, so it's a premature answer, but that would be the expected plan.
Q: And in the course of your treatment of patients with this type of injury, do the diagnostic tests vary when in terms of the times they are taken? In other words, those were taken in '88 and '89. Do you expect a different result if this was—if similar testing was taken in '90?
A: I can't answer that. I don't know.

MR. NICITA: I have no further questions.
MR. LARSEN: I just have a few.

EXAMINATION BY MR. LARSEN (Further)

Q: You were just being asked about the overlay issue. Actually, Doctor, did you, on your examination, elicit any responses by Mr. Smith that would have been inconsistent with injury to L4-S1 vertebrae or disks?
A: No.
Q: And regarding further surgery, the last myelogram we have is December of '88, and there was a computer tomography on January 6 of 1989. In your opinion, would it be advisable prior to actually conducting any surgery, further surgery on Mr. Smith's back, to update any test findings from those dates?
A: It would certainly be appropriate to consider doing that. When I last saw him on December 3rd, an M.R.I. scan was pending and that would probably be the next resort to a preoperative test.
Q: One of the purposes for a myelogram is to isolate areas of injury to disk material which would be amenable to surgery?
A: The purpose for a myelogram would be to verify that his findings on these studies would corroborate what you have seen on examination. In other words, you would like to see studies that show a right-sided problem when a patient complains of right-sided problems, and not vice versa.
Q: Do you have an opinion or knowledge as to the going cost at this time, or reasonable cost, for the type of surgery that Mr. Smith would be asked to undergo?
MR. NICITA: Objection. Irrelevant.
A: No, I don't.
Q: Do you know, Doctor, if Mr. Smith did have such further surgery, whether there would be any guarantees of successfully getting back to his job responsibilities as a carpenter?
A: Most likely not, and I stated from my own perspective having undergone two operations of this magnitude, I would forever limit him to going back to the normal facets of a carpenter.
Q: Might he at some point achieve a light-duty status where he might do some walking and standing?
A: Yes.
Q: And being status post successful second surgery, would you have an indication of any limits on lifting and carrying?
A: That's variable, depending on the surgeon. We all have our own limits. Mine are not set where Dr. Lynne would set his, but in my opinion, there would be a permanent reduction in the amount of lifting that would be allowed.
MR. LARSEN: Thank you, Doctor. I have no further questions.
MR. NICITA: Nothing.
(The deposition was adjourned at 5:38 P.M.)

STATE OF RHODE ISLAND

ss. Providence, Rhode Island

COUNTY OF PROVIDENCE

BE IT KNOWN THAT I, Grace T. Van Melca, Shorthand Reporter and Notary Public, reported stenographically the foregoing deposition pursuant to notice at the time and place stated in the caption hereof; that I was then and there a Notary Public in and for the State of Rhode Island; that by witness before testifying was duly sworn to tell the truth, the whole truth, and nothing but the truth; that the testimony of said witness was reduced to typewriting under my direction; that the foregoing pages contain a full, true, and correct transcription of the notes of said deposition.

I FURTHER CERTIFY that I am not of counsel nor attorney for either or any party to said action or otherwise interested in the event thereof, and that I am not related to either or any of the parties to said cause.

IN WITNESS WHEREOF, I have hereunto subscribed my name and affixed my seal of office this 31st day of December, 1990.

____

NOTARY PUBLIC

MY COMMISSION EXPIRES:
June 30, 1991

Appendix K Referral Organizations

TASA Directory of Expertise
Technical Advisory Service for Attorneys
www.tasanet.com
Phone: (800) 523-2319; (610) 275-8272
Fax: (800) 329-8272
E-mail: experts@tasanet.com
1166 DeKalb Pike, Blue Bell, PA 19422-1853
Registry/referral service, tens of thousands of experts listed in over 7,800 categories. TASA experts are searchable online. Established 1961.

American Medical Forensic Specialists, Inc.
www.amfs.com
Phone: (800) 275-8903; (510) 549-1693
Fax: (510) 486-1255
E-mail medicalexperts@amfs.com
2991 Shattuck Ave., Suite 302, Berkeley, CA 94705-1872
Panel of experts, contact for application.

Consolidated Consultants, Co.
www.freereferall.com
Phone: (800) 683-9847; (619) 422-5559
Fax: (619) 422-8101
Contact: Steve Van Rickley
E-mail: steve_vr@msn.com
739 Twin Oaks Ave., Chula Vista, CA 91910
National referral services to attorneys, insurance companies, and others seeking forensic expert witnesses. Contact for rates.

Diligence, Inc.
www.diligenceinc.com
Phone: (818) 888-6748
Fax: (818) 888-5370
Contact: Vincent Croal
E-mail: vince@diligenceinc.com
21241 Ventura Blvd., Suite 250, Woodland Hills, CA 91364-2121
Referral service. No charge for listing in their database. General rate is a percentage of the fee charged for services.

Expert Link
National Forensics Center
www.expertwitnesslink.com/home.htm
Phone: (800) 526-5177; (609) 883-0550
E-mail: forenexpts@worldnet.att.net
P.O. Box 3161, Princeton, NJ 08643
Referral service.

Expert Resources, Inc.
Phone: (800) 383-4857; (309) 688-4857
Fax: (309) 688-0915
Contact: Christina King
4700 N. Prospect Road, #1B, Peoria Heights, IL 61614
Registry/broker. Nationwide database of 3,000+ experts. Contact for pricing.

Experts Unlimited
Phone: (800) 432-2083
Fax: (312) 649-0588
Contact: Dean C. Dauw, PhD
1212 Lake Shore Drive, #34CN, Chicago, IL 60610
Registry/broker. Contact for information.

EXPERTS-On-Line
www.experts-on-line.com
Phone: (818) 704-0854
Fax: (818) 704-9644
E-mail: experts@experts-on-line.com
20501 Ventura Blvd., Suite 311,
Woodland Hills, CA 91364
Referral service. Listing and searching are free. Service charges a one-time fee for the initial listing, then takes a percentage of the expert's fees. Over 700 categories. Register online.

Forensic Expert Advisers, Inc.
Maureen Shepherd
Phone: (714) 754-4332
Fax: (714) 754-7432
3305 S. Woodland Pl., Santa Ana, CA 92707
Registry/broker.

Legal Expert Network
Melvin Kramer, MPH
Phone: (410) 653-5121
7904 Starburst Dr., Baltimore, MD 21208-3033
Registry/broker. National general search firm.

Lexpert Research Services
www.lexpertresearch.com
Phone: (310) 589-5546
Fax: (310) 589-2559
E-mail: info@lexpertresearch.com
P.O. Box 4362, Malibu, CA 90264
Referral service for law, business, and economics professors.

Maritime and Aviation Consultants
www.mac-experts.com
Phone: (360) 574-1101
Fax: (360) 574-1101
Contact: Kirk Greiner
E-mail: cptkirk@pacificer.com
15112 NE 30th Ave., Vancouver WA 98686-1669
Registry/brokerage. Fee to be listed in the database. Contact for further pricing info.

Medi-Legal Services
Phone: (619) 579-2135
Fax: (619) 444-6473
P.O. Box 1464, El Cajon, CA 92022

Medical Advisors, Inc.
Gary Steinberg
Phone: (215) 654-0650
Fax: (215) 654-0650
501 Office Center Dr., #248, Fort Washington, PA 19034
Registry/brokerage.

Medical Experts—A Physician Referral Center
www.docinsler.com
Phone: (800) 321-MDJD
Contact: Michael S. Insler, MD, JD
E-mail MINSLE@lsumc.edu
5649 Marcia Avenue, New Orleans, LA 70124
Referral service.

MedicoLegal Consultants, Inc.
www.mlegal.com
Phone: (888) 661-3593
Fax: (808) 667-6229
E-mail: mlegal@aloha.net
880 Front Street, Suite 657, Lahaina, HI 96761-1636
MedicoLegal also has a Los Angeles office. Referral service, placements from the MLC panel. Application fee. MLC takes a percentage of the fees.

National Consultant Referrals, Inc.—Talent Bank
www.referrals.com
Phone: (800) 221-3104
Fax: (619) 523-2184
E-mail: kline@referrals.com
4918 N. Harbor Drive, Suite 103, San Diego, CA 92106
Referral agency.

Psybar, LLC
www.psybar.com
Phone: (612) 866-1000
Fax: (612) 707-9159
Contact: Dr. Sheridan Fenwick or Dr. David Fisher
E-mail: PsyBar@aol.com
5749 Nicollet Avenue South, Minneapolis, MN 55419-2414
Network of psychiatrists and psychologists who provide expert services. Contact to become an affiliate.

TAB Consultant Registry
Technical Assistance Bureau, Inc.
www.tabexperts.com
Phone: (800) 260-8174
Fax: (314) 273-5779
E-mail: tabexperts@cwixmail.com
11469 Olive Boulevard, Suite 108, St. Louis, MO 63141
Referral service. Free listing in the registry. Contact for percentages. Register at the Web site. Offices in MD, MO, and CA.

The Legal Expert Network
The Legal Expert Network, Ltd.
www.expertnetwork.com
Phone: (800) 597-5371
E-mail: len@expertnetwork.com
40 East Hamburg Street, Baltimore, MD 21230
Referral service. One-time fee to list in the database, percentage of the expert's fees.

Unirisk—Expert Witness Services
www.unirisk.com
Phone: (415) 461-8870
Fax: (415) 464-4974
Contact: Warren Heiman
E-mail: info@unirisk.com
700 Larskspur Landing Circle, Larkspur, CA 94939
Pool of experts, neither a referral agency nor a directory. Contact for information regarding joining.

Technical Network Consulting Service
www.techmedexperts.com
Phone: (800) 355-1329; (610) 941-3981
Fax: (610) 941 9730
620 Sentry Parkway, Suite 130, Blue Bell, PA 19422
Referral service/registry. Contact for pricing information.

medQuest, Ltd.
www.medquestltd.com
Phone: (800) 633-6251; (212) 725-8000
Fax: (212) 725-5090
E-mail: info@medQuestLtd.com
116 East 30th Street, New York, NY, 10016

Expert Medical Witnesses, Inc.
www.expertmedicalwitnesses.com
Phone: (888) 944-8456; (814) 944-2566
Fax: (814) 944-4384
E-mail: admin@expertmedicalwitnesses.com
85 Logan Blvd., Altoona, PA 16602
Referral service, hundreds of experts, nationwide referrals.

Registered Nurse Experts, Inc.
www.rnexperts.com
Phone: (800) 759-6938
E-mail: vicki@rnexperts.com
14024 SW 104 Court, Miami, FL 33176

Also, it is very important to explore the professional organizations within your field or relating to your field. Many of these maintain referral networks or provide referral services to their members.

Appendix L Online and Print Directories

Online Directories

ExpertPages.com
ExpertPages is a unit of Advice & Counsel
www.expertpages.com
Phone: (800) ITS LEGAL; (415) 388-5000
Fax: (888) 487-5342; (415) 388-5005
E-mail: admin@expertpages.com
P.O. Box 1739, Mill Valley, CA 94942-1739
Very large and easily searchable online expert directory. Experts pay a yearly fee and an additional fee for more topics. Free Web site hosting. Easy to register online.

Southwestern Directory of Expert Witnesses and Consultants
California Directory of Expert Witnesses
Great Lakes Directory of Expert Witnesses
Southeastern Directory of Expert Witnesses
Midwest Directory of Expert Witnesses
Texas Lawyer and American Lawyer Media
www.texlaw.com
Phone: (800) 456-5484, ext. 138; (214) 744-7738
Fax: (214) 741-2325
E-mail: deweber@amlaw.com
900 Jackson Street, Suite 500, Dallas, TX 75202
Regional online directories, listing is included with the purchase of a listing in the print version of the respective regional directory. Also includes expert's resume in the Expert Witness Referral Service.

Expert Witness Network
Expert Witness Network
www.witness.net
Phone: (207) 885-1555; cell: (207) 329-5790
Fax: (207) 885-1555
E-mail: witness@javanet.com
P.O. Box 9421, South Portland, ME 04116-9421
Experts can list a brief description and link to their existing Web site. This list is searchable by attorneys/members of the EWN. Also features a searchable CV database. Contact EWN for more information.

AELE—Directory of Criminal Justice Experts and Litigation Consultants
Americans for Effective Law Enforcement, Inc.
www.aele.org
Phone: (773) 763-2800
Fax: (773) 763-3225
E-mail: aele@aol.com
5519 N. Cumberland Ave., #1008, Chicago, IL 60656-1498
Online directory.

Artel Resources Expert Witness Directory
Artel Resources
www.artelsources.com/experts.html
E-mail: webmaster@artelsources.com
List of links to existing Web pages. Monthly or yearly listings. Will also host Web site.

ASTM Directory of Scientific and Technical Consultants and Expert Witnesses
American Society for Testing and Materials
www.astm.org
Phone: (610) 832-9611
Fax: (610) 832-9555
Contact: Ellen McGlinchey
E-mail: emcglinc@astm.org
100 Barr Harbor Drive, West Consahocken, PA 19428-2959
Online directory, also a print version. Over 600 experts listed, yearly listing includes link to the expert's existing Web site.

ATLA Mart, Expert Witnesses/Consultants Index
Association of Trial Lawyers of America
www.atlamart.com
Phone: (202) 944 -2870
Contact: Judy Lewis
Email: judy.lewis@atlahq.org
An online store that provides products and services to lawyers. Advertising rates vary.

Attorney Referral Network
www.attorneyreferral.net/expert.htm
E-mail: webmaster@attorneyreferral.net
1225 West Main, Suite 102, Norman, OK 73069
Online directory. Few experts listed, but a large directory of attorneys. Add a link to a Web site and a 50-word description for one-time fee.

Best Directory of Recommended Insurance Attorneys & Adjusters
A.M. Best & Co.
www.ambest.com/legal/index.html
Phone: (908) 439-2200, ext. 5673
E-mail: legal_claims@ambest.com
Annual print directory of insurance attorneys and adjusters, as well as expert service providers. Also searchable online. Contact for pricing information.

Community of Science Expertise
Community of Science, Inc.
www.cos.com
Phone: (410) 563-5382, x225
Contact: Edwin Van Dusen, VP, Information Products
E-mail: evd@cos.com
1629 Thames Street, Suite 200, Baltimore, MD 21231
This site simply has a section called COS Expertise. It allows member scientists to create and post online CVs. Subscribers can search this database. Not directed toward expert witnesses. Advertised as "By scientists, for scientists." However, the scientific expert might use this resource.

Counsel Quest
Counsel Quest, a law.com company
www.counselquest.com
E-mail: info@counselquest.com
Huge legal resource site that includes an expert witness directory. Free listing. Best to register online at www.counselquest.com/z-expert.htm or send an e-mail.

CyberAttorney's Experts Online
CyberAttorney
www.cyberattorney.com
Phone: (818) 833-7884
E-mail: info@cyberattorney.com
12828 Victory Blvd., Suite 325, N. Hollywood, CA 91606
Online directory. Numerous categories. Fees vary, based on category and geographic area. More extensive full listing available on an annual basis.

DRI—Expert Witness Database
Defense Research Institute
www.driewb.org
Phone: (312) 795-1101
Fax: (312) 795-0747
E-mail: dri@dri.org
150 N. Michigan Ave, Suite 300, Chicago, IL 60601
DRI maintains a database of over 50,000 experts. Searchable by members only. Listing is free, no referral fees. DRI maintains the database as a service to the defense bar. Contact DRI for form to submit CV, Attn: Expert Witness Staff.

Expert 4 Law—Experts & Consultants
Expert 4 Law, sponsored by the LA County Bar Association
www.expert4law.org
Contact: Melissa Algaze
Phone: (213) 896-6470, ext. 6
E-mail: forensics@lacba.com
Expert4Law—The Legal Marketplace. Includes several categories of legal service providers. Yearly listings, links available.

Expert Marketplace
The PEN Group, in conjunction with Dun & Bradstreet
www.expertmarketplace.com
Phone: (800) 983-9737; (303) 790-7474
Fax: (303) 790-1805
E-mail: ask@expert-market.com
7395 South Peoria Street, Englewood, CO 80112
Internet directory that lists financial and technical consultants. Not directed toward litigation support, but expert witnesses are listed. Listing is free, with a fee/referral program for more extensive listings and benefits.

ExpertLaw.com
www.expertlaw.com
E-mail: webmaster@expertlaw.com
Large, searchable expert witness database. Free listings in the form of a link to existing Web site. To add a site, follow the "add an expert" link at the bottom of each relevant category page in the directory.

FindLaw
www.findlaw.com
E-mail: write@findlaw.com
FindLaw is a very large legal resource site that includes an expert directory. Free listing. Register online—follow the "add U.R.L." link. Experts can also create a free Web site in the "firms online" section.

Forensic Services Directory
National Forensic Center
www.expertwitnesslink.com/home.htm
Phone: (800) 526-5177; (609) 883-0550
Fax: (609) 883-7622
Contact: Betty Lipscher
E-mail: forenexpts@worldnet.att.net
P.O. Box 3161, Princeton, NJ 08643
Yearly membership in the center includes a listing in the directory, as well as a listing in Lexis/Nexis and NFC's ExpertLink.

HIEROS GAMOS—Experts Database
Hieros Gamos
www.hg.org
E-mail: lexmundi@lexmundi.org
1800 West Loop South, Houston, TX 77027
This is an enormous legal info site that includes an expert database. HG offers self-listing—experts go to the site and add themselves.

Horizon's Expert Witness List
Horizon Professional Services
www.sonic.net/thom/expert/
Phone: (707) 575-3939
E-mail: webmaster@ca-experts.com
2154 Hastings Court, Suite 101,
Santa Rosa, CA 95405-8377
Online directory oriented toward California. Free posting of Web site/e-mail link. Yearly fee to post CV or links in additional categories.

I.D.E.A.L., Inc. Legal Support Index
I.D.E.A.L., Inc.
www.i-deal.com
Phone: (877) 443-3257
E-mail: service@i-deal.com
911 Duluth Hwy., Building D, Suite 3232, Lawrenceville, GA 30043
Legal resource site with expert database.

Larry Anderson's Expert Witness Page
Larry Anderson
home.earthlink.net/~laanderson/experts.htm
E-mail: laanderson@earthlink.net
Large expert list maintained by an individual. E-mail and ask if he will add you to the site. Also includes an excellent directory of directories.

The Round Table Group
www.round.table.com
Phone: (312) 214-4990
Fax: (312) 416-7982
980 N. Michigan Ave., 14th Floor,
Chicago, IL 60611
Contact: Vince LaConte
E-mail: laconte@roundtable.com
Round Table Group is an international consortium of academic experts and thought leaders in a number of specialized business-related fields.

LawInfo.com—Expert Witness Database
lawinfo.com
Phone: (888) 943-9759
Fax: (800) 220-4546
Contact: Gordon Davis
E-mail: gdavis@lawinfo.com
4403 Manchester Ave, Encinitas, CA 92024
Large legal resource site. Expert directory includes over 2,500 categories. Annual listing includes creation and hosting of Web page as well as inclusion in the database. Also offers an "expert starter" package—a Web site and e-mail—for a yearly fee.

Legal Expert Pages
www.legalexpertpages.com/
Online directory, easy to search, difficult to contact. So far, only technical consultants.

National Directory of Expert Witnesses Online
Claims Providers of America
www.claims.com
Phone: (800) 735-6660
Fax: (530) 796-3631
Contact: James Patterson
E-mail: jhp@claims.com
P.O. Box 395, Esparto, CA 95627
Very large print and online directory. Yearly fee for basic listings that appear in print and online.

National Registry of Experts
www.expert-registry.com
Phone: (800) 576-7264
Fax: (909) 781-4221
E-mail: pcmi@pcmi-experts.com
4101 Almond Street, Riverside, CA 92501
Online directory, not a referral service. Contact for pricing.

Noble Group—Directory of Experts
The Noble Group
www.experts.com
Phone: (800) 640-5959; (650) 391-7790
Fax: (650) 570-5178
E-mail: gwhitman@quake.net
P.O. Box 8208, Foster City, CA 94404
Online directory. Yearly fee for basic listing, one-time set up fee, includes link to existing Web site.

A Pennsylvania Attorney's Guide to Expert Witnesses and Consultants
PaLAWnet, in conjunction with American Lawyer Media
www.palawnet.com/exp/index.htm
Phone: (215) 557-2391
E-mail: info@palawnet.com
Expert witness directory.

Rominger Legal—Expert Witness & Consultant Dircctory
Rominger Legal
www.romingerlegal.com/
E-mail: kromin1351@aol.com
A legal research site with an extensive expert directory.

IEEE-USA Electrotechnology Consultants Database
Institute of Electrical and Electronics Engineers, United States of America
www.ieeeusa-consultants.org
Contact: Chris Currie
1828 L Street, NW, Suite 1202
Washington, DC 20036-5104
Phone: (202) 785-0017
Fax: (202) 785-0835
E-mail: c.currie@ieee.org

The Internet Directory of Expert Witnesses
www.expertwitness.com
Phone: (714) 624-8521
E-mail: diana@expertwitness.com
Online directory, over 600 experts. Home page plus link in directory or a simple link and brief description. Yearly fee.

Legal Nurses Online
www.legalnurses.com
Phone: (805) 966-2068
E-mail: morganrn@legalnurses.com
P.O. Box 91913, Santa Barbara, CA 93190

UNIVERSAL LAW Consultant and Expert Witness Directory
Universal Law
www.universal-law.com
E-mail: contact@universal-law.com
Small directory of consultants, experts and mediators. One-time fee to link a Web site to this directory.

WashLaw WEB
Washburn University School of Law
www.washlaw.edu
Contact: Joe Hewitt
E-mail: zzhewitt@washburn.edu
List of experts and legal consultants maintained by the law library. Free listing. Use the "add your site" link on the home page.

Yahoo's Legal Consultants Index
Yahoo!
www.yahoo.com
Follow links to Business and Economy, Companies, Law, Consulting, and Expert Witnesses to locate. Follow instructions at the "how to suggest a site" link at the bottom of the page to add a site. Free, but inclusion is at Yahoo's discretion.

Expert-Source.com
www.expert-source.com
E-mail: jason@expert-source.com
Online directory, yearly fee for listing. Sign up online.

LawyersWeeklyExperts.com
Lawyers Weekly
www.lawyersweeklyexperts.com
41 West St., Boston, MA 02111

Print Directories

ABA Register of Expert Witnesses
The American Bar Association
www.abanet.org
Phone: (800) 285-2221
Fax: (312) 988-5568
E-mail: info@abanet.org
Print directory. Contact ABA for pricing.

Southwestern Directory of Expert Witnesses and Consultants
California Directory of Expert Witnesses
Great Lakes Directory of Expert Witnesses
Southeastern Directory of Expert Witnesses
Midwest Directory of Expert Witnesses
Texas Lawyer and American Lawyer Media
www.texlaw.com
Phone: (800) 456-5484, ext. 138; (214) 744-7738
Fax: (214) 741-2325
E-mail: deweber@amlaw.com
900 Jackson Street, Suite 500, Dallas, TX 75202
Regional print directories that correlate with the online versions. Also includes experts' resumes in the Expert Witness Referral Service.

ASTM Directory of Scientific and Technical Consultants and Expert Witnesses
American Society for Testing and Materials
www.astm.org
Phone: (610) 832-9611
Fax: (610) 832-9555
Contact: Ellen McGlinchey
E-mail: emcglinc@astm.org
100 Barr Harbor Drive, West Consahocken, PA 19428-2959

Best Directory of Recommended Insurance Attorneys & Adjusters
A.M. Best & Co.
www.ambest.com/legal/index.html
Phone: (908) 439-2200, ext. 5673
E-mail: legal_claims@ambest.com
Annual print directory of insurance attorneys and adjusters, as well as expert service providers. Also searchable online. Contact for pricing information.

Consultants and Consulting Organizations Directory
The Gale Group
www.gale.com
Phone: (800) 877-GALE
Fax: (800) 414-5043
E-mail: galeord@gale.com
Print directory. Contact the Gale Group for more information.

Lawyer's Desk Reference
Published by West Group
Phone: (800) 221-9428
This directory lists hundreds of experts in specific categories. Contact for pricing information.

Martindale-Hubbell Buyer's Guide
Martindale-Hubbell, member of Reed Elsevier Group
www.marhub.com
Phone: (800) 526-4902
Fax: (908) 665 2894
Contact: Linda Rosen
121 Chanlon Road, New Providence, NJ 07974
Print directory of services for the legal profession. Yearly listing includes listing on Lexis/Nexis.

National Directory of Expert Witnesses
Claims Providers of America
www.claims.com
Phone: (800) 735-6660
Fax: (530) 796-3631
Contact: James Patterson
E-mail: jhp@claims.com
P.O. Box 395, Esparto, CA 95627
Very large print and online directory. Basic listings appear in print and online for yearly fee.

Forensic Services Directory
National Forensic Center
www.expertwitnesslink.com/home.htm
Phone: (800) 526-5177; (609) 883-0550
Fax: (609)-883-7622
Contact: Betty Lipscher
E-mail: forenexpts@worldnet.att.net
P.O. Box 3161, Princeton, NJ 08643
The Forensic Services Directory is a 1,400+-page hardcover book. It contains the names, addresses, and specialties of approximately 4000-5,000 experts plus specialized sources of expert knowledge. This directory has been published since 1980 and is also available online through an exclusive arrangement with WESTLAW and LEXIS-NEXIS.

Jury Verdict Researcher Verdict and Settlement Database
LRP
Contact: Jackie Peddigree
Department 205; 747 Dreshner Rd., P.O. Box 980, Horsham, PA 19044-0980
Service locates cases and the names of expert witnesses for attorneys. Send resume to above address for inclusion in the database at no charge.

Appendix M Legal Journals and Other Publications

The expert might advertise in or submit articles to the following publications.

For the Defense
Defense Research Institute
150 N. Michigan Ave, Suite 300
Chicago, IL 60601
Phone: (312) 795-1101
Fax: (312) 795-0747

California Bar Journal
555 Franklin Street
San Francisco, CA 94102-4498
Phone: (415) 561-8804
Fax: (415) 561-8247
E-mail: Cbjnl@aol.com

Advertising representative is:
The R.W. Walker Company, Inc.
Southern California: (310) 450-9001
Northern California: (510) 888-1104
Outside California: (310) 450-9001

ABA Journal
750 N. Lake Shore Dr.
Chicago, IL 60611
Phone: (312) 988 5998; (312) 988-6018
Fax: (312) 988-6014
E-mail: abajournal@abanet.org

American Lawyer Media
345 Park Avenue South
New York, NY 10010
Phone: (800) 888-8300
Fax: (212) 481-8110

American Lawyer Media publishes numerous journals for the legal community, many of which are listed below. Visit www.americanlawyermedia.com, www.lawnewsnetwork.com, or www.law.com, for information regarding advertising in print and online legal publications. For article submissions, the expert might need to contact the specific publication.

For advertising in *American Lawyer Media* publications, contact:

Kevin J. Vermeulen
Vice President, Group Publisher
Phone: (212) 545-6269
Fax: (212) 481-8074
E-mail: kevinv@amlaw.com

The National Law Journal
www.nlj.com

The American Lawyer
Amlaw Tech
Corporate Counsel Magazine
IP Worldwide
www.ipmag.com
IP Magazine c/o The Recorder
10 United Nations Plaza, 3rd Floor
San Francisco, CA 94102

Law Technology News
www.lawtechnews.com
Editorial Contact: (800) 537-2128, ext. 9149; (212) 313-9149
E-mail: mbay@amlaw.com

Fulton County Daily Report
www.dailyreportonline.com
190 Pryor Street, S.W.
Atlanta, GA 30303
Phone: (404) 521-1227
Fax: (404) 523-5924

Pennsylvania Law Weekly
www.palawnet.com

Delaware Law Weekly
www.delawnet.com

To place a classified ad in *Delaware Law Weekly*, *The Legal Intelligencer*, or *The Pennsylvania Law Weekly*, call Fran Adler at (215) 557-2341, Kevin Cartwright at (215) 557-2452, Anne Ginsberg at (215) 557-2457 or e-mail franm@palawnet.com.

California Law Week
The Recorder (San Francisco & Bay Area)
Web partner for both publications: www.callaw.com.

James Beckner
Classified Advertising Manager
10 UN Plaza, 3rd Floor
San Francisco, CA 94102-3368
Phone: (415) 749-5429
Fax:(415) 749-5430
E-mail: jbeckner@therecorder.com

Sandy Gibbons
Legal Advertising Manager
The Recorder
625 Polk Street, Suite 500
San Francisco, CA 94102-3368
Phone: (415) 749-5418
Fax: (415) 749-5435
E-mail: sgibbons@therecorder.com

The Connecticut Law Tribune
One Post Road, Suite 100
Fairfield, CT 06430
Phone: (203) 256-3600
Fax: (203) 255-3319
E-mail: clt@counsel.com

Illinois Law
www.statelaw.com
E-mail: illinois@statelaw.com

Legal Times
www.legaltimes.com
1730 M Street, N.W., Suite 802
Washington, D.C. 20036
Phone: (800) 933-4317; (202) 457-0686
Fax: (202) 457-0718
E-mail: advertising@legaltimes.com

New Jersey Law Journal
www.njlawjournal.com
P.O. Box 20081
Newark, NJ 07101-6081
Phone: (973) 642-0075
E-mail: njljclassifieds@amlaw.com

New York Law Journal
www.nylj.com
345 Park Avenue South
New York, NY 10010
Phone: (212) 779-9200
Fax: (212) 696-4287
Contact: Steve Lincoln (212) 545-6271
E-mail: stevel@ljx.com
Regarding classified advertising, call (800) 888-8300 or (212) 545-5999

Texas Lawyer
www.texlaw.com
900 Jackson St., Suite 500
Dallas, TX 75202
Phone: (214) 744-9300; (800) 456-5484
Fax: (214) 741-2325
Advertising Director: Pat Rafferty (214) 744-7711
Expert Witness Advertising Director: Dennis Weber (214) 744-7720

Lawyers Weekly USA
www.lawyersweekly.com
Lawyers Weekly
41 West Street
Boston, MA 02111

Advertising Department:
(800) 444-5297, ext. 8164

or
Jeff Bryan
(800) 444-5297, ext. 8219
E-mail: jbryan@lawyersweekly.com

Use the above contact for advertising in all *Lawyers Weekly* publications, including the following:

Massachusetts Lawyers Weekly
Rhode Island Lawyers Weekly
41 West Street
Boston, MA 02111
Phone: (617) 451-7300

Ohio Lawyers Weekly
504 Superior Ave.
Cleveland, OH 44114
Phone: (800) 935-LAWS

Virginia Lawyers Weekly
106 North Eighth Street
Richmond, VA 23219
Phone: (804) 783-0770; (800) 456-LAWS

North Carolina Lawyers Weekly
107 Fayetteville Street Mall
Raleigh, NC 27601
Phone: (919) 829-9333, (800) 876-LAWS

Missouri Lawyers Weekly
515 Olive Street
Suite 1606
St. Louis, MO 63101
Phone: (314) 621-8500

Michigan Lawyers Weekly
333 S. Washington Street, Suite 300
Lansing, MI 48933
Phone: (517) 374-6200; (800) 678-5297

Trial Magazine
Association of Trial Lawyers of America
www.atlanet.org

In North Dakota, South Dakota, Minnesota, Wisconsin, Nebraska, Iowa, Michigan, Indiana, Illinois, Kansas, Oklahoma, Missouri, Kentucky, Louisiana, Alabama, Tennessee, Georgia, Mississippi, and Arkansas contact:

Jan Mason
203 N. Wabash Ave., Suite 1512
Chicago, IL 60601
Phone: (312) 346-3076
Fax: (312) 346-4824
E-mail: MedRepCons@aol.com

In Maine, Vermont, Massachusetts, Rhode Island, Connecticut, New Hampshire, New York, New Jersey, Pennsylvania, Ohio, and Delaware contact:

Joe Murphy
P.O. Box 1422
Fairfield, CT 06432
Phone: (203) 254-9595
Fax: (203) 259-4447
E-mail: adsales25@aol.com

In Washington, Oregon, California, Nevada, Arizona, Utah, Montana, Idaho, Wyoming, New Mexico, Colorado, Texas, Hawaii, and Alaska contact:

John Pellettieri
17900 Sherman Way, Suite 234
Reseda, CA 91335
Phone: (818) 781-7320
Fax: (818) 781-7321

In Washington, DC, Maryland, Virginia, West Virginia, North Carolina, South Carolina, and Florida contact:

Judy Lewis
1050 31st Street, NW
Washington, DC 20007

Phone: (800) 424 2725, ext. 223;
(202) 944-2870
Fax: (202) 625-7313
E-mail judy.lewis@atlahq.org

Mealey Publications
(Mealey's Litigation Reports)
www.mealeys.com
P.O. Box 62090
King of Prussia, PA 19406-0230
Phone: (610) 768-7800; (800) MEALEYS
Fax: (610) 768-0880
E-mail: news@mealeys.com

Appendix N Key Internet Sites

Legal Research Sites

The following legal research sites are very comprehensive—any one of them is an excellent place to begin a search for legal resources and information. The first section lists actual research services where the site itself maintains the information. The second section lists indices—sites that organize and present lists of links to legal resources.

Services

Legal Information Institute at Cornell
www.law.cornell.edu
A comprehensive free research site, an excellent resource.

WESTLAW
www.westlaw.com
The major subscription-based online legal research service used by attorneys. Expansive and complete.

Lexis/Nexis
www.lexis.com
Along with Westlaw, a comprehensive research site containing numerous databases. Used by the legal profession and journalists, among others.

Loislaw.com
www.loislaw.com
Comprehensive online legal research system. Portions are free, the bulk is subscription-based.

Lect Law
www.lectlaw.com
A free research site, entertaining and quite large.

Indices

The following are large compilations of links to resources.

Heiros Gamos
www.hg.org

Findlaw
www.findlaw.com

LawInfo
www.lawinfo.com

CounselQuest
www.counselquest.com

Washburn University School of Law Library
www.washlaw.edu
An effort to provide links to all known law-related materials on the Internet.

The World Wide Web Virtual Library: Law
www.law.indiana.edu/law/lawindex.html
A compilation of legal sites generated by Indiana Law School.

Yahoo: Law
www.yahoo.com/Law
This Web index contains numerous links to law-related sites.

Law.com
www.law.com

ABA Law Link
www.abanet.org/lawlink

ALSO
www.lawsource.com/also

Attorney's Toolbox
www.mother.com/~randy/tools.html

Lawlists
www.kentlaw.edu

LawCrawler
www.lawcrawler.com
Search engine for legal sites.

State and Local Government, Library of Congress Internet Resource Page
www.lcweb.loc.gov

Federal Judicial Center
www.fjc.gov

The National Law Net
www.lawsites.com

Law Lists Guide
www.lib.uchicago.edu/~llou/lawhlists/info.html
This guide is an index of lists and usenet groups related to law on the Internet.

Legal dot Net™
www.legal.net
An online legal resource database service.

Legislative Research Sources

U.S. Senate
www.senate.gov/
Locate senators' e-mail addresses, conduct word searches, links.

Government, Law, and Society
www.english-www.hss.cmu.edu/govt
Information about government law.

United States Code
www.law.house.gove/usc.htm

Updated Revisions to the U.S.C.
www.law.house.gov/tbl_cd.txt

U.S. Constitution
www.law.cornell.educ/constitution/constitution.overview.html

Center for Legislative Archives
www.nara.gov/nara/legislative
Records of the United States Senate and the United States House of Representatives.

C-Span
www.c-span.org/
Congressional schedules, hearings, and votes.

Legal Libraries

University of Colorado Law School Library
www.colorado.edu/Law/lawlib

Cornell Law Library
www.law.cornell.edu/library/default.html

Emory University Law Library
www.law.emory.edu/LAW/law.html

Georgetown University Law Library
www.ll.georgetown.edu/

Indiana University Law Library
www.law.indiana.edu/law/v-lib/lawindex.html

Stanford Law Library
www.stanford.edu/

Yale Law Library
elsinore.cis.yale.edu/lawweb/library.htm

Legal Journals, Magazines, and Newsletters Online

Guide to Online Law Journals
www.law.indiana.edu/law/v-lib/journals.html

Journal of Online Law
www.law.cornell.edu/jol/jol.table.html

American Lawyer Media's Law News Network
www.lawnewsnetwork.com

Lawyers Weekly
www.lawyersweekly.com

Net Watchers—A Cyberlaw Magazine
www.ionet.net/~mdyer/netwatch.html

The Internet Lawyer
internetlawyer.com

National Bar and Specialty Legal Associations

American Bar Association
www.abanet.org

Association of Trial Lawyers of America
www.atlanet.org

Defense Research Institute
www.dri.org

National Institute for Trial Advocacy
www.nita.org

Federal Bar Association
www.fedbar.org

National Bar Association
www.nationalbar.org

National Lawyers Association
www.nla.org

American Agricultural Law Association
www.aglaw-assn.org/

American Association of Law Libraries
www.aallnet.org/

American Corporate Counsel Association
www.acca.com/

American Immigration Lawyers Association
www.aila.org/

American Intellectual Property Law Association
www.aipla.org/

Association of Federal Defense Attorneys
www.afda.org/

Cyberspace Bar Association
www.cyberbar.net/

Hispanic National Bar Association
www.incacorp.com/hnba

Judge Advocates Association
www.jaa.org/

Law Practice & Technology Association
www.lawsch.uga.edu/~lpta/

National Academy of Elder Law Attorneys
www.naela.com/

National Organization of Bar Counsel
www.nobc.org/

National Asian Pacific American Bar Association
www.napaba.org/

National Association of Bar Executives
www.abanet.org/barserv/nabe.html

National Association of Legal Assistants
www.nala.org/

National Bar Association
www.nationalbar.org

National Federation of Paralegals Association
www.paralegals.org/

Association of Healthcare Medical Lawyers
www.healthcare-medlawyers.org

Black Entertainment & Sports Lawyers Association
www.besla.org

The Cyberlaw Association
www.cyberlawassociation.com

National Lawyers Association
www.nla.org

Federation of Insurance & Corporate Counsel
www.thefederation.org

International Association of Defense Counsel
www.iadclaw.org

State & Local Bar Associations

Alabama

Alabama State Bar
www.alabar.org

The Birmingham Bar Association
www.birminghambar.org

Mobile Bar Association
www.mobilebar.com

Tuscaloosa County Bar Association
www.dbtech.net/tuscaloosabar/index.html

Alabama Defense Lawyers Association
www.adla.org

Alaska

Alaska Bar Association
www.alaskabar.org

Arizona

State Bar of Arizona
www.azbar.org

Los Abogados (The Hispanic Bar Association of Maricopa County)
www.losabogados.org/

Arkansas

Arkansas Bar Association
www.arkbar.com

Arkansas Trial Lawyers Association
www.arktla.org

California

The State Bar of California
www.calbar.org

The California Bar Association's Web site, www.calbar.org, maintains a comprehensive list of all California bar associations—local, minority, and specialty.

Association of Business Trial Lawyers
(several geographic divisions)
www.abtl.org

Association of Defense Council of Northern California
www.adcnc.org

Consumer Attorneys of California
www.caoc.com

Local Bar Associations
Go to www.calbar.org for a listing of contact information.

Alameda County Bar Association
www.acbanet.org

Beverly Hills Bar Association
www.bhba.org

Charles Lincoln Bar Association
www.charlesLincoln.org

Contra Costa County Bar Association
www.cccba.org

Lawyers Club of Los Angeles
www.sidebar.com/lawyers

Lawyers Club of San Diego
www.lawyersclubsandiego.com

Los Angeles County Bar Association
www.lacba.org

Marin County Bar Association
www.marinbar.com

Palo Alto Area Bar Association
www.lawscape.com/paaba/index.html

Sacramento County Bar Association
www.sacbar.org

San Bernardino County Bar Association
Web site1.lanminds.com/sbcba

San Diego County Bar Association
www.sddt.com/law

San Fernando Valley Bar Association
www.sfvba.org

Bar Association of San Francisco
www.sfbar.org

San Mateo County Bar Association
www.webmaster.com/smcba/index/html

Southwest Riverside County Bar Association
www.lawref.com/assoc/9b.html

Sunnyvale-Cupertino Bar Association
www.lawscape.com/suncupbar/links.htm

Ventura County Bar Association
www.vcba.org

<u>Colorado</u>
Colorado Bar Association
www.cobar.org
Lists local bar associations.

Colorado Trial Lawyers Association
www.ctla.net

Connecticut
Connecticut State Bar
www.ctbar.org

Connecticut Trial Lawyers Association
www.ct-tla.org

Delaware
Delaware State Bar Association
www.dsba.org

Delaware Trial Lawyers Association
www.dtla.org

District of Columbia
The District of Columbia Bar
www.dcbar.org

Trial Lawyers Association of Metro Washington, DC
nturalcrls@aol.com

Florida
Florida Bar Association
www.flabar.org

Academy of Florida Trial Lawyers
www.aftl.org

Florida Defense Lawyers Association
www.fdla.org

Attorneys Bar Association of Florida
www.bridge.net

Broward County Bar Association
www.browardbar.org

Clearwater Bar Association
www.clwbar.org

Orange County Bar Association
www.obar.org

Palm Beach County Bar Association
www.palmbeachbar.org

Georgia
State Bar of Georgia
www.gabar.org

Georgia Trial Lawyers Association
www.gtla.org

Georgia Defense Lawyers Association
www.gdla.org

Atlanta Bar Association
www.atlantabar.org

Decatur Bar Association
www.decaturbar.org

Georgia Association for Women Lawyers
www.law.emory.edu/GAWL/gawl.htm

Cobb County Bar Association
www.kuesterlaw.com/cobb/

Hawaii
Hawaii State Bar Association
www.hsba.org

Consumer Lawyers of Hawaii
www.clh.org

Idaho
Idaho State Bar
www2.state.id.us/isb/

Idaho State Trial Lawyers Association
www.itla.org

Illinois
Illinois State Bar Association
www.illinoisbar.org

Illinois Association of Defense Trial Counsel
www.iadtc.org

Indiana
Indiana State Bar Association
www.state.in.us/isba

Iowa
Iowa State Bar Association
www.iowabar.org

Kansas
Kansas Bar Association
www.ksbar.org

Kansas Trial Lawyers Association
www.ink.org/public/ktla/

Kansas Association of Defense Counsel (KADC)
www.kadc.org

Kentucky
Kentucky Bar Association
www.kybar.org

Louisiana
Louisiana State Bar Association
www.lsba.org

Baton Rouge Bar Association
www.brba.org

Louisiana Young Lawyers
www.younglawyers.org

Louisiana Trial Lawyers Association
www.ltla.org

New Orleans Bar Association
www.gnofn.org/~noba

Lafayette Parish Bar Association
www.lafayettebar.org

Maine
Maine State Bar Association
www.mainebar.org

Maine Trial Lawyers Association
www.mtla.org

Maryland
Maryland State Bar Association
www.msba.org

Anne Arundel Bar Association
www.aabar.org

Baltimore County Bar Association
www.bcba.org

Bar Association of Montgomery County
www.montbar.org

Prince George's County Bar Association
www.mdlaw.net

Massachusetts
Massachusetts Bar Association
www.massbar.org

Boston Bar Association
www.bostonbar.org

Women's Bar Association of Massachusetts
www.1weekly.com/wba.htm

Michigan
Michigan State Bar Association
www.michbar.org

Michigan Defense Trial Counsel
www.mdtc.org

Minnesota
Minnesota State Bar Association
www.mnbar.org

Minnesota Defense Lawyers Association
www.mdla.org

Minnesota Trial Lawyers Association
www.mtla.com

Mississippi
The Mississippi Bar
www.msbar.org

Mississippi Trial Lawyers Association
www.mstla.com

Missouri
Missouri State Bar Association
www.mobar.org

Bar Association of Metropolitan St. Louis
www.bamsl.org

Missouri Association of Trial Attorneys
www.matanet.org

Montana
State Bar of Montana
www.montanabar.org

Montana Trial Lawyers Association
www.monttla.com

Nebraska
Nebraska State Bar Association
www.nebar.com

Nebraska Association of Trial Attorneys
www.nebraskatrial.com

Nevada
State Bar of Nevada
www.nvbar.org

Nevada Trial Lawyers Association
www.ntla.org

New Hampshire
New Hampshire State Bar Association
www.nhbar.org

New Hampshire Trial Lawyers Association
www.nhtla.org

New Jersey
New Jersey State Bar Association
www.njsba.com

Association of Trial Lawyers of America—NJ
www.atlanj.org

New Jersey Defense Association
www.members.aol.com/NJDAEMAIL/njdaweb.html

Essex County Bar Association
www.law.shu.edu

Mercer County Bar Association
www.mercerbar.com

New Mexico
State Bar of New Mexico
www.technet.nm.org/sbnm/

New York
New York State Bar Association
www.nysba.org
Contains a list of local bar associations' Web sites in New York State.

Association of the Bar of New York City
www.abcny.org

New York County Lawyers' Association
www.nycla.org

New York State Trial Lawyers Association
www.nystla.org

Albany County Bar Association
www.web-ex.com/acba

Bar Association of Nassau County
www.nassaubar.org

Cortland County Bar Association
www.odyssey.net/subscribers/fvisco/bar

Delaware County Bar Association
www.hancock.net/~dcba/dcba.html

Dutchess County Bar Association
www1.mhv.net/~dcba/dcba3.htm

Bar Association of Erie County
www.eriebar.org

Greene County Bar Association
members.aol.com/dewoodin/gcba1.htm

Onondaga County Bar Association
www.onbar.org/

Queens County Bar Association
infoshop.com/qcba/

Queens Bench Bar Association
www.queensbench.org

Queens Women's Bar Association
www.wbasny.org/queens.htm

Richmond County Bar Association
www.richmondcountybar.org/

Suffolk County Bar Association
villagenet.com/~scba/

Women's Bar Association of the State of New York
www.wbasny.org/

North Carolina

North Carolina Bar Association
www.barlinc.org

North Carolina Academy of Trial Lawyers
www.ncatl.org

North Carolina Association of Defense Attorneys
www.ncada.org

Ohio

Ohio State Bar
www.ohiobar.org

Ohio Academy of Trial Lawyers
www.oatlaw.org

Akron Bar Association
www.akronbar.org

Cincinnati Bar Association
www.cincybar.org/

Columbus Bar Association
www.cbalaw.org

Cleveland Bar Association
www.clevelandbar.org

Toledo Bar Association
www.toledobarassoc.com

Oklahoma

Oklahoma Bar Association
www.okbar.org

Oklahoma Trial Lawyers Association
www.otla.org

Tulsa County Bar Association
www.tulsabar.com

Oklahoma Indian Bar Association
www.free.websight.com/indian

Oregon
Oregon State Bar
www.osbar.org

Oregon Trial Lawyers Association
www.otla-online.org

Multnomah Bar Association
www.mbabar.org

Pennsylvania
Pennsylvania State Bar Association
www.pa-bar.org

Pennsylvania Trial Lawyers Association
www.patla.org

Philadelphia Bar Association
www.philabar.org

Philadelphia Trial Lawyers Association
www.philatla.org

Pennsylvania Defense Institute
www.padefense.org

Pennsylvania Bar Institute
www.pbi.org
Contains links to Pennsylvania local bar associations' Web sites.

Rhode Island
Rhode Island State Bar Association
www.ribar.com

South Carolina
South Carolina Bar Association
www.scbar.org

Charleston County Bar Association
www.charlestonbar.org

South Carolina Defense Trial Attorneys
www.scdtaa.com

South Dakota
South Dakota State Bar Association
www.sdbar.org

South Dakota Defense Lawyers Association
www.rapidnet.com/sddla

Tennessee
Tennessee Bar Association
www.tba.org

Texas
State Bar of Texas
www.texasbar.com

Dallas Bar Association
www.dallasbar.com

Houston Bar Association
www.hba.org

The San Antonio Trial Lawyers Association
www.satla.org

Texas Trial Lawyers Association
www.ttla.com

Texas Association of Defense Counsel
www.tadc.org

Utah
Utah State Bar
www.utahbar.org

Utah Trial Lawyers Association
www.utla.org

Vermont
Vermont State Bar Association
www.vtbar.org

Vermont Trial Lawyers Association
www.vtla.org

<u>**Virginia**</u>
Virginia Bar Association
www.vba.org

Virginia State Bar
www.vsb.org

Virginia Trial Lawyers Association
www.vtla.com

Virginia Association of Defense Attorneys
www.vada.org

<u>**Washington**</u>
Washington State Bar Association
www.wsba.org

Washington State Trial Lawyers Association
www.wstla.org

Washington Defense Trial Lawyers Association
www.wdtl.org

King County Bar Association
www.owt.com/kcba/

Spokane County Bar Association
www.spokanebar.org

Tacoma Pierce County Bar Association
www.co.pierce.wa.us

Whatcom County Bar Association
www.viewit.com/whatcombar

<u>**West Virginia**</u>
West Virginia State Bar Association
www.wvbar.org

Defense Trial Counsel of West Virginia
www.dtcwv.org

West Virginia Trial Lawyers Association
www.wvtla.org

<u>**Wisconsin**</u>
The State Bar of Wisconsin
www.wisbar.org

Milwaukee Bar Association
www.milwbar.org

Wisconsin Academy of Trial Lawyers
www.watl.org

Civil Trial Counsel of Wisconsin
www.ctcw.org

<u>**Wyoming**</u>
Wyoming State Bar Association
www.wyomingbar.org

<u>***Virtual Libraries***</u>
The Argus Clearinghouse
www.clearinghouse.net

Infomine
hlib-www.ucr.edu/

Internet Public Library
www.ipl.org

Librarians' Index to the Internet
sunsite.berkeley.edu/internetindex

World Wide Web Virtual Library
vlib.stanford.edu/Overview.html

<u>***Sites for Locating Library Catalogs***</u>
LIBWEB at Berkeley will find all types of libraries.
sunsite.berkeley.edu/libweb

LIBCAT gives valuable tips on searching library catalogs.
www.metronet.lib.mn.us/lc/lc1.html

webCATS will only find Web-based libraries.
www.lights.com/webcats

Specialized Databases

FACSNET
www.facsnet.org/report_tools/car/cardirec.htm
Directory of proprietary databases.

MEDLINE—National Library of Medicine
www.nlm.nih.gov/databases/freemedl.html

SEC EDGAR Archive
Contains the full text of 10-K and other reports that public companies are required by law to submit to the SEC.
www.sec.gov/cgi-bin/srch-edgar

The IBM Patent Server
www.patents.ibm.com/ibm.html
Index of patent descriptions since 1971.

Expert Witness Directories

ExpertPages.com
www.expertpages.com

Southwestern Directory of Expert Witnesses and Consultants
California Directory of Expert Witnesses
Great Lakes Directory of Expert Witnesses
Southeastern Directory of Expert Witnesses
Midwest Directory of Expert Witnesses

Texas Lawyer and American Lawyer Media
www.texlaw.com

Expert Witness Network
Expert Witness Network
www.witness.net

AELE—Directory of Criminal Justice Experts and Litigation Consultants
Americans for Effective Law Enforcement, Inc.
www.aele.org

Artel Resources Expert Witness Directory
Artel Resources
www.artelsources.com/experts.html

ASTM Directory of Scientific and Technical Consultants and Expert Witnesses
American Society for Testing and Materials
www.astm.org

ATLA Mart, Expert Witnesses/Consultants Index
Association of Trial Lawyers of America
www.atlamart.com

Attorney Referral Network
www.attorneyreferral.net/expert.htm

Best Directory of Recommended Insurance Attorneys & Adjusters
A.M. Best & Co.
www.ambest.com/legal/index.html

Community of Science Expertise
Community of Science, Inc.
www.cos.com

Counsel Quest
Counsel Quest, a law.com company
www.counselquest.com

CyberAttorney's Experts Online
CyberAttorney
www.cyberattorney.com

DRI Expert Witness Database
Defense Research Institute
www.driewb.org

Expert 4 Law Experts & Consultants
Expert 4 Law, sponsored by the LA County Bar Association
www.expert4law.org

Expert Marketplace
The PEN Group, in conjunction with Dun & Bradstreet
www.expertmarketplace.com

ExpertLaw.com
www.expertlaw.com

FindLaw
www.findlaw.com

Forensic Services Directory
National Forensic Center
www.expertwitnesslink.com/home.htm

HIEROS GAMOS—Experts Database
Hieros Gamos
www.hg.org

Horizon's Expert Witness List
Horizon Professional Services
www.sonic.net/thom/expert/

I.D.E.A.L., Inc. Legal Support Index
I.D.E.A.L., Inc.
www.i-deal.com

Larry Anderson's Expert Witness Page
home.earthlink.net/~laanderson/experts.htm

The Round Table Group
www.round.table.com

LawInfo.com Expert Witness Database
lawinfo.com

Legal Expert Pages
www.legalexpertpages.com/

National Directory of Expert Witnesses Online
Claims Providers of America
www.claims.com

National Registry of Experts
www.expert-registry.com

Noble Group Directory of Experts
The Noble Group
www.experts.com

A Pennsylvania Attorney's Guide to Expert Witnesses and Consultants
PaLAWnet, in conjunction with American Lawyer Media
www.palawnet.com/exp/index.htm

Rominger Legal Expert Witness & Consultant Directory
Rominger Legal
www.romingerlegal.com/

IEEE-USA Electrotechnology Consultants Database
Institute of Electrical and Electronics Engineers—United States of America
www.ieeeusa-consultants.org

The Internet Directory of Expert Witnesses
www.expertwitness.com

Legal Nurses Online
www.legalnurses.com

UNIVERSAL LAW Consultant and Expert Witness Directory
Universal Law
www.universal-law.com

WashLaw WEB
Washburn University School of Law
www.washlaw.edu

Yahoo's Legal Consultants Index
Yahoo!
www.yahoo.com

Expert-Source.com
www.expert-source.com

Referral Agencies, Registries, and Panels

TASA Directory of Expertise
Technical Advisory Service for Attorneys
www.tasanet.com

Consolidated Consultants, Co.
www.freereferall.com

Diligence, Inc.
www.diligenceinc.com

Expert Link
National Forensics Center
www.expertwitnesslink.com/home.htm

EXPERTS-On-Line
Experts-On-Line
www.experts-on-line.com

Lexpert Research Services
www.lexpertresearch.com

Maritime and Aviation Consultants
www.mac-experts.com

Medical Experts—A Physician Referral Center
www.docinsler.com

MedicoLegal Consultants, Inc.
mlegal.com

National Consultant Referrals, Inc. Talent Bank
NCR, Inc.
www.referrals.com

Psybar, LLC
www.psybar.com

TAB Consultant Registry
Technical Assistance Bureau, Inc.
www.tabexperts.com

The Legal Expert Network
The Legal Expert Network, Ltd.
www.expertnetwork.com

Unirisk—Expert Witness Services
www.unirisk.com

Technical Network Consulting Service
www.techmedexperts.com

medQuest, Ltd.
www.medquestltd.com

Expert Medical Witnesses, Inc.
www.expertmedicalwitnesses.com

Appendix O Bar Associations and Other Legal Associations

<u>**National Associations**</u>

American Bar Association
www.abanet.org
750 N. Lake Shore Drive
Chicago, IL 60611
abasvcctr@abanet.org

Association of Trial Lawyers of America
www.atlanet.org
1050 31st Street, NW
Washington, DC 20007
Phone: (800) 424-2725; (202) 965-3500
E-mail: help@atlahq.org.

Defense Research Institute
www.dri.org
150 N. Michigan Ave, Ste. 300
Chicago, IL 60601
Phone: (312) 795-1101; Fax: (312) 795-0747

Federal Bar Association
www.fedbar.org
2215 M Street, NW
Washington, DC 20037
Phone: (202) 785-1614; Fax: (202) 785-1568
E-mail: fba@fedbar.org

National Bar Association
www.nationalbar.org
1225 W Street, NW
Washington, DC 20001-4217
Phone: (202) 842-3900
E-mail: nba@nationalbar.org

National Lawyers Association
www.nla.org
City Center Square, P.O. Box 26005
Kansas City, MO 64196
Phone: (816) 471-2994; (800) 471-2994; Fax: (816) 471-2995
E-mail: nla@primenet.com

Association of Federal Defense Attorneys
www.afda.org

Association of Healthcare Medical Lawyers
www.healthcare-medlawyers.org

Black Entertainment & Sports Lawyers Association
www.besla.org

The Cyberlaw Association
www.cyberlawassociation.com

CyberSpace Bar Association
www.cyberbar.net/index.html

Hispanic National Bar Association
www.hnba.com

National Asian Pacific American Bar Association
www.napaba.org

National Association of Trial Lawyer Executives
www.pwr.com/legal/natle/

Federation of Insurance & Corporate Counsel
www.thefederation.org

International Association of Defense Counsel
www.iadclaw.org

State Associations

Many local and specialty bar associations are not listed here. Please consult Appendix N for a more comprehensive list of Web sites, or contact the corresponding state bar association.

Alabama

Alabama State Bar
www.alabar.org
Dexter Avenue, P.O. Box 671
Montgomery, AL 36104
Phone: (334) 269-1515; Fax: (334) 261-6310
E-mail Executive Director: exec@alabar.org

Alabama Trial Lawyers Association
770 Washington Avenue, Suite 170
Montgomery, AL 36104
Phone: (334) 262-4974; Fax: (334) 262-1452
E-mail: atla@mont.mindspring.com

The Birmingham Bar Association
www.birminghambar.org
2021 Second Avenue North
Birmingham, AL 35203
Phone: (205) 251-8006
E-mail: bethc@scott.net

Mobile Bar Association
www.mobilebar.com

Tuscaloosa County Bar Association
www.dbtech.net/tuscaloosabar/index.html

Alabama Defense Lawyers Association
www.adla.org
30 South Perry Street, Montgomery, AL 36104
E-mail: adla@adla.org

Alaska

Alaska Bar Association
www.alaskabar.org
P.O. Box 100279
Anchorage, AK 99510-0279
Phone: 907-272-7469; Fax: 907-272-2932
E-mail: alaskabar@alaskabar.org

Arizona

State Bar of Arizona
www.azbar.org
111 W. Monroe Street, Ste. 1800
Phoenix, AZ 85003-1742
Phone: (602) 340-7200; Fax: (602) 271-4930
E-mail: azbar@azbar.org

Maricopa County Bar Association
303 E. Palm Lane
Phoenix, AZ 85004-9890
Phone: (602) 257-4200; Fax: (602) 257-0522

Arkansas

Arkansas Bar Association
www.arkbar.com
400 W. Markham, Suite 401
Little Rock, AR 72201
Phone: (501) 375-4605; (800) 609-5668; Fax: (501) 375-4901
E-mail: arkbar@ipa.net

Arkansas Trial Lawyers Association
www.arktla.org
Phone: (501) 376-2852

California

The State Bar of California
www.calbar.org
San Francisco, Main Office
180 Howard Street
San Francisco, CA 94105-1639
Phone: (415) 538-2000
The California Bar Association's Web site, www.calbar.org, maintains a comprehensive list of all California

bar associations—local, minority, and specialty.

Association of Business Trial Lawyers
(several geographic divisions)
www.abtl.org

Association of Defense Council of Northern California
www.adcnc.org

Consumer Attorneys of California
http.//caoc.com

<u>California Local Bar Associations</u>
Alameda County Bar Association
James I. Fisher, President
Lanferman Fisher, et al.
3100 Mowry Avenue, #300
Fremont, CA 94538-1509
Phone: (510) 494-5500; Fax: (510) 494-5510

Alameda County Bar Association
Bari Susan Robinson, Executive Director
360 22nd Street, Ste. 800
Oakland, CA 94612
Phone: (510) 893-7160; Fax: (510) 893-3119

Amador County Bar
Joseph J. Scoleri III, President
Barker & Associates
205 Court Street
Jackson, CA 95642
Phone: (209) 223-0877; Fax: (209) 223-0831

Antelope Valley Bar Association
James C. Lillicrap, President
43770 15th Street, W, #100
Lancaster, CA 93534
Phone: (661) 948-3434; Fax: (661) 256-6608

Bar Association of San Francisco
Mark I. Schickman, President
Fox & Grove, Chartered
240 Stockton, Ste. 900
San Francisco, CA 94108-5306
Phone: (415) 956-1360

Bar Association of San Francisco
Drucilla S. Ramey, Executive Director
685 Market Street
San Francisco, CA 94105
Phone: (415) 764-1600

Berkeley-Albany Bar Association
Susan B. Luten, President
2140 Shattuck Avenue, #1206
Berkeley, CA 94704
Phone: (510) 548-5500; Fax: (510) 548-6363

Beverly Hills Bar Association
Linda Wight Mazur, President
W. Farbinger Enterprises, Inc.
11684 Ventura Blvd, #324
Studio City, CA 91604
Phone: (818) 753-5202; Fax: (818) 753-5204

Beverly Hills Bar Association
Bert Z. Tigerman, Executive Director
300 S. Beverly Drive, #201
Beverly Hills, CA 90212
Phone: (310) 553-6644; (310) 284-8290

Burbank Bar Association
Candace Kay Ladley, President
222 East Olive Avenue
Burbank, CA 91502
Phone: (818) 841-2266; Fax: (818) 843-5822

Burbank Bar Association
Charles W. Adams, Executive Director
222 East Olive Avenue
Burbank, CA 91502
Phone: (818) 843-0931; Fax: (818) 843-5852

Butte County Bar Association
Dirk Deverne Potter, President
515 Wall Street
Chico, CA 95928
Phone: (530) 342-1848; Fax: (530) 894-5043

Calaveras County Bar Association
Sandra Kraft, President
116 Court Street, P.O. Box 1818
San Andreas, CA 95249
Phone: (209) 795-0217; Fax (209) 795-0217

California Association of Local Bars
Josef Anthony Vittal, President
Vittal & Sternberg
1900 Ave. of the Stars, 25FL
Los Angeles, CA 90067-4506
Phone: (310) 282-8914; Fax: (310) 551-2710

California Organization of Small Bars Association
Todd Salmon, President
200 Oceangate, Ste 520
Long Beach, CA 90802
Phone: (310) 437-0841

Century City Bar Association
Myles Berman, President
Myles L. Berman Law Office
9255 Sunset Blvd, #720
Los Angeles, CA 90069
Phone: (310) 273-9501; Fax: (310) 273-8085

Century City Bar Association
Rebecca Lee, Executive Director
516 S. Fuller Avenue
Los Angeles, CA 90036
Phone: (310) 358-3330; Fax: (213) 935-6622

Colusa County Bar Association
Tedd A. Mehr, President
P.O. Box 1286, 249 5th Street
Colusa, CA 95932

Contra Costa County Bar Association
Michael Kenneth Brown, President
Morgan Miller & Blair
1676 N. California Blvd., #200
Walnut Creek, CA 94596
Phone: (925) 937-3600; Fax: (925) 943-1106

Contra Costa County Bar Association
Lisa Graves Reep, Executive Director
1001 Galaxy Way, Ste. 102
Concord, CA 94520-5734
Phone: (925) 687-0237; Fax: (925) 686-9867

Culver Marina Bar Association
Anthony V. Salerno, President
4676 Admiralty Way, #300
Marina Del Rey, CA 90292
Phone: (310) 574-5318; Fax: (310) 216-0781

Del Norte County Bar Association
Donald D. McElfresh, President
P.O. Box 187
Crescent City, CA 95531
Phone: (707) 464-6567; Fax: (707) 464-6567

Desert Bar Association
John Goodloe Evans, President
5 E. Citrus, #208
Redlands, CA 92373
Phone: (909) 307-1876; Fax: (909) 307-1878

Eastern Alameda County Bar Association
Thomas G. Borst, President
Law Ofc. Leonard D. Weller
2 Annabel Lane, #200
San Ramon, CA 94583
Phone: (925) 275-0855; Fax: (925) 830-8787

Eastern Bar Association of Los Angeles County
Mary M. Weigert, Executive Director
1175 East Garvey Avenue, Ste. 105
Covina, CA 91724-3618
Phone: (626) 967-3115; Fax: (626) 915-4755

Eastern Madera County Bar Association
Dale J. Blea, President
P.O. Box 3207
Oakhurst, CA 93644
Phone: (559) 658-2999

El Dorado County Bar Association
David M. Johnson, President
3161 Cameron Park Drive, #209
Cameron Park, CA 95682-7979
Phone: (530) 672-1773; Fax: (530) 672-1573

Foothill Bar Association
Desiree A. O'Brien, President
Deputy Atty. General's Off.
300 S. Spring St., #500
Los Angeles, CA 90013
Phone: (213) 897-2578; Fax: (213) 897-2804

Foothills Bar/San Diego
Thomas Miller Buchenau, President
275 E. Douglas Avenue, #108
El Cajon, CA 92020 4546
Phone: (619) 441-1100; Fax: (619) 579-5761

Fresno County Bar Association
Vicki Holm-Savaria, Executive Director
2014 Tulare Street, Ste. 420
Fresno, CA 93721
Phone: (559) 264-2619; Fax: (559) 264-8726

Fresno County Bar Association
Anthony Patrick Capozzi, President
1233 W. Shaw Avenue, #102
Fresno, CA 93711
Phone: (559) 221-0200; Fax: (559) 221-7997

Glendale Bar Association
Jeffrey Allen Kopczynski, President
345 N. Cedar Street
Glendale, CA 92106
Phone: (818) 500-1631; Fax: (818) 246-9745

Glendale Bar Association
Kathy Bond, Executive Director
512 East Wilson Avenue, Ste. 307
Glendale, CA 91206
Phone: (818) 956-1633; Fax: (818) 956-1654

Glenn County Bar Association
Leonard G. Krup, President
134 West Sycamore Street
Willows, CA 95988
Phone: (530) 934-5416; Fax: (530) 934-3508

Harbor Bar Association
Carmen Anthony Trutanich, President
Jaffe Trutanich et al.
222 West 6th Street, #920
San Pedro, CA 90731-3354
Phone: (310) 548-0410; Fax: (310) 548-4813

Hemet/Mt. San Jacinto Bar Association
Jude Thaddeus Augustus Powers, President
950 N. State St., #C
Hemet, CA 92543-1485
Phone: (909) 929-6969; Fax: (909) 652-7102

Hollywood Bar Association
Frank O. Ponce, President
211 N. State St., #110
Hemet, CA 92543
Phone: (909) 925-7662

Humboldt County Bar Association
Dennis Craig Reinholtsen, President
P.O. Box 105
Eureka, CA 95502
Phone: (707) 445-4140; Fax: (707) 443-2470

Imperial County Bar Association
Kris M. Malec, President
Anderholt Walker, et al
654 Main Street
El Centro, CA 92243
Phone: (619) 352-1311; Fax: (760) 353-3410

Inglewood Bar Association
Hollis McCray-Clark, President
Clark & McCray-Clark
850 Wilshire Blvd., Ste. 404
Beverly Hills, CA 90211
Phone: (213) 850-6785

Inyo County Bar Association
Gerard B. Harvey, President
148 N. Main, Suite 201
Bishop, CA 93514
Phone: (760) 873-1064; Fax: (760) 873-5515

Kern County Bar Association
James Richard Hulsy, President
412 Truxtun Avenue
P.O. Box 825
Bakersfield, CA 93302
Phone: (661) 324-9475; Fax: (661) 324-9506

Kern County Bar Association
Suellen Irene Hubbard Anderson, Executive Director
P.O. Box 1926
1675 Chester Avenue
Bakersfield, CA 93303
Phone: (661) 334-4700; Fax: (661) 334-4701

Kings County Bar Association
John M. Melikian, President
Maroot Hardcastle, et al.
429 North Redington Street
Hanford, CA 93230
Phone: (209) 584-0131

Lake County Bar Association
Susan Krones, President
DA/Family Support
926 South Forbes Street
Lakeport, CA 95453
Phone: (707) 263-2316

Lassen County Bar Association
James E. Pardee, President
215 South Lassen Street
P.O. Box 609
Susanville, CA 96130
Phone: (916) 257-6162

Long Beach Bar Association
Frank R. Newell, President
11 Golden Shore Drive, #400
Long Beach, CA 90802-4218
Phone: (310) 435-7471

Long Beach Bar Association
Keila E. Loaiza, Executive Director
11 Golden Shore Drive, #230
Long Beach, CA 90802
Phone: (310) 432-5913

Los Angeles County Bar Association
Sheldon H. Sloan, President
1801 Avenue of Stars, #417
Los Angeles, CA 90067-5906
Phone: (310) 201-0622

Los Angeles County Bar Association
Richard Walch, Executive Director
P.O. Box 55020
Los Angeles, CA 90055-2020
Phone: (213) 896-6424

Madera County Bar Association
Frank Ramirez, President
Hernandez & Ramirez
6103 North 1st Street, #102
Fresno, CA 93710
Phone: (209) 449-8150

Marin County Bar Association
Marta Osterloh, President
Marin County Civic Center, Room 161
San Rafael, CA 94903
Phone: (415) 499-6321

Marin County Bar Association
Lynne Pfeifer, Executive Director
1010 B Street, Suite 419
San Rafael, CA 94901
Phone: (415) 453-8181

Mariposa County Bar Association
Quinn R. Baranski, President
Office of the District Attorney
P.O. Box 748
Mariposa, CA 95338
Phone: (209) 966-8258

Mendocino County Bar Association
Maryann Villwock, President
308 South School Street
Ukiah, CA 95482
Phone: (707) 468-8017

Merced County Bar Association
Michael Fagalde, President
1640 N Street, Suite 200
Merced, CA 95344
Phone: (209) 723-4372

Modoc County Bar Association
Frances Barclay, President
P.O. Box 171
Alturas, CA 96101
Phone: (916) 233-4222

Mono County Bar Association
R. Mark Carney, President
Sherwin Professional Plaza
P.O. Box 2127
Mammoth Lakes, CA 93546
Phone: (619) 934-4558

Monterey County Bar Association
Frank W. Dice, President
150 West Gabilan
Salinas, CA 93902-0270
Phone: (408) 757-6163

Monterey County Bar Association
Susan Goodrich, Executive Director
411 Pacific Street, Suite 308
Monterey, CA 93940
Phone: (408) 375-1693

Morgan Hill/GilThom Bar
Kevin Patrick Courtney, President
P.O. Box 1845
Morgan Hill, CA 95037
Phone: (408) 779-5101

Morongo Basin Bar Association
Dee Davis, President
P.O. Box 1869
Yucca Valley, CA 92286-1869
Phone: (619) 365-8384

Napa County Bar Association
Ellen York, President
822 Brolon Street
Napa, CA 94559
Phone: (707) 224-7971

Nevada County Bar Association
Paul Manka, President
107 Court Street
Nevada City, CA 95959
Phone: (916) 265-9176

Newport Harbor Bar/Orange County
Stuart Loren Grant, President
1300 Dove, Suite 200
Newport Beach, CA 92660
Phone: (714) 851-3933

Northern San Diego County Bar Association
Cheryl L. Tomac, President
400 South Melrose Drive, #214
Vista, CA 92083
Phone: (619) 941-9494

Northern San Diego County Bar Association
Lawrence Martinez, Executive Director
P.O. Box 2381
Vista, CA 92085
Phone: (619) 758-5833

Northern San Mateo County Bar
Abigail Marshall, President
P.O. Box 1639
Pacifica, CA 94040
Phone: (415) 355-3193

Northern Santa Barbara County Bar
David Merrill Bixby, President
937 East Main Street, Suite 206
Santa Maria, CA 93454
Phone: (805) 928-8323

Orange County Bar Association
Jennifer L. Keller, President
Earley & Keller
19100 Von Karman Avenue, #950
Irvine, CA 92715
Phone: (714) 476-8900

Orange County Bar Association
Donna H. Fouste, Executive Director
P.O. Box 17777
Irvine, CA 92623
Phone: (714) 440-6700

Palo Alto Area Bar Association
Jeffrey A. Snyder, President
245 Lytton Avenue, #300
Palo Alto, CA 94301
Phone: (415) 327-4200

Palo Alto Area Bar Association
Trina Lovercheck, Executive Director
405 Sherman Avenue
Palo Alto, CA 94306
Phone: (415) 326-8322

Pasadena Bar Association
Todd J. Muir, President
Collins Collins Muir, et al.
P.O. Box 93490
Pasadena, CA 91119-3409
Phone: (818) 793-1163

Pasadena Bar Association
Geri L. Manning, Executive Director
301 West Colorado Blvd., #524
Pasadena, CA 91101
Phone: (818) 793-1422

Placer County Bar Association
Geri Bray, President
1445 Lincoln Way
Auburn, CA 95603
Phone: (916) 823-3501

Plumas County Bar Association
Robert D. McIlThom, President
46 Harbison Street, #A
P.O. Box 3136
Quincy, CA 95971
Phone: (530) 283-5155; Fax: (530) 283-2534

Ramona Bar Association
Patricia Thompson, President
709 D Street, Suite 205
Ramona, CA 92065
Phone: (619) 789-9446

Riverside County Bar
Steven L. Harmon, President
3685 Main Street, Suite 250
Riverside, CA 92501
Phone: (909) 787-6800

Riverside County Bar
Louise Biddle, Executive Director
4129 Main Street, #100
Riverside, CA 92501
Phone: (909) 682-1015

Sacramento County Bar Association
Gary Loveridge, President
Sutter Health
P.O. Box 160727
Sacramento, CA 95816-0727
Phone: (916) 554-6780

Sacramento County Bar Association
Robert M. Stone, Executive Director
901 H Street, Suite 101
Sacramento, CA 95814
Phone: (916) 448-1087

San Benito County Bar Association
Arthur Cantu, President
Court House, Room 206
Fifth & Monterey Streets
Hollister, CA 95023
Phone: (408) 637-2585

San Bernardino County Bar
Bryan C. Hartnell, President
25757 Redlands Boulevard
Redlands, CA 92373
Phone: (909) 796-6881

San Bernardino County Bar
Lowell Jameson, Exec. Director
555 North Arrowhead Avenue
San Bernardino, CA 92401-1201
Phone: (909) 885-1986

San Diego County Bar
Hayden J. Trubitt, President
Brobeck Phleger & Harrison
550 West C Street, #1300
San Diego, CA 92101
Phone: (619) 234-1966

San Diego County Bar
Dalton Menhall, Exec. Director
1333 Seventh Avenue
San Diego, CA 92101
Phone: (619) 231-0781

San Fernando Valley Bar
David Hagen, President
17525 Ventura Blvd., #201
Encino, CA 91316
Phone: (818) 501-6161

San Fernando Valley Bar
Elizabeth Post, Exec. Director
5435 Balboa Blvd., Suite 205
Encino, CA 91316
Phone: (818) 995-6665

San Gabriel Valley Bar
Cecilia S. Wu, President
Wasserman Comden, et al.
801 South Garfield Avenue, #100
Alhambra, CA 91801
Phone: (818) 308-9588

San Gabriel Valley Bar
Mary M. Weigert, Exec. Director
1175 East Garvey Ave., Suite 105
Covina, CA 91724-3618
Phone: (818) 966-5532

San Joaquin County Bar
William Fattarsi, President
102 South San Joaquin St., Room 1
Stockton, CA 95202
Phone: (209) 468-2730

San Joaquin County Bar
L. Adelle Barrette, Exec. Director
6 South El Dorado, Suite 504
Stockton, CA 95202
Phone: (209) 984-0125

San Luis Obispo County Bar
Steven J. Adamski, President
Sinsheimer, Schiebelhut & Baggett
P.O. Box 61
San Luis Obispo, CA 93401
Phone: (805) 541-2800

San Mateo County Bar
Cameron Miller, President
250-A Twin Dolphin Dr.
Redwood City, CA 94065
Phone: (415) 595-0444

San Mateo County Bar
John Kevin McInerney, Exec. Director
303 Bradford Street, Suite A
Redwood City, CA 94063
Phone: (415) 363-4230

Santa Barbara County Bar
Jamie F. Raney, President
Fell Marking, et al.
222 East Carillo Street
Santa Barbara, CA 93101
Phone: (805) 963-0755

Santa Barbara County Bar
Margret E. Mowrer, Exec. Director
1111 Garden Street, Suite 106
Santa Barbara, CA 93101
Phone: (805) 962-3443

Santa Clara County Bar
Roberta S. Hayashi, President
Berliner Cohen
10 Almaden Blvd., 11th Floor
San Jose, CA 95113
Phone: (408) 286-5800

Santa Clara County Bar
Christine Burdick, Exec. Director
4 North Second Street, Suite 400
San Jose, CA 95113
Phone: (408) 287-2557

Santa Cruz County Bar
James Hober, President
300 Summerhill Drive
Scotts Valley, CA 95066
Phone: (408) 461-0258

Santa Cruz County Bar
Linda M. Martin, Exec. Director
340 Soquel Avenue, Suite 209
Santa Cruz, CA 95062
Phone: (408) 423-5031

Santa Monica Bar Association
Avery M. Cooper, President
2530 Wilshire Blvd., 3rd Floor
Santa Monica, CA 90404
Phone: (310) 829-9918

Santa Monica Bar Association
Elaine S. Glass, Exec. Director
1707 Fourth Street, Suite 209
Santa Monica, CA 90401
Phone: (310) 394-6979

Shasta Trinity Counties Bar
Cherry Challe, President
Gray & Proudy
1755 East Street
Redding, CA 96001
Phone: (916) 246-9099

Siskiyou County Bar
Jerry O. Crow, President
P.O. Box 429
Yreka, CA 96032
Phone: (916) 468-2016

Solano County Bar
Robert Fracchia, President
Dobbins, Weir, et al.
500 Main Street
Vacaville, CA 95688
Phone: (707) 448-6894

Solano County Bar
Sidney Wojan, Exec. Director
744 Empire Street, Suite 100
Fairfield, CA 94533
Phone: (707) 422-0127

Sonoma County Bar
Rose Zoia, President
P.O. Box 1656
Glen Ellen, CA 95442
Phone: (707) 576-0198

Sonoma County Bar
Dan Schurman, Exec. Director
115 Talbot Avenue
Santa Rosa, CA 95404
Phone: (707) 542-1190

South Bay Bar/Los Angeles
William J. Beverly, President
Beverly & Hart
3424 Carson Street, #400
Torrance, CA 90503
Phone: (310) 793-7766

South Bay Bar/Los Angeles
Jeanne Rhodes, Exec. Director
P.O. Box 3825
825 Maple Avenue
Torrance, CA 90503
Phone: (310) 320-9350

South Bay Bar/San Diego
Mary C. Downey, President
Vuong Downey & Louie
3709 Convoy Street, #208
San Diego, CA 92111
Phone: (619) 278-3737

South Bay Bar/San Diego
Irene Whitney, Exec. Director
230 Glover Avenue, Suite 1
Chula Vista, CA 92010
Phone: (619) 422-5377

South Lake Tahoe Bar
Paul I. Palant, President
3351 Lake Tahoe Blvd., Suite 11
South Lake Tahoe, CA 96150-7920
Phone: (916) 544-0431

Southeast District Bar Association
Javier B. Ramirez, President
12749 Norwalk Blvd., #206
Norwalk, CA 90650
Phone: (310) 869-2589

Southeast District Bar Association
Connie Garcia, Exec. Director
12720 Norwalk Blvd., Suite 112
Norwalk, CA 90650
Phone: (310) 864-4713

Southern Orange County Bar
Jean Miller, President
260 St. Ann's Drive
Laguna Beach, CA 92651
Phone: (714) 494-2591

Southwest Riverside County Bar
J. S. Munoz, President
28581 Front Street, Suite 108
Temecula, CA 92591
Phone: (909) 694-5711

Stanislaus County Bar
Nancy Smith, President
California Rural Legal Assistance
1020 15th Street, Suite 11
Modesto, CA 95354
Phone: (209) 577-3811

Stanislaus County Bar
Roberta Burge, Exec. Director
914 13th Street
Modesto, CA 95354
Phone: (209) 571-5729

Sunnyvale-Cupertino Bar
Michael A. Nichols, President
599 North Mathilda Avenue, Suite 245
Sunnyvale, CA 94086
Phone: (408) 733-9221

Sunnyvale-Cupertino Bar
Joyce Kovacs, Exec. Director
1111 El Camino, #109-193
Sunnyvale, CA 94087
Phone: (408) 486-9220

Tahoe-Truckee Bar
Robert L. Tamietti, President
10020 Church Street
Truckee, CA 96161
Phone: (916) 587-8700

Tahoe-Truckee Bar
Jean Roznos, Exec. Director
P.O. Box 2614
Truckee, CA 96160
Phone: (916) 587-0342

Tehama County Bar
Nelson Buck, President
P.O. Box 8189
Red Bluff, CA 96080

Tulare County Bar
Teresa Saucedo, President
Tulare County Counsel's Office
2900 Burrel Avenue
Visalia, CA 93291
Phone: (209) 733-6263

Tulare County Bar
Dorothy McDermott, Exec. Director
208 West Main Street, Suite 2
Visalia, CA 93291
Phone: (209) 732-2513

Tuolumne County Bar
Donald Inch Segerstrom, Jr., President
84 North Washington Street
Sonora, CA 95370
Phone: (209) 532-8363

Ventura County Bar
David Shain, President
300 Esplanade Drive
Oxnard, CA 93030
Phone: (805) 983-2800

Ventura County Bar
Steve Henderson, Exec. Director
4475 Market Street, Suite B
Ventura, CA 93003
Phone: (805) 650-7599

Washington Township Bar
Steven Citti, President
39500 Stevenson Place, #210
Fremont, CA 94539
Phone: (510) 797-7656

West Orange County Bar
John Cogorno, President
14121 Beach Blvd.
Westminster, CA 92683
Phone: (714) 892-2936

West Valley Bar
Joyce Ferris-Metcalf, President
District Attorney's Office
70 West Hedding Street, 6 West
San Jose, CA 95110
Phone: (408) 299-7457

Western San Bernardino Bar
Patricia Teunisse, President
120 West Bonita Avenue, #203
San Dimas, CA 91773
Phone: (909) 599-8181

Western San Bernardino Bar
Colleen Baffa, Exec. Director
10532 Acacia, Suite B-10
Haven Executive Park
Rancho Cucamonga, CA 91730
Phone: (909) 945-2980

Westwood Bar
Paul M. Enriquez, President
10920 Wilshire Blvd., #650
Los Angeles, CA 90210
Phone: (310) 208-2889

Whittier Bar
Carolyn Martin, President
13330 Philadelphia Street
Whittier, CA 90601
Phone: (310) 464-1130

Wilshire Bar Association
Laura Conti, President
15260 Ventura Blvd., Suite 680
Sherman Oaks, CA 91403
Phone: (818) 789-7079

Wilshire Bar Association
Linda Shaw, Exec. Director
P.O. Box 75338
Los Angeles, CA 90075-0338
Phone: (213) 488-0050

Yolo County Bar
William D. Kopper, President
417 E Street
Davis, CA 95616
Phone: (916) 758-0757

Yuba-Sutter Bar
James L. Curry, President
613 D Street
Marysville, CA 95901
Phone: (916) 743-4664

California Trial Lawyers Associations

Alameda/Contra Costa Trial Lawyers
David McClain, President
Law Offices of Steven Kazan
171 12th Street, Suite 300
Oakland, CA 94607
Phone: (510) 465-7728

San Francisco Trial Lawyers
Michael Kelly, President
Walkup Melodia, et al.
650 California, 30th Floor
San Francisco, CA 94108
Phone: (415) 981-7210

San Francisco Trial Lawyers
Diane Rito, Exec. Director
c/o SFLRA
World Trade Center, Suite 230
San Francisco, CA 94111
Phone: (415) 956-6401

Colorado

Colorado Bar Association
www.cobar.org
(Lists local bar associations.)
1900 Grant Street, Ninth Floor
Denver, CO 80203
Phone: (303) 860-1115; Fax: (303) 894-0821
E-mail: comments@cobar.org

Colorado Trial Lawyers Association
www.ctla.net

Connecticut

Connecticut State Bar
www.ctbar.org
101 Corporate Place,
Rocky Hill, CT 06067
Phone: (860) 721-0025; Fax: (860) 257-4125
E-mail: ctbar@ctbar.org

Connecticut Trial Lawyers Association
www.ct-tla.org
Phone: (860) 522-4345

Delaware

Delaware State Bar Association
www.dsba.org
1201 Orange Street, Suite 1100
Wilmington, DE 19801
Phone: (302) 658-5279; (800) 292-7869 (from Kent & Sussex Counties);
Fax: (302) 658-5212

Delaware Trial Lawyers Association
www.dtla.org
715 King Street, Second Floor
Wilmington, DE 19801
Phone: (302) 421-2800; Fax: (302) 421-2803
E-mail: jt@dtla.org

District of Columbia

The Bar Association of the District of Columbia (Voluntary Bar Association)
Phone: (202) 223-6600
E-mail: BAofDC@aol.com

The District of Columbia Bar
www.dcbar.org
1250 H Street NW, Sixth Floor
Washington, DC 20005-5937
Phone: 202-737-4700; Fax: 202-626-3471
E-mail: info@dcbar.org

Trial Lawyers Association of Metro Washington, DC
nturalcrls@aol.com

Florida

Florida Bar Association
www.flabar.org
650 Apalachee Parkway
Tallahassee, FL 32399-2300
Phone: (850) 561-5600; Fax: 850/561-5826
E-mail: flabar@flabar.org

Academy of Florida Trial Lawyers
www.aftl.org
218 South Monroe Street
Tallahassee, FL 32301
Phone: (850) 224-9403; Fax: (850) 224-4254
E-mail: AFTL@AFTL.org

Florida Defense Lawyers Association
www.fdla.org
James A. Dixon, Jr., Exec. Director
902 N. Gadsden St., P.O. Box 13767
Tallahassee, FL 32317-3767
Phone: (850) 224-1025; Fax: (850) 222-9166

Georgia

State Bar of Georgia
www.gabar.org
800 The Hurt Building,
50 Hurt Plaza
Atlanta, GA 30303-2934
Phone: (404) 527-8700; (800) 334-6865; Fax: (404) 527-8717

Georgia Trial Lawyers Association
www.gtla.org
1250 The Hurt Building,
50 Hurt Plaza, S.E.
Atlanta, GA 30303-2916
Phone: (404) 522-8487; Fax: (404) 522-3705
E-mail: contact@gtla.org

Georgia Defense Lawyers Association
www.gdla.org
P.O. Box 246
Macon, GA 31298-5399
Phone: (912)755-9813
E-mail: gdlashurley@mindspring.com; bkb@boviskyle.com; jablaw@msn.com

Hawaii

Hawaii State Bar Association
1136 Union Mall, PH 1
Honolulu, HI 96813
Phone: (808) 537-1868; Neighbor Islands: (888) 808-4722; Fax: (808) 521-7936

Consumer Lawyers of Hawaii
www.clh.org
1088 Bishop Street, Suite 1111
Honolulu, HI 96813
Phone: (808) 599-2769; Fax: (808) 599-2859; Cell/Pager/Voice Mail: (808) 381-4740
E-mail: clh@pixi.com

Idaho

Idaho State Bar
P.O. Box 895
Boise, ID 83701
Phone: (208) 334-4500; Fax: (208) 334-4515

Idaho State Trial Lawyers Association
1517 W. Hays, Boise, ID
P.O. Box 1777
Boise, ID 83701
Phone: (208) 345-1890; Fax: (208) 345-1894
E-mail: itla@itla.org

Illinois

Illinois State Bar Association
Springfield, IL 62701
Phone: (217) 525-1760; In Illinois: (800) 252-8908; Fax: (217) 525-0712

Illinois Association of Defense Trial Counsel
www.iadtc.org
IDC (c/o SAS Unlimited)
103 N. Main Street, Suite A, P.O. Box 318
Athens, IL 62613
Phone: (800) 232-0169; (217) 636-7970; Fax: (217) 636-8812
E-mail: iadtcoffice@iadtc.org

Illinois Trial Lawyers Association
110 W. Edwards Street; P.O. Box 5000
Springfield, IL
Phone: (217) 7890-0755; (800) 252-8501
E-mail: iltla@aol.com

Indiana

Indiana State Bar Association
www.state.in.us/isba
Indiana Bar Center, 230 E. Ohio St.
Indianapolis, IN 46204-2119
Phone: (800) 266-2581; Voice Mail: (317) 639-5465; Fax: (317) 266-2588
E-mail: isbaadmin@inbar.org

Indiana Trial Lawyers Association
150 West Market St., ISTA Building
Indianapolis, IN 46204
Phone: (800) 395-4852; (317) 634-8841; Fax: (317) 634-4898

Iowa

Iowa State Bar Association
www.iowabar.org
521 E. Locust, Suite 300
Des Moines, IA, 50309-1939
Phone: (515) 243-3179; Fax: (515) 243-2511

Kansas

Kansas Bar Association
www.ksbar.org
1200 Harrison St., P.O. Box 1037
Topeka, KS 66612
Phone: (913) 234-5696; Fax: (913) 234-3813

Kansas Trial Lawyers Association
www.ink.org/public/ktla/

Kansas Association of Defense Counsel (KADC)
www.kadc.org
700 SW Jackson, Suite 702
Topeka, KS 66603
Phone: (785) 232-9091; Fax: (785) 357-6629
E-mail: jbarbee@kadc.org

Kentucky
Kentucky Bar Association
www.kybar.org
514 West Main Street
Frankfurt, KY 40601-1883
Phone: (502) 564-3795; Fax: (502) 564-3225
E-mail: webmaster@kybar.org

Louisiana
Louisiana State Bar Association
601 St. Charles Avenue
New Orleans, LA 70130
Phone: (504) 566-1600; Fax: (504) 566-0930

Louisiana Trial Lawyers Association
www.ltla.org
442 Europe Street
Baton Rouge, LA 70802
Phone: (800) 354-6267; (504) 383-5554
E-mail: info@ltla.org

New Orleans Bar Association
www.gnofn.org/~noba

New Orleans Bar Association
228 Saint Charles Ave., Suite 1223
New Orleans, LA 70130-2612
Phone: (504) 525-7453; Fax: (504) 525-6549

Maine
Maine State Bar Association
www.mainebar.org
124 State Street, P.O. Box 788
Augusta, ME 04330
Phone: (207) 622-7523; Fax: (207) 623-0083
E-mail: info@mainebar.org

Maine Trial Lawyers Association
www.mtla.org
P.O. Box 428
Augusta, ME 04332-04228
Phone: (207) 623-2661; Fax: (207) 621-0118
E-mail: mtla@ime.net

Maryland
Maryland State Bar Association
www.msba.org
Maryland Bar Center
Baltimore, MD 21201
Phone: (410) 685-7878; (800) 492-1964; Fax: (410) 837-0518

Baltimore County Bar Association
www.bcba.org
111 N. Calvert Street, Suite 625
Baltimore, MD, 21202
Phone: (410) 337-9103

Bar Association of Montgomery County
www.montbar.org
27 W. Jefferson Street
Rockville, MD, 20850
Phone: (301) 424-3454; Fax: (301) 217-9327

Maryland Trial Lawyers Association
E-mail: 102161.1617@compuserve.com

Massachusetts
Massachusetts Bar Association
www.massbar.org
20 West Street
Boston, MA 02111-1218
Phone: (617) 542-3602; Fax: (617) 426-4344
E-mail: webmaster@massbar.org

Boston Bar Association
www.bostonbar.org
16 Beacon Street
Boston, MA 02108
Phone: (617) 742-0615; Fax: (617) 523-0127

Massachusetts Academy of Trial Attorneys
E-mail: mata@ljextra.com

Michigan

Michigan State Bar Association
www.michbar.org
306 Townsend Street
Lansing, MI 48933-2083
Phone: (517) 372-9030; Fax: (517) 372-2410

Michigan Defense Trial Counsel
www.mdtc.org
700 N. Washington Ave.
Lansing, MI 48906
Phone: (517) 482-7538; Fax: (517) 485-4129

Minnesota

Minnesota State Bar Association
www.mnbar.org
514 Nicollet Mall, Suite 300
Minneapolis, MN 55402
Phone: (612) 333-1183; Fax: (612) 333-4927

Minnesota Defense Lawyers Association
www.mdla.org
Suite 812, 401 Second Avenue South
Minneapolis, MN 55401
Phone: (612) 338-2717; Fax: (612) 338-9148
E-mail: director@mdla.org

Minnesota Trial Lawyers Association
www.mtla.com

Mississippi

The Mississippi Bar
www.msbar.org
643 N. State Street, P.O. Box 2168
Jackson, MS 39225-2168
Phone: (601) 948-4471; Fax: (601) 355-8635
E-mail: msbar@msbar.org

Mississippi Trial Lawyers Association
www.mstla.com
P.O. Box 1992
Jackson, MS 39205
Phone: (601) 948-8631; Fax: (601) 948-8633

Missouri

Missouri State Bar Association
www.mobar.org
326 Monroe, P.O. Box 119
Jefferson City, MO 65102
Phone: (314) 635-4128; Fax: (314) 635-2811
E-mail: mobar@mobar.org

Bar Association of Metropolitan St. Louis
www.bamsl.org
One Metropolitan Square, Suite 1400
St. Louis, MO 63102
Phone: (314) 421-4134; Fax: (314) 421-0013

Missouri Association of Trial Attorneys
www.matanet.org

Montana

State Bar of Montana
www.montanabar.org
46 N. Last Chance Gulch, Suite 2A, P.O. Box 577
Helena, MT 59624
Phone: (406) 442-7660; Fax: (406) 442-7763

Montana Trial Lawyers Association
www.monttla.com

Nebraska

Nebraska State Bar Association
www.nebar.com
635 S. 14th Street, 2nd Floor,
P.O. Box 81809
Lincoln, NE 68501
Phone: (402) 475-7091; Fax: (402) 475-7098

Nebraska Association of Trial Attorneys
www.nebraskatrial.com

Nevada

State Bar of Nevada
www.nvbar.org
600 E. Charleston Blvd.
Las Vegas, NV 89104
Phone: (702) 382-2200; Fax: (702) 385-2878

Nevada Trial Lawyers Association
www.ntla.org

New Hampshire

New Hampshire State Bar Association
www.nhbar.org
112 Pleasant Street
Concord, NH 03301
Phone: (603) 224-6942; Fax: (603) 224-2910

New Hampshire Trial Lawyers Association
www.nhtla.org

New Jersey

New Jersey State Bar Association
www.njsba.com
New Jersey Law Center,
One Constitution Square
New Brunswick, NJ 08901-1500
Phone: (908) 249-5000; Fax: (908) 249-2815

Association of Trial Lawyers of America, NJ
www.atlanj.org
E-mail: info@atlanj.org

Bergen County Bar
61 Hudson Street
Hackensack, NJ 07601
Phone: (201) 488-0044; Fax: (201) 488-0073

New Jersey Defense Association
members.aol.com/NJDAEMAIL/njdaweb.html
Maryanne R. Steedle, Exec. Director
P.O. Box 463, Linwood, NJ 08221
Phone: (609) 927-1180; Fax: (609) 927-4540
E-mail: NJDAE-MAIL@aol.com

New Mexico

State Bar of New Mexico
www.technet.nm.org/sbnm/
121 Tijeras Street, NE, P.O. Box 25883
Albuquerque, NM 87102
Phone: (505) 842-6132; Fax: (505) 843-8765

New York

New York State Bar Association
www.nysba.org
One Elk Street
Albany, NY 12207
Phone: (518) 487-5557; Fax: (518) 487-5564

Association of the Bar of NYC
www.abcny.org

New York County Lawyers' Association
www.nycla.org

New York State Trial Lawyers Association
www.nystla.org
132 Nassau Street, 2nd Floor
New York, NY 10038
Phone: (212) 349-5890; Fax: (212) 608-2310
E-mail: webmaster@nystla.org

North Carolina

North Carolina Bar Association
www.barlinc.org
800 Weston Pkwy.
Cary, NC 27519
Phone: (919) 677-0561; Fax: (919) 677-0761

North Carolina Academy of Trial Lawyers
www.ncatl.org
1312 Annapolis Dr., P.O. Box 10918
Raleigh, NC 27605
Phone: (800) 688-1413; (919) 832-1413; Fax: (919) 832-6361
E-mail: webmaster@ncatl.org

North Carolina Association of Defense Attorneys
www.ncada.org
P.O. Box 4830
Cary, NC 27519-4830
Phone: (919) 677-0561; Fax: (919) 677-0761

North Dakota

State Bar Association of North Dakota
P.O. Box 2136
Bismarck, ND 58502-2136
Phone: (701) 255-1404; Fax: (701) 224-1621

Ohio

Ohio State Bar
www.ohiobar.org
1700 Lake Shore Dr., P.O. Box 16562
Columbus, OH 43216-6562
Phone: (614) 487-2050; Fax: (614) 487-1008

Ohio Academy of Trial Lawyers
www.oatlaw.org
395 E. Broad Street, Suite 200
Columbus, OH 43215
Phone: (614) 341-6800; Fax: (614) 341-6810
E-mail: webmaster@oatlaw.org

Oklahoma

Oklahoma Bar Association
www.okbar.org
1901 N. Lincoln
Oklahoma City, OK 73105
Phone: (405) 524-2365; Fax: (405) 524-1115

Oklahoma Trial Lawyers Association
www.otla.org

Tulsa County Bar Association
www.tulsabar.com

Oregon

Oregon State Bar
www.osbar.org
5200 S.W. Meadows Road
Lake Oswego, OR 97035
Phone: (503) 620-0222; Fax: (503) 684-1366
E-mail: osbar@osbar.org

Oregon Trial Lawyers Association
www.otla-online.org
1020 S.W. Taylor, Suite 400
Portland, OR 97205
Phone: (503) 223-5587; Fax: (503) 223-4101
E-mail: otla@otla-online.org

Pennsylvania
Pennsylvania State Bar Association
www.pa-bar.org
100 South Street, P.O. Box 186
Harrisburg, PA 17108-0186
Phone: (717) 238-6715; Fax: (717) 238-1204

Pennsylvania Trial Lawyers Association
www.patla.org
121 South Broad Street, Suite 800
Philadelphia, PA 19107-4594
Phone: (215) 546-6451; Fax: (215) 546-5430
E-mail: patla@patla.org

Philadelphia Bar Association
www.philabar.org
1101 Market St., 11th Floor
Philadelphia, PA 19107-2911
Phone: (215) 238-6300
E-mail: philabar@philabar.org

Philadelphia Trial Lawyers Association
www.philatla.org
121 South Broad Street, Suite 800
Philadelphia, PA 19107-4594
Phone: (215) 732-2256
E-mail: ptla@concentric.net

Pennsylvania Defense Institute
133 State Street
Harrisburg, PA 17101
Phone: (717) 238-7806; (800) 734-0737; Fax: (717) 238-2766
E-mail: rbagley@localnet.com

Puerto Rico
Puerto Rico Bar Association
P.O. Box 1900
San Juan, PR 00902
Phone: (809) 721-3358; Fax: (809) 725-0330

Rhode Island
Rhode Island State Bar Association
www.ribar.com
115 Cedar Street
Providence, RI 02903
Phone: (401) 421-5740; Fax: (401) 421-2703

Rhode Island Trial Lawyers Association
E-mail: rita@ici.net

South Carolina
South Carolina Bar Association
www.scbar.org
950 Taylor Street, P.O. Box 608
Columbia, SC 29202
Phone: (803) 799-6653; Fax: (803) 799-4118

South Carolina Trial Lawyers Association
E-mail: LFrank822@aol.com

Charleston County Bar Association
www.charlestonbar.org

South Carolina Defense Trial Attorneys
3008 Millwood Avenue
Columbia, SC 29206
Phone: (800) 445-8629; Fax: (803) 252-5646
E-mail: info@scdtaa.com

South Dakota
South Dakota State Bar Association
www.sdbar.org
222 E. Capitol
Pierre, SD 57501
Phone: (605) 224-7554; Fax: (605) 224-0282

South Dakota Defense Lawyers Association
www.rapidnet.com/sddla
Pres: Patricia A. Meyers, Rapid City, SD
Fax: (605) 343-4262
E-mail: cphlaw@sdbar.org

Tennessee
Tennessee Bar Association
www.tba.org
3622 West End Avenue
Nashville, TN 37205-2403
Phone: (615) 383-7421; Fax: (615) 297-8058

Tennessee Trial Lawyers Association
TennTLA@aol.com

Texas
State Bar of Texas
www.texasbar.com
1414 Colorado, P.O. Box 12487
Austin, TX 78711-2487
Phone: (512) 463-1463; Fax: (512) 473-2295

Dallas Bar Association
www.dallasbar.com
2101 Ross Avenue
Dallas, TX 75201
Phone: (214) 220-7400; Fax: (214) 220-7465

Houston Bar Association
www.hba.org
1300 First City Tower, 1001 Fannin
Houston, TX 77002-6708
Phone: (713) 759-1133; Fax: (713) 759-1710

The San Antonio Trial Lawyers Association
www.satla.org
E-mail: admin@satla.org

Texas Trial Lawyers Association
www.ttla.com
Phone: (512) 476-3852

Texas Association of Defense Counsel
www.tadc.org
400 W. 15th St., Suite 315
Austin, TX 78701
Phone: (512) 476-5225; Fax: (512) 476-5394

Utah
Utah State Bar
www.utahbar.org
645 S. 200 East
Salt Lake City, UT 84111-3834
Phone: (801) 531-9077; Fax: (801) 531-0660
E-mail: info@utahbar.org

Utah Trial Lawyers Association
www.utla.org
645 South 200 East, #103
Salt Lake City, UT 84111
Phone: (801) 531-7514; Fax: (801) 531-1207

Vermont
Vermont State Bar Association
www.vtbar.org
35-37 Court Street, P.O. Box 100
Montpelier, VT 05602
Phone: (802) 223-2020; Fax: (802) 223-1573

Vermont Trial Lawyers Association
www.vtla.org
E-mail: vtla@vtla.org

<u>**Virginia**</u>
Virginia Bar Association
www.vba.org
7th & Franklin Building, 701 E. Franklin St., Suite 1120
Richmond, VA 23219
Phone: (804) 644-0041; Fax: (804) 644-0052

Virginia State Bar
www.vsb.org
707 E. Main Street, Suite 1500
Richmond, VA 23219-2803
Phone: (804) 775-0500; Fax: (804) 775-0501

Virginia Trial Lawyers Association
www.vtla.com
E-mail: vtla@vtla.com

Virginia Association of Defense Attorneys
www.vada.org
707 E. Main St., Suite 1605
Richmond, VA 23219
Phone: (804) 649-1002; Fax: (804) 649-1004
E-mail: vada@richmond.infi.net

<u>**Washington**</u>
Washington State Bar Association
www.wsba.org
500 Westin Bldg., 2001 6th Avenue
Seattle, WA 98121-2599
Phone: (206) 727-8200; Fax: (206) 727-8320

Washington State Trial Lawyers Association
www.wstla.org
1809 7th Ave. #1500
Seattle, WA 98101-1328
Phone: (206) 464-1011
E-mail: wstla@wstla.org

Washington Defense Trial Lawyers Association
www.wdtl.org
1601 Fifth Avenue, Suite 2400
Seattle WA 98101
Phone: (206) 521-6559; Fax: (206) 521-6501
E-mail: info@wdtl.org

<u>**West Virginia**</u>
West Virginia State Bar Association
www.wvbar.org
2006 Kanawha Boulevard East
Charleston, WV 25311
Phone: (304) 558-2456; Fax: (304) 558-2467

West Virginia Bar Association (Voluntary)
Route 1, Box 18, P.O. Box 180A
Charleston, WV 25339
Phone: (304) 342-1474

Defense Trial Counsel of West Virginia
www.dtcwv.org

West Virginia Trial Lawyers Association
www.wvtla.org
Boulevard Tower, Suite 207,
1018 Kanawha Boulevard East
Charleston, WV 25301
Phone: (304) 344-0692; Fax: (304) 343-7926
E-mail: egnor@wvtla.org

<u>**Wisconsin**</u>
The State Bar of Wisconsin
www.wisbar.org
P.O. Box 7158
Madison, WI 53707-7158
Phone: (608) 257-3838; (800) 362-8096 (statewide); (800) 728-7788 (nationwide); (800) 444-9404 (auto-attendant); Fax: (608) 257-5502

Milwaukee Bar Association
www.milwbar.org
424 East Wells Street
Milwaukee, WI 53202
Phone: (414) 274-6760; Fax: (414) 274-6765

Wisconsin Academy of Trial Lawyers
www.watl.org
44 East Mifflin Street, Suite 103
Madison, WI 53703-2897
Phone: (608) 257-5741; Fax: (608) 255-9285
E-mail: contact@watl.org

Civil Trial Counsel of Wisconsin
www.ctcw.org
P.O. Box 169
Madison, WI 53701
Phone: (608) 283-2586; Fax: (608) 283-2589
E-mail: hough@hfomadison.com

Wyoming

Wyoming State Bar Association
www.wyomingbar.org
500 Randall Avenue, P.O. Box 109
Cheyenne, WY 82001
Phone: (307) 632-9061; Fax: (307) 632-3737

Appendix P Federal Rules of Evidence

ARTICLE I. GENERAL PROVISIONS
Rule 101. Scope
Rule 102. Purpose and Construction
Rule 103. Rulings on Evidence
Rule 104. Preliminary Questions
Rule 105. Limited Admissibility
Rule 106. Remainder of or Related Writings or Recorded Statements
ARTICLE II. JUDICIAL NOTICE
Rule 201. Judicial Notice of Adjudicative Facts
ARTICLE III. PRESUMPTIONS IN CIVIL ACTIONS AND PROCEEDINGS
Rule 301. Presumptions in General Civil Actions and Proceedings
Rule 302. Applicability of State Law in Civil Actions and Proceedings
ARTICLE IV. RELEVANCY AND ITS LIMITS
Rule 401. Definition of "Relevant Evidence"
Rule 402. Relevant Evidence Generally Admissible; Irrelevant Evidence Inadmissible
Rule 403. Exclusion of Relevant Evidence on Grounds of Prejudice, Confusion, or Waste of Time
Rule 404. Character Evidence Not Admissible To Prove Conduct; Exceptions; Other Crimes
Rule 405. Methods of Proving Character
Rule 406. Habit; Routine Practice
Rule 407. Subsequent Remedial Measures
Rule 408. Compromise and Offers to Compromise
Rule 409. Payment of Medical and Similar Expenses
Rule 410. Inadmissibility of Pleas, Plea Discussions, and Related Statements
Rule 411. Liability Insurance
Rule 412. Sex Offense Cases; Relevance of Alleged Victim's Past Sexual Behavior or Alleged Sexual Predisposition
Rule 413. Evidence of Similar Crimes in Sexual Assault Cases
Rule 414. Evidence of Similar Crimes in Child Molestation Cases
Rule 415. Evidence of Similar Acts in Civil Cases Concerning Sexual Assault or Child Molestation
ARTICLE V. PRIVILEGES
Rule 501. General Rule
ARTICLE VI. WITNESSES
Rule 601. General Rule of Competency
Rule 602. Lack of Personal Knowledge
Rule 603. Oath or Affirmation
Rule 604. Interpreters
Rule 605. Competency of Judge as Witness
Rule 606. Competency of Juror as Witness
Rule 607. Who May Impeach
Rule 608. Evidence of Character and Conduct of Witness
Rule 609. Impeachment by Evidence of Conviction of Crime

ARTICLE I. GENERAL PROVISIONS

Rule 101. Scope

These rules govern proceedings in the courts of the United States and before United States bankruptcy judges and United States magistrate judges, to the extent and with the exceptions stated in rule 1101.

Rule 102. Purpose and Construction

These rules shall be construed to secure fairness in administration, elimination of unjustifiable expense and delay, and promotion of growth and development of the law of evidence to the end that the truth may be ascertained and proceedings justly determined.

Rule 103. Rulings on Evidence
(a) Effect of erroneous ruling.
Error may not be predicated upon a ruling which admits or excludes evidence unless a substantial right of the party is affected, and
(1) *Objection*. In case the ruling is one admitting evidence, a timely objection or motion to strike appears of record, stating the specific ground of objection, if the specific ground was not apparent from the context; or
(2) *Offer of proof*. In case the ruling is one excluding evidence, the substance of the evidence was made known to the court by offer or was apparent from the context within which questions were asked.
(b) Record of offer and ruling.
The court may add any other or further statement which shows the character of the evidence, the form in which it was offered, the objection made, and the ruling thereon. It may direct the making of an offer in question and answer form.
(c) Hearing of jury.
In jury cases, proceedings shall be conducted, to the extent practicable, so as to prevent inadmissible evidence from being suggested to the jury by any means, such as making statements or offers of proof or asking questions in the hearing of the jury.
(d) Plain error.
Nothing in this rule precludes taking notice of plain errors affecting substantial rights although they were not brought to the attention of the court.
Rule 104. Preliminary Questions
(a) Questions of admissibility generally.
Preliminary questions concerning the qualification of a person to be a witness, the existence of a privilege, or the admissibility of evidence shall be determined by the court, subject to the provisions of subdivision (b). In making its determination it is not bound by the rules of evidence except those with respect to privileges.
(b) Relevancy conditioned on fact.
When the relevancy of evidence depends upon the fulfillment of a condition of fact, the court shall admit it upon, or subject to, the introduction of evidence sufficient to support a finding of the fulfillment of the condition.
(c) Hearing of jury.
Hearings on the admissibility of confessions shall in all cases be conducted out of the hearing of the jury. Hearings on other preliminary matters shall be so conducted when the interests of justice require, or when an accused is a witness and so requests.
(d) Testimony by accused.
The accused does not, by testifying upon a preliminary matter, become subject to cross-examination as to other issues in the case.
(e) Weight and credibility.
This rule does not limit the right of a party to introduce before the jury evidence relevant to weight or credibility.
Rule 105. Limited Admissibility
When evidence which is admissible as to one party or for one purpose but not admissible as to another party or for another purpose is admitted, the court, upon request, shall restrict the evidence to its proper scope and instruct the jury accordingly.

Rule 106. Remainder of or Related Writings or Recorded Statements
When a writing or recorded statement or part thereof is introduced by a party, an adverse party may require the introduction at that time of any other part or any other writing or recorded statement which ought in fairness to be considered contemporaneously with it.

ARTICLE II. JUDICIAL NOTICE

Rule 201. Judicial Notice of Adjudicative Facts
(a) Scope of rule.
This rule governs only judicial notice of adjudicative facts.
(b) Kinds of facts.
A judicially noticed fact must be one not subject to reasonable dispute in that it is either (1) generally known within the territorial jurisdiction of the trial court or (2) capable of accurate and ready determination by resort to sources whose accuracy cannot reasonably be questioned.
(c) When discretionary.
A court may take judicial notice, whether requested or not.
(d) When mandatory.
A court shall take judicial notice if requested by a party and supplied with the necessary information.
(e) Opportunity to be heard.
A party is entitled upon timely request to an opportunity to be heard as to the propriety of taking judicial notice and the tenor of the matter noticed. In the absence of prior notification, the request may be made after judicial notice has been taken.
(f) Time of taking notice.
Judicial notice may be taken at any stage of the proceeding.
(g) Instructing jury.
In a civil action or proceeding, the court shall instruct the jury to accept as conclusive any fact judicially noticed. In a criminal case, the court shall instruct the jury that it may, but is not required to, accept as conclusive any fact judicially noticed.

ARTICLE III. PRESUMPTIONS IN CIVIL ACTIONS AND PROCEEDINGS

Rule 301. Presumptions in General Civil Actions and Proceedings
In all civil actions and proceedings not otherwise provided for by Act of Congress or by these rules, a presumption imposes on the party against whom it is directed the burden of going forward with evidence to rebut or meet the presumption, but does not shift to such party the burden of proof in the sense of the risk of nonpersuasion, which remains throughout the trial upon the party on whom it was originally cast.
Rule 302. Applicability of State Law in Civil Actions and Proceedings
In civil actions and proceedings, the effect of a presumption respecting a fact which is an element of a claim or defense as to which State law supplies the rule of decision is determined in accordance with State law.

ARTICLE IV. RELEVANCY AND ITS LIMITS

Rule 401. Definition of "Relevant Evidence"
"Relevant evidence" means evidence having any tendency to make the existence of any fact that is of consequence to the determination of the action more probable or less probable than it would be without the evidence.

Rule 402. Relevant Evidence Generally Admissible; Irrelevant Evidence Inadmissible

All relevant evidence is admissible, except as otherwise provided by the Constitution of the United States, by Act of Congress, by these rules, or by other rules prescribed by the Supreme Court pursuant to statutory authority. Evidence which is not relevant is not admissible.

Rule 403. Exclusion of Relevant Evidence on Grounds of Prejudice, Confusion, or Waste of Time

Although relevant, evidence may be excluded if its probative value is substantially outweighed by the danger of unfair prejudice, confusion of the issues, or misleading the jury, or by considerations of undue delay, waste of time, or needless presentation of cumulative evidence.

Rule 404. Character Evidence Not Admissible To Prove Conduct; Exceptions; Other Crimes

(a) Character evidence generally.

Evidence of a person's character or a trait of character is not admissible for the purpose of proving action in conformity therewith on a particular occasion, except:

(1) *Character of accused.* Evidence of a pertinent trait of character offered by an accused, or by the prosecution to rebut the same;

(2) *Character of victim.* Evidence of a pertinent trait of character of the victim of the crime offered by an accused, or by the prosecution to rebut the same, or evidence of a character trait of peacefulness of the victim offered by the prosecution in a homicide case to rebut evidence that the victim was the first aggressor;

(3) *Character of witness.* Evidence of the character of a witness, as provided in rules 607, 608, and 609.

(b) Other crimes, wrongs, or acts.

Evidence of other crimes, wrongs, or acts is not admissible to prove the character of a person in order to show action in conformity therewith. It may, however, be admissible for other purposes, such as proof of motive, opportunity, intent, preparation, plan, knowledge, identity, or absence of mistake or accident, provided that upon request by the accused, the prosecution in a criminal case shall provide reasonable notice in advance of trial, or during trial if the court excuses pretrial notice on good cause shown, of the general nature of any such evidence it intends to introduce at trial.

Rule 405. Methods of Proving Character

(a) Reputation or opinion.

In all cases in which evidence of character or a trait of character of a person is admissible, proof may be made by testimony as to reputation or by testimony in the form of an opinion. On cross-examination, inquiry is allowable into relevant specific instances of conduct.

(b) Specific instances of conduct.

In cases in which character or a trait of character of a person is an essential element of a charge, claim, or defense, proof may also be made of specific instances of that person's conduct.

Rule 406. Habit; Routine Practice

Evidence of the habit of a person or of the routine practice of an organization, whether corroborated or not and regardless of the presence of eyewitnesses, is relevant to prove that the conduct of the person or organization on a particular occasion was in conformity with the habit or routine practice.

Rule 407. Subsequent Remedial Measures
When, after an injury or harm allegedly caused by an event, measures are taken that, if taken previously, would have made the injury or harm less likely to occur, evidence of the subsequent measures is not admissible to prove negligence, culpable conduct, a defect in a product, a defect in a product's design, or a need for a warning or instruction. This rule does not require the exclusion of evidence of subsequent measures when offered for another purpose, such as proving ownership, control, or feasibility of precautionary measures, if controverted, or impeachment.
Rule 408. Compromise and Offers to Compromise
Evidence of (1) furnishing or offering or promising to furnish, or (2) accepting or offering or promising to accept, a valuable consideration in compromising or attempting to compromise a claim which was disputed as to either validity or amount, is not admissible to prove liability for or invalidity of the claim or its amount. Evidence of conduct or statements made in compromise negotiations is likewise not admissible. This rule does not require the exclusion of any evidence otherwise discoverable merely because it is presented in the course of compromise negotiations. This rule also does not require exclusion when the evidence is offered for another purpose, such as proving bias or prejudice of a witness, negating a contention of undue delay, or proving an effort to obstruct a criminal investigation or prosecution.
Rule 409. Payment of Medical and Similar Expenses
Evidence of furnishing or offering or promising to pay medical, hospital, or similar expenses occasioned by an injury is not admissible to prove liability for the injury.
Rule 410. Inadmissibility of Pleas, Plea Discussions, and Related Statements
Except as otherwise provided in this rule, evidence of the following is not, in any civil or criminal proceeding, admissible against the defendant who made the plea or was a participant in the plea discussions:
(1) a plea of guilty which was later withdrawn;
(2) a plea of nolo contendere;
(3) any statement made in the course of any proceedings under Rule 11 of the Federal Rules of Criminal Procedure or comparable state procedure regarding either of the foregoing pleas; or
(4) any statement made in the course of plea discussions with an attorney for the prosecuting authority which do not result in a plea of guilty or which result in a plea of guilty later withdrawn.
However, such a statement is admissible (i) in any proceeding wherein another statement made in the course of the same plea or plea discussions has been introduced and the statement ought in fairness be considered contemporaneously with it, or (ii) in a criminal proceeding for perjury or false statement if the statement was made by the defendant under oath, on the record and in the presence of counsel.
Rule 411. Liability Insurance
Evidence that a person was or was not insured against liability is not admissible upon the issue whether the person acted negligently or otherwise wrongfully. This rule does not require the exclusion of evidence of insurance against liability when offered for another purpose, such as proof of agency, ownership, or control, or bias or prejudice of a witness.

Rule 412. Sex Offense Cases; Relevance of Alleged Victim's Past Sexual Behavior or Alleged Sexual Predisposition

(a) Evidence generally inadmissible.

The following evidence is not admissible in any civil or criminal proceeding involving alleged sexual misconduct except as provided in subdivisions (b) and (c):

(1) Evidence offered to prove that any alleged victim engaged in other sexual behavior.

(2) Evidence offered to prove any alleged victim's sexual predisposition.

(b) Exceptions.

(1) In a criminal case, the following evidence is admissible, if otherwise admissible under these rules:

(A) evidence of specific instances of sexual behavior by the alleged victim offered to prove that a person other than the accused was the source of semen, injury, or other physical evidence;

(B) evidence of specific instances of sexual behavior by the alleged victim with respect to the person accused of the sexual misconduct offered by the accused to prove consent or by the prosecution; and

(C) evidence the exclusion of which would violate the constitutional rights of the defendant.

(2) In a civil case, evidence offered to prove the sexual behavior or sexual predisposition of any alleged victim is admissible if it is otherwise admissible under these rules and its probative value substantially outweighs the danger of harm to any victim and of unfair prejudice to any party. Evidence of an alleged victim's reputation is admissible only if it has been placed in controversy by the alleged victim.

(c) Procedure to determine admissibility.

(1) A party intending to offer evidence under subdivision (b) must --

(A) file a written motion at least 14 days before trial specifically describing the evidence and stating the purpose for which it is offered unless the court, for good cause requires a different time for filing or permits filing during trial; and

(B) serve the motion on all parties and notify the alleged victim or, when appropriate, the alleged victim's guardian or representative.

(2) Before admitting evidence under this rule the court must conduct a hearing in camera and afford the victim and parties a right to attend and be heard. The motion, related papers, and the record of the hearing must be sealed and remain under seal unless the court orders otherwise.

Rule 413. Evidence of Similar Crimes in Sexual Assault Cases

(a) In a criminal case in which the defendant is accused of an offense of sexual assault, evidence of the defendant's commission of another offense or offenses of sexual assault is admissible, and may be considered for its bearing on any matter to which it is relevant.

(b) In a case in which the Government intends to offer evidence under this rule, the attorney for the Government shall disclose the evidence to the defendant, including statements of witnesses or a summary of the substance of any testimony that is expected to be offered, at least fifteen days before the scheduled date of trial or at such later time as the court may allow for good cause.

(c) This rule shall not be construed to limit the admission or consideration of evidence under any other rule.

(d) For purposes of this rule and Rule 415, "offense of sexual assault" means a crime under Federal law or the law of a State (as defined in section 513 of title 18, United States Code) that involved--
(1) any conduct proscribed by chapter 109A of title 18, United States Code;
(2) contact, without consent, between any part of the defendant's body or an object and the genitals or anus of another person;
(3) contact, without consent, between the genitals or anus of the defendant and any part of another person's body;
(4) deriving sexual pleasure or gratification from the infliction of death, bodily injury, or physical pain on another person; or
(5) an attempt or conspiracy to engage in conduct described in paragraphs (1)-(4).

Rule 414. Evidence of Similar Crimes in Child Molestation Cases

(a) In a criminal case in which the defendant is accused of an offense of child molestation, evidence of the defendant's commission of another offense or offenses of child molestation is admissible, and may be considered for its bearing on any matter to which it is relevant.
(b) In a case in which the Government intends to offer evidence under this rule, the attorney for the Government shall disclose the evidence to the defendant, including statements of witnesses or a summary of the substance of any testimony that is expected to be offered, at least fifteen days before the scheduled date of trial or at such later time as the court may allow for good cause.
(c) This rule shall not be construed to limit the admission or consideration of evidence under any other rule.
(d) For purposes of this rule and Rule 415, "child" means a person below the age of fourteen, and "offense of child molestation" means a crime under Federal law or the law of a State (as defined in section 513 of title 18, United States Code) that involved—
(1) any conduct proscribed by chapter 109A of title 18, United States Code, that was committed in relation to a child;
(2) any conduct proscribed by chapter 110 of title 18, United States Code;
(3) contact between any part of the defendant's body or an object and the genitals or anus of a child;
(4) contact between the genitals or anus of the defendant and any part of the body of a child;
(5) deriving sexual pleasure or gratification from the infliction of death, bodily injury, or physical pain on a child; or
(6) an attempt or conspiracy to engage in conduct described in paragraphs (1)-(5).

Rule 415. Evidence of Similar Acts in Civil Cases Concerning Sexual Assault or Child Molestation

(a) In a civil case in which a claim for damages or other relief is predicated on a party's alleged commission of conduct constituting an offense of sexual assault or child molestation, evidence of that party's commission of another offense or offenses of sexual assault or child molestation is admissible and may be considered as provided in Rule 413 and Rule 414 of these rules.
(b) A party who intends to offer evidence under this Rule shall disclose the evidence to the party against whom it will be offered, including statements of witnesses or a summary of the substance of any testimony that is expected to be offered, at least fifteen days before the scheduled date of trial or at such later time as the court may allow for good cause.

(c) This rule shall not be construed to limit the admission or consideration of evidence under any other rule.

ARTICLE V. PRIVILEGES

Rule 501. General Rule

Except as otherwise required by the Constitution of the United States or provided by Act of Congress or in rules prescribed by the Supreme Court pursuant to statutory authority, the privilege of a witness, person, government, State, or political subdivision thereof shall be governed by the principles of the common law as they may be interpreted by the courts of the United States in the light of reason and experience. However, in civil actions and proceedings, with respect to an element of a claim or defense as to which State law supplies the rule of decision, the privilege of a witness, person, government, State, or political subdivision thereof shall be determined in accordance with State law.

ARTICLE VI. WITNESSES

Rule 601. General Rule of Competency

Every person is competent to be a witness except as otherwise provided in these rules. However, in civil actions and proceedings, with respect to an element of a claim or defense as to which State law supplies the rule of decision, the competency of a witness shall be determined in accordance with State law.

Rule 602. Lack of Personal Knowledge

A witness may not testify to a matter unless evidence is introduced sufficient to support a finding that the witness has personal knowledge of the matter. Evidence to prove personal knowledge may, but need not, consist of the witness' own testimony. This rule is subject to the provisions of rule 703, relating to opinion testimony by expert witnesses.

Rule 603. Oath or Affirmation

Before testifying, every witness shall be required to declare that the witness will testify truthfully, by oath or affirmation administered in a form calculated to awaken the witness' conscience and impress the witness' mind with the duty to do so.

Rule 604. Interpreters

An interpreter is subject to the provisions of these rules relating to qualification as an expert and the administration of an oath or affirmation to make a true translation.

Rule 605. Competency of Judge as Witness

The judge presiding at the trial may not testify in that trial as a witness. No objection need be made in order to preserve the point.

Rule 606. Competency of Juror as Witness

(a) At the trial.

A member of the jury may not testify as a witness before that jury in the trial of the case in which the juror is sitting. If the juror is called so to testify, the opposing party shall be afforded an opportunity to object out of the presence of the jury.

(b) Inquiry into validity of verdict or indictment.

Upon an inquiry into the validity of a verdict or indictment, a juror may not testify as to any matter or statement occurring during the course of the jury's deliberations or to the effect of anything upon that or any other juror's mind or emotions as influencing the juror to assent to or dissent from the verdict or indictment or concerning the juror's mental processes in connection therewith, except that a juror may testify on the question whether extraneous prejudicial information was improperly brought to the jury's attention or whether any outside influence was improperly brought to bear upon any juror. Nor may a juror's affidavit or evidence of any statement by the juror concerning a matter about which the juror would be precluded from testifying be received for these purposes.

Rule 607. Who May Impeach

The credibility of a witness may be attacked by any party, including the party calling the witness.

Rule 608. Evidence of Character and Conduct of Witness

(a) Opinion and reputation evidence of character.

The credibility of a witness may be attacked or supported by evidence in the form of opinion or reputation, but subject to these limitations: (1) the evidence may refer only to character for truthfulness or untruthfulness, and (2) evidence of truthful character is admissible only after the character of the witness for truthfulness has been attacked by opinion or reputation evidence or otherwise.

(b) Specific instances of conduct.

Specific instances of the conduct of a witness, for the purpose of attacking or supporting the witness' credibility, other than conviction of crime as provided in rule 609, may not be proved by extrinsic evidence. They may, however, in the discretion of the court, if probative of truthfulness or untruthfulness, be inquired into on cross-examination of the witness (1) concerning the witness' character for truthfulness or untruthfulness, or (2) concerning the character for truthfulness or untruthfulness of another witness as to which character the witness being cross-examined has testified.

The giving of testimony, whether by an accused or by any other witness, does not operate as a waiver of the accused's or the witness' privilege against self-incrimination when examined with respect to matters which relate only to credibility.

Rule 609. Impeachment by Evidence of Conviction of Crime

(a) General rule.

For the purpose of attacking the credibility of a witness,

(1) evidence that a witness other than an accused has been convicted of a crime shall be admitted, subject to Rule 403, if the crime was punishable by death or imprisonment in excess of one year under the law under which the witness was convicted, and evidence that an accused has been convicted of such a crime shall be admitted if the court determines that the probative value of admitting this evidence outweighs its prejudicial effect to the accused; and

(2) evidence that any witness has been convicted of a crime shall be admitted if it involved dishonesty or false statement, regardless of the punishment.

(b) Time limit.

Evidence of a conviction under this rule is not admissible if a period of more than ten years has elapsed since the date of the conviction or of the release of the witness from the confinement imposed for that conviction, whichever is the later date, unless the court determines, in the interests of justice, that the probative value of the conviction supported by specific facts and circumstances substantially outweighs its prejudicial effect. However, evidence of a conviction more than 10 years old as calculated herein, is not admissible unless the proponent gives to the adverse party sufficient advance written notice of intent to use such evidence to provide the adverse party with a fair opportunity to contest the use of such evidence.

(c) Effect of pardon, annulment, or certificate of rehabilitation.
Evidence of a conviction is not admissible under this rule if (1) the conviction has been the subject of a pardon, annulment, certificate of rehabilitation, or other equivalent procedure based on a finding of the rehabilitation of the person convicted, and that person has not been convicted of a subsequent crime which was punishable by death or imprisonment in excess of one year, or (2) the conviction has been the subject of a pardon, annulment, or other equivalent procedure based on a finding of innocence.
(d) Juvenile adjudications.
Evidence of juvenile adjudications is generally not admissible under this rule. The court may, however, in a criminal case allow evidence of a juvenile adjudication of a witness other than the accused if conviction of the offense would be admissible to attack the credibility of an adult and the court is satisfied that admission in evidence is necessary for a fair determination of the issue of guilt or innocence.
(e) Pendency of appeal.
The pendency of an appeal therefrom does not render evidence of a conviction inadmissible. Evidence of the pendency of an appeal is admissible.

Rule 610. Religious Beliefs or Opinions

Evidence of the beliefs or opinions of a witness on matters of religion is not admissible for the purpose of showing that by reason of their nature the witness' credibility is impaired or enhanced.

Rule 611. Mode and Order of Interrogation and Presentation

(a) Control by court.
The court shall exercise reasonable control over the mode and order of interrogating witnesses and presenting evidence so as to (1) make the interrogation and presentation effective for the ascertainment of the truth, (2) avoid needless consumption of time, and (3) protect witnesses from harassment or undue embarrassment.
(b) Scope of cross-examination.
Cross-examination should be limited to the subject matter of the direct examination and matters affecting the credibility of the witness. The court may, in the exercise of discretion, permit inquiry into additional matters as if on direct examination.
(c) Leading questions.
Leading questions should not be used on the direct examination of a witness except as may be necessary to develop the witness' testimony. Ordinarily leading questions should be permitted on cross-examination. When a party calls a hostile witness, an adverse party, or a witness identified with an adverse party, interrogation may be by leading questions.

Rule 612. Writing Used to Refresh Memory

Except as otherwise provided in criminal proceedings by section 3500 of title 18, United States Code, if a witness uses a writing to refresh memory for the purpose of testifying, either—
(1) while testifying, or
(2) before testifying, if the court in its discretion determines it is necessary in the interests of justice,
an adverse party is entitled to have the writing produced at the hearing, to inspect it, to cross-examine the witness thereon, and to introduce in evidence those portions which relate to the testimony of the witness. If it is claimed that the writing contains matters not related to the subject matter of the testimony the court shall examine the

writing in camera, excise any portions not so related, and order delivery of the remainder to the party entitled thereto. Any portion withheld over objections shall be preserved and made available to the appellate court in the event of an appeal. If a writing is not produced or delivered pursuant to order under this rule, the court shall make any order justice requires, except that in criminal cases when the prosecution elects not to comply, the order shall be one striking the testimony or, if the court in its discretion determines that the interests of justice so require, declaring a mistrial.

Rule 613. Prior Statements of Witnesses

(a) Examining witness concerning prior statement.

In examining a witness concerning a prior statement made by the witness, whether written or not, the statement need not be shown nor its contents disclosed to the witness at that time, but on request the same shall be shown or disclosed to opposing counsel.

(b) Extrinsic evidence of prior inconsistent statement of witness.

Extrinsic evidence of a prior inconsistent statement by a witness is not admissible unless the witness is afforded an opportunity to explain or deny the same and the opposite party is afforded an opportunity to interrogate the witness thereon, or the interests of justice otherwise require. This provision does not apply to admissions of a party-opponent as defined in rule 801(d)(2).

Rule 614. Calling and Interrogation of Witnesses by Court

(a) Calling by court.

The court may, on its own motion or at the suggestion of a party, call witnesses, and all parties are entitled to cross-examine witnesses thus called.

(b) Interrogation by court.

The court may interrogate witnesses, whether called by itself or by a party.

(c) Objections.

Objections to the calling of witnesses by the court or to interrogation by it may be made at the time or at the next available opportunity when the jury is not present.

Rule 615. Exclusion of Witnesses

At the request of a party the court shall order witnesses excluded so that they cannot hear the testimony of other witnesses, and it may make the order of its own motion. This rule does not authorize exclusion of (1) a party who is a natural person, or (2) an officer or employee of a party which is not a natural person designated as its representative by its attorney, or (3) a person whose presence is shown by a party to be essential to the presentation of the party's cause, or (4) a person authorized by statute to be present.

ARTICLE VII. OPINIONS AND EXPERT TESTIMONY

Rule 701. Opinion Testimony by Lay Witnesses

If the witness is not testifying as an expert, the witness' testimony in the form of opinions or inferences is limited to those opinions or inferences which are (a) rationally based on the perception of the witness and (b) helpful to a clear understanding of the witness' testimony or the determination of a fact in issue.

NOTES TO RULE 701

Notes of Advisory Committee on Rules.

The rule retains the traditional objective of putting the trier of fact in possession of an accurate reproduction of the event.

Limitation (a) is the familiar requirement of firsthand knowledge or observation.

Limitation (b) is phrased in terms of requiring testimony to be helpful in resolving issues. Witnesses often find difficulty in expressing themselves in language which is not that of an opinion or conclusion. While the courts have made concessions in certain recurring situations, necessity as a standard for permitting opinions and conclusions has proved too elusive and too unadaptable to particular situations for purposes of satisfactory judicial administration. McCormick § 11. Moreover, the practical impossibility of determinating by rule what is a "fact," demonstrated by a century of litigation of the question of what is a fact for purposes of pleading under the Field Code, extends into evidence also. 7 Wigmore § 1919. The rule assumes that the natural characteristics of the adversary system will generally lead to an acceptable result, since the detailed account carries more conviction than the broad assertion, and a lawyer can be expected to display his witness to the best advantage. If he fails to do so, cross-examination and argument will point up the weakness. See Ladd, Expert Testimony, 5 Vand.L.Rev. 414, 415-417 (1952). If, despite these considerations, attempts are made to introduce meaningless assertions which amount to little more than choosing up sides, exclusion for lack of helpfulness is called for by the rule.

The language of the rule is substantially that of Uniform Rule 56(1). Similar provisions are California Evidence Code § 800; Kansas Code of Civil Procedure § 60-456(a); New Jersey Evidence Rule 56(1).

Rule 702. Testimony by Experts

If scientific, technical, or other specialized knowledge will assist the trier of fact to understand the evidence or to determine a fact in issue, a witness qualified as an expert by knowledge, skill, experience, training, or education, may testify thereto in the form of an opinion or otherwise.

NOTES TO RULE 702

Notes of Advisory Committee on Rules.

An intelligent evaluation of facts is often difficult or impossible without the application of some scientific, technical, or other specialized knowledge. The most common source of this knowledge is the expert witness, although there are other techniques for supplying it.

Most of the literature assumes that experts testify only in the form of opinions. The assumption is logically unfounded. The rule accordingly recognizes that an expert on the stand may give a dissertation or exposition of scientific or other principles relevant to the case, leaving the trier of fact to apply them to the facts. Since much of the criticism of expert testimony has centered upon the hypothetical question, it seems wise to recognize that opinions are not indispensable and to encourage the use of expert testimony in non-opinion form when counsel believes the trier can itself draw the requisite inference. The use of opinions is not abolished by the rule, however. It will continue to be permissible for the experts to take the further step of suggesting the inference which should be drawn from applying the specialized knowledge to the facts. See *Rules 703 to 705*.

Whether the situation is a proper one for the use of expert testimony is to be determined on the basis of assisting the trier. "There is no more certain test for determining when experts may be used than the common sense inquiry whether the untrained layman would be qualified to determine intelligently and to the best possible degree the particular issue without enlightenment from those having a specialized understanding of the subject involved in the dispute." Ladd, *Expert Testimony*, 5 VAND.L.REV. 414, 418 (1952). When opinions are excluded, it is because they are unhelpful and therefore superfluous and a waste of time. 7 WIGMORE § 1918.

The rule is broadly phrased. The fields of knowledge which may be drawn upon are not limited merely to the "scientific" and "technical" but extend to all "specialized" knowledge. Similarly, the expert is viewed, not in a narrow sense, but as a person qualified by "knowledge, skill, experience, training or education." Thus within the scope of the rule are not only experts in the strictest sense of the word, e.g., physicians, physicists, and architects, but also the large group sometimes called "skilled" witnesses, such as bankers or landowners testifying to land values.

Rule 703. Bases of Opinion Testimony by Experts

The facts or data in the particular case upon which an expert bases an opinion or inference may be those perceived by or made known to the expert at or before the hearing. If of a type reasonably relied upon by experts in the particular field in forming opinions or inferences upon the subject, the facts or data need not be admissible in evidence.

NOTES TO RULE 703

Notes of Advisory Committee on Rules.

Facts or data upon which expert opinions are based may, under the rule, be derived from three possible sources. The first is the firsthand observation of the witness, with opinions based thereon traditionally allowed. A treating physician affords an example. Rheingold, The Basis of Medical Testimony, 15 Vand.L.Rev. 473, 489 (1962). Whether he must first relate his observations is treated in Rule 705. The second source, presentation at the trial, also reflects existing practice. The technique may be the familiar hypothetical question or having the expert attend the trial and hear the testimony establishing the facts. Problems of determining what testimony the expert relied upon, when the latter technique is employed and the testimony is in conflict, may be resolved by resort to Rule 705. The third source contemplated by the rule consists of presentation of data to the expert outside of court and other than by his own perception. In this respect the rule is designed to broaden the basis for expert opinions beyond that current in many jurisdictions and to bring the judicial practice into line with the practice of the experts themselves when not in court. Thus a physician in his own practice bases his diagnosis on information from numerous sources and of considerable variety, including statements by patients and relatives, reports and opinions from nurses, technicians and other doctors, hospital records, and X rays. Most of them are admissible in evidence, but only with the expenditure of substantial time in producing and examining various authenticating witnesses. The physician makes life-and-death decisions in reliance upon them. His validation, expertly performed and subject to cross-examination, ought to suffice for judicial purposes. Rheingold, supra, at 531; McCormick § 15. A similar provision is California Evidence Code § 801(b).

The rule also offers a more satisfactory basis for ruling upon the admissibility of public opinion poll evidence. Attention is directed to the validity of the techniques employed rather than to relatively fruitless inquiries whether hearsay is involved. See Judge Feinberg's careful analysis in Zippo Mfg. Co. v. Rogers Imports, Inc., 216 F.Supp. 670 (S.D.N.Y. 1963) See also Blum et al, The Art of Opinion Research: A Lawyer's Appraisal of an Emerging Service, 24 U.Chi.L.Rev. 1 (1956); Bonynge, Trademark Surveys and Techniques and Their Use in Litigation, 48 A.B.A.J. 329 (1962); Zeisel, The Uniqueness of Survey Evidence, 45 Cornell L.Q. 322 (1960); Annot., 76 A.L.R.2d 919.

If it be feared that enlargement of permissible data may tend to break down the rules of exclusion unduly, notice should be taken that the rule requires that the facts or data "be of a type reasonably relied upon by experts in the particular field." The language would not warrant admitting in evidence the opinion of an "accidentologist" as to the point of impact in an automobile collision based on statements of bystanders, since this requirement is not satisfied. See Comment, Cal.Law Rev.Comm'n, Recommendation Proposing an Evidence Code 148-150 (1965).

Rule 704. Opinion on Ultimate Issue

(a) Except as provided in subdivision (b), testimony in the form of an opinion or inference otherwise admissible is not objectionable because it embraces an ultimate issue to be decided by the trier of fact.

(b) No expert witness testifying with respect to the mental state or condition of a defendant in a criminal case may state an opinion or inference as to whether the defendant did or did not have the mental state or condition constituting an element of the crime charged or of a defense thereto. Such ultimate issues are matters for the trier of fact alone.

NOTES TO RULE 704

Notes of Advisory Committee on Rules.

The basic approach to opinions, lay and expert, in these rules is to admit them when helpful to the trier of fact. In order to render this approach fully effective and to allay any doubt on the subject, the so-called "ultimate issue" rule is specifically abolished by the instant rule.

The older cases often contained strictures against allowing witnesses to express opinions upon ultimate issues, as a particular aspect of the rule against opinions. The rule was unduly restrictive, difficult of application, and generally served only to deprive the trier of fact of useful information. 7 Wigmore §§ 1920, 1921; McCormick § 12. The basis usually assigned for the rule, to prevent the witness from "usurping the province of the jury," is aptly characterized as "empty rhetoric." 7 Wigmore § 1920, p. 17. Efforts to meet the felt needs of particular situations led to odd verbal circumlocutions which were said not to violate the rule. Thus a witness could express his estimate of the criminal responsibility of an accused in terms of sanity or insanity, but not in terms of ability to tell right from wrong or other more modern standard. And in cases of medical causation, witnesses were sometimes required to couch their opinions in cautious phrases of "might or could," rather than "did," though the result was to deprive many opinions of the positiveness to which they were entitled, accompanied by the hazard of a ruling of insufficiency to support a verdict. In other instances the rule was simply disregarded, and, as concessions to need, opinions were allowed upon such matters as intoxication, speed, handwriting, and value, although more precise coincidence with an ultimate issue would scarcely be possible.

Many modern decisions illustrate the trend to abandon the rule completely. People v. Wilson, 25 Cal.2d 341, 153 P.2d 720 (1944), whether abortion necessary to save life of patient; Clifford-Jacobs Forging Co. v. Industrial Comm., 19 Ill.2d 236, 166 N.E.2d 582 (1960), medical causation; Dowling v. L. H. Shattuck, Inc., 91 N.H. 234, 17 A.2d 529 (1941), proper method of shoring ditch; Schweiger v. Solbeck, 191 Or. 454, 230 P.2d 195 (1951), cause of landslide. In each instance the opinion was allowed.

The abolition of the ultimate issue rule does not lower the bars so as to admit all opinions. Under Rules 701 and 702, opinions must be helpful to the trier of fact, and Rule 403 provides for exclusion of evidence which wastes time. These provisions afford ample assurances against the admission of opinions which would merely tell the jury what result to reach, somewhat in the manner of the oath-helpers of an earlier day. They also stand ready to exclude opinions phrased in terms of inadequately explored legal criteria. Thus the question, "Did T have capacity to make a will?" would be excluded, while the question, "Did T have sufficient mental capacity to know the nature and extent of his property and the natural objects of his bounty and to formulate a rational scheme of distribution?" would be allowed. McCormick § 12.

For similar provisions see Uniform Rule 56(4); California Evidence Code § 805; Kansas Code of Civil Procedures § 60-456(d); New Jersey Evidence Rule 56(3).

Rule 705. Disclosure of Facts or Data Underlying Expert Opinion

The expert may testify in terms of opinion or inference and give reasons therefor without first testifying to the underlying facts or data, unless the court requires otherwise. The expert may in any event be required to disclose the underlying facts or data on cross-examination.

NOTES TO RULE 705

Notes of Advisory Committee on Rules.

The hypothetical question has been the target of a great deal of criticism as encouraging partisan bias, affording an opportunity for summing up in the middle of the case, and as complex and time consuming. Ladd, Expert Testimony, 5 Vand.L.Rev. 414, 426-427 (1952). While the rule allows counsel to make disclosure of the underlying facts or data as a preliminary to the giving of an expert opinion, if he chooses, the instances in which he is required to do so are reduced. This is true whether the expert bases his opinion on data furnished him at secondhand or observed by him at firsthand.

The elimination of the requirement of preliminary disclosure at the trial of underlying facts or data has a long background of support. In 1937 the Commissioners on Uniform State Laws incorporated a provision to this effect in the Model Expert Testimony Act, which furnished the basis for Uniform Rules 57 and 58. Rule 4515, N.Y. CPLR (McKinney 1963), provides:

"Unless the court orders otherwise, questions calling for the opinion of an expert witness need not be hypothetical in form, and the witness may state his opinion and reasons without first specifying the data upon which it is based. Upon cross-examination, he may be required to specify the data. . .,".

See also California Evidence Code § 802; Kansas Code of Civil Procedure §§ 60-456, 60-457; New Jersey Evidence Rules 57, 58.

If the objection is made that leaving it to the cross-examiner to bring out the supporting data is essentially unfair, the answer is that he is under no compulsion to bring out any facts or data except those unfavorable to the opinion. The answer assumes that the cross-examiner has the advance knowledge which is essential for effective cross-examination. This advance knowledge has been afforded, though imperfectly, by the traditional foundation requirement. Rule 26(b)(4) of the Rules of Civil Procedure, as revised, provides for substantial discovery in this area, obviating in large measure the obstacles which have been raised in some instances to discovery of findings, underlying data, and even the identity of the experts. Friedenthal, Discovery and Use of an Adverse Party's Expert Information, 14 Stan.L.Rev. 455 (1962).

These safeguards are reinforced by the discretionary power of the judge to require preliminary disclosure in any event.

Notes of Advisory Committee on 1993 amendments to Rules.
This rule, which relates to the manner of presenting testimony at trial, is revised to avoid an arguable conflict with revised Rules 26(a)(2)(B) and 26(a)(1) of the Federal Rules of Civil Procedure or with revised Rule 16 of the Federal Rules of Criminal Procedure, which require disclosure in advance of trial of the basis and reasons for an expert's opinions.

If a serious question is raised under Rule 702 or 703 as to the admissibility of expert testimony, disclosure of the underlying facts or data on which opinions are based may, of course, be needed by the court before deciding whether, and to what extent, the person should be allowed to testify. This rule does not preclude such an inquiry.

Rule 706. Court Appointed Experts

(a) Appointment.

The court may on its own motion or on the motion of any party enter an order to show cause why expert witnesses should not be appointed, and may request the parties to submit nominations. The court may appoint any expert witnesses agreed upon by the parties, and may appoint expert witnesses of its own selection. An expert witness shall not be appointed by the court unless the witness consents to act. A witness so appointed shall be informed of the witness' duties by the court in writing, a copy of which shall be filed with the clerk, or at a conference in which the parties shall have opportunity to participate. A witness so appointed shall advise the parties of the witness' findings, if any; the witness' deposition may be taken by any party; and the witness may be called to testify by the court or any party. The witness shall be subject to cross-examination by each party, including a party calling the witness.

(b) Compensation.

Expert witnesses so appointed are entitled to reasonable compensation in whatever sum the court may allow. The compensation thus fixed is payable from funds which may be provided by law in criminal cases and civil actions and proceedings involving just compensation under the fifth amendment. In other civil actions and proceedings the compensation shall be paid by the parties in such proportion and at such time as the court directs, and thereafter charged in like manner as other costs.

(c) Disclosure of appointment.

In the exercise of its discretion, the court may authorize disclosure to the jury of the fact that the court appointed the expert witness.

(d) Parties' experts of own selection.

Nothing in this rule limits the parties in calling expert witnesses of their own selection.

NOTES TO RULE 706

Notes of Advisory Committee on Rules.
The practice of shopping for experts, the venality of some experts, and the reluctance of many reputable experts to involve themselves in litigation, have been matters of deep concern. Though the contention is made that court appointed experts acquire an aura of infallibility to which they are not entitled. Levy, Impartial Medical Testimony—Revisited, 34 Temple L.Q. 416 (11961), the trend is increasingly to provide for their use. While experience indicates that actual appointment is a relatively infrequent occurrence, the assumption may be made that the availability of the procedure in itself decreases the need for resorting to it. The ever-present possibility that the judge may appoint an expert in a given case

must inevitably exert a sobering effect on the expert witness of a party and upon the person utilizing his services.

The inherent power of a trial judge to appoint an expert of his own choosing is virtually unquestioned. Scott v. Spanjer Bros., Inc., 298 F.2d 928 (2d Cir. 1962); Danville Tobacco Assn. v. Bryant-Buckner Associates, Inc., 333 F.2d 202 (4th Cir. 1964); Sink, The Unused Power of a Federal Judge to Call His Own Expert Witnesses, 29 S.Cal.L.Rev. 195 (1956); 2 Wigmore § 563, 9 Id. § 2484; Annot., 95 A.L.R.2d 383. Hence the problem becomes largely one of detail.

The New York plan is well known and is described in Report by Special Committee of the Association of the Bar of the City of New York: Impartial Medical Testimony (1956). On recommendation of the Section of Judicial Administration, local adoption of an impartial medical plan was endorsed by the American Bar Association. 82 A.B.A.Rep. 184-185 (1957). Descriptions and analyses of plans in effect in various parts of the country are found in Van Dusen, A United States District Judge's View of the Impartial Medical Expert System, 322 F.R.D. 498 (1963); Wick and Kightlinger, Impartial Medical Testimony Under the Federal Civil Rules: A Tale of Three Doctors, 34 Ins. Counsel J. 115 (1967); and numerous articles collected in Klein, Judicial Administration and the Legal Profession 393 (1963). Statutes and rules include California Evidence Code §§ 730-733; Illinois Supreme Court Rule 215(d), Ill.Rev.Stat.1969, c. 110A, § 215(d); Burns Indiana Stats. 1956, § 9-1702; Wisconsin Stats.Annot.1958, § 957.27.

In the federal practice, a comprehensive scheme for court appointed experts was initiated with the adoption of Rule 28 of the Federal Rules of Criminal Procedure in 1946. The Judicial Conference of the United States in 1953 considered court appointed experts in civil cases, but only with respect to whether they should be compensated from public funds, a proposal which was rejected. Report of the Judicial Conference of the United States 23 (1953). The present rule expands the practice to include civil cases.

Subdivision (a) is based on Rule 28 of the Federal Rules of Criminal Procedure, with a few changes, mainly in the interest of clarity. Language has been added to provide specifically for the appointment either on motion of a party or on the judge's own motion. A provision subjecting the court appointed expert to deposition procedures has been incorporated. The rule has been revised to make definite the right of any party, including the party calling him, to cross-examine.

Subdivision (b) combines the present provision for compensation in criminal cases with what seems to be a fair and feasible handling of civil cases, originally found in the Model Act and carried from there into Uniform Rule 60. See also California Evidence Code §§ 730-731. The special provision for Fifth Amendment compensation cases is designed to guard against reducing constitutionally guaranteed just compensation by requiring the recipient to pay costs. See Rule 71A(l) of the Rules of Civil Procedure.

Subdivision (c) seems to be essential if the use of court appointed experts is to be fully effective.

Uniform Rule 61 so provides.

Subdivision (d) is in essence the last sentence of Rule 28(a) of the Federal Rules of Criminal Procedure.

ARTICLE VIII. HEARSAY

Rule 801. Definitions

The following definitions apply under this article:
(a) Statement.
A "statement" is (1) an oral or written assertion or (2) nonverbal conduct of a person, if it is intended by the person as an assertion.
(b) Declarant.
A "declarant" is a person who makes a statement.
(c) Hearsay.
"Hearsay" is a statement, other than one made by the declarant while testifying at the trial or hearing, offered in evidence to prove the truth of the matter asserted.
(d) Statements which are not hearsay.
A statement is not hearsay if--
(1) *Prior statement by witness.* The declarant testifies at the trial or hearing and is subject to cross-examination concerning the statement, and the statement is (A) inconsistent with the declarant's testimony, and was given under oath subject to the penalty of perjury at a trial, hearing, or other proceeding, or in a deposition, or (B) consistent with the declarant's testimony and is offered to rebut an express or implied charge against the declarant of recent fabrication or improper influence or motive, or (C) one of identification of a person made after perceiving the person; or
(2) *Admission by party-opponent.* The statement is offered against a party and is
(A) the party's own statement, in either an individual or a representative capacity or
(B) a statement of which the party has manifested an adoption or belief in its truth, or
(C) a statement by a person authorized by the party to make a statement concerning the subject, or
(D) a statement by the party's agent or servant concerning a matter within the scope of the agency or employment, made during the existence of the relationship, or
(E) a statement by a coconspirator of a party during the course and in furtherance of the conspiracy.
The contents of the statement shall be considered but are not alone sufficient to establish the declarant's authority under subdivision (C), the agency or employment relationship and scope thereof under subdivision (D), or the existence of the conspiracy and the participation therein of the declarant and the party against whom the statement is offered under subdivision (E).

Rule 802. Hearsay Rule

Hearsay is not admissible except as provided by these rules or by other rules prescribed by the Supreme Court pursuant to statutory authority or by Act of Congress.

Rule 803. Hearsay Exceptions; Availability of Declarant Immaterial

The following are not excluded by the hearsay rule, even though the declarant is available as a witness:
(1) **Present sense impression**. A statement describing or explaining an event or condition made while the declarant was perceiving the event or condition, or immediately thereafter.
(2) **Excited utterance**. A statement relating to a startling event or condition made while the declarant was under the stress of excitement caused by the event or condition.

(3) **Then existing mental, emotional, or physical condition**. A statement of the declarant's then existing state of mind, emotion, sensation, or physical condition (such as intent, plan, motive, design, mental feeling, pain, and bodily health), but not including a statement of memory or belief to prove the fact remembered or believed unless it relates to the execution, revocation, identification, or terms of declarant's will.
(4) **Statements for purposes of medical diagnosis or treatment**. Statements made for purposes of medical diagnosis or treatment and describing medical history, or past or present symptoms, pain, or sensations, or the inception or general character of the cause or external source thereof insofar as reasonably pertinent to diagnosis or treatment.
(5) **Recorded recollection**. A memorandum or record concerning a matter about which a witness once had knowledge but now has insufficient recollection to enable the witness to testify fully and accurately, shown to have been made or adopted by the witness when the matter was fresh in the witness' memory and to reflect that knowledge correctly. If admitted, the memorandum or record may be read into evidence but may not itself be received as an exhibit unless offered by an adverse party.
(6) **Records of regularly conducted activity**. A memorandum, report, record, or data compilation, in any form, of acts, events, conditions, opinions, or diagnoses, made at or near the time by, or from information transmitted by, a person with knowledge, if kept in the course of a regularly conducted business activity, and if it was the regular practice of that business activity to make the memorandum, report, record, or data compilation, all as shown by the testimony of the custodian or other qualified witness, unless the source of information or the method or circumstances of preparation indicate lack of trustworthiness. The term "business" as used in this paragraph includes business, institution, association, profession, occupation, and calling of every kind, whether or not conducted for profit.
(7) **Absence of entry in records kept in accordance with the provisions of paragraph (6)**. Evidence that a matter is not included in the memoranda reports, records, or data compilations, in any form, kept in accordance with the provisions of paragraph (6), to prove the nonoccurrence or nonexistence of the matter, if the matter was of a kind of which a memorandum, report, record, or data compilation was regularly made and preserved, unless the sources of information or other circumstances indicate lack of trustworthiness.
(8) **Public records and reports**. Records, reports, statements, or data compilations, in any form, of public offices or agencies, setting forth (A) the activities of the office or agency, or (B) matters observed pursuant to duty imposed by law as to which matters there was a duty to report, excluding, however, in criminal cases matters observed by police officers and other law enforcement personnel, or (C) in civil actions and proceedings and against the Government in criminal cases, factual findings resulting from an investigation made pursuant to authority granted by law, unless the sources of information or other circumstances indicate lack of trustworthiness.
(9) **Records of vital statistics**. Records or data compilations, in any form, of births, fetal deaths, deaths, or marriages, if the report thereof was made to a public office pursuant to requirements of law.
(10) **Absence of public record or entry**. To prove the absence of a record, report, statement, or data compilation, in any form, or the nonoccurrence or nonexistence

of a matter of which a record, report, statement, or data compilation, in any form, was regularly made and preserved by a public office or agency, evidence in the form of a certification in accordance with rule 902, or testimony, that diligent search failed to disclose the record, report, statement, or data compilation, or entry.
(11) **Records of religious organizations**. Statements of births, marriages, divorces, deaths, legitimacy, ancestry, relationship by blood or marriage, or other similar facts of personal or family history, contained in a regularly kept record of a religious organization.
(12) **Marriage, baptismal, and similar certificates**. Statements of fact contained in a certificate that the maker performed a marriage or other ceremony or administered a sacrament, made by a clergyman, public official, or other person authorized by the rules or practices of a religious organization or by law to perform the act certified, and purporting to have been issued at the time of the act or within a reasonable time thereafter.
(13) **Family records**. Statements of fact concerning personal or family history contained in family Bibles, genealogies, charts, engravings on rings, inscriptions on family portraits, engravings on urns, crypts, or tombstones, or the like.
(14) **Records of documents affecting an interest in property**. The record of a document purporting to establish or affect an interest in property, as proof of the content of the original recorded document and its execution and delivery by each person by whom it purports to have been executed, if the record is a record of a public office and an applicable statute authorizes the recording of documents of that kind in that office.
(15) **Statements in documents affecting an interest in property**. A statement contained in a document purporting to establish or affect an interest in property if the matter stated was relevant to the purpose of the document, unless dealings with the property since the document was made have been inconsistent with the truth of the statement or the purport of the document.
(16) **Statements in ancient documents**. Statements in a document in existence twenty years or more the authenticity of which is established.
(17) **Market reports, commercial publications**. Market quotations, tabulations, lists, directories, or other published compilations, generally used and relied upon by the public or by persons in particular occupations.
(18) **Learned treatises**. To the extent called to the attention of an expert witness upon cross-examination or relied upon by the expert witness in direct examination, statements contained in published treatises, periodicals, or pamphlets on a subject of history, medicine, or other science or art, established as a reliable authority by the testimony or admission of the witness or by other expert testimony or by judicial notice. If admitted, the statements may be read into evidence but may not be received as exhibits.
(19) **Reputation concerning personal or family history**. Reputation among members of a person's family by blood, adoption, or marriage, or among a person's associates, or in the community, concerning a person's birth, adoption, marriage, divorce, death, legitimacy, relationship by blood, adoption, or marriage, ancestry, or other similar fact of personal or family history.
(20) **Reputation concerning boundaries or general history**. Reputation in a community, arising before the controversy, as to boundaries of or customs affecting lands in the community, and reputation as to events of general history important to the community or State or nation in which located.

(21) **Reputation as to character**. Reputation of a person's character among associates or in the community.
(22) **Judgment of previous conviction**. Evidence of a final judgment, entered after a trial or upon a plea of guilty (but not upon a plea of *nolo contendere*), adjudging a person guilty of a crime punishable by death or imprisonment in excess of one year, to prove any fact essential to sustain the judgment, but not including, when offered by the Government in a criminal prosecution for purposes other than impeachment, judgments against persons other than the accused. The pendency of an appeal may be shown but does not affect admissibility.
(23) **Judgment as to personal, family or general history, or boundaries**. Judgments as proof of matters of personal, family or general history, or boundaries, essential to the judgment, if the same would be provable by evidence of reputation.
(24) [Transferred to Rule 807]

Rule 804. Hearsay Exceptions; Declarant Unavailable

(a) Definition of unavailability.
"Unavailability as a witness" includes situations in which the declarant—
(1) is exempted by ruling of the court on the ground of privilege from testifying concerning the subject matter of the declarant's statement; or
(2) persists in refusing to testify concerning the subject matter of the declarant's statement despite an order of the court to do so; or
(3) testifies to a lack of memory of the subject matter of the declarant's statement; or
(4) is unable to be present or to testify at the hearing because of death or then existing physical or mental illness or infirmity; or
(5) is absent from the hearing and the proponent of a statement has been unable to procure the declarant's attendance (or in the case of a hearsay exception under subdivision (b)(2), (3), or (4), the declarant's attendance or testimony) by process or other reasonable means.
A declarant is not unavailable as a witness if exemption, refusal, claim of lack of memory, inability, or absence is due to the procurement or wrongdoing of the proponent of a statement for the purpose of preventing the witness from attending or testifying.
(b) Hearsay exceptions.
The following are not excluded by the hearsay rule if the declarant is unavailable as a witness:
(1) *Former testimony*. Testimony given as a witness at another hearing of the same or a different proceeding, or in a deposition taken in compliance with law in the course of the same or another proceeding, if the party against whom the testimony is now offered, or, in a civil action or proceeding, a predecessor in interest, had an opportunity and similar motive to develop the testimony by direct, cross, or redirect examination.
(2) *Statement under belief of impending death*. In a prosecution for homicide or in a civil action or proceeding, a statement made by a declarant while believing that the declarant's death was imminent, concerning the cause or circumstances of what the declarant believed to be impending death.
(3) *Statement against interest*. A statement which was at the time of its making so far contrary to the declarant's pecuniary or proprietary interest, or so far tended to subject the declarant to civil or criminal liability, or to render invalid a claim by the declarant against another, that a reasonable person in the declarant's position would not have made the statement unless believing it to be true. A statement tending to

expose the declarant to criminal liability and offered to exculpate the accused is not admissible unless corroborating circumstances clearly indicate the trustworthiness of the statement.

(4) *Statement of personal or family history.* (A) A statement concerning the declarant's own birth, adoption, marriage, divorce, legitimacy, relationship by blood, adoption, or marriage, ancestry, or other similar fact of personal or family history, even though declarant had no means of acquiring personal knowledge of the matter stated; or (B) a statement concerning the foregoing matters, and death also, of another person, if the declarant was related to the other by blood, adoption, or marriage or was so intimately associated with the other's family as to be likely to have accurate information concerning the matter declared.

(5) [Transferred to Rule 807]

(6) Forfeiture by wrongdoing. A statement offered against a party that has engaged or acquiesced in wrongdoing that was intended to, and did, procure the unavailability of the declarant as a witness.

Rule 805. Hearsay Within Hearsay

Hearsay included within hearsay is not excluded under the hearsay rule if each part of the combined statements conforms with an exception to the hearsay rule provided in these rules.

Rule 806. Attacking and Supporting Credibility of Declarant

When a hearsay statement, or a statement defined in Rule 801(d)(2),(C),(D), or (E), has been admitted in evidence, the credibility of the declarant may be attacked, and if attacked may be supported, by any evidence which would be admissible for those purposes if declarant had testified as a witness. Evidence of a statement or conduct by the declarant at any time, inconsistent with the declarant's hearsay statement, is not subject to any requirement that the declarant may have been afforded an opportunity to deny or explain. If the party against whom a hearsay statement has been admitted calls the declarant as a witness, the party is entitled to examine the declarant on the statement as if under cross-examination.

Rule 807. Residual Exception

A statement not specifically covered by Rule 803 or 804 but having equivalent circumstantial guarantees of trustworthiness, is not excluded by the hearsay rule, if the court determines that (A) the statement is offered as evidence of a material fact; (B) the statement is more probative on the point for which it is offered than any other evidence which the proponent can procure through reasonable efforts; and (C) the general purposes of these rules and the interests of justice will best be served by admission of the statement into evidence. However, a statement may not be admitted under this exception unless the proponent of it makes known to the adverse party sufficiently in advance of the trial or hearing to provide the adverse party with a fair opportunity to prepare to meet it, the proponent's intention to offer the statement and the particulars of it, including the name and address of the declarant.

ARTICLE IX. AUTHENTICATION AND IDENTIFICATION

Rule 901. Requirement of Authentication or Identification

(a) General provision.

The requirement of authentication or identification as a condition precedent to admissibility is satisfied by evidence sufficient to support a finding that the matter in question is what its proponent claims.

(b) Illustrations.
By way of illustration only, and not by way of limitation, the following are examples of authentication or identification conforming with the requirements of this rule:
(1) *Testimony of witness with knowledge*. Testimony that a matter is what it is claimed to be.
(2) *Nonexpert opinion on handwriting*. Nonexpert opinion as to the genuineness of handwriting, based upon familiarity not acquired for purposes of the litigation.
(3) *Comparison by trier or expert witness*. Comparison by the trier of fact or by expert witnesses with specimens which have been authenticated.
(4) *Distinctive characteristics and the like*. Appearance, contents, substance, internal patterns, or other distinctive characteristics, taken in conjunction with circumstances.
(5) *Voice identification*. Identification of a voice, whether heard firsthand or through mechanical or electronic transmission or recording, by opinion based upon hearing the voice at any time under circumstances connecting it with the alleged speaker.
(6) *Telephone conversations*. Telephone conversations, by evidence that a call was made to the number assigned at the time by the telephone company to a particular person or business, if (A) in the case of a person, circumstances, including self-identification, show the person answering to be the one called, or (B) in the case of a business, the call was made to a place of business and the conversation related to business reasonably transacted over the telephone.
(7) *Public records or reports*. Evidence that a writing authorized by law to be recorded or filed and in fact recorded or filed in a public office, or a purported public record, report, statement, or data compilation, in any form, is from the public office where items of this nature are kept.
(8) *Ancient documents or data compilation*. Evidence that a document or data compilation, in any form, (A) is in such condition as to create no suspicion concerning its authenticity, (B) was in a place where it, if authentic, would likely be, and (C) has been in existence 20 years or more at the time it is offered.
(9) *Process or system*. Evidence describing a process or system used to produce a result and showing that the process or system produces an accurate result.
(10) *Methods provided by statute or rule*. Any method of authentication or identification provided by Act of Congress or by other rules prescribed by the Supreme Court pursuant to statutory authority.

Rule 902. Self-authentication

Extrinsic evidence of authenticity as a condition precedent to admissibility is not required with respect to the following:
(1) **Domestic public documents under seal**. A document bearing a seal purporting to be that of the United States, or of any State, district, Commonwealth, territory, or insular possession thereof, or the Panama Canal Zone, or the Trust Territory of the Pacific Islands, or of a political subdivision, department, officer, or agency thereof, and a signature purporting to be an attestation or execution.
(2) **Domestic public documents not under seal**. A document purporting to bear the signature in the official capacity of an officer or employee of any entity included in paragraph (1) hereof, having no seal, if a public officer having a seal and having official duties in the district or political subdivision of the officer or employee certifies under seal that the signer has the official capacity and that the signature is genuine.

(3) **Foreign public documents**. A document purporting to be executed or attested in an official capacity by a person authorized by the laws of a foreign country to make the execution or attestation, and accompanied by a final certification as to the genuineness of the signature and official position (A) of the executing or attesting person, or (B) of any foreign official whose certificate of genuineness of signature and official position relates to the execution or attestation or is in a chain of certificates of genuineness of signature and official position relating to the execution or attestation. A final certification may be made by a secretary of an embassy or legation, consul general, consul, vice consul, or consular agent of the United States, or a diplomatic or consular official of the foreign country assigned or accredited to the United States. If reasonable opportunity has been given to all parties to investigate the authenticity and accuracy of official documents, the court may, for good cause shown, order that they be treated as presumptively authentic without final certification or permit them to be evidenced by an attested summary with or without final certification.
(4) **Certified copies of public records**. A copy of an official record or report or entry therein, or of a document authorized by law to be recorded or filed and actually recorded or filed in a public office, including data compilations in any form, certified as correct by the custodian or other person authorized to make the certification, by certificate complying with paragraph (1), (2), or (3) of this rule or complying with any Act of Congress or rule prescribed by the Supreme Court pursuant to statutory authority.
(5) **Official publications**. Books, pamphlets, or other publications purporting to be issued by public authority.
(6) **Newspapers and periodicals**. Printed materials purporting to be newspapers or periodicals.
(7) **Trade inscriptions and the like**. Inscriptions, signs, tags, or labels purporting to have been affixed in the course of business and indicating ownership, control, or origin.
(8) **Acknowledged documents**. Documents accompanied by a certificate of acknowledgment executed in the manner provided by law by a notary public or other officer authorized by law to take acknowledgments.
(9) **Commercial paper and related documents**. Commercial paper, signatures thereon, and documents relating thereto to the extent provided by general commercial law.
(10) **Presumptions under Acts of Congress**. Any signature, document, or other matter declared by Act of Congress to be presumptively or prima facie genuine or authentic.

Rule 903. Subscribing Witness' Testimony Unnecessary

The testimony of a subscribing witness is not necessary to authenticate a writing unless required by the laws of the jurisdiction whose laws govern the validity of the writing.

ARTICLE X. CONTENTS OF WRITINGS, RECORDINGS, AND PHOTOGRAPHS

Rule 1001. Definitions

For purposes of this article the following definitions are applicable:
(1) **Writings and recordings**. "Writings" and "recordings" consist of letters, words, or numbers, or their equivalent, set down by handwriting, typewriting, printing,

photostating, photographing, magnetic impulse, mechanical or electronic recording, or other form of data compilation.
(2) **Photographs**. "Photographs" include still photographs, X-ray films, video tapes, and motion pictures.
(3) **Original**. An "original" of a writing or recording is the writing or recording itself or any counterpart intended to have the same effect by a person executing or issuing it. An "original" of a photograph includes the negative or any print therefrom. If data are stored in a computer or similar device, any printout or other output readable by sight, shown to reflect the data accurately, is an "original".
(4) **Duplicate**. A "duplicate" is a counterpart produced by the same impression as the original, or from the same matrix, or by means of photography, including enlargements and miniatures, or by mechanical or electronic re-recording, or by chemical reproduction, or by other equivalent techniques which accurately reproduces the original.

Rule 1002. Requirement of Original

To prove the content of a writing, recording, or photograph, the original writing, recording, or photograph is required, except as otherwise provided in these rules or by Act of Congress.

Rule 1003. Admissibility of Duplicates

A duplicate is admissible to the same extent as an original unless (1) a genuine question is raised as to the authenticity of the original or (2) in the circumstances it would be unfair to admit the duplicate in lieu of the original.

Rule 1004. Admissibility of Other Evidence of Contents

The original is not required, and other evidence of the contents of a writing, recording, or photograph is admissible if—
(1) **Originals lost or destThomed**. All originals are lost or have been destThomed, unless the proponent lost or destThomed them in bad faith; or
(2) **Original not obtainable**. No original can be obtained by any available judicial process or procedure; or
(3) **Original in possession of opponent**. At a time when an original was under the control of the party against whom offered, that party was put on notice, by the pleadings or otherwise, that the contents would be a subject of proof at the hearing, and that party does not produce the original at the hearing; or
(4) **Collateral matters**. The writing, recording, or photograph is not closely related to a controlling issue.

Rule 1005. Public Records

The contents of an official record, or of a document authorized to be recorded or filed and actually recorded or filed, including data compilations in any form, if otherwise admissible, may be proved by copy, certified as correct in accordance with rule 902 or testified to be correct by a witness who has compared it with the original. If a copy which complies with the foregoing cannot be obtained by the exercise of reasonable diligence, then other evidence of the contents may be given.

Rule 1006. Summaries

The contents of voluminous writings, recordings, or photographs which cannot conveniently be examined in court may be presented in the form of a chart, summary, or calculation. The originals, or duplicates, shall be made available for examination or copying, or both, by other parties at reasonable time and place. The court may order that they be produced in court.

Rule 1007. Testimony or Written Admission of Party
Contents of writings, recordings, or photographs may be proved by the testimony or deposition of the party against whom offered or by that party's written admission, without accounting for the nonproduction of the original.
Rule 1008. Functions of Court and Jury
When the admissibility of other evidence of contents of writings, recordings, or photographs under these rules depends upon the fulfillment of a condition of fact, the question whether the condition has been fulfilled is ordinarily for the court to determine in accordance with the provisions of rule 104. However, when an issue is raised (a) whether the asserted writing ever existed, or (b) whether another writing, recording, or photograph produced at the trial is the original, or (c) whether other evidence of contents correctly reflects the contents, the issue is for the trier of fact to determine as in the case of other issues of fact.

ARTICLE XI: MISCELLANEOUS RULES

Rule 1101. Applicability of Rules
(a) Courts and judges.
These rules apply to the United States district courts, the District Court of Guam, the District Court of the Virgin Islands, the Disrict Court for the Northern Mariana Islands, the United States courts of appeals, the United States Claims Court, and to the United States bankruptcy judges and United States magistrate judges, in the actions, cases, and proceedings and to the extent hereinafter set forth. The terms "judge" and "court" in these rules include United States bankruptcy judges and United States magistrate judges.
(b) Proceedings generally.
These rules apply generally to civil actions and proceedings, including admiralty and maritime cases, to criminal cases and proceedings, to contempt proceedings except those in which the court may act summarily, and to proceedings and cases under title 11, United States Code [11 USCS §§ 1 et seq.].
(c) Rule of privilege.
The rule with respect to privileges applies at all stages of all actions, cases, and proceedings.
(d) Rules inapplicable.
The rules (other than with respect to privileges) do not apply in the following situations:
(1) *Preliminary questions of fact.* The determination of questions of fact preliminary to admissibility of evidence when the issue is to be determined by the court under rule 104.
(2) *Grand jury.* Proceedings before grand juries.
(3) *Miscellaneous proceedings.* Proceedings for extradition or rendition; preliminary examinations in criminal cases; sentencing, or granting or revoking probation; issuance of warrants for arrest, criminal summonses, and search warrants; and proceedings with respect to release on bail or otherwise.
(e) Rules applicable in part.
In the following proceedings these rules apply to the extent that matters of evidence are not provided for in the statutes which govern procedure therein or in other rules prescribed by the Supreme Court pursuant to statutory authority: the trial of misdemeanors and other petty offenses before United States magistrate judge; review of agency actions when the facts are subject to trail de novo under section

107(2)(F) of title 5, United States Code; review of orders of the Secretary of Agriculture under section 2 of the Act entitled "An Act to authorize association of producers of agricultural products" approved February 18, 1922 (7 U.S.C. 292), and under section 6 and 7(c) of the Perishable Agricultural Commodities Act, 1930 (7 U.S.C. 499f, 499g(c))); naturalization and revocation of naturalization under sections 310--318 of the Immigration and Nationality Act (8 U.S.C. 1421--1429); prize proceedings in admiralty under sections 7651--7681 of title 10, United States Code; review of orders of the Secretary of the Interior under section 2 of the Act entitled "An Act authorizing associations of producers of aquatic products" approved June 25, 1934 (15 U.S.C. 533); review of orders of petroleum control boards under section 5 of the Act entitled "An act to regulate interstate and foreign commerce in petroleum and its products by prohibiting the shipment in such commerce of petroleum and its products produced in violation of State law, and for other purposes", approved February 22, 1935 (15 U.S.C. 715d); actions for fines, penalties, or forfeitures under part V of title IV of the Tariff Act of 1930 (19 U.S.C. 1581--1624), or under the Anti-Smuggling Act (19 U.S.C. 1701--1711); criminal libel for condemnation, exclusion of imports, or other proceedings under the Federal Food, Drug, and Cosmetic Act (21 U.S.C. 301--392); disputes between seamen under sections 4079, 4080, and 4081 of the Revised Statutes (22 U.S.C. 256--258); habeas corpus under sections 2241--2254 of title 28, United States Code; motions to vacate, set aside or correct sentence under section 2255 of title 28, United States Code; actions for penalties for refusal to transport destitute seamen under section 4578 of the Revised Statutes (46 U.S.C. 679); actions against the United States under the Act entitled "An Act authorizing suits against the United States in admiralty for damage caused by and salvage service rendered to public vessels belonging to the United States, and for other purposes", approved March 3, 1925 (46 U.S.C. 781--790), as implemented by section 7730 of title 10, United States Code.

Rule 1102. Amendments

Amendments to the Federal Rules of Evidence may be made as provided in section 2072 of title 28 of the United States Code.

Rule 1103. Title

These rules may be known and cited as the Federal Rules of Evidence.

Appendix Q Select Federal Rules of Civil Procedure

(Underlined Rules are reprinted in this appendix.)

I. SCOPE OF RULES—ONE FORM OF ACTION

1. Scope of Rules
2. One Form of Action

II. COMMENCEMENT OF ACTION; SERVICE OF PROCESS, PLEADINGS, MOTIONS, AND ORDERS

3. Commencement of Action
4. Summons

4.1. Service of Other Process

5. Service and Filing of Pleadings and Other Papers
6. Time

III. PLEADINGS AND MOTIONS

7. Pleadings Allowed; Form of Motions
8. General Rules of Pleading
9. Pleading Special Matters
10. Form of Pleadings
11. Signing of Pleadings, Motions, and Other Papers; Representations to Court; Sanctions
12. Defenses and Objections--When and How Presented--By Pleading or Motion—Motion for Judgment on the Pleadings
13. Counterclaim and Cross-Claim
14. Third-Party Practice
15. Amended and Supplemental Pleadings
16. Pretrial Conferences; Scheduling, Management

IV. PARTIES

17. Parties Plaintiff and Defendant; Capacity
18. Joinder of Claims and Remedies
19. Joinder of Persons Needed for Just Adjudication
20. Permissive Joinder of Parties
21. Misjoinder and Non-Joinder of Parties
22. Interpleader
23. Class Actions

23.1. Derivative Actions by Shareholders

23.2. Actions Relating to Unincorporated Associations

24. Intervention
25. Substitution of Parties

V. DEPOSITIONS AND DISCOVERY

26. General Provisions Governing Discovery; Duty of Disclosure
27. Depositions Before Action or Pending Appeal
28. Persons Before Whom Depositions May Be Taken
29. Stipulations Regarding Discovery Procedure
30. Deposition Upon Oral Examination
31. Depositions Upon Written Questions

I. SCOPE OF RULES—ONE FORM OF ACTION

Rule 1. Scope and Purpose of Rules

These rules govern the procedure in the United States district courts in all suits of a civil nature whether cognizable as cases at law or in equity or in admiralty, with the exceptions stated in Rule 81. They shall be construed and administered to secure the just, speedy, and inexpensive determination of every action.

Rule 2. One Form of Action

There shall be one form of action to be known as "civil action."

II. COMMENCEMENT OF ACTION; SERVICE OF PROCESS, PLEADINGS, MOTIONS, AND ORDERS

Rule 3. Commencement of Action

A civil action is commenced by filing a complaint with the court.

Rule 5. Service and Filing of Pleadings and Other Papers

(a) Service: When Required.

Except as otherwise provided in these rules, every order required by its terms to be served, every pleading subsequent to the original complaint unless the court otherwise orders because of numerous defendants, every paper relating to discovery required to be served upon a party unless the court otherwise orders, every written motion other than one which may be heard ex parte, and every written notice, appearance, demand, offer of judgment, designation of record on appeal, and similar paper shall be served upon each of the parties. No service need be made on parties in default for failure to appear except that pleadings asserting new or additional claims for relief against them shall be served upon them in the manner provided for service of summons in Rule 4.

In an action begun by seizure of property, in which no person need be or is named as defendant, any service required to be made prior to the filing of an answer, claim, or appearance shall be made upon the person having custody or possession of the property at the time of its seizure.

(b) Same: How Made.
Whenever under these rules service is required or permitted to be made upon a party represented by an attorney the service shall be made upon the attorney unless service upon the party is ordered by the court. Service upon the attorney or upon a party shall be made by delivering a copy to the attorney or party or by mailing it to the attorney or party at the attorney's or party's last known address or, if no address is known, by leaving it with the clerk of the court. Delivery of a copy within this rule means: handing it to the attorney or to the party; or leaving it at the attorney's or party's office with a clerk or other person in charge thereof; or, if there is no one in charge, leaving it in a conspicuous place therein; or, if the office is closed or the person to be served has no office, leaving it at the person's dwelling house or usual place of abode with some person of suitable age and discretion then residing therein. Service by mail is complete upon mailing.
(c) Same: Numerous Defendants.
In any action in which there are unusually large numbers of defendants, the court, upon motion or of its own initiative, may order that service of the pleadings of the defendants and replies thereto need not be made as between the defendants and that any cross-claim, counterclaim, or matter constituting an avoidance or affirmative defense contained therein shall be deemed to be denied or avoided by all other parties and that the filing of any such pleading and service thereof upon the plaintiff constitutes due notice of it to the parties. A copy of every such order shall be served upon the parties in such manner and form as the court directs.
(d) Filing; Certificate of Service.
All papers after the complaint required to be served upon a party, together with a certificate of service, shall be filed with the court within a reasonable time after service, but the court may on motion of a party or on its own initiative order that depositions upon oral examination and interrogatories, requests for documents, requests for admission, and answers and responses thereto not be filed unless on order of the court or for use in the proceeding.
(e) Filing with the Court Defined.
The filing of papers with the court as required by these rules shall be made by filing them with the clerk of the court, except that the judge may permit the papers to be filed with the judge, in which event the judge shall note thereon the filing date and forthwith transmit them to the office of the clerk. A court may by local rule permit papers to be filed, signed, or verified by electronic means that are consistent with technical standards, if any, which the Judicial Conference of the United States establishes. A paper filed by electronic means in compliance with a local rule constitutes a written paper for the purpose of applying these rules. The clerk shall not refuse to accept for filing any paper presented for that purpose solely because it is not presented in proper form as required by these rules or by any local rules or practices.

III. PLEADINGS AND MOTIONS

Rule 7. Pleadings Allowed; Form of Motions
(a) Pleadings.
There shall be a complaint and an answer; a reply to a counterclaim denominated as such; an answer to a cross-claim, if the answer contains a cross-claim; a third-party complaint, if a person who was not an original party is summoned under the provisions of Rule 14; and a third-party answer, if a third-party complaint is served.

No other pleading shall be allowed, except that the court may order a reply to an answer or a third-party answer.

(b) Motions and Other Papers.

(1) An application to the court for an order shall be by motion which, unless made during a hearing or trial, shall be made in writing, shall state with particularity the grounds therefor, and shall set forth the relief or order sought. The requirement of writing is fulfilled if the motion is stated in a written notice of the hearing of the motion.

(2) The rules applicable to captions and other matters of form of pleadings apply to all motions and other papers provided for by these rules.

(3) All motions shall be signed in accordance with Rule 11.

(c) Demurrers, Pleas, etc.,

Abolished. Demurrers, pleas, and exceptions for insufficiency of a pleading shall not be used.

Rule 11. Signing of Pleadings, Motions, and Other Papers; Representations to Court; Sanctions

(a) Signature.

Every pleading, written motion, and other paper shall be signed by at least one attorney of record in the attorney's individual name, or, if the party is not represented by an attorney, shall be signed by the party. Each paper shall state the signer's address and telephone number, if any. Except when otherwise specifically provided by rule or statute, pleadings need not be verified or accompanied by affidavit. An unsigned paper shall be stricken unless omission of the signature is corrected promptly after being called to the attention of attorney or party.

(b) Representations to Court.

By presenting to the court (whether by signing, filing, submitting, or later advocating) a pleading, written motion, or other paper, an attorney or unrepresented party is certifying that to the best of the person's knowledge, information, and belief, formed after an inquiry reasonable under the circumstances,—

(1) it is not being presented for any improper purpose, such as to harass or to cause unnecessary delay or needless increase in the cost of litigation;

(2) the claims, defenses, and other legal contentions therein are warranted by existing law or by a nonfrivolous argument for the extension, modification, or reversal of existing law or the establishment of new law;

(3) the allegations and other factual contentions have evidentiary support or, if specifically so identified, are likely to have evidentiary support after a reasonable opportunity for further investigation or discovery; and

(4) the denials of factual contentions are warranted on the evidence or, if specifically so identified, are reasonably based on a lack of information or belief.

(c) Sanctions.

If, after notice and a reasonable opportunity to respond, the court determines that subdivision (b) has been violated, the court may, subject to the conditions stated below, impose an appropriate sanction upon the attorneys, law firms, or parties that have violated subdivision (b) or are responsible for the violation.

(1) How Initiated.

(A) By Motion. A motion for sanctions under this rule shall be made separately from other motions or requests and shall describe the specific conduct alleged to violate subdivision (b). It shall be served as provided in Rule 5, but shall not be filed with or presented to the court unless, within 21 days after service of the motion (or such other period as the court may prescribe), the challenged paper, claim, defense, contention, allegation, or denial is not withdrawn or appropriately corrected. If warranted, the court may award to the party prevailing on the motion the reasonable expenses and attorney's fees incurred in presenting or opposing the motion. Absent exceptional circumstances, a law firm shall be held jointly responsible for violations committed by its partners, associates, and employees.

(B) On Court's Initiative. On its own initiative, the court may enter an order describing the specific conduct that appears to violate subdivision (b) and directing an attorney, law firm, or party to show cause why it has not violated subdivision (b) with respect thereto.

(2) Nature of Sanction; Limitations. A sanction imposed for violation of this rule shall be limited to what is sufficient to deter repetition of such conduct or comparable conduct by others similarly situated. Subject to the limitations in subparagraphs (A) and (B), the sanction may consist of, or include, directives of a nonmonetary nature, an order to pay a penalty into court, or, if imposed on motion and warranted for effective deterrence, an order directing payment to the movant of some or all of the reasonable attorneys' fees and other expenses incurred as a direct result of the violation.

(A) Monetary sanctions may not be awarded against a represented party for a violation of subdivision (b)(2).

(B) Monetary sanctions may not be awarded on the court's initiative unless the court issues its order to show cause before a voluntary dismissal or settlement of the claims made by or against the party which is, or whose attorneys are, to be sanctioned.

(3) Order. When imposing sanctions, the court shall describe the conduct determined to constitute a violation of this rule and explain the basis for the sanction imposed.

(d) Inapplicability to Discovery.

Subdivisions (a) through (c) of this rule do not apply to disclosures and discovery requests, responses, objections, and motions that are subject to the provisions of Rules 26 through 37.

Rule 12. Defenses and Objections—When and How Presented—By Pleading or Motion—Motion for Judgment on the Pleadings

(a) When Presented.

(1) Unless a different time is prescribed in a statute of the United States, a defendant shall serve an answer

(A) within 20 days after being served with the summons and complaint, or

(B) if service of the summons has been timely waived on request under Rule 4(d), within 60 days after the date when the request for waiver was sent, or within 90 days after that date if the defendant was addressed outside any judicial district of the United States.

(2) A party served with a pleading stating a cross-claim against that party shall serve an answer thereto within 20 days after being served. The plaintiff shall serve a reply to a counterclaim in the answer within 20 days after service of the answer, or, if a reply is ordered by the court, within 20 days after service of the order, unless the order otherwise directs.

(3) The United States or an officer or agency thereof shall serve an answer to the complaint or to a cross-claim, or a reply to a counterclaim, within 60 days after the service upon the United States attorney of the pleading in which the claim is asserted.

(4) Unless a different time is fixed by court order, the service of a motion permitted under this rule alters the periods of time as follows:

(A) if the court denies the motion or postpones its disposition until the trial on the merits, the responsive pleading shall be served within 10 days after notice of the court's action; or

(B) if the court grants a motion for a more definite statement, the responsive pleading shall be served within 10 days after the service of the more definite statement.

(b) How Presented.

Every defense, in law or fact, to a claim for relief in any pleading, whether a claim, counterclaim, cross-claim, or third-party claim, shall be asserted in the responsive pleading thereto if one is required, except that the following defenses may at the option of the pleader be made by motion: (1) lack of jurisdiction over the subject matter, (2) lack of jurisdiction over the person, (3) improper venue, (4) insufficiency of process, (5) insufficiency of service of process, (6) failure to state a claim upon which relief can be granted, (7) failure to join a party under Rule 19. A motion making any of these defenses shall be made before pleading if a further pleading is permitted. No defense or objection is waived by being joined with one or more other defenses or objections in a responsive pleading or motion. If a pleading sets forth a claim for relief to which the adverse party is not required to serve a responsive pleading, the adverse party may assert at the trial any defense in law or fact to that claim for relief. If, on a motion asserting the defense numbered (6) to dismiss for failure of the pleading to state a claim upon which relief can be granted, matters outside the pleading are presented to and not excluded by the court, the motion shall be treated as one for summary judgment and disposed of as provided in Rule 56, and all parties shall be given reasonable opportunity to present all material made pertinent to such a motion by Rule 56.

(c) Motion for Judgment on the Pleadings.

After the pleadings are closed but within such time as not to delay the trial, any party may move for judgment on the pleadings. If, on a motion for judgment on the pleadings, matters outside the pleadings are presented to and not excluded by the court, the motion shall be treated as one for summary judgment and disposed of as provided in Rule 56, and all parties shall be given reasonable opportunity to present all material made pertinent to such a motion by Rule 56.

(d) Preliminary Hearings.

The defenses specifically enumerated (1)-(7) in subdivision (b) of this rule, whether made in a pleading or by motion, and the motion for judgment mentioned in subdivision (c) of this rule shall be heard and determined before trial on application of any party, unless the court orders that the hearing and determination thereof be deferred until the trial.

(e) Motion For More Definite Statement.
If a pleading to which a responsive pleading is permitted is so vague or ambiguous that a party cannot reasonably be required to frame a responsive pleading, the party may move for a more definite statement before interposing a responsive pleading. The motion shall point out the defects complained of and the details desired. If the motion is granted and the order of the court is not obeyed within 10 days after notice of the order or within such other time as the court may fix, the court may strike the pleading to which the motion was directed or make such order as it deems just.

(f) Motion To Strike.
Upon motion made by a party before responding to a pleading or, if no responsive pleading is permitted by these rules, upon motion made by a party within 20 days after the service of the pleading upon the party or upon the court's own initiative at any time, the court may order stricken from any pleading any insufficient defense or any redundant, immaterial, impertinent, or scandalous matter.

(g) Consolidation of Defenses in Motion.
A party who makes a motion under this rule may join with it any other motions herein provided for and then available to the party. If a party makes a motion under this rule but omits therefrom any defense or objection then available to the party which this rule permits to be raised by motion, the party shall not thereafter make a motion based on the defense or objection so omitted, except a motion as provided in subdivision (h)(2) hereof on any of the grounds there stated.

(h) Waiver or Preservation of Certain Defense.

(1) A defense of lack of jurisdiction over the person, improper venue, insufficiency of process, or insufficiency of service of process is waived (A) if omitted from a motion in the circumstances described in subdivision (g), or (B) if it is neither made by motion under this rule nor included in a responsive pleading or an amendment thereof permitted by Rule 15(a) to be made as a matter of course.

(2) A defense of failure to state a claim upon which relief can be granted, a defense of failure to join a party indispensable under Rule 19, and an objection of failure to state a legal defense to a claim may be made in any pleading permitted or ordered under Rule 7(a), or by motion for judgment on the pleadings, or at the trial on the merits.

(3) Whenever it appears by suggestion of the parties or otherwise that the court lacks jurisdiction of the subject matter, the court shall dismiss the action.

Rule 13. Counterclaim and Cross-Claim

(a) Compulsory Counterclaims.
A pleading shall state as a counterclaim any claim which at the time of serving the pleading the pleader has against any opposing party, if it arises out of the transaction or occurrence that is the subject matter of the opposing party's claim and does not require for its adjudication the presence of third parties of whom the court cannot acquire jurisdiction. But the pleader need not state the claim if (1) at the time the action was commenced the claim was the subject of another pending action, or (2) the opposing party brought suit upon the claim by attachment or other process by which the court did not acquire jurisdiction to render a personal judgment on that claim, and the pleader is not stating any counterclaim under this Rule 13.

(b) Permissive Counterclaims.
A pleading may state as a counterclaim any claim against an opposing party not arising out of the transaction or occurrence that is the subject matter of the opposing party's claim.
(c) Counterclaim Exceeding Opposing Claim.
A counterclaim may or may not diminish or defeat the recovery sought by the opposing party. It may claim relief exceeding in amount or different in kind from that sought in the pleading of the opposing party.
(d) Counterclaim Against the United States.
These rules shall not be construed to enlarge beyond the limits now fixed by law the right to assert counterclaims or to claim credits against the United States or an officer or agency thereof.
(e) Counterclaim Maturing or Acquired After Pleading.
A claim which either matured or was acquired by the pleader after serving a pleading may, with the permission of the court, be presented as a counterclaim by supplemental pleading.
(f) Omitted Counterclaim.
When a pleader fails to set up a counterclaim through oversight, inadvertence, or excusable neglect, or when justice requires, the pleader may by leave of court set up the counterclaim by amendment.
(g) Cross-Claim Against Co-Party.
A pleading may state as a cross-claim any claim by one party against a co-party arising out of the transaction or occurrence that is the subject matter either of the original action or of a counterclaim therein or relating to any property that is the subject matter of the original action. Such cross-claim may include a claim that the party against whom it is asserted is or may be liable to the cross-claimant for all or part of a claim asserted in the action against the cross-claimant.
(h) Joinder of Additional Parties.
Persons other than those made parties to the original action may be made parties to a counterclaim or cross-claim in accordance with the provisions of Rules 19 and 20.
(i) Separate Trials; Separate Judgments.
If the court orders separate trials as provided in Rule 42(b), judgment on a counterclaim or cross-claim may be rendered in accordance with the terms of Rule 54(b) when the court has jurisdiction so to do, even if the claims of the opposing party have been dismissed or otherwise disposed of.
Rule 14. Third-Party Practice
(a) When Defendant May Bring in Third Party.
At any time after commencement of the action a defending party, as a third-party plaintiff, may cause a summons and complaint to be served upon a person not a party to the action who is or may be liable to the third-party plaintiff for all or part of the plaintiff's claim against the third-party plaintiff. The third-party plaintiff need not obtain leave to make the service if the third-party plaintiff files the third-party complaint not later than 10 days after serving the original answer. Otherwise the third-party plaintiff must obtain leave on motion upon notice to all parties to the action. The person served with the summons and third-party complaint, hereinafter called the third-party defendant, shall make any defenses to the third-party plaintiff's claim as provided in Rule 12 and any counterclaims against the third-party plaintiff and cross-claims against other third-party defendants as provided in Rule 13. The third-party defendant may assert against the plaintiff any defenses

which the third-party plaintiff has to the plaintiff's claim. The third-party defendant may also assert any claim against the plaintiff arising out of the transaction or occurrence that is the subject matter of the plaintiff's claim against the third-party plaintiff. The plaintiff may assert any claim against the third-party defendant arising out of the transaction or occurrence that is the subject matter of the plaintiff's claim against the third-party plaintiff, and the third-party defendant thereupon shall assert any defenses as provided in Rule 12 and any counterclaims and cross-claims as provided in Rule 13. Any party may move to strike the third-party claim, or for its severance or separate trial. A third-party defendant may proceed under this rule against any person not a party to the action who is or may be liable to the third-party defendant for all or part of the claim made in the action against the third-party defendant. The third-party complaint, if within the admiralty and maritime jurisdiction, may be in rem against a vessel, cargo, or other property subject to admiralty or maritime process in rem, in which case references in this rule to the summons include the warrant of arrest, and references to the third-party plaintiff or defendant include, where appropriate, the claimant of the property arrested.

(b) When Plaintiff May Bring in Third Party.

When a counterclaim is asserted against a plaintiff, the plaintiff may cause a third party to be brought in under circumstances which under this rule would entitle a defendant to do so.

(c) Admiralty and Maritime Claims.

When a plaintiff asserts an admiralty or maritime claim within the meaning of Rule 9(h), the defendant or claimant, as a third-party plaintiff, may bring in a third-party defendant who may be wholly or partly liable, either to the plaintiff or to the third-party plaintiff, by way of remedy over, contribution, or otherwise on account of the same transaction, occurrence, or series of transactions or occurrences. In such a case the third-party plaintiff may also demand judgment against the third-party defendant in favor of the plaintiff, in which event the third-party defendant shall make any defenses to the claim of the plaintiff as well as to that of the third-party plaintiff in the manner provided in Rule 12 and the action shall proceed as if the plaintiff had commenced it against the third-party defendant as well as the third-party plaintiff.

Rule 16. Pretrial Conferences; Scheduling; Management

(a) Pretrial Conferences; Objectives.

In any action, the court may in its discretion direct the attorneys for the parties and any unrepresented parties to appear before it for a conference or conferences before trial for such purposes as

(1) expediting the disposition of the action;

(2) establishing early and continuing control so that the case will not be protracted because of lack of management;

(3) discouraging wasteful pretrial activities;

(4) improving the quality of the trial through more thorough preparation, and;

(5) facilitating the settlement of the case.

(b) Scheduling and Planning.

Except in categories of actions exempted by district court rule as inappropriate, the district judge, or a magistrate judge when authorized by district court rule, shall, after receiving the report from the parties under Rule 26(f) or after consulting with the attorneys for the parties and any unrepresented parties by a scheduling conference, telephone, mail, or other suitable means, enter a scheduling order that limits the time

(1) to join other parties and to amend the pleadings;
(2) to file motions; and
(3) to complete discovery.

The scheduling order may also include

(4) modifications of the times for disclosures under Rules 26(a) and 26(e)(1) and of the extent of discovery to be permitted;
(5) the date or dates for conferences before trial, a final pretrial conference, and trial; and
(6) any other matters appropriate in the circumstances of the case.

The order shall issue as soon as practicable but in any event within 90 days after the appearance of a defendant and within 120 days after the complaint has been served on a defendant. A schedule shall not be modified except upon a showing of good cause and by leave of the district judge or, when authorized by local rule, by a magistrate judge.

(c) Subjects for Consideration at Pretrial Conferences.

At any conference under this rule consideration may be given, and the court may take appropriate action, with respect to

(1) the formulation and simplification of the issues, including the elimination of frivolous claims or defenses;
(2) the necessity or desirability of amendments to the pleadings;
(3) the possibility of obtaining admissions of fact and of documents which will avoid unnecessary proof, stipulations regarding the authenticity of documents, and advance rulings from the court on the admissibility of evidence;
(4) the avoidance of unnecessary proof and of cumulative evidence, and limitations or restrictions on the use of testimony under Rule 702 of the Federal Rules of Evidence;
(5) the appropriateness and timing of summary adjudication under Rule 56;
(6) the control and scheduling of discovery, including orders affecting disclosures and discovery pursuant to Rule 26 and Rules 27 through 37;
(7) the identification of witnesses and documents, the need and schedule for filing and exchanging pretrial briefs, and the date or dates for further conferences and for trial;
(8) the advisability of referring matters to a magistrate judge or master;
(9) settlement and the use of special procedures to assist in resolving the dispute when authorized by statute or local rule;
(10) the form and substance of the pretrial order;
(11) the disposition of pending motions;
(12) the need for adopting special procedures for managing potentially difficult or protracted actions that may involve complex issues, multiple parties, difficult legal questions, or unusual proof problems;
(13) an order for a separate trial pursuant to Rule 42(b) with respect to a claim, counterclaim, cross-claim, or third-party claim, or with respect to any particular issue in the case;

(14) an order directing a party or parties to present evidence early in the trial with respect to a manageable issue that could, on the evidence, be the basis for a judgment as a matter of law under Rule 50(a) or a judgment on partial findings under Rule 52(c);

(15) an order establishing a reasonable limit on the time allowed for presenting evidence; and

(16) such other matters as may facilitate the just, speedy, and inexpensive disposition of the action.

At least one of the attorneys for each party participating in any conference before trial shall have authority to enter into stipulations and to make admissions regarding all matters that the participants may reasonably anticipate may be discussed. If appropriate, the court may require that a party or its representatives be present or reasonably available by telephone in order to consider possible settlement of the dispute.

(d) Final Pretrial Conference.

Any final pretrial conference shall be held as close to the time of trial as reasonable under the circumstances. The participants at any such conference shall formulate a plan for trial, including a program for facilitating the admission of evidence. The conference shall be attended by at least one of the attorneys who will conduct the trial for each of the parties and by any unrepresented parties.

(e) Pretrial Orders.

After any conference held pursuant to this rule, an order shall be entered reciting the action taken. This order shall control the subsequent course of the action unless modified by a subsequent order. The order following a final pretrial conference shall be modified only to prevent manifest injustice.

(f) Sanctions.

If a party or party's attorney fails to obey a scheduling or pretrial order, or if no appearance is made on behalf of a party at a scheduling or pretrial conference, or if a party or party's attorney is substantially unprepared to participate in the conference, or if a party or party's attorney fails to participate in good faith, the judge, upon motion or the judge's own initiative, may make such orders with regard thereto as are just, and among others any of the orders provided in Rule 37(b)(2) (B), (C), (D). In lieu of or in addition to any other sanction, the judge shall require the party or the attorney representing the party or both to pay the reasonable expenses incurred because of any noncompliance with this rule, including attorney's fees, unless the judge finds that the noncompliance was substantially justified or that other circumstances make an award of expenses unjust.

V. DEPOSITIONS AND DISCOVERY

Rule 26. General Provisions Governing Discovery; Duty of Disclosure

(a) Required Disclosures; Methods to Discover Additional Matter.

(1) Initial Disclosures.

Except to the extent otherwise stipulated or directed by order or local rule, a party shall, without awaiting a discovery request, provide to other parties:

(A) the name and, if known, the address and telephone number of each individual likely to have discoverable information relevant to disputed facts alleged with particularity in the pleadings, identifying the subjects of the information;

(B) a copy of, or a description by category and location of, all documents, data compilations, and tangible things in the possession, custody, or control of the party that are relevant to disputed facts alleged with particularity in the pleadings;

(C) a computation of any category of damages claimed by the disclosing party, making available for inspection and copying as under Rule 34 the documents or other evidentiary material, not privileged or protected from disclosure, on which such computation is based, including materials bearing on the nature and extent of injuries suffered; and

(D) for inspection and copying as under Rule 34 any insurance agreement under which any person carrying on an insurance business may be liable to satisfy part or all of a judgment which may be entered in the action or to indemnify or reimburse for payments made to satisfy the judgment.

Unless otherwise stipulated or directed by the court, these disclosures shall be made at or within 10 days after the meeting of the parties under subdivision (f). A party shall make its initial disclosures based on the information then reasonably available to it and is not excused from making its disclosures because it has not fully completed its investigation of the case or because it challenges the sufficiency of another party's disclosures or because another party has not made its disclosures.

(2) Disclosure of Expert Testimony.

(A) In addition to the disclosures required by paragraph (1), a party shall disclose to other parties the identity of any person who may be used at trial to present evidence under Rules 702, 703, or 705 of the Federal Rules of Evidence.

(B) Except as otherwise stipulated or directed by the court, this disclosure shall, with respect to a witness who is retained or specially employed to provide expert testimony in the case or whose duties as an employee of the party regularly involve giving expert testimony, be accompanied by a written report prepared and signed by the witness. The report shall contain a complete statement of all opinions to be expressed and the basis and reasons therefor; the data or other information considered by the witness in forming the opinions; any exhibits to be used as a summary of or support for the opinions; the qualifications of the witness, including a list of all publications authored by the witness within the preceding ten years; the compensation to be paid for the study and testimony; and a listing of any other cases in which the witness has testified as an expert at trial or by deposition within the preceding four years.

(C) These disclosures shall be made at the times and in the sequence directed by the court. In the absence of other directions from the court or stipulation by the parties, the disclosures shall be made at least 90 days before the trial date or the date the case is to be ready for trial or, if the evidence is intended solely to contradict or rebut evidence on the same subject matter identified by another party under paragraph (2)(B), within 30 days after the disclosure made by the other party. The parties shall supplement these disclosures when required under subdivision (e)(1).

(3) Pretrial Disclosures.

In addition to the disclosures required in the preceding paragraphs, a party shall provide to other parties the following information regarding the evidence that it may present at trial other than solely for impeachment purposes:

(A) the name and, if not previously provided, the address and telephone number of each witness, separately identifying those whom the party expects to present and those whom the party may call if the need arises;

(B) the designation of those witnesses whose testimony is expected to be presented by means of a deposition and, if not taken stenographically, a transcript of the pertinent portions of the deposition testimony; and

(C) an appropriate identification of each document or other exhibit, including summaries of other evidence, separately identifying those which the party expects to offer and those which the party may offer if the need arises.

Unless otherwise directed by the court, these disclosures shall be made at least 30 days before trial. Within 14 days thereafter, unless a different time is specified by the court, a party may serve and file a list disclosing (i) any objections to the use under Rule 32(a) of a deposition designated by another party under subparagraph (B) and (ii) any objection, together with the grounds therefor, that may be made to the admissibility of materials identified under subparagraph (C). Objections not so disclosed, other than objections under Rules 402 and 403 of the Federal Rules of Evidence, shall be deemed waived unless excused by the court for good cause shown.

(4) Form of Disclosures; Filing.

Unless otherwise directed by order or local rule, all disclosures under paragraphs (1) through (3) shall be made in writing, signed, served, and promptly filed with the court.

(5) Methods to Discover Additional Matter.

Parties may obtain discovery by one or more of the following methods: depositions upon oral examination or written questions; written interrogatories; production of documents or things or permission to enter upon land or other property under Rule 34 or 45(a)(1) (C), for inspection and other purposes; physical and mental examinations; and requests for admission.

(b) Discovery Scope and Limits.

Unless otherwise limited by order of the court in accordance with these rules, the scope of discovery is as follows:

(1) In General.

Parties may obtain discovery regarding any matter, not privileged, which is relevant to the subject matter involved in the pending action, whether it relates to the claim or defense of the party seeking discovery or to the claim or defense of any other party, including the existence, description, nature, custody, condition, and location of any books, documents, or other tangible things and the identity and location of persons having knowledge of any discoverable matter. The information sought need not be admissible at the trial if the information sought appears reasonably calculated to lead to the discovery of admissible evidence.

(2) Limitations.

By order or by local rule, the court may alter the limits in these rules on the number of depositions and interrogatories and may also limit the length of depositions under Rule 30 and the number of requests under Rule 36. The frequency or extent of use of the discovery methods otherwise permitted under these rules and by any local rule shall be limited by the court if it determines that: (i) the discovery sought is unreasonably cumulative or duplicative, or is obtainable from some other source that is more convenient, less burdensome, or less expensive; (ii) the party seeking discovery has had ample opportunity by discovery in the action to obtain the information sought; or (iii) the burden or expense of the proposed discovery outweighs its likely benefit, taking into account the needs of the case, the amount in controversy, the parties' resources, the importance of the issues at stake in the litigation, and the importance of the proposed discovery in resolving the issues. The court may act upon its own initiative after reasonable notice or pursuant to a motion under subdivision (c).

(3) Trial Preparation: Materials.

Subject to the provisions of subdivision (b)(4) of this rule, a party may obtain discovery of documents and tangible things otherwise discoverable under subdivision (b)(1) of this rule and prepared in anticipation of litigation or for trial by or for another party or by or for that other party's representative (including the other party's attorney, consultant, surety, indemnitor, insurer, or agent) only upon a showing that the party seeking discovery has substantial need of the materials in the preparation of the party's case and that the party is unable without undue hardship to obtain the substantial equivalent of the materials by other means. In ordering discovery of such materials when the required showing has been made, the court shall protect against disclosure of the mental impressions, conclusions, opinions, or legal theories of an attorney or other representative of a party concerning the litigation.

A party may obtain without the required showing a statement concerning the action or its subject matter previously made by that party. Upon request, a person not a party may obtain without the required showing a statement concerning the action or its subject matter previously made by that person. If the request is refused, the person may move for a court order. The provisions of Rule 37(a)(4) apply to the award of expenses incurred in relation to the motion. For purposes of this paragraph, a statement previously made is (A) a written statement signed or otherwise adopted or approved by the person making it, or (B) a stenographic, mechanical, electrical, or other recording, or a transcription thereof, which is a substantially verbatim recital of an oral statement by the person making it and contemporaneously recorded.

(4) Trial Preparation: Experts.

(A) A party may depose any person who has been identified as an expert whose opinions may be presented at trial. If a report from the expert is required under subdivision (a)(2)(B), the deposition shall not be conducted until after the report is provided.

(B) A party may, through interrogatories or by deposition, discover facts known or opinions held by an expert who has been retained or specially employed by another party in anticipation of litigation or preparation for trial and who is not expected to be called as a witness at trial, only as provided in Rule 35(b) or upon a showing of exceptional circumstances under which it is impracticable for the party seeking discovery to obtain facts or opinions on the same subject by other means.

(C) Unless manifest injustice would result, (i) the court shall require that the party seeking discovery pay the expert a reasonable fee for time spent in responding to discovery under this subdivision; and (ii) with respect to discovery obtained under subdivision (b)(4)(B) of this rule the court shall require the party seeking discovery to pay the other party a fair portion of the fees and expenses reasonably incurred by the latter party in obtaining facts and opinions from the expert.

(5) Claims of Privilege or Protection of Trial Preparation Materials. When a party withholds information otherwise discoverable under these rules by claiming that it is privileged or subject to protection as trial preparation material, the party shall make the claim expressly and shall describe the nature of the documents, communications, or things not produced or disclosed in a manner that, without revealing information itself privileged or protected, will enable other parties to assess the applicability of the privilege or protection.

(c) Protective Orders.

Upon motion by a party or by the person from whom discovery is sought, accompanied by a certification that the movant has in good faith conferred or attempted to confer with other affected parties in an effort to resolve the dispute without court action, and for good cause shown, the court in which the action is pending or alternatively, on matters relating to a deposition, the court in the district where the deposition is to be taken may make any order which justice requires to protect a party or person from annoyance, embarrassment, oppression, or undue burden or expense, including one or more of the following:

(1) that the disclosure or discovery not be had;

(2) that the disclosure or discovery may be had only on specified terms and conditions, including a designation of the time or place;

(3) that the discovery may be had only by a method of discovery other than that selected by the party seeking discovery;

(4) that certain matters not be inquired into, or that the scope of the disclosure or discovery be limited to certain matters;

(5) that discovery be conducted with no one present except persons designated by the court;

(6) that a deposition, after being sealed, be opened only by order of the court;

(7) that a trade secret or other confidential research, development, or commercial information not be revealed or be revealed only in a designated way; and

(8) that the parties simultaneously file specified documents or information enclosed in sealed envelopes to be opened as directed by the court.

If the motion for a protective order is denied in whole or in part, the court may, on such terms and conditions as are just, order that any party or other person provide or permit discovery. The provisions of Rule 37(a)(4) apply to the award of expenses incurred in relation to the motion.

(d) Timing and Sequence of Discovery.

Except when authorized under these rules or by local rule, order, or agreement of the parties, a party may not seek discovery from any source before the parties have met and conferred as required by subdivision (f). Unless the court upon motion, for the convenience of parties and witnesses and in the interests of justice, orders otherwise, methods of discovery may be used in any sequence, and the fact that a party is conducting discovery, whether by deposition or otherwise, shall not operate to delay any other party's discovery.

(e) Supplementation of Disclosures and Responses.

A party who has made a disclosure under subdivision (a) or responded to a request for discovery with a disclosure or response is under a duty to supplement or correct the disclosure or response to include information thereafter acquired if ordered by the court or in the following circumstances:

(1) A party is under a duty to supplement at appropriate intervals its disclosures under subdivision (a) if the party learns that in some material respect the information disclosed is incomplete or incorrect and if the additional or corrective information has not otherwise been made known to the other parties during the discovery process or in writing. With respect to testimony of an expert from whom a report is required under subdivision (a)(2)(B) the duty extends both to information contained in the report and to information provided through a deposition of the expert, and any additions or other changes to this information shall be disclosed by the time the party's disclosures under Rule 26(a)(3) are due.

(2) A party is under a duty seasonably to amend a prior response to an interrogatory, request for production, or request for admission if the party learns that the response is in some material respect incomplete or incorrect and if the additional or corrective information has not otherwise been made known to the other parties during the discovery process or in writing.

(f) Meeting of Parties; Planning for Discovery.

Except in actions exempted by local rule or when otherwise ordered, the parties shall, as soon as practicable and in any event at least 14 days before a scheduling conference is held or a scheduling order is due under Rule 16(b), meet to discuss the nature and basis of their claims and defenses and the possibilities for a prompt settlement or resolution of the case, to make or arrange for the disclosures required by subdivision (a)(1), and to develop a proposed discovery plan. The plan shall indicate the parties' views and proposals concerning:

(1) what changes should be made in the timing, form, or requirement for disclosures under subdivision (a) or local rule, including a statement as to when disclosures under subdivision (a)(1) were made or will be made;

(2) the subjects on which discovery may be needed, when discovery should be completed, and whether discovery should be conducted in phases or be limited to or focused upon particular issues;

(3) what changes should be made in the limitations on discovery imposed under these rules or by local rule, and what other limitations should be imposed; and

(4) any other orders that should be entered by the court under subdivision (c) or under Rule 16(b) and (c).

The attorneys of record and all unrepresented parties that have appeared in the case are jointly responsible for arranging and being present or represented at the meeting, for attempting in good faith to agree on the proposed discovery plan, and for submitting to the court within 10 days after the meeting a written report outlining the plan.

(g) Signing of Disclosures, Discovery Requests, Responses, and Objections.

(1) Every disclosure made pursuant to subdivision (a)(1) or subdivision (a)(3) shall be signed by at least one attorney of record in the attorney's individual name, whose address shall be stated. An unrepresented party shall sign the disclosure and state the party's address. The signature of the attorney or party constitutes a certification that to the best of the signer's knowledge, information, and belief, formed after a reasonable inquiry, the disclosure is complete and correct as of the time it is made.

(2) Every discovery request, response, or objection made by a party represented by an attorney shall be signed by at least one attorney of record in the attorney's individual name, whose address shall be stated. An unrepresented party shall sign the request, response, or objection and state the party's address. The signature of the attorney or party constitutes a certification that to the best of the signer's knowledge, information, and belief, formed after a reasonable inquiry, the request, response, or objection is:

(A) consistent with these rules and warranted by existing law or a good faith argument for the extension, modification, or reversal of existing law;

(B) not interposed for any improper purpose, such as to harass or to cause unnecessary delay or needless increase in the cost of litigation; and

(C) not unreasonable or unduly burdensome or expensive, given the needs of the case, the discovery already had in the case, the amount in controversy, and the importance of the issues at stake in the litigation.

If a request, response, or objection is not signed, it shall be stricken unless it is signed promptly after the omission is called to the attention of the party making the request, response, or objection, and a party shall not be obligated to take any action with respect to it until it is signed.

(3) If without substantial justification a certification is made in violation of the rule, the court, upon motion or upon its own initiative, shall impose upon the person who made the certification, the party on whose behalf the disclosure, request, response, or objection is made, or both, an appropriate sanction, which may include an order to pay the amount of the reasonable expenses incurred because of the violation, including a reasonable attorney's fee.

Rule 29. Stipulations Regarding Discovery Procedure
Unless otherwise directed by the court, the parties may by written stipulation (1) provide that depositions may be taken before any person, at any time or place, upon any notice, and in any manner and when so taken may be used like other depositions, and (2) modify other procedures governing or limitations placed upon discovery, except that stipulations extending the time provided in Rules 33, 34, and 36 for responses to discovery may, if they would interfere with any time set for completion of discovery, for hearing of a motion, or for trial, be made only with the approval of the court.

Rule 30. Deposition Upon Oral Examination

(a) When Depositions May Be Taken; When Leave Required.

(1) A party may take the testimony of any person, including a party, by deposition upon oral examination without leave of court except as provided in paragraph (2). The attendance of witnesses may be compelled by subpoena as provided in Rule 45.

(2) A party must obtain leave of court, which shall be granted to the extent consistent with the principles stated in Rule 26(b)(2), if the person to be examined is confined in prison or if, without the written stipulation of the parties.

(A) a proposed deposition would result in more than ten depositions being taken under this rule or Rule 31 by the plaintiffs, or by the defendants, or by third-party defendants;

(B) the person to be examined already has been deposed in the case; or

(C) a party seeks to take a deposition before the time specified in Rule 26(d) unless the notice contains a certification, with supporting facts, that the person to be examined is expected to leave the United States and be unavailable for examination in this country unless deposed before that time.

(b) Notice of Examination: General Requirements; Method of Recording; Production of Documents and Things; Deposition of Organization; Deposition by Telephone.

(1) A party desiring to take the deposition of any person upon oral examination shall give reasonable notice in writing to every other party to the action. The notice shall state the time and place for taking the deposition and the name and address of each person to be examined, if known, and, if the name is not known, a general description sufficient to identify the person or the particular class or group to which the person belongs. If a subpoena duces tecum is to be served on the person to be examined, the designation of the materials to be produced as set forth in the subpoena shall be attached to, or included in, the notice.

(2) The party taking the deposition shall state in the notice the method by which the testimony shall be recorded. Unless the court orders otherwise, it may be recorded by sound, sound-and-visual, or stenographic means, and the party taking the deposition shall bear the cost of the recording. Any party may arrange for a transcription to be made from the recording of a deposition taken by nonstenographic means.

(3) With prior notice to the deponent and other parties, any party may designate another method to record the deponent's testimony in addition to

the method specified by the person taking the deposition. The additional record or transcript shall be made at that party's expense unless the court otherwise orders.

(4) Unless otherwise agreed by the parties, a deposition shall be conducted before an officer appointed or designated under Rule 28 and shall begin with a statement on the record by the officer that includes (A) the officer's name and business address; (B) the date, time and place of the deposition; (C) the name of the deponent; (D) the administration of the oath or affirmation to the deponent; and (E) an identification of all persons present. If the deposition is recorded other than stenographically, the officer shall repeat items (A) through (C) at the beginning of each unit of recorded tape or other recording medium. The appearance or demeanor of deponents or attorneys shall not be distorted through camera or sound-recording techniques. At the end of the deposition, the officer shall state on the record that the deposition is complete and shall set forth any stipulations made by counsel concerning the custody of the transcript or recording and the exhibits, or concerning other pertinent matters.

(5) The notice to a party deponent may be accompanied by a request made in compliance with Rule 34 for the production of documents and tangible things at the taking of the deposition. The procedure of Rule 34 shall apply to the request.

(6) A party may in the party's notice and in a subpoena name as the deponent a public or private corporation or a partnership or association or governmental agency and describe with reasonable particularity the matters on which examination is requested. In that event, the organization so named shall designate one or more officers, directors, or managing agents, or other persons who consent to testify on its behalf, and may set forth, for each person designated, the matters on which the person will testify. A subpoena shall advise a non-party organization of its duty to make such a designation. The persons so designated shall testify as to matters known or reasonably available to the organization. This subdivision (b)(6) does not preclude taking a deposition by any other procedure authorized in these rules.

(7) The parties may stipulate in writing or the court may upon motion order that a deposition be taken by telephone or other remote electronic means. For the purposes of this rule and Rules 28(a), 37(a)(1), and 37(b)(1), a deposition taken by such means is taken in the district and at the place where the deponent is to answer questions.

(c) Examination and Cross-Examination; Record of Examination; Oath; Objections.

Examination and cross-examination of witnesses may proceed as permitted at the trial under the provisions of the Federal Rules of Evidence except Rules 103 and 615. The officer before whom the deposition is to be taken shall put the witness on oath or affirmation and shall personally, or by someone acting under the officer's direction and in the officer's presence, record the testimony of the witness. The testimony shall be taken stenographically or recorded by any other method authorized by subdivision (b)(2) of this rule. All objections made at the time of the examination to the qualifications of the officer taking the deposition, to the manner of taking it, to the evidence presented, to the conduct of any party, or to any other aspect of the proceedings shall be noted by the officer upon the record of the deposition; but the examination shall proceed, with the testimony being taken subject to the objections. In lieu of participating in the oral examination, parties may serve written questions in a sealed envelope on the party taking the deposition and the party taking the deposition shall transmit them to the officer, who shall propound them to the witness and record the answers verbatim.

(d) Schedule and Duration; Motion to Terminate or Limit Examination.

(1) Any objection to evidence during a deposition shall be stated concisely and in a non-argumentative and non-suggestive manner. A party may instruct a deponent not to answer only when necessary to preserve a privilege, to enforce a limitation on evidence directed by the court, or to present a motion under paragraph (3).

(2) By order or local rule, the court may limit the time permitted for the conduct of a deposition, but shall allow additional time consistently with Rule 26(b)(2) if needed for a fair examination of the deponent or if the deponent or another party impedes or delays the examination. If the court finds such an impediment, delay, or other conduct that has frustrated the fair examination of the deponent, it may impose upon the persons responsible an appropriate sanction, including the reasonable costs and attorney's fees incurred by any parties as a result thereof.

(3) At any time during a deposition, on motion of a party or of the deponent and upon a showing that the examination is being conducted in bad faith or in such manner as unreasonably to annoy, embarrass, or oppress the deponent or party, the court in which the action is pending or the court in the district where the deposition is being taken may order the officer conducting the examination to cease forthwith from taking the deposition, or may limit the scope and manner of the taking of the deposition as provided in Rule 26(c). If the order made terminates the examination, it shall be resumed thereafter only upon the order of the court in which the action is pending. Upon demand of the objecting party or deponent, the taking of the deposition shall be suspended for the time necessary to make a motion for an order. The provisions of Rule 37(a)(4) apply to the award of expenses incurred in relation to the motion.

(e) Review by Witness; Changes; Signing.

If requested by the deponent or a party before completion of the deposition, the deponent shall have 30 days after being notified by the officer that the transcript or recording is available in which to review the transcript or recording and, if there are changes in form or substance, to sign a statement reciting such changes and the reasons given by the deponent for making them. The officer shall indicate in the certificate prescribed by subdivision (f)(1) whether any review was requested and, if so, shall append any changes made by the deponent during the period allowed.

(f) Certification and Filing by Officer; Exhibits; Copies; Notices of Filing.

(1) The officer shall certify that the witness was duly sworn by the officer and that the deposition is a true record of the testimony given by the witness. This certificate shall be in writing and accompany the record of the deposition. Unless otherwise ordered by the court, the officer shall securely seal the deposition in an envelope or package indorsed with the title of the action and marked 'Deposition of [here insert name of witness]' and shall promptly file it with the court in which the action is pending or

send it to the attorney who arranged for the transcript or recording, who shall store it under conditions that will protect it against loss, destruction, tampering, or deterioration. Documents and things produced for inspection during the examination of the witness, shall, upon the request of a party, be marked for identification and annexed to the deposition and may be inspected and copied by any party, except that if the person producing the materials desires to retain them the person may (A) offer copies to be marked for identification and annexed to the deposition and to serve thereafter as originals if the person affords to all parties fair opportunity to verify the copies by comparison with the originals, or (B) offer the originals to be marked for identification, after giving to each party an opportunity to inspect and copy them, in which event the materials may then be used in the same manner as if annexed to the deposition. Any party may move for an order that the original be annexed to and returned with the deposition to the court, pending final disposition of the case.

(2) Unless otherwise ordered by the court or agreed by the parties, the officer shall retain stenographic notes of any deposition taken stenographically or a copy of the recording of any deposition taken by another method. Upon payment of reasonable charges therefor, the officer shall furnish a copy of the transcript or other recording of the deposition to any party or to the deponent.

(3) The party taking the deposition shall give prompt notice of its filing to all other parties.

(g) Failure to Attend or to Serve Subpoena; Expenses.

(1) If the party giving the notice of the taking of a deposition fails to attend and proceed therewith and another party attends in person or by attorney pursuant to the notice, the court may order the party giving the notice to pay to such other party the reasonable expenses incurred by that party and that party's attorney in attending, including reasonable attorney's fees.

(2) If the party giving the notice of the taking of a deposition of a witness fails to serve a subpoena upon the witness and the witness because of such failure does not attend, and if another party attends in person or by attorney because that party expects the deposition of that witness to be taken, the court may order the party giving the notice to pay to such other party the reasonable expenses incurred by that party and that party's attorney in attending, including reasonable attorney's fees.

Rule 31. Depositions Upon Written Questions

(a) Serving Questions; Notice.

(1) A party may take the testimony of any person, including a party, by deposition upon written questions without leave of court except as provided in paragraph (2). The attendance of witnesses may be compelled by the use of subpoena as provided in Rule 45.

(2) A party must obtain leave of court, which shall be granted to the extent consistent with the principles stated in Rule 26(b)(2), if the person to be examined is confined in prison or if, without the written stipulation of the parties.

(A) a proposed deposition would result in more than ten depositions being taken under this rule or Rule 30 by the plaintiffs, or by the defendants, or by third-party defendants;

(B) the person to be examined has already been deposed in the case; or

(C) a party seeks to take a deposition before the time specified in Rule 26(d).

(3) A party desiring to take a deposition upon written questions shall serve them upon every other party with a notice stating (1) the name and address of the person who is to answer them, if known, and if the name is not known, a general description sufficient to identify the person or the particular class or group to which the person belongs, and (2) the name or descriptive title and address of the officer before whom the deposition is to be taken. A deposition upon written questions may be taken of a public or private corporation or a partnership or association or governmental agency in accordance with the provisions of Rule 30(b)(6).

(4) Within 14 days after the notice and written questions are served, a party may serve cross questions upon all other parties. Within 7 days after being served with cross questions, a party may serve redirect questions upon all other parties. Within 7 days after being served with redirect questions, a party may serve recross questions upon all other parties. The court may for cause shown enlarge or shorten the time.

(b) Officer to Take Responses and Prepare Record.

A copy of the notice and copies of all questions served shall be delivered by the party taking the deposition to the officer designated in the notice, who shall proceed promptly, in the manner provided by Rule 30(c), (e), and (f), to take the testimony of the witness in response to the questions and to prepare, certify, and file or mail the deposition, attaching thereto the copy of the notice and the questions received by the officer.

(c) Notice of Filing.

When the deposition is filed the party taking it shall promptly give notice thereof to all other parties.

Rule 32. Use of Depositions in Court Proceedings

(a) Use of Depositions.

(1) Any deposition may be used by any party for the purpose of contradicting or impeaching the testimony of deponent as a witness, or for any other purpose permitted by the Federal Rules of Evidence.

(2) The deposition of a party or of anyone who at the time of taking the deposition was an officer, director, or managing agent, or a person designated under Rule 30(b)(6) or 31(a) to testify on behalf of a public or private corporation, partnership or association or governmental agency which is a party may be used by an adverse party for any purpose.

(3) The deposition of a witness, whether or not a party, may be used by any party for any purpose if the court finds:

(A) that the witness is dead; or

(B) that the witness is at a greater distance than 100 miles from the place of trial or hearing, or is out of the United States, unless it appears that the absence of the witness was procured by the party offering the deposition; or

(C) that the witness is unable to attend or testify because of age, illness, infirmity, or imprisonment; or

(D) that the party offering the deposition has been unable to procure the attendance of the witness by subpoena; or
(E) upon application and notice, that such exceptional circumstances exist as to make it desirable, in the interest of justice and with due regard to the importance of presenting the testimony of witnesses orally in open court, to allow the deposition to be used.

A deposition taken without leave of court pursuant to a notice under Rule 30(a)(2)(C) shall not be used against a party who demonstrates that, when served with the notice, it was unable through the exercise of diligence to obtain counsel to represent it at the taking of the deposition; nor shall a deposition be used against a party who, having received less than 11 days notice of a deposition, has promptly upon receiving such notice filed a motion for a protective order under Rule 26(c)(2) requesting that the deposition not be held or be held at a different time or place and such motion is pending at the time the deposition is held.

(b) Objections to Admissibility.

Subject to the provisions of Rule 28(b) and subdivision (d)(3) of this rule, objection may be made at the trial or hearing to receiving in evidence any deposition or part thereof for any reason which would require the exclusion of the evidence if the witness were then present and testifying.

(c) Form of presentation.

Except as otherwise directed by the court, a party offering deposition testimony pursuant to this rule may offer it in stenographic or nonstenographic form, but, if in nonstenographic form, the party shall also provide the court with a transcript of the portions so offered. On request of any party in a case tried before a jury, deposition testimony offered other than for impeachment purposes shall be presented in nonstenographic form, if available, unless the court for good cause orders otherwise.

(d) Effect of Errors and Irregularities in Depositions.

(1) As to Notice.

All errors and irregularities in the notice for taking a deposition are waived unless written objection is promptly served upon the party giving the notice.

(2) As to Disqualification of Officer.

Objection to taking a deposition because of disqualification of the officer before whom it is to be taken is waived unless made before the taking of the deposition begins or as soon thereafter as the disqualification becomes known or could be discovered with reasonable diligence.

(3) As to Taking of Deposition.

(A) Objections to the competency of a witness or to the competency, relevancy, or materiality of testimony are not waived by failure to make them before or during the taking of the deposition, unless the ground of the objection is one which might have been obviated or removed if presented at that time.

(B) Errors and irregularities occurring at the oral examination in the manner of taking the deposition, in the form of the questions or answers, in the oath or affirmation, or in the conduct of parties, and errors of any kind which might be obviated, removed, or cured if promptly presented, are waived unless seasonable objection thereto is made at the taking of the deposition.

(C) Objections to the form of written questions submitted under Rule 31 are waived unless served in writing upon the party propounding them within the time allowed for serving the succeeding cross or other questions and within 5 days after service of the last questions authorized.

(4) As to Completion and Return of Deposition.

Errors and irregularities in the manner in which the testimony is transcribed or the deposition is prepared, signed, certified, sealed, indorsed, transmitted, filed, or otherwise dealt with by the officer under Rules 30 and 31 are waived unless a motion to suppress the deposition or some part thereof is made with reasonable promptness after such defect is, or with due diligence might have been, ascertained.

Rule 33. Interrogatories to Parties

(a) Availability.

Without leave of court or written stipulation, any party may serve upon any other party written interrogatories, not exceeding 25 in number including all discrete subparts, to be answered by the party served or, if the party served is a public or private corporation or a partnership or association or governmental agency, by any officer or agent, who shall furnish such information as is available to the party. Leave to serve additional interrogatories shall be granted to the extent consistent with the principles of Rule 26(b)(2). Without leave of court or written stipulation, interrogatories may not be served before the time specified in Rule 26(d).

(b) Answers and Objections.

(1) Each interrogatory shall be answered separately and fully in writing under oath, unless it is objected to, in which event the objecting party shall state the reasons for objection and shall answer to the extent the interrogatory is not objectionable.

(2) The answers are to be signed by the person making them, and the objections signed by the attorney making them.

(3) The party upon whom the interrogatories have been served shall serve a copy of the answers, and objections if any, within 30 days after the service of the interrogatories. A shorter or longer time may be directed by the court or, in the absence of such an order, agreed to in writing by the parties subject to Rule 29.

(4) All grounds for an objection to an interrogatory shall be stated with specificity. Any ground not stated in a timely objection is waived unless the party's failure to object is excused by the court for good cause shown.

(5) The party submitting the interrogatories may move for an order under Rule 37(a) with respect to any objection to or other failure to answer an interrogatory.

(c) Scope; Use at Trial.

Interrogatories may relate to any matters which can be inquired into under Rule 26(b)(1), and the answers may be used to the extent permitted by the rules of evidence.

An interrogatory otherwise proper is not necessarily objectionable merely because an answer to the interrogatory involves an opinion or contention that relates to fact or the application of law to fact, but the court may order that such an interrogatory need not be answered until after designated discovery has been completed or until a pre-trial conference or other later time.

(d) Option to Produce Business Records.

Where the answer to an interrogatory may be derived or ascertained from the business records of the party upon whom the interrogatory has been served or from an examination, audit or inspection of such business records, including a compilation, abstract or summary thereof, and the burden of deriving or ascertaining the answer is substantially the same for the party serving the interrogatory as for the party served, it is a sufficient answer to such interrogatory to specify the records from which the answer may be derived or ascertained and to afford to the party serving the interrogatory reasonable opportunity to examine, audit or inspect such records and to make copies, compilations, abstracts or summaries. A specification shall be in sufficient detail to permit the interrogating party to locate and to identify, as readily as can the party served, the records from which the answer may be ascertained.

Rule 34. Production of Documents and Things and Entry Upon Land for Inspection and Other Purposes

(a) Scope.

Any party may serve on any other party a request (1) to produce and permit the party making the request, or someone acting on the requestor's behalf, to inspect and copy, any designated documents (including writings, drawings, graphs, charts, photographs, phonorecords, and other data compilations from which information can be obtained, translated, if necessary, by the respondent through detection devices into reasonably usable form), or to inspect and copy, test, or sample any tangible things which constitute or contain matters within the scope of Rule 26(b) and which are in the possession, custody or control of the party upon whom the request is served; or (2) to permit entry upon designated land or other property in the possession or control of the party upon whom the request is served for the purpose of inspection and measuring, surveying, photographing, testing, or sampling the property or any designated object or operation thereon, within the scope of Rule 26(b).

(b) Procedure.

The request shall set forth, either by individual item or by category, the items to be inspected, and describe each with reasonable particularity. The request shall specify a reasonable time, place, and manner of making the inspection and performing the related acts. Without leave of court or written stipulation, a request may not be served before the time specified in Rule 26(d).

The party upon whom the request is served shall serve a written response within 30 days after the service of the request. A shorter or longer time may be directed by the court or, in the absence of such an order, agreed to in writing by the parties, subject to Rule 29. The response shall state, with respect to each item or category, that inspection and related activities will be permitted as requested, unless the request is objected to, in which event the reasons for the objection shall be stated. If objection is made to part of an item or category, the part shall be specified and inspection permitted of the remaining parts. The party submitting the request may move for an order under Rule 37(a) with respect to any objection to or other failure to respond to the request or any part thereof, or any failure to permit inspection as requested.

A party who produces documents for inspection shall produce them as they are kept in the usual course of business or shall organize and label them to correspond with the categories in the request.

(c) Persons Not Parties.

A person not a party to the action may be compelled to produce documents and things or to submit to an inspection as provided in Rule 45.

Rule 35. Physical and Mental Examination of Persons

(a) Order for Examination.

When the mental or physical condition (including the blood group) of a party or of a person in the custody or under the legal control of a party, is in controversy, the court in which the action is pending may order the party to submit to a physical or mental examination by a suitably licensed or certified examiner or to produce for examination the person in the party's custody or legal control. The order may be made only on motion for good cause shown and upon notice to the person to be examined and to all parties and shall specify the time, place, manner, conditions, and scope of the examination and the person or persons by whom it is to be made.

(b) Report of Examiner.

(1) If requested by the party against whom an order is made under Rule 35(a) or the person examined, the party causing the examination to be made shall deliver to the requesting party a copy of the detailed written report of the examiner setting out the examiner's findings, including results of all tests made, diagnoses and conclusions, together with like reports of all earlier examinations of the same condition. After delivery the party causing the examination shall be entitled upon request to receive from the party against whom the order is made a like report of any examination, previously or thereafter made, of the same condition, unless, in the case of a report of examination of a person not a party, the party shows that the party is unable to obtain it. The court on motion may make an order against a party requiring delivery of a report on such terms as are just, and if an examiner fails or refuses to make a report the court may exclude the examiner's testimony if offered at trial.

(2) By requesting and obtaining a report of the examination so ordered or by taking the deposition of the examiner, the party examined waives any privilege the party may have in that action or any other involving the same controversy, regarding the testimony of every other person who has examined or may thereafter examine the party in respect of the same mental or physical condition.

(3) This subdivision applies to examinations made by agreement of the parties, unless the agreement expressly provides otherwise. This subdivision does not preclude discovery of a report of an examiner or the taking of a deposition of the examiner in accordance with the provisions of any other rule.

(c) Definitions.

For the purpose of this rule, a psychologist is a psychologist licensed or certified by a State or the District of Columbia.

Rule 37. Failure to Make or Cooperate in Discovery; Sanctions

(a) Motion for Order Compelling Disclosure or Discovery.

A party, upon reasonable notice to other parties and all persons affected thereby, may apply for an order compelling disclosure or discovery as follows:

(1) Appropriate Court.
An application for an order to a party shall be made to the court in which the action is pending. An application for an order to a person who is not a party shall be made to the court in the district where the discovery is being, or is to be, taken.
(2) Motion.

(A) If a party fails to make a disclosure required by Rule 26(a), any other party may move to compel disclosure and for appropriate sanctions. The motion must include a certification that the movant has in good faith conferred or attempted to confer with the party not making the disclosure in an effort to secure the disclosure without court action.

(B) If a deponent fails to answer a question propounded or submitted under Rules 30 or 31, or a corporation or other entity fails to make a designation under Rule 30(b)(6) or 31(a), or a party fails to answer an interrogatory submitted under Rule 33, or if a party, in response to a request for inspection submitted under Rule 34, fails to respond that inspection will be permitted as requested or fails to permit inspection as requested, the discovering party may move for an order compelling answer, or a designation, or an order compelling inspection in accordance with the request. The motion must include a certification that the movant has in good faith conferred or attempted to confer with the person or party failing to make the discovery in an effort to secure the information or material without court action. When taking a deposition on oral examination, the proponent of the question may complete or adjourn the examination before applying for an order.

(3) Evasive or Incomplete Disclosure, Answer, or Response.
For purposes of this subdivision an evasive or incomplete disclosure, answer, or response is to be treated as a failure to disclose, answer, or respond.
(4) Expenses and Sanctions.

(A) If the motion is granted or if the disclosure or requested discovery is provided after the motion was filed, the court shall, after affording an opportunity to be heard, require the party or deponent whose conduct necessitated the motion or the party or attorney advising such conduct or both of them to pay to the moving party the reasonable expenses incurred in making the motion, including attorney's fees, unless the court finds that the motion was filed without the movant's first making a good faith effort to obtain the disclosure or discovery without court action, or that the opposing party's nondisclosure, response, or objection was substantially justified, or that other circumstances make an award of expenses unjust.

(B) If the motion is denied, the court may enter any protective order authorized under Rule 26(c) and shall, after affording an opportunity to be heard, require the moving party or the attorney filing the motion or both of them to pay to the party or deponent who opposed the motion the reasonable expenses incurred in opposing the motion, including attorney's fees, unless the court finds that the making of the motion was substantially justified or that other circumstances make an award of expenses unjust.

(C) If the motion is granted in part and denied in part, the court may enter any protective order authorized under Rule 26(c) and may, after affording an opportunity to be heard, apportion the reasonable expenses incurred in relation to the motion among the parties and persons in a just manner.

(b) Failure to comply with order.

(1) Sanctions by Court in District Where Deposition is Taken.

If a deponent fails to be sworn or to answer a question after being directed to do so by the court in the district in which the deposition is being taken, the failure may be considered a contempt of that court.

(2) Sanctions by Court in Which Action Is Pending.

If a party or an officer, director, or managing agent of a party or a person designated under Rule 30(b)(6) or 31(a) to testify on behalf of a party fails to obey an order to provide or permit discovery, including an order made under subdivision (a) of this rule or Rule 35, or if a party fails to obey an order entered under Rule 26(f), the court in which the action is pending may make such orders in regard to the failure as are just, and among others the following:

(A) An order that the matters regarding which the order was made or any other designated facts shall be taken to be established for the purposes of the action in accordance with the claim of the party obtaining the order;

(B) An order refusing to allow the disobedient party to support or oppose designated claims or defenses, or prohibiting that party from introducing designated matters in evidence;

(C) An order striking out pleadings or parts thereof, or staying further proceedings until the order is obeyed, or dismissing the action or proceeding or any part thereof, or rendering a judgment by default against the disobedient party;

(D) In lieu of any of the foregoing orders or in addition thereto, an order treating as a contempt of court the failure to obey any orders except an order to submit to a physical or mental examination;

(E) Where a party has failed to comply with an order under Rule 35(a) requiring that party to produce another for examination, such orders as are listed in paragraphs (A), (B), and (C) of this subdivision, unless the party failing to comply shows that that party is unable to produce such person for examination.

In lieu of any of the foregoing orders or in addition thereto, the court shall require the party failing to obey the order or the attorney advising that party or both to pay the reasonable expenses, including attorney's fees, caused by the failure, unless the court finds that the failure was substantially justified or that other circumstances make an award of expenses unjust.

(c) Failure to Disclose; False or Misleading Disclosure; Refusal to Admit.

(1) A party that without substantial justification fails to disclose information required by Rule 26(a) or 26(e)(1) shall not, unless such

failure is harmless, be permitted to use as evidence at a trial, at a hearing, or on a motion any witness or information not so disclosed. In addition to or in lieu of this sanction, the court, on motion and after affording an opportunity to be heard, may impose other appropriate sanctions. In addition to requiring payment of reasonable expenses, including attorney's fees, caused by the failure, these sanctions may include any of the sanctions authorized under subparagraphs (A), (B), and (C) of subdivision (b)(2) of this rule and may include informing the jury of the failure to make the disclosure.

(2) If a party fails to admit the genuineness of any document or the truth of any matter as requested under Rule 36, and if the party requesting the admissions thereafter proves the genuineness of the document or the truth of the matter, the requesting party may apply to the court for an order requiring the other party to pay the reasonable expenses incurred in making that proof, including reasonable attorney's fees. The court shall make the order unless it finds that (A) the request was held objectionable pursuant to Rule 36(a), or (B) the admission sought was of no substantial importance, or (C) the party failing to admit had reasonable ground to believe that the party might prevail on the matter, or (D) there was other good reason for the failure to admit.

(d) Failure of Party to Attend at Own Deposition or Serve Answers to Interrogatories or Respond to Request for Inspection.

If a party or an officer, director, or managing agent of a party or a person designated under Rule 30(b)(6) or 31(a) to testify on behalf of a party fails (1) to appear before the officer who is to take the deposition, after being served with a proper notice, or (2) to serve answers or objections to interrogatories submitted under Rule 33, after proper service of the interrogatories, or (3) to serve a written response to a request for inspection submitted under Rule 34, after proper service of the request, the court in which the action is pending on motion may make such orders in regard to the failure as are just, and among others it may take any action authorized under subparagraphs (A), (B), and (C) of subdivision (b)(2) of this rule. Any motion specifying a failure under clause (2) or (3) of this subdivision shall include a certification that the movant has in good faith conferred or attempted to confer with the party failing to answer or respond in an effort to obtain such answer or response without court action. In lieu of any order or in addition thereto, the court shall require the party failing to act or the attorney advising that party or both to pay the reasonable expenses, including attorney's fees, caused by the failure unless the court finds that the failure was substantially justified or that other circumstances make an award of expenses unjust.

The failure to act described in this subdivision may not be excused on the ground that the discovery sought is objectionable unless the party failing to act has a pending motion for a protective order as provided by Rule 26(c).

(e) [Abrogated]

(f) [Repealed]

(g) Failure to Participate in the Framing of a Discovery Plan.

If a party or a party's attorney fails to participate in the development and submission of a proposed discovery plan as required by Rule 26(f), the court may, after opportunity for hearing, require such party or attorney to pay to any other party the reasonable expenses, including attorney's fees, caused by the failure.

VI. TRIALS

Rule 38. Jury Trial of Right

(a) Right Preserved.

The right of trial by jury as declared by the Seventh Amendment to the Constitution or as given by a statute of the United States shall be preserved to the parties inviolate.

(b) Demand.

Any party may demand a trial by jury of any issue triable of right by a jury by (1) serving upon the other parties a demand therefor in writing at any time after the commencement of the action and not later than 10 days after the service of the last pleading directed to the issue, and (2) filing the demand as required by Rule 5(d). Such demand may be indorsed upon a pleading of the party.

(c) Same: Specification of Issues.

In the demand a party may specify the issues which the party wishes so tried; otherwise the party shall be deemed to have demanded trial by jury for all the issues so triable. If the party has demanded trial by jury for only some of the issues, any other party within 10 days after service of the demand or such lesser time as the court may order, may serve a demand for trial by jury of any other or all of the issues of fact in the action.

(d) Waiver.

The failure of a party to serve and file a demand as required by this rule constitutes a waiver by the party of trial by jury. A demand for trial by jury made as herein provided may not be withdrawn without the consent of the parties.

(e) Admiralty and Maritime Claims.

These rules shall not be construed to create a right to trial by jury of the issues in an admiralty or maritime claim within the meaning of Rule 9(h).

Rule 41. Dismissal of Actions

(a) Voluntary Dismissal: Effect Thereof.

(1) By Plaintiff; By Stipulation.

Subject to the provisions of Rule 23(e), of Rule 66, and of any statute of the United States, an action may be dismissed by the plaintiff without order of court (i) by filing a notice of dismissal at any time before service by the adverse party of an answer or of a motion for summary judgment, whichever first occurs, or (ii) by filing a stipulation of dismissal signed by all parties who have appeared in the action. Unless otherwise stated in the notice of dismissal or stipulation, the dismissal is without prejudice, except that a notice of dismissal operates as an adjudication upon the merits when filed by a plaintiff who has once dismissed in any court of the United States or of any state an action based on or including the same claim.

(2) By Order of Court.

Except as provided in paragraph (1) of this subdivision of this rule, an action shall not be dismissed at the plaintiff's instance save upon order of the court and upon such terms and conditions as the court deems proper. If a counterclaim has been pleaded by a defendant prior to the service upon the defendant of the plaintiff's motion to dismiss, the action shall not be dismissed against the defendant's objection unless the counterclaim can remain pending for independent adjudication by the court. Unless otherwise specified in the order, a dismissal under this paragraph is without prejudice.

(b) Involuntary Dismissal: Effect Thereof.
For failure of the plaintiff to prosecute or to comply with these rules or any order of court, a defendant may move for dismissal of an action or of any claim against the defendant. Unless the court in its order for dismissal otherwise specifies, a dismissal under this subdivision and any dismissal not provided for in this rule, other than a dismissal for lack of jurisdiction, for improper venue, or for failure to join a party under Rule 19, operates as an adjudication upon the merits.
(c) Dismissal of Counterclaim, Cross-Claim, or Third-Party Claim.
The provisions of this rule apply to the dismissal of any counterclaim, cross-claim, or third-party claim. A voluntary dismissal by the claimant alone pursuant to paragraph (1) of subdivision (a) of this rule shall be made before a responsive pleading is served or, if there is none, before the introduction of evidence at the trial or hearing.
(d) Costs of Previously-Dismissed Action.
If a plaintiff who has once dismissed an action in any court commences an action based upon or including the same claim against the same defendant, the court may make such order for the payment of costs of the action previously dismissed as it may deem proper and may stay the proceedings in the action until the plaintiff has complied with the order.
Rule 43. Taking of Testimony
(a) Form.
In every trial, the testimony of witnesses shall be taken in open court, unless a federal law, these rules, the Federal Rules of Evidence, or other rules adopted by the Supreme Court provide otherwise. The court may, for good cause shown in compelling circumstances and upon appropriate safeguards, permit presentation of testimony in open court by contemporaneous transmission from a different location.
(b) [Abrogated]
(c) [Abrogated]
(d) Affirmation in Lieu of Oath.
Whenever under these rules an oath is required to be taken, a solemn affirmation may be accepted in lieu thereof.
(e) Evidence on Motions.
When a motion is based on facts not appearing of record the court may hear the matter on affidavits presented by the respective parties, but the court may direct that the matter be heard wholly or partly on oral testimony or deposition.
(f) Interpreters.
The court may appoint an interpreter of its own selection and may fix the interpreter's reasonable compensation. The compensation shall be paid out of funds provided by law or by one or more of the parties as the court may direct, and may be taxed ultimately as costs, in the discretion of the court.
Rule 45. Subpoena
(a) Form; Issuance.

(1) Every subpoena shall

(A) state the name of the court from which it is issued; and

(B) state the title of the action, the name of the court in which it is pending, and its civil action number; and

(C) command each person to whom it is directed to attend and give testimony or to produce and permit inspection and copying of designated books, documents or tangible things in the possession, custody or control of that person, or to permit inspection of premises, at a time and place therein specified; and

(D) set forth the text of subdivisions (c) and (d) of this rule. A command to produce evidence or to permit inspection may be joined with a command to appear at trial or hearing or at deposition, or may be issued separately.

(2) A subpoena commanding attendance at a trial or hearing shall issue from the court for the district in which the hearing or trial is to be held. A subpoena for attendance at a deposition shall issue from the court for the district designated by the notice of deposition as the district in which the deposition is to be taken. If separate from a subpoena commanding the attendance of a person, a subpoena for production or inspection shall issue from the court for the district in which the production or inspection is to be made.

(3) The clerk shall issue a subpoena, signed but otherwise in blank, to a party requesting it, who shall complete it before service. An attorney as officer of the court may also issue and sign a subpoena on behalf of

(A) a court in which the attorney is authorized to practice; or

(B) a court for a district in which a deposition or production is compelled by the subpoena, if the deposition or production pertains to an action pending in a court in which the attorney is authorized to practice.

(b) Service.

(1) A subpoena may be served by any person who is not a party and is not less than 18 years of age. Service of a subpoena upon a person named therein shall be made by delivering a copy thereof to such person and, if the person's attendance is commanded, by tendering to that person the fees for one day's attendance and the mileage allowed by law. When the subpoena is issued on behalf of the United States or an officer or agency thereof, fees and mileage need not be tendered. Prior notice of any commanded production of documents and things or inspection of premises before trial shall be served on each party in the manner prescribed by Rule 5(b).

(2) Subject to the provisions of clause (ii) of subparagraph (c)(3)(A) of this rule, a subpoena may be served at any place within the district of the court by which it is issued, or at any place without the district that is within 100 miles of the place of the deposition, hearing, trial, production, or inspection specified in the subpoena or at any place within the state where a state statute or rule of court permits service of a subpoena issued by a state court of general jurisdiction sitting in the place of the deposition, hearing, trial, production, or inspection specified in the subpoena. When a statute of the United States provides therefor, the court upon proper application and cause shown may authorize the service of a subpoena at any other place. A subpoena directed to a witness in a foreign country who is a national or resident of the United States shall issue under the circumstances and in the manner and be served as provided in Title 28, U.S.C. § 1783.

(3) Proof of service when necessary shall be made by filing with the clerk of the court by which the subpoena is issued a statement of the date and

manner of service and of the names of the persons served, certified by the person who made the service.

(c) Protection of Persons Subject to Subpoenas.

(1) A party or an attorney responsible for the issuance and service of a subpoena shall take reasonable steps to avoid imposing undue burden or expense on a person subject to that subpoena. The court on behalf of which the subpoena was issued shall enforce this duty and impose upon the party or attorney in breach of this duty an appropriate sanction, which may include, but is not limited to, lost earnings and a reasonable attorney's fee.

(2)

(A) A person commanded to produce and permit inspection and copying of designated books, papers, documents or tangible things, or inspection of premises need not appear in person at the place of production or inspection unless commanded to appear for deposition, hearing or trial.

(B) Subject to paragraph (d)(2) of this rule, a person commanded to produce and permit inspection and copying may, within 14 days after service of the subpoena or before the time specified for compliance if such time is less than 14 days after service, serve upon the party or attorney designated in the subpoena written objection to inspection or copying of any or all of the designated materials or of the premises. If objection is made, the party serving the subpoena shall not be entitled to inspect and copy the materials or inspect the premises except pursuant to an order of the court by which the subpoena was issued. If objection has been made, the party serving the subpoena may, upon notice to the person commanded to produce, move at any time for an order to compel the production. Such an order to compel production shall protect any person who is not a party or an officer of a party from significant expense resulting from the inspection and copying commanded.

(3)

(A) On timely motion, the court by which a subpoena was issued shall quash or modify the subpoena if it

(i) fails to allow reasonable time for compliance;

(ii) requires a person who is not a party or an officer of a party to travel to a place more than 100 miles from the place where that person resides, is employed or regularly transacts business in person, except that, subject to the provisions of clause (c)(3)(B)(iii) of this rule, such a person may in order to attend trial be commanded to travel from any such place within the state in which the trial is held, or

(iii) requires disclosure of privileged or other protected matter and no exception or waiver applies, or

(iv) subjects a person to undue burden.

(B) If a subpoena

(i) requires disclosure of a trade secret or other confidential research, development, or commercial information, or

(ii) requires disclosure of an unretained expert's opinion or information not describing specific events or occurrences in dispute and resulting from the expert's study made not at the request of any party, or

(iii) requires a person who is not a party or an officer of a party to incur substantial expense to travel more than 100 miles to attend trial, the court may, to protect a person subject to or affected by the subpoena, quash or modify the subpoena or, if the party in whose behalf the subpoena is issued shows a substantial need for the testimony or material that cannot be otherwise met without undue hardship and assures that the person to whom the subpoena is addressed will be reasonably compensated, the court may order appearance or production only upon specified conditions.

(d) Duties in Responding to Subpoena.

(1) A person responding to a subpoena to produce documents shall produce them as they are kept in the usual course of business or shall organize and label them to correspond with the categories in the demand.

(2) When information subject to a subpoena is withheld on a claim that it is privileged or subject to protection as trial preparation materials, the claim shall be made expressly and shall be supported by a description of the nature of the documents, communications, or things not produced that is sufficient to enable the demanding party to contest the claim.

(e) Contempt.

Failure by any person without adequate excuse to obey a subpoena served upon that person may be deemed a contempt of the court from which the subpoena issued. An adequate cause for failure to obey exists when a subpoena purports to require a non-party to attend or produce at a place not within the limits provided by clause (ii) of subparagraph (c)(3)(A).

Rule 47. Selection of Jurors

(a) Examination of Jurors.

The court may permit the parties or their attorneys to conduct the examination of prospective jurors or may itself conduct the examination. In the latter event, the court shall permit the parties or their attorneys to supplement the examination by such further inquiry as it deems proper or shall itself submit to the prospective jurors such additional questions of the parties or their attorneys as it deems proper.

(b) Peremptory Challenges.

The court shall allow the number of peremptory challenges provided by 28 U.S.C. 1870.

(c) Excuse.

The court may for good cause excuse a juror from service during trial or deliberation.

Rule 48. Number of Jurors—Participation in Verdict
The court shall seat a jury of not fewer than six and not more than twelve members and all jurors shall participate in the verdict unless excused from service by the court pursuant to Rule 47(c). Unless the parties otherwise stipulate, (1) the verdict shall be unanimous and (2) no verdict shall be taken from a jury reduced in size to fewer than six members.
Rule 49. Special Verdicts and Interrogatories
(a) Special Verdicts.
The court may require a jury to return only a special verdict in the form of a special written finding upon each issue of fact. In that event the court may submit to the jury written questions susceptible of categorical or other brief answer or may submit written forms of the several special findings which might properly be made under the pleadings and evidence; or it may use such other method of submitting the issues and requiring the written findings thereon as it deems most appropriate. The court shall give to the jury such explanation and instruction concerning the matter thus submitted as may be necessary to enable the jury to make its findings upon each issue. If in so doing the court omits any issue of fact raised by the pleadings or by the evidence, each party waives the right to a trial by jury of the issue so omitted unless before the jury retires the party demands its submission to the jury. As to an issue omitted without such demand the court may make a finding; or, if it fails to do so, it shall be deemed to have made a finding in accord with the judgment on the special verdict.
(b) General Verdict Accompanied by Answer to Interrogatories.
The court may submit to the jury, together with appropriate forms for a general verdict, written interrogatories upon one or more issues of fact the decision of which is necessary to a verdict. The court shall give such explanation or instruction as may be necessary to enable the jury both to make answers to the interrogatories and to render a general verdict, and the court shall direct the jury both to make written answers and to render a general verdict. When the general verdict and the answers are harmonious, the appropriate judgment upon the verdict and answers shall be entered pursuant to Rule 58. When the answers are consistent with each other but one or more is inconsistent with the general verdict, judgment may be entered pursuant to Rule 58 in accordance with the answers, notwithstanding the general verdict, or the court may return the jury for further consideration of its answers and verdict or may order a new trial. When the answers are inconsistent with each other and one or more is likewise inconsistent with the general verdict, judgment shall not be entered, but the court shall return the jury for further consideration of its answers and verdict or shall order a new trial.
Rule 50. Judgment as a Matter of Law in Jury Trials; Alternative Motion for New Trial; Conditional Rulings
(a) Judgment as a Matter of Law.

(1) If during a trial by jury a party has been fully heard on an issue and there is no legally sufficient evidentiary basis for a reasonable jury to find for that party on that issue, the court may determine the issue against that party and may grant a motion for judgment as a matter of law against that party with respect to a claim or defense that cannot under the controlling law be maintained or defeated without a favorable finding on that issue.

(2) Motions for judgment as a matter of law may be made at any time before submission of the case to the jury. Such a motion shall specify the

judgment sought and the law and the facts on which the moving party is entitled to the judgment.

(b) Renewing Motion for Judgment After Trial; Alternative Motion for New Trial; Conditional Rulings.

If, for any reason, the court does not grant a motion for judgment as a matter of law made at the close of all the evidence, the court is considered to have submitted the action to the jury subject to the court's later deciding the legal questions raised by the motion. The movant may renew its request for judgment as a matter of law by filing a motion no later than 10 days after entry of judgment—and may alternatively request a new trial or join a motion for a new trial under Rule 59. In ruling on a renewed motion, the court may:

(1) if a verdict was returned:

(A) allow the judgment to stand,

(B) order a new trial, or

(C) direct entry of judgment as a matter of law; or

(2) if no verdict was returned:

(A) order a new trial, or

(B) direct entry of judgment as a matter of law.

(c) Granting Renewed Motion for Judgment as a Matter of Law; Conditional Rulings; New Trial Motion.

(1) If the renewed motion for judgment as a matter of law is granted, the court shall also rule on the motion for a new trial, if any, by determining whether it should be granted if the judgment is thereafter vacated or reversed, and shall specify the grounds for granting or denying the motion for the new trial. If the motion for a new trial is thus conditionally granted, the order thereon does not affect the finality of the judgment. In case the motion for a new trial has been conditionally granted and the judgment is reversed on appeal, the new trial shall proceed unless the appellate court has otherwise ordered. In case the motion for a new trial has been conditionally denied, the appellee on appeal may assert error in that denial; and if the judgment is reversed on appeal, subsequent proceedings shall be in accordance with the order of the appellate court.

(2) Any motion for a new trial under Rule 59 by a party against whom judgment as a matter of law is rendered shall be filed no later than 10 days after entry of the judgment.

(d) Same: Denial of Motion for Judgment as a Matter of Law.

If the motion for judgment as a matter of law is denied, the party who prevailed on that motion may, as appellee, assert grounds entitling the party to a new trial in the event the appellate court concludes that the trial court erred in denying the motion for judgment. If the appellate court reverses the judgment, nothing in this rule precludes it from determining that the appellee is entitled to a new trial, or from directing the trial court to determine whether a new trial shall be granted.

Rule 51. Instructions to Jury: Objection

At the close of the evidence or at such earlier time during the trial as the court reasonably directs, any party may file written requests that the court instruct the jury on the law as set forth in the requests. The court shall inform counsel of its proposed action upon the requests prior to their arguments to the jury. The court, at its election, may instruct the jury before or after argument, or both. No party may assign as error the giving or the failure to give an instruction unless that party objects thereto before the jury retires to consider its verdict, stating distinctly the matter objected to and the grounds of the objection. Opportunity shall be given to make the objection out of the hearing of the jury.

VII. JUDGMENT

Rule 54. Judgments; Costs

(a) Definintion; Form.

"Judgment" as used in these rules includes a decree and any order from which an appeal lies. A judgment shall not contain a recital of pleadings, the report of a master, or the record of prior proceedings.

(b) Judgment Upon Multiple Claims or Involving Multiple Parties.

When more than one claim for relief is presented in an action, whether as a claim, counterclaim, cross-claim, or third-party claim, or when multiple parties are involved, the court may direct the entry of a final judgment as to one or more but fewer than all of the claims or parties only upon an express determination that there is no just reason for delay and upon an express direction for the entry of judgment. In the absence of such determination and direction, any order or other form of decision, however desgnated, which adjudicates fewer than all the claims or the rights and liabilities of fewer than all the parties shall not terminate the action as to any of the claims or parties, and the order or other form of decision is subject to revision at any time before the entry of judgment adjudicating all the claims and the rights and liabilities of all the parties.

(c) Demand for Judgment.

A judgment by default shall not be different in kind from or exceed in amount that prayed for in the demand for judgment. Except as to a party against whom a judgment is entered by default, every final judgment shall grant the relief to which the party in whose favor it is rendered is entitled, even if the party has not demanded such relief in the party's pleadings.

(d) Costs; Attorney's Fees.

(1) Costs Other than Attorneys' Fees.

Except when express provision therefor is made either in a statute of the United States or in these rules, costs other than attorneys' fees shall be allowed as of course to the prevailing party unless the court otherwise directs; but costs against the United States, its officers, and agencies shall be imposed only to the extent permitted by law. Such costs may be taxed by the clerk on one day's notice. On motion served within 5 days thereafter, the action of the clerk may be reviewed by the court.

(2) Attorneys' Fees.

(A) Claims for attorneys' fees and related nontaxable expenses shall be made by motion unless the substantive law governing the action provides for the recovery of such fees as an element of damages to be proved at trial.

(B) Unless otherwise provided by statute or order of the court, the motion must be filed and served no later than 14 days after entry of judgment; must specify the judgment and the statute, rule, or other grounds entitling the moving party to the award; and must state the amount or provide a fair estimate of the amount sought. If directed by the court, the motion shall also disclose the terms of

any agreement with respect to fees to be paid for the services for which claim is made.
(C) On request of a party or class member, the court shall afford an opportunity for adversary submissions with respect to the motion in accordance with Rule 43(e) or Rule 78. The court may determine issues of liability for fees before receiving submissions bearing on issues of evaluation of services for which liability is imposed by the court. The court shall find the facts and state its conclusions of law as provided in Rule 52(a), and a judgment shall be set forth in a separate document as provided in Rule 58.
(D) By local rule the court may establish special procedures by which issues relating to such fees may be resolved without extensive evidentiary hearings. In addition, the court may refer issues relating to the value of services to a special master under Rule 53 without regard to the provisions of subdivision (b) thereof and may refer a motion for attorneys' fees to a magistrate judge under Rule 72(b) as if it were a dispositive pretrial matter.
(E) The provisions of subparagraphs (A) through (D) do not apply to claims for fees and expenses as sanctions for violations of these rules or under 28 U.S.C. § 1927.

Rule 55. Default

(a) Entry.

When a party against whom a judgment for affirmative relief is sought has failed to plead or otherwise defend as provided by these rules and that fact is made to appear by affidavit or otherwise, the clerk shall enter the party's default.

(b) Judgment.

Judgment by default may be entered as follows:

(1) By the Clerk.

When the plaintiff's claim against a defendant is for a sum certain or for a sum which can by computation be made certain, the clerk upon request of the plaintiff and upon affidavit of the amount due shall enter judgment for that amount and costs against the defendant, if the defendant has been defaulted for failure to appear and is not an infant or incompetent person.

(2) By the Court.

In all other cases the party entitled to a judgment by default shall apply to the court therefor; but no judgment by default shall be entered against an infant or incompetent person unless represented in the action by a general guardian, committee, conservator, or other such representative who has appeared therein. If the party against whom judgment by default is sought has appeared in the action, the party (or, if appearing by representative, the party's representative) shall be served with written notice of the application for judgment at least 3 days prior to the hearing on such application. If, in order to enable the court to enter judgment or to carry it into effect, it is necessary to take an account or to determine the amount of damages or to establish the truth of any averment by evidence or to make an investigation of any other matter, the court may conduct such hearings or order such references as it deems necessary and proper and shall accord a right of trial by jury to the parties when and as required by any statute of the United States.

(c) Setting Aside Default.
For good cause shown the court may set aside an entry of default and, if a judgment by default has been entered, may likewise set it aside in accordance with Rule 60(b).
(d) Plaintiffs, Counterclaimants, Cross-Claimants.
The provisions of this rule apply whether the party entitled to the judgment by default is a plaintiff, a third-party plaintiff, or a party who has pleaded a cross-claim or counterclaim. In all cases a judgment by default is subject to the limitations of Rule 54(c).
(e) Judgment Against the United States.
No judgment by default shall be entered against the United States or an officer or agency thereof unless the claimant establishes a claim or right to relief by evidence satisfactory to the court.
Rule 56. Summary Judgment
(a) For Claimant.
A party seeking to recover upon a claim, counterclaim, or cross-claim or to obtain a declaratory judgment may, at any time after the expiration of 20 days from the commencement of the action or after service of a motion for summary judgment by the adverse party, move with or without supporting affidavits for a summary judgment in the party's favor upon all or any part thereof.
(b) For Defending Party.
A party against whom a claim, counterclaim, or cross-claim is asserted or a declaratory judgment is sought may, at any time, move with or without supporting affidavits for a summary judgment in the party's favor as to all or any part thereof.
(c) Motion and Proceedings Thereon.
The motion shall be served at least 10 days before the time fixed for the hearing. The adverse party prior to the day of hearing may serve opposing affidavits. The judgment sought shall be rendered forthwith if the pleadings, depositions, answers to interrogatories, and admissions on file, together with the affidavits, if any, show that there is no genuine issue as to any material fact and that the moving party is entitled to a judgment as a matter of law. A summary judgment, interlocutory in character, may be rendered on the issue of liability alone although there is a genuine issue as to the amount of damages.
(d) Case Not Fully Adjudicated on Motion.
If on motion under this rule judgment is not rendered upon the whole case or for all the relief asked and a trial is necessary, the court at the hearing of the motion, by examining the pleadings and the evidence before it and by interrogating counsel, shall if practicable ascertain what material facts exist without substantial controversy and what material facts are actually and in good faith controverted. It shall thereupon make an order specifying the facts that appear without substantial controversy, including the extent to which the amount of damages or other relief is not in controversy, and directing such further proceedings in the action as are just. Upon the trial of the action the facts so specified shall be deemed established, and the trial shall be conducted accordingly.
(e) Form of Affidavits; Further Testimony; Defense Required.
Supporting and opposing affidavits shall be made on personal knowledge, shall set forth such facts as would be admissible in evidence, and shall show affirmatively that the affiant is competent to testify to the matters stated therein. Sworn or certified copies of all papers or parts thereof referred to in an affidavit shall be attached thereto or served therewith. The court may permit affidavits to be

supplemented or opposed by depositions, answers to interrogatories, or further affidavits. When a motion for summary judgment is made and supported as provided in this rule, an adverse party may not rest upon the mere allegations or denials of the adverse party's pleading, but the adverse party's response, by affidavits or as otherwise provided in this rule, must set forth specific facts showing that there is a genuine issue for trial. If the adverse party does not so respond, summary judgment, if appropriate, shall be entered against the adverse party.

(f) When Affidavits are Unavailable.

Should it appear from the affidavits of a party opposing the motion that the party cannot for reasons stated present by affidavit facts essential to justify the party's opposition, the court may refuse the application for judgment or may order a continuance to permit affidavits to be obtained or depositions to be taken or discovery to be had or may make such other order as is just.

(g) Affidavits Made in Bad Faith.

Should it appear to the satisfaction of the court at any time that any of the affidavits presented pursuant to this rule are presented in bad faith or solely for the purpose of delay, the court shall forthwith order the party employing them to pay to the other party the amount of the reasonable expenses which the filing of the affidavits caused the other party to incur, including reasonable attorney's fees, and any offending party or attorney may be adjudged guilty of contempt.

Rule 59. New Trials; Amendment of Judgments

(a) Grounds.

A new trial may be granted to all or any of the parties and on all or part of the issues (1) in an action in which there has been a trial by jury, for any of the reasons for which new trials have heretofore been granted in actions at law in the courts of the United States; and (2) in an action tried without a jury, for any of the reasons for which rehearings have heretofore been granted in suits in equity in the courts of the United States. On a motion for a new trial in an action tried without a jury, the court may open the judgment if one has been entered, take additional testimony, amend findings of fact and conclusions of law or make new findings and conclusions, and direct the entry of a new judgment.

(b) Time for Motion.

Any motion for a new trial shall be filed no later than 10 days after entry of the judgment.

(c) Time for Serving Affidavits.

When a motion for new trial is based upon affidavits, they shall be filed with the motion. The opposing party has 10 days after service to file opposing affidavits, but that period may be extended for up to 20 days, either by the court for good cause or by the parties' written stipulation. The court may permit reply affidavits.

(d) On Initiative of Court.

No later than 10 days after entry of judgment the court, on its own, may order a new trial for any reason that would justify granting one on a party's motion. After giving the parties notice and an opportunity to be heard, the court may grant a timely motion for a new trial for a reason not stated in the motion. When granting a new trial on its own initiative or for a reason not stated in a motion, the court shall specify the grounds in its order.

(e) Motion to Alter or Amend a Judgment.

Any motion to alter or amend a judgment shall be filed no later than 10 days after entry of the judgment.

Rule 60. Relief from Judgment or Order

(a) Clerical Mistakes.

Clerical mistakes in judgments, orders or other parts of the record and errors therein arising from oversight or omission may be corrected by the court at any time of its own initiative or on the motion of any party and after such notice, if any, as the court orders. During the pendency of an appeal, such mistakes may be so corrected before the appeal is docketed in the appellate court, and thereafter while the appeal is pending may be so corrected with leave of the appellate court.

(b) Mistakes; Inadvertence; Excusable Neglect; Newly Discovered Evidence; Fraud, Etc.

On motion and upon such terms as are just, the court may relieve a party or a party's legal representative from a final judgment, order, or proceeding for the following reasons: (1) mistake, inadvertence, surprise, or excusable neglect; (2) newly discovered evidence which by due diligence could not have been discovered in time to move for a new trial under Rule 59(b); (3) fraud (whether heretofore denominated intrinsic or extrinsic), misrepresentation, or other misconduct of an adverse party; (4) the judgment is void; (5) the judgment has been satisfied, released, or discharged, or a prior judgment upon which it is based has been reversed or otherwise vacated, or it is no longer equitable that the judgment should have prospective application; or (6) any other reason justifying relief from the operation of the judgment. The motion shall be made within a reasonable time, and for reasons (1), (2), and (3) not more than one year after the judgment, order, or proceeding was entered or taken. A motion under this subdivision (b) does not affect the finality of a judgment or suspend its operation. This rule does not limit the power of a court to entertain an independent action to relieve a party from a judgment, order, or proceeding, or to grant relief to a defendant not actually personally notified as provided in Title 28, U.S.C., § 1655, or to set aside a judgment for fraud upon the court. Writs of coram nobis, coram vobis, audita querela, and bills of review and bills in the nature of a bill of review, are abolished, and the procedure for obtaining any relief from a judgment shall be by motion as prescribed in these rules or by an independent action.

Rule 61. Harmless Error

No error in either the admission or the exclusion of evidence and no error or defect in any ruling or order or in anything done or omitted by the court or by any of the parties is ground for granting a new trial or for setting aside a verdict or for vacating, modifying, or otherwise disturbing a judgment or order, unless refusal to take such action appears to the court inconsistent with substantial justice. The court at every stage of the proceeding must disregard any error or defect in the proceeding which does not affect the substantial rights of the parties.

Appendix R Model Fee Schedules and Agreements

FORENSIC ENGINEERS & TECHNOLOGISTS
John M. Orlowski, P.E., CSP, BCFE, Director

11 Vanderbilt Avenue,
Suite 120
Norwood, MA 02062-5056
Phone: 617.762.8377
Fax: 617.762.1862

FEE SCHEDULE

TECHNICAL CONSULTING (excluding Depositions, Court Appearances or other legal testimony:

- F.E.T. Principals $175 per hour
  - Senior Forensic Engineer $160 per hour
  - Senior Specialist $150 per hour
  - Staff Consultant $125 per hour
  - Technician $100 per hour
  - Consultants with unique qualifications necessary for a particular assignment will be charged at rates agreed to by client.

TECHNICAL CONSULTING AT DEPOSITIONS, COURT APPEARANCES: 150 percent of the above rates, up to a maximum add-on of $75.00 per hour. Invoicing for depositions, court appearances or other legal testimony will be for a minimum of four hours per day.

PURCHASES NECESSARY FOR COMPLETION OF ASSIGNMENT: (Included are laboratory fees, materials, tradesmen and specialized commercial services.) Cost plus 20 percent.

TRAVEL EXPENSES:

- Travel time is billed at TECHNICAL CONSULTING rates - office to site (or lodging).
  - Out of pocket travel expenses such as air fare, lodging, meals, and car rental are plus a 20 percent handling charge.
  - Automobile mileage is billed at current IRS allowance.

TERMS: F.E.T. requires a $1,250.00 retainer prior to beginning work on new case assignments. F.E.T. requires a $2,500.00 retainer prior to appearing for depositions, court appearances or other legal testimony. We bill against the retainer. We will refund, or invoice additionally depending on the time and cost expended. Retainer amounts quoted are for Eastern Massachusetts case assignments. Retainers for other areas will be based on travel requirements and expenses. The disclosure fee is $1,250.00. Review and signing of Affidavits and similar documents will be billed one hour minimum.

ADDITIONAL COMMENTS:

1. Special tasks or areas of investigation might be recommended by F.E.T. staff after initial evaluation of the assignment. Costs for and potential gains from these tasks will be discussed with the client and will require approval before they are undertaken.

2. Rates are subject to change. However, rates in effect at the time assignment is accepted will hold for 90 days or until completion of assignment, whichever is earlier.

SCHEDULE OF FEES AND CONDITIONS
William Marletta, PhD, CSP
Consulting Services

A. Expert consulting time (report preparation, analysis, consultations, telephone conferences, interviews, inspection, photography, research, review of materials, testing, preparation, including travel (portal to portal)) will be billed at a rate of $220.00 per hour plus expenses. Any time related to the case or project which is beyond the scope of an initial telephone interview of the consultant may be considered billable time.

B. A minimum **retainer of $750.00** will be required **in advance** for all work for un-established accounts and the retainer will be credited against the final bill. A retainer is required prior to any work being initiated.

C. Estimates of time anticipated to be spent will be gladly provided upon request.

D. Upon presentation of reports, any balance due must be paid. Past due invoices shall be charged interest at the rate of 1.5% per month (annual rate of 18%). Prepayment is required for deposition and court testimony. All invoices are due when rendered.

E. Depositions and travel time are charged at an hourly rate of $220.00 plus expenses (minimum 10 hours). An advance payment of (10) hours, $2200, is required, at least five working days prior to the deposition, which is credited towards the total bill. Billing is made for preparation time, travel time, expenses incurred, time being deposed, waiting time, and time expended to read and correct transcript if required. Cancellation of a scheduled deposition, with less than 48 hours notice, shall result in a minimum billing of two hours.

F. Court room testimony time, travel time and court room waiting time will be charged as a minimum of 10 hours for the first day ($2200). (Testimony fee will normally include one hour of telephone preparation time.) Cancellation of court room testimony at less than 48 hours notice will result in a minimum billing of 2 hours. Cancellation of court room testimony at less than 24 hours notice will result in a minimum billing of 4 hours. Same day cancellation will result in full day fee of $2200.

G. Scheduled air time over two hours and thirty minutes (2:30 minutes one way) shall be business class. If business class is not available, such travel shall be first class.

H. Reasonable and customary expenses for photography, travel, air fare, photograph enlargements, etc. may be billed in addition to hourly rates. Estimates of expenses anticipated to be spent will be gladly provided upon request.

I. Checks can be made payable to William Marletta PhD, CSP. Social security number is 123-45-6789.

Appendix S Model Bills

FORENSIC ENGINEERS & TECHNOLOGISTS
John M. Orlowski, P.E., CSP, BCFE, Director

11 Vanderbilt Avenue,
Suite 120
Norwood, MA 02062-5056
Phone: 617.762.8377
Fax: 617.762.1862

September 19, 2000

Leonard Logan
555 Deer Park Lane
Suite 123
New York, NY 10038

RE: Mary Jones vs. ABC Company, Inc.
Date of Accident: 5/10/94
CIV.Number: 95-4354 (BSJ)

INVOICE NO. 1-2059.1 **IRS Identification Number: 12-345-6789**

SERVICES RENDERED:

-06/20/97:Generate case file	0.1 hrs.
-07/14/97:Review documents	1.3 hrs.
-07/15/97:Review documents	3.6 hrs.
-08/26/97:Review documents	1.3 hrs.
-08/28/97:Review documents	0.6 hrs.
-08/29/97:Review documents	2.1 hrs.
-08/30/97:Review documents; outline report	1.0 hrs.
-09/01/97:Write report	4.0 hrs.
-09/02/97:Write report	3.5 hrs.
-09/03/97:Write report	2.1 hrs.
-09/05/97:Edit/type report	0.6 hrs.
-09/08/97:T/C's with Attorneys Hobbes & Ally	0.3 hrs. N/C
-09/08/97:Further revise and fax report	0.3 hrs.
-09/10/97:Three T/C's with Attorney Ally	1.0 hrs.
-09/11/97:Revise report	1.3 hrs.
-09/15/97:T/C with Karen Cho	0.2 hrs. N/C
-09/17/97:T/C's with Attorney Ally; revise report	0.6 hrs. N/C
-09/17/97:Letter to Attorney Hobbes	0.2 hrs. N/C
-09/19/97:Review and sign reports	0.1 hrs. N/C

PROFESSIONAL SERVICES: $3,990.00
John M. Orlowski, P.E., CSP, BCFE: 22.8 hrs. @ $175.00/hr.

TOTAL DUE: **$3,990.00**

FORENSIC ENGINEERS & TECHNOLOGISTS
John M. Orlowski, P.E., CSP, BCFE, Director

11 Vanderbilt Avenue,
Suite 120
Norwood, MA 02062-5056
Phone: 617.762.8377
Fax: 617.762.1862

INVOICE NO.: **IRS Identification Number:** 12-345-6789

RETAINER FOR CONSULTING SERVICES	$1,250.00
TOTAL DUE:	**$1,250.00**

NOTE: We will bill against the retainer. We will refund or invoice additionally depending on the time and cost expended.

Work will begin on receipt of retainer.

MODEL BILLS

WILLIAM MARLETTA, PhD, CSP
SAFETY CONSULTANT
143 CEDAR POINT DR.
WEST ISLIP, NY 11795
PH.: 516.321.8772
FAX: 516.321.8773

June 3, 1999

RE:______________________

Dear Mr. _______________:

This bill is for professional services rendered by William Marletta, PhD, CSP as follows:

1. Onsite inspection, September 10, 1998, physical measurements, photography, including travel time (Washington, D.C.) — 9.5 hrs.

11:30 AM-1:30 PM	Travel from West Islip to LaGuardia Airport
1:30 PM-2:30 PM	NYC to Washington, DC air travel
2:30 PM-5:00 PM	Onsite inspection, physical measurements, photography
5:00 PM-6:30 PM	Travel to Washington National Airport
6:30 PM-7:30 PM	Washington National Airport to LaGuardia Airport
7:30 PM-9:00 PM	LaGuardia Airport to West Islip

2.	Review of materials provided	.5 hrs.
3.	Research and review of codes and standards	1.0 hrs.
4.	Research Kennedy Western University, review of expert report and telephone conferences (Actual 3.00 hrs.)	1.5 hrs.
5.	Draft Report preparation, case analysis, standby until settlement (Actual 6.00 hrs.)	4.0 hrs.

TOTAL:	16.5 hrs
16.5 hrs. @ $220.00 =	$3,630.00
35 Black & white photographs @ $7.00 ea. (time lapse and flash)	$ 245.00
Color photographs	$ 21.00
Travel expenses (mileage, airport parking)	$ 38.00
Airline Travel Expenses (copy of invoice attached)	$ 306.50
TOTAL:	$4,240.50
Less Retainers ($750 initial, $1600 inspection)	($2,350.00)
BALANCE DUE:	**$1,890.50**

SS#: 012-34-5678

Gray Smith's Office
Architecture & Community Development
Expert Analysis & Testimony

Philadelphia, PA 19107
Penthouse
1324 Locust Street
215.546.4985
215.546.4960 - Fax

Gray Smith, AIA, AICP
Ernest Lawyer, Esq.
Ketchum & Cheatum, LLP
1800 Tall Building, Suite 720
Philadelphia, PA 19000

April 30, 1999
For Period: 03/26/99-04/29/99

RE: Good Guy v. Bad Guy, Inc.

Date	**Service**	**Hours**	**Rate**	**Amount**
4/15/99	telephone correspondence, review documents	0.5	$225	$112.5
4/15/99	review documents, supp. report	3.5	$225	$787.5
4/19/99	written correspondence	0.75	$225	$168.75
4/22/99	testimony at trial	3	$325	$975
4/22/99	travel, trial prep.	6	$225	$1350
4/23/99	travel, trial prep.	6	$225	$1350
4/23/99	testimony at trial	2	$325	$650
4/24/99	trial prep.	1	$225	$225
4/26/99	travel, trial prep.	6	$225	$1350

Terms: Net Due Upon Receipt

GSO Tax ID #123-45-6789 **BILLED THIS MONTH: $9,243.75**

Gray Smith's Office
Architecture & Community Development
Expert Analysis & Testimony

Philadelphia, PA 19107
Penthouse
1324 Locust Street
215.546.4985
215.546.4960 - Fax

Gray Smith, AIA, AICP
Ernest Lawyer, Esq.
Ketchum & Cheatum, LLP
1800 Tall Building, Suite 720
Philadelphia, PA 19000

4/30/99
Total Amount Due: $17.956.25

Date	Summary of Bills, Payments, & Fin. Charges	Amount	Balance
03/31/99	Balance Forward		$ 412.50
	Good Guy v. Bad Guy, Inc.		
04/09/99	Inv. #155	$10,800.00	$11,212.50
04/24/99	PMT #3534	$- 2,500.00	$ 8,712.50
04/30/99	Inv. #165	$ 9,243.75	$17,956.25

Current	1-30 Days Past Due	31-60 Days Past Due	61-90 Days Past Due	Over 90 Days Past Due	Total Amount Due
$9,243.75	$8,712.50	0.00	0.00	0.00	$17,956.25

Invoice

Jane Doe, MD
1 Main Street
Anywhere, USA 12345
Taxpayer ID# 123-45-6789

Invoice # 000001 Date: 8.30.00

Terms: On Receipt

BILL TO:

Mary Client
Employers Insurance
100 Main Street
Augusta, ME 04031

RE: John D. Sample
Your File No.: A1234-97
Date of Evaluation: August 1, 1997

Payment Due Upon Receipt

Service
Time
Rate per hour
Fee

Medical record review
1.0
$250.00
$250.00

Interview
0.5
$250.00
$125.00

Physical examination
0.5
$250.00
$125.00

Review of studies
0.25
$250.00
$62.50

Report preparation
1.25
$250.00
$312.50

Telephone conversation
0.25
$250.00
$62.50

Total Due

$937.50

Appendix T Model CVs

Harold J. Bursztajn, MD

CURRICULUM VITAE

PERSONAL INFORMATION

- Born November 18, 1950, Lodz, Poland
- Married
- Tax ID #123-45-6789

EDUCATION

- 1968: Diploma, Eastside High School, Paterson, NJ
- 1972: A.B. Princeton University, Princeton, NJ
- 1977: M.D. Harvard Medical School, Boston, MA

POSTDOCTORAL TRAINING

- Internships and Residencies:
    - *1977-1978: *Resident in Pediatrics*, Children's Hospital Medical Center
    - *1979-1982: *Resident in Psychiatry*, Massachusetts Mental Health Center
    - *1981-1982: *Chief Resident*, Program in Psychiatry and the Law, Massachusetts Mental Health Center
- Fellowships and Other Education:
    - *1975-1976: *Special Fellow*, Department of Preventive and Social Medicine, Harvard Medical School
    - *1978-1980: *Research Fellow*, Division of Family Medicine and Primary Care, Harvard Medical School
    - *1981: *Special Student*, Harvard Law School
    - *1981: *Candidate*, Boston Psychoanalytic Institute
    - *1989: *Advanced Candidate*, Boston Psychoanalytic Institute

LICENSURE AND CERTIFICATION

- 1978: Massachusetts, #43038
- 1982: New Hampshire, #6572
- 1984: American Board of Psychiatry and Neurology, #26278
- 1994: American Board of Psychiatry and Neurology Added Qualifications in Forensic Psychiatry, #38

ACADEMIC APPOINTMENTS

- 1982-1984: *Clinical Instructor*, Department of Psychiatry, Harvard Medical School
- 1984-1990: *Assistant Clinical Professor*, Department of Psychiatry, Harvard Medical School
- 1990-: *Associate Clinical Professor*, Department of Psychiatry, Harvard Medical School

HOSPITAL APPOINTMENTS

- 1978-1979: Metropolitan State Hospital, Waltham, MA
- 1979-1982: Massachusetts General Hospital, Boston, MA
- 1982-1986: Hampstead Hospital, Hampstead, NH
- 1985-: Massachusetts Mental Health Center, Boston, MA
- 1986-: Mount Auburn Hospital, Cambridge, MA
- 1989-: Beth Israel Hospital, Boston, MA

OTHER PROFESSIONAL POSITIONS AND MAJOR VISITING APPOINTMENTS

- 1968-1972: *Health Consultant*, Model Cities Program, Paterson, NJ
- 1978-1979: *Acting Medical Director*, Concord Unit, Metropolitan State Hospital
- 1983-: *Co-Director*, Program in Psychiatry and the Law of Harvard Medical School Department at the Massachusetts Mental Health Center
- 1985 (July): *Acting Medical Director*, Hampstead Hospital, Hampstead, NH
- 1994-: *Consultant,* National Institutes of Health, Bethesda, M.D.

AWARDS AND HONORS

- 1968-1972: *University Scholar*, Princeton University
- 1972: *Phi Beta Kappa*
- 1972: *magna cum laude,* Department of Philosophy, Princeton University
- 1977: *cum laude* Honors Thesis, Harvard Medical School
- 1981: *Co-winner*, Solomon Award, Massachusetts Mental Health Center
- 1983: *Second Place*, Solomon Award, Massachusetts Mental Health Center
- 1998: *Honorary mention*, Article: Medical Negligence and Informed Consent in the Managed Care Era, The American College of Physician Executives

COMMITTEE ASSIGNMENTS

- 1972-1977: Recruiter, socioeconomically disadvantaged students, Harvard Medical School
- 1974-1976: Harvard Medical School Admissions Committee, Subcommittee II, student member
- 1974-1977: Boston Alumni School Committee of Princeton University
- 1982-1986: Hampstead Hospital, Peer Review Committee
- 1984: International Advisory Committee, International Congress on Psychiatry, Law and Ethics, Israel
- 1988-: Campaign for the Third Century Committee, Harvard Medical School
- 1988-1989: Harvard Medical School Admissions Committee, Subcommittee II, faculty member
- 1988-1989: Ethics Committee, Mount Auburn Hospital
- 1990-: Committee on Institute Analysis, Boston Psychoanalytic Institute

- 1990-: Massachusetts Board of Registration, Medicine, Consultant and Supervisor
- 1991-: Charter Supporter, United States Holocaust Memorial Hospital
- 1996-: Rappeport Fellowship Committee, American Academy of Psychiatry & the Law
- 1997-: Subtaskforce on Competency to Stand Trial. American Academy of Psychiatry and the Law
- 1998-: Advisory and Expert Panel Member, State Justice Institute (SJI) Benchbook Project on Psychiatric and Psychological Evidence. American Bar Association
- 1999-: Advisory Board, The International Center for Health Concerns
- 1999-: Gender Issues Committee, American Academy of Psychiatry & the Law

MEMBERSHIPS, OFFICES, AND COMMITTEE ASSIGNMENTS IN SOCIETIES

- 1972-: Phi Beta Kappa
- 1975-: The Hastings Center Institute and Society, Ethics and the Life Sciences; Associate member
- 1976-: Society for Health and Human Values
- 1979-: Society for Medical Decision Making
- 1980-: American Academy of Psychiatry and the Law
- 1981-: American Society of Law and Medicine
- 1981-: American Psychiatric Association
- 1984-: American Psychoanalytic Association
- 1994-: American Academy of Forensic Sciences
- 1995-: American College of Physician Executives
- 1997-: The Academy of Experts
- 1997-: American Hospital Association
- 1998-: Physicians for Human Rights

MAJOR RESEARCH INTERESTS

1. Psychiatry, medical decision making, ethics, and the law
2. Informed consent and risk management
3. Trauma and the life cycle
4. Forensic neuropsychiatric evaluation of disability and diminished capacity

PRINCIPAL CLINICAL, HOSPITAL SERVICE RESPONSIBILITIES AND PROFESSIONAL ACTIVITY

- Presently: Private Practice, Cambridge, MA
  Consultant to attorneys and institutions
- *Co-Director*, Program in Psychiatry and the Law of Harvard Medical School Department at the Massachusetts Mental Health Center

TEACHING EXPERIENCE

- 1982-1983: Psychiatric Decision-Making Seminar - Harvard Medical School Core
- 1982-: Psychiatry, the Law, and the Practice of Medicine: North House Seminar 113, Harvard University

- 1982-: Ethics Rounds, Massachusetts Mental Health Center, New England Deaconess Hospital, Mount Auburn Hospital
- 1983-: Program in Psychiatry and the Law Research Seminar, Massachusetts Mental Health Center, Co-Director
- 1991-: Extension Division, Boston Psychoanalytic Institute-Clinical Ethics, Risk Management, and the Psychoanalytic Perspective

EDITORIAL
- 1988-: Editorial Board-Adult Development, Book Review Board of the American Journal of Psychotherapy
- Occasional Article, Book and Video Reviewer:
    - American Academy of Psychiatry and the Law
    - American Journal of Psychiatry
    - Archives of Internal Medicine
    - Bioscience
    - Boston Psychoanalytic Society Newsletter
    - Contemporary Psychiatry
    - The Forensic Examiner
    - General Hospital Psychiatry
    - Hospital and Community Psychiatry
    - Journal of Child and Adolescent Psychopharmacology
    - Journal of Clinical Ethics
    - Journal of Health Politics, Policy and Law
    - Medical Decision Making
    - Merloyd Lawrence Books: Addison-Wesley
    - New England Journal of Medicine
    - Oxford Medical Publications
    - Patient Care
    - Routledge, Chapman & Hall: Methuen Inc.

BIBLIOGRAPHY
Original Reports
1. Bursztajn HJ. The role of a training protocol in formulating patient instructions as to terminal care choices. J Med Educ. 1977; 52:347-348.

2. Bursztajn HJ, Hamm RM. Medical maxims: two views of science. Yale J Biol Med. 1979; 52:483-486.

3. Bursztajn HJ, Hamm RM. The clinical utility of utility assessment. Med Decision Making. 1982; 2:162-165.

4. Wulsin LR, Bursztajn HJ, Gutheil TG. Unexpected clinical features of the Tarasoff decision: the therapeutic alliance and the "duty to warn." Am J Psychiatry. 1983; 140:601-603.

5. Gutheil TG, Bursztajn HJ, Hamm RM, Brodsky A. Subjective data and suicide assessment in the light of recent legal developments. Part I: Malpractice prevention and the use of subjective data. Int J Law Psychiatry. 1983; 6:317-329.

6. Bursztajn HJ, Gutheil TG, Hamm RM, Brodsky A. Subjective data and suicide assessment in the light of recent legal developments. Part II: Clinical uses of legal standards in the interpretation of subjective data. Int J Law Psychiatry. 1983; 6:331-350.

7. Gutheil TG, Bursztajn HJ, Brodsky A. Malpractice prevention through the sharing of uncertainty: informed consent and the therapeutic alliance. N Engl J Med. 1984; 311:49-51. Reprinted in 'Grand Rounds on Medical Malpractice' article 3.2, p.131-133.

8. Bursztajn HJ, Hamm RM, Gutheil TG, Brodsky A. The decision-analytic approach to medical malpractice law: formal proposals and informal syntheses. Med Decision Making. 1984; 4:401-414.

9. Hamm RM, Clark JA, Bursztajn HJ. Psychiatrists' thorny judgments: describing and improving decision-making processes. Med Decision Making. 1984; 4:425-447.

10. Bursztajn HJ, Barsky AJ. Facilitating patient acceptance of a psychiatric referral. Arch Intern Med. 1985; 145:73-75.

11. Bursztajn HJ. More law and less protection: "critogenesis," "legal iatrogenesis," and medical decision-making. J Geriat Psychiatry. 1985; 18:143-153.

12. Bursztajn HJ, Gutheil TG, Mills M, Hamm RM, Brodsky A. Process analysis of judges' commitment decisions: a preliminary empirical study. Am J Psychiatry. 1986; 143:170-174.

13. Gutheil TG, Bursztajn HJ, Brodsky A. The multidimensional assessment of dangerousness: competence assessment in patient care and liability prevention. Bull Am Acad Psychiatry Law. 1986; 14:123-129.

14. Bursztajn HJ, Gutheil TG, Warren MJ, Brodsky A. Depression, self-love, time, and the "right" to suicide. Gen Hospital Psychiatry. 1986; 8:91-95.

15. Bursztajn HJ. Ethicogenesis. Gen Hospital Psychiatry. 1986; 8:422-424.

16. Gutheil TG, Bursztajn HJ. Clinicians' guidelines for assessing and presenting subtle forms of patient incompetence in legal settings. Am J Psychiatry. 1986; 143:1020-1023.

17. Pavlo AM, Bursztajn HJ, Gutheil TG, Levi LM. Weighing religious beliefs in determining competence. Hospital and Community Psychiatry. 1987; 38:350-352.

18. Pavlo AM, Bursztajn HJ, Gutheil TG. Christian Science and competence to make treatment choices: clinical challenges in assessing values. Int J Law Psychiatry. 1987; 395-401.

19. Gutheil TG, Bursztajn HJ, Kaplan AN, Brodsky A. Participation in competency assessment and treatment decisions: the role of a psychiatrist-attorney team. Mental Physical Disabilities Law Reporter. 1987; 11:446-449.

20. Bursztajn HJ, Gutheil TG, Hamm RM, Brodsky A, Mills M. Parens Patriae considerations in the commitment process. Psychiatric Quart. 1988; 59:3:165-181.

21. Bursztajn HJ, Gutheil TG, Brodsky A, Swagerty E. Magical thinking, suicide, and malpractice litigation. Bull Am Acad Psychiatry Law, 1988; 16:369-376.

22. Bursztajn HJ, Harding HP, Gutheil TG, Brodsky A. Beyond cognition: the role of disordered affective states in impairing competence to consent to treatment. Bull Am Acad Psychiatry Law. 1991; 19:383-388.

23. Bursztajn HJ, Chanowitz B, Kaplan E, Gutheil TG, Hamm RM, Alexander V. Medical and judicial perceptions of the risks associated with use of antipsychotic medication. Bull Am Acad Psychiatry Law. 1991; 19:271-275.

24. Bursztajn HJ, Chanowitz B, Gutheil TG, Hamm RM. Micro-effects of language on risk perception in drug prescribing behavior. Bull Am Acad Psychiatry Law. 1992; 20:59-66.

25. Deaton RJS, Illingworth PML, Bursztajn HJ. Unanswered questions about the criminalization of therapist-patient sex. Am J Psychotherapy. 1992; 46:526-531.

26. Bursztajn HJ. From PSDA to PTSD: The patient self-determination act and post-traumatic stress disorder. J Clinical Ethics. 1993; 4:71-74.9

27. Pitman RK, Orr SP, Bursztajn HJ. Vinal v. New England Telephone: admission of PTSD psychophysiologic test results in a civil trial. AAPL Newsletter. 1993; 18(3): 67-69.

28. Bursztajn HJ, Scherr AE, Brodsky A. The rebirth of forensic psychiatry in light of recent historical trends in criminal responsibility. Psychiat Clinics N Am. 1994; 17:611-635.

29. Bursztajn HJ, Brodsky A. Authenticity and autonomy in the managed care era: forensic psychiatric perspectives. J Clinical Ethics. 1994; 5:237-242.

30. Bursztajn HJ, Brodsky A. Clear, convincing, and authentic advance directives in the context of managed care? J Clinical Ethics. 1994; 5:364-366.

31. Bursztajn HJ. Reflections on my father's experience with doctors during the Shoah (1939-1945). J Clinical Ethics. 1996; 7:100-102.

32. Bursztajn HJ, Brodsky A. A new resource for managing malpractice risks in managed care. Archives of Internal Medicine. 1996; 156:2057-2063.

33. Bursztajn HJ, Saunders LS, Brodsky A. Medical negligence and informed consent in the managed care era. Health Lawyer. 1997; 9(5): 14-17.

34. Bursztajn HJ, Hamm RM, Gutheil TG. Beyond the black letter of the law: an empirical study of a judge's decision-making process in civil commitment hearings. Bull Am Acad Psychiatry Law. 1997; 25:79-94.

35. Bursztajn HJ, Brodsky A. Ethical and legal dimensions of benzodiazepine prescription. Psychiatric Annals. 1998; 28(3): 121-128.

36. Bursztajn HJ, Gutheil TG, Brodsky A. Ethics and the triage model in managed care hospital psychiatry. Psychiatric Times. 1998; 15(9): 33-40.

37. Bursztajn HJ, Sobel R. Accountability without health care data banks. Health Affairs. 1998; 17(6): 252-253.

38. Bursztajn HJ. Melatonin therapy: from benzodiazepine-dependent insomnia to authenticity and autonomy. Archives of Internal Medicine. 1999; 159 (20): 2393-2395.

39. Bursztajn HJ, Brodsky A. Captive patients, captive doctors: clinical dilemmas and interventions in caring for patients in managed health care. General Hospital Psychiatry. 1999, 21., 239-248.

40. Bursztajn HJ, Berman S. What is in a neuropsychiatric diagnosis? Evidence-Based Mental Health. In Press.

Book Chapters

1. Feinbloom RI, Bursztajn HJ, Hamm RM, Brodsky A. Bringing the family into family practice. In. Brazelton TB, Vaughn VC III, eds. The family: Setting Priorities. New York: Science and Medicine Publishing Co, 1979; 169-179.

2. Bursztajn HJ, Hamm RM, Gutheil TG. The technological target: involving the patient in clinical choices. In: Reiser SJ, Anbar M, eds. The Machine at the Bedside: Strategies for Using Technology in Patient Care. Cambridge, England: Cambridge University Press, 1984; 177-191.

3. Bursztajn HJ, Gutheil TG, Cummins B. Legal issues in inpatient psychiatry. In: Sederer LI, ed. Inpatient Psychiatry. 2d ed, Baltimore: Williams and Wilkins, 1986; 338-356.

4. Bursztajn HJ, Gutheil TG, Cummins B. Legal issues in inpatient psychiatry. In: Sederer LI, ed. Inpatient Psychiatry. 3d ed., Baltimore: Williams and Wilkins, 1991; 379-406.

5. Bursztajn HJ, Hamm RM, Brodsky A, Alexander V, Levi L. Probability, decision analysis, and conscious gambling. In: Gutheil TG, Bursztajn HJ, Brodsky A, Alexander V, eds. Decision making in psychiatry and the law. Baltimore: Williams & Wilkins, 1991; 37-52.

6. Bursztajn HJ, Hamm RM, Brodsky A, Gutheil TG, Alexander V. Subjective assessment in clinical decision making and malpractice liability. In: Gutheil TG, Bursztajn HJ, Brodsky A, Alexander V, eds. Decision Making in Psychiatry and the Law. Baltimore: Williams & Wilkins, 1991; 53-68.

7. Bursztajn HJ, Gutheil TG, Brodsky A. Affective disorders, competence, and decision-making. In: Gutheil TG, Bursztajn HJ, Brodsky A, Alexander V, eds. Decision Making in Psychiatry and the Law. Baltimore: Williams & Wilkins, 1991; 153-170.

8. Gutheil TG, Bursztajn HJ, Brodsky A, Alexander V. Managing uncertainty: the therapeutic alliance, informed consent, and liability. In: Gutheil TG, Bursztajn HJ, Brodsky A, Alexander V, eds. Decision Making in Psychiatry and the Law. Baltimore: Williams & Wilkins, 1991; 69-88.

9. Alexander V, Bursztajn HJ, Brodsky A, Hamm RM, Gutheil TG, Levi L. Involuntary commitment. In: Gutheil TG, Bursztajn HJ, Brodsky A, Alexander V, eds. Decision Making in Psychiatry and the Law. Baltimore: Williams & Wilkins, 1991; 89-112.

10. Kaplan E, Bursztajn HJ, Alexander V, Hamm RM, Brodsky A, Barnard D, Kaplan AN. Making treatment decisions. In: Gutheil TG, Bursztajn HJ, Brodsky A, Alexander V, eds. Decision Making in Psychiatry and the Law. Baltimore: Williams & Wilkins, 1991; 113-132.

11. Alexander V, Bursztajn HJ, Brodsky A, Gutheil TG. Deciding for others; autonomy and protection in tension. In: Gutheil TG, Bursztajn HJ, Brodsky A, Alexander V, eds. Decision Making in Psychiatry and the Law. Baltimore: Williams & Wilkins, 1991; 133-152.

12. Warren M, Commons ML, Gutheil TG, Swagerty EL, Bursztajn HJ, Brodsky A. Suicide, magical thinking, and liability. In: Gutheil TG, Bursztajn HJ, Brodsky A, Alexander V, eds. Decision Making in Psychiatry and the Law. Baltimore: Williams & Wilkins, 1991; 189-208.

13. Hauser MJ, Commons ML, Bursztajn HJ, Gutheil TG. Fear of malpractice liability and its role in clinical decision-making. In: Gutheil TG, Bursztajn HJ, Brodsky A, Alexander V, eds. Decision Making in Psychiatry and the Law. Baltimore: Williams & Wilkins, 1991; 209-226.

14. Canning S, Hauser MJ, Gutheil TG, Bursztajn HJ. Communications in psychiatric practice: Decision-making and the use of the telephone. In: Gutheil TG, Bursztajn HJ, Brodsky A, Alexander V, eds. Decision Making in Psychiatry and the Law. Baltimore: Williams & Wilkins, 1991; 227-238.

15. Commons ML, Sonnert G, Gutheil TG, Bursztajn HJ. Ethics and decisions about suicide. In: Gutheil TG, Bursztajn HJ, Brodsky A, Alexander V, eds. Decision Making in Psychiatry and the Law. Baltimore: Williams & Wilkins, 1991; 239-256.

16. Deaton RJS, Colenda CC, Bursztajn HJ. Medical-legal issues. In: Stoudemire A, Fogel BS, eds. Psychiatric Care of the Medical Patient. New York: Oxford University Press, 1993; 929-938.

17. Deaton R, Bursztajn HJ. Antipsychotic medication: regulation through the right to refuse. In: Schwartz HI, ed. Psychiatric Practice Under Fire. Washington, DC: American Psychiatric Press, Inc., 1994; 85-101.

18. Bursztajn HJ. One axiom and eight corollaries for managing legal issues in an inpatient psychiatric setting. In: Docherty JP, ed. Inpatient Psychiatry in the 1990s. San Francisco: Jossey-Bass Publishers, 1994; 95-107.

19. Bursztajn HJ, Brodsky A. Competence and insanity. In: Jacobson JL, Jacobson AM, eds. Psychiatric Secrets. Philadelphia: Hanley & Belfus, Inc., 1996; 501-515.

20. Bursztajn HJ, Brodsky A. Patients who sue and clinicians who are sued in the managed-care era. In: Lifson LE, Simon RI, eds. The Mental Health Practitioner and the Law. Cambridge, MA: Harvard University Press, 1998; 237-249.

21. Bursztajn HJ, Brodsky A. Ethical and effective testimony during direct examination and cross-examination post-Daubert. In: Lifson LE, Simon RI, eds. The Mental Health Practitioner and the Law. Cambridge, MA: Harvard University Press, 1998; 262-280.

22. Bursztajn HJ. Responses to a defective managed care product: medical negligence, lack of informed consent, and choicelessness. In: 2000 Wiley Expert Witness Update. New York: Aspen Law Business/Panel Publishers, 2000; 239-264.

Books

1. Reiser SJ, Bursztajn HJ, Gutheil TG, Appelbaum PS. Divided Staffs, Divided Selves: A Case Approach to Mental Health Ethics. Cambridge, England: Cambridge University Press, 1987.

2. Bursztajn HJ, Feinbloom RI, Hamm RM, Brodsky A. Medical Choices, Medical Chances: How Patients, Families, and Physicians Can Cope With Uncertainty. New York: Delacorte, 1981; New York: Routledge, Chapman & Hall, 1990.

3. Gutheil TG, Bursztajn HJ, Brodsky A, Alexander V, eds. Decision Making in Psychiatry and the Law. Baltimore: Williams & Wilkins, 1991.

COURSE CO-DIRECTOR AND FACULTY

- Harvard Medical School, Department of Continuing Education and Massachusetts Mental Health Center:
  - "Ethical Issues in Clinical Practice," September 1990
  - "Sex Between Clinicians and Patients: Clinical, Legal and Medico-Legal Perspectives," September 1990

"Malpractice Prevention for the 1990s: An Update on the Issues and Practical Approaches," January 1991
"The Clinician in Court: A Survival Guide," January 1992
"Dangers and Pitfalls of Forensic Practice," January 1992
"Liability Prevention for Medical and Surgical Practitioners: Trends and Update," January, 1993.
"Doctors and Nurses in Court: A Basic Survival Guide," January, 1993.
"Malpractice in the 1990s: Trends and Update," February, 1993.
"The Clinician in Court: A Survival Guide," February, 1993.

- Massachusetts Bar Association, Continuing Legal Education Course:
  "Nuts and Bolts of Using Medical Experts at Trial," November 1990

FACULTY

- Harvard Medical School, Department of Continuing Education and Massachusetts Mental Health Center:
  "Intensive Diagnostic Interviewing," 1990-

RECENT PRESENTATIONS

1. "Prevention of Violence and Suicide by the High Risk Patient," Mount Auburn Hospital Grand Rounds, Cambridge, MA, September 15, 1992.

2. "Malpractice Prevention," Brookside Hospital Grand Rounds, Nashua, New Hampshire, March 15, 1993.

3. "Post-Traumatic Stress Disorder in the Courtroom," Panel, American Psychiatric Association, San Francisco, California, May 26, 1993.

4. "Psychiatry Issues," Medical Malpractice Seminar for Office of Legal Education, Executive Office for United States Attorneys, Salt Lake City, Utah, July 1993.

5. "Liability for Sexual Misconduct of Government Providers," with Thomas G. Gutheil, M.D., Workshop, Office of Legal Education, Executive Office for United States Attorneys, Salt Lake City, Utah, July 13, 1993.

6. "Competency to Confess to a Criminal Act," American Academy of Forensic Sciences, Boston, Massachusetts, 1993.

7. "Malpractice Prevention in High Risk Doctor-Patient Encounters," Lawrence General Hospital, Lawrence, Massachusetts, January 18, 1994.

8. "Forensic Psychiatric Assessment of Mental Damages," Discussant, Panel, American Psychiatric Association, Philadelphia, Pennsylvania, May 24, 1994.

9. "What is Forensic Psychiatry?: A Guide for Judges." New Hampshire Bar Association Meeting, January 27, 1995.

10. "Diminished Capacity in the Criminal Justice System." Seventh Annual Bridgewater State Hospital Conference, April 7, 1995.

11. "Fact vs. Expert Witness." Workshop, The Clinician in Court: A Survival Guide, Harvard Medical School Department of Continuing Education, April 8, 1995.

12. "Medical Choices, Managed Care and Uncertainty." Medical Staff Conference, Emerson Hospital, Concord, MA, June 9, 1995.

13. "Behavioral Strategies for Malpractice Prevention in a Managed Care Era." Medical Grand Rounds, Marlborough Hospital, Marlborough, MA, November 30, 1995.

14. "Violence Against Attorneys, Judges, and Litigants in the Family Law Courtroom." Boston Bar Association, Family Law Section, December 1995.

15. "Violence in the Courtroom." Annual Conference of Massachusetts Probate and Family Court Judges, Stockbridge, MA, May 10, 1996.

16. "How to be an Ethical and Effective Medical Witness, Post-Daubert." National Expert Witness and Litigation Seminar, Hyannis, MA, June 20, 1996.

17. "Effective and Ethical Testimony for Mental Health Professionals." Testifying and Consulting Experts, San Francisco, CA, September 1996.

18. "Being an Ethical and Effective Medical Expert." Testifying and Consulting Experts, San Francisco, CA, September 1996.

19. "Dimensions of a Forensic Psychiatric Home Page." American Academy of Psychiatry and the Law, San Juan, Puerto Rico, October 1996.

20. "From the Shoah to Managed Health: What One Forensic Psychiatrist has Learned about Clinical Ethics." YIVO Institute and New School for Social Research, New York, NY, November 1996.

21. "Preventing Malpractice Litigation in Managed Health Care Settings." Harvard Medical School Department of Continuing Education, November 22, 1996.

22. "Ethical and Effective Testimony for Physicians Accused of Malpractice." Harvard Medical School Department of Continuing Education, November 23, 1996.

23. "Ethical and Decision Making Issues in Primary Care Medicine in a Managed Care Context." Vermont Technical College, Vermont Ethics Network, February 10, 1997.

24. "Surreptitious LSD Administration: Ethical, Toxicologic and Psychiatric Impact on Product Liability Issues." American Academy of Forensic Sciences, February 19, 1997.

25. "Medical Historical Perspectives Regarding Managed Care and Medical Necessity: True and False." Chairman of Symposium on Ethical Issues in Managed Health Care. American Psychiatric Association Annual Meeting, San Diego, CA, May 19, 1997

26. "Medical Necessity, Managed Health Care Denial of Benefits, and the Nuremberg Code." Panel: "Medical Ethics: Who Gets the Care?" Moderator: Professor Uwe E. Reinhardt, PhD, Princeton University 250th Anniversary Symposium, Princeton, NJ, May 29, 1997.

27. "Capital Punishment in the Mcveigh Case." BBC World Services. Cambridge, MA, June 13, 1997.

28. "Managed Health Care: Protecting the Quality of Care in the Clinic and the Courtroom." Saints Memorial Medical Center, Lowell, MA, July 9, 1997.

29. "Why Do They Do It? Motivation of Violent Criminals." National Association of Legal Secretaries Annual Meeting and Educational Conference, Boston, MA, July 26, 1997.

30. "Substituting Alliance for Alienation: Supporting the Human Side in Changing Health Care." Advanced Risk Management Seminar, New England Health Care Assembly, Falmouth, MA, July 28, 1997.

31. "High Risk Patients and Families in Chronic Illness Situations." Physicians' Meeting, Spaulding Rehabilitation Hospital, Boston, MA, October 8, 1997.

32. "Protecting Yourself from Potential Litigation from Employees and Patients." Harvard School of Public Health conference: "Leadership in Evolving Health Care Systems." Boston, MA, November 4, 1997.

33. "Forensic Psychiatry and Brain Imaging." Harvard Medical School, Advanced Workshop, "Liability Prevention" postgraduate course, Boston, MA, November 22, 1997.

34. "Sexual Harassment Post Daubert." Presidential Panel, American Academy of Forensic Sciences, San Francisco, CA, February, 1998.

35. "Exploring the Consequences of a National Health Care Data Base: Cyberspace Medicine." Harvard Law School Berkman Center: "Privacy and Cyber/Spaces: Government Databanks and Identification. Medical and Other Instances," Cambridge, MA, May 13, 1998.

36. "Values in the Physician Patient Managed Health Care Relationship." American Psychiatric Association Annual Meeting, Toronto, Canada, June 1, 1998.

37. "Employment Disability and Accommodation Dilemmas." American Psychiatric Association Annual Meeting, Toronto, Canada, June 4, 1998.

38. "Sexual Misconduct in Managed Health Care Settings." Boston Psychoanalytic Society and Institute: "Sexual Misconduct by Psychotherapists, other Health Care Professionals, and Clergy: Prevention and Treatment of Boundary Violations by Professionals." Chestnut Hill, MA, October 4, 1998.

39. "Boundary Violations: How are they defined in the patient-physician relationship?" Massachusetts Medical Society, Waltham, MA, October 7, 1998.

40. "Risk Management: How to reduce medical malpractice suits," Sheraton-Newton Hotel, October 10-11, 1998.

41. "Post-Daubert Sexual Harassment Expert," 1998 Annual Meeting Program, American Academy of Psychiatry and the Law, New Orleans, Louisiana, October 22, 1998.

42. "Functional Brain Imaging and Criminal Behavior," with Lisa Acosta, BA, 1998 Annual Meeting Program, American Academy of Psychiatry and the Law, New Orleans, Louisiana, October 23, 1998.

43. "Protecting Yourself from Potential Litigation from Employees and Patients." Harvard School of Public Health: "Leadership in Evolving Health Care Systems." Boston, MA, November 4, 1998.

44. "Ethical and Legal Issues in Managed Health Care." Mount Auburn Hospital, Cambridge, MA, November 11, 1998.

45. "Ethical & Technical Effects of Daubert on Expert's Opinions." Harvard Medical School: "The Mental Health Clinician in Court: A Survival Guide." Boston, MA, November 21, 1998.

46. "Managed Care, Standards of Care & Informed Consent: How to Present Your Medical Opinion." Harvard Medical School: "Medical and Surgical Practitioners in Court: A Survival Guide." Boston, MA, November 21, 1998.

47. "When am I Going To Be Sued: How Can Physicians, Lawyers, and Surgeons Prevent Malpractice, Sexual Misconduct, and Employee Litigation." Lawrence General Hospital, Lawrence, MA, January 13, 1999.

48. "Forensic Psychiatry and Brain Imaging Testimony Post-Daubert." New England School of Law: "Criminal and Civil Issues Concerning the Mentally Ill: Lawyers, Courts & Mental Health Professionals." Boston, MA, January 1999.

49. "An Essential Guide to Ethical and Effective Conflict Resolution via an Objective Expert's Deposition." SEAK Inc. "National Medical Witness Summit." Fort Lauderdale, FL, February 20-21, 1999.

50. "Boundary Violations: How to Avoid the Slippery Slope." The Massachusetts Medical Society. Holyoke, MA, March 10, 1999.

51. "Clinical Responses to Managed Health Care." American Psychiatric Association, Washington, D.C., May 18, 1999.

52. "Beyond the Court Appointed Custody Expert Post-Daubert." American Psychological Association Convention: " Abusive Practices in Divorce Cases: Clinical, Legal and Ethical Dilemmas." Boston, MA, August 23, 1999.

53. "Clinical Ethics and Shared Decision-Making with Patients and Their Families." Healthcare Educational and Research Fund and Saratoga Hospital, Saratoga, NY, September 18, 1999

54. "Working with High-Risk Patients and Families to Turn Alienation into Patient Loyalty." Healthcare Educational and Research Fund and Saratoga Hospital, Saratoga, NY, September 18, 1999

55. "Brain Imaging and Child Development." Watertown Public School, Watertown, MA, November 4, 1999.

56. "Premises Liability: Ethical and Effective Psychological and Psychiatric Evaluation Post-Daubert." ICLE, Atlanta, Georgia, November 5, 1999.

POPULAR PUBLICATIONS

1. Gutheil TG, Bursztajn HJ, Brodsky A. Liability prevention through informed consent with some new approaches for the clinician. Risk Management Foundation Forum. 1986; 7:8-9.

2. Bursztajn HJ. Flight: the eloquence of silence. Harvard Medical Alumni Bulletin. 1989; 62:3:45-47.

3. Bursztajn HJ. The phobic in court. Lawyers Weekly, December 7, 1992.

4. Bursztajn HJ. The role of a forensic psychiatrist in legal proceedings. Journal of the Massachusetts Academy of Trial Attorneys, Vol. 1, No. 2, October, 1993.

5. Bursztajn HJ. New developments in the role of Post-Traumatic Stress Disorder in civil and criminal law. Journal of the Massachusetts Academy of Trial Attorneys, Vol. 1, No. 3, January, 1994.

6. Bursztajn HJ. Traumatic memories as evidence: true or false? Journal of the Massachusetts Academy of Trial Attorneys, March 15, 1994.

7. Bursztajn HJ. The role of the forensic psychiatrist in civil proceedings. (New Hampshire) Trial Bar News 16, Summer 1994:84-86.

8. Bursztajn HJ. Psychiatric experts in victim litigation. Crime Victims' Litigation Quarterly, Vol. 2, No. 1, February 1995.

9. Bursztajn HJ. Supervisory negligence litigation in context. Journal of the Massachusetts Academy of Trial Attorneys, Vol. 2, No. 2, October, 1994.

10. Bursztajn HJ, Saunders LS, Brodsky A. National certification for forensic psychiatrists: A preview of the post-*Daubert* expert. Journal of the Massachusetts Academy of Trial Attorneys, Vol. 2, No. 4, April, 1995.

11. Saunders LS, Bursztajn HJ, Brodsky A. Recovered memory and managed care: HB 236's post-*Daubert* "science" junket. Trial Bar News 17, Spring 1995:27-37.

12. Bursztajn HJ, Joshi PT, Sutherland SM, Tomb DA (Article Consultants). Recognizing posttraumatic stress. Patient Care, March 30, 1995.

13. Bursztajn HJ, Hilliard JT. Violence Against Attorneys and Judges: Protecting Yourself Before and After a Threat. Journal of the Massachusetts Academy of Trial Attorneys, July, 1995.

14. Bursztajn HJ, Saunders LS, Brodsky A. Daubert without prejudice: Achieving relevance and reliability without randomness. J Mass Acad Trial Attys, January 1996:54-58.

15. Bursztajn HJ, Saunders LS, Brodsky A. Keeping a jury involved during a long trial. Criminal Justice, Vol. 11, 1997:8-9.

16. Bursztajn, HJ. Criminalizing doctor-assisted suicide isn't a cure. The Boston Globe, January 9, 1997.

17. Bursztajn HJ, Brodsky A. Responsibility without scapegoating. Health Decisions, A Publication of The Vermont Ethics Network, May 1997.

18. Bernstine EG, Bursztajn HJ, Wilkens J. Effective use of scientific evidence: lessons from the Simpson trial. J Mass Acad Trial Attys. Winter 1997:22-28.

19. Bernstine EG, Bursztajn, HJ, Wilkens J. Emotional justice: further lessons from the Simpson trial. Journal of the Massachusetts Academy of Trial Attorneys. Spring 1997: 18-26.

20. Bursztajn HJ. Preventing neo-nazi cult violence in our schools. Jewishfamily.com. 1999.

LETTERS TO THE EDITOR

1. Bursztajn HJ. Efficacy research and psychodynamic psychiatry. Am J Psychiatry. 1991; 148:817-818.

2. Bursztajn HJ. Competency to make a will. Am J Psychiatry. 1992; 149:10:1415.

3. Bursztajn HJ. Protecting Patients from clinician-patient sexual contact. Am J Psychiatry. 1992; 149:9:1276.

4. Bursztajn HJ. An overview of sexual harassment. Am J Psychiatry. 1995; 152:3:478.

5. Bursztajn HJ. Psychotherapist versus expert witness. Am J Psychiatry. 1998; 155:2:307.

6. Bursztajn HJ. Recovered Memories. Psychiatric Services. 1998; 49:5:699-700.

7. Bursztajn HJ. On the goals of the Freud Library of Congress Museum Exhibition. New York Times Magazine. November 1, 1998:Section 6:20.

RECENT BOOK REVIEWS

1. Bursztajn HJ. Managing Care, Not Dollars: The Continuum of Mental Health Services. Am J Psychiatry. 1998; 155:7:985.

2. Bursztajn HJ. Managing Managed Care. Am J Psychiatry. 1999; 156:1:148.

MODEL CVS

QUALIFICATIONS OF

DAVID A. DODGE, C.S.P.

P.O. Box 600, Standish, ME 04084 | **Phone 207-642-5459**
e-mail: penhome@mix-net.net | **Fax 207-642-2506**

EXPERIENCE

1986 to Present	Safety and Forensic Consulting Safety Consultant performing accident analysis in the areas of safety, worker/machinery accidents, products liability and boiler pressure failure and design. Loss Control Consultant to many insurance companies performing risk evaluation and accident investigation.
1984 to 1986	Medical and Technical Consultants Same safety consultations as described above. Establishment of products and employee safety programs for industry.
1982 to 1983	Authorized National Board Inspector for General Electric's South Portland, Maine, facility monitoring the quality control of pressure vessels for the nuclear power plant industry. Technical Safety Consultant and Authorized Inspector to the Energy Testing Laboratory of Maine.
1976 to 1981	Safety Consultant/Manager for Commercial Union Insurance Company in the State of Maine, responsibilities included Bath Iron Works, Great Northern Paper Company, and Scott Paper Company.
1975 to 1976	Safety Consultant/Manager for Commercial Union Insurance Company, Syracuse, New York. Established and monitored safety program of Standard Brands, Inc., construction project including over 75 subcontractors.
1974 to 1975	High Pressure Boiler Design, Riley Stoker Corp., Worcester, Massachusetts.

1971 to 1973 — Safety Consultant for Commercial Union Insurance Company, accident investigation and safety inspection, Boston, Massachusetts.

EDUCATION

Maine Maritime Academy, Castine, Maine.
Graduated: 1971
B.S. Marine Engineering

Industrial Safety
Northeastern University, Boston, Massachusetts

National Board/A.S.M.E. High Pressure Boiler and Pressure
Boiler and Pressure Vessel Welded Repair

Ohio Arson School
Columbus, Ohio

Industrial Safety
University of Massachusetts, Amherst, Massachusetts

Industrial Safety
Syracuse University, Syracuse, New York

Annual Education Requirements for Certified Safety Professional Certification

TECHNICAL ACCOMPLISHMENTS

- Certified Safety Professional Test Question Examiner
- American National Standard Institute Committee Member - Lock Out/Tag Out Safety Standard (Z244)
- Formulation of User and Installation Manuals and Labeling for Fundamental Energies, Inc., to comply with Consumer Product Safety Commission regulations
- Technical Safety Consultant and Authorized Inspector to the Energy Testing Laboratory of Maine
- Authorized National Board Inspector for General Electric's South Portland, Maine, Facility monitoring the quality control of pressure vessels for the nuclear power plant industry
- Author of the paper "Product Safety and Liability Prevention"
- Author of the book Safety Manual for Municipalities
- Authored Safety Manual for the State of Maine Correctional Woodworking Program
- Authored Safety Manual for the State of Maine
- Authored Safety Procedures for the State of New Hampshire, Department of Transportation
- Lecturer, "Confined Space Entry", University of Southern Maine
- Lecturer, "Hazardous Materials Recognition", University of Southern Maine
- Developed and taught "Product Safety", University of Southern Maine
- Developed instructions and warnings for Prestone, Inc.

PROFESSIONAL CERTIFICATIONS AND MEMBERSHIPS

- Certified Safety Professional. (Designations in Products Safety, Safety Management and Comprehensive Safety Aspects)
- Registered Professional Engineer (P.E.), Masschusetts
- Associate in Risk Management (A.R.M.)
- Member, American Society of Safety Engineering
- Member, Maine Safety Council
- Formerly Commissioned, National Board of Boiler and Pressure Vessel Inspectors
- Former U.S. Coast Guard Licensee, Third Assistant Engineer
- Third Class Engineer, State of Maine
- Former Certified Boiler and Pressure Vessel Inspector; Maine, Massachusetts, and New York
- Member, International Association of Arson Investigators
- Crane Inspections and Certification Bureau - Inspection Certification
- Former Member, Maine State Occupational Safety and Health Board
- Former Member, Energy Testing Laboratory of Maine, Board of Directors

William Marletta Ph.D, CSP

SAFETY CONSULTANT
143 Cedar Point Drive
West Islip, New York 11795
PHONE: 516-321-8772 FAX: 516-321-8773

EDUCATION:

Ph. D. in Occupational Safety and Health New York University, New York, New York, July 1994
Dissertation "The Effects of Humidity & Wetness on Pedestrian Slip Resistance. . ."

M. A. Occupational Health and Safety, January 1985, 3.89 GPA
New York University, New York, New York

A. B. Applied Science - Fire Protection Technology, with Distinction, 4.0 GPA, January 1980,
Suffolk Community College, Selden, New York

B. A. Biological Sciences, January 1977, 3.29 GPA
Indiana University, Bloomington, Indiana

PROFESSIONAL HONORS:
Certified Safety Professional (CSP) #7214, by exam in Comprehensive Practice, 1984
New York State Certification #98-0093 "*Workplace Safety and Loss Prevention Consultant*" Industrial Code Rule 59
Board of Certified Safety Professionals (BCSP) Exam Instructor 1987-90
Fellow of the ASTM (American Society of Testing and Materials) "Award of Merit" presented in 1999
Member of the American Society of Testing and Materials (ASTM) 1986-99
Chairman ASTM F13 Committee "*Safety and Traction for Footwear*" 1992-7 (Sec. 1990-91); Chair Traction F13.1 (98-99)
Member of ASTM C21 Committee "*Ceramic Whitewares*" & ASTM F06 Committee "*Resilient Floor Coverings*" 1986-99
Member of ASTM F15 Subcommittee "*Consumer Products Safety Standards*" 1986
Certified Hazard Control Manager (CHCM) - Masters Level 1983
National Recipient of the ASSE National Edgar Monsanto Queeny "*Safety Professional of the Year 1996*" Award
"*Safety Professional of the Year 1991*" American Society of Safety Engineers (ASSE) LI
Consultant to USDOL OSHA/ SENRAC Committee. Conducted research under contract to propose a Federal Standard specifying criteria for the slip resistance level of structural steel and decking in construction
Consultant to the American Insurance Association (AISG, Inc.) with over 250 subscriber insurance companies providing national seminars and expertise for practical approaches to Slip, Trip, and Fall Prevention

Consultant to Florsheim/HiTest Safety Shoes on slip resistance - Tractional design, composition, COF evaluation
Consultant and member of NFPA Committee on Fire Department Apparatus (1901) (slip performance research)
Consultant to Coastal Video - Slip, Trip and Fall Prevention Video
US Patent 5,768,786 Co inventor of hand held machine guarding brake, with fail safe design, rotating & fixed guard
Footwear Session Chairperson (1995) International Symposium on Slip Resistance NIST, Gaithersburg, MD
Professional Member of the American Society of Safety Engineers # 4706230 (ASSE) 1982 /1986
President (ASSE) LI 1993-94; President Elect (ASSE) LI 1992-93; Vice President (ASSE) LI 1991-90
Chairman of Education American Society of Safety Engineers ASSE LI Chapter 1988-90; Treasurer (ASSE) LI 90-91
Co-Chairman of Education - American Society of Safety Engineers ASSE - LI 1987-88
Co-Chairman Membership Committee ASSE LI Chapter 1986-88
Co-Chairman Risk Management / Insurance Committee ASSE LI Chapter 1985-86
Chairman Risk Management / Insurance Committee ASSE LI Chapter 1986-87
Member ANSI A117.1 *"Providing Accessibility & Usability for Physically Handicapped People"* (represent ASSE 97-99)
Member ANSI A117.1 Committee *"Interpretation Review Panel"* (3 person panel) 1/99
Professional Development Conference Chairman ASSE - LI 1990-1; Nat Assembly Delegate ASSE LI 1987-90 & 98-99
Member of American National Standard Institute (ANSI) 1993/ (Member ANSI *"Board of Standards Review"* 1994-99)
Member ANSI A1264.1 Committee *"Workplace Floor and Wall Openings, Stairs, and Railings Systems"/ "Slip Resistance"*
Member of American Industrial Hygiene Association (AIHA) 1986
Member of National Fire Protection Association (NFPA) 1986; Member of New York Academy of Sciences (1994-99)
Member of World Safety Organization (WSO) - 1986 /WSO Certified Safety Executive (CSE)
PHI ETA SIGMA - National Honor Society (Indiana University) 1977
PHI ALPHA SIGMA - National Honor Society (Suffolk Community College) 1980
Author and Producer of Film "NOISE YOUR EARS YOUR FUTURE" 1988
Trained OSHA Inspectors in LI Area Office *"Walking & Working Surfaces"*
Author of reference chapter *"Trip, Slip and Fall Prevention"* and other published works in the area of slip resistance.

WORK EXPERIENCE:

11/85 to present William Marletta, Ph.D, CSP
WILLIAM MARLETTA SAFETY CONSULTANTS

William Marletta is the principal of a diversified safety consulting firm providing a wide range of safety consulting services to industrial, commercial & construction industries. As a safety consultant, Dr. Marletta is specialized in slip, trip, fall and machine guarding accident prevention. Safety services include safety loss analysis, hazard identification, OSHA type inspections, accident reconstruction, safety program development and evaluation, and safety training. Dr. Marletta is a safety specialist regarding stairs, ramps, walks, flooring, construction and industry fall protection, ladders, scaffolds, slip resistance testing and evaluation, speed bumps, and similar floor surface transitions providing consultation, expert opinion and/or testimony.

11/85 to 7/90 VICE PRESIDENT
Technical and Medical Forensic Consultants Inc.
151 Hempstead Turnpike
West Hempstead, New York 11552

Self-employed safety consultant contracted to TMFC as a safety specialist regarding slip, trip, fall and machine guarding accident prevention. Safety specialist regarding stairs, ramps, walks and floor surfaces. Also providing expert opinion and/or testimony for litigation cases to TMFC clients.

11/84 - 11/85 SENIOR DIRECTOR
Ogden Risk Management Control Services
One Mass Tech Center
East Boston Massachusetts 02128

Responsible for the development of a risk management consulting company for a $ 2.4 billion dollar a year diversified conglomerate. Reported directly to a divisional president with responsibility for safety program development encompassing 54 Ogden companies. Specialized experience identifying, evaluating, and controlling slip and fall hazards in major airport operations, food service catering operations, floor and building maintenance services and heavy public exposure areas. Coordinated contract engineering services for over 1000 locations including Allied Maintenance, Progresso, Allied Aviation Services Fueling, Allied Aviation Services, Avondale Shipyards, Ortner Freight Car, Tillie Lewis Foods, and Danly Press.

2/83 - 11/84 REGIONAL TECHNICAL CONSULTANT
Commercial Union Insurance Companies
Wall Street Plaza
New York, New York 10005

Responsible for the technical quality all casualty risk control engineering in the Eastern region (7 offices). Provided consulting in risk management, loss control, safety program development and evaluation. Experienced with large loss investigations, accident reconstruction, hazard identification and control.

6/80 - 2/83 RISK CONTROL ACCOUNT CONSULTANT
Commercial Union Insurance Companies

Promoted to the company's senior field service position. Primarily functioned as an account coordinator initiating, developing, and monitoring corporate safety and loss control service to national and international accounts.

3/78 - 6/80 SR. REPRESENTATIVE LOSS PREVENTION ENGINEERING
Utica Mutual Insurance Company
200 Garden City Plaza
Garden City, New York 11530

Multi - line commercial insurance loss control inspection servicing with strong concentrations in printers, binderies, schools, fleets and machine shops. Experienced in general liability, construction safety, fire inspections, hazard identification, accident cause analysis, and safety program evaluation. Inspected more than 1500 sites.

3/77 - 3/78 ENGINEERING INSPECTOR
Bowe, Walsh, and Associates - Engineers
32 North Park Avenue
Bayshore, New York 11706

Field Engineering inspector with the consulting engineering firm for the construction of the Suffolk County Sewer District. Responsibilities included making recommendations for the improvement of public and crew safety, compliance with OSHA and fire laws, reporting of damages, blueprint design modifications, and the recording of all construction activities.

MODEL CVS

William Marletta, PhD, CSP

PUBLISHED WORKS, PRESENTATIONS, RESEARCH PROJECTS, SYMPOSIUMS

Marletta, W., Chapter 12 *"Trip, Slip and Fall Prevention,"* The Work Environment, editor Doan Hansen PhD, Lewis Publishers, 1991

Marletta, W., *"The Effects of Expectation"*, Long Island Annual Journal, 1991

Marletta, W. interviewed in Chain Store Age Executive, "Slip/ Fall Liability for Upscale Retailers" (discussion of mats and floor care) November 1992

Marletta, W. (Doctoral Dissertation), *"The Effects of Humidity and Wetness on Pedestrian Slip Resistance Evaluated with Slip Testing Devices on Selected Sole and Floor Surface Materials"*, New York University, 1994

Marletta, W. & English W., Project Research under contract for the US DOL, Ironworkers of America, *"An Investigation of Surface Slip Resistance on Structural Steel,"* published by The Center to Protect Workers Rights, October 1995

Marletta, W. & English W., *"The Right Paint Can Prevent Slips and Falls"* National Safety Council, November 1995, pg. 78-81.

Marletta, W., *"The Effect of Surface Texture on Coefficient of Friction Variability Between Selected Slip Testers,"* Proceedings American Academy of Forensic Sciences, Annual Meeting, Seattle, Washington, February 13-18, 1995

Marletta, W., *"The Effects of Wetness on Coefficient of Friction Measurement Evaluated with Three Slip Testers with Varied Residence Times on Selected Materials,"* Proceeding of the 1995 Fourteenth Southern Biomedical Engineering Conference sponsored by the Louisiana State University Medical School, 1995.

Marletta, W. *"Slips, Trips, and Falls - Evaluation and Control"* Seminar Series for the American Insurance Association, 1995 - Seminars (May 23, 1995 NYC; June 13, 1995; Chicago, September 26, 1995, Dallas; September 28, 1995; November 7, 1995, Atlanta:

Marletta, W. International Symposium on Slip Resistance: The Interaction of Man, Footwear, and Walking Surfaces, October 30-31, 1995, Footwear Session Moderator.

Marletta, W.; Brungraber, R; English, W.; Fleisher, D.; Gray, E.; Kohr,; Marpet; Schieb, D., *"Bucknell University F13 Workshop to Evaluate Various Slip Resistance Measuring Devices"*, ASTM Standardization News, May 1992

Guest Lecturer, Suffolk Community College, *"Slip Trip and Fall Prevention - Evaluation of Stairs & Ramps", Spring 1996*

SUNY Environmental Health and Safety Association (SEHSA) lecturer on *"Slip, Trip and Fall Prevention for Campus Safety"*, October 23, 1997

American Society of Safety Engineers (ASSE) LI Chapter speaker *"Safety Issues with Scaffolds, OSHA, NYS Rules and Regulations, New York State Labor Law"* March 10, 1998, Marriot Windwatch, Islandia, New York

American Society of Safety Engineers (ASSE) LI Chapter speaker *"Slip, Trip and Fall Prevention"* Sheraton Hotel, Smithtown, New York

ASSE National 34th Annual Professional Development Conference (PDC, San Diego) Session Speaker *"Slip, Trip and Fall Prevention" 6/96*

ASSE National 35th Annual Professional Development Conference (PDC, Seattle) Session Speaker *"Slip, Trip and Fall Prevention - ASTM Standards and the OSHA SENRAC Slip Resistance on Steel Construction Study"* 6/97

ASSE National 36th Annual Professional Development Conference (PDC, New Orleans) Session Speaker *"Slip Resistance on Walking/ Working Surfaces Current Trends... Proposed A1264.2 ANSI Standard ... Impact & Implication of Standard." 6/98*

National Fire Protection Association (NFPA) Committee on Fire Apparatus, Safety Task Group Presentation of Charlotte Test Results (Orlando) *"Tread Plate Slip Resistance for the Firefighter Study"* 1998

National Fire Protection Association (NFPA) Committee on Fire Apparatus, Committee Meeting Guest Presentation (Louisville, KY) *"Tread Plate Slip Resistance for the Firefighter Study"* September, 1998

Cable Televised presentation developed by Charlotte Fire Department for the National Fire Protection Association (NFPA) Committee on Fire Apparatus, describing the *"Tread Plate Slip Resistance for the Firefighter Study"* 1998

Marletta Interviewed in Occupational, Safety and Health Magazine, *"Confined Spaces - Rise and Fall"* (Ladder Safety), David May, February 1999.

Guest Lecturer Suffolk Community College, *"Trip, Slip and Fall Prevention"*, April 1999

National Fire Protection Association (NFPA) Committee on Fire Apparatus, Safety Task Group. Marletta presented task group with suggested improvements for standard on slip resistance resulting in emergency re-balloting of the standard, November 3rd, Reno, Nevada

American Society of Home Inspectors, (ASHA) New England Chapter November 18th, 1999. Dr. William Marletta conducted Full Day Seminar *on "Trips, Slips, and Falls for the Home Inspector*"

Appendix U Model Forensic Reports

(Note: The attachments and appendices referenced in the reports in this appendix have not been included.)

IN THE UNITED STATES DISTRICT COURT
FOR THE SOUTHERN DISTRICT OF TEXAS
LINCOLN DIVISION

LYNN STEPHENS, Plaintiff	* * *	
vs.	*	CIVIL ACTION H-94-4168
	* *	
THE CITY OF LINCOLN, ET AL., Defendants	* *	

PRELIMINARY
REPORT OF MELVIN L. TUCKER

QUALIFICATIONS

My name is Melvin L. Tucker and I retired as the Chief of Police of Tallahassee, Florida, on December 31, 1993, where I had served from October 15, 1979. During a twenty-five year law enforcement career I served as a Chief of Police in four cities, in three states and as an Agent for the Federal Bureau of Investigation.

I served as the Chairman of the North Carolina Criminal Justice Education and Training Council from 1977 until 1979, and as Vice-Chairman of the Florida Criminal Justice Standards and Training Commission from 1981 until 1984.

I served as an adjunct faculty member in criminal justice at Western Carolina University, Florida State University, Florida A&M University, and other institutions.

I have held several law enforcement certifications, including the advanced certificate from the State of North Carolina. I currently hold a Florida Law Enforcement Certificate and a Board Certificate from the National Academy of Police Specialists.

I completed my bachelors degree at the University of South Florida, Tampa, Florida and my masters degree at Appalachian State University, Boone, North Carolina. I have authored over twenty articles that have been published in public administration and criminal justice professional journals. (See CV attached)

I have served as a consultant and expert witness on numerous matters relating to police practices. I have published, conducted training, and taught in the areas of law enforcement standards, policies, issues, and training requirements.

My expert witness testimony has been evenly divided between plaintiff and defense.

I am familiar with the issues involved with women in policing, having managed a department which, in 1993, was 18% female. I have supervised investigations into allegations of sexual harassment and have disciplined officers as a result of sustained complaints of sexual harassment. During my career I frequently observed the phenomenon known commonly in the field of law enforcement as the "code of silence" or the "blue curtain" and have been called upon to testify, as a consultant, concerning this phenomenon before a grand jury investigating corruption in a municipal police department.

My fee for the analysis in this case is $2,500.00 which is my standard fee for this type of work.

EXPERT TESTIMONY

I have provided deposition or trial testimony in the following cases in the past four years:

1. Marceline Lasater, et al
vs.
City of Tyler, Texas, et al

2. Margaret A. Georgiadis
vs.
Amneal Corporation and David Petroski
Marion County, Florida

3. Ken Hall
v.
City of Sarasota, Florida Police Department, et al
Sarasota, Florida

4. Frederick E. Hendricks
vs.
State of Florida DHS&MV
Volusia County, Florida

5. Wayne Howell
v.
Carolina Beach, N.C.
Wilmington, N.C.

6. James R. Sasser
v.
Tallahassee Police Department
Tallahassee, Florida

7. Sidney Herlich
v.
Lake Worth Police Department
Lake Worth, Florida

8. Wyner
v.
DeWald, et al
West Palm Beach, Florida

9. Gaila Triggs
v.
Park Inn International, et al
Lee County, Florida

10. Dave M. Mathewson
v.
Florida Game & Fresh Water Fish Commission et al
Tampa, Florida

11. Stalvey
v.
City of Waycross
Waycross, Georgia

12. Claudc Jones
v.
City of Douglas
Douglas, Georgia

13. Steven L. Shephard
v.
City of Folly Beach, et al
Folly Beach, South Carolina

14. Larry Gabbard
v.
Eastern Airlines, Inc.
Alachua County, Florida

15. Thomas R. Zutell And John Kale
v.
Ralph A. Dahlstrom, Jr.
Gainesville, Florida

16. Styles
v.
Tallahassee Housing Authority
Tallahassee, Florida

17. Kastogianis
v.
Pillsbury and Burger King
West Palm Beach, Florida

18. Kirkland
v.
Gadsden County Sheriff's Department
Quincy, Florida

MATERIALS REVIEWED

I reviewed the following materials in developing my opinion(s) in this case:

1. Plaintiff's First Amended Complaint;
2. Defendants' Answers;
3. The Sexual Harassment Policies for the Lincoln Police Department before and after Officer Stephens's charge of sexual harassment;
4. A transcript of the deposition of Leigh Anne Smith;
5. A transcript of the deposition of Mary Johnston;
6. A transcript of the deposition of William Thomas;
7. The Lincoln Police Department Internal Affairs Division investigation in this case;
8. The personnel file of Plaintiff Lynn Stephens;
9. The personnel file of Defendant George Johnston;
10. The personnel file of defendant William Thomas; and
11. Lincoln Police Department General Orders (numbers 200-25, 300-8, 200-8,200-3 and 300-14).

The materials that I comprehensively reviewed in this case are materials that are typically relied upon by consultants and experts in analyzing law enforcement issues.

BRIEF SUMMARY OF DISPOSITIVE FACTS

The following facts have been obtained from documentation provided by counsel and I have relied upon them in consideration of this case:

Lynn Stephens was employed with the City of Lincoln Police Department in May, 1986. In August, 1989 she was assigned to the Lincoln Police Department Mounted Patrol Unit of the Special Operations Division where her immediate supervisors were Sergeant George Johnston and Lieutenant William Thomas.

During her tenure with the Mounted Patrol Officer Stephens was frequently subjected to acts and statements from both Johnston and Thomas which constituted sexual harassment.

In February, 1993 Sergeant Johnston put his hands on Officer Stephens's shoulders and kissed her on her right ear. She immediately relayed her shock and disgust to Sergeant Johnston in the presence of another employee who witnessed the event. Officer Stephens did not report these incidents to Lieutenant Thomas

(Johnston's supervisor) as she was experiencing the same type of conduct from him and had no confidence he would take corrective action.

In May, 1993 an allegation of race discrimination in the Mounted Patrol Unit was made by Officer Jon Turner. During an investigation into the complaint of Officer Turner, the conduct of Johnston and Thomas regarding the sexual harassment of Officer Stephens came to light and was also investigated. The following violations were sustained against Lieutenant Thomas:

1. Improper conduct and behavior (urinating and lowering pants in public);
2. Interfering in cases or operations (for attempting to intimidate a witness);
3. Insubordination (for failing to follow a direct order to not interfere with the investigation);
4. Sexual harassment (for improper acts or statements to Officer Stephens);
5. Respect for fellow employees (for acts or statements made in front of employees of the Mounted Patrol Unit); and
6. Truthfulness(for denying allegations that were witnessed and confirmed by more than one employee).

The following violations were sustained against Sergeant Johnston:

1. Sexual harassment (for acts and statements made to Officer Stephens);
2. Respect for fellow employees (for conduct toward Officer Stephens and Officer Karen Larsen); and
3. Truthfulness (for denying allegations made that were witnessed and confirmed by more than one employee).

Sergeant Johnston and Lieutenant Thomas were each suspended for ninety days without pay and transferred out of the Mounted Patrol Unit for their misconduct. This action was less than the Administrative Disciplinary Committee, convened by the Lincoln Police Department, recommended to the Chief of Police (demotion to Sergeant for Thomas and demotion to patrol officer for Johnston in addition to transfer and suspension).

Because of her complaint against two fellow officers (breaking the code of silence) Officer Stephens was subjected to "blackballing" by some of her fellow employees in the Mounted Patrol and retaliation efforts by Thomas, Johnston, and his wife Mary Johnston. As one example of "blackballing" Sergeant Patrick Foley held a roll call session in the lobby at the Mounted Patrol Units quarters while Officer Stephens was waiting in the roll call room. Before this time roll call had never been held in the lobby. (Leigh Anne Smith deposition pages 50 & 51)

Because of her complaint against two fellow officers Officer Stephens was subjected to retaliation by George Johnston, Mary Johnston, and William Thomas. As an example, Mary Johnston conducted a three week investigation of Officer Stephens (including video-taping Stephens at her off-duty employment) with the knowledge of her husband, George Johnston. (Mary Johnston deposition page 60)

Opinion(s)

The basis and reasons for my opinion(s) are premised upon my education, training, experience, knowledge of law enforcement standards, analysis and study in the field, through consulting professional literature, through seminars, and the facts of the case presented and the materials reviewed. My opinion(s) are based upon a synthesis of the above.

I presently hold the following preliminary opinion(s) to a reasonable degree of professional certainty:

1. As a result of the failure of the supervisors of the Lincoln Police Department and its Chief to enforce its own directive, General Order 200-8 (Supervisor's Responsibilities), Officer Lynn Stephens was subjected to a violation of the law (sexual harassment) by Sergeant George Johnston and Lieutenant William Thomas while she was assigned as an officer in the Mounted Patrol Unit under the immediate supervision of Sergeant Johnston and the unit command of Lieutenant William Thomas.

2. Chief Tim Duncan's failure to insure the Lincoln Police Departments own directive system was followed (General Order 200-3 titled INVESTIGATION OF ALLEGED MISCONDUCT BY OFFICERS) in the investigation into the sexual harassment of Officer Stephens (that all complaints of serious misconduct be investigated by the Internal Affairs Division as a Class 1 complaint) sent a message to the employees of the Lincoln Police Department that sexual harassment is not considered a serious act of misconduct.

3. Chief Tim Duncan's decision to suspend for ninety days and to transfer Johnston and Thomas, but not to demote Johnston and Thomas as the Departments' Administrative Disciplinary Committee had recommended, re-enforced the message already sent to the employees of the Lincoln Police Department that sexual harassment allegations would not be treated as seriously by the administration of the department as their Directives require or their employees (membership of Administrative Disciplinary Committee) expected.

Chief Duncan's failure to terminate Thomas when another complaint was sustained against him after he returned to work from his ninety day suspension (as Chief Duncan had warned Thomas he would do) and the Departments performance evaluation of Thomas (very good) during the time period of his suspension again re-enforced this message.

By neglecting to reflect the disciplinary actions taken against Lieutenant Thomas on Thomas performance evaluation that covered the time period in which he was suspended for sexually harassing Officer Stephens, Chief Duncan and the supervisors of the Lincoln Police Department failed to insure General Order 300-8 (Performance Evaluations) was followed and properly enforced.

By failing to provide counseling (corrective action) for Thomas and Johnston, in addition to the ninety day suspension (punishment), about their misconduct in the sexual harassment of Officer Stephens, as required by General Order 300-8, Chief Duncan and the Lincoln Police Department placed female employees in the divisions where Thomas and Johnston were transferred to possible risk of sexual harassment.

4. Chief Duncan's failure to take decisive, clear, and visible action as to the Department's values when it became apparent that Officer Stephens was being subjected to "blackballing" and "retaliation" sent a message to the employees of the

Lincoln Police Department that the custom and policy of the Department would continue to be the "code of silence" and officers who file complaints against other officers will not be supported by the leadership of the department.

5. The phenomenon known as "code of silence" or blue curtain" in the field of law enforcement has been recognized and discussed in criminal justice literature over the past quarter century. The "code of silence" is known to thrive if the leadership of the department does not make it clear, by policy and practice, that the value statement of the organization is to rebuke the few miscreants whose conduct falls below standards and to support the majority of officers who are doing their jobs effectively and lawfully.

6. That the "code of silence" existed in the Lincoln Police Department during the time when Officer Stephens was being sexually harassed and subjected to retaliation for her complaint against fellow officers is not only evidenced by the testimony of witnesses such as Leigh Anne Smith (deposition page 39 of volume 1 and page 14 of volume 2) wherein she stated that "she has experienced it herself" but is also evidenced by the Lincoln Police Departments own official documents (Page 17 of the Investigative Summary of Stephens Sexual Harassment Complaint) wherein it is stated "Mounted Patrol was considered a highly desirable assignment and the reluctance of some witnesses to "rock the boat" was understandable". This statement clearly supports the contention that to tell the truth may cost you the loss of assignment to a desirable job.

Further evidence that the "code of silence" was a custom and policy of the Lincoln Police Department is the fact that no officer, employee, or supervisor in the Mounted Patrol Unit came forward after Sergeant George Johnston warned all officers at a roll call session, after the investigation into the race discrimination and sexual harassment allegations had begun, to "stick together and they can't get any of us" and to "stick to your story no matter what happens" (Leigh Anne Smith deposition page 33) even though his conduct was in violation of Lincoln Police Department General Order 200-8 titled <u>SUPERVISORS' RESPONSIBILITIES</u>.

I may have additional opinions and reasoning depending upon the review of additional materials and what is asked of me at trial.

Respectfully Submitted,

Melvin L. Tucker

Dr. David W. Richardson, D.O.
111 E. Main St., Suite 201
Coastal City, FL 12345

October 3, 1995

Mary Smith, Esq.
Smith, Thomas, and Hart
600 Constitution Avenue
Suite 1200
Coastal City, FL 12345

RE: Amy Garson (File No. 98-4512)

This workers' compensation case involves a back injury. The examinee has not yet reached maximum medical improvement and recommendations are made as to her clinical management. The physician is unable to conclude that the totality of the examinee's difficulties are causally related to the reported injury.

This 33-year-old, right-handed woman was referred for an independent medical evaluation by the above client. The IME process was explained to the examinee, and she understands that no patient/treating physician relationship exists and that a report will be sent to the requesting client. History was provided by the examinee, who was a cooperative, fair to good historian and completed the questionnaire. She was driven 3½ hours to the appointment by her sister and arrived on time. Her sister waited in the reception area. The patient reported that the long ride aggravated her back.

The client provided clinical records of Jean Loren, MD Coastal Imaging; and Betsy Coens, RPT. No records prior to May 15, 1995 or subsequent to September 13, 1995 were available for review. Significant missing records included those of pre-existing status.

To ensure accuracy, the clinical synopsis was reviewed in the presence of the examinee. The issues requested in the referral are addressed in the Conclusions.

HISTORY

Pre-existing Status

Ms. Garson admits to a low back injury in 1990, when she was pregnant. She was bending forward to remove a food tray from the lower level of a cart. She suffered low back strain, for which she received short-term treatment. She was out of work for 8 months; however, most of this was due to her pregnancy and a death in the family. She indicates that after several weeks her low back improved. Subsequently she noticed "on and off lameness," especially "if I overdid it." However, she denies any significant episodes requiring her to miss time from work.

She states that prior to the injury of May 1995 she was not experiencing significant problems.

Injury

She reports that on May 2, 1995 she was transferring a client from bed to walker and then wheelchair. The client had gotten up to the walker but started to fall. Ms. Garson was able to help her into the wheelchair, but had to bear her full weight. She felt something "pull" across her low back. She continued working that shift and didn't feel too bad; however, by the end of the shift she had mildly increased low back pain. The following day her pain was worse. She had difficulty continuing her job, and called her family physician for an appointment.

Initial Clinical Encounter

She was seen on May 15, 1995 by Jean Loren, MD. The patient presented complaining of low back pain but also indicated the left side of the abdomen was bothering her, near the site of a hernia repair. The doctor refers to "on and off 3 weeks." It is not clear if this is in regard to the hernia site or the low back pain. She recommended the patient remain out of work for rest, but due to financial constraints the patient could not do so, and they finally agreed to reduce her to four days per week. However, she did remain on her usual activities.

Clinical Synopsis

Within a couple of weeks she began experiencing increasing pain to the right buttocks, radiating to the leg intermittently. She states this went as far as the ankle but was not associated with paresthesias, bladder or bowel dysfunction, and there was no pain with valsalva. She was referred to physical therapy and attended twice, but there was no insurance reimbursement so she discontinued. Because the patient is living in Canada she has Canadian Medicare, and in early July this coverage began paying for her physical therapy. She returned to treatments twice a week, consisting of ultrasound, hot packs, and stretching exercises. She continues attending physical therapy one to two times per week, but has not received instruction or progressive exercises. She continues receiving passive modalities. She does some stretching at home on a nightly basis.

At this point she doesn't feel that her symptoms are particularly improved. She remains under the care of Dr. Loren and has not seen other providers for consultation or assessment.

Clinical Management Summary

Health Care Providers

Jean Loren, MD is identified as the primary treating doctor. The last appointment was September 5, 1995 and the next is scheduled for October 4, 1995. Dr. Loren is also her primary care physician.

Evaluation Summary

X-ray, LS spine, June 9, 1995: "Some disc space narrowing at L4-5 but no other significant findings . . . and . . . little if any degenerative changes. There is only a minimal curvature of the spine convex to the right." Films were reviewed and there appeared to be no sign of spondylolysis or spondylolisthesis. Disc space appeared well-maintained. I do not agree with the radiologist's impression that there was narrowing at L4-5. If there is narrowing here, it certainly is minimal.

Treatment Summary

Physical therapy: As noted above.

Medications: Currently Flexeril 10 mg up to three times per day. She consistently takes this in the evening, but finds it causes too much drowsiness when she works. She previously used Darvocet but has discontinued it because it made her sick.

Other: Currently none; previously heat, ice, and walking.

Current Status

The examinee's major concern is whether she will improve. She feels she has remained the same. The pain is located primarily in the low back with occasional radiation to the right posterior buttocks, posterolateral thigh, into the lateral calf as far as the ankle, and is described as aching in the low back and at times burning in the buttocks. There are no left lower extremity symptoms.

Aggravating Factors: Almost all activities.

Relieving Factors: Doing nothing.

The pain is nearly constant (present 50-80% of the time). On a scale from 0 (no pain) to 10 (excruciating pain), initially it was a 9. During the past month it averaged a 7, with a low of 6 and a high of 9. Today the pain is an 8.

She denies any history of paresthesias/numbness or tingling, and weakness in the leg or foot. She notes occasional morning stiffness in the lower back "if I do to[o] much" the previous day. She has no history of headaches. She admits to depression, but states this is primarily related to other personal stresses not her back. There is no history of suicidal ideation. She admits to secondary insomnia due to low back pain. There has been no history of increased pain with coughing, sneezing, or bowel movement.

Functional Status

She estimates she can sit or walk for a maximum of 30 minutes at a time and stand for up to 20 minutes, but she is not sure how much she can lift. She reports major difficulties sweeping, vacuuming, and driving a car. She indicates minor problems lifting a gallon of milk or a light bag of groceries, bending, pulling or pushing, climbing stairs, and kneeling. She is unsure about her ability to lift heavy weights and heavy bags of groceries, reach above shoulder level, and climb ladders. Her most difficult tasks are sweeping, vacuuming, and riding for long distances in a car.

Occupational History

At the time of the injury the examinee had been employed by Elder Care Nursing Home since April 1988. She was working full-time (38-75 hours a week) as a CNA. According to the description provided by the examinee, this involved caring for the residents. The physical demands included sitting or standing for up to half an hour at a time, walking for up to 5 hours, repetitive use of the hands, frequent lifting, and awkward positioning. The heaviest object she usually had to lift was a resident.

She previously worked as a cashier in a grocery store and in a fish factory. She is a high school graduate and has a current driver's license.

The examinee was "not put out of work but cut back from a 5 day . . . to a 4 day work week" since May 15, 1995.

Social History

The examinee has been married for 8 years but is currently separated. She has three children living with her, ages 4, 8, and 12. During the day she rests, watches TV, cleans house (she is unable to do heavy chores), and works as described above. She briefly describes an average day as follows: "I get up [at 4:30 AM] and get ready for work. Then I get my 3 children ready for school. Then I go to work. Then I come home, change and rest for a while. Then I do housework, cook supper, do laundry. Get kids ready for bed. Watch T.V. Then I get ready and go to bed [at 8:00]." She reports having no specific hobbies.

She has smoked one pack of cigarettes a day for 11 years, for an 11 pack-year history. She drinks approximately 2 alcoholic beverages per week, and denies having had any problems with alcohol or other drugs. She consumes 5 caffeinated beverages per day. She does have health insurance.

Past Medical History

Unrelated surgery:	Tonsillectomy, C-section, exploratory surgery, tubal ligation.
Other hospitalizations:	Noncontributory.
Drug allergies:	None.
Unrelated medications:	None.
Review of systems:	Positive for fatigue.
Family history:	Positive for grandparents with arthritis.

PHYSICAL EXAMINATION

Observations

The examinee is a white female who appeared healthy. She reported her weight as 186 lbs. and her height as 5 ft. 6 in.

Behavioral Examination

The examinee was pleasant, cooperative, and attentive. Her affect was normal and she maintained eye contact. She appeared comfortable during the interview and exam, sitting continuously for 20 minutes. No behavioral dysfunction or non-physiologic findings were observed.

Structural Examination

In the standing neutral position cervical, thoracic, and lumbar curves were well-maintained. Gait was normal, with no antalgia. She was able to heel and toe walk, and demonstrated normal balance.

Examination focused on the low back and lower extremities.

Brief inspection of the upper quarter indicated normal range of the cervical spine and bilateral shoulders, as well as elbows, wrists, and digits. There was no pain to palpation throughout the shoulder girdle or upper thoracic paraspinal regions. DTRs were 2/4 at the Johnstonps, brachioradialis, and triceps.

Low Back Examination

There were no surgical scars. There was no generalized tenderness. Tenderness was reported at the lumbosacral junction, primarily on the right SI region extending to the sciatic notch and piriformis area. There was no significant pain at the coccyx or left gluteal area.

Lumbar Motion (degrees)	Normal	Angle
Flexion forward	60	60
Extension backward	25	28
Right lateral flexion	25	24
Left lateral flexion	25	24

Lumbar motion was normal. Range of motion measurements were made with an inclinometer. Sacroiliac testing was positive on the right. Somatic dysfunction was identified at the right sacroiliac joint. There was pain reported at the right piriformis region with palpation.

Lower Extremity Neurologic Examination

Patellar reflexes were +2/4 L, +2/4 R; Achilles were +2/4 L, +2/4 R.

Manual muscle strength testing throughout the bilateral lower extremities disclosed no focal areas of weakness. There was no gross evidence of atrophy. To gross inspection there appeared to be slight calf atrophy on the left (unaffected) side compared to the right. There is no history of trauma to the left leg, and no dysfunction.

Sensory examination with sharp/soft discrimination was normal throughout all dermatomes. Straight-leg raising was negative seated and supine on the left. On the right the patient noted increased minor back discomfort at 90° seated and at about 75° supine; however, there was associated hamstring tension.

There was full and symmetric hip motion bilaterally. There was normal knee motion bilaterally, with no signs of crepitus or instability.

Palpation and inspection were unremarkable.

PAIN STATUS INVENTORIES

Pain Drawing

The examinee completed a pain drawing (enclosed), using symbols to describe sensations. This drawing received a normal score.

Pain Disability Index

The Pain Disability Index uses rating scales to measure the extent of perceived disability in seven areas of life. The results are as follows:

Area	Perceived Disability
Family/home responsibilities	70%
Recreation	70%
Social activity	70%
Occupation	70%
Sexual activity	80%
Self-care	70%
Life-support activities	50%

The total score is 48 out of a possible 70, for a total index of 69% (a high level of perceived disability).

McGill Pain Questionnaire

The examinee completed the McGill Pain Questionnaire (Short Form), rating 15 pain descriptors on a scale from 0 (none) to 3 (severe). The sum of eleven sensory descriptors was 8, averaging 0.7. The sum of four affective descriptors was 6, averaging 1.5. The total of all descriptors was 14. The descriptors were primarily affective, suggesting an exaggerating pain patient. The overall pain intensity was rated at 3 (distressing) on a scale of 0-5.

Multidimensional Pain Inventory

The results of the University of Pittsburgh School of Medicine Multidimensional Pain Inventory were computer analyzed. The examinee rated the impact of the pain in several areas on a 0-6 scale. The report (appended) gives scores and statistical analysis, along with a graphic representation of the results compared with a control group.

This profile is classified as that of a dysfunctional individual. Compared with the control group, these individuals report a higher severity of pain, greater interference with their lives, a higher degree of psychological distress, a lower perceived ability to control their lives, and lower activity levels. They are labeled dysfunctional because the pain has affected a broad range of their functioning.

CES-D

The Center for Epidemiologic Studies Depressed Mood Scale was administered. The examinee scored 35, suggesting a depressed mood.

Oswestry Function Test

Her score on the Oswestry Function Test was 25 out of a possible 50 (50th percentile), indicating a perception of severe disability.

CONCLUSIONS

Diagnoses

1. Low back pain (724.2).
   - 1.1. Sciatica, right side.
   - 1.2. Somatic dysfunction, right sacroiliac and piriformis area.
   - 1.3. Doubt radiculopathy.

2. Obesity (278.0)/Deconditioning (728.2).

3. Tobacco use (305.1).

4. Nonrestorative sleep disorder.

5. Probable depression.

Ms. Garson was pleasant and cooperative with today's evaluation. Her physical findings would support a chronic low back problem, primarily localized to the right sacroiliac and sciatic region. It appears that piriformis spasm and sacroiliac somatic dysfunction are contributing to sciatica, causing low back pain. Despite the subjective complaints, over all her physical findings are relatively mild. She continues to work 30 hours per week in a fairly demanding job, and maintains her household with three young children as a single parent.

The patient achieved an elevated score on the CES-D test. While this test cannot diagnose depression, certainly the results suggest a depressed mood and she may in fact be clinically depressed. This does not appear related to her low back injury.

Causation

Based upon the available information, to a reasonable degree of medical certainty, there is a possible causal relationship between the current complaints and the occupational injury reported. More likely than not her ongoing complaints are due to a combination of cumulative work trauma, obesity, Deconditioning, and lack of appropriate rest during her "off" time. I would rate all of these factors as equally contributory to her condition.

Prognosis

Prognosis would seem good to excellent considering her apparent high motivation level.

Maximum Medical Improvement

Maximum medical improvement (MMI) is defined as the date after which further recovery and restoration of function can no longer be anticipated, based upon reasonable medical probability. She has not reached MMI.

Work Capacity

This examinee has at least a moderate to heavy work capacity as defined in the *Dictionary of Occupational Titles*, U.S. Department of Labor. Moderate work is defined as exerting up to 50 lbs. of force occasionally and/or up to 20 lbs. of force frequently and/or up to 10 lbs. of force constantly to move objects. Heavy work is defined as exerting up to 100 lbs. of force occasionally and/or up to 50 lbs. of force frequently and/or up to 20 lbs. of force constantly to move objects.

The examinee can work part- to full-time, 4-5 days a week. She should alternate between sitting and standing based upon comfort. She can lift up to 45-50 lbs. occasionally and up to 20-25 lbs. frequently, depending upon the circumstances. Factors include the height of the lift, the distance from the body, and the bulk. She may have greater capabilities, particularly with conditioning. She can occasionally bend and twist.

In my opinion she is capable of continuing to perform her current job at her current capacity. I would expect her capacity to increase as her symptoms improve. Please see recommendations.

I would be pleased to review any written functional job descriptions or videotapes of jobs, to make arrangements to view work being considered, and/or to discuss any issues concerning work capability or the return to work process.

Appropriateness of Care

Her care has been consistent with the usual standards of care for this problem.

Recommendations

Diagnostic

I think the primary problem is sciatica related to musculoligamentous irritation. I would recommend ruling out nerve impingement through an EMG/nerve conduction study. I think this would provide more information and be more cost-effective than an MRI. It will probably require the services of a neurologist. I am not sure if there is one in her immediate area; if not, she could obtain this at Neurology Associates in Presque Isle, or might have to travel to Bangor.

Therapeutic

She seems to have chronic irritability at the right SI joint as well as piriformis area. This should be an area of focus by the physical therapist. The examinee seems to be following a fairly simple routine of low back exercises, and while these might be somewhat beneficial, a more specific program aimed at the piriformis area would probably be more beneficial.

The examinee also might be a candidate for osteopathic manipulative therapy of 4-6 visits. The goal of this treatment would be to increase mobilization of the sacroiliac and piriformis area, helping to speed recovery.

She should be encouraged to lose weight and quit smoking.

The patient notes poor sleep. This may be contributing to her poor recovery. I would suggest a trial of low-dose tricyclic antidepressant medication to treat this; in fact, increasing this medication to therapeutic levels for depression might be beneficial as well.

The above analysis is based upon the subjective complaints, the history given by the examinee, the medical records and tests provided, the results of pain status inventories, and the physical findings. It is assumed that the material provided is correct. If more information becomes available at a later date, an additional report may be requested. Such information may or may not change the opinions rendered in this evaluation.

The examiner's opinions are based upon reasonable medical probability and are totally independent of the requesting agent. Medicine is both an art and a science, and although an individual may appear to be fit for return to duty, there is no guarantee that the person will not be reinjured or suffer additional injury. If applicable, employers should follow the process established in the Americans with Disabilities Act, Title 1. Comments on appropriateness of care are professional opinions based upon the specifics of this case, and should not be generalized to the involved providers or disciplines. The opinions expressed do not constitute a recommendation that specific claims or administrative functions be made or enforced.

Thank you for asking me to see this examinee in consultation. If you have any further questions, please do not hesitate to contact me.

Respectfully submitted,

David W. Richardson, DO
Occupational Medicine

DWR/ge
Enclosures: Work Capacity Report

cc: Jean Loren, MD

FORENSIC ENGINEERS & TECHNOLOGISTS

John M. Orlowski, P.E., CSP, BCFE, Director

11 Vanderbilt Avenue, Suite 120
Norwood, Massachusetts 02062-5056
PHONE: (617)762-8377
FAX: (617)762-1862

September 15, 1997

TECHNICAL REPORT TO
Thom Hobbes, Esquire
139 Leeds Avenue
Suite 500
New York, New York 10038

RE: Jean Smith
Vs: A.B. Stamp Company, Inc.
Date of Accident: 5/10/94
CIV. Number: 95-4354 (BSJ)
F.E.T. File Number: 2059.1

1.0 INTRODUCTION

1.1 Jean Smith was employed by ACME Metal Stamping Company, Inc., 4551 Furman Avenue, Bronx, NY, when his accident occurred.

He was operating a mechanical punch press at the time. A press is a machine used to supply force for the reshaping of materials, primarily metal. A die is a member placed in the press. It consists of a punch and a lower die. Its purpose is to supply a mold for the metal to conform to. Mr. Smith was inserting strip stock from a reel into the stamping die when the press suddenly and unexpectedly began cycling. As a result, Mr. Smith sustained a crush injury to his right hand. There was no point-of-operation guard on the press at the time of Mr. Smith's accident.

Thom S. Hobbes, Esquire, has requested that Forensic Engineers & Technologists review the circumstances of the accident and determine if any unsafe conditions existed that caused the injury to Mr. Smith's right hand.

The undersigned reviewed the following documents prior to formulating the opinions contained within the report:

a) A. B. Stamp Rolling Key Clutch Service and operation manuals A-111 and A-111-B
b) A. B. Stamp Catalog 2-C
c) A. B. Stamp Service Manual A-110-1
d) A letter from A. B. Stamp to "Stamp Power Press Owners and Employers Using Stamp Presses RE: Stamp Rolling Key Clutches and Latch Brackets", dated November 12, 1975
e) An undated letter, with attachments, entitled "B11.1 AS WE SEE IT"

f) A letter from Paul N. Jobs of A. B. Stamp to Mr. Arnold, Plant Manager of ACME Stamping, Inc., dated November 17, 1981
g) 61 laser photocopies of the subject press
h) A photocopy of two Warning Signs, presumably generated by A. B. Stamp
i) UDAL promotional literature describing interlocking guards for Power Presses
j) British Guarding Statistical Data dated April 1982
k) Power Presses Safe Practices Pamphlet No. 18, published by the NSC 1929
l) First report of Proceedings of the Joint Standing Committee on Safety in the use of Power Presses dated 1950
m) Safety Code for Power Presses and Foot and Hand Presses B11-1926
n) A. B. Stamp "Safety Precautions and Suggestions"
o) Defendant A. B. Stamp Company's Responses and Objections to Plaintiff's First Request for Production of Documents
p) Verified Complaint
q) Plaintiff's Answers to First Set of Contention Interrogatories of Defendant
r) Plaintiff's Answers to Interrogatories Pursuant to Rule 46(a)
s) Press inspection report dated October 24, 1995
t) Data on press owned by ACME Stamping Co., Inc.
u) Two A. B. Stamp assembly drawings entitled "One Stroke Latch"
v) Two volume deposition transcript of Jean Smith
w) Deposition transcript of Steven Arnold, Part 1
x) Deposition transcript of Daniel Nichols.

2.0 MACHINE DESCRIPTION

2.1 A mechanical punch press generates high forces, typically measured in tons, to rework metal. A rotating flywheel generates the kinetic energy necessary to reform the stock. The kinetic energy is transmitted from the flywheel to a slide or ram. A clutch is used to deliver and control the surge of force that is required for the working of metal. When the clutch is engaged, the flywheel transmits torque to an eccentric shaft. The eccentric shaft, in turn, imparts vertical motion to a slide or ram. The punch is generally assembled to the slide. As work is performed on the metal stock, the flywheel speed will correspondingly decrease. An electric motor is used to restore and maintain the necessary flywheel speed.

A press equipped with a mechanical clutch can be operated in either a single stroke or continuous mode. When the press is operating single stroke, the flywheel makes one 360° revolution, and the die will close and open once. When the press is single stroked, the clutch must accelerate all rotating and translating members from zero to full speed, as well as transmit the necessary torque. The brake, conversely, must decelerate the moving parts so the slide may be stopped. Note that at the conclusion of each stroke the flywheel continues to turn. The clutch simply disengages the fly wheel from the shaft.

When the press is operating continuously, the clutch maintains engagement and transmits the necessary torque from the flywheel to the eccentric shaft.

The press that caused Mr. Smith's injury was manufactured by the A. B. Stamp Company. The machine was purchased new by ACME Stamping Co., Inc. in 1936. The press was designated serial number 104759, model number 21. The ACME designation for the equipment was press number 8. The press was operated with a foot treadle. The equipment was furnished without point of operation guards. Stamp press serial number 104759 was furnished with a Rolling Key Clutch. The Rolling Key Clutch was a positive mechanical clutch designed to be used in either a single stroke or continuous operating mode. The clutch functions by engaging or disengaging two "rolling keys."

A latch is used to engage and disengage the clutch. To engage the clutch, the latch head is rotated counter-clockwise allowing the clutch spring to roll the key into engagement with the wheel bushing. The bushing is keyed to the flywheel hub, thereby locking the flywheel to the crankshaft.[1]

For single stroke operation, a throwout cam on the crankshaft disengages the clutch near the top of each stroke. The foot treadle must be released and reapplied for each stroke of the press. For continuous operation, the treadle rod must be relocated. The press will continue to operate as long as the treadle is depressed when in the continuous mode.

A John Humm Guard had been added to the press by ACME. This guard had been disconnected from the press and only part of a John Humm component remained when Mr. Smith was injured. This component did not cause or contribute to Mr. Smith's injury.

3.0 INCIDENT

3.1 Mr. Smith was manufacturing clips, or what he referred to as brackets, when his accident occurred. The clips were about one inch wide by one and one half inches long and were made from 20 gauge steel. The steel strip was coiled on a reel. The reel was located at the right side of the press.

[1]Refer to Appendices B-1 and B-2.

The procedure was as follows: Mr. Smith inserted strip stock from the reel into the die with his right hand. He would remove his hand and activate the foot treadle. The press would make a single stroke forming the clip. The completed part was ejected from the die by a jet of air.

Mr. Smith was injured when he was inserting the coiled strip stock into the die. Suddenly, and with no warning, the press began operating continuously while in the single stroke mode. As a result, Mr. Smith sustained a severe crush injury to his right hand.

4.0 ANALYSIS

4.1 Cycling of the press is controlled by the latch. When the latch head is rotated counter-clockwise, OR OTHERWISE REMOVED FROM CONTACT WITH THE CLUTCH HOOK, the press will cycle.

In the original A. B. Stamp design, the latch was "secured" in position with a hex nut. This is item 130 in Appendix B-1. This design was defective in that no positive means was provided to insure that the latch maintained a precise dimensional relation to the clutch hook. A means to do so was available and feasible in 1936. This was essential to the safe operation of the press. Any movement of the latch, even lateral displacement, would cause the press to cycle.

The hex nut assembled to the latch was insufficient to prevent movement. The loosening effects of vibrations on threaded fasteners has been well documented. It was foreseeable that the nut would loosen over time. To insure that the latch maintained position, a positive locking means should have been furnished.

At some point, A. B. Stamp personnel apparently realized what they should have previously known. That loosening of the latch hex nut could result in catastrophe for a press operator or set-up man. A. B. Stamp did in fact redesign the latch bracket to include a spring loaded stop pin. The function of the stop pin was to prevent lateral movement of the latch when the hex nut became loose. When queried about the effects of a loose nut at his deposition, Daniel Nichols, formerly Manager of Product Reliability for A. B. Stamp, stated the following:

A. If the latch were to come out, if the machine were in operation, the machine would continue to cycle and would only stop when the motor was stopped.

A. B. Stamp did in fact issue a recommendation that the "old style" latch bracket be replaced with the "new style" latch bracket. The letter was dated November 12, 1975. The two page letter, with attachment entitled "Single Tripping Latch Bracket," is included in this report as Appendix C. A comparison of Appendix B-1 and C-3 depicts the redesign referred to in the letter. Note that in addition to a redesign of the latch bracket, A. B. Stamp recommended that a cotter pin be installed in the nut to prevent loosening. The diameter and length of the cotter pin was not specified, nor was the size of the drilled hole delineated. The only instructions were:

"the Cotter pin should be the largest diameter that fits the drilled hole, and long enough to bend partially around the nut."

In our opinion, this letter was woefully inadequate in its attempt to communicate the extreme hazards associated with operating the press with the original, defective latch bracket design. The letter recommended only that the old style bracket be replaced. Further, the consequences of failing to adhere to the recommendations are not even addressed in the letter. This is incomprehensible considering that severe injury could result in not following the recommendations.

The letter should have been designed as a warning. The letter should have used the word *Warning*. The purpose of warnings is to control or modify the behavior of the user in order to avoid bodily injury. The warning must communicate the hazard and specify the consequence if not heeded. This was not done in the A. B. Stamp letter of November 12, 1975. Furthermore, A. B. Stamp should have forwarded the warning *Certified Mail Return Receipt Registered* to insure that A. B. Stamp Press owners and users did in fact receive the warning. The latch bracket redesign was critical to safety. As such, it was incumbent on A. B. Stamp personnel to follow-up each letter and offer whatever assistance necessary to insure that the presses were converted to safe operation.

The evidence indicates that ACME Metal Spinning and Stamping Company, Inc., did not act on the recommendations of the A. B. Stamp letter of November 12, 1975. Daniel Nichols inspected the accident press on October 24, 1995. At that time the press was equipped with the old style bracket. The documents reviewed indicate that the only latch bracket ordered by ACME, was on June 29, 1954. This was well prior to the A. B. Stamp letter of November 12, 1975.

Mr. Nichols testified at his deposition that the latch nut had a cotter pin in place on October 24, 1995. However, there is no evidence to indicate or suggest that the cotter pin was in place on the day that Mr. Smith sustained his injury. The evidence, in fact, suggests otherwise. Given the absence of any maintenance records describing the installation of the cotter pin, given the defective condition of the latch bracket, and given Mr. Smith's description of the press suddenly operating continuously while in the single stroke mode, it is our opinion that the nut was not equipped with a cotter pin when Mr. Smith's accident occurred. It is our further opinion, to a reasonable degree of engineering certainty, that the defective latch bracket design was a proximate cause of Mr. Smith's injury.

4.2 A mechanical power press utilizes great forces to perform work on metal stock. The area where work is accomplished is called the point-of-operation. The point-of-operation presents extreme hazards to an operator. This is due to the high forces involved and the proximity to the die area in which an operator must work. The worker must frequently place stock in the die area. An inadvertent press stroke, due to either a press malfunction or operator error, can be catastrophic. Many fingers, hands, and worse have been lost because a press manufacturer shipped a press without effective safeguarding. When a press is equipped with a foot treadle or foot control, the only means of safeguarding the point-of-operation is with barrier guards. Foot operation without guarding is inherently dangerous and should be prohibited. Foot operation without a guard allows, and even encourages, the operator to place his or her hands in the point-of-operation with frequent catastrophic results. An American Standard was approved by the American Engineering Standards Committee, under the sponsorship of the National Safety Council, on November 11, 1926, regarding safety standards for presses. This standard was entitled B11-1926. The following was extracted from Rule 110 of the standard:

Rule 110. Safeguarding classification.

One or more means of safeguarding the press hazards at the point of operation shall be provided and used on every press, depending upon the method of feeding, and in accordance with the following:

The complete standard is included in this report as Appendix D.

This intent of B11-1926 was that the press manufacturer include the safeguarding delineated by the standard. This is correct and appropriate. The press manufacturers possess the engineering knowledge to design and build presses. They understand how the equipment functions and know, or should know, how their machinery will be used. Safeguarding is one of the least complex components of the machine. It certainly follows that the manufacturer has the technical expertise to design, fabricate and test effective safeguarding.

Later standards have reallocated the responsibility for safeguarding a power press from the manufacturer to the user of a press. The American National Standards Institute (ANSI) B11.1 Committee states that it is the employer's responsibility to guard presses. In my opinion this is wrong. Manufacturers have a duty to provide a safe machine. The delegation of this duty to others should not be permitted.

The reason for this reallocation of responsibility is that safety standards are typically "industry driven." As such, the standards attempt to unconditionally shift the onus for safety away from the manufacturer. This is done by inserting into the standards explicit "responsibility" statements identifying the employer as the party responsible for providing equipment safeguarding. This use of the standards is unjustified. The immunity that this gratuitous allocation of responsibility grants manufacturers, encourages the shipment of unsafe machinery.

This subject has been addressed by the undersigned in "Engineering Aspects of Guarding of Machinery and Equipment."[2] The following was reproduced from that publication:

> **[1] The Machinery Manufacturer. The manufacturer of a machine such as a mechanical power press must be knowledgeable in state-of-the-art safety and guarding technology and must be thoroughly versed in the latest safety protocols, standards, and federal regulations. Most importantly, the manufacturer must incorporate this knowledge in his machine design and construction. All equipment must conform to, or exceed, current state-of-the-art. The manufacturer must apply his safe guarding knowledge to all foreseeable uses and foreseeable misuses of the equipment. He must endeavor to build a machine that is as safe as is feasible and practical. He must not ship unguarded equipment simply because it is industry practice to do so. Unguarded press equipment is still being produced and shipped today (1993), and continues to injure and maim operators.**
>
> **The B11 American National Standards Committee would have one believe that point-of-operation safeguarding, the single most important factor in the elimination of point-of-operation injuries, can only be determined by the employer. They state that a production system consists of the press as one component, dies (tooling) as another component, feeding methods (including point-of-operation scrap removal) as a third component, and the fourth component, point-of-operation safeguarding. They conclude that the vital fourth component, point-of-operation safeguarding can be evaluated for effectiveness only after the first three components and operator involvements are known. Since the first three components are, in many instances determined by the employer, the**

[2]Release 66 of Products Liability, edited by Frumer and Friedman, published by Matthew Bender, New York, NY.

> **B11 committees have accordingly assigned responsibility for safeguarding to the employer.**
>
> **While it is agreed that the multitude of parts sizes, feed devices and die configurations renders it difficult for the manufacturer to supply a totally effective barrier guard for all conditions, it certainly is feasible for the press builder to furnish a barrier guard with adjustment capabilities to enclose the space through which the press slide moves, with allowance for estimated die configuration. The final adjustment would of course be the responsibility of the press user.**
>
> **Figure 18 illustrates a mechanical punch press equipped with a universal guard. An adjustable barrier guard will not safeguard all situations and requires modifications in some cases. However, it can assist an employer in providing point-of-operation guarding, since many such employees do not have the expertise to design and manufacture an adequate guard.**

Figure 18 from ANSI B11.1-1988 has been included in this report as Appendix E.

Where barrier guards are used to protect workers from injury, it is strongly recommended that the guards be interlocked. An interlocked barrier guard should perform one of three functions:

> **a) Prevent operation of the press if the guard is not in place.**
> **b) Prevent access to the point-of-operation until all press motion ceases.**
> **c) or, immediately shut down the press if the guard is opened or removed.**

It is the manufacturer's further responsibility to provide warnings and instructions to insure that guards are in place, and interlocks functioning, prior to operating the press.

5.0 FINDINGS

5.1 It is my opinion, to a reasonable degree of engineering certainty, that the A. B. Stamp Press that caused Jean Smith's injury was defective and unreasonably dangerous. It is my further opinion that the defective and unreasonably dangerous condition of the press was a proximate cause of Mr. Smith's injury.

My findings are as follows:

a) The A. B. Stamp Press, serial number 104759, was sold to ACME Metal Spinning and Stamping

Company, Inc., with a defectively designed and manufactured latch and latch bracket. The defect caused the press, suddenly and without warning, to begin operating continuously while in the single stroke mode.

b) The manufacturer failed to adequately notify and warn users about the extreme hazards associated with the defective latch bracket.

c) The manufacturer failed to furnish the press with an appropriate point-of-operation interlocked barrier guard.

d) The manufacturer failed to provide suitable warnings and instructions to insure that guards are in place, and interlocks functioning, prior to operating the press.

Submitted by:

John M. Orlowski, P.E., CSP, BCFE
Director

Appendix V Model Consulting Agreement

This Agreement is made effective as of __________________, by and between <Client Organization>, of <Client Address>, __________________________, ___ __________, and Consultant, of <Consultant address>, __________________________, ___ __________.

In this Agreement, the party who is contracting to receive services shall be referred to as "Client," and the party who will be providing the services shall be referred to as "Consultant."

Consultant has a background in medicine and is willing to provide services to Client based on this background.

Client desires to have services provided by Consultant.

Therefore, the parties agree as follows:

1. **DESCRIPTION OF SERVICES.** Beginning on __________________, Consultant will provide the following services (collectively, the "Services"): review of medical files, answering specific medical questions asked by client, meeting individually with claims adjusters to provide medical advice on cases, participating in case conferences, and providing medical training to staff.

2. **PERFORMANCE OF SERVICES.** The manner in which the Services are to be performed and the specific hours to be worked by Consultant shall be determined by Consultant. Client will rely on Consultant to work as many hours as may be reasonably necessary to fulfill Consultant's obligations under this Agreement.

3. **PAYMENT.** Client will pay a fee of $______ per hour to Consultant for the Services. This fee shall be payable monthly, no later than the first day of the month following the period during which the Services were performed. Upon termination of this Agreement, payments under this paragraph shall cease; provided, however, that Consultant shall be entitled to payments for periods or partial periods that occurred prior to the date of termination and for which Consultant has not yet been paid.

4. **EXPENSE REIMBURSEMENT.** Consultant shall be entitled to reimbursement from Client for all reasonable expenses, including but not limited to, travel, telephone, fax, and photocopying expense.

5. **NEW PROJECT APPROVAL.** Consultant and Client recognize that Consultant's Services will include working on various projects for Client. Consultant shall obtain the approval of Client prior to the commencement of a new project.

6. TERM/TERMINATION. This Agreement shall be effective for a period of one year and shall automatically renew for successive terms of the same duration, unless either party provides 60 days written notice to the other party prior to the termination of the applicable initial term or renewal term.

7. RELATIONSHIP OF PARTIES. It is understood by the parties that Consultant is an independent contractor with respect to Client, and not an employee of Client. Client will not provide fringe benefits, including health insurance benefits, paid vacation, or any other employee benefit, for the benefit of Consultant.

8. DISCLOSURE. Consultant is required to disclose any outside activities or interests, including ownership or participation in the development of prior inventions, that conflict or may conflict with the best interests of Client. Prompt disclosure is required under this paragraph if the activity or interest is related, directly or indirectly, to any activity that Consultant may be involved with on behalf of Client.

9. INJURIES. Consultant acknowledges Consultant's obligation to obtain appropriate insurance coverage for the benefit of Consultant (and Consultant's employees, if any). Consultant waives any rights to recovery from Client for any injuries that Consultant (and/or Consultant's employees) may sustain while performing services under this Agreement and that are a result of the negligence of Consultant or Consultant's employees.

10. INDEMNIFICATION. Client agrees to indemnify and hold Consultant harmless from all claims, losses, expenses, and fees including attorney fees, costs, and judgments that may be asserted against Consultant that result from the acts or omissions of Client, Client's employees, if any, and Client's agents.

11. ASSIGNMENT. Consultant's obligations under this Agreement may not be assigned or transferred to any other person, firm, or corporation without the prior written consent of Client.

12. CONFIDENTIALITY. Client recognizes that Consultant has and will have the following information:

- products
- future plans
- business affairs
- process information
- trade secrets
- technical information
- customer lists
- product design information

and other proprietary information (collectively, "Information") which are valuable, special, and unique assets of Client and need to be protected from improper disclosure. In consideration for the disclosure of the Information, Consultant agrees that Consultant will not at any time or in any manner, either directly or indirectly, use any Information for Consultant's own benefit, or divulge, disclose, or communicate in any manner any Information to any third party without the prior written consent of Client. Consultant will protect the Information and treat it as strictly confidential. A violation of this paragraph shall be a material violation of this Agreement.

13. RETURN OF RECORDS. Upon termination of this Agreement, Consultant shall deliver all records, notes, data, memoranda, models, and equipment of any nature that are in Consultant's possession or under Consultant's control and that are Client's property or relate to Client's business.

14. NOTICES. All notices required or permitted under this Agreement shall be in writing and shall be deemed delivered when delivered in person or deposited in the United States mail, postage prepaid, addressed as follows:

IF for Client:

<Client Organization>
<Client Address>

IF for Consultant:

<Consultant>
<Consultant Address>

Such address may be changed from time to time by either party by providing written notice to the other in the manner set forth above.

15. ENTIRE AGREEMENT. This Agreement contains the entire agreement of the parties and there are no other promises or conditions in any other agreement whether oral or written. This Agreement supersedes any prior written or oral agreements between the parties.

16. AMENDMENT. This Agreement may be modified or amended if the amendment is made in writing and is signed by both parties.

17. SEVERABILITY. If any provision of this Agreement shall be held to be invalid or unenforceable for any reason, the remaining provisions shall continue to be valid and enforceable. If a court finds that any provision of this Agreement is invalid or unenforceable, but that by limiting such provision it would become valid and enforceable, then such provision shall be deemed to be written, construed, and enforced as so limited.

18. WAIVER OF CONTRACTUAL RIGHT. The failure of either party to enforce any provision of this Agreement shall not be construed as a waiver or limitation of that party's right to subsequently enforce and compel strict compliance with every provision of this Agreement.

19. APPLICABLE LAW. This Agreement shall be governed by the laws of the State of ________________________.

Party receiving services:
<Client Organization>

By: ____

____

Party providing services:
<Consultant>

By: ____

____

Appendix W Model Marketing Letters

(Note: Each of the following letters can be adapted as e-mail correspondence.)

[Date]

Steven Babitsky, Esq.
13 Falmouth Heights Road
Falmouth, MA 02540

Dear Attorney Babitsky,

Enclosed is a recent article of mine which appeared in Forensic Accident Investigations. I thought that it might be of interest to you.

If you have any questions on the article, machine guarding, or our services in the fields of product liability cases, slip and fall, vehicular accident reconstruction, and other personal injury cases, please feel free to call upon me.

Thank you.

Sincerely,

John M. Nichols, PE, CSP, BCFE

P.S.:	For additional information and my CV, see my Web site: www.jnichols.com

[Date]

Steven Babitsky, Esq.
13 Falmouth Heights Road
Falmouth, MA 02540

Dear Attorney Babitsky,

Your colleague, Jim Mangraviti, Esq., advised me that I should write to you. I met Jim at a recent meeting of the Barnstable County Bar Association, where I gave a presentation on symptom magnification.

The purpose of this letter is to advise you of our capabilities in performing independent medical evaluations. We understand the challenges you face in clarifying issues associated with injuries and illness. I have received special training in the performance of independent medical evaluations and have the knowledge, skills and abilities to assist you and your clients.

We can assist you by:

Providing comprehensive independent medical evaluations responding to your specific issues,
Clarifying the specific diagnoses associated with a case,
Assessing causation, to a reasonable degree of medical probability,
Evaluating maximal medical improvement and permanent impairment,
Specifying medical restrictions and suggesting appropriate modified duties,
Assessing appropriateness of care,
Offering recommendations when requested,
Preparing a thorough written report, and
Being available for depositions and testimony, if needed.

My curriculum vitae and a sample report are enclosed. Please call me if you have any questions or comments.

Sincerely yours,

Joseph Banks, M.D.

[Date]

Steven Babitsky, Esq.
13 Falmouth Heights Road
Falmouth, MA 02540

Dear Attorney Babitsky,

When your firm needs a forensic psychiatrist—who are you going to call?

I am a board certified, Harvard-trained psychiatrist who testifies on behalf of both plaintiffs and defendants.

I am available to offer assistance in the following areas:

Criminal cases
Personal injury
Custody cases
Medical malpractice
Workers' compensation
Testamentary capacity

A sample written opinion and curriculum vitae will be furnished upon request.

I have enclosed a Rolodex card for your convenience.

Thank you.

Sincerely,

Raymond R. Robinson, MD

P.S.: For additional information, see my Web site: www.rrrmd.com

Appendix X Fee Survey

The amounts being charged by experts vary by specialty and region of the country. A 1998 survey of 266 medical experts conducted by SEAK, Inc. revealed the following.

Primary Specialty	Testify Rate/Hour
Anesthesiology	$400.00
Chiropractic	$439.29
Chiropractic Neurology	$250.00
Chiropractic Orthopedics	$327.78
Emergency Medicine	$500.00
Family Practice	$564.29
General Surgery	$775.00
Hand Surgery	$700.00
Internal Medicine	$508.33
Neurology	$515.91
Neuropsychiatry	$200.00
Neurosurgery	$347.50
Occupational Medicine	$339.29
Ophthalmology	$300.00
Orthopedics	$661.44
Otolaryngology	$300.00
Pain Management	$400.00
Pain Medicine	$450.00
Physical Medicine & Rehabilitation	$579.53
Physical Therapy	$225.00
Preventative Medicine	$500.00
Psychiatry	$357.14
Pulmonary Medicine	$325.00
ALL	**$534.96**

Appendix Y Attorneys' Rules of Ethics

Because of their role in society and their close involvement in the administration of law, lawyers are subject to special standards, regulations, and liabilities. Sometimes called legal ethics, sometimes professional responsibility, the topic is perhaps most comprehensively described as the law governing lawyers.

Because lawyers are admitted to practice by states this topic is largely one of state law. However, because federal courts and federal agencies set their own practice rules, the topic has a federal component, too.

Rules of professional conduct are often promulgated by the state bar, which has a division dedicated to attorney ethical oversight. Attorneys can be disciplined by the state bar for violation of these rules—discipline usually ranges from an admonition to disbarment. In some jurisdictions, these rules are also incorporated into the codified law, or the codified law has separate provisions governing professional conduct. Violation of these laws may result in civil or criminal penalty.

For rules in specific jurisdictions, as well as decisions handed down by the body in each respective jurisdiction responsible for attorney discipline, begin your research at the following two sites:

www.law.cornell.edu/ethics/
www.legalethics.com

The American Bar Association has published a collection of Model Rules of Professional Conduct (Model Rules). Over the years, many jurisdictions have adopted rules of professional conduct similar to—and often identical to—these model rules. Moreover, the rules in states that have not adopted the Model Rules are quite similar in language and concept to the Model Rules.

As an example, we have reprinted Rule 3:07 of the Massachusetts Canons of Ethics and Disciplinary Rules Regulating the Practice of Law. This contains the Massachusetts Rules of Professional Conduct. All lawyers admitted to practice in Massachusetts are bound by these Rules of Professional Conduct, which have been adopted by the Massachusetts Supreme Judicial Court. The purpose of the Rules is to set forth minimum ethical standards for the practice of law. It is the responsibility of the Board of Bar Overseers and the Office of the Bar Counsel (administrative agencies in Massachusetts created by the Supreme Judicial Court) to see that the Rules of Professional Conduct are observed.

In order for a lawyer to be found to have committed misconduct, it must be shown that his or her acts have violated the Rules of Professional Conduct. Charges of misconduct must be supported by the facts.

RULE 3:07
MASSACHUSETTS RULES OF PROFESSIONAL CONDUCT*

*Including amendments through 10/27/99.

Index to the Rules

Preamble and Scope

Preamble: A Lawyer's Responsibilities

A lawyer is a representative of clients, an officer of the legal system, and a public citizen having special responsibility for the quality of justice.

1. As a representative of clients, a lawyer performs various functions. As advisor, a lawyer provides a client with an informed understanding of the client's legal rights and obligations and explains their practical implications. As advocate, a lawyer zealously asserts the client's position under the rules of the adversary system. As negotiator, a lawyer seeks a result advantageous to the client but consistent with requirements of honest dealing with others. A lawyer acts as evaluator by examining a client's legal affairs and reporting about them to the client or to others.
2. In all professional functions a lawyer should be competent, prompt, and diligent. A lawyer should maintain communication with a client concerning the representation. A lawyer should keep in confidence information relating to representation of a client except so far as disclosure is required or permitted by the Rules of Professional Conduct or other law.
3. A lawyer's conduct should conform to the requirements of the law, both in professional service to clients and in the lawyer's business and personal affairs. A lawyer should use the law's procedures only for legitimate purposes and not to harass or intimidate others. A lawyer should demonstrate respect for the legal system and for those who serve it, including judges, other lawyers, and public officials. While it is a lawyer's duty, when necessary, to challenge the rectitude of official action, it is also a lawyer's duty to uphold legal process.
4. As a public citizen, a lawyer should seek improvement of the law, the administration of justice, and the quality of service rendered by the legal profession. As a member of a learned profession, a lawyer should cultivate knowledge of the law beyond its use for clients, employ that knowledge in reform of the law, and work to strengthen legal education. A lawyer should be mindful of deficiencies in the administration of justice and of the fact that the poor, and sometimes persons who are not poor, cannot afford adequate legal assistance, and should therefore devote professional time and civic influence in their behalf. A lawyer should aid the legal profession in pursuing these objectives and should help the bar regulate itself in the public interest.
5. Many of a lawyer's professional responsibilities are prescribed in the Rules of Professional Conduct, as well as in substantive and procedural law. However, a lawyer is also guided by personal conscience and the approbation of professional peers. A lawyer should strive to attain the highest level of skill, to improve the law and the legal profession, and to exemplify the legal profession's ideals of public service.
6. A lawyer's responsibilities as a representative of clients, an officer of the legal system, and a public citizen are usually harmonious. Thus, when an opposing party is well represented, a lawyer can be a zealous advocate on behalf of a client and at the same time assume that justice is being done. So also, a lawyer can be sure that preserving client confidences ordinarily serves the public interest because people are more likely to seek legal advice, and thereby heed their legal obligations, when they know their communications will be private.
7. In the nature of law practice, however, conflicting responsibilities are encountered. Virtually all difficult ethical problems arise from conflict between a lawyer's responsibilities to clients, to the legal system, and to the lawyer's own interest in remaining an upright

person while earning a satisfactory living. The Rules of Professional Conduct prescribe terms for resolving such conflicts. Within the framework of these Rules, many difficult issues of professional discretion can arise. Such issues must be resolved through the exercise of sensitive professional and moral judgment guided by the basic principles underlying the Rules.

8. The legal profession is largely self-governing. Although other professions also have been granted powers of self-government, the legal profession is unique in this respect because of the close relationship between the profession and the processes of government and law enforcement. This connection is manifested in the fact that ultimate authority over the legal profession is vested largely in the courts.

9. To the extent that lawyers meet the obligations of their professional calling, the occasion for government regulation is obviated. Self-regulation also helps maintain the legal profession's independence from government domination. An independent legal profession is an important force in preserving government under law, for abuse of legal authority is more readily challenged by a profession whose members are not dependent on government for the right to practice.

10. The legal profession's relative autonomy carries with it special responsibilities of self-government. The profession has a responsibility to assure that its regulations are conceived in the public interest and not in furtherance of parochial or self-interested concerns of the bar. Every lawyer is responsible for observance of the Rules of Professional Conduct. A lawyer should also aid in securing their observance by other lawyers. Neglect of these responsibilities compromises the independence of the profession and the public interest which it serves.

11. Lawyers play a vital role in the preservation of society. The fulfillment of this role requires an understanding by lawyers of their relationship to our legal system. The Rules of Professional Conduct, when properly applied, serve to define that relationship.

Client-Lawyer Relationship

Rule 1.1 Competence

A lawyer shall provide competent representation to a client. Competent representation requires the legal knowledge, skill, thoroughness, and preparation reasonably necessary for the representation.

Rule 1.2 Scope of Representation

(a) A lawyer shall seek the lawful objectives of his or her client through reasonably available means permitted by law and these rules. A lawyer does not violate this rule, however, by acceding to reasonable requests of opposing counsel which do not prejudice the rights of his or her client, by being punctual in fulfilling all professional commitments, by avoiding offensive tactics, or by treating with courtesy and consideration all persons involved in the legal process. A lawyer shall abide by a client's decision whether to accept an offer of settlement of a matter. In a criminal case, the lawyer shall abide by the client's decision, after consultation with the lawyer, as to a plea to be entered, whether to waive jury trial, and whether the client will testify.

(b) A lawyer's representation of a client, including representation by appointment, does not constitute an endorsement of the client's political, economic, social, or moral views or activities.

(c) A lawyer may limit the objectives of the representation if the client consents after consultation.

(d) A lawyer shall not counsel a client to engage, or assist a client, in conduct that the lawyer knows is criminal or fraudulent, but a lawyer may discuss the legal consequences of any proposed course of conduct with a client and may counsel or assist a client to make a good faith effort to determine the validity, scope, meaning, or application of the law.

(e) When a lawyer knows that a client expects assistance not permitted by the rules of professional conduct or other law, the lawyer shall consult with the client regarding the relevant limitations on the lawyer's conduct.

Rule 1.3 Diligence

A lawyer shall act with reasonable diligence and promptness in representing a client. The lawyer should represent a client zealously within the bounds of the law.

Rule 1.4 Communication

(a) A lawyer shall keep a client reasonably informed about the status of a matter and promptly comply with reasonable requests for information.

(b) A lawyer shall explain a matter to the extent reasonably necessary to permit the client to make informed decisions regarding the representation.

Rule 1.5 Fees

(a) A lawyer shall not enter into an agreement for, charge, or collect an illegal or clearly excessive fee. The factors to be considered in determining whether a fee is clearly excessive include the following:

(1) the time and labor required, the novelty and difficulty of the questions involved, and the skill requisite to perform the legal service properly;

(2) the likelihood, if apparent to the client, that the acceptance of the particular employment will preclude other employment by the lawyer;

(3) the fee customarily charged in the locality for similar legal services;

(4) the amount involved and the results obtained;

(5) the time limitations imposed by the client or by the circumstances;

(6) the nature and length of the professional relationship with the client;

(7) the experience, reputation, and ability of the lawyer or lawyers performing the services; and

(8) whether the fee is fixed or contingent.

(b) When the lawyer has not regularly represented the client, the basis or rate of the fee shall be communicated to the client, preferably in writing, before or within a reasonable time after commencing the representation.

(c) A fee may be contingent on the outcome of the matter for which the service is rendered, except in a matter in which a contingent fee is prohibited by paragraph (d) or other law. Except for contingent fee arrangements concerning the collection of commercial accounts and of insurance company subrogation claims, a contingent fee agreement shall be in writing and signed in duplicate by both the lawyer and the client within a reasonable time after the making of the agreement. One such copy (and proof that the duplicate copy has been delivered or mailed to the client) shall be retained by the lawyer for a period of seven years after the conclusion of the contingent fee matter. The writing shall state:

(1) the name and address of each client;

(2) the name and address of the lawyer or lawyers to be retained;

(3) the nature of the claim, controversy, and other matters with reference to which the services are to be performed;

(4) the contingency upon which compensation to be paid, and whether and to what extent the client is to be liable to pay compensation otherwise than from amounts collected for him or her by the lawyer;

(5) the method by which the fee is to be determined, including the percentage or percentages that shall accrue to the lawyer out of amounts collected; and

(6) the method by which litigation and other expenses are to be deducted from the recovery and whether such expenses are to be deducted before or after the contingent fee is calculated.

Upon conclusion of a contingent fee matter for which a writing is required under this paragraph, the lawyer shall provide the client with a written statement stating the outcome of the matter and, if there is a recovery, showing the remittance to the client and the method of its determination.

(d) A lawyer shall not enter into an arrangement for, charge, or collect:

(1) any fee in a domestic relations matter, the payment or amount of which is contingent upon the securing of a divorce or upon the amount of alimony or support, or property settlement in lieu thereof; or

(2) a contingent fee for representing a defendant in a criminal case.

(e) A division of a fee between lawyers who are not in the same firm may be made only if, after informing the client that a division of fees will be made, the client consents to the joint participation and the total fee is reasonable. This limitation does not prohibit payment to a former partner or associate pursuant to a separation or retirement agreement.

(f) The following form of contingent fee agreement may be used to satisfy the requirements of paragraph (c). The authorization of this form shall not prevent the use of other forms consistent with this rule.

CONTINGENT FEE AGREEMENT

To be Executed in Duplicate

Date:______________, 19__

The Client ____

(Name) (Street & Number) (City or Town)

retains the Lawyer____

(Name) (Street & Number) (City or Town)

to perform the legal services mentioned in paragraph (1) below. The lawyer agrees to perform them faithfully and with due diligence.

(1) The claim, controversy, and other matters with reference to which the services are to be performed are:

(2) The contingency upon which compensation is to be paid is:

(3) The client is not to be liable to pay compensation or court costs and expenses of litigation otherwise than from amounts collected for the client by the lawyer, except as follows:

(4) Compensation (including that of any associated counsel) to be paid to the lawyer by the client on the foregoing contingency shall be the following percentage of the (gross) (net) [indicate which] amount collected. [Here insert the percentages to be charged in the event of collection. These may be on a flat rate basis or in a descending scale in relation to amount collected.]

This agreement and its performance are subject to Rule 1.5 of the Rules of Professional Conduct adopted by the Massachusetts Supreme Judicial Court.

WE EACH HAVE READ THE ABOVE AGREEMENT BEFORE SIGNING IT.

Witnesses to signatures

(To client) ____

(Signature of Client)

(To lawyer)____

(Signature of Lawyer)

(If more space is needed separate sheets may be attached and initialed.)

Rule 1.6 Confidentiality of Information

(a) A lawyer shall not reveal confidential information relating to representation of a client unless the client consents after consultation, except for disclosures that are impliedly authorized in order to carry out the representation, and except as stated in paragraph (b).

(b) A lawyer may reveal, and to the extent required by Rule 3.3, Rule 4.1(b), or Rule 8.3 must reveal, such information:

(1) to prevent the commission of a criminal or fraudulent act that the lawyer reasonably believes is likely to result in death or substantial bodily harm, or in substantial injury to the financial interests or property of another, or to prevent the wrongful execution or incarceration of another;

(2) to the extent the lawyer reasonably believes necessary to establish a claim or defense on behalf of the lawyer in a controversy between the lawyer and the client, to establish a defense to a criminal charge or civil claim against the lawyer based upon conduct in which the client was involved, or to respond to allegations in any proceeding concerning the lawyer's representation of the client;

(3) to the extent the lawyer reasonably believes necessary to rectify client fraud in which the lawyer's services have been used, subject to Rule 3.3(e);

(4) when permitted under these rules or required by law or court order.

(c) A lawyer participating in a lawyer assistance program, as hereinafter defined, shall treat the person so assisted as a client for the purposes of this rule. Lawyer assistance means assistance provided to a lawyer, judge, other legal professional, or law student by a lawyer participating in an organized nonprofit effort to provide assistance in the form of (a) counseling as to practice matters (which shall not include counseling a law student in a law school clinical program) or (b) education as to personal health matters, such as the treatment and rehabilitation from a mental, emotional, or psychological disorder, alcoholism, substance abuse, or other addiction, or both. A lawyer named in an order of the Supreme Judicial Court or the Board of Bar Overseers concerning the monitoring or terms of probation of another attorney shall treat that other attorney as a client for the purposes of this rule. Any lawyer participating in a lawyer assistance program may require a person acting under the lawyer's supervision or control to sign a nondisclosure form approved by the Supreme Judicial Court. Nothing in this paragraph (c) shall require a bar association-sponsored ethics advisory committee, the Office of Bar Counsel, or any other governmental agency advising on questions of professional responsibility to treat persons so assisted as clients for the purpose of this rule.

Rule 1.7 Conflict of Interest: General Rule

(a) A lawyer shall not represent a client if the representation of that client will be directly adverse to another client, unless:

(1) the lawyer reasonably believes the representation will not adversely affect the relationship with the other client; and

(2) each client consents after consultation.

(b) A lawyer shall not represent a client if the representation of that client may be materially limited by the lawyer's responsibilities to another client or to a third person, or by the lawyer's own interests, unless:

(1) the lawyer reasonably believes the representation will not be adversely affected; and

(2) the client consents after consultation. When representation of multiple clients in a single matter is undertaken, the consultation shall include explanation of the implications of the common representation and the advantages and risks involved.

Rule 1.8 Conflict of Interest: Prohibited Transactions

(a) A lawyer shall not enter into a business transaction with a client or knowingly acquire an ownership, possessory, security, or other pecuniary interest adverse to a client unless:

(1) the transaction and terms on which the lawyer acquires the interest are fair and reasonable to the client and are fully disclosed and transmitted in writing to the client in a manner which can be reasonably understood by the client;

(2) the client is given a reasonable opportunity to seek the advice of independent counsel in the transaction; and

(3) the client consents in writing thereto.

(b) A lawyer shall not use confidential information relating to representation of a client to the disadvantage of the client or for the lawyer's advantage or the advantage of a third person, unless the client consents after consultation, except as Rule 1.6 or Rule 3.3 would permit or require.

(c) A lawyer shall not prepare an instrument giving the lawyer or a person related to the lawyer as parent, child, sibling, or spouse any substantial gift from a client, including a testamentary gift, except where the client is related to the donee.

(d) Prior to the conclusion of representation of a client, a lawyer shall not make or negotiate an agreement giving the lawyer literary or media rights to a portrayal or account based in substantial part on information relating to the representation.

(e) A lawyer shall not provide financial assistance to a client in connection with pending or contemplated litigation, except that:

(1) a lawyer may advance court costs and expenses of litigation, the repayment of which may be contingent on the outcome of the matter; and

(2) a lawyer representing an indigent client may pay court costs and expenses of litigation on behalf of the client.

(f) A lawyer shall not accept compensation for representing a client from one other than the client unless:

(1) the client consents after consultation;

(2) there is no interference with the lawyer's independence of professional judgment or with the client-lawyer relationship; and

(3) information relating to representation of a client is protected as required by Rule 1.6.

(g) A lawyer who represents two or more clients shall not participate in making an aggregate settlement of the claims of or against the clients, or in a criminal case an aggregated agreement as to guilty or nolo contendere pleas, unless each client consents after consultation, including disclosure of the existence and nature of all the claims or pleas involved and of the participation of each person in the settlement.

(h) A lawyer shall not make an agreement prospectively limiting the lawyer's liability to a client for malpractice unless permitted by law and the client is independently represented in making the agreement, or settle a claim for such liability with an unrepresented client or former client without first advising that person in writing that independent representation is appropriate in connection therewith.

(i) A lawyer related to another lawyer as parent, child, sibling, or spouse shall not represent a client in a representation directly adverse to a person whom the lawyer knows is represented by the other lawyer except upon consent by the client after consultation regarding the relationship.

(j) A lawyer shall not acquire a proprietary interest in the cause of action or subject matter of litigation the lawyer is conducting for a client, except that the lawyer may:
(1) acquire a lien granted by law to secure the lawyer's fee or expenses; and
(2) contract with a client for a reasonable contingent fee in a civil case.

Rule 1.9 Conflict of Interest: Former Client

(a) A lawyer who has formerly represented a client in a matter shall not thereafter represent another person in the same or a substantially related matter in which that person's interests are materially adverse to the interests of the former client unless the former client consents after consultation.
(b) A lawyer shall not knowingly represent a person in the same or a substantially related matter in which a firm with which the lawyer formerly was associated had previously represented a client
(1) whose interests are materially adverse to that person; and
(2) about whom the lawyer had acquired information protected by Rules 1.6 and 1.9(c) that is material to the matter, unless the former client consents after consultation.
(c) A lawyer who has formerly represented a client in a matter or whose present or former firm has formerly represented a client in a matter shall not thereafter, unless the former client consents after consultation:
(1) use confidential information relating to the representation to the disadvantage of the former client, to the lawyer's advantage, or to the advantage of a third person, except as Rule 1.6, Rule 3.3, or Rule 4.1 would permit or require with respect to a client; or
(2) reveal confidential information relating to the representation except as Rule 1.6 or Rule 3.3 would permit or require with respect to a client.

Rule 1.10 Imputed Disqualification: General Rule

(a) While lawyers are associated in a firm, none of them shall knowingly represent a client when any one of them practicing alone would be prohibited from doing so by Rules 1.7, 1.8(c), or 1.9. A lawyer employed by the Public Counsel Division of the Committee for Public Counsel Services and a lawyer assigned to represent clients by the Private Counsel Division of that Committee are not considered to be associated. Lawyers are not considered to be associated merely because they have each individually been assigned to represent clients by the Committee for Public Counsel Services through its Private Counsel Division.
(b) When a lawyer has terminated an association with a firm, the firm is not prohibited from thereafter representing a person with interests materially adverse to those of a client represented by the formerly associated lawyer and not currently represented by the firm, unless:
(1) the matter is the same or substantially related to that in which the formerly associated lawyer represented the client; and
(2) any lawyer remaining in the firm has information protected by Rules 1.6 and 1.9(c) that is material to the matter.
(c) A disqualification prescribed by this rule may be waived by the affected client under the conditions stated in Rule 1.7.
(d) When a lawyer becomes associated with a firm, the firm may not undertake to or continue to represent a person in a matter that the firm knows or reasonably should know is the same or substantially related to a matter in which the newly associated lawyer (the "personally disqualified lawyer"), or a firm with which that lawyer was associated, had previously represented a client whose interests are materially adverse to that person unless:
(1) the personally disqualified lawyer has no information protected by Rule 1.6 or Rule 1.9 that is material to the matter ("material information"); or

(2) the personally disqualified lawyer (i) had neither substantial involvement nor substantial material information relating to the matter and (ii) is screened from any participation in the matter in accordance with paragraph (e) of this Rule and is apportioned no part of the fee therefrom.
(e) For the purposes of paragraph (d) of this Rule and of Rules 1.11 and 1.12, a personally disqualified lawyer in a firm will be deemed to have been screened from any participation in a matter if:
(1) all material information which the personally disqualified lawyer has been isolated from the firm;
(2) the personally disqualified lawyer has been isolated from all contact with the client relating to the matter, and any witness for or against the client;
(3) the personally disqualified lawyer and the firm have been precluded from discussing the matter with each other;
(4) the former client of the personally disqualified lawyer or of the firm with which the personally disqualified lawyer was associated receives notice of the conflict and an affidavit of the personally disqualified lawyer and the firm describing the procedures being used effectively to screen the personally disqualified lawyer, and attesting that (i) the personally disqualified lawyer will not participate in the matter and will not discuss the matter or the representation with any other lawyer or employee of his or her current firm, (ii) no material information was transmitted by the personally disqualified lawyer before implementation of the screening procedures and notice to the former client; and (iii) during the period of the lawyer's personal disqualification those lawyers or employees who do participate in the matter will be apprised that the personally disqualified lawyer is screened from participating in or discussing the matter; and
(5) the personally disqualified lawyer and the firm with which he is associated reasonably believe that the steps taken to accomplish the screening of material information are likely to be effective in preventing material information from being disclosed to the firm and its client.

In any matter in which the former client and the person being represented by the firm with which the personally disqualified lawyer is associated are not before a tribunal, the firm, the personally disqualified lawyer, or the former client may seek judicial review in a court of general jurisdiction of the screening procedures used, or may seek court supervision to ensure that implementation of the screening procedures has occurred and that effective actual compliance has been achieved.

Rule 1.11 Successive Government and Private Employment

(a) Except as law may otherwise expressly permit, a lawyer shall not represent a private client in connection with a matter in which the lawyer participated personally and substantially as a public officer or employee, unless the appropriate government agency consents after consultation. No lawyer in a firm with which that lawyer is associated may knowingly undertake or continue representation in such a matter unless:
(1) the disqualified lawyer is screened from any participation in the matter and is apportioned no part of the fee therefrom; and
(2) written notice is promptly given to the appropriate government agency to enable it to ascertain compliance with the provisions of this rule.
(b) Except as law may otherwise expressly permit, a lawyer having information that the lawyer knows is confidential government information about a person acquired when the lawyer was a public officer or employee, may not represent a private client whose interests are adverse to that person in a matter in which the information could be used to the material

disadvantage of that person. A firm with which that lawyer is associated may undertake or continue representation in the matter only if the disqualified lawyer is screened from any participation in the matter and is apportioned no part of the fee therefrom.

(c) Except as law may otherwise expressly permit, a lawyer serving as a public officer or employee shall not:

(1) participate in a matter in which the lawyer participated personally and substantially while in private practice or nongovernmental employment, unless under applicable law no one is, or by lawful delegation may be, authorized to act in the lawyer's stead in the matter; or

(2) negotiate for private employment with any person who is involved as a party or as lawyer for a party in a matter in which the lawyer is participating personally and substantially, except that a lawyer serving as a law clerk to a judge, other adjudicative officer, arbitrator, or mediator may negotiate for private employment as permitted by Rule 1.12(b) and subject to the conditions stated in Rule 1.12(b).

(d) As used in this rule, the term "matter" includes:

(1) any judicial or other proceeding, application, request for a ruling or other determination, contract, claim, controversy, investigation, charge, accusation, arrest, or other particular matter involving a specific party or parties, and

(2) any other matter covered by the conflict of interest rules of the appropriate government agency.

(e) As used in this rule, the term "confidential government information" means information which has been obtained under governmental authority and which, at the time this rule is applied, the government is prohibited by law from disclosing to the public or has a legal privilege not to disclose, and which is not otherwise available to the public.

Rule 1.12 Former Judge or Arbitrator

(a) Except as stated in paragraph (d), a lawyer shall not represent anyone in connection with a matter in which the lawyer participated personally and substantially as a judge or other adjudicative officer, arbitrator, mediator, or law clerk to such a person, unless all parties to the proceeding consent after consultation.

(b) A lawyer shall not negotiate for employment with any person who is involved as a party or as lawyer for a party in a matter in which the lawyer is participating personally and substantially as a judge or other adjudicative officer, arbitrator, or mediator. A lawyer serving as a law clerk to a judge, other adjudicative officer, arbitrator or mediator may negotiate for employment with a party or lawyer involved in a matter in which the clerk is participating personally and substantially, but only after the lawyer has notified the judge, other adjudicative officer, arbitrator, or mediator.

(c) If a lawyer is disqualified by paragraph (a), no lawyer in a firm with which that lawyer is associated may knowingly undertake or continue representation in the matter unless:

(1) the disqualified lawyer is screened from any participation in the matter and is apportioned no part of the fee therefrom; and

(2) written notice is promptly given to the appropriate tribunal to enable it to ascertain compliance with the provisions of this rule.

(d) An arbitrator selected as a partisan of a party in a multimember arbitration panel is not prohibited from subsequently representing that party.

following the date of retirement, resignation or most recent service as a retired judge pursuant to G.L. c. 32, §§ 65E-65G."

[2] Law clerks who serve before they are admitted to the bar are subject to the limitations stated in Rule 1.12(b).

Rule 1.13 Organization as Client

(a) A lawyer employed or retained by an organization represents the organization acting through its duly authorized constituents.

(b) If a lawyer for an organization knows that an officer, employee, or other person associated with the organization is engaged in action, intends to act or refuses to act in a matter related to the representation that is a violation of a legal obligation to the organization, or a violation of law which reasonably might be imputed to the organization, and is likely to result in substantial injury to the organization, the lawyer shall proceed as is reasonably necessary in the best interest of the organization. In determining how to proceed, the lawyer shall give due consideration to the seriousness of the violation and its consequences, the scope and nature of the lawyer's representation, the responsibility in the organization and the apparent motivation of the person involved, the policies of the organization concerning such matters, and any other relevant considerations. Any measures taken shall be designed to minimize disruption of the organization and the risk of revealing information relating to the representation to persons outside the organization. Such measures may include among others:

(1) asking reconsideration of the matter;

(2) advising that a separate legal opinion on the matter be sought for presentation to appropriate authority in the organization; and

(3) referring the matter to higher authority in the organization, including, if warranted by the seriousness of the matter, referral to the highest authority that can act in behalf of the organization as determined by applicable law.

(c) If, despite the lawyer's efforts in accordance with paragraph (b), the highest authority that can act on behalf of the organization insists upon action, or a refusal to act, that is clearly a violation of law and is likely to result in substantial injury to the organization, the lawyer may resign in accordance with Rule 1.16 and may make such disclosures as are consistent with Rule 1.6, Rule 3.3, Rule 4.1, and Rule 8.3.

(d) In dealing with an organization's directors, officers, employees, members, shareholders, or other constituents, a lawyer shall explain the identity of the client when it is apparent that the organization's interests are adverse to those of the constituents with whom the lawyer is dealing.

(e) A lawyer representing an organization may also represent any of its directors, officers, employees, members, shareholders, or other constituents, subject to the provisions of Rule 1.7. If the organization's consent to the dual representation is required by Rule 1.7, the consent shall be given by an appropriate official of the organization other than the individual who is to be represented, or by the shareholders.

Rule 1.14 Client Under a Disability

(a) When a client's ability to make adequately considered decisions in connection with the representation is impaired, whether because of minority, mental disability, or for some other reason, the lawyer shall, as far as reasonably possible, maintain a normal client-lawyer relationship with the client.

(b) If a lawyer reasonably believes that a client has become incompetent or that a normal client-lawyer relationship cannot be maintained as provided in paragraph (a) because the client lacks sufficient capacity to communicate or to make adequately considered decisions in connection with the representation, and if the lawyer reasonably believes that the client is at risk of substantial harm, physical, mental, financial, or otherwise, the lawyer may take the following action. The lawyer may consult family members, adult protective agencies, or other individuals or entities that have authority to protect the client, and, if it reasonably appears necessary, the lawyer may seek the appointment of a guardian ad litem, conservator, or a guardian, as the case may be. The lawyer may consult only those individuals or entities reasonably necessary to protect the client's interests and may not consult any individual or entity that the lawyer believes, after reasonable inquiry, will act in a fashion adverse to the interests of the client. In taking any of these actions the lawyer may disclose confidential information of the client only to the extent necessary to protect the client's interests.

Rule 1.15 Safekeeping Property

(a) A lawyer shall hold property of clients or third persons that is in a lawyer's possession in connection with a representation separate from the lawyer's own property. Funds shall be kept in a separate account maintained in the State where the lawyer's office is situated, or elsewhere with the consent of the client or third person. Other property shall be identified as such and appropriately safeguarded. Complete records of the receipt, maintenance, and disposition of such account funds and other property shall be kept by the lawyer from the time of receipt to the time of final distribution and shall be preserved for a period of six years after termination of the representation.

(b) Upon receiving funds or other property in which a client or third person has an interest, a lawyer shall promptly notify the client or third person. Except as stated in this rule or otherwise permitted by law or by agreement with the client, a lawyer shall promptly deliver to the client or third person any funds or other property that the client or third person is entitled to receive and, upon request by the client or third person, shall promptly render a full accounting regarding such property.

(c) When in the course of representation a lawyer is in possession of property in which both the lawyer and another person claim interests, the property shall be kept separate by the lawyer until there is an accounting and severance of their interests. If a dispute arises concerning their respective interests, the portion in dispute shall be kept separate by the lawyer until the dispute is resolved.

(d) All funds held in trust by a lawyer or law firm, other than advances for costs and expenses, shall be deposited in accounts clearly identified as "trust accounts," "escrow accounts," "client funds accounts," "conveyancing accounts," or "IOLTA accounts," or with words of similar import indicating the fiduciary nature of the account. All funds required to be deposited in an IOLTA account by this rule must be maintained in this Commonwealth. Such accounts are referred to herein and in Rules 1.15(e) and (f) as "trust accounts." Lawyers or law firms maintaining trust accounts shall take all steps necessary to inform the depository institution of the purpose and identity of such accounts. Funds held in trust include funds held for clients and in any other fiduciary capacity in connection with a representation, whether as trustee, agent, guardian, executor, or otherwise. Whenever "client" or "clients" is referred to in this rule, it shall be intended to refer to any person or entity on whose behalf a lawyer or law firm holds funds in trust. Trust accounts in this Commonwealth shall be maintained only in financial institutions that are in accordance with Rule 1.15(f). No funds belonging to the lawyer or law firm shall be deposited in trust accounts except as follows:

(1) Funds reasonably sufficient to pay bank charges may be deposited therein.

(2) Funds belonging in part to a client and in part presently or potentially to the lawyer or law firm must be deposited therein, but the portion belonging to the lawyer or law firm must be withdrawn at the earliest reasonable time after the lawyer's or law firm's interest in

that portion becomes fixed. If the right of the lawyer or law firm to receive such portion is disputed by the client, the disputed portion shall not be withdrawn until the dispute is resolved.

(e) Each lawyer who has a law office in this Commonwealth and who holds trust funds shall deposit such funds, as appropriate, in one of two types of interest-bearing accounts; either (i) a pooled account ("IOLTA account") for all trust funds which in the judgment of the lawyer are nominal in amount, or are to be held for a short period of time, or (ii) for all other trust funds, an individual account with the interest payable as directed by the client. The foregoing deposit requirements apply to funds received by lawyers in connection with real estate transactions and loan closings; provided, however, that a trust account in a lending bank in the name of a lawyer representing the lending bank and used exclusively for depositing and disbursing funds in connection with that particular bank's loan transactions, shall not be required but is permitted to be established as an IOLTA account. All IOLTA accounts shall be established in compliance with the following provisions:

(1) The IOLTA account shall be established with any bank, savings and loan association, or credit union authorized by Federal or State law to do business in Massachusetts and insured by the Federal Deposit Insurance Corporation or similar State insurance programs for State-chartered institutions. At the direction of the lawyer, funds in the IOLTA account in excess of $100,000 may be temporarily reinvested in repurchase agreements fully collateralized by U.S. Government obligations. Funds in the IOLTA account shall be subject to withdrawal upon request and without delay.

(2) Lawyers or law firms creating and maintaining an IOLTA account shall direct the depository institution:

(i) to remit interest or dividends, net of any service charges or fees, on the average monthly balance in the account, or as otherwise computed in accordance with an institution's standard accounting practice, at least quarterly, to the IOLTA Committee;

(ii) to transmit with each remittance to the IOLTA Committee a statement showing the name of the lawyer who or law firm which deposited the funds; and

(iii) at the same time to transmit to the depositing lawyer or law firm a report showing the amount paid, the rate of interest applied, and the method by which the interest was computed.

(3) Lawyers shall certify their compliance with this rule as required by S.J.C. Rule 4:02, subsection (2).

(4) This court shall appoint members of a permanent IOLTA Committee to fixed terms on a staggered basis. The representatives appointed to the committee shall oversee the operation of a comprehensive IOLTA program, including:

(i) the receipt of all IOLTA funds and their disbursement, net of actual expenses, to the designated charitable entities, as follows: sixty-seven percent (67%) to the Massachusetts Legal Assistance Corporation and the remaining thirty-three percent (33%) to other designated charitable entities in such proportions as the Supreme Judicial Court may order;

(ii) the education of lawyers as to their obligation to create and maintain IOLTA accounts under Rule 1.15(e);

(iii) the encouragement of the banking community and the public to support the IOLTA program;

(iv) the obtaining of tax rulings and other administrative approval for a comprehensive IOLTA program as appropriate;

(v) the preparation of such guidelines and rules, subject to court approval, as may be deemed necessary or advisable for the operation of a comprehensive IOLTA program;

(vi) establishment of standards for reserve accounts by the recipient charitable entities for the deposit of IOLTA funds which the charitable entity intends to preserve for future use; and

(vii) reporting to the court in such manner as the court may direct.

(5) The Massachusetts Legal Assistance Corporation and other designated charitable entities shall receive IOLTA funds from the IOLTA Committee and distribute such funds for approved purposes. The Massachusetts Legal Assistance Corporation may use IOLTA funds to further its corporate purpose and other designated charitable entities may use IOLTA funds either for (a) improving the administration of justice or (b) delivering civil legal services to those who cannot afford them.

(6) The Massachusetts Legal Assistance Corporation and other designated charitable entities shall submit an annual report to the court describing their IOLTA activities for the year and providing a statement of the application of IOLTA funds received pursuant to this rule.

(f) All trust accounts shall be established in compliance with the following provisions on dishonored check notification:

(1) A lawyer or law firm shall maintain trust accounts [as defined in Rule 1.15(d)] only in financial institutions which have filed with the Board of Bar Overseers an agreement, in a form provided by the Board, to report to the Board in the event any properly payable instrument is presented against any trust account that contains insufficient funds, and the financial institution dishonors the instrument for that reason.

(2) Any such agreement shall apply to all branches of the financial institution and shall not be cancelled except upon thirty days notice in writing to the Board.

(3) The Board shall publish annually a list of financial institutions which have signed agreements to comply with this rule, and shall establish rules and procedures governing amendments to the list.

(4) The dishonored check notification agreement shall provide that all reports made by the financial institution shall be identical to the notice of dishonor customarily forwarded to the depositor, and should include a copy of the dishonored instrument, if such a copy is normally provided to depositors. Such reports shall be made simultaneously with the notice of dishonor and within the time provided by law for such notice, if any.

(5) Every lawyer practicing or admitted to practice in this Commonwealth shall, as a condition thereof, be conclusively deemed to have consented to the reporting and production requirements mandated by this rule.

(6) The following definitions shall be applicable to this subparagraph:

(i) "Financial institution" includes (a) any bank, savings and loan association, credit union, or savings bank, and (b) with the written consent of the client, any other business or person which accepts for deposit funds held in trust by lawyers.

(ii) "Notice of dishonor" refers to the notice which a financial institution is required to give, under the laws of this Commonwealth, upon presentation of an instrument which the institution dishonors.

(iii) "Properly payable" refers to an instrument which, if presented in the normal course of business, is in a form requiring payment under the laws of this Commonwealth.

Rule 1.16 Declining or Terminating Representation

(a) Except as stated in paragraph (c), a lawyer shall not represent a client or, where representation has commenced, shall withdraw from the representation of a client if:

(1) the representation will result in violation of the rules of professional conduct or other law;

(2) the lawyer's physical or mental condition materially impairs the lawyer's ability to represent the client; or
(3) the lawyer is discharged.
(b) Except as stated in paragraph (c), a lawyer may withdraw from representing a client if withdrawal can be accomplished without material adverse effect on the interests of the client, or if:
(1) the client persists in a course of action involving the lawyer's services that the lawyer reasonably believes is criminal or fraudulent;
(2) the client has used the lawyer's services to perpetrate a crime or fraud;
(3) a client insists upon pursuing an objective that the lawyer considers repugnant or imprudent;
(4) the client fails substantially to fulfil an obligation to the lawyer regarding the lawyer's services and has been given reasonable warning that the lawyer will withdraw unless the obligation is fulfilled;
(5) the representation will result in an unreasonable financial burden on the lawyer or has been rendered unreasonably difficult by the client; or
(6) other good cause for withdrawal exists.
(c) If permission for withdrawal from employment is required by the rules of a tribunal, a lawyer shall not withdraw from employment in a proceeding before that tribunal without its permission.
(d) Upon termination of representation, a lawyer shall take steps to the extent reasonably practicable to protect a client's interests, such as giving reasonable notice to the client, allowing time for employment of other counsel, surrendering papers and property to which the client is entitled, and refunding any advance payment of fee that has not been earned.
(e) A lawyer must make available to a former client, within a reasonable time following the client's request for his or her file, the following:
(1) all papers, documents, and other materials the client supplied to the lawyer. The lawyer may at his or her own expense retain copies of any such materials.
(2) all pleadings and other papers filed with or by the court or served by or upon any party. The client may be required to pay any copying charge consistent with the lawyer's actual cost for these materials, unless the client has already paid for such materials.
(3) all investigatory or discovery documents for which the client has paid the lawyer's out-of-pocket costs, including but not limited to medical records, photographs, tapes, disks, investigative reports, expert reports, depositions, and demonstrative evidence. The lawyer may at his or her own expense retain copies of any such materials.
(4) if the lawyer and the client have not entered into a contingent fee agreement, the client is entitled only to that portion of the lawyer's work product (as defined in subparagraph (6) below) for which the client has paid.
(5) if the lawyer and the client have entered into a contingent fee agreement, the lawyer must provide copies of the lawyer's work product (as defined in subparagraph (6) below). The client may be required to pay any copying charge consistent with the lawyer's actual cost for the copying of these materials.
(6) for purposes of this paragraph (e), work product shall consist of documents and tangible things prepared in the course of the representation of the client by the lawyer or at the lawyer's direction by his or her employee, agent, or consultant, and not described in paragraphs (2) or (3) above. Examples of work product include without limitation legal research, records of witness interviews, reports of negotiations, and correspondence.

(7) notwithstanding anything in this paragraph (e) to the contrary, a lawyer may not refuse, on grounds of nonpayment, to make available materials in the client's file when retention would prejudice the client unfairly.

Rule 1.17 Sale of Law Practice

A lawyer or legal representative may sell, and a lawyer or law firm may purchase, with or without consideration, a law practice, including good will, if the following conditions are satisfied:

(a) [RESERVED]

(b) [RESERVED]

(c) Actual written notice is given to each of the seller's clients regarding:

(1) the proposed sale;

(2) the terms of any proposed change in the fee arrangement authorized by paragraph (d);

(3) the client's right to retain other counsel or to take possession of the file; and

(4) the fact that the client's consent to the transfer of that client's representation will be presumed if the client does not take any action or does not otherwise object within ninety (90) days of receipt of the notice.

If a client cannot be given notice, the representation of that client may be transferred to the purchaser only upon entry of an order so authorizing by a court having jurisdiction. The seller may disclose to the court in camera information relating to the representation only to the extent necessary to obtain an order authorizing the transfer of a file.

(d) The fees charged clients shall not be increased by reason of the sale. The purchaser may, however, refuse to undertake the representation unless the client consents to pay the purchaser fees at a rate not exceeding the fees charged by the purchaser for rendering substantially similar services prior to the initiation of the purchase negotiations.

Counselor

Rule 2.1 Advisor

In representing a client, a lawyer shall exercise independent professional judgment and render candid advice. In rendering advice, a lawyer may refer not only to law but to other considerations, such as moral, economic, social, and political factors, that may be relevant to the client's situation.

Rule 2.2 Intermediary [Reserved]

Rule 2.3 Evaluation for Use by Third Persons

(a) A lawyer may undertake an evaluation of a matter affecting a client for the use of someone other than the client if:

(1) the lawyer reasonably believes that making the evaluation is compatible with other aspects of the lawyer's relationship with the client; and

(2) the client consents after consultation.

(b) Except as disclosure is required in connection with a report of an evaluation, information relating to the evaluation is otherwise protected by Rule 1.6.

Advocate

Rule 3.1 Meritorious Claims and Contentions

A lawyer shall not bring or defend a proceeding, or assert or controvert an issue therein, unless there is a basis for doing so that is not frivolous, which includes a good faith argument for an extension, modification, or reversal of existing law. A lawyer for the defendant in a criminal proceeding, or the respondent in a proceeding that could result in incarceration, may nevertheless so defend the proceeding as to require that every element of the case be established.

Rule 3.2 Expediting Litigation

A lawyer shall make reasonable efforts to expedite litigation consistent with the interests of the client.

Rule 3.3 Candor Toward the Tribunal

(a) A lawyer shall not knowingly:

(1) make a false statement of material fact or law to a tribunal;

(2) fail to disclose a material fact to a tribunal when disclosure is necessary to avoid assisting a criminal or fraudulent act by the client, except as provided in Rule 3.3(e);

(3) fail to disclose to the tribunal legal authority in the controlling jurisdiction known to the lawyer to be directly adverse to the position of the client and not disclosed by opposing counsel; or

(4) offer evidence that the lawyer knows to be false, except as provided in Rule 3.3(e). If a lawyer has offered, or the lawyer's client or witnesses testifying on behalf of the client have given, material evidence and the lawyer comes to know of its falsity, the lawyer shall take reasonable remedial measures.

(b) The duties stated in paragraph (a) continue to the conclusion of the proceeding, including all appeals, and apply even if compliance requires disclosure of information otherwise protected by Rule 1.6.

(c) A lawyer may refuse to offer evidence that the lawyer reasonably believes is false.

(d) In an ex parte proceeding, a lawyer shall inform the tribunal of all material facts known to the lawyer which will enable the tribunal to make an informed decision, whether or not the facts are adverse.

(e) In a criminal case, defense counsel who knows that the defendant, the client, intends to testify falsely may not aid the client in constructing false testimony, and has a duty strongly to discourage the client from testifying falsely, advising that such a course is unlawful, will have substantial adverse consequences, and should not be followed. If a lawyer discovers this intention before accepting the representation of the client, the lawyer shall not accept the representation; if the lawyer discovers this intention before trial, the lawyer shall seek to withdraw from the representation, requesting any required permission. Disclosure of privileged or prejudicial information shall be made only to the extent necessary to effect the withdrawal. If disclosure of privileged or prejudicial information is necessary, the lawyer shall make an application to withdraw ex parte to a judge other than the judge who will preside at the trial and shall seek to be heard in camera and have the record of the proceeding, except for an order granting leave to withdraw, impounded. If the lawyer is unable to obtain the required permission to withdraw, the lawyer may not prevent the client from testifying. If a criminal trial has commenced and the lawyer discovers that the client intends to testify falsely at trial, the lawyer need not file a motion to withdraw from the case if the lawyer reasonably believes that seeking to withdraw will prejudice the client. If, during the client's testimony or after the client has testified, the lawyer knows that the client has testified falsely, the lawyer shall call upon the client to rectify the false testimony and, if the client refuses or is unable to do so, the lawyer shall not reveal the false testimony to the tribunal. In no event may the lawyer examine the client in such a manner as to elicit any testimony from the client the lawyer knows to be false, and the lawyer shall not argue the probative value of the false testimony in closing argument or in any other proceedings, including appeals.

Rule 3.4 Fairness to Opposing Party and Counsel

A lawyer shall not:

(a) unlawfully obstruct another party's access to evidence or unlawfully alter, or conceal a document or other material having potential evidentiary value. A lawyer shall not counsel or assist another person to do any such act;

(b) falsify evidence, counsel or assist a witness to testify falsely, or offer an inducement to a witness that is prohibited by law;

(c) knowingly disobey an obligation under the rules of a tribunal except for an open refusal based on an assertion that no valid obligation exists;

(d) in pretrial procedure, make a frivolous discovery request or fail to make reasonably diligent effort to comply with a legally proper discovery request by an opposing party;

(e) in trial, allude to any matter that the lawyer does not reasonably believe is relevant or that will not be supported by admissible evidence, assert personal knowledge of facts in issue except when testifying as a witness, or state a personal opinion as to the justness of a cause, the credibility of a witness, the culpability of a civil litigant, or the guilt or innocence of an accused;

(f) request a person other than a client to refrain from voluntarily giving relevant information to another party unless:

(1) the person is a relative or an employee or other agent of a client; and

(2) the lawyer reasonably believes that the person's interests will not be adversely affected by refraining from giving such information;

(g) pay, offer to pay, or acquiesce in the payment of compensation to a witness contingent upon the content of his or her testimony or the outcome of the case. But a lawyer may advance, guarantee, or acquiesce in the payment of:

(1) expenses reasonably incurred by a witness in attending or testifying

(2) reasonable compensation to a witness for loss of time in attending or testifying

(3) a reasonable fee for the professional services of an expert witness;

(h) present, participate in presenting, or threaten to present criminal or disciplinary charges solely to obtain an advantage in a private civil matter; or

(i) in appearing in a professional capacity before a tribunal, engage in conduct manifesting bias or prejudice based on race, sex, religion, national origin, disability, age, or sexual orientation against a party, witness, counsel, or other person. This paragraph does not preclude legitimate advocacy when race, sex, religion, national origin, disability, age, or sexual orientation, or another similar factor is an issue in the proceeding.

Rule 3.5 Impartiality and Decorum of the Tribunal

A lawyer shall not:

(a) seek to influence a judge, juror, prospective juror, or other official by means prohibited by law;

(b) communicate ex parte with such a person except as permitted by law;

(c) engage in conduct intended to disrupt a tribunal; or

(d) after discharge of the jury from further consideration of a case with which the lawyer was connected, initiate any communication with a member of the jury without leave of court granted for good cause shown. If a juror initiates a communication with such a lawyer, directly or indirectly, the lawyer may respond provided that the lawyer shall not ask questions of or make comments to a member of that jury that are intended only to harass or embarrass the juror or to influence his or her actions in future jury service. In no circumstances shall such a lawyer inquire of a juror concerning the jury's deliberation processes.

Rule 3.6 Trial Publicity

(a) A lawyer who is participating or has participated in the investigation or litigation of a matter shall not make an extrajudicial statement that a reasonable person would expect to be disseminated by means of public communication if the lawyer knows or reasonably should know that it will have a substantial likelihood of materially prejudicing an adjudicative proceeding in the matter.

(b) Notwithstanding paragraph (a), a lawyer may state:

(1) the claim, offense, or defense involved, and, except when prohibited by law, the identity of the persons involved;

(2) the information contained in a public record;

(3) that an investigation of the matter is in progress;

(4) the scheduling or result of any step in litigation;

(5) a request for assistance in obtaining evidence and information necessary thereto;

(6) a warning of danger concerning the behavior of a person involved, when there is reason to believe that there exists the likelihood of substantial harm to an individual or to the public interest; and

(7) in a criminal case, in addition to subparagraphs (1) through (6):

(i) the identity, residence, occupation, and family status of the accused;

(ii) if the accused has not been apprehended, information necessary to aid in apprehension of that person;

(iii) the fact, time, and place of arrest; and

(iv) the identity of investigating and arresting officers or agencies and the length of the investigation.

(c) Notwithstanding paragraph (a), a lawyer may make a statement that a reasonable lawyer would believe is required to protect a client from the substantial undue prejudicial effect of recent publicity not initiated by the lawyer or the lawyer's client. A statement made pursuant to this paragraph shall be limited to such information as is necessary to mitigate the recent adverse publicity.

(d) No lawyer associated in a firm or government agency with a lawyer subject to paragraph (a) shall make a statement prohibited by paragraph (a).

(e) This rule does not preclude a lawyer from replying to charges of misconduct publicly made against him or her or from participating in the proceedings of a legislative, administrative, or other investigative body.

Rule 3.7 Lawyer as Witness

(a) A lawyer shall not act as advocate at a trial in which the lawyer is likely to be a necessary witness except where:

(1) the testimony relates to an uncontested issue;

(2) the testimony relates to the nature and value of legal services rendered in the case; or

(3) disqualification of the lawyer would work substantial hardship on the client.

(b) A lawyer may act as advocate in a trial in which another lawyer in the lawyer's firm is likely to be called as a witness unless precluded from doing so by Rule 1.7 or Rule 1.9.

Rule 3.8 Special Responsibilities of a Prosecutor

The prosecutor in a criminal case shall:

(a) refrain from prosecuting a charge that the prosecutor knows is not supported by probable cause;

(b) make reasonable efforts to assure that the accused has been advised of the right to, and the procedure for obtaining, counsel and has been given reasonable opportunity to obtain counsel;
(c) not seek to obtain from an unrepresented accused a waiver of important pretrial rights, such as the right to a preliminary hearing, unless a court first has obtained from the accused a knowing and intelligent written waiver of counsel;
(d) make timely disclosure to the defense of all evidence or information known to the prosecutor that tends to negate the guilt of the accused or mitigates the offense, and, in connection with sentencing, disclose to the defense and to the tribunal all unprivileged mitigating information known to the prosecutor, except when the prosecutor is relieved of this responsibility by a protective order of the tribunal;
(e) exercise reasonable care to prevent investigators, law enforcement personnel, employees, or other persons assisting or associated with the prosecutor in a criminal case from making an extrajudicial statement that the prosecutor would be prohibited from making under Rule 3.6;
(f) not subpoena a lawyer in a grand jury or other criminal proceeding to present evidence about a past or present client unless:
(1) the prosecutor reasonably believes:
(i) the information sought is not protected from disclosure by any applicable privilege;
(ii) the evidence sought is essential to the successful completion of an ongoing investigation or prosecution; and
(iii) there is no other feasible alternative to obtain the information; and
(2) the prosecutor obtains prior judicial approval after an opportunity for an adversarial proceeding;
(g) except for statements that are necessary to inform the public of the nature and extent of the prosecutor's action and that serve a legitimate law enforcement purpose, refrain from making extrajudicial comments that have a substantial likelihood of heightening public condemnation of the accused;
(h) not assert personal knowledge of the facts in issue, except when testifying as a witness;
(i) not assert a personal opinion as to the justness of a cause, as to the credibility of a witness, as to the culpability of a civil litigant, or as to the guilt or innocence of an accused; but the prosecutor may argue, on analysis of the evidence, for any position or conclusion with respect to the matters stated herein; and
(j) not intentionally avoid pursuit of evidence because the prosecutor believes it will damage the prosecution's case or aid the accused.

Rule 3.9 Advocate in Nonadjudicative Proceedings

A lawyer representing a client before a legislative or administrative tribunal in a nonadjudicative proceeding shall disclose that the appearance is in a representative capacity and shall conform to the provisions of Rules 3.3(a) through (c), 3.4(a) through (c), and 3.5(a) through (c).

Transactions with Persons other than Clients

Rule 4.1 Truthfulness in Statements to Others

In the course of representing a client a lawyer shall not knowingly:
(a) make a false statement of material fact or law to a third person; or

(b) fail to disclose a material fact to a third person when disclosure is necessary to avoid assisting a criminal or fraudulent act by a client, unless disclosure is prohibited by Rule 1.6.

Rule 4.2 Communication with Person Represented by Counsel

In representing a client, a lawyer shall not communicate about the subject of the representation with a person the lawyer knows to be represented by another lawyer in the matter, unless the lawyer has the consent of the other lawyer or is authorized by law to do so.

Rule 4.3 Dealing with Unrepresented Person

(a) In dealing on behalf of a client with a person who is not represented by counsel, a lawyer shall not state or imply that the lawyer is disinterested. When the lawyer knows or reasonably should know that the unrepresented person misunderstands the lawyer's role in the matter, the lawyer shall make reasonable efforts to correct the misunderstanding.

(b) During the course of representation of a client, a lawyer shall not give advice to a person who is not represented by a lawyer, other than the advice to secure counsel, if the interests of such person are or have a reasonable possibility of being in conflict with the interests of the client.

Rule 4.4 Respect for Rights of Third Persons

In representing a client, a lawyer shall not use means that have no substantial purpose other than to embarrass, delay, or burden a third person, or use methods of obtaining evidence that violate the legal rights of such a person.

Law Firms and Associations

Rule 5.1 Responsibilities of a Partner or Supervisory Lawyer

(a) A partner in a law firm shall make reasonable efforts to ensure that the firm has in effect measures giving reasonable assurance that all lawyers in the firm conform to the Rules of Professional Conduct.

(b) A lawyer having direct supervisory authority over another lawyer shall make reasonable efforts to ensure that the other lawyer conforms to the Rules of Professional Conduct.

(c) A lawyer shall be responsible for another lawyer's violation of the Rules of Professional Conduct if:

(1) the lawyer orders or, with knowledge of the specific conduct, ratifies the conduct involved; or

(2) the lawyer is a partner in the law firm in which the other lawyer practices, or has direct supervisory authority over the other lawyer, and knows of the conduct at a time when its consequences can be avoided or mitigated but fails to take reasonable remedial action.

Rule 5.2 Responsibilities of a Subordinate Lawyer

(a) A lawyer is bound by the Rules of Professional Conduct notwithstanding that the lawyer acted at the direction of another person.

(b) A subordinate lawyer does not violate the Rules of Professional Conduct if that lawyer acts in accordance with a supervisory lawyer's reasonable resolution of an arguable question of professional duty.

Rule 5.3 Responsibilities Regarding Nonlawyer Assistants

With respect to a nonlawyer employed or retained by or associated with a lawyer:

(a) a partner in a law firm shall make reasonable efforts to ensure that the firm has in effect measures giving reasonable assurance that the person's conduct is compatible with the professional obligations of the lawyer;

(b) a lawyer having direct supervisory authority over the nonlawyer shall make reasonable efforts to ensure that the person's conduct is compatible with the professional obligations of the lawyer; and

(c) a lawyer shall be responsible for conduct of such a person that would be a violation of the Rules of Professional Conduct if engaged in by a lawyer if:

(1) the lawyer orders or, with the knowledge of the specific conduct, ratifies the conduct involved; or

(2) the lawyer is a partner in the law firm in which the person is employed, or has direct supervisory authority over the person, and knows of the conduct at a time when its consequences can be avoided or mitigated but fails to take reasonable remedial action.

Rule 5.4 Professional Independence of a Lawyer

(a) A lawyer or law firm shall not share legal fees with a nonlawyer, except that:

(1) an agreement by a lawyer with the lawyer's firm, partner, or associate may provide for the payment of money, over a reasonable period of time after the lawyer's death, to the lawyer's estate or to one or more specified persons;

(2) a lawyer who purchases the practice of a deceased, disabled, or disappeared lawyer may, pursuant to the provisions of Rule 1.17, pay to the estate or other representative of that lawyer the agreed-upon purchase price;

(3) a lawyer or law firm may include nonlawyer employees in a compensation or retirement plan, even though the plan is based in whole or in part on a profit-sharing arrangement; and

(4) a lawyer or law firm may agree to share a statutory or tribunal-approved fee award, or a settlement in a matter eligible for such an award, with a qualified legal assistance organization that referred the matter to the lawyer or law firm, if (i) the organization is one that is not for profit, (ii) the organization is tax-exempt under federal law, (iii) the fee award or settlement is made in connection with a proceeding to advance one or more of the purposes by virtue of which the organization is tax-exempt, and (iv) the client consents, after being informed that a division of fees will be made, to the sharing of the fees and the total fee is reasonable.

(b) A lawyer shall not form a partnership with a nonlawyer if any of the activities of the partnership consist of the practice of law.

(c) A lawyer shall not permit a person who recommends, employs, or pays the lawyer to render legal services for another to direct or regulate the lawyer's professional judgment in rendering such legal services.

(d) A lawyer shall not practice with or in the form of a professional corporation or association authorized to practice law for a profit, if:

(1) a nonlawyer owns any interest therein, except that a fiduciary representative of the estate of a lawyer may hold the stock or interest of the lawyer for a reasonable time during administration;

(2) a nonlawyer is a corporate director or officer thereof; or

(3) a nonlawyer has the right to direct or control the professional judgment of a lawyer.

Rule 5.5 Unauthorized Practice of Law

A lawyer shall not:

(a) practice law in a jurisdiction where doing so violates the regulation of the legal profession in that jurisdiction; or

(b) assist a person who is not a member of the bar in the performance of activity that constitutes the unauthorized practice of law.

Rule 5.6 Restrictions on Right to Practice
A lawyer shall not participate in offering or making:
(a) a partnership or employment agreement that restricts the right of a lawyer to practice after termination of the relationship, except an agreement concerning benefits upon retirement; or
(b) an agreement in which a restriction on the lawyer's right to practice is part of the settlement of a controversy.
Rule 5.7 Responsibilities Regarding Law-Related Services
(a) A lawyer shall be subject to the Rules of Professional Conduct with respect to the provision of law-related services, as defined in paragraph (b), if the law-related services are provided:
(1) by the lawyer in circumstances that are not distinct from the lawyer's provision of legal services to clients; or
(2) by a separate entity controlled by the lawyer individually or with others if the lawyer fails to take reasonable measures to assure that a person obtaining the law-related services knows that the services of the separate entity are not legal services and that the protections of the client-lawyer relationship do not exist.
(b) The term "law-related services" denotes services that might reasonably be performed in conjunction with and in substance are related to the provision of legal services, and that are not prohibited as unauthorized practice of law when provided by a nonlawyer.

Public Service
Rule 6.1 Voluntary Pro Bono Publico Service
A lawyer should provide annually at least 25 hours of *pro bono publico* legal services for the benefit of persons of limited means. In providing these professional services, the lawyer should:
(a) provide all or most of the 25 hours of *pro bono publico* legal services without compensation or expectation of compensation to persons of limited means, or to charitable, religious, civic, community, governmental, and educational organizations in matters that are designed primarily to address the needs of persons of limited means. The lawyer may provide any remaining hours by delivering legal services at substantially reduced compensation to persons of limited means or by participating in activities for improving the law, the legal system, or the legal profession that are primarily intended to benefit persons of limited means; or,
(b) contribute from $250 to 1% of the lawyer's annual taxable, professional income to one or more organizations that provide or support legal services to persons of limited means.
Rule 6.2 Accepting Appointments
A lawyer shall not seek to avoid appointment by a tribunal to represent a person except for good cause, such as:
(a) representing the client is likely to result in violation of the Rules of Professional Conduct or other law;
(b) representing the client is likely to result in an unreasonable financial burden on the lawyer; or
(c) the client or the cause is so repugnant to the lawyer as to be likely to impair the client-lawyer relationship or the lawyer's ability to represent the client.

Rule 6.3 Membership in Legal Services Organization

A lawyer may serve as a director, officer, or member of a legal services organization, apart from the law firm in which the lawyer practices, notwithstanding that the organization serves persons having interests adverse to a client of the lawyer. The lawyer shall not knowingly participate in a decision or action of the organization:

(a) if participating in the decision or action would be incompatible with the lawyer's obligations to a client under Rule 1.7; or

(b) where the decision or action could have a material adverse effect on the representation of a client of the organization whose interests are adverse to a client of the lawyer.

Rule 6.4 Law Reform Activities Affecting Client Interests

A lawyer may serve as a director, officer, or member of an organization involved in reform of the law or its administration notwithstanding that the reform may affect the interests of a client of the lawyer. When the lawyer knows that the interests of a client may be materially benefitted by a decision in which the lawyer participates, the lawyer shall disclose that fact but need not identify the client.

Information about Legal Services

Rule 7.1 Communications Concerning a Lawyer's Services

A lawyer shall not make a false or misleading communication about the lawyer or the lawyer's services. A communication is false or misleading if it contains a material misrepresentation of fact or law, or omits a fact necessary to make the statement considered as a whole not materially misleading.

Rule 7.2 Advertising

(a) Subject to the requirements of Rule 7.1, a lawyer may advertise services through public media, such as a telephone directory, legal directory including an electronic or computer-accessed directory, newspaper or other periodical, outdoor advertising, radio or television, or through written communication not involving solicitation prohibited in Rule 7.3.

(b) A copy or recording of an advertisement or written communication shall be kept for two years after its last dissemination along with a record of when and where it was used.

(c) A lawyer shall not give anything of value to a person for recommending the lawyer's services, except that a lawyer may:

(1) pay the reasonable costs of advertisements or communications permitted by this Rule;

(2) pay the usual charges of a not-for-profit lawyer referral service or legal service organization;

(3) pay for a law practice in accordance with Rule 1.17; and

(4) pay referral fees permitted by Rule 1.5(e);

(5) share a statutory fee award or court-approved settlement in lieu thereof with a qualified legal assistance organization in accordance with Rule 5.4(a)(4).

(d) Any communication made pursuant to this rule shall include the name of the lawyer, group of lawyers, or firm responsible for its content.

Rule 7.3 Solicitation of Professional Employment

(a) In soliciting professional employment, a lawyer shall not coerce or harass a prospective client and shall not make a false or misleading communication.

(b) A lawyer shall not solicit professional employment if:

(1) the lawyer knows or reasonably should know that the physical, mental, or emotional state of the prospective client is such that there is a substantial potential that the person cannot exercise reasonable judgment in employing a lawyer, provided, however, that this prohibition shall not apply to solicitation not for a fee; or

(2) the prospective client has made known to the lawyer a desire not to be solicited.

(c) Except as provided in paragraph (e), a lawyer shall not solicit professional employment for a fee from a prospective client known to be in need of legal services in a particular matter by written communication, including audio or video cassette or other electronic communication, unless the lawyer retains a copy of such communication for two years.

(d) Except as provided in paragraph (e), a lawyer shall not solicit professional employment for a fee from a prospective client in person or by personal communication by telephone, electronic device, or otherwise.

(e) The following communications shall be exempt from the provisions of paragraphs (c) and (d) above:

(1) communications to members of the bar of any state or jurisdiction;

(2) communications to individuals who are (A) the grandparents of the lawyer or the lawyer's spouse, (B) descendants of the grandparents of the lawyer or the lawyer's spouse, or (C) the spouse of any of the foregoing persons;

(3) communications to prospective clients with whom the lawyer had a prior attorney-client relationship; and

(4) communications with organizations engaged in trade or commerce as defined in G.L. c. 93A, § 1(b), non-profit entities, or governmental entities for purposed related to the solicitation of professional employment from such entities.

(f) A lawyer shall not give anything of value to any person or organization to solicit professional employment for the lawyer from a prospective client. However, this rule does not prohibit a lawyer or a partner or associate or any other lawyer affiliated with the lawyer or the lawyer's firm from requesting referrals from a lawyer referral service operated, sponsored, or approved by a bar association or from cooperating with any other qualified legal assistance organization.

Rule 7.4 Communication of Fields of Practice

(a) Lawyers may hold themselves out publicly as specialists in particular services, fields, and areas of law if the holding out does not include a false or misleading communication. Such holding out includes (1) a statement that the lawyer concentrates in, specializes in, is certified in, has expertise in, or limits practice to a particular service, field, or area of law, (2) directory listings, including electronic, computer-accessed or other similar types of directory listings, by particular service, field, or area of law, and (3) any other association of the lawyer's name with a particular service, field, or area of law.

(b) Lawyers who hold themselves out as "certified" in a particular service, field, or area of law must name the certifying organization and must state that the certifying organization is "a private organization, whose standards for certification are not regulated by the Commonwealth of Massachusetts," if that is the case, or, if the certifying organization is a governmental body, must name the governmental body.

(c) Except as provided in this paragraph, lawyers who associate their names with a particular service, field, or area of law imply an expertise and shall be held to the standard of performance of specialists in that particular service, field, or area. Lawyers may limit responsibility with respect to a particular service, field, or area of law to the standard of an ordinary lawyer by holding themselves out in a fashion that does not imply expertise, such as by advertising that they "handle" or "welcome" cases, "but are not specialists in" a specific service, field, or area of law.

Rule 7.5 Firm Names and Letterheads

(a) A lawyer shall not use a firm name, letterhead, or other professional designation that violates Rule 7.1. A trade name may be used by a lawyer in private practice if it does not imply a connection with a government agency or with a public or charitable legal services organization and is not otherwise in violation of Rule 7.1.

(b) A law firm with offices in more than one jurisdiction may use the same name in each jurisdiction, but identification of the lawyers in an office of the firm shall indicate the jurisdictional limitations on those not licensed to practice in the jurisdiction where the office is located.

(c) The name of a lawyer holding a public office shall not be used in the name of a law firm, or in communications on its behalf, during any substantial period in which the lawyer is not actively and regularly practicing with the firm.

(d) Lawyers may state or imply that they practice in a partnership or other organization only when that is the fact.

Maintaining the Integrity of the Profession

Rule 8.1 Bar Admission and Disciplinary Matters

An applicant for admission to the bar, or a lawyer in connection with a bar admission application or in connection with a disciplinary matter, shall not:

(a) knowingly make a false statement of material fact; or

(b) fail to disclose a fact necessary to correct a misapprehension known by the person to have arisen in the matter, or knowingly fail to respond to a lawful demand for information from an admissions or disciplinary authority, except that this rule does not require disclosure of information otherwise protected by Rule 1.6.

Rule 8.2 Judicial and Legal Officials

A lawyer shall not make a statement that the lawyer knows to be false or with reckless disregard as to its truth or falsity concerning the qualifications or integrity of a judge or a magistrate, or of a candidate for appointment to judicial or legal office.

Rule 8.3 Reporting Professional Misconduct

(a) A lawyer having knowledge that another lawyer has committed a violation of the Rules of Professional Conduct that raises a substantial question as to that lawyer's honesty, trustworthiness or fitness as a lawyer in other respects, shall inform the Bar Counsel's office of the Board of Bar Overseers.

(b) A lawyer having knowledge that a judge has committed a violation of applicable rules of judicial conduct that raises a substantial question as to the judge's fitness for office shall inform the Commission on Judicial Conduct.

(c) This rule does not require disclosure of information otherwise protected by Rule 1.6 or information gained by a lawyer or judge while serving as a member of lawyer assistance program as defined in Rule 1.6(c), to the extent that such information would be confidential if it were communicated by a client.

Rule 8.4 Misconduct

It is professional misconduct for a lawyer to:

(a) violate or attempt to violate the Rules of Professional Conduct, knowingly assist or induce another to do so, or do so through the acts of another;

(b) commit a criminal act that reflects adversely on the lawyer's honesty, trustworthiness, or fitness as a lawyer in other respects;
(c) engage in conduct involving dishonesty, fraud, deceit, or misrepresentation;
(d) engage in conduct that is prejudicial to the administration of justice;
(e) state or imply an ability to influence improperly a government agency or official;
(f) knowingly assist a judge or judicial officer in conduct that is a violation of applicable rules of judicial conduct or other law;
(g) fail without good cause to cooperate with the Bar Counsel or the Board of Bar Overseers as provided in Supreme Judicial Court Rule 4:01, § 3; or
(h) engage in any other conduct that adversely reflects on his or her fitness to practice law.

Rule 8.5 Disciplinary Authority

(a) A lawyer admitted to practice in this jurisdiction is subject to the disciplinary authority of this jurisdiction, regardless of where the lawyer's conduct occurs. A lawyer may be subject to the disciplinary authority of both this jurisdiction and another jurisdiction where the lawyer is admitted for the same conduct.
(b) [RESERVED].

Definitions; Title

Rule 9.1 Definitions

The following definitions are applicable to the Rules of Professional Conduct:
(a) "Bar association" includes an association of specialists in particular services, fields, and areas of law.
(b) "Belief" or "believes" denotes that the person involved actually supposed the fact in question to be true. A person's belief may be inferred from circumstances.
(c) "Consult" or "consultation" denotes communication of information reasonably sufficient to permit the client to appreciate the significance of the matter in question.
(d) "Firm" or "law firm" denotes a lawyer or lawyers in a private firm, lawyers employed in the legal department of a corporation or other organization, and lawyers employed in a legal services organization. The term includes a partnership, including a limited liability partnership, a corporation, a limited liability company, or an association treated as a corporation, authorized by law to practice law for profit.
(e) "Fraud" or "fraudulent" denotes conduct having a purpose to deceive and not merely negligent misrepresentation or failure to apprise another of relevant information.
(f) "Knowingly," "known," or "knows" denotes actual knowledge of the fact in question. A person's knowledge may be inferred from circumstances.
(g) "Partner" denotes a member of a partnership and a shareholder in a law firm organized as a professional corporation.
(h) "Person" includes a corporation, an association, a trust, a partnership, and any other organization or legal entity.
(i) "Qualified legal assistance organization" means a legal aid, public defender, or military assistance office; or a bona fide organization that recommends, furnishes or pays for legal services to its members or beneficiaries, provided the office, service, or organization receives no profit from the rendition of legal services, is not designed to procure financial benefit or legal work for a lawyer as a private practitioner, does not infringe the individual member's freedom as a client to challenge the approved counsel or to select outside counsel at the client's expense, and is not in violation of any applicable law.

(j) "Reasonable" or "reasonably" when used in relation to conduct by a lawyer denotes the conduct of a reasonably prudent and competent lawyer.
(k) "Reasonable belief" or "reasonably believes" when used in reference to a lawyer denotes that the lawyer believes the matter in question and that the circumstances are such that the belief is reasonable.
(l) "Reasonably should know" when used in reference to a lawyer denotes that a lawyer of reasonable prudence and competence would ascertain the matter in question.
(m) "State" includes the District of Columbia, Puerto Rico, and federal territories or possessions.
(n) "Substantial" when used in reference to degree or extent denotes a material matter of clear and weighty importance.
(o) "Tribunal" includes a court or other adjudicatory body.

Rule 9.2 Title

These rules may be known and cited as the Massachusetts Rules of Professional Conduct (Mass. R. Prof. C.).

Promulgated 426 Mass. 1302 (1997)

Amended:
effective 1/1/98
effective 3/1/98
27 M.L.W. 853 (12/21/98), effective 1/1/99)
430 Mass. 1301 (1999), effective 10/1/99
___ Mass. 130_ (1999), effective 12/1/99.

Index